Theory and Structure in International Political Economy

International Organization Readers

Issues and Agents in International Political Economy, 1999

Theory and Structure in International Political Economy, 1999

THEORY AND STRUCTURE
IN
INTERNATIONAL POLITICAL ECONOMY
An *International Organization* Reader

edited by
Charles Lipson and Benjamin J. Cohen

The MIT Press
Cambridge, Massachusetts and London, England

The contents of this book were first published in *International Organization* (ISSN 0162-2889), a publication of The MIT Press under the sponsorship of the IO Foundation. Except as otherwise noted, copyright for each article is owned jointly by the IO Foundation and of the Massachusetts Institute of Technology.

Joseph M. Grieco, "Anarchy and the Limits of Cooperation: A Realist Critique of the Newest Liberal Institutionalism," IO 42 (3) (summer 1988); Andrew Moravcsik, "A Liberal Theory of International Politics," IO 51 (4) (autumn 1997); Alexander Wendt, "Anarchy Is What States Make of It," IO 46 (2) (spring 1992); Philip G. Cerny, "Globalization and the Changing Logic of Collective Action," IO 49 (4) (autumn 1995); Robert O. Keohane "The Demand for International Regimes," IO 36 (2) (spring 1982); Stephan Haggard and Beth A. Simmons, "Theories of International Regimes," IO 41 (3) (summer 1987); Ronald B. Mitchell, "Regime Design Matters: International Oil Pollution and Treaty Compliance," IO 48 (3) (summer 1994); John G. Ruggie, "International Regimes, Transactions, and Change: Embedded Liberalism in the Postwar Economic Order," IO 36 (2) (spring 1982); Arthur A. Stein, "The Hegemon's Dilemma: Great Britain, the United States, and the International Economic Order," IO 38 (2) (spring 1984); Lisa L. Martin, "Interests, Power, and Multilateralism," IO 46 (4) (autumn 1992); Robert D. Putnam, "Diplomacy and Domestic Politics: The Logic of Two-Level Games," IO 42 (3) (summer 1988); Joanne Gowa, "Public Goods and Political Institutions: Trade and Monetary Policy Processes in the United States," IO 42 (1) (winter 1988); Peter F. Cowhey, "Domestic Institutions and the Credibility of International Commitments," IO 47 (2) (spring 1993).

Library of Congress Cataloging-in-Publication Data

Theory and structure in international political economy / edited by
Charles Lipson and Benjamin J. Cohen.
   p. cm.—(*International organization* reader)
Includes bibliographical references.
ISBN 0-262-12215-4 (hc : alk. paper).—ISBN 0-262-62127-4 (pbk. : alk. paper)
  1. International economic relations. 2. International relations. I. Lipson, Charles. II. Cohen, Benjamin J. III. Series: *International Organization* readers.
HF1359.T445   1999
337—dc21   98-50265
                                                       CIP

Contents

Contributors

Volume Editors

Charles Lipson is Associate Professor of Political Science and Co-Director of the Program on International Politics, Economics, and Security at the University of Chicago, Chicago, Illinois.

Benjamin J. Cohen is Louis G. Lancaster Professor of International Political Economy at the University of California, Santa Barbara.

Contributors

Philip G. Cerny is Professor of International Political Economy at the University of Leeds, Leeds, United Kingdom.

Peter F. Cowhey is Professor in the Graduate School of International Relations and Pacific Studies, University of California, San Diego.

Joanne Gowa is Professor of Politics at Princeton University, Princeton, New Jersey.

Joseph M. Grieco is Professor of Political Science at Duke University, Durham, N.C.

Stephan Haggard is Professor in the Graduate School of International Relations and Pacific Studies at the University of California, San Diego, and Director of the University of California's Institute on Global Conflict and Cooperation.

Robert O. Keohane is James B. Duke Professor of Political Science, Duke University, Durham, N.C.

Lisa L. Martin is Professor of Government at Harvard University, Cambridge, Massachusetts.

Ronald B. Mitchell is Assistant Professor of Political Science at the University of Oregon, Eugene, Oregon.

Andrew Moravcsik is Associate Professor of Government at the Center for European Studies, Harvard University, Cambridge, Massachusetts.

Robert D. Putnam is Stanfield Professor for International Peace and Director of the Saguaro Seminar: Civic Engagement in America at the Kennedy School of Government at Harvard University, Cambridge, Massachusetts.

John Gerard Ruggie currently serves as chief adviser for strategic planning to United Nations Secretary-General Kofi Annan, at the rank of Assistant Secretary-General. He is on leave as Burgess Professor of Political Science and International Affairs at Columbia University, where he was Dean of the School of International and Public Affairs from 1991–96.

Beth Simmons is Associate Professor of Political Science at University of California, Berkeley.

Arthur A. Stein is Professor of Political Science at the University of California, Los Angeles.

Alexander Wendt is Associate Professor of Government at Dartmouth College, Hanover, New Hampshire.

Abstracts

Anarchy and the Limits of Cooperation: A Realist Critique of the Newest Liberal Institutionalism (1988)
by Joseph M. Grieco

The newest liberal institutionalism asserts that, although it accepts a major realist proposition that international anarchy impedes cooperation among states, it can nevertheless affirm the central tenets of the liberal institutionalist tradition that states can achieve cooperation and that international institutions can help them work together. However, this essay's principal argument is that neoliberal institutionalism misconstrues the realist analysis of international anarchy and therefore it misunderstands realism's analysis of the inhibiting effects of anarchy on the willingness of states to cooperate. This essay highlights the profound divergences between realism and the newest liberal institutionalism. It also argues that the former is likely to be proven analytically superior to the latter.

Taking Preferences Seriously: A Liberal Theory of International Politics (1997)
by Andrew Moravcsik

This article reformulates liberal international relations (IR) theory in nonideological and non-utopian form appropriate to empirical social science. Liberal IR theory elaborates the basic insight that state-society relations—the relationship between governments and the domestic and transnational social context in which they are embedded—are the most fundamental determinant of state behavior in world politics. In the liberal view state-society relations influence state behavior by shaping "national preferences"—the fundamental social purposes that underlie state strategies—not, as realism argues, the configuration of national capabilities and not, as institutionalist regime theory maintains, the configuration of information and institutions. This article codifies this basic liberal insight in the form of three core analytical propositions, derives from these propositions three variants of liberal theory, and demonstrates that the existence of a coherent liberal theory has significant theoretical, methodological, and empirical implications. These implications include the existence of significant omitted variable bias in recent realist and constructivist studies, and the analytical priority of liberal theory, which emerges as the most fundamental among major IR theories because it defines and explains the conditions under which realist and institutionalist, as well as constructivist, factors matter.

Anarchy Is What States Make of It: The Social Construction of Power Politics (1992)
by Alexander Wendt

The claim that international institutions can transform state interests is central to neoliberal challenges to the realist assumption that "process" (interaction and learning among states) cannot fundamentally affect system "structure" (anarchy and the distribution of capabilities). Systematic development of this claim, however, has been hampered by the neoliberals' commitment to rational choice theory, which treats interests as exogenously given and thus offers only a weak form of institutional analysis. A growing body of international relations scholarship points to ways in which the identities and interests of states are socially constructed by knowledgeable practice. This article builds a bridge between this scholarship and neoliberalism by developing a theory of identity- and interest-formation in support of the neoliberal claim that international institutions can transform state interests. Its substantive focus is the realist view that anarchies are necessarily self-help systems, which justifies disinterest in processes of identity- and interest-formation. Self-help is a function not of anarchy but of process and, as such, is itself an institution that determines the meaning of anarchy and the distribution of power for state action. The article concludes with an examination of how this institution can be transformed by practices of sovereignty, by an evolution of cooperation, and by critical strategic practice.

Globalization and the Changing Logic of Collective Action (1995)
by Philip G. Cerny

Globalization transforms collective action in domestic and international politics. As the scale of markets widens and as economic organization becomes more complex, the institutional scale of political structures can become insufficient for the provision of an appropriate range of public goods. A process of this sort occurred prior to the emergence of the modern nation-state, which itself constituted a paradigmatic response to this predicament. Today, however, a complex process of globalization of goods and assets is undermining the effectiveness of state-based collective action. Overlapping "playing fields" are developing, made up of increasingly heterogeneous—transnational, local, and intermediate—arenas. The residual state retains great cultural force, and innovative projects for reinventing government are being tried. Nevertheless, the state's effectiveness as a civil association has eroded significantly, and this may lead to a crisis of legitimacy.

The Demand for International Regimes (1982)
by Robert O. Keohane

International regimes can be understood as results of rational behavior by the actors—principally states—that create them. Regimes are demanded in part because they facilitate the making of agreements, by providing information and reducing transactions costs in world politics. Increased interdependence among issues—greater "issue density"—will lead to increased demand for regimes. Insofar as regimes succeed in providing high quality information, through such processes as the construction of generally accepted norms or the development of transgovernmental relations, they create demand for their own continuance, even if the structural conditions (such as hegemony) under which they were first supplied, change. Analysis of the demand for international regimes thus helps us to understand lags between structural change and regime change, as well as to assess the significance of transgovernmental policy networks. Several assertions of structural theory seem problematic in light of this analysis. Hegemony may not be a necessary condition for stable international regimes; past patterns of institutionalized cooperation may be able to compensate, to some extent, for increasing fragmentation of power.

Theories of International Regimes (1987)
by Stephan Haggard and Beth A. Simmons

Over the last decade, international regimes have become a major focus of empirical research and theoretical debate within international relations. This article provides a critical review of this literature. We survey contending definitions of regimes and suggest dimensions along which regimes vary over time or across cases; these dimensions might be used to operationalize "regime change." We then examine four approaches to regime analysis: structural, game-theoretic, functional, and cognitive. We conclude that the major shortcoming of the regimes literature is its failure to incorporate domestic politics adequately. We suggest a research program that begins with the central insights of the interdependence literature which have been ignored in the effort to construct "systemic" theory.

Regime Design Matters: Intentional Oil Pollution and Treaty Compliance (1994)
by Ronald B. Mitchell

Whether a treaty elicits compliance from governments or nonstate actors depends upon identifiable characteristics of the regime's compliance systems. Within the international regime controlling intentional oil pollution, a provision requiring tanker owners to install specified equipment produced dramatically higher levels of compliance than a provision requiring tanker operators to limit their discharges. Since both provisions entailed strong economic incentives for violation and regulated the same countries over the same time period, the variance in compliance clearly can be attributed to different features of the two subregimes. The equipment requirements' success stemmed from establishing an integrated compliance system that increased transparency, provided for potent and credible sanctions, reduced implementation costs to governments by building on existing infrastructures, and prevented violations rather than merely deterring them.

International Regimes, Transactions, and Change: Embedded Liberalism in the Postwar Economic Order (1982)
by John Gerard Ruggie

The prevailing model of international economic regimes is strictly positivistic in its epistemological orientation and stresses the distribution of material power capabilities in its explanatory logic. It is inadequate to account for the current set of international economic regimes and for the differences between past and present regimes. The model elaborated here departs from the prevailing view in two respects, while adhering to it in a third. First, it argues that regimes comprise not simply what actors say and do, but also what they understand and find acceptable within an intersubjective framework of meaning. Second, it argues that in the economic realm such a framework of meaning cannot be deduced from the distribution of material power capabilities, but must be sought in the configuration of state-society relations that is characteristic of the regime-making states. Third, in incorporating these notions into our understanding of the formation and transformation of international economic regimes, the formulation self-consciously strives to remain at the systemic level and to avoid becoming reductionist in attributing cause and effect relations. The article can therefore argue that the prevailing view is deficient on its own terms and must be expanded and modified. Addressing the world of actual international economic regimes, the article argues that the *pax Britannica* and the *pax Americana* cannot be equated in any meaningful sense, and that the postwar regimes for money and trade live on notwithstanding premature announcements of their demise.

The Hegemon's Dilemma: Great Britain, the United States, and the International Economic Order (1984)
by Arthur A. Stein

Liberal international trade regimes do not emerge from the policies of one state, even a hegemonic one. Trade liberalization among major trading states is, rather, the product of tariff bargains. Thus, hegemons need followers and must make concessions to obtain agreements. The liberal trade regimes that emerged in both the 19th and the 20th centuries were founded on asymmetric bargains that permitted discrimination, especially against the hegemon. The agreements that lowered tariff barriers led to freer trade not free trade; resulted in subsystemic rather than global orders; and legitimated mercantilistic and protectionist practices of exclusion and discrimination, and thus did not provide a collective good. Moreover, these trade agreements (and trade disputes as well) had inherently international political underpinnings and did not reflect economic interests alone. Trade liberalization also required a certain internal strength on the part of the government. Furthermore, only a complete political rupturing of relations, such as occurs in wartime, can destroy such a regime. A hegemon's decline cannot do so alone. These arguments are developed in a historical reassessment of the evolution of the international trading order since 1820. Eras commonly seen as liberal, such as the 1860s, are shown to have included a good deal of protection, and eras seen as protectionist, such as the 1880s, are shown to have been much more liberal than is usually believed.

Interests, Power, and Multilateralism (1992)
by Lisa L. Martin

Multilateralism characterizes, to varying degrees, patterns of interaction among states and the formal organizations they construct. The utility of multilateral norms or organizations varies with the type of cooperation problem states confront. Thus, the functional logic of international cooperation leads to hypotheses about the conditions under which the institution of multilateralism may be a feasible and efficient solution, as in coordination problems, and those under which it will not, as in collaboration problems. Within these constraints, powerful states choose institutions that will serve their interests, with multilateral arrangements becoming more attractive as the future is valued more highly. Multilateral institutions should be stable in circumstances of changing distributions of power, relative to more hierarchical institutions. The vulnerability of patterns of international cooperation to various exogenous changes depends on the type of strategic interaction underlying state behavior.

Diplomacy and Domestic Politics: The Logic of Two-Level Games (1988)
by Robert D. Putnam

Domestic politics and international relations are often inextricably entangled, but existing theories (particularly "state-centric" theories) do not adequately account for these linkages. When national leaders must win ratification (formal or informal) from their constituents for an international agreement, their negotiating behavior reflects the simultaneous imperatives of both a domestic political game and an international game. Using illustrations from Western economic summitry, the Panama Canal and Versailles Treaty negotiations, IMF stabilization programs, the European Community, and many other diplomatic contexts, this article offers a theory of ratification. It addresses the role of domestic preferences and coalitions, domestic political institutions and practices, the strategies and tactics of negotiators, uncertainty, the domestic reverberation of international pressures, and the interests of the chief negotiator. This theory of "two-level games" may also be applicable to many other political phenomena, such as dependency, legislative committees, and multiparty coalitions.

Public Goods and Political Institutions: Trade and Monetary Policy Processes in the United States (1988)
by Joanne Gowa

Basic analytic premises vary widely in the existing literature on the U.S. foreign economic policy process. In an effort to clarify ongoing debate, this article applies to the arena of foreign economic policymaking the logic of collective action, as affected by the specific institutions of the U.S. policy process. This approach requires a conception of American trade and international monetary policy as political goods whose susceptibility to collective action is a function both of characteristics inherent in those goods and of the institutional framework within which they are produced.

An analysis of incentives for collective action rises red flags for issue-area typologies and for state and society models of the policy process. Emphasis on the variable publicness of trade and monetary policy tends to vitiate the logic of state and society distinctions; attention to the role of political institutions in establishing the public or "quasi" public character of goods in the political marketplace partly—but only partly—resurrects it. The U.S. case raises warning flags for both because it makes clear that the defining characteristics of issues are neither obvious nor immutable, and it simultaneously demonstrates how easily allegedly "weak" states can metamorphose into "strong" states as the public character of political goods varies.

Domestic Institutions and the Credibility of International Commitments: Japan and the United States (1993)
by Peter F. Cowhey

The domestic politics of great powers significantly influence the fate of such multilateral regimes as the General Agreement on Tariffs and Trade and the North Atlantic Treaty Organization. Unless great powers can make credible commitments to support those regimes, few countries will offer more than token support. Domestic political constraints may bind national leaders to good faith adherence to multilateral regimes even if international circumstances do not compel adherence. Domestic politics also influence the ability of other countries to monitor national adherence to agreements. Case studies of U.S. and Japanese responses to multilateral regimes show how the nature of the national electoral system, the division of powers in the government, and the transparency of the national political system influence credibility and lead to special features of multilateral economic and security regimes.

Preface

Charles Lipson and Benjamin J. Cohen

On most days, the headlines report a dizzying range of international stories. Japan is negotiating with China over rights to trade and invest in that huge market. The United States is grumbling about European agricultural subsidies, which hurt farmers in the American Midwest. A German auto firm, hoping to increase its exports to the United States and Canada, has just cut the ribbon on a new factory in Mexico; its workers back in Europe complain they are losing good jobs to low-wage countries. High-technology firms in the Silicon Valley are also concerned about less-developed countries but for a different reason; they are losing royalties because their software is being pirated. They demand action from Congress and the World Trade Organization. Another news story considers a conference on global warming, bringing together biologists, meteorologists, and government planners. Sitting on the sidelines are business executives and workers, worried that more restrictive environmental rules will come at their expense.

In one way or another, all these news stories deal with the very essence of international politics. They tell of commercial transactions across borders, the emergence of new issues and new constituencies, and the development of strong economic ties among individuals and firms in different countries. But how can such a wide range of issues and such a diverse group of actors be drawn together into a coherent depiction of international affairs? What are the basic relationships? What is the fundamental structure?

These questions go to the heart of the field of international political economy. The study of international political economy may be conducted at either of two levels: fundamental theory and structure or concrete issues and actors. International Organization has been at the forefront of intellectual development at both levels, producing much of the literature that has successfully stimulated and shaped thinking by specialists in the field. A companion to this volume, Issues and Agents in International Political Economy, reproduces key contributions at the latter level. This volume provides a sample of influential articles focusing more broadly on matters of basic theory and structure, offering powerful generalizations and insights for students and scholars alike.

The broad theoretical orientation of the volume is particularly clear in the first section, which is organized around four contrasting perspectives on international *politics and political economy. Joseph Grieco states the realist position in Chapter 1. Although realism is widely used to analyze security issues, Grieco makes a strong argument that its insights apply equally well to international political economy. Realist theories, including Grieco's, are sharply contested by other approaches, as the next three chapters make clear. Andrew Moravcsik, Alexander Wendt, and Philip Cerny each develop a distinctive theoretical position with broad relevance to issues in international political economy. What they have in common is their rejection of realism's heavy emphasis on security issues and national military power.*

Moravcsik (Chapter 2) seeks to construct a theory of international politics grounded in the basic tenets of liberal political philosophy, with its emphasis on individuals and voluntary associations. Moravcsik argues that it is these social actors—and not the state itself—that should be considered the basic actors in international politics. Wendt (Chapter 3) argues that "anarchy"—one of the central concepts in international relations—has been misunderstood. He concludes that states have the capacity to reconceive their relationships, to make their anarchic environment more or less hostile. Cerny (Chapter 4) shifts the emphasis away from states as the exclusive actors in international affairs. He contends that multinational firms and banks also play a vital role in many economic issues. They not only influence government policies but also may be important international actors in their own right. Cerny concludes that the vast expansion of multinational business and the ease of modern communications amount to a fundamental transformation, which he calls "globalization."

Section II deals with one of the most developed subfields of international political economy: theories of international regimes. In many ways this is a continuation of the earlier section on theoretical perspectives, but we have given it its own section because it is the subject of so much important work. It is also a topic closely associated with International Organization, *where many of the seminal articles were published.*

Regimes, in Stephen Krasner's well-known definition, are "sets of implicit or explicit principles, norms, rules, and decision-making procedures around which actors' expectations converge in a given area of international relations."[1] That definition, and the 1982 special issue of International Organization *in which it appeared, have had an important impact on research in international political economy. To begin with, they shifted attention away from specific international organizations like the UN and toward broader patterns of international order and change. They also stimulated a vast outpouring of serious empirical work, built around common definitions and conceptions.*

Indeed, one major reason why regime theory has been so important is that so many empirical studies have fleshed out the argument and refined it. They show that international cooperation and governance structures are important in a wide range of issues, particularly key aspects of the world economy like trade and monetary relations. These studies challenge the notion that only one international structure exists

---

1. Krasner 1983, 2.

or that only military resources matter. They emphasize instead how state capabilities vary across different issues and produce very different institutional arrangements.

In Section II we include several major contributions to this literature. Robert Keohane (Chapter 5) asks why states might want to construct regimes rather than simply make specific agreements as needed. His argument is that it is easier and cheaper to negotiate individual agreements once the overarching rules and proce-dures are in place. Since it is costly to construct these basic rules and procedures, however, it makes sense to develop them in those issues where many more individual agreements are expected. In Chapter 6, Stephan Haggard and Beth Simmons evalu-ate the entire research effort on regimes and critique the major findings and debates in the field. Ronald Mitchell's study of pollution by oil tankers (Chapter 7) shows how policymakers design regimes to deal with particular problems.

Section III turns to the place of multilateral organizations in the world's economy and to the role of the leading states within these organizations. Some scholars have argued that the world economy is typically more open and stable when it is domi-nated by one major power—a "hegemon." The theory of hegemonic stability, as it is known, has been hotly contested. Important contributions to that debate appear here in chapters by John Ruggie (Chapter 8) and Arthur Stein (Chapter 9). Ruggie ob-serves that too much of the analysis has been about raw power, too little about the purposes that leading actors pursue. He shows that America's goals since World War II have been fundamentally different from those of nineteenth-century Britain, which is usually named as the other leading economic power of modern times. Ruggie's point is that we cannot understand the basic features of international political economy unless we also understand these purposes and beliefs. The world economy, he con-cludes, is embedded in this wider political context, made up of purposes and mean-ings as well as power.

Stein extends this comparison between the United States and Great Britain, focus-ing on a paradox of international leadership. The more successful these leading states are in establishing an open world economy, the more they foster economic growth in rival countries. The result, Stein says, is a dilemma for the hegemon. Should it continue its liberal international policies even if others benefit dispropor-tionately?

Lisa Martin (Chapter 10) is concerned with other aspects of international organi-zation. She is particularly interested in showing how multilateral organizations must confront different kinds of problems. It is the strategic logic of these different prob-lems, she argues, that shapes the organizations themselves.

The last three chapters (Section IV) turn to the connection between the world economy and domestic politics—clearly, an important two-way linkage. Not only do domestic interests shape international politics, but the reverse is also true: the wider context of international politics shapes domestic interests. That is, domestic actors and institutions are deeply affected by events in the wider world, by imports and exports, by devaluations, by foreign investment and loans, and by economic growth or recession abroad. Because these linkages are so complex, theorists typically focus on a few crucial aspects.

One of the most influential studies is by Robert Putnam, who concentrates on the linkage between domestic and international economic negotiations (Chapter 11). Putnam's central insight is that successful diplomatic negotiations must win approval at home, just as many domestic policies can succeed only if they receive support abroad. This means that negotiations must often seek solutions in two "games" at once: in national politics and at the diplomatic negotiating table.

Joanne Gowa (Chapter 12) and Peter Cowhey (Chapter 13) focus on structural features of domestic politics that affect international political economy. Gowa asks why trade politics is so dominated by interest groups while monetary relations, which are equally important, are rarely the object of lobbyists. The answer, she explains, is that trade politics can be divided into small slices—slices that directly affect a small number of actors who have powerful incentives to make their views known. International monetary affairs, on the other hand, deals with a few large issues (such as the value of currencies) that affect millions of actors. Mobilizing constituents and lobbying politicians in all issues is costly; and in large, indivisible issues like exchange rates, few actors have strong enough individual incentives to do so. In short, a serious collective-action problem exists in monetary affairs that has no counterpart in trade.

Peter Cowhey analyzes another feature of domestic politics: the ability of governments to make credible international promises. This issue is important because almost all international agreements rest, at bottom, on national promises. Rarely are there third parties willing and able to step in and enforce others' bargains. Cowhey's point is that some domestic political arrangements make for more credible promises. Promises are most believable and reliable when they are hard to reverse. According to Cowhey, that scenario is more likely in democracies with divided powers like the United States than in parliamentary systems like Japan.

Taken together, these chapters show the range and vigor of theoretical work in international political economy.

References

Stephen D. Krasner, ed. 1983. *International Regimes*. Ithaca, N.Y.: Cornell University Press. (Originally published as *International Organization* 36 (2)).

I.
Contending Theoretical Perspectives

International political economy stands at the intersection of world politics and economics. Theories about it are designed to clarify underlying structures, relationships among key actors, and the pattern of outcomes—and to do all that in simple, powerful ways.

Such theories inevitably speak to the largest and most profound questions about all international relations. Consider the growing economic ties among nations. The rise of such interdependence affects domestic producers, consumers, states, and interstate relations. Crucial areas of government, such as the formulation of monetary policy, may slip away from effective national control. What were once purely domestic issues, such as minimum wages and working conditions, are less easily regulated because they bear on international competitiveness. As a result, when we analyze economic interdependence, we must also analyze how countries cope with such diverse challenges to their sovereignty. Likewise, to study the politics of modern exchange rates, we must examine vast global markets, where central banks, commercial banks, and multinational corporations constantly buy and sell currencies. These are basic questions that bear on all theories of international relations.

When considering issues like these, does it make sense to simplify our theories by limiting them to nation-states? Or should we broaden them to include a wider range of actors such as firms, banks, interest groups, and international organizations, even if that makes the theory much more complicated? How should we understand the creation of international order in issues like these? How broad in scope should our theories be? Should they, for example, focus tightly on specific issues like trade, investment, or exchange rates? Or should we cast our net wider, trying to understand common themes about order and change as they apply to the entire global economy?

Theories of international political economy—indeed, all theories of international politics—must confront serious questions like these. The chapters in this section represent four very different approaches to these questions. Perhaps the best way to understand these approaches is to look first at "realism," the oldest and most developed theory of international relations.

With a heritage drawn from Thucydides, Machiavelli, and Hobbes, realism emphasizes the role of power politics and military force. Its modern formulation develops these themes in more scientific terms, with a special emphasis on the distribution of global power resources. For that reason, it is often called "structural realism," or neorealism.

For all realists, the world is a dangerous place. It is anarchic in the straightfor-ward sense that no world government can set rules for and impose punishments on nations, firms, or individuals. This view is closely connected to the importance of state sovereignty. In a world dominated by security concerns and power politics, sovereign states are the only actors of real importance.

The absence of world government has other crucial implications. It means, for instance, that all states must develop their own means of self-protection. They may make alliances, realists say, but they cannot prudently rely on others. Because states have similar security needs and must rely on themselves, they cannot specialize as domestic actors can. In modern economies, firms and workers are highly specialized, bound together by extensive networks of exchange. Not so in the harsh world of international anarchy. It pushes states away from such interdependence, away from specialization, and toward similarity, in both state characteristics and policy choices. That, at least, is the theoretical argument.

What does differentiate states is their power resources. All states may have to defend themselves, but not all are equally well equipped to do so. For structural realists, we can characterize world politics succinctly by looking at the global distribution of power resources. Crucial differences exists between a world dominated by two powers, such as the superpowers during the Cold War, and one where several Great Powers compete and cooperate, such as the Concert of Europe in the nineteenth century.

For realists, it is this basic structure of world politics—bipolarity versus multipo-larity, for instance—that guides the interactions of states and determines outcomes. Of course, states may want to pursue their own distinctive goals. That desire is hardly surprising; they have different governments, ideologies, religions, interest groups, and so on. But whatever their individual aims, they are tightly constrained by the underlying structure of international politics and the unrelenting demands of anarchy. International interactions are thus the product of global structure, defined as the distribution of power and resources.

Although realism was developed to answer perennial questions about war and national security, it has important implications for the study of international political economy. It implies, for example, that

- *Anarchy is a harsh, unchanging condition of international life.*

- *States are by far the most important international actors; other actors, such as multinational enterprises, pale by comparison; for simplicity's sake, they can be ignored entirely.*

- *States, constrained by international structure, have little real choice over their policies and even less control over outcomes.*

- *A single international structure, based mainly on state military capabilities, shapes interactions across a wide range of issues.*

- *Governance is extremely weak at the international level, and institutions have little impact.*

- *Connections across national boundaries, such as those of multinational firms, international religions, or common ethnicity, are not especially important to world politics.*

Each of these assertions is controversial, and all of them are vigorously debated in the first section of this volume. Indeed, the entire field of international political economy has developed as a sustained engagement with these basic theoretical issues. Who are the key actors in international politics? What kinds of resources do they bring to bear? How feasible is international cooperation? Why is cooperation prevalent in some issues but not others? Why is cooperation found at some times, among some states, but not others? How much scope is there for policy choices? Are these choices ultimately determined by the tight constraints of international structure or by the preferences of domestic actors?

The first chapter, by Joseph M. Grieco, is important because it clearly explains the key features of modern realism and then teases out one particularly important implication about cooperation. If self-help and security concerns are as important as realists say, states will not only seek their own advantage, they will also be concerned about whether potential rivals gain more. Grieco does not argue that "absolute gains" are irrelevant. He acknowledges their importance. But, as a realist, he says that security competition also highlights the significance of "relative gains" (that is, gains or losses relative to a potential adversary). He concludes that this attention to relative gains is yet another obstacle to international cooperation. As he puts it, "Realism's identification of the relative gains problem for cooperation is based on its insight that states in anarchy fear for their survival as independent actors. According to realists, states worry that today's friend may be tomorrow's enemy."

Andrew Moravcsik (Chapter 2) responds not merely with a critique but with an alternative theory, drawing on the rich tradition of liberal political philosophy. Like many critics of realism, Moravcsik argues that states are not so tightly bound by international structures. They have not only distinctive preferences but also room to make real choices. The task of theory is to understand why states make the choices they do and, equally important, how choices made by different states interact to produce international outcomes. Moravcsik calls this ambitious agenda a "liberal theory" because it is grounded in the pulling and hauling of domestic politics.

Moravcsik builds his theory around three key assumptions. First, the fundamental actors are not states but individuals, firms, and private groups. Second, some of these social actors are favored in the formation of state policies. Social pressures, transmitted through government institutions, are the foundation of states' preferences. Third, in choosing which actions to take, states must also consider other states' preferences and likely behavior. In other words, they do not simply translate their individual preferences into action; they must consider what others are doing and how their choices might interact.

Alexander Wendt (Chapter 3) is less concerned about how states choose policies than in how they form their identities as actors. The key point for Wendt is that states form their self-conceptions not in isolation but through interactions with each other. "Identities," he says, "are inherently relational." For instance, the war for Texas in 1848 did much to frame the identities of both Mexico and the United States. The loss of Alsace and Lorraine in 1870–71 played a powerful role in determining the identities of both France and Germany and their deep-seated opposition. If national conceptions are determined through interactions like these, it is misleading to think that anarchy is a uniform, unchanging constraint on states. True, states may lack global government. But theirs is not an unchanging anarchy; it is shaped by their own actions and by their understandings of themselves and each other. Wendt explicitly rejects the neorealist claim that "self-help is given by anarchic structure exogenously to process."

Different international processes and understandings can lead to very different collective outcomes. That may well produce the world neorealists depict: a harsh competitive environment of self-help. But it need not. States, Wendt argues, can transform their understandings of themselves and each other and produce more benign and cooperative international environments. Because this approach emphasizes states' ability to construct and interpret their social environment, it is usually called "constructivism" or "interpretivism." Wendt puts one of its central themes elegantly: "Anarchy," he says, "is what states make of it."

For all its criticism of structural approaches, Wendt's analysis does share at least one perspective with neorealism. Both are focused on the state. Moravcsik moves away from that focus since individuals and interest groups are central to his liberal theory. These social actors are the fundamental sources of foreign policy. But once policies are chosen, it is states—and only states—that act at the international level.

That view is unduly narrow, says Philip Cerny (Chapter 4). What is striking about modern international politics, he contends, is the global reach of so many societal actors, at least in recent years. With cheap, instantaneous communications and lower barriers to commerce, firms, groups, and individuals have developed more and more contacts across national boundaries. The issue, however, is not just that firms and groups increasingly act at the international level. The international level itself is transformed in a process labeled "globalization." The rising volume and significance of cross-border transactions change the political environment in very basic ways.

Globalization is so important, Cerny says, that it constitutes a third industrial revolution. It is grounded in new ways of organizing production, such as flexible manufacturing, lean management with less bureaucracy, intensive use of information technology, and reliance on new, global financial markets. Taken together, these changes are as fundamental as the first industrial revolution based on textiles, steam engines, and railroads, or the second industrial revolution, based on large-scale production of chemicals, petroleum, electricity, and automobiles. Like those earlier changes, the newest changes in the world economy will have a profound effect on the role of states as well as on interstate relations.

Cerny's and Moravcsik's arguments bear on one of the central issues in international political economy: who are the actors in world politics? Debate over this issue has raged since the 1971 publication of a special issue of International Organization *devoted to transnational actors.[1]*

These, then, are four distinctive approaches to international political economy: neorealism, liberalism, constructivism, and globalism. All of them are debated and explored in the pages of International Organization.

References

Joseph S. Nye, Jr., and Robert O. Keohane, eds. 1971. Transnational Relations and World Politics. *International Organization* 25 (3). Special issue.

1. Keohane and Nye 1971.

Anarchy and the limits of cooperation: a realist critique of the newest liberal institutionalism
Joseph M. Grieco

Realism has dominated international relations theory at least since World War II.[1] For realists, international anarchy fosters competition and conflict among states and inhibits their willingness to cooperate even when they share common interests. Realist theory also argues that international institutions are unable to mitigate anarchy's constraining effects on inter-state cooperation. Realism, then, presents a pessimistic analysis of the prospects for international cooperation and of the capabilities of international institutions.[2]

For their helpful comments on this essay, I thank Louise Hodgden, Ole Holsti, Robert Jervis, Robert Keohane, Stephen Krasner, Joseph Nye, Stephen Van Evera, Kenneth Waltz, and especially John Mearsheimer. For their financial support during preparation of earlier drafts, I am grateful to the German–Marshall Fund of the United States and the Center for International Affairs at Harvard University. Of course, I remain responsible for all statements in the essay.

1. Major realist works include: E. H. Carr, *The Twenty Years Crisis, 1919–1939: An Introduction to the Study of International Relations* (London and New York: Harper Torchbooks, 1964); Hans J. Morgenthau, *Politics Among Nations: The Struggle for Power and Peace*, 5th ed. (New York: Knopf, 1973); Raymond Aron, *International Relations: A Theory of Peace and War*, trans. Richard Howard and Annette Baker Fox (Garden City, N.J.: Doubleday, 1973); Kenneth N. Waltz, *Man, the State, and War: A Theoretical Analysis* (New York: Columbia University Press, 1959); Waltz, *Theory of International Politics* (Reading, Mass.: Addison-Wesley, 1979); Robert Gilpin, *U.S. Power and the Multinational Corporation: The Political Economy of Foreign Direct Investment* (New York: Basic Books, 1975); and Gilpin, *War and Change in World Politics* (Cambridge: Cambridge University Press, 1981). This essay does not distinguish between realism and "neorealism," because on crucial issues—the meaning of international anarchy, its effects on states, and the problem of cooperation—modern realists like Waltz and Gilpin are very much in accord with classical realists like Carr, Aron, and Morgenthau. For an alternative view, see Richard Ashley, "The Poverty of Neorealism," in Robert O. Keohane, ed., *Neorealism and Its Critics* (New York: Columbia University Press, 1986), pp. 255–300.

2. Richard Rosecrance provided the insight that realism presents an essentially pessimistic view of the human condition: this is noted by Robert Gilpin, "The Richness of the Tradition of Political Realism," in Keohane, ed., *Neorealism and Its Critics*, p. 304. This pessimism in realist theory is most clearly evident in Hans J. Morgenthau, *Scientific Man vs. Power Politics* (Chicago: University of Chicago Press, 1946), especially pp. 187–203.

International Organization 42, 3, Summer 1988, pp. 485–507

The major challenger to realism has been what I shall call liberal institutionalism. Prior to the current decade, it appeared in three successive presentations—functionalist integration theory in the 1940s and early 1950s, neofunctionalist regional integration theory in the 1950s and 1960s, and interdependence theory in the 1970s.[3] All three versions rejected realism's propositions about states and its gloomy understanding of world politics. Most significantly, they argued that international institutions can help states cooperate. Thus, compared to realism, these earlier versions of liberal institutionalism offered a more hopeful prognosis for international cooperation and a more optimistic assessment of the capacity of institutions to help states achieve it.

International tensions and conflicts during the 1970s undermined liberal institutionalism and reconfirmed realism in large measure. Yet, that difficult decade did not witness a collapse of the international system, and, in the light of continuing modest levels of inter-state cooperation, a new liberal institutionalist challenge to realism came forward during the early 1980s.[4] What is distinctive about this newest liberal institutionalism is its claim that it accepts a number of core realist propositions, including, apparently, the realist argument that anarchy impedes the achievement of international cooperation. However, the core liberal arguments—that realism overemphasizes conflict and underestimates the capacities of international institutions to promote cooperation—remain firmly intact. The new liberal institutionalists basically argue that even if the realists are correct in believing that anarchy constrains the willingness of states to cooperate, states nevertheless can work together and can do so especially with the assistance of international institutions.

This point is crucial for students of international relations. If neoliberal

3. For functionalist international theory, see David Mitrany, *A Working Peace System* (Chicago: Quadrangle Press, 1966); see also Ernst B. Haas, *Beyond the Nation-State: Functionalism and International Organization* (Stanford, Calif.: Stanford University Press, 1964). On neofunctionalism, see Haas, *The Uniting of Europe: Political, Economic, and Social Forces, 1950–1957* (Stanford, Calif.: Stanford University Press, 1958); Haas, "Technology, Pluralism, and the New Europe," in Joseph S. Nye, Jr., ed., *International Regionalism* (Boston: Little, Brown, 1968), pp. 149–76; and Joseph S. Nye, Jr., "Comparing Common Markets: A Revised Neo-Functional Model," in Leon N. Lindberg and Stuart A. Scheingold, eds., *Regional Integration: Theory and Research* (Cambridge: Harvard University Press, 1971), pp. 192–231. On interdependence theory, see Richard C. Cooper, "Economic Interdependence and Foreign Policies in the 1970's," *World Politics* 24 (January 1972), pp. 158–81; Edward S. Morse, "The Transformation of Foreign Policies: Modernization, Interdependence, and Externalization," *World Politics* 22 (April 1970), pp. 371–92; and Robert O. Keohane and Joseph S. Nye, Jr., *Power and Interdependence: World Politics in Transition* (Boston: Little, Brown, 1977).

4. See Robert Axelrod, *The Evolution of Cooperation* (New York: Basic Books, 1984); Axelrod and Robert O. Keohane, "Achieving Cooperation Under Anarchy: Strategies and Institutions," *World Politics* 38 (October 1985), pp. 226–54; Keohane, *After Hegemony: Cooperation and Discord in the World Political Economy* (Princeton, N.J.: Princeton University Press, 1984); Charles Lipson, "International Cooperation in Economic and Security Affairs," *World Politics* 37 (October 1984), pp. 1–23; and Arthur Stein, "Coordination and Collaboration: Regimes in an Anarchic World," in Stephen D. Krasner, ed., *International Regimes* (Ithaca, N.Y.: Cornell University Press, 1983), pp. 115–40.

institutionalists are correct, then they have dealt realism a major blow while providing the intellectual justification for treating their own approach, and the tradition from which it emerges, as the most effective for understanding world politics.

This essay's principal argument is that, in fact, neoliberal institutionalism misconstrues the realist analysis of international anarchy and therefore it misunderstands the realist analysis of the impact of anarchy on the preferences and actions of states. Indeed, the new liberal institutionalism fails to address a major constraint on the willingness of states to cooperate which is generated by international anarchy and which is identified by realism. As a result, the new theory's optimism about international cooperation is likely to be proven wrong.

Neoliberalism's claims about cooperation are based on its belief that states are atomistic actors. It argues that states seek to maximize their individual *absolute* gains and are indifferent to the gains achieved by others. Cheating, the new theory suggests, is the greatest impediment to cooperation among rationally egoistic states, but international institutions, the new theory also suggests, can help states overcome this barrier to joint action. Realists understand that states seek absolute gains and worry about compliance. However, realists find that states are *positional*, not atomistic, in character, and therefore realists argue that, in addition to concerns about cheating, states in cooperative arrangements also worry that their partners might gain more from cooperation than they do. For realists, a state will focus both on its absolute and relative gains from cooperation, and a state that is satisfied with a partner's compliance in a joint arrangement might nevertheless exit from it because the partner is achieving relatively greater gains. Realism, then, finds that there are at least two major barriers to international cooperation: state concerns about cheating and state concerns about relative achievements of gains. Neoliberal institutionalism pays attention exclusively to the former, and is unable to identify, analyze, or account for the latter.

Realism's identification of the relative gains problem for cooperation is based on its insight that states in anarchy fear for their survival as independent actors. According to realists, states worry that today's friend may be tomorrow's enemy in war, and fear that achievements of joint gains that advantage a friend in the present might produce a more dangerous *potential* foe in the future. As a result, states must give serious attention to the gains of partners. Neoliberals fail to consider the threat of war arising from international anarchy, and this allows them to ignore the matter of relative gains and to assume that states only desire absolute gains. Yet, in doing so, they fail to identify a major source of state inhibitions about international cooperation.

In sum, I suggest that realism, its emphasis on conflict and competition notwithstanding, offers a more complete understanding of the problem of international cooperation than does its latest liberal challenger. If that is true, then realism is still the most powerful theory of international politics.

1. Realism and liberal institutionalism

Realism encompasses five propositions. First, states are the major actors in world affairs.[5] Second, the international environment severely penalizes states if they fail to protect their vital interests or if they pursue objectives beyond their means; hence, states are "sensitive to costs" and behave as unitary–rational agents.[6] Third, international anarchy is the principal force shaping the motives and actions of states.[7] Fourth, states in anarchy are preoccupied with power and security, are predisposed towards conflict and competition, and often fail to cooperate even in the face of common interests.[8] Finally, international institutions affect the prospects for cooperation only marginally.[9]

Liberal institutionalists sought to refute this realist understanding of world politics.[10] First, they rejected realism's proposition about the centrality of states.[11] For functionalists, the key new actors in world politics appeared

5. Morgenthau, *Politics Among Nations*, p. 10; see also Waltz, *Theory of International Politics*, p. 95.

6. Waltz, "Reflections on *Theory of International Politics:* A Response to My Critics," in Keohane, ed., *Neorealism and Its Critics*, p. 331.

7. Waltz, *Man, State, and War*, pp. 224–38; and Waltz, *Theory of International Politics*, pp. 79–128; Stanley Hoffmann, *The State of War: Essays in the Theory and Practice of International Politics* (New York: Praeger, 1965), pp. 27, 54–87, 129; Aron, *Peace and War*, pp. 6–10.

8. Aron, *Peace and War*, p. 5; Gilpin, "Political Realism," p. 304.

9. Waltz, *Theory of International Politics*, pp. 115–16; see also Morgenthau, *Politics Among Nations*, p. 512; and Stanley Hoffmann, "International Organization and the International System," in Leland M. Goodrich and David A. Kay, eds., *International Organization: Politics and Process* (Madison: University of Wisconsin Press, 1973), p. 50.

10. Liberal institutionalist theories may be distinguished from three other variants of liberal theory. One of these, trade liberalism, articulated by Richard Cobden and John Bright, finds that international commerce facilitates greater inter-state cooperation: for Cobden, see Arnold Wolfers and Laurence W. Martin, eds., *The Anglo-American Tradition in Foreign Affairs* (New Haven, Conn.: Yale University Press, 1956), pp. 192–205; with respect to both Cobden and Bright, see also Waltz, *Man, State, and War*, pp. 98–99, 103–7. A second variant, democratic structural liberalism, posited by Immanuel Kant and Woodrow Wilson, finds that democracies based on national self-determination are conducive to greater international cooperation. For Wilson, see Wolfers and Martin, eds., *Anglo-American Tradition*, pp. 263–79; for Kant and Wilson, see Waltz, *Man, State, and War*, pp. 101–3, 109–11, 117–19; and Michael W. Doyle, "Liberalism and World Politics," *American Political Science Review* 80 (December 1986), pp. 1151–69. Finally, a liberal transactions approach suggests that private international interactions promote international integration: see Karl Deutsch et al., *Political Community and the North Atlantic Area* (Princeton, N.J.: Princeton University Press, 1957); and Bruce Russett, *Community and Contention* (Cambridge, Mass.: MIT Press, 1963). Citing an unpublished study by Keohane, Nye recently refers to the first two variants as commercial and democratic liberalism, respectively, and suggests that the third might be termed sociological liberalism. See Joseph S. Nye, Jr., "Neorealism and Neoliberalism," *World Politics* 40 (January 1988), p. 246.

11. In a way quite different from liberal institutionalist theories, world systems analysis also challenges realism's focus on states. It suggests that they are not ultimate causes of world events but instead are themselves resultants of the development of a single world capitalist economy. See Immanuel Wallerstein, "The Rise and Future Demise of the World Capitalist System," in Wallerstein, *The Capitalist World System* (Cambridge: Cambridge University Press, 1979), pp. 1–37; and Wallerstein, *The Modern World System*, vol. 1 (New York: Academic Press, 1974).

to be specialized international agencies and their technical experts; for neo-functionalists, they were labor unions, political parties, trade associations, and supranational bureaucracies; and for the interdependence school, they were multinational corporations and transnational and transgovernmental coalitions.[12] Second, liberal institutionalists attacked the realist view that states are unitary or rational agents.[13] Authority was already decentralized within modern states, functionalists argued, and it was undergoing a similar process internationally.[14] Modern states, according to interdependence theorists, were increasingly characterized by "multiple channels of access," which, in turn, progressively enfeebled the grip on foreign policy previously held by central decision makers.[15]

Third, liberals argued that states were becoming less concerned about power and security. Internationally, nuclear weapons and mobilized national populations were rendering war prohibitively costly.[16] Moreover, increases in inter-nation economic contacts left states increasingly dependent upon one another for the attainment of such national goals as growth, full employment, and price stability.[17] Domestically, industrialization had created the present "social century": the advanced democracies (and, more slowly, socialist and developing countries) were becoming welfare states less oriented towards power and prestige and more towards economic growth and social security.[18] Thus, liberals rejected realism's fourth proposition that

12. See Mitrany, *Working Peace System*, pp. 17, 85–87, 133–34; Haas, *Beyond the Nation-State*, pp. 32–40; Haas, *Uniting of Europe*, pp. 16–31, 113–239, 283–340; Nye, "Comparing Common Markets," pp. 195–206; and Robert O. Keohane and Joseph S. Nye, Jr., "Introduction," and "Conclusion," in Keohane and Nye, eds., *Transnational Relations and World Politics* (Cambridge: Harvard University Press, 1972), pp. ix–xxix, 371–98.

13. A substantial body of literature that is not based on liberalism nevertheless shares the latter's skepticism about the unity and rationality of states. It finds that subsystemic forces, such as organizational and bureaucratic politics, small group dynamics, crisis decision-making, and individual psychology, all undermine state coherence and rationality. See Graham T. Allison, *Essence of Decision: Explaining the Cuban Missile Crisis* (Boston: Little, Brown, 1971); Irving J. Janis, *Groupthink*, 2d ed. (Boston: Houghton Mifflin, 1980); Ole R. Holsti, *Crisis Escalation War* (Montreal: McGill University Press, 1970); John D. Steinbruner, *The Cybernetic Theory of Decision* (Princeton, N.J.: Princeton University Press, 1974); Alexander L. and Juliette L. George, *Woodrow Wilson and Colonel House: A Personality Study* (New York: Dover, 1964); and Robert Jervis, *Perception and Misperception in World Politics* (Princeton, N.J.: Princeton University Press, 1976).

14. Mitrany, *Working Peace System*, pp. 54–55, 63, 69–73, 88, 134–38.

15. See Mitrany, *Working Peace System*, pp. 20, 32–38; Haas, "The New Europe," pp. 152, 155–56; Keohane and Nye, "Introduction," p. xxv, and "Conclusion," pp. 375–78; Morse, "Transformation," pp. 387–89; Cooper, "Interdependence," pp. 177, 179; and Keohane and Nye, *Power and Interdependence*, pp. 33–35, 226–29.

16. Mitrany, *Working Peace System*, p. 13; Morse, "Transformation," pp. 380–81; Keohane and Nye, *Power and Interdependence*, pp. 27–29, 228.

17. Mitrany, *Working Peace System*, pp. 131–37; Haas, "The New Europe," pp. 161–62; Cooper, "Interdependence," pp. 161–68, 173–74; Keohane and Nye, *Power and Interdependence*, pp. 26, 228.

18. See Mitrany, *Working Peace System*, pp. 41–42, 95–96, 136–37, 144–45; Haas, "The New Europe," pp. 155–58; Morse, "Transformation," pp. 383–85; and Keohane and Nye, *Power and Interdependence*, p. 227.

states are fundamentally disinclined to cooperate, finding instead that states increasingly viewed one another not as enemies, but instead as partners needed to secure greater comfort and well-being for their home publics.[19]

Finally, liberal institutionalists rejected realism's pessimism about international institutions. For functionalist theory, specialized agencies like the International Labor Organization could promote cooperation because they performed valuable tasks without frontally challenging state sovereignty.[20] For neofunctionalist theory, supranational bodies like the European Economic Community were "the appropriate regional counterpart to the national state which no longer feels capable of realizing welfare goals within its own narrow borders."[21] Finally, interdependence theory suggested that "in a world of multiple issues imperfectly linked, in which coalitions are formed transnationally and transgovernmentally, the potential role of international institutions in political bargaining is greatly increased."[22]

Postwar events, and especially those of the 1970s, appeared to support realist theory and to invalidate liberal institutionalism. States remained autonomous in setting foreign policy goals; they retained the loyalty of government officials active in "transgovernmental networks"; and they recast the terms of their relationships with such seemingly powerful transnational actors as high-technology multinational corporations.[23] Industrialized states varied in their economic performance during the 1970s in the face of similar challenges (oil shortages, recession, and inflation). Scholars linked these differences in performance to divergences, and not convergence, in their domestic political–economic structures.[24] A number of events during the 1970s and early 1980s also demonstrated that the use of force continued to be a pervasive feature of world politics: increases in East–West tensions

19. Neofunctionalists suggested that, for West European states, "the argument is no longer over the slice of the pie to go to each; it is increasingly over the means for increasing the overall size of the pastry." See Haas, "The New Europe," p. 158; see also pp. 160–62, 166–67. See also Mitrany, *Working Peace System*, pp. 92–93; Morse, "Transformation," pp. 383–85; and Cooper, "Interdependence," pp. 164–67, 170–72, 179.

20. Mitrany, *Working Peace System*, pp. 133–37, 198–211; see also Haas, *Beyond the Nation-State*.

21. Haas, "The New Europe," p. 159.

22. Keohane and Nye, *Power and Interdependence*, p. 35; see also pp. 36, 232–34, 240–42.

23. See Stephen D. Krasner, *Defending the National Interest: Raw Materials Investments and U.S. Foreign Policy* (Princeton, N.J.: Princeton University Press, 1978); Robert W. Russell, "Transgovernmental Interaction in the International Monetary System, 1960–1972," *International Organization* 27 (Autumn 1973), pp. 431–64; and Joseph M. Grieco, *Between Dependency and Autonomy: India's Experience with the International Computer Industry* (Berkeley: University of California Press, 1984).

24. See Peter J. Katzenstein, ed., *Between Power and Plenty: Foreign Economic Policies of Advanced Industrialized States* (Madison: University of Wisconsin Press, 1978); Katzenstein, *Small States in World Markets: Industrial Policy in Europe* (Ithaca, N.Y.: Cornell University Press, 1985); John Zysman, *Political Strategies for Industrial Order: State, Market, and Industry in France* (Berkeley: University of California Press, 1977); Zysman, *Governments, Markets, and Growth: Financial Systems and the Politics of Industrial Change* (Ithaca, N.Y.: Cornell University Press, 1983); and Peter Gourevitch, *Politics in Hard Times: Comparative Responses to International Economic Crises* (Ithaca, N.Y.: Cornell University Press, 1986), pp. 181–217.

and the continuation of the Soviet–American arms competition; direct and indirect military intervention and counter-intervention by the superpowers in Africa, Central America, and Southwest Asia; and the Yom Kippur and Iran–Iraq wars.[25] International institutions appeared to be unable to reshape state interests; instead, they were often embroiled in and paralyzed by East–West and North–South disputes.[26] Finally, supranationalism in West Europe was replaced by old-fashioned intergovernmental bargaining, and the advanced democracies frequently experienced serious trade and monetary conflicts and sharp discord over economic relations with the Soviet Union.[27]

And yet, international cooperation did not collapse during the 1970s as it had during the 1930s.[28] In finance, private banks and governments in developed countries worked with the International Monetary Fund to contain the international debt crisis.[29] In trade, the advanced states completed the Tokyo Round negotiations under the General Agreement on Tariffs and

25. On the continuing utility of force in the nuclear age, see Alexander L. George and Richard Smoke, *Deterrence in American Foreign Policy: Theory and Practice* (New York: Columbia University Press, 1974); Barry M. Blechman and Stephen S. Kaplan, *Force Without War: U.S. Armed Forces as a Political Instrument* (Washington, D.C.: Brookings Institution, 1978); Stephen S. Kaplan, *Diplomacy of Power: Soviet Armed Forces as a Political Instrument* (Washington, D.C.: Brookings Institution, 1981); and Richard Betts, *Nuclear Blackmail and Nuclear Balance* (Washington, D.C.: Brookings Institution, 1987).

26. East–West disputes in a specialized international agency are examined in Walter Galenson, *The International Labor Organization: An American View* (Madison: University of Wisconsin Press, 1981). North–South struggles within international institutions are discussed in Stephen D. Krasner, *Structural Conflict: The Third World Against Global Liberalism* (Berkeley: University of California Press, 1985).

27. On the problem of European integration, see Donald J. Puchala, "Domestic Politics and Regional Harmonization in the European Communities," *World Politics* 27 (July 1975), pp. 496–520; and Paul Taylor, *The Limits of European Integration* (New York: Columbia University Press, 1983). Trends towards a "new protectionism" supported realist arguments that the erosion of America's hegemonic position would produce a less open international economy. See Gilpin, *U.S. Power*, and Stephen D. Krasner, "State Power and the Structure of International Trade," *World Politics* 28 (April 1976), pp. 317–45. On trade conflicts during the 1970s, see John H. Jackson, "The Crumbling Institutions of the Liberal Trade System," *Journal of World Trade Law* 12 (March–April 1978), pp. 93–106; Bela and Carol Balassa, "Industrial Protection in the Developed Countries," *World Economy* 7 (June 1984), pp. 179–86; and Miles Kahler, "European Protectionism in Theory and Practice," *World Politics* 37 (July 1985), pp. 475–502. On monetary disputes, see Susan Strange, *International Monetary Relations of the Western World, 1959–1971*, vol. 2 of Andrew Shonfield, ed. *International Economic Relations of the Western World, 1959–1971* (Oxford: Oxford University Press for the Royal Institute of International Affairs, 1976), pp. 320–53; and Benjamin J. Cohen, "Europe's Money, America's Problems," *Foreign Policy*, No. 35 (Summer 1979), pp. 31–47. On disputes over economic ties with the Soviet Union, see Stephen Woolcock, *Western Policies on East-West Trade*, Chatham House Papers No. 15 (London: Routledge & Kegan Paul for the Royal Institute of International Affairs, 1982); and Bruce W. Jentleson, *Pipeline Politics: The Complex Political Economy of East–West Energy Trade* (Ithaca, N.Y.: Cornell University Press, 1986).

28. Stephen D. Krasner, "Preface," in Krasner, ed., *International Regimes*, p. viii.

29. See Charles Lipson, "Bankers' Dilemmas: Private Cooperation in Rescheduling Sovereign Debts," *World Politics* 38 (October 1985), pp. 200–25; also see Miles Kahler, ed., *The Politics of International Debt* (Ithaca, N.Y.: Cornell University Press, 1986).

Trade.[30] In energy, the advanced states failed to coordinate responses to the oil crises of 1973–1974 and 1979, but cooperated effectively—through the International Energy Agency—following the outbreak of the Iran–Iraq war in 1980.[31] Finally, in high technology, the European states initiated and pursued during the 1970s a host of joint projects in high technology such as Airbus Industrie, the ARIANE rocket program, and the ESPRIT information technology effort.[32] Governments had not transformed their foreign policies, and world politics were not in transition, but *states* achieved cooperation through *international institutions* even in the harsh 1970s. This set the stage for a renewed, albeit truncated, liberal challenge to realism in the 1980s.

2. The new liberal institutionalism

In contrast to earlier presentations of liberal institutionalism, the newest liberalism accepts realist arguments that states are the major actors in world affairs and are unitary–rational agents. It also claims to accept realism's emphasis on anarchy to explain state motives and actions. Robert Axelrod, for example, seeks to address this question: "Under what conditions will cooperation emerge in a world of egoists without central authority?"[33] Similarly, Axelrod and Robert Keohane observe of world politics that "there is no common government to enforce rules, and by the standards of domestic society, international institutions are weak."[34]

Yet neoliberals argue that realism is wrong to discount the possibilities for international cooperation and the capacities of international institutions. Neoliberals claim that, contrary to realism and in accordance with traditional

30. See Gilbert Winham, *International Trade and the Tokyo Round Negotiation* (Princeton, N.J.: Princeton University Press, 1986); see also Charles Lipson, "The Transformation of Trade: The Sources and Effects of Regime Change," in Krasner, ed., *International Regimes*, pp. 233–72; and Jock A. Finlayson and Mark W. Zacher, "The GATT and the Regulation of Trade Barriers: Regime Dynamics and Functions," in Krasner, ed., *International Regimes*, pp. 273–314.

31. See Robert J. Lieber, *The Oil Decade: Conflict and Cooperation in the West* (New York: Praeger, 1983); Daniel Badger and Robert Belgrave, *Oil Supply and Price: What Went Right in 1980?* (Paris: Atlantic Institute for International Affairs, May 1982); and Keohane, *After Hegemony*, pp. 217–40.

32. See Bruce L. R. Smith, "A New Technology Gap in Europe?" *SAIS Review* 6 (Winter–Spring 1986), pp. 219–36; and Walter A. McDougall, "Space-Age Europe: Gaullism, Euro-Gaullism, and the American Dilemma," *Technology and Culture* 26 (April 1985), pp. 179–203.

33. Axelrod, *Evolution of Cooperation*, p. 3; also see pp. 4, 6.

34. Axelrod and Keohane, "Achieving Cooperation," p. 226. Stein argues that his theory of international regimes "is rooted in the classic characterization of international politics as relations between sovereign entities dedicated to their own self-preservation, ultimately able to depend only upon themselves, and prepared to resort to force"; see Stein, "Coordination and Collaboration," p. 116. Lipson notes that Axelrod's ideas are important because they "obviously bear on a central issue in international relations theory: the emergence and maintenance of cooperation among sovereign, self-interested states, operating without any centralized authority"; see Lipson, "International Cooperation," p. 6.

liberal views, institutions can help states work together.[35] Thus, neoliberals argue, the prospects for international cooperation are better than realism allows.[36] These points of convergence and divergence among the three perspectives are summarized in Table 1.

Neoliberals begin with assertions of acceptance of several key realist propositions; however, they end with a rejection of realism and with claims of affirmation of the central tenets of the liberal institutionalist tradition. To develop this argument, neoliberals first observe that states in anarchy often face mixed interests and, in particular, situations which can be depicted by Prisoner's Dilemma.[37] In the game, each state prefers mutual cooperation to mutual noncooperation (CC>DD), but also successful cheating to mutual cooperation (DC>CC) and mutual defection to victimization by another's cheating (DD>CD); overall, then, DC>CC>DD>CD. In these circumstances, and in the absence of a centralized authority or some other countervailing force to bind states to their promises, each defects regardless of what it expects the other to do.

However, neoliberals stress that countervailing forces often do exist— forces that cause states to keep their promises and thus to resolve the Prisoner's Dilemma. They argue that states may pursue a strategy of tit-for-tat and cooperate on a conditional basis—that is, each adheres to its promises so long as partners do so. They also suggest that conditional cooperation is more likely to occur in Prisoner's Dilemma if the game is highly iterated, since states that interact repeatedly in either a mutually beneficial or harmful manner are likely to find that mutual cooperation is their best long-term strategy. Finally, conditional cooperation is more attractive to states if the

35. Keohane notes in *After Hegemony* (p. 9) that "I begin with Realist insights about the role of power and the effects of hegemony" but that "my central arguments draw more on the Institutionalist tradition, arguing that cooperation can under some conditions develop on the basis of complementary interests, and that institutions, broadly defined, affect the patterns of cooperation that emerge." Keohane also notes (p. 26) that "what distinguishes my argument from structural Realism is my emphasis on the effects of international institutions and practices on state behavior."

36. Keohane indicates in *After Hegemony* (pp. 14, 16) that he does not seek the wholesale rejection of realism. However, on the issue of the prospects for cooperation, like the question of international institutions, he does seek to refute realism's conclusions while employing its assumptions. He notes (p. 29) that "[s]tarting with similar premises about motivations, I seek to show that Realism's pessimism about welfare-increasing cooperation is exaggerated," and he proposes (p. 67) "to show, on the basis of their own assumptions, that the characteristic pessimism of Realism does not follow." Keohane also suggests (p. 84) that rational-choice analysis "helps us criticize, in its own terms, Realism's bleak picture of the inevitability of either hegemony or conflict." Finally, he asserts (p. 84) that rational-choice theory, "combined with sensitivity to the significance of international institutions," allows for an awareness of both the strengths and weaknesses of realism, and in so doing "[w]e can strip away some of the aura of verisimilitude that surrounds Realism and reconsider the logical and empirical foundations of its claims to our intellectual allegiance."

37. On the importance of Prisoner's Dilemma in neoliberal theory, see Axelrod, *Evolution of Cooperation*, p. 7; Keohane, *After Hegemony*, pp. 66–69; Axelrod and Keohane, "Achieving Cooperation," p. 231; Lipson, "International Cooperation," p. 2; and Stein, "Coordination and Collaboration," pp. 120–24.

TABLE 1. *Liberal institutionalism, neoliberal institutionalism, and realism: summary of major propositions*

Proposition	Liberal institutionalism	Neoliberal institutionalism	Realism
States are the only major actors in world politics	No; other actors include: —specialized international agencies —supranational authorities —interest groups —transgovernmental policy networks —transnational actors (MNCs, etc.)	Yes (but international institutions play a major role)	Yes
States are unitary–rational actors	No; state is fragmented	Yes	Yes
Anarchy is a major shaping force for state preferences and actions	No; forces such as technology, knowledge, welfare-orientation of domestic interests are also salient	Yes (apparently)	Yes
International institutions are an independent force facilitating cooperation	Yes	Yes	No
Optimistic/pessimistic about prospects for cooperation	Optimistic	Optimistic	Pessimistic

costs of verifying one another's compliance, and of sanctioning cheaters, are low compared to the benefits of joint action. Thus, conditional cooperation among states may evolve in the face of international anarchy and mixed interests through strategies of reciprocity, extended time horizons, and reduced verification and sanctioning costs.

Neoliberals find that one way states manage verification and sanctioning problems is to restrict the number of partners in a cooperative arrangement.[38] However, neoliberals place much greater emphasis on a second factor—international institutions. In particular, neoliberals argue that institutions reduce verification costs, create iterativeness, and make it easier to punish cheaters. As Keohane suggests, "in general, regimes make it more sensible to cooperate by lowering the likelihood of being double-crossed."[39] Similarly, Keohane and Axelrod assert that "international regimes do not substitute for reciprocity; rather, they reinforce and institutionalize it. Regimes incorporating the norm of reciprocity delegitimize defection and thereby make it more costly."[40] In addition, finding that "coordination conventions" are often an element of conditional cooperation in Prisoner's Dilemma, Charles Lipson suggests that "in international relations, such conventions, which are typically grounded in ongoing reciprocal exchange, range from international law to regime rules."[41] Finally, Arthur Stein argues that, just as societies "create" states to resolve collective action problems among individuals, so too "regimes in the international arena are also created to deal with the collective suboptimality that can emerge from individual [state] behavior."[42] Hegemonic power may be necessary to establish cooooperation among states, neoliberals argue, but it may endure after hegemony with the aid of institutions. As Keohane concludes, "When we think about cooperation after hegemony, we need to think about institutions."[43]

3. Realism and the failure of the new liberal institutionalism

The new liberals assert that they can accept key realist views about states and anarchy and still sustain classic liberal arguments about institutions and international cooperation. Yet, in fact, realist and neoliberal perspectives on states and anarchy differ profoundly, and the former provides a more complete understanding of the problem of cooperation than the latter.

Neoliberals assume that states have only one goal in mixed-interest in-

38. See Keohane, *After Hegemony*, p. 77; Axelrod and Keohane, "Achieving Cooperation," pp. 234–38. For a demonstration, see Lipson, "Bankers' Dilemmas."
39. Keohane, *After Hegemony*, p. 97.
40. Axelrod and Keohane, "Achieving Cooperation," p. 250.
41. Lipson, "International Cooperation," p. 6.
42. Stein, "Coordination and Collaboration," p. 123.
43. Keohane, *After Hegemony*, p. 246.

teractions: to achieve the greatest possible individual gain. For example, Axelrod suggests that the key issue in selecting a "best strategy" in Prisoner's Dilemma—offered by neoliberals as a powerful model of the problem of state cooperation in the face of anarchy and mixed interests—is to determine "what strategy will yield a player the highest possible score."[44] Similarly, Lipson observes that cheating is attractive in a single play of Prisoner's Dilemma because each player believes that defecting "can maximize his own reward," and, in turning to iterated plays, Lipson retains the assumption that players seek to maximize individual payoffs over the long run.[45] Indeed, reliance upon conventional Prisoner's Dilemma to depict international relationships and upon iteration to solve the dilemma unambiguously requires neoliberalism to adhere to an individualistic payoff maximization assumption, for a player responds to an iterated conventional Prisoner's Dilemma with conditional cooperation *solely out of a desire to maximize its individual long-term total payoffs.*

Moreover, neoliberal institutionalists assume that states define their interests in strictly individualistic terms. Axelrod, for example, indicates that his objective is to show how actors "who pursue their own interests" may nevertheless work together.[46] He also notes that Prisoner's Dilemma is useful to study states in anarchy because it is assumed in the game that "the object is to do as well as possible, regardless of how well the other player does."[47] Similarly, Lipson suggests that Prisoner's Dilemma "clearly parallels the Realist conception of sovereign states in world politics" because each player in the game "is assumed to be a self-interested, self-reliant maximizer of his own utility."[48]

Finally, Keohane bases his analysis of international cooperation on the assumption that states are basically atomistic actors. He suggests that states in an anarchical context are, as microeconomic theory assumes with respect to business firms, "rational egoists." Rationality means that states possess "consistent, ordered preferences, and . . . calculate costs and benefits of alternative courses of action in order to maximize their utility in view of these preferences." In turn, he defines utility maximization atomistically; egoism, according to Keohane, "means that their [i.e., state] utility functions are independent of one another: they do not gain or lose utility simply because of the gains or losses of others."[49]

44. Axelrod, *Evolution of Cooperation*, pp. 6, 14. Stein acknowledges that he employs an absolute-gains assumption and that the latter "is very much a liberal, not mercantilist, view of self-interest; it suggests that actors focus on their own returns and compare different outcomes with an eye to maximizing their own gains." See Stein, "Coordination and Collaboration," p. 134. It is difficult to see how Stein can employ a "liberal" assumption of state interest and assert that his theory of regimes, as noted earlier in note 34, is based on the "classic [realist?] characterization" of international politics.

45. Lipson, "International Cooperation," pp. 2, 5.
46. Axelrod, *Evolution of Cooperation*, p. 9.
47. Ibid., p. 22.
48. Lipson, "International Cooperation," p. 2.
49. Keohane, *After Hegemony*, p. 27.

Neoliberalism finds that states attain greater utility—that is, a higher level of satisfaction—as they achieve higher individual payoffs. Also, in keeping with the concept of rational egoism, a utility function specified by the new theory for one state would not be "linked" to the utility functions of others. Hence, if a state enjoys utility, U, in direct proportion to its payoff, V, then the neoliberal institutionalist specification of that state's utility function would be $U = V$.[50]

Overall, "rational egoist" states care only about their own gains. They do not care whether partners achieve or do not achieve gains, or whether those gains are large or small, or whether such gains are greater or less than the gains they themselves achieve. The major constraint on their cooperation in mixed interest international situations is the problem of cheating.

And yet, realist theory rejects neoliberalism's exclusive focus on cheating. Differences in the realist and neoliberal understanding of the problem of cooperation result from a fundamental divergence in their interpretations of the basic meaning of international anarchy. Neoliberal institutionalism offers a well-established definition of anarchy, specifying that it means "the lack of common government in world politics."[51] Neoliberalism then proceeds to identify one major effect of international anarchy. Because of anarchy, according to neoliberals, individuals or states believe that no agency is available to "enforce rules," or to "enact or enforce rules of behavior," or to "force them to cooperate with each other."[52] As a result, according to neoliberal theory, "cheating and deception are endemic" in international relations.[53] Anarchy, then, means that states may wish to cooperate, but, aware that cheating is both possible and profitable, *lack a central agency to enforce promises*. Given this understanding of anarchy, neoliberal institutional theory correctly identifies the problem of cheating and then proceeds to investigate how institutions can ameliorate that particular problem.

For realists, as for neoliberals, international anarchy means the absence of a common inter-state government. Yet, according to realists, states do not believe that the lack of a common government only means that no agency can reliably enforce promises. Instead, realists stress, states recognize that, in anarchy, *there is no overarching authority to prevent others from using*

---

50. On payoffs and utility functions, see Anatol Rapoport, *Fights, Games and Debates* (Ann Arbor: University of Michigan Press, 1960), p. 121, and Michael Taylor, *Anarchy and Cooperation* (London: Wiley, 1976), pp. 70–74.

51. Axelrod and Keohane, "Achieving Cooperation," p. 226; see also Keohane, *After Hegemony*, p. 7; Lipson, "International Cooperation," pp. 1–2; Axelrod, *Evolution of Cooperation*, pp. 3–4; and Stein, "Coordination and Collaboration," p. 116.

52. See Axelrod and Keohane, "Achieving Cooperation," p. 226; Keohane, *After Hegemony*, p. 7; and Axelrod, *Evolution of Cooperation*, p. 6.

53. Axelrod and Keohane, "Achieving Cooperation," p. 226. Similarly, Lipson notes that while institutionalized mechanisms (such as governments) that guarantee the enforcement of contracts are available in civil society, "the absence of reliable guarantees is an essential feature of international relations and a major obstacle to concluding treaties, contracts, and agreements." The resulting problem, according to Lipson, is that "constraints on opportunism are weak." See Lipson, "International Cooperation," p. 4. Also see Keohane, *After Hegemony*, p. 93, and Stein, "Coordination and Collaboration," p. 116.

violence, or the threat of violence, to destroy or enslave them. As Kenneth Waltz suggests, in anarchy, wars can occur "because there is nothing to prevent them," and therefore "in international politics force serves, not only as the *ultima ratio*, but indeed as the first and constant one."[54] Thus, some states may sometimes be driven by greed or ambition, but anarchy and the danger of war cause all states always to be motivated in some measure by fear and distrust.[55]

Given its understanding of anarchy, realism argues that individual well-being is not the key interest of states; instead, it finds that *survival* is their core interest. Raymond Aron, for example, suggested that "politics, insofar as it concerns relations among states, seems to signify—in both ideal and objective terms—simply the survival of states confronting the potential threat created by the existence of other states."[56] Similarly, Robert Gilpin observes that individuals and groups may seek truth, beauty, and justice, but he emphasizes that "all these more noble goals will be lost unless one makes provision for one's security in the power struggle among groups."[57]

Driven by an interest in survival, states are acutely sensitive to any erosion of their relative capabilities, which are the ultimate basis for their security and independence in an anarchical, self-help international context. Thus, realists find that the major goal of states in any relationship is not to attain the highest possible individual gain or payoff. Instead, *the fundamental goal of states in any relationship is to prevent others from achieving advances in their relative capabilities.* For example, E. H. Carr suggested that "the most serious wars are fought in order to make one's own country militarily stronger or, *more often*, to prevent another from becoming militarily stronger."[58] Along the same lines, Gilpin finds that the international system "stimulates, and may compel, a state to increase its power; at the least, it necessitates that the prudent state prevent relative increases in the power of competitor states."[59] Indeed, states may even forgo increases in their absolute capabilities if doing so prevents others from achieving even greater gains. This is because, as Waltz suggests, "the first concern of states is not to maximize power but to maintain their position in the system."[60]

54. See Waltz, *Man, State, and War*, p. 232; and Waltz, *Theory of International Politics*, p. 113. Similarly, Carr suggests that war "lurks in the background of international politics just as revolution lurks in the background of domestic politics." See Carr, *Twenty Years Crisis*, p. 109. Finally, Aron observes that international relations "present one original feature which distinguishes them from all other social relations: they take place within the shadow of war." See Aron, *Peace and War*, p. 6.
55. See Gilpin, "Political Realism," pp. 304–5.
56. Aron, *Peace and War*, p. 7; also see pp. 64–65.
57. Gilpin, "Political Realism," p. 305. Similarly, Waltz indicates that "in anarchy, security is the highest end. Only if survival is assured can states safely seek such other goals as tranquility, profit, and power." See Waltz, *Theory of International Politics*, p. 126; also see pp. 91–92, and Waltz, "Reflections," p. 334.
58. Carr, *Twenty-Years Crisis*, p. 111, emphasis added.
59. Gilpin, *War and Change*, pp. 87–88.
60. Waltz, *Theory of International Politics*, p. 126; see also Waltz, "Reflections," p. 334.

States seek to prevent increases in others' relative capabilities. As a result, states always assess their performance in any relationship in terms of the performance of others.[61] Thus, I suggest that states are positional, not atomistic, in character. Most significantly, *state positionality may constrain the willingness of states to cooperate*. States fear that their partners will achieve relatively greater gains; that, as a result, the partners will surge ahead of them in relative capabilties; and, finally, that their increasingly powerful partners in the present could become all the more formidable foes at some point in the future.[62]

State positionality, then, engenders a "relative gains problem" for cooperation. That is, a state will decline to join, will leave, or will sharply limit its commitment to a cooperative arrangement if it believes that partners are achieving, or are likely to achieve, relatively greater gains. It will eschew cooperation even though participation in the arrangement was providing it, or would have provided it, with large absolute gains. Moreover, a state concerned about relative gains may decline to cooperate even if it is confident that partners will keep their commitments to a joint arrangement. Indeed, if a state believed that a proposed arrangement would provide all parties absolute gains, but would also generate gains favoring partners, then greater certainty that partners would adhere to the terms of the arrangement would only accentuate its relative gains concerns. Thus, a state worried about relative gains might respond to greater certainty that partners would keep their promises with a lower, rather than a higher, willingness to cooperate.

I must stress that realists do not argue that positionality causes all states to possess an offensively oriented desire to maximize the difference in gains arising from cooperation to their own advantage. They do not, in other words, attribute to states what Stein correctly calls a mercantilist definition of self-interest.[63] Instead, realists argue that states are more likely to concentrate on the danger that relative gains may advantage partners and thus

---

61. On the tendency of states to compare performance levels, see Oran Young, "International Regimes: Toward a New Theory of Institutions," *World Politics* 39 (October 1986), p. 118. Young suggests that realists assume that states are "status maximizers" and attribute to states the tendency to compare performance levels because each seeks "to attain the highest possible rank in the hierarchy of members of the international community." The present writer offers a different understanding of realism: while realism acknowledges that *some* states may be positional in the sense noted by Young, its fundamental insight is that *all* states are positional and compare performance levels because they fear that *others* may attain a higher ranking in an issue-area.

62. As Waltz suggests, "When faced with the possibility of cooperating for mutual gains, states that feel insecure must ask how the gain will be divided. They are compelled to ask not "Will both of us gain?" but "Who will gain more?" If an expected gain is to be divided, say, in the ratio of two to one, one state may use its disproportionate gain to implement a policy intended to damage or destroy the other." See Waltz, *Theory of International Politics*, p. 105.

63. Stein, "Coordination and Collaboration," p. 134.

may foster the emergence of a more powerful potential adversary.[64] Realism, then, finds that states are positional, but it also finds that state positionality is more defensive than offensive in nature.

In addition, realists find that defensive state positionality and the relative gains problem for cooperation essentially reflect the persistence of uncertainty in international relations. States are uncertain about one another's future *intentions*; thus, they pay close attention to how cooperation might affect relative *capabilities* in the future.[65] This uncertainty results from the inability of states to predict or readily to control the future leadership or interests of partners. As Robert Jervis notes, "Minds can be changed, new leaders can come to power, values can shift, new opportunities and dangers can arise."[66]

Thus, realism expects a state's utility function to incorporate *two distinct terms*. It needs to include the state's individual payoff, V, reflecting the realist view that states are motivated by absolute gains. Yet it must also include a term integrating both the state's individual payoff and the partner's payoff, W, in such a way that gaps favoring the state add to its utility while, more importantly, gaps favoring the partner detract from it. One function that depicts this realist understanding of state utility is $U = V - k(W - V)$, with k representing the state's coefficient of sensitivity to gaps in payoffs either to its advantage or disadvantage.[67]

64. In her review of Axelrod, Joanne Gowa cites the 1979 Waltz passage employed in note 62 and, following Taylor's terminology in *Anarchy and Cooperation* (pp. 73–74), suggests that a state may display "negative altruism." Furthermore, according to Gowa, a state "may seek to maximize a utility function that depends both on increases in its own payoffs *and* on increases in the difference between its payoffs and those of another state." See Joanne Gowa, "Anarchy, Egoism, and Third Images: *The Evolution of Cooperation* and International Relations," *International Organization* 40 (Winter 1986), p. 178. This portrays realist thinking in a manner similar to that suggested by Young and cited above in note 61. However, this understanding of state utility cannot be readily based on Waltz, for his core insight, and that of the realist tradition, is not that all states necessarily seek a balance of advantages in their favor (although some may do this) but rather that all fear that relative gains may favor and thus strengthen others. From a realist viewpoint, some states may be negative altruists, but *all* states will be "defensive positionalists." Waltz emphasizes that he does not believe that all states necessarily seek to maximize their power: see his statement cited in note 60 and see especially his "Response to My Critics," p. 334.

65. Waltz, for example, observes that "the impediments to collaboration may not lie in the character and the immediate intention of either party. Instead, the condition of insecurity—at the least, the uncertainty of each about the other's future intentions and actions—works against their cooperation." See Waltz, *Theory of International Politics*, p. 105.

66. Robert Jervis, "Cooperation Under the Security Dilemma," *World Politics* 30 (January 1978), p. 168.

67. Similar to the concept of a state "sensitivity coefficient" to gaps in jointly produced gains is the concept of a "defense coefficient" in Lewis Richardson's model of arms races. The latter serves as an index of one state's fear of another: the greater the coefficient, the stronger the state's belief that it must match increases in the other's weapons inventory with increases in its own. See Lewis F. Richardson, *Arms and Insecurity: A Mathematical Study of the Causes and Origins of War*, eds. Nicolas Rachevsky and Ernesto Trucco (Pittsburgh and Chicago: Boxwood Press and Quadrangle Books, 1960), pp. 14–15.

This realist specification of state utility can be contrasted with that inferred from neoliberal theory, namely, $U = V$. In both cases, the state obtains utility from the receipt of absolute payoffs. However, while neoliberal institutional theory assumes that state utility functions are independent of one another and that states are indifferent to the payoffs of others, realist theory argues that state utility functions are at least partially interdependent and that one state's utility can affect another's.[68] We may also observe that this realist-specified function does not suggest that any payoff achieved by a partner detracts from the state's utility. Rather, *only gaps in payoffs to the advantage of a partner do so.*

The coefficient for a state's sensitivity to gaps in payoffs—k—will vary, but it will always be greater than zero. In general, k will increase as a state transits from relationships in what Karl Deutsch termed a "pluralistic security community" to those approximating a state of war.[69] The level of k will be greater if a state's partner is a long-term adversary rather than a long-time ally; if the issue involves security rather than economic well-being; if the state's relative power has been on the decline rather than on the rise; if payoffs in the particular issue-area are more rather than less easily converted into capabilities within that issue-area; or if these capabilities and the influence associated with them are more rather than less readily transferred to other issue-areas.[70] Yet, given the uncertainties of international politics, a state's level of k will be greater than zero even in interactions with allies, for gaps in payoffs favoring partners will always detract from a state's utility to some degree.[71]

Faced with both problems—cheating and relative gains—states seek to ensure that partners in common endeavors comply with their promises and that their collaboration produces "balanced" or "equitable" achievements of gains. According to realists, states define balance and equity as distributions of gains that roughly maintain pre-cooperation balances of capabilities. To attain this balanced relative achievement of gains, according to Hans Morgenthau, states offer their partners "concessions"; in exchange, they expect to receive approximately equal "compensations." As an ex-

---

68. Robert Jervis also argues that realist theory posits at least partially interdependent state utility functions. See Jervis, "Realism, Game Theory, and Cooperation," *World Politics* 40 (April 1988), pp. 334–36.

69. A pluralistic security community, according to Deutsch and his associates, "is one in which there is real assurance that the members of that community will not fight each other physically, but will settle their disputes in some other way," and in which the members retain separate governments; the examples they provide are Canada—United States and Norway—Sweden. See Deutsch et al., *Political Community*, pp. 5–7.

70. Contextual influences on state sensitivities to gaps in gains are explored in Joseph M. Grieco, "Realist Theory and the Problem of International Cooperation: Analysis with an Amended Prisoner's Dilemma Model," *Journal of Politics* 50 (August 1988) pp. 600–24.

71. In contrast, Keohane finds that that relative gains concerns may impede cooperation only in cases in which states pursue "positional goods" such as "status"; see Keohane, *After Hegemony*, p. 54. Similarly, Lipson expects that states will be sensitive to relative gains only in security relationships; see Lipson, "International Cooperation," pp. 14–16.

ample of this balancing tendency, Morgenthau offers the particular case of "cooperation" among Prussia, Austria, and Russia in their partitions of Poland in 1772, 1793, and 1795. He indicates that in each case, "the three nations agreed to divide Polish territory in such a way that the distribution of power among themselves would be approximately the same after the partitions as it had been before."[72] For Morgenthau, state balancing of joint gains is a universal characteristic of the diplomacy of cooperation. He attributes this to the firmly grounded practice of states to balance power, and argues that "given such a system, no nation will agree to concede political advantages to another nation without the expectation, which may or may not be well founded, of receiving *proportionate* advantages in return."[73]

In sum, neoliberals find that anarchy impedes cooperation through its generation of uncertainty in states about the compliance of partners. For neoliberals, the outcome a state most fears in mixed interest situations is to be cheated. Yet, successful unilateral cheating is highly unlikely, and the more probable neoliberal "worst case" is for all states to defect and to find themselves less well off than if they had all cooperated. For neoliberal institutionalists, then, anarchy and mixed interests often cause states to suffer the opportunity costs of not achieving an outcome that is mutually more beneficial. Keohane and Axelrod argue that games like Prisoner's Dilemma, Stag Hunt, Chicken, and Deadlock illustrate how many international relationships offer both the danger that "the myopic pursuit of self-interest can be disastrous" and the prospect that "both sides can potentially benefit from cooperation—if they can only achieve it."[74]

Realists identify even greater uncertainties for states considering cooperation: which among them could achieve the greatest gains, and would imbalanced achievements of gains affect relative capabilities? In addition, a state that knows it will not be cheated still confronts another risk that is at least as formidable: perhaps a partner will achieve disproportionate gains, and, thus strengthened, might someday be a more dangerous enemy than if they had never worked together. For neoliberal theory, the problem of cooperation in anarchy is that states may fail to achieve it; in the final analysis, the worst possible outcome is a lost opportunity. For realist theory, state efforts to cooperate entail these dangers plus the much greater risk, for some states, that cooperation might someday result in lost independence or security.

Realism and neoliberal institutionalism offer markedly different views concerning the effects of international anarchy on states. These differences are summarized in Table 2. Compared to realist theory, neoliberal institutionalism understates the range of uncertainties and risks states believe they

---

72. Morgenthau, *Politics Among Nations*, p. 179.
73. Ibid., p. 180, emphasis added.
74. Axelrod and Keohane, "Achieving Cooperation," p. 231; see also Stein, "Coordination and Collaboration," pp. 123–24.

TABLE 2. *Anarchy, state properties, and state inhibitions about cooperation: summary of neoliberal and realist views*

Basis of Comparison	Neoliberal institutionalism	Political realism
Meaning of anarchy	No central agency is available to enforce promises	No central agency is available to enforce promises *or* to provide protection
State properties		
Core interest	To advance in utility defined individualistically	To enhance prospects for survival
Main goal	To achieve greatest possible absolute gains	To achieve greatest gains *and* smallest gap in gains favoring partners
Basic character	Atomistic ("rational egoist")	Defensively positional
Utility function	Independent: U = V	Partially interdependent: U = V − k (W − V)
State inhibitions concerning cooperation		
Range of uncertainties associated with cooperation	Partners' compliance	Compliance *and* relative achievement of gains *and* uses to which gaps favoring partners may be employed
Range of risks associated with cooperation	To be cheated and to receive a low payoff	To be cheated *or* to experience decline in relative power if others achieve greater gains
Barriers to cooperation	State concerns about partners' compliance	State concerns about partners' compliance *and* partners' relative gains

must overcome to cooperate with others. Hence, realism provides a more comprehensive theory of the problem of cooperation than does neoliberal institutionalism.

4. Conclusion

Neoliberal institutionalism is not based on realist theory; in fact, realism specifies a wider range of systemic-level constraints on cooperation than does neoliberalism. Thus, the next scholarly task is to conduct empirical tests of the two approaches. It is widely accepted—even by neoliberals— that realism has great explanatory power in national security affairs. However, international political economy would appear to be neoliberalism's preserve. Indeed, economic relationships among the advanced democracies would provide opportunities to design "crucial experiments" for the two theories.[75] That is, they would provide the opportunity to observe behavior confirming realist expectations in circumstances least likely to have generated such observations unless realism is truly potent, while at the same time they might disconfirm neoliberal claims in circumstances most likely to have produced observations validating neoliberal theory.[76]

According to neoliberal theory, two factors enhance prospects for the achievement and maintenance of political-economic cooperation among the advanced democracies. First, these states have the broadest range of common political, military, and economic interests.[77] Thus, they have the greatest hopes for large absolute gains through joint action. This should work against realism and its specification of the relative gains problem for cooperation. That is, states which have many common interests should have the fewest worries that they might become embroiled in extreme conflicts in the future and, as a result, they should have the fewest concerns about relative achievements of gains arising from their common endeavors. Neoliberal theory emphasizes another background condition: the economic arrangements of advanced democracies are "nested" in larger political-strategic alliances. Nesting, according to the theory, accentuates iterativeness and so promotes compliance.[78] This condition should also place realist theory at a disadvantage. If states are allies, they should be unconcerned that possible gaps in economic gains might advantage partners. Indeed, they should take comfort in the latter's success, for in attaining greater economic gains these partners become stronger military allies.

We can identify a number of efforts by advanced democracies to cooperate in economic issue-areas that were characterized by high common interests and nesting. In the trade field, such efforts would include the Tokyo Round codes on non-tariff barriers and efforts by the Nordic states to construct regional free-trade arrangements. In the monetary field, there are the ex-

75. A crucial experiment seeks real world observations confirming one theory's empirical expectations in circumstances most unlikely to have done so unless the theory is very powerful, while simultaneously disconfirming a competitive theory's empirical expectations in circumstances most likely to have provided such confirming observations. On the methodology of crucial experiments, see Arthur L. Stinchcombe, *Constructing Social Theories* (New York: Harcourt, Brace, 1968), pp. 20–28; and Harry Eckstein, "Case Study and Theory in Political Science," in Fred I. Greenstein and Nelson W. Polsby, eds., *Strategies of Inquiry*, vol. 7 of the *Handbook of Political Science* (Reading, Mass.: Addison-Wesley, 1975), pp. 118–20.

76. Such a crucial experiment would demonstrate realism's superiority over neoliberalism. On the other hand, if neoliberal theorists wanted to design a crucial experiment to demonstrate the superiority of their approach, they would focus not on North–North economic relations but rather on North–South relations or, better still, on East–West military interactions.

77. See Keohane, *After Hegemony*, pp. 6–7.

78. On the "nesting" of international regimes, see Keohane, *After Hegemony*, pp. 90–91; and Vinod K. Aggarwal, *Liberal Protection: The International Politics of Organized Textile Trade* (Berkeley: University of California Press, 1985).

periences of the European Community with exchange-rate coordination—the Economic and Monetary Union and the European Monetary System. Finally, in the field of high technology, one might examine European collaboration in commercial aviation (Airbus Industrie) or data processing (the Unidata computer consortium).[79] If these cooperative arrangements varied in terms of their success (and indeed such variance can be observed), and the less successful or failed arrangements were characterized not by a higher incidence of cheating but by a greater severity of relative gains problems, then one could conclude that realist theory explains variation in the success or failure of international cooperation more effectively than neoliberal institutional theory. Moreover, one could have great confidence in this assessment, for it would be based on cases which were most hospitable to neoliberalism and most hostile to realism.

However, additional tests of the two theories can and should be undertaken. For example, one might investigate realist and neoliberal expectations as to the *durability* of arrangements states prefer when they engage in joint action. Neoliberal theory argues that cheating is less likely to occur in a mixed interest situation that is iterated; hence, it suggests that "the most direct way to encourage cooperation is to make the relationship more durable."[80] If, then, two states that are interested in cooperation could choose

79. I am completing a study of the relative gains problem in the case of the Tokyo Round trade codes. Available studies suggest that the Economic and Monetary Union broke down during 1972–76 as a result of concerns by Britain, France, Ireland, and Italy that they had taken on disproportionate burdens and that West Germany was achieving disproportionate gains: see Loukas Tsoukalis, *The Politics and Economics of European Monetary Integration* (London: Allen & Unwin, 1977), p. 157. Its successor, the European Monetary System, was designed to ensure greater balance in the gains and losses among partners: see Peter Coffey, *The European Monetary System: Past, Present, and Future* (Dordrecht, Neth., and Boston: Martinus Nijhoff, 1984), pp. 21–26, 126–27. In the case of Scandinavian trade cooperation, Norway shifted from opposition during the 1950s and much of the 1960s to support at the end of the latter decade as it became less concerned about its capacity to achieve a satisfactory share of trade gains with Sweden: see Barbara Haskel, *The Scandinavian Option: Opportunities and Opportunity Costs in Postwar Scandinavian Foreign Policies* (Oslo: Universitetsforlaget, 1976), pp. 124–27. Much of the literature on the problem of regional integration among developing countries also emphasizes the importance of relative gains issues. See, for example, Lynn K. Mytelka, "The Salience of Gains in Third-World Integrative Systems," *World Politics* 25 (January 1973), pp. 236–46; W. Andrew Axline, "Underdevelopment, Dependence, and Integration: The Politics of Regionalism in the Third World," *International Organization* 31 (Winter 1977), pp. 83–105; and Constantine V. Vaitsos, "Crisis in Regional Economic Cooperation (Integration) Among Developing Countries: A Survey, "*World Development* 6 (June 1978), pp. 747–50. For case studies of the problem of relative gains in developing country regional efforts to cooperate, see Richard I. Fagan, *Central American Economic Integration: The Politics of Unequal Benefits* (Berkeley: Institute of International Studies, 1970); Lynn Krieger Mytelka, *Regional Development in a Global Economy: The Multinational Corporation, Technology, and Andean Integration* (New Haven, Conn.: Yale University Press, 1979), pp. 39–61; and Arthur Hazlewood, "The End of the East African Community," *Journal of Common Market Studies* 18 (September 1979), especially pp. 44–48 and 53–54.

80. Axelrod, *Evolution of Cooperation*, p. 129; also see Keohane, *After Hegemony*, pp. 257–59, in which he argues that there are "costs of flexibility" and that states commit themselves to regimes and thereby forgo a measure of flexibility in the future to attain cooperation in the present; and Axelrod and Keohane, "Achieving Cooperation," p. 234, in which they argue that international regimes promote cooperation because they "link the future with the present."

between two institutional arrangements that offered comparable absolute gains but that differed in their expected durability—one arrangement might, for example, have higher exit costs than the other—neoliberalism would expect the states to prefer the former over the latter, for each state could then be more confident that the other would remain in the arrangement. Realism generates a markedly different hypothesis. If two states are worried or uncertain about relative achievements of gains, then each will prefer a less durable cooperative arrangement, for each would want to be more readily able to exit from the arrangement if gaps in gains did come to favor the other.

A second pair of competing hypotheses concerns the *number of partners* states prefer to include in a cooperative arrangement. Advocates of neoliberalism find that a small number of participants facilitates verification of compliance and sanctioning of cheaters. Hence, they would predict that states with a choice would tend to prefer a smaller number of partners. Realism would offer a very different hypothesis. A state may believe that it might do better than some partners in a proposed arrangement but not as well as others. If it is uncertain about which partners would do relatively better, the state will prefer more partners, for larger numbers would enhance the likelihood that the relative achievements of gains advantaging (what turn out to be) better-positioned partners could be offset by more favorable sharings arising from interactions with (as matters develop) weaker partners.

A third pair of competing empirical statements concerns the effects of *issue linkages* on cooperation. Neoliberalism's proponents find that tightly knit linkages within and across issue-areas accentuate iterativeness and thus facilitate cooperation.[81] Realism, again, offers a very different proposition. Assume that a state believes that two issue-areas are linked, and that it believes that one element of this linkage is that changes in relative capabilities in one domain affect relative capabilities in the other. Assume also that the state believes that relative achievements of jointly produced gains in one issue-area would advantage the partner. This state would then believe that cooperation would provide additional capabilities to the partner not only in the domain in which joint action is undertaken, but also in the linked issue-area. Cooperation would therefore be unattractive to this state in direct proportion to its belief that the two issue-areas were interrelated. Thus, issue linkages may impede rather than facilitate cooperation.

These tests are likely to demonstrate that realism offers the most effective understanding of the problem of international cooperation.[82] In addition, further analysis of defensive state positionality may help pinpoint policy strategies that facilitate cooperation. If relative gains concerns do act as a

---

81. See Keohane, *After Hegemony*, pp. 91–92, 103–6; and Axelrod and Keohane, "Achieving Cooperation," pp. 239–43.

82. This, however, would certainly not mark the end of the liberal institutionalist challenge to realism. There are at least two related clusters of modern literature that are firmly rooted

constraint on cooperation, then we should identify methods by which states have been able to address such concerns through unilateral bargaining strategies or through the mechanisms and operations of international institutions. For example, we might investigate states' use of side-payments to mitigate the relative gains concerns of disadvantaged partners.[83] Thus, with its understanding of defensive state positionality and the relative gains problem for collaboration, realism may provide guidance to states as they seek security, independence, and mutually beneficial forms of international cooperation.

---

in the liberal institutionalist tradition, that attempt no compromise with realism, and that present an understanding of world politics markedly at odds with realist theory. The first cluster argues that international institutions embody and reinforce norms and beliefs that are held in common among states and that facilitate and guide their cooperative endeavors. The key works in this cluster include John Gerard Ruggie, "International Responses to Technology: Concepts and Trends," *International Organization* 29 (Summer 1975), pp. 557–83; Ruggie, "International Regimes, Transactions, and Change: Embedded Liberalism in the Postwar Economic Order," in Krasner, ed., *International Regimes*, pp. 195–231; Friedrich Kratochwil, "The Force of Prescriptions," *International Organization* 38 (Autumn 1984), pp. 685–708; John Gerard Ruggie and Friedrich Kratochwil, "International Organization: The State of the Art on an Art of the State," *International Organization* 40 (Autumn 1986), pp. 753–76; and Donald J. Puchala and Raymond F. Hopkins, "International Regimes: Lessons from Inductive Analysis," in Krasner, ed., *International Regimes*, pp. 61–92. The second cluster suggests that international institutions help states develop, accept, and disseminate consensual theoretical and empirical knowledge that can reinforce or introduce international norms leading to cooperation. Haas presented this argument in *Beyond the Nation State*, pp. 12–13, 47–48, 79–85; also see Haas, "Is There a Hole in the Whole? Knowledge, Technology, Interdependence and the Construction of International Regimes," *International Organization* 29 (Summer 1975), pp. 827–76; Haas, Mary Pat Williams, and Don Babai, *Scientists and World Order: The Uses of Technical Information in International Organizations* (Berkeley: University of California Press, 1977); Haas, "Why Collaborate? Issue-Linkage and International Regimes," *World Politics* 32 (April 1980), pp. 357–405; Haas, "Words Can Hurt You; Or, Who Said What to Whom About Regimes," in Krasner, ed., *International Regimes*, pp. 23–59; and Beverly Crawford and Stefanie Lenway, "Decision Modes and International Regime Change: Western Collaboration on East–West Trade," *World Politics* 37 (April 1985), pp. 375–402.

83. On the general concept of side-payments, see R. Duncan Luce and Howard Raiffa, *Games and Decisions: Introduction and Critical Survey* (New York: Wiley, 1957), pp. 168–69; and William H. Riker, *The Theory of Political Coalitions* (New Haven, Conn.: Yale University Press, 1962), pp. 34, 108–23. Deutsch and his associates determined that the capacity of advantaged regions to extend symbolic and material side-payments to disadvantaged regions was essential to national integration and amalgamation in such cases as Switzerland and Germany. See Deutsch et al., *Political Community*, p. 55. Similarly, special subsidies were provided to Italy and Ireland to attract them to the European Monetary System. See George Zis, "The European Monetary System, 1979–84: An Assessment," *Journal of Common Market Studies* 23 (September 1984), p. 58. In addition, Norway was attracted to the proposed Nordek arrangement during 1968–70 partly because Sweden offered to provide the bulk of the funds for a Nordic development bank that would be used in large measure to support Norwegian industrial projects. See Claes Wiklund, "The Zig-Zag Course of the Nordek Negotiations," *Scandinavian Political Studies* 5 (1970), p. 322; and Haskel, *Scandinavian Option*, p. 127. Finally, West Germany has sought to ameliorate U.S. concerns about relative burden-sharing in NATO through special "offset" programs aimed at reducing U.S. foreign exchange expenditures associated with its European commitment. See Gregory F. Treverton, *The "Dollar Drain" and American Forces in Germany: Managing the Political Economics of the Atlantic Alliance* (Athens, Ohio: Ohio University Press, 1978).

Taking preferences seriously:
a liberal theory of
international politics
Andrew Moravcsik

This article reformulates liberal international relations (IR) theory in a nonideological and nonutopian form appropriate to empirical social science. Liberal IR theory elaborates the insight that state-society relations—the relationship of states to the domestic and transnational social context in which they are embedded—have a fundamental impact on state behavior in world politics. Societal ideas, interests, and institutions influence state behavior by shaping state preferences, that is, the fundamental social purposes underlying the strategic calculations of governments. For liberals, the configuration of state preferences matters most in world politics—not, as realists argue, the configuration of capabilities and not, as institutionalists (that is, functional regime theorists) maintain, the configuration of information and institutions. This article codifies this basic liberal insight in the form of three core theoretical assumptions, derives from them three variants of liberal theory, and demonstrates that the existence of a coherent liberal theory has significant theoretical, methodological, and empirical implications. Restated in this way, liberal theory deserves to be treated as a paradigmatic alternative empirically coequal with and analytically more fundamental than the two dominant theories in contemporary IR scholarship: realism and institutionalism.

For detailed comments and criticisms, I am grateful above all to Anne-Marie Slaughter, who was there from the beginning, and to Lea Brilmayer, Lawrence Broz, Marc Busch, James Caporaso, Dale Copeland, David Dessler, Jeffry Frieden, Martha Finnemore, Charles Glazer, Michael Griesdorf, Stefano Guzzini, Ernst Haas, Stanley Hoffmann, Stephen Holmes, Ted Hopf, Alan Houston, David Lumsdaine, Robert Keohane, Yuen Khong, Larry Kramer, David Long, Steven Lukes, James Marquart, Lisa Martin, Jonathan Mercer, Henry Nau, Kalypso Nicolaïdis, James Nolt, Joseph Nye, John Odell, Kenneth Oye, Robert Paarlberg, Daniel Philpott, Gideon Rose, Judith Shklar, David Skidmore, Allison Stanger, Janice Stein, Andrew Wallace, Celeste Wallander, Stephen Walt, Alexander Wendt, Mark Zacher, Fareed Zakaria, Michael Zürn, and three anonymous referees. I thank also two other critics: Peter Katzenstein encouraged a more direct comparison with constructivist approaches and John Mearsheimer invited me to state the liberal case vis-à-vis realism in a series of public debates. I am also indebted to participants in seminars at the Program on International Politics, Economics, and Security (PIPES), University of Chicago; University of Konstanz; University of Toronto; University of California, San Diego; Olin Institute and Center for International Affairs, Harvard University; International Jurisprudence Colloquium, New York University Law School; Fletcher School, Tufts University; and the European University Institute. For research support, I thank Amit Sevak, Brian Portnoy, and PIPES. For more detailed and documented versions of this article, see Moravcsik 1992.

International Organization 51, 4, Autumn 1997, pp. 513–53

Grounding liberal theory in a set of core social scientific assumptions helps overcome a disjuncture between contemporary empirical research on world politics and the language employed by scholars to describe IR as a field. Liberal hypotheses stressing variation in state preferences play an increasingly central role in IR scholarship. These include explanations stressing the causal importance of state-society relations as shaped by domestic institutions (for example, the "democratic peace"), by economic interdependence (for example, endogenous tariff theory), and by ideas about national, political, and socioeconomic public goods provision (for example, theories about the relationship between nationalism and conflict). Liberal hypotheses do not include, for reasons clarified later, functional regime theory. Yet the conceptual language of IR theory has not caught up with contemporary research. IR theorists continue to speak as if the dominant theoretical cleavage in the field were the dichotomy between realism and ("neoliberal") institutionalism. The result: liberal IR theory of the kind outlined earlier is generally ignored as a major paradigmatic alternative.

Worse, its lack of paradigmatic status has permitted critics to caricature liberal theory as a normative, even utopian, ideology. Postwar realist critics such as Hans Morgenthau and E. H. Carr took rhetorical advantage of liberalism's historical role as an ideology to contrast its purported altruism ("idealism," "legalism," "moralism," or "utopianism") with realism's "theoretical concern with human nature as it actually is [and] historical processes as they actually take place."[1] Forty years later, little has changed. Robert Gilpin's influential typology in international political economy juxtaposes a positive mercantilist view ("politics determines economics") against a narrower and conspicuously normative liberal one ("economics *should* determine politics"). Kenneth Waltz, a realist critic, asserts that "if the aims . . . of states become matters of . . . central concern, then we are forced back to the descriptive level; and from simple descriptions no valid generalizations can be drawn."[2]

Liberals have responded to such criticisms not by proposing a unified set of positive social scientific assumptions on which a nonideological and nonutopian liberal theory can be based, as has been done with considerable success for realism and institutionalism, but by conceding its theoretical incoherence and turning instead to intellectual history. It is widely accepted that any nontautological social scientific theory must be grounded in a set of positive assumptions from which arguments, explanations, and predictions can be derived.[3] Yet surveys of liberal IR theory either collect disparate views held by "classical" liberal publicists or define liberal theory teleologically, that is, according to its purported optimism concerning the potential for peace, cooperation, and international institutions in world history. Such studies offer an indispensable source of theoretical and normative inspiration. Judged by the more narrowly social scientific criteria adopted here, however, they do not justify reference to a distinct "liberal" IR theory.

Leading liberal IR theorists freely concede the absence of coherent microfoundational assumptions but conclude therefrom that a liberal IR theory in the social scien-

---

1. See Morgenthau 1960, 4; Keohane 1989, 68, n. 17; and Howard 1978, 134.
2. See Waltz 1979, 65, 27; Gilpin 1975, 27 (emphasis in original); and Gilpin 1987.
3. See Bueno de Mesquita 1996, 64–65; and Keohane 1986.

tific sense *cannot* exist. Robert Keohane, an institutionalist sympathetic to liberalism, maintains that "in contrast to Marxism and Realism, Liberalism is not committed to ambitious and parsimonious structural theory." Michael Doyle, a pioneer in analyzing the "democratic peace," observes that liberal IR theory, unlike others, lacks "canonical" foundations. Mark Zacher and Richard Matthew, sympathetic liberals, assert that liberalism should be considered an "approach," not a theory, since "its propositions cannot be . . . deduced from its assumptions."[4] Accurate though this may be as a characterization of intellectual history and current theory, it is second-best social science.

I seek to move beyond this unsatisfactory situation by proposing a set of core assumptions on which a general restatement of positive liberal IR theory can be grounded. In the first section of the article I argue that the basic liberal insight about the centrality of state-society relations to world politics can be restated in terms of three positive assumptions, concerning, respectively, the nature of fundamental social actors, the state, and the international system.

Drawing on these assumptions, I then elaborate three major variants of liberal theory—each grounded in a distinctive causal mechanism linking social preferences and state behavior. Ideational liberalism stresses the impact on state behavior of conflict and compatibility among collective social values or identities concerning the scope and nature of public goods provision. Commercial liberalism stresses the impact on state behavior of gains and losses to individuals and groups in society from transnational economic interchange. Republican liberalism stresses the impact on state behavior of varying forms of domestic representation and the resulting incentives for social groups to engage in rent seeking.[5]

Finally, I demonstrate that the identification of coherent theoretical assumptions is not simply an abstract and semantic matter. It has significant methodological, theoretical, and empirical implications. The utility of a paradigmatic restatement should be evaluated on the basis of four criteria, each relevant to the empirical researcher: superior parsimony, coherence, empirical accuracy, and multicausal consistency.

First, a theoretical restatement should be *general and parsimonious,* demonstrating that a limited number of microfoundational assumptions can link a broad range of previously unconnected theories and hypotheses. This restatement does so by showing how *liberalism provides a general theory of IR linking apparently unrelated areas of inquiry.* The theory outlined here applies equally to liberal and nonliberal states, economic and national security affairs, conflictual and nonconflictual situations, and the behavior both of individual states ("foreign policy") and of aggregations of states ("international relations"). Liberal theory, moreover, explains important phenomena overlooked by alternative theories, including the substantive content of foreign policy, historical change, and the distinctiveness of interstate relations among modern Western states.

---

4. See Keohane 1990, 166, 172–73; Doyle 1986, 1152; Zacher and Matthew 1992, 2; Matthew and Zacher 1995, 107–11, 117–20; Hoffmann 1987, 1995; and Nye 1988.
5. For other such distinctions, see Keohane 1990; and Doyle 1983.

Second, a theoretical restatement should be *rigorous and coherent,* offering a clear definition of its own boundaries. This restatement does so by demonstrating that *institutionalist theories of regimes—commonly treated as liberal due to ideological and historical connotations—are in fact based on assumptions closer to realism than to liberalism.* This helps to explain why IR theorists have found it difficult to distill a set of coherent microfoundational assumptions for liberal theory.

Third, a theoretical restatement should *demonstrate empirical accuracy vis-à-vis other theories;* it should expose anomalies in existing work, forcing reconsideration of empirical findings and theoretical positions. This restatement of liberal theory meets this criterion by *revealing significant methodological biases in empirical evaluations of realist theories of "relative gains-seeking" and constructivist analyses of ideas and IR due to the omission of liberal alternatives.* If these biases were corrected, liberal accounts might well supplant many widely accepted realist and institutionalist, as well as constructivist, explanations of particular phenomena in world politics.

Fourth, a theoretical restatement should *demonstrate multicausal consistency.* By specifying the antecedent conditions under which it is valid and the precise causal links to policy outcomes, a theory should specify rigorously how it can be synthesized with other theories into a multicausal explanation consistent with tenets of fundamental social theory. This restatement does so by reversing the nearly universal presumption among contemporary IR theorists that "systemic" theories like realism and institutionalism should be employed as an analytical "first cut," with theories of "domestic" preference formation brought in only to explain anomalies—a prescription that is both methodologically biased and theoretically incoherent. In its place, this restatement dictates the reverse: *Liberal theory is analytically prior to both realism and institutionalism because it defines the conditions under which their assumptions hold.*

If this proposed reformulation of liberal IR theory meets these four criteria, as I argue it does, there is good reason to accord it a paradigmatic position empirically coequal with and analytically prior to realism and institutionalism, as well as constructivism, in theory and research on world politics.

Core Assumptions of Liberal IR Theory

Liberal IR theory's fundamental premise—that the relationship between states and the surrounding domestic and transnational society in which they are embedded critically shapes state behavior by influencing the social purposes underlying state preferences—can be restated in terms of three core assumptions. These assumptions are appropriate foundations of any social theory of IR: they specify the nature of societal actors, the state, and the international system.

Assumption 1: The Primacy of Societal Actors

The fundamental actors in international politics are individuals and private groups, who are on the average rational and risk-averse and who organize exchange and collective action to promote differentiated interests under constraints imposed by material scarcity, conflicting values, and variations in societal influence.

Liberal theory rests on a "bottom-up" view of politics in which the demands of individuals and societal groups are treated as analytically prior to politics. Political action is embedded in domestic and transnational civil society, understood as an aggregation of boundedly rational individuals with differentiated tastes, social commitments, and resource endowments. Socially differentiated individuals define their material and ideational interests independently of politics and then advance those interests through political exchange and collective action.[6] Individuals and groups are assumed to act rationally in pursuit of material and ideal welfare.[7]

For liberals, the definition of the interests of societal actors is theoretically central. Liberal theory rejects the utopian notion that an *automatic* harmony of interest exists among individuals and groups in society; scarcity and differentiation introduce an inevitable measure of competition. Where social incentives for exchange and collective action are perceived to exist, individuals and groups exploit them: the greater the expected benefits, the stronger the incentive to act. In pursuing these goals, individuals are on the average risk-averse; that is, they strongly defend existing investments but remain more cautious about assuming cost and risk in pursuit of new gains. What is true about people on the average, however, is not necessarily true in every case: some individuals in any given society may be risk-acceptant or irrational.

Liberal theory seeks to generalize about the social conditions under which the behavior of self-interested actors converges toward cooperation or conflict. Conflictual societal demands and the willingness to employ coercion in pursuit of them are associated with a number of factors, three of which are relevant to this discussion: divergent fundamental beliefs, conflict over scarce material goods, and inequalities in political power. Deep, irreconcilable differences in beliefs about the provision of public goods, such as borders, culture, fundamental political institutions, and local social practices, promote conflict, whereas complementary beliefs promote harmony and cooperation. Extreme scarcity tends to exacerbate conflict over resources by increasing the willingness of social actors to assume cost and risk to obtain them. Relative abundance, by contrast, lowers the propensity for conflict by providing the opportunity to satisfy wants without inevitable conflict and giving certain individuals and groups more to defend. Finally, where inequalities in societal influence are large, conflict is more likely. Where social power is equitably distributed, the costs and benefits of actions are more likely to be internalized to individuals—for example, through the existence of complex, cross-cutting patterns of mutually beneficial interaction or strong and legitimate domestic political institutions—and the incentive for selective or arbitrary coercion is dampened. By contrast, where power asymmetries permit groups to evade the costs of redistributing goods, incentives arise for exploitative, rent-seeking behavior, even if the result is inefficient for society as a whole. [8]

---

6. This does not imply a "pre-social" conception of the individual unencumbered by nation, community, family, or other collective identities but only that these identities enter the political realm when individuals and groups engage in political exchange on the basis of them; see, for example, Coleman 1990.

7. Kant 1991, 44.

8. Milgrom and Roberts 1990, 86–87.

Assumption 2: Representation and State Preferences

States (or other political institutions) represent some subset of domestic society, on the basis of whose interests state officials define state preferences and act purposively in world politics.

In the liberal conception of domestic politics, the state is not an actor but a representative institution constantly subject to capture and recapture, construction and reconstruction by coalitions of social actors. Representative institutions and practices constitute the critical "transmission belt" by which the preferences and social power of individuals and groups are translated into state policy. Individuals turn to the state to achieve goals that private behavior is unable to achieve efficiently.[9] Government policy is therefore constrained by the underlying identities, interests, and power of individuals and groups (inside and outside the state apparatus) who constantly pressure the central decision makers to pursue policies consistent with their preferences.

This is not to adopt a narrowly pluralist view of domestic politics in which all individuals and groups have equal influence on state policy, nor one in which the structure of state institutions is irrelevant. No government rests on universal or unbiased political representation; every government represents some individuals and groups more fully than others. In an extreme hypothetical case, representation might empower a narrow bureaucratic class or even a single tyrannical individual, such as an ideal-typical Pol Pot or Josef Stalin. Between theoretical extremes of tyranny and democracy, many representative institutions and practices exist, each of which privileges particular demands; hence the nature of state institutions, alongside societal interests themselves, is a key determinant of what states do internationally.

Representation, in the liberal view, is not simply a formal attribute of state institutions but includes other stable characteristics of the political process, formal or informal, that privilege particular societal interests. Clientalistic authoritarian regimes may distinguish those with familial, bureaucratic, or economic ties to the governing elite from those without. Even where government institutions are formally fair and open, a relatively inegalitarian distribution of property, risk, information, or organizational capabilities may create social or economic monopolies able to dominate policy. Similarly, the way in which a state recognizes individual rights may shape opportunities for voice.[10] Certain domestic representational processes may tend to select as leaders individuals, groups, and bureaucracies socialized with particular attitudes toward information, risk, and loss. Finally, cost-effective exit options, such as emigration, noncompliance, or the transfer of assets to new jurisdictions or uses, insofar as they constrain governments, may be thought of as substitutes for formal representation.[11]

---

9. Representative political institutions and practices result from prior contracts and can generally be taken for granted in explaining foreign policy; but where the primary interests and allegiances of individuals and private groups are transferred to subnational or supranational institutions empowered to represent them effectively, a liberal analysis would naturally shift to these levels.

10. Doyle 1997, 251–300.

11. North and Thomas 1973, 87.

Societal pressures transmitted by representative institutions and practices alter "state preferences." This term designates an ordering among underlying substantive outcomes that may result from international political interaction. Here it is essential—particularly given the inconsistency of common usage—to avoid conceptual confusion by keeping state "preferences" distinct from national "strategies," "tactics," and "policies," that is, the particular transient bargaining positions, negotiating demands, or policy goals that constitute the everyday currency of foreign policy. State preferences, as the concept is employed here, comprise a set of fundamental interests defined across "states of the world." Preferences are by definition causally independent of the strategies of other actors and, therefore, prior to specific interstate political interactions, including external threats, incentives, manipulation of information, or other tactics. By contrast, strategies and tactics—sometimes also termed "preferences" in game-theoretical analyses—are policy options defined across intermediate political aims, as when governments declare an "interest" in "maintaining the balance of power," "containing" or "appeasing" an adversary, or exercising "global leadership."[12] Liberal theory focuses on the consequences for state behavior of shifts in fundamental preferences, not shifts in the strategic circumstances under which states pursue them.

Representative institutions and practices determine not merely which social coalitions are represented in foreign policy, but how they are represented. Two distinctions are critical. First, states may act in either a unitary or "disaggregated" way. In many traditional areas of foreign policy, "politics stops at the water's edge," and there is strong coordination among national officials and politicians. In other areas, the state may be "disaggregated," with different elements—executives, courts, central banks, regulatory bureaucracies, and ruling parties, for example—conducting semiautonomous foreign policies in the service of disparate societal interests.[13] Second, domestic decision making may be structured so as to generate state preferences that satisfy a strong rationality condition, such as transitivity or strict expected utility maximization, or so as to satisfy only the weaker rationality criterion of seeking efficient means. Recently, formal theorists have derived specific conditions under which nonunitary state behavior can be analyzed "as if" it were unitary and rational, implying that much superficially "nonrational" or "nonunitary" behavior should actually be understood in terms of shifting state preferences.[14]

Taken together, assumptions 1 and 2 imply that states do not automatically maximize fixed, homogeneous conceptions of security, sovereignty, or wealth per se, as realists and institutionalists tend to assume. Instead they are, in Waltzian terms, "functionally differentiated"; that is, they pursue particular interpretations and combinations of security, welfare, and sovereignty preferred by powerful domestic groups

---

12. The phrase "country A changed its preferences in response to an action by country B" is thus a misuse of the term as defined here, implying less than consistently rational behavior; see Sebenius 1991, 207.

13. See Slaughter 1995; and Keohane and Nye 1971.

14. Achen 1995.

enfranchised by representative institutions and practices.[15] As Arnold Wolfers, John Ruggie, and others have observed, the nature and intensity of national support for any state purpose—even apparently fundamental concerns like the defense of political and legal sovereignty, territorial integrity, national security, or economic welfare— varies decisively with the social context.[16] It is not uncommon for states knowingly to surrender sovereignty, compromise security, or reduce aggregate economic welfare. In the liberal view, trade-offs among such goals, as well as cross-national differences in their definition, are inevitable, highly varied, and causally consequential.[17]

Assumption 3: Interdependence and the International System

The configuration of interdependent state preferences determines state behavior.

For liberals, state behavior reflects varying patterns of state preferences. States require a "purpose," a perceived underlying stake in the matter at hand, in order to provoke conflict, propose cooperation, or take any other significant foreign policy action. The precise nature of these stakes drives policy. This is not to assert that each state simply pursues its ideal policy, oblivious of others; instead, each state seeks to realize *its* distinctive preferences under varying constraints imposed by the preferences of *other states*. Thus liberal theory rejects not just the realist assumption that state preferences must be treated as if naturally conflictual, but equally the institutionalist assumption that they should be treated as if they were partially convergent, compromising a collective action problem.[18] To the contrary, liberals causally privilege variation in the configuration of state preferences, while treating configurations of capabilities and information as if they were either fixed constraints or endogenous to state preferences.

The critical theoretical link between state preferences, on the one hand, and the behavior of one or more states, on the other, is provided by the concept of policy interdependence. Policy interdependence is defined here as the set of costs and benefits created for foreign societies when dominant social groups in a society seek to realize their preferences, that is, the pattern of transnational externalities resulting from attempts to pursue national distinctive purposes. Liberal theory assumes that the pattern of interdependent state preferences imposes a binding constraint on state behavior.

Patterns of interdependence or externalities induced by efforts to realize state preferences can be divided into three broad categories, corresponding to the strategic situation (the pattern of policy externalities) that results.[19] Where preferences are naturally compatible or harmonious, that is, where the externalities of unilateral poli-

---

15. Ruggie 1983, 265.

16. Ruggie 1982, 1983.

17. On the contradictions within Waltz's effort to avoid these ambiguities, see Baldwin 1997, 21–22.

18. Keohane 1984, 10; 1986, 193. Note that these are all "as if" assumptions. The world must be consistent with them, but need not fulfill them precisely.

19. See Stein 1982; Snidal 1985; and Martin 1992.

cies are optimal for others (or insignificant), there are strong incentives for coexistence with low conflict.

Where, by contrast, underlying state preferences are zero-sum or deadlocked, that is, where an attempt by dominant social groups in one country to realize their preferences through state action *necessarily* imposes costs (negative externalities) on dominant social groups in other countries, governments face a bargaining game with few mutual gains and a high potential for interstate tension and conflict. The decisive precondition for costly attempts at coercion, for example, is neither a particular configuration of power, as realists assert, nor of uncertainty, as institutionalists maintain, but a configuration of preferences conflictual enough to motivate willingness to accept high cost and risk.[20] In other words, intense conflict requires that an aggressor or revisionist state advance demands to which other states are unwilling to submit. Revisionist preferences—underlying, socially grounded interests in revising the status quo—are distinct from revisionist "strategies," that is, a need to alter the status quo to protect enduring interests under new strategic circumstances. Liberals focus on the former, realists (and institutionalists) on the latter. Hence while both theories predict security conflict, they do so under different circumstances. For example, increased military spending in response to an adversary's arms buildup is a change in strategy with fixed preferences consistent with realism; increased spending initiated by a new ruling elite ideologically committed to territorial aggrandizement is a preference-induced change in strategy consistent with liberalism.[21]

Where, finally, motives are mixed such that an exchange of policy concessions through coordination or precommitment can improve the welfare of both parties relative to unilateral policy adjustment (i.e., a collective action problem), states have an incentive to negotiate policy coordination. Games like coordination, assurance, prisoner's dilemma, and suasion have distinctive dynamics, as well as impose precise costs, benefits, and risks on the parties. Within each qualitative category, incentives vary further according to the intensity of preferences.

For liberals, the form, substance, and depth of cooperation depends directly on the nature of these patterns of preferences. Hence where "Pareto-inefficient" outcomes are observed—trade protection is a commonly cited example—liberals turn first to countervailing social preferences and unresolved domestic and transnational distributional conflicts, whereas institutionalists and realists, respectively, turn to uncertainty and particular configurations of interstate power.[22]

Liberal Theory as Systemic Theory

These liberal assumptions, in particular the third—in essence, "what states want is the primary determinant of what they do"—may seem commonsensical, even tautological. Yet mainstream IR theory has uniformly rejected such claims for the past

---

20. Note that some rationalist analyses dismiss such risk-acceptant preferences as "irrational"; see Fearon 1995.
21. For example, Van Evera 1990–91, 32.
22. Grieco's study of NTB regulation is discussed later.

half-century. At the heart of the two leading contemporary IR theories, realism and institutionalism, is the belief that state behavior has *ironic* consequences.[23] Power politics and informational uncertainty constrain states to pursue second- and third-best strategies strikingly at variance with their underlying preferences.[24] Thus varying state preferences should be treated as if they were irrelevant, secondary, or endogenous. In his classic definition of realism Morgenthau contrasts it to "two popular fallacies: the concern with motives and the concern with ideological preferences."[25] Neorealist Waltz's central objection to previous, "reductionist" theories is that in world politics "results achieved seldom correspond to the intentions of actors"; hence "no valid generalizations can logically be drawn" from an examination of intentions.[26] Though the interests it assumes are different, Keohane's institutionalism relies on a similar as if assumption: it "takes the existence of mutual interests as given and examines the conditions under which they will lead to cooperation."[27] In short, Powell observes that "structural theories . . . lack a theory of preferences over outcomes."[28] What states do is primarily determined by strategic considerations—what they can get or what they know—which in turn reflect their international political environment. In short, variation in means, not ends, matters most.[29]

Liberal theory reverses this assumption: *Variation in ends, not means, matters most.* Realists and institutionalists, as well as formal theorists who seek to integrate the two, criticize this core liberal assumption because it appears at first glance to rest on what Waltz terms a "reductionist" rather than a "systemic" understanding of IR. In other words, liberalism appears to be a purely "domestic" or "unit-level" theory that ignores the international environment. In particular, realists are skeptical of this view because it appears at first glance to be grounded in the utopian expectation that every state can do as it pleases. This commonplace criticism is erroneous for two important reasons.

First, state preferences may reflect patterns of transnational *societal* interaction. While state preferences are (by definition) invariant in response to changing inter-state political and strategic circumstances, they may vary in response to a changing transnational *social* context. In the political economy for foreign economic policy,

---

23. What about Marxism? Marxism provides distinctive normative insights (Doyle 1997), but its non-teleological positive assumptions—the centrality of domestic economic interests, the importance of transnational interdependence, the state as a representative of dominant social forces—are quite compatible with this restatement of liberalism. For examples, see the contribution by Frieden and Rogowski in Keohane and Milner 1996.

24. Waltz 1979, 60–67, 93–97.

25. The resulting "autonomy of the political" in geopolitics gives realism its "distinctive intellectual and moral attitude"; see Morgenthau 1960, 5–7. The fact that Morgenthau distinguished nonrealist elements of his own thought illustrates a further danger of defining realism not in terms of social scientific assumptions, but in terms of its intellectual history, that is, assuming that everything a "realist" wrote constitutes a coherent realist theory; see Morgenthau 1960, 5, 227.

26. Waltz follows Morgenthau almost verbatim: "Neo-realism establishes the autonomy of international politics and thus makes a theory about it possible"; see Waltz 1979, 29, and also 65–66, 79, 90, 108–12, 196–98, 271.

27. See Keohane 1984, 6; and Hellmann and Wolf 1993.

28. Powell 1994, 318.

29. Ruggie 1983, 107–10.

for example, social demands are derived not simply from "domestic" economic assets and endowments, but from the relative position of those assets and endowments in global markets. Similarly, the position of particular values in a transnational cultural discourse may help define their meaning in each society. In this regard, liberalism does not draw a strict line between domestic and transnational levels of analysis.[30]

A second and more Waltzian reason why the charge of "reductionism" is erroneous is that according to liberal theory the expected behavior of any single state—the strategies it selects and the systemic constraints to which it adjusts—reflect not simply its own preferences, but the configuration of preferences of *all* states linked by patterns of significant policy interdependence. National leaders must always think systemically about their position within a structure composed of the preferences of other states. Since the pattern of and interdependence among state preferences, like the distribution of capabilities and the distribution of information and ideas, lies outside the control of any single state, it conforms to Waltz's own definition of systemic theory, whereby interstate interactions are explained by reference to "how [states] stand in relation to one another."[31] Hence the causal preeminence of state preferences does not imply that states always get what they want.

One implication of liberalism's systemic, structural quality is that, contra Waltz, it can explain not only the "foreign policy" goals of individual states but the "systemic" outcomes of interstate interactions. That systemic predictions can follow from domestic theories of preferences should be obvious simply by inspecting the literature on the democratic peace.[32] In addition, by linking social purpose to the symmetry and relative intensity of state preferences, liberalism offers *a distinctive conception of political power* in world politics—something traditionally considered unique to realist theory.

The liberal conception of power is based on an assumption *more* consistent with basic theories of bargaining and negotiation than those underlying realism: namely that the willingness of states to expend resources or make concessions is itself primarily a function of preferences, not capabilities. In this view—the foundation of Nash bargaining analysis, which has been extended to IR by Albert Hirshman, Keohane, Joseph Nye, and others—bargaining outcomes reflect the nature and relative intensity of actor preferences.[33] The "win-set," the "best alternative to negotiated agreement," the pattern of "asymmetrical interdependence," the relative opportunity cost of forgoing an agreement—all these core terms in negotiation analysis refer to different aspects of the relationship of bargaining outcomes on the preference functions of the actors. The capability-based power to threaten central to realism enters the equation in specific circumstances and only through linkage to threats and side-payments. Even where capability-based threats and promises are employed, preference-based determinants of the tolerance for bearing bargaining costs, including differential tem-

---

30. For example, see Gourevitch 1976.
31. Ruggie 1983, 90–91.
32. For a more general argument, see Elman 1996, especially 58–59.
33. See Harsanyi 1977; Hirshman 1945; and Keohane and Nye 1987, 733.

poral discount rates, risk-acceptance, and willingness to accept punishment, remain central.[34]

The liberal claim that the pattern of interdependence among state preferences is a primary determinant not just of individual foreign policies, but of systemic outcomes, is commonsensical. Nations are rarely prepared to expend their entire economic or defense capabilities, or to mortgage their entire domestic sovereignty, in pursuit of any single foreign policy goal. Few wars are total, few peaces Carthaginian. Treating the willingness of states to expend resources in pursuit of foreign policy goals as a strict function of existing capabilities thus seems unrealistic. On the margin, the binding constraint is instead generally "resolve" or "determination"—the *willingness* of governments to mobilize and expend social resources for foreign policy purposes.

Extensive empirical evidence supports this assumption. Even in "least likely" cases, where political independence and territorial integrity are at stake and military means are deployed, relative capabilities do not necessarily determine outcomes. A "strong preference for the issue at stake can compensate for a deficiency in capabilities," as demonstrated by examples like the Boer War, Hitler's remilitarization of the Rhineland, Vietnam, Afghanistan, and Chechnya. In each case the relative intensity of state preferences reshaped the outcome to the advantage of the "weak."[35] Such examples suggest that the liberal view of power politics, properly understood, generates plausible explanations not just of harmony and cooperation among nations, but of the full range of phenomena central to the study of world politics, from peaceful economic exchange to brutal guerrilla warfare.

Variants of Liberal Theory

Like their realist and institutionalist counterparts, the three core liberal assumptions introduced earlier are relatively thin or content-free. Taken by themselves, they do not define a single unambiguous model or set of hypotheses, not least because they do not specify precise sources of state preferences. Instead they support three separate variants of liberal theory, termed here ideational, commercial, and republican liberalism. Each rests on a distinctive specification of the central elements of liberal theory: social demands, the causal mechanisms whereby they are transformed into state preferences, and the resulting patterns of national preferences in world politics. Ideational liberalism focuses on the compatibility of social preferences across fundamental collective goods like national unity, legitimate political institutions, and socioeconomic regulation. Commercial liberalism focuses on incentives created by opportunities for transborder economic transactions. Republican liberalism focuses on the nature of domestic representation and the resulting possibilities for rent-seeking behavior.

---

34. See Raiffa 1982; Sebenius 1991; Evans, Jacobson, and Putnam 1993; and Keohane and Nye 1977.
35. See Morrow 1988, 83–84; and Mack 1975.

Ideational Liberalism: Identity and Legitimate Social Order

Drawing on a liberal tradition dating back to John Stuart Mill, Giuseppe Mazzini, and Woodrow Wilson, ideational liberalism views the configuration of domestic social identities and values as a basic determinant of state preferences and, therefore, of interstate conflict and cooperation. "Social identity" is defined as the set of preferences shared by individuals concerning the proper scope and nature of public goods provision, which in turn specifies the nature of legitimate domestic order by stipulating which social actors belong to the polity and what is owed them.[36] Liberals take no distinctive position on the origins of social identities, which may result from historical accretion or be constructed through conscious collective or state action, nor on the question of whether they ultimately reflect ideational or material factors.[37]

Three essential elements of domestic public order often shaped by social identities are geographical borders, political decision-making processes, and socioeconomic regulation. Each can be thought of as a public or club good; the effectiveness of each typically requires that it be legislated universally across a jurisdiction.[38] Recall that for liberals, even the defense of (or, less obvious but no less common, the willing compromise of) territorial integrity, political sovereignty, or national security is not an end in itself, but a means of realizing underlying preferences defined by the demands of societal groups. According to assumption 2, social actors provide support to the government in exchange for institutions that accord with their identity-based preferences; such institutions are thereby "legitimate." Foreign policy will thus be motivated in part by an effort to realize social views about legitimate borders, political institutions, and modes of socioeconomic regulation.

The consequences of identity-based preferences for IR depend, according to assumption 3, on the nature of transnational externalities created by attempts to realize them. Where national conceptions of legitimate borders, political institutions, and socioeconomic equality are compatible, thus generating positive or negligible externalities, harmony is likely. Where national claims can be made more compatible by reciprocal policy adjustment, cooperation is likely.[39] Where social identities are incompatible and create significant negative externalities, tension and zero-sum conflict is more likely. Parallel predictions about international politics follow from each of the three essential sources of ideational preferences: national, political, and socioeconomic identity.[40] Let us briefly consider each.

---

36. This concept is similar but narrower than Ruggie's "legitimate social purpose" and Katzenstein's "collective identity"; see Ruggie 1983; Katzenstein 1996a, 6.

37. Here is a point of tangency with recent constructivist work; see Katzenstein 1996a, 5; Finnemore 1996, 27–28; and Wendt 1996, 7. Whether the *fundamental* sources of societal preferences are ideational is the focus of a debate among general social theorists for which IR theorists lack any distinctive comparative advantage.

38. Fearon 1995.

39. Oye 1986.

40. Liberal theory need not and in general does not claim that shared identities emerge from chance interactions among "atomistic" individuals, or that nationality must reflect "timeless" factors like language, religion, or ethnicity. Identities need only be translated into political preferences through individual and group commitments; compare Finnemore 1996, 147.

The first fundamental type of social identity central to the domestic legitimacy of foreign policy comprises the set of *fundamental societal preferences concerning the scope of the "nation," which in turn suggest the legitimate location of national borders and the allocation of citizenship rights.* The roots of national identity may reflect a shared set of linguistic, cultural, or religious identifications or a shared set of historical experiences—often interpreted and encouraged by both private groups and state policy. In explaining conflict and cooperation over borders and citizenship, realism stresses the role of relative power, and institutionalism stresses the role of shared legal norms, whereas ideational liberalism stresses the extent to which borders coincide with the national identities of powerful social groups.[41] Where borders coincide with underlying patterns of identity, coexistence and even mutual recognition are more likely. Where, however, inconsistencies between borders and underlying patterns of identity exist, greater potential for interstate conflict exists. In such circumstances, some social actors and governments are likely to have an interest in uniting nationals in appropriate jurisdictions, perhaps through armed aggression or secession; other governments may intervene militarily to promote or hinder such efforts. More than twenty years before conflict reemerged in the former Yugoslavia, Myron Weiner termed the resulting disruptive international behavior—a recurrent complex of aggression, exacerbation of nationalist ideologies, offensive alliance formation, and risk acceptance in foreign policy—the "Macedonian syndrome."[42]

Strong empirical evidence supports the proposition that disjunctures between borders and identities are important determinants of international conflict and cooperation. In early modern Europe, interstate conflict reflected in part the competition between two communal religious identities—each of which, at least until domestic and international norms of tolerance spread, was perceived as a threat to the other.[43] Over the last century and a half, from mid-nineteenth-century nationalist uprisings to late-twentieth-century national liberation struggles, the desire for national autonomy constitutes the most common issue over which wars have been fought and great power intervention has taken place; the Balkan conflicts preceding World War I and succeeding the Cold War are only the most notorious examples.[44] The post–World War II peace in Western Europe and the reintegration of Germany into Europe were assisted by the reestablishment of borders along ethnic lines in the Saar and Alsace-Lorraine, as well as much of Eastern Europe. Even leading realists now concede—though it in no way follows from realist premises—that disputes between "intermingled or divided nationalities" are the most probable catalyst for war in Eastern Europe and the former Soviet Union.[45]

---

41. See Jackson 1990; and Gilpin 1989.

42. See Weiner 1971; and Pillar 1983, 24–26.

43. Philpott 1996.

44. Holsti 1991. Even those who stress the absence of credible commitment mechanisms in explaining nationalist conflicts concede the importance of underlying identities; see Fearon 1996, 56.

45. To be sure, Mearsheimer heroically asserts that nationalism is a "second-order force in international politics," with a "largely . . . international" cause, namely multipolarity; see Mearsheimer 1990, 21. This is testable: Is violent nationalism more of an international problem in Central and Eastern Europe than in Western Europe, as liberalism predicts, or an equal problem in both areas, as realism predicts?

A second fundamental type of social identity central to foreign policymaking is *the commitment of individuals and groups to particular political institutions.* Realism accords theoretical weight to domestic regime type only insofar as it influences the distribution of capabilities, institutionalism only insofar as it contributes to the certainty of coordination and commitment. Ideational liberalism, by contrast, maintains that differences in perceptions of domestic political legitimacy translate into patterns of underlying preferences and thus variation in international conflict and cooperation. Where the realization of legitimate domestic political order in one jurisdiction threatens its realization in others, a situation of negative externalities, conflict is more likely. Where the realization of national conceptions of legitimate decision making reinforce or can be adjusted to reinforce one another, coexistence or cooperation is more likely.[46]

Plausible examples abound. Thucydides accords an important role to conflict between oligarchs and democrats in alliance formation during the Peloponnesian War. In the seventeenth and eighteenth centuries, absolutist kings fought to establish dynastic claims and religious rule; in the nineteenth century, they cooperated to preserve monarchical rule against societal pressures for reform.[47] The twentieth century has witnessed a struggle between governments backing fascist, communist, and liberal ideologies, as well as more recently a resurgence of religious claims and the emergence of a group of developed countries that share democratic norms of legitimate dispute resolution—a plausible explanation for the "democratic peace" phenomenon.[48] A more complex pattern, consistent with the preceding assumptions, may emerge when individual domestic actors—most often national executives—exploit the legitimacy of particular international policies as a "two-level" instrument to increase their influence over the domestic polity. This is a constant theme in modern world politics, from Bismarck's manipulation of domestic coalitions to the current use of monetary integration by today's European leaders to "strengthen the state" at home.[49]

A third fundamental type of social identity central to foreign policy *is the nature of legitimate socioeconomic regulation and redistribution.* Modern liberal theory (as opposed to the laissez faire libertarianism sometimes invoked by critics as quintessentially "liberal") has long recognized that societal preferences concerning the nature and level of regulation impose legitimate limits on markets.[50] In a Polanyian vein, Ruggie recently reminds us that domestic and international markets are embedded in local social compromises concerning the provision of regulatory public goods.[51] Such compromises underlie varying national regulations on immigration, social welfare, taxation, religious freedom, families, health and safety, environmental and

---

46. Governments may actually have altruistic preferences (see Lumsdaine 1993) or may seek to create an international environment conducive to the realization of domestic values (see Moravcsik 1995).
47. See Nolt 1990; and Barkin and Cronin 1994.
48. Russett 1993, 30–38.
49. See Evans, Jacobson, and Putnam 1994; Wehler 1985; and Moravcsik 1994.
50. Holmes 1995.
51. Ruggie 1992.

consumer protection, cultural promotion, and many other public goods increasingly discussed in international economic negotiations.

In the liberal view, state preferences concerning legitimate socioeconomic practices shape interstate behavior when their realization imposes significant transborder externalities. Evidence from the European Community (EC) suggests that substantial prior convergence of underlying values is a necessary prerequisite for cooperation in regulatory issue areas like environmental and consumer protection, many tax and social policies, immigration, and foreign policy, as well as for significant surrenders of sovereign decision making to supranational courts and bureaucracies. Regulatory pluralism limits international cooperation, in particular economic liberalization. Courts, executives, and parliaments mutually recognize "legitimate differences" of policy in foreign jurisdictions.[52] Concerns about the proper balance between policy coordination and legitimate domestic regulation are giving rise to even more complex forms of cooperation. Hence regulatory issues play an increasingly important role in international economic negotiations such as the 1992 initiative of the EC, the Uruguay Round of GATT, NAFTA, and the U.S.–Japan Structural Impediments Initiative.[53]

Commercial Liberalism: Economic Assets and Cross-Border Transactions

Commercial liberalism explains the individual and collective behavior of states based on the patterns of market incentives facing domestic and transnational economic actors. At its simplest, the commercial liberal argument is broadly functionalist: Changes in the structure of the domestic and global economy alter the costs and benefits of transnational economic exchange, creating pressure on domestic governments to facilitate or block such exchanges through appropriate foreign economic and security policies.

It is tempting, particularly for critics, to associate commercial liberal theory with ideological support for free trade. Yet as theory rather than ideology, commercial liberalism does *not* predict that economic incentives automatically generate universal free trade and peace—a utopian position critics who treat liberalism as an ideology often wrongly attribute to it—but instead stresses the interaction between aggregate incentives for certain policies and obstacles posed by domestic and transnational distributional conflict.[54] The greater the economic benefits for powerful private actors, the greater their incentive, other things being equal, to press governments to facilitate such transactions; the more costly the adjustment imposed by economic interchange, the more opposition is likely to arise. Rather than assuming that market structure always creates incentives for cooperation among social actors as well as states, or focusing exclusively on those issue areas where it does, as do some liberal

52. Burley 1992.
53. Ruggie 1995.
54. Compare Gilpin 1975, 27.

ideologies, liberal IR theory focuses on market structure as a variable creating incentives for both openness and closure.

Accordingly, many commercial liberal analyses start with aggregate welfare gains from trade resulting from specialization and functional differentiation, then seek to explain divergences from foreign economic and security policies that would maximize those gains. To explain the rejection of aggregate gains, commercial liberals from Adam Smith to contemporary "endogenous" tariff theorists look to domestic and international distributional conflicts. The resulting commercial liberal explanation of relative-gains seeking in foreign economic policy is quite distinct from that of realism, which emphasizes security externalities and relative (hegemonic) power, or that of institutionalism, which stresses informational and institutional constraints on interstate collective action.[55]

One source of pressure for protection is domestic distributional conflict, which arises when the costs and benefits of national policies are not internalized to the same actors, thus encouraging rent-seeking efforts to seek personal benefit at the expense of aggregate welfare. In this view, uncompetitive, monopolistic, or undiversified sectors or factors lose the most from liberalization and have an incentive to oppose it, inducing a systematic divergence from laissez faire policies. Smith himself reminds us that "the contrivers of [mercantilism are] the producers, whose interest has been so carefully attended to . . . our merchants and manufacturers"—a view echoed by many liberals since.[56] Recent research supports the view that protectionist pressure from rent-seeking groups is most intense precisely where distributional concerns of concentrated groups are strongest, for example, when industries are uncompetitive or irreversible investments (asset specificity) impose high adjustment costs on concentrated interests. Free trade is more likely where strong competitiveness, extensive intra-industry trade, or trade in intermediate goods, large foreign investments, and low asset specificity internalize the net benefits of free trade to powerful actors, thus reducing the influence of net losers from liberalization.[57]

The distributional consequences of global market imperfections create a second sort of disjuncture between the aggregate benefits of economic interdependence and national policies. Modern trade theory identifies incentives for strategic behavior where increasing returns to scale, high fixed costs, surplus capacity, or highly concentrated sources of supply render international markets imperfectly competitive. Firms hoping to create (or break into) a global oligopoly or monopoly, for example, may have an incentive to engage in predatory dumping abroad while seeking domestic protection and subsidization at home, even though this imposes costs on domestic consumers and foreign producers. Such policies can create substantial international conflict, since government intervention to assist firms can improve welfare for society as a whole, though usually not for all societies involved.[58]

55. Grieco 1988; Gowa 1989; and Keohane 1984.
56. Ekelund and Tollison 1981, 25.
57. Milner 1988.
58. Keohane and Milner 1996, 39.

Commercial liberalism has important implications for security affairs as well. Trade is generally a less costly means of accumulating wealth than war, sanctions, or other coercive means, not least due to the minimization of collateral damage. Yet governments sometimes have an incentive to employ coercive means to create and control international markets. To explain this variation, domestic distributional issues and the structure of global markets are again critical. Commercial liberals argue that the more diversified and complex the existing transnational commercial ties and production structures, the less cost-effective coercion is likely to be.[59] Cost-effective coercion was most profitable in an era where the main sources of economic profit, such as farmland, slave labor, raw materials, or formal monopoly, could be easily controlled in conquered or colonial economies. Yet economic development tends to increase the material stake of social actors in *existing* investments, thereby reducing their willingness to assume the cost and risk of coercion through war or sanctions.[60] As production becomes more specialized and efficient and trading networks more diverse and complex, political extraction (for example, war and embargoes) become more disruptive, and profitable monopolies over commercial opportunities become more difficult to establish. Both cross-cultural anthropological evidence and modern cross-national evidence link warfare to the existence of monopolizable resources; over the past century, it has remained the major determinant of boundary disputes.[61] Yet the advent of modern industrial networks, particularly those based on postindustrial informational exchange, has increased the opportunity costs of coercive tactics ranging from military aggression to coercive nationalization.[62]

Republican Liberalism: Representation and Rent Seeking

While ideational and commercial liberal theory, respectively, stress demands resulting from particular patterns of underlying societal identities and economic interests, republican liberal theory emphasizes the ways in which domestic institutions and practices aggregate those demands, transforming them into state policy. The key variable in republican liberalism is the mode of domestic political representation, which determines whose social preferences are institutionally privileged. When political representation is biased in favor of particularistic groups, they tend to "capture" government institutions and employ them for their ends alone, systematically passing on the costs and risks to others. The precise policy of governments depends on which domestic groups are represented. The simplest resulting prediction is that policy is biased in favor of the governing coalition or powerful domestic groups.

A more sophisticated extension of this reasoning focuses on rent seeking. When particularistic groups are able to formulate policy without necessarily providing offsetting gains for society as a whole, the result is likely to be inefficient, suboptimal

59. Van Evera 1990.
60. Realist theory, with its assumptions of a unitary state and fixed preferences, simply presumes that the greater the wealth and power of a state, the less the marginal cost of deploying it, thus reducing power to capabilities. Liberal theory suggests different predictions. The two are testable.
61. See Huth 1996; and Keeley 1996.
62. See Van Evera 1990, 14–16, 28–29; and Kaysen 1990, 53.

policies from the aggregate perspective—one form of which may be costly international conflict.[63] While many liberal arguments are concerned with the seizure of state institutions by administrators (rulers, armies, and bureaucracies), similar arguments apply to privileged societal groups that "capture" the state, according to assumption 2, or simply act independently of it. If, following assumption 1, most individuals and groups in society, while acquisitive, tend also to be risk-averse (at least where they have something to lose), the more unbiased the range of domestic groups represented, the less likely they will support policies that impose high net costs or risks on a broad range of social actors. Thus aggressive behavior—the voluntary recourse to costly or risky foreign policy—is most likely in undemocratic or inegalitarian polities where privileged individuals can easily pass costs on to others.[64]

This does not, of course, imply the existence of a one-to-one correspondence between the breadth of domestic representation and international political or economic cooperation, for two reasons. First, in specific cases, elite preferences may be more convergent than popular ones. If commercial or ideational preferences are conflictual, for example where hypernationalist or mercantilist preferences prevail, a broadening of representation may have the opposite effect—a point to which I will return. Elites, such as those leaders that constructed the Concert of Europe or similar arrangements among African leaders today, have been attributed to their convergent interests in maintaining themselves in office. Second, the extent of bias in representation, not democratic participation per se, is the theoretically critical point. Direct representation may overrepresent concentrated, organized, short-term, or otherwise arbitrarily salient interests. Predictable conditions exist under which governing elites may have an incentive to represent long-term social preferences more unbiasedly than does broad opinion.[65]

Despite these potential complexities and caveats, republican liberalism nonetheless generates parsimonious predictions where conflictual policies impose extremely high costs and risks on the majority of individuals in domestic society. With respect to extreme but historically common policies like war, famine, and radical autarky, fair representation tends to inhibit international conflict. In this way, republican liberal theory has helped to explain phenomena as diverse as the "democratic peace," modern anti-imperialism, and international trade and monetary cooperation. Given the prima facie plausibility of the assumption that major war imposes net costs on society as a whole, it is not surprising that the prominent republican liberal argument concerns the "democratic peace," which one scholar has termed "as close as anything we have to a law in international relations"—one that applies to tribal societies as well as to modern states.[66] Liberal democratic institutions tend not to provoke such wars because influence is placed in the hands of those who must expend blood and treasure and the leaders they choose.[67]

---

63. Ekelund and Tollison 1981.
64. Milgrom and Roberts 1990.
65. See Keohane and Milner 1996, 52–53; and Wooley 1992.
66. Levy 1988, 662.
67. By analogy to Hirshleifer 1987.

Often overlooked is the theoretical corollary of "democratic peace" theory: a republican liberal theory of war that stresses abnormally risk-acceptant leaders and rent-seeking coalitions. Substantial evidence shows that the aggressors who have provoked modern great power wars tend either to be risk-acceptant individuals in the extreme or individuals well able to insulate themselves from the costs of war or both. Most leaders initiating twentieth-century great power wars lost them; Adolf Hitler and Saddam Hussein, for example, initiated conflicts against coalitions far more powerful than their own.[68] In the same vein, Jack Snyder has recently deepened Hobson's classic rent-seeking analysis of imperialism—whereby the military, uncompetitive foreign investors and traders, jingoistic political elites, and others who benefit from imperialism are particularly well-placed to influence policy—by linking unrepresentative and extreme outcomes to logrolling coalitions. Consistent with this analysis, the highly unrepresentative consequences of partial democratization, combined with the disruption of rapid industrialization and incomplete political socialization, suggest that democratizing states, if subject to these influences, may be particularly war prone. Such findings may challenge some variants of liberal ideology but are consistent with liberal theory.[69]

The link between great-power military aggression and small-group interests in nonrepresentative states implies neither unceasing belligerence by autocratic regimes nor unquestioning pacifism by democratic ones. Enlightened despotism or democratic aggression remains possible. The more precise liberal prediction is thus that despotic power, bounded by neither law nor representative institutions, tends to be wielded in a more *arbitrary* manner by a wider range of individuals, leading both to a wider range of expected outcomes and a more conflictual average. Nonetheless, liberal theory predicts that democratic states may provoke preventive wars in response to direct or indirect threats, against very weak states with no great power allies, or in peripheral areas where the legal and political preconditions for trade and other forms of profitable transnational relations are not yet in place.[70]

Scholars also often overlook precise analogs to the "democratic peace" in matters of political economy. The liberal explanation for the persistence of illiberal commercial policies, such as protection, monetary instability, and sectoral subsidization, where such policies manifestly undermine the general welfare of the population, is pressure from powerful domestic groups.[71] Thus in the liberal view the creation and maintenance of regimes assuring free trade and monetary stability result not primarily from common threats to national security or appropriate international institutions, but from the ability of states to overcome domestic distributional conflicts in a way supportive of international cooperation. This may ultimately reflect the economic benefits of doing so, as commercial liberal theory suggests, but it can also be decisively helped or hindered by biases in representative institutions. Where such biases favor sheltered groups, and substantial misrepresentation of this type is seen as endemic to

68. See Kaysen 1990, 59; and Mueller 1991, 23–44.
69. See Mansfield and Snyder 1995; Snyder 1991; and Van Evera 1990, 18, 20.
70. Hopkins 1980.
71. For an overview, see Keohane and Milner 1996.

most contemporary representative institutions, rent-seeking groups are likely to gain protection through tariffs, subsidies, favorable regulation, or competitive devaluation. Where policymakers are insulated from such pressures, which may involve less democratic but more representative institutions, or where free trade interests dominate policy, open policies are more viable.[72]

Broader Implications of Liberal Theory

Do labels matter? I have explored three variants of liberal theory that share a set of assumptions. What is gained by subsuming them under a single rubric, as proposed here?

To demonstrate its utility for empirical research and theoretical inquiry, a paradigmatic restatement such as this must meet four criteria. First, its assumptions should highlight unexplored conceptual connections among previously unrelated liberal hypotheses. Second, it should clearly define its own conceptual boundaries in a manner conforming to fundamental social theory, in this case clearly distinguishing liberal hypotheses from ideologically or historically related hypotheses based on different social scientific assumptions. Third, it should reveal anomalies in previous theories and methodological weaknesses in previous testing, creating new presumptions about the proper theories and methods that structure empirical research. Fourth, it should define how the theory in question can be combined rigorously rather than randomly with other theories to form coherent multicausal explanations.

Liberalism as a General Theory: Parsimony and Coherence

One advantage of this restatement is that it suggests a theory of world politics that parsimoniously connects a wide range of distinctive and previously unrelated hypotheses concerning areas unexplained by existing theories. These hypotheses are not limited to cooperation among liberal states, but subsume liberal and nonliberal polities, conflictual and cooperative situations, security and political economy issues, and both individual foreign policy and aggregate behavior. Its key causal mechanisms can be generalized to many issue areas. Thus liberal theory challenges the conventional presumption that realism is the most encompassing and parsimonious of major IR theories. Although not all liberal theories are easy to specify, hypotheses about endogenous tariff setting, the democratic peace, and nationalist conflict suggest that liberalism generates many empirical arguments as powerful, parsimonious, and "efficient" as those of realism.[73]

Not only does liberal theory apply across a wide domain of circumstances, but its three variants—ideational, commercial, and republican liberalism—are stronger taken

---

72. See Wooley 1992; Bailey et al. 1997; contributions by Garrett and Lange and by Haggard and Maxfield in Keohane and Milner 1996; and Moravcsik 1994.
73. On the efficiency criterion, see King, Keohane, and Verba 1994, 182–87.

together than separately. Not only do they share assumptions and causal mechanisms, but their empirical implications aggregate in interesting ways. It is widely accepted, for example, that economic development has a strong influence on the viability of democratic governance, with its pacific implications; liberal democratic governments tend in turn to support commerce, which promotes economic development.[74] Karl Deutsch, Ernst Haas, and Nye, among many others, have explored how economic interaction can lead to transnational communication and the dissemination of scientific information, which may in turn promote secularizing cognitive and ideological change.[75]

Liberal theories can be analytically reinforcing even where they do not make parallel predictions. Anomalies within one variant of liberal theory may be resolved by considering other variants. Positive movement along one liberal dimension—patterns of national identity, democratic participation, or transnational economic transactions—may condone or exacerbate the negative distortions along another liberal dimension.[76] Norman Angell, whose commercial liberal claims are often parodied by secondhand critics, maintained that his well-known "unprofitability of war" thesis in no way implies "the impossibility of war," a doctrine he dismissed for republican liberal reasons as a "ridiculous myth."[77] Where representative bias permits rent-seeking groups to control policy, aggregate incentives for welfare-improving trade are likely to have less effect. Indeed, recent studies reveal that the correlation between economic interdependence and peace holds only (or most strongly) among liberal states.[78] Conversely, where democratization heightens socioeconomic inequality, nationalist cleavages, uneven patterns of gains, and losses due to interdependence or extreme heterogeneity of interests—as may have occurred in the former Yugoslavia—it may exacerbate international economic and political conflict.[79] Such interaction effects among liberal factors offer a promising area for more detailed analysis.

Liberal theory also illuminates at least three major phenomena for which realism and institutionalism offer few, if any, predictions—another indicator of greater parsimony. First, *liberal theory provides a plausible theoretical explanation for variation in the substantive content of foreign policy.* Neither realism nor institutionalism explains the changing substantive goals and purposes over which states conflict and cooperate; both focus instead on formal causes, such as relative power or issue density, and formal consequences, such as conflict and cooperation per se.[80] By contrast, liberal theory provides a plausible explanation not just for conflict and cooperation,

74. Huntington 1991, 46–72.

75. See Deutsch 1954; Haas 1989; and Nye 1988.

76. Realist critics tend to overlook this. Howard's brilliant polemic against liberal theories of war often employs one liberal theory to debunk another; for example, the existence of nationalist irredentism is evidence against the claim that greater economic development and democratization lead to peace; see Howard 1986, 98–99, 130–31; compare Mansfield and Snyder 1995.

77. Angell 1933, 53, 268–70.

78. Oneal 1996.

79. Fearon 1996.

80. Yet Ruggie concedes too much when he observes that "power may predict the form of the international order, but not its *content,*" because liberal theory does help predict bargaining outcomes and institutional form; see Ruggie 1982, 382.

but for the substantive content of foreign policy. Major elements of international order emphasized, but not explained, in recent criticisms of realism and institutionalism include the difference between Anglo-American, Nazi, and Soviet plans for the post–World War II world; U.S. concern about a few North Korean, Iraqi, or Chinese nuclear weapons, rather than the greater arsenals held by Great Britain, Israel, and France; the substantial differences between the compromise of "embedded liberalism" underlying Bretton Woods and arrangements under the Gold Standard; divergences between economic cooperation under the EC and the Council for Mutual Economic Assistance; and the greater protectionism of the Organization for Economic Cooperation and Development's agricultural policy, as compared to its industrial trade policy.[81] Liberal IR theory offers plausible, parsimonious hypotheses to explain each of these phenomena.[82]

Second, *liberal theory offers a plausible explanation for historical change in the international system.* The static quality of both realist and institutionalist theory— their lack of an explanation for fundamental long-term change in the nature of international politics—is a recognized weakness. In particular, global economic development over the past five hundred years has been closely related to greater per capita wealth, democratization, education systems that reinforce new collective identities, and greater incentives for transborder economic transactions.[83] Realist theory accords these changes no theoretical importance. Theorists like Waltz, Gilpin, and Paul Kennedy limit realism to the analysis of unchanging patterns of state behavior or the cyclical rise and decline of great powers. Liberal theory, by contrast, forges a direct causal link between economic, political, and social change and state behavior in world politics. Hence, over the modern period the principles of international order have been decreasingly linked to dynastic legitimacy and increasingly tied to factors directly drawn from the three variants of liberal theory: national self-determination and social citizenship, the increasing complexity of economic integration, and liberal democratic governance.[84]

Third, *liberal theory offers a plausible explanation for the distinctiveness of modern international politics.* Among advanced industrial democracies, a stable form of interstate politics has emerged, grounded in reliable expectations of peaceful change, domestic rule of law, stable international institutions, and intensive societal interaction. This is the condition Deutsch terms a "pluralistic security community" and Keohane and Nye term "complex interdependence."[85]

Whereas realists (and constructivists) offer no general explanation for the emergence of this distinctive mode of international politics, liberal theory argues that the emergence of a large and expanding bloc of pacific, interdependent, normatively satisfied states has been a precondition for such politics. Consider, for example, the current state of Europe. Unlike realism, liberal theory explains the utter lack of com-

---

81. See Ruggie 1982; and Wendt 1994.
82. Moravcsik 1992, forthcoming.
83. Huntington 1991.
84. See Barkin and Cronin 1994; and Keohane and Nye, 1971.
85. See Deutsch 1957; and Keohane and Nye 1977, chap. 2.

petitive alliance formation among the leading democratic powers today. For example, the absence of serious conflict among Western powers over Yugoslavia—the "World War I scenario"—reflects in large part a shared perception that the geopolitical stakes among democratic governments are low. Similarly, liberalism makes more sense of the sudden reversal of East–West relations, a shift made possible by the widespread view among Russian officials (so interview data reveal) that Germany is ethnically satisfied, politically democratic, and commercially inclined.[86]

The Conceptual Limits of Liberalism: Why Functional Regime Theory Is Not Liberal

A second advantage of the reformulation is to clarify the fundamental divergence between theories of state preferences and modern theories of international regimes. This divergence helps explain why liberals have failed to identify a coherent set of social scientific assumptions underlying existing "liberal" IR theory.

Those who choose to define liberal theory in terms of its intellectual history naturally conflate the belief in institutions with a concern about the societal sources of state preferences. Liberalism as an ideology and partisan movement has often been associated in the popular mind with advocacy of international law and organization, despite the views of many leading liberals.[87] Others link these two arguments ideologically: Both seem to suggest an optimistic, ameliorative trend in modern world politics. Whatever the reason, contemporary "functional" theories of international regimes are often referred to as forms of "neoliberal institutionalism," though it is fair to note that Keohane, originator of "functional regime theory," has abandoned the term. Daniel Deudney and G. John Ikenberry's attempted restatement of liberalism goes furthest, asserting flatly that "the peace of the West does not derive simply or mainly from the fact that its polities are all democracies," but from international institutions.[88]

Imre Lakatos reminds us, however, that the coherence of scientific theories is measured not by their conclusions, but by the consistency of their "hard-core" assumptions. By this standard, neoliberal institutionalist theory has relatively little in common with liberal theory as elaborated here, because most of the analytic assumptions and basic causal variables employed by institutionalist theory are more realist than liberal. Like realism, institutionalism takes state preferences as fixed or exogenous, seeks to explain state policy as a function of variation in the geopolitical environment—albeit for institutionalists information and institutions and for realists material capabilities—and focuses on the ways in which anarchy leads to suboptimal outcomes.

---

86. Wallander 1993.

87. Nearly all treatments of liberal IR theory combine institutionalist and preference-based strains in this way; see Doyle 1997; Keohane 1990; Russett 1993; Matthews and Zacher 1995, 133–37; Risse-Kappen 1996, 365; and Deudney 1995, 191–228. Despite a serious misreading of Kant, the English school trichotomy, which distinguishes Grotius from Kant, is more consistent; for example, see Wight 1991.

88. Deudney and Ikenberry 1994. For a liberal critique, see Moravcsik 1996.

Liberalism, by contrast, shares none of these assumptions. It permits state preferences to vary while holding power and information constant, explains policy as a function of the societal context, and focuses on how domestic conflict, not international anarchy, imposes suboptimal outcomes. Therefore, contemporary regime theory ought more properly to be termed "modified structural realism" (as it was initially) or "institutionalism" (as some now prefer), rather than "neoliberal institutionalism."[89] This division permits us to speak of a coherent set of social scientific assumptions underlying both. Rather than treated as parts of the same theoretical tradition, the two theories should be tested against one another or carefully crafted into explicitly multicausal explanations—options explored in more detail in the next two sections.

This is not to imply, however, that liberal theory is of no utility in analyzing international regimes. To the contrary, it contributes to such analysis in at least two distinctive ways. First, liberal theory explains when and why the configuration of state preferences assumed by institutionalists—a mixed-motive collective action problem that can be overcome by the centralized manipulation of information through common rules—is likely to emerge. Since, moreover, particular institutional structures solve specific collective action problems, the configuration of preferences permits us to predict detailed characteristics of international regimes.[90]

Second, liberal theory deepens the institutionalist account of regime stability. Realists argue that regime stability and expansion are functions of enduring hegemonic power; institutionalists maintain that the high interstate transaction costs of regime creation or renegotiation explain regime stability, even if patterns of functional benefits would recommend renegotiation. Liberal theory suggests an alternative hypothesis: namely that international regimes are stable when societal individuals and groups adjust so as to make domestic policy reversal (or even stagnation) costly—as neofunctionalist regional integration theorists have long argued. This account is consistent with the transaction cost foundations of institutionalist reasoning but grounded in societal "lock in" effects and the resulting stability of state preferences, not the costs of interstate bargaining, monitoring, and sanctioning. Such "social embeddedness" may take the form of fixed investments by private firms, ideological commitments by political parties concerned about their reputation, costly institutional adaptation by domestic bureaucracies, or government investment in military defense.[91]

The liberal view of regimes as "socially embedded" can be extended to suggest endogenous causes of regime change over time. International regimes that induce greater societal demands for cooperation are more likely to deepen or expand over time, whereas those that do not are likely to be fragile. One example is the liberal account of international law, which suggests that international rules and norms are most effectively implemented as "horizontal commitments" enforced by national courts and parliaments, not "vertical commitments" enforced by supranational ac-

---

89. Keohane 1985, 1989.
90. Martin 1993.
91. On institutional adaptation, see Keohane 1991.

tors, and that such horizontal commitments can generate self-sustaining momentum over time by empowering particular domestic groups.[92]

Methodological Implications of Liberal Theory: The Danger of Omission

A third potential advantage of reformulating a social scientific theory is to increase its salience, thus compelling empirical studies to give serious consideration to hypotheses drawn from it and discouraging omitted variable bias.[93] Powerful liberal hypotheses exist to account for many major phenomena in world politics, yet surprisingly few studies directly confront realist and institutionalist (or constructivist) hypotheses with their liberal counterparts. Instead, empirical studies tend to treat realism (or occasionally institutionalism or "rationalism") as an exclusive baseline. The result is not just incomplete analysis. It is omitted variable bias that inflates the empirical support for new theoretical propositions due to the exclusion of (correlated) liberal ones. Two recent examples—one realist, one constructivist—demonstrate the considerable empirical significance of this bias.[94]

The first example comes from perhaps the most prominent debate in recent realist theory—namely, that surrounding Joseph Grieco's "relative-gains" critique of institutionalism. Based on an analysis of the implementation of nontariff barrier (NTB) provisions negotiated in the Tokyo Round of GATT, Grieco seeks to demonstrate that security concerns about relative gains, not fears of future cheating, motivate noncooperation, even in foreign economic policy.[95] Yet in focusing on institutionalism, Grieco ignores liberal explanations for noncooperation based on domestic institutions, ideas, and distributional conflict among domestic economic interests.[96] Subsequent interventions in the relative-gains debate by formal theorists, which have done much to clarify the strategic conditions under which particular strategies are likely to emerge, exacerbate this neglect by seeking to make a virtue of omission. Emerson Niou and Peter Ordeshook see preferences as "tangential to a theory of international systems. . . . We can conduct this discussion without references to goals."[97] As a result, the relative-gains debate has remained extraordinarily narrow. Both Grieco and those he criticizes treat national interests as fixed and seek only to determine *which* external political constraint—capabilities or information—constitutes the primary determinant of state behavior.

This neglect of liberal hypotheses would be of only abstract significance had it not led all participants in the relative-gains debate to overlook the explanation of noncooperation that most analysts of international trade policy, not to mention nearly all who actually conduct negotiations of this kind, consider decisive—namely, pressure

92. See Slaughter 1995; Burley and Mattli 1993; and Moravcsik 1995.
93. Tetlock and Belkin 1996, 34.
94. King, Keohane, and Verba 1994, 168–82.
95. See Grieco 1988, 1990; and Baldwin 1993.
96. Grieco concedes this; see Grieco 1990, 486–88 n.
97. See Niou and Ordeshook 1994; Powell 1994, 318; and Snidal 1991.

from particularistic domestic groups with intense distributional concerns. Liberal preference-based explanations dominate the specialized economic, political science, and policy literature on trade, particularly in precisely those three areas where Grieco finds "relative gains": government procurement, industrial standard-setting, and administrative protection. Yet Grieco codes these three critical cases of interstate bargaining failure as confirming his account, without considering alternative motivations nor, except in one minor case, providing any direct evidence of national security concerns. Studies in other areas that do test liberal theories against realist alternatives reveal that pressure from economic special interests tends to dominate security concerns, even in "least likely" cases like military procurement.[98] Since there is good reason to suspect omitted variable bias, our theoretical understanding of relative gains seeking would have been far more reliable (but also surely far less realist!) if the initial research design had included liberal hypotheses.

A second example of omitted variable bias is drawn from recent efforts to develop a constructivist approach to IR. Constructivism, though not yet formulated as a theory, is a welcome effort to broaden IR debates by focusing on ideational socialization. Yet, like realist claims about relative gains, constructivist arguments are generally employed so as to prevent confrontation with preexisting liberal theory. The theoretical introduction to a recent collection of constructivist essays, *The Culture of National Security,* for example, identifies "two major analytical perspectives on IR": Waltzian neorealism and the "neoliberal" regime theory of Keohane and Robert Axelrod. With only a few exceptions, recent constructivist work employs this dichotomy, therefore neglecting liberal theories focusing on the relationship between conflict and democratic government, economic interdependence, and domestic coalitions—theories recognized as among the most powerful in contemporary security studies.[99]

This is unfortunate. There are good a priori reasons to suspect that omitted variable bias is inflating the empirical support for any constructivist claim that remains untested against a liberal hypothesis. Not only do both liberal and constructivist arguments focus on variation in state preferences, but we know that the receptiveness to particular ideas is closely correlated with authoritative domestic institutions, patterns of interdependence, and existing patterns of cultural identity. "Systemic" constructivist claims—the view that national ideas and identities result from the socializing "feedback" effects of previous international political interactions—are particularly vulnerable to such bias, because domestic preferences are the critical causal link between systemic socialization and state policy. Without a theory of domestic preference formation, how can a constructivist specify which feedback processes of socialization matter, let alone when and how they matter? Sociologists have long since concluded that "new institutionalist" analyses of this kind are crippled unless con-

---

98. Moravcsik 1993.
99. Typical of the literature are Katzenstein 1996, 3, 12–13, 25, 37; and Wendt 1996. Finnemore is a welcome exception, whereas Risse-Kappen and Legro attempt syntheses; see Finnemore 1996; Risse-Kappen 1996; and Legro 1996.

joined with a reliable theory of actors and agency.[100] In short, in order to theorize rigorously about systemic social construction, we *first* require a liberal theory.

Existing liberal hypotheses, moreover, offer a general account of variation in socialization—a theory of when the transnational transmission of ideas matters— something for which "systemic" constructivists as of yet lack an explanation. Socialization effects, liberals predict, will reflect the extent of convergence or divergence among preexisting domestic institutions and ideas. For example, socialization toward convergent norms stems from convergent domestic institutions and ideas. Liberal institutions and norms may be particularly conducive to the promotion of peace and cooperation, but the argument implies that the convergence of certain other sorts of *nonliberal* values, such as monarchy in the Concert of Europe or "Asian values" in ASEAN, may also have significant, if generally less striking, effects on world politics.

Consider, for example, the current revival of interest among constructivists in Deutsch's analysis of how transnational communication creates "pluralistic security communities" (PSGs) in which groups of states "cease to contemplate" military conflict. PSGs are said to demonstrate the importance of the socializing power of transnational ideas, the importance of "common . . . we-feeling" rather than "convergent" interests.[101] Yet Deutsch himself viewed liberal factors—an autonomous civil society with individual mobility, the rule of law, and competitive politics—as preconditions for transformative effects of high levels of international transactions and communication. Is it just coincidence that of the of the twelve successful post-1750 PSGs identified by Deutsch, ten or eleven were composed of liberal or nearly liberal states?[102]

This analysis poses two general challenges to constructivism. First, it suggests that liberal variables are more fundamental than constructivist ones, because they define the conditions under which high rates of communication and transaction alter state behavior. Second, it raises the possibility that domestic liberal factors may explain *both* peace and transactions, rendering the correlation between international communication and peace not just secondary, but spurious.[103] Without directly confronting liberal theory, we cannot dismiss either possibility. Surely our understanding of world politics would be better served by more rigorous empirical confrontation between constructivism and liberalism. Better yet would be a sophisticated synthesis, as found in the "liberal constructivist" research program advocated by Thomas Risse-Kappen. This approach—a "constructivist interpretation of liberal theory"—backs away from the notion that values result from interstate socialization and argues instead in a liberal vein that ideas and communication matter when they are most congruent with existing domestic values and institutions.[104]

These examples demonstrate why it is essential to treat liberalism as a constant theoretical baseline against which either realist or constructivist hypotheses are

100. DiMaggio 1988, 10ff.
101. Adler and Barnett, forthcoming.
102. Deutsch 1957, 29–30, 36, 66–69, 123–24.
103. Oneal et al. 1996, 13.
104. For example, see Risse-Kappen 1996, 365; Legro 1996; Johnston 1995; Burley and Mattli 1993; Moravcsik 1995; and Sikkink 1993.

tested—that is, as a fundamental paradigmatic alternative in IR. Failure to control for underlying variation in state preferences has confounded recent attempts, quantitative and qualitative, to test monocausal realist theory in many other areas. These include the study of deterrence, hegemonic influence, alliance formation, international negotiation, international monetary cooperation, multilateral cooperation, economic sanctions, and European integration.[105] Similar criticisms could be directed at functional regime theory; baseline predictions about the precise form and the subsequent consequences of international regimes could be derived from liberal theory.[106] Failure to do so poses a clear threat to valid empirical inference.

We already see realists and constructivists "borrowing" liberal hypotheses, even where it undermines the "hard core" of theories. Realist Stephen Walt suggests that "intentions" should be included alongside power, proximity, and offense dominance in their specification of "threat." Constructivist Alexander Wendt is in retreat from his "holistic" or "top-down" claim that state identities are ideationally constructed by interaction of states (not societies) within the international system. Now he accepts a view heavily dependent on "unit-level changes in the structure of state-society relations," embedded in domestic (as well as international) institutions, which leads him to embrace phenomena for which well-established liberal theories have long provided widely accepted explanations, for example, the democratic peace, U.S. fear of nuclear weapons in the hands of rogue states but not democratic allies, and the "distinctiveness of the West."[107] The prognosis: Unbiased tests would very likely supplant numerous accepted realist, institutionalist, and constructivist explanations of state behavior with liberal accounts.

In the long run, comparative theory testing should be aimed at a clearer definition of the empirical domain within which each major theory performs best. Detailed predictions concerning these empirical domains go beyond the scope of this essay, since they require issue-specific analysis of at least three theories. We can nonetheless conclude that oft-cited generalizations about the scope of realism and liberalism need to be revised fundamentally. Liberal theory remains important, even primary, even in what are currently considered "least likely" cases, for example, where there exist direct threats to national security, high levels of interstate conflict, and large numbers of nonliberal states. The restatement proposed here aims to facilitate empirical research that would move us beyond these simplistic assertions about the limited explanatory domain of liberal theory.

Liberalism and Theory Synthesis: The Priority of Preferences

The previous section demonstrates that, as a monocausal theory, liberalism offers a theoretically coherent and empirically promising alternative to realism and institu-

---

105. See Fearon, forthcoming; Walt 1987, 21–28; Baldwin 1985; and Moravcsik, forthcoming. An instructive example is Martin, who finds liberal and institutionalist factors to be so closely correlated that quantitative analysis cannot distinguish them—a result consistent with the existence of potential for significant omitted variable bias; see Martin 1992.

106. Martin 1993.

107. See Walt 1987; Elman 1996, 33; Wendt 1996, 1–4, 6, 11, 28–30, 33–40, 109ff, 328–33, 344ff, 400ff.

tionalism, as well as to constructivism. Yet it is not always appropriate to employ a monocausal theory. If foreign policymaking is a process of constrained choice by purposive states, a view shared by realist, institutionalist, and liberal theory, there may well be cases in which a *combination* of preferences and constraints shapes state behavior. In such cases, a multicausal synthesis, one that treats these theories not as substitutes but as complements, is required. If so, what synthetic model should properly be employed? Fundamental theories should be formulated so as to provide rigorous means of defining their proper relationship to other theories.

A fourth important advantage of this theoretical restatement is that it offers a clearer and more internally consistent model for multicausal theory synthesis in IR than currently exists. It does so, moreover, by reversing the nearly universal presumption among IR theorists that "liberalism makes sense as an explanatory theory within the constraints pointed out by . . . Realism."[108] Waltz, Keohane, and many others recommend that we synthesize theories by employing realism first (with preferences assumed to be invariant) and then introducing competing theories of domestic politics, state-society relations, and preference change as needed to explain residual variance.[109]

Yet this conventional procedure lacks any coherent methodological or theoretical justification. Methodologically, the procedure overtly introduces omitted variable bias by arbitrarily privileging realist explanations of any phenomena that might be explained by both realist and liberal theories, without ever testing the latter explanation. Theoretically, the procedure is grounded in an incoherent underlying model. The assumption of state rationality, central to realism, institutionalism, and most variants of liberalism, ought to imply precisely the opposite: Once we accept that both preferences and constraints are causally important, *liberal theory enjoys analytical priority in any synthesis.*

To see why this is so and what it implies, one need only note that the assumption of rationality or purposive behavior central to realism (like the "bounded rationality" claims of institutionalism) implies action on the basis of a prior, specific, and consistent set of preferences. Unless we know what these preferences are (that is, unless we know the extent to which states value the underlying stakes), we cannot assess realist or institutionalist claims linking variation in the particular means available to states (whether coercive capabilities or institutions) on interstate conflict or cooperation. Preferences determine the nature and intensity of the game that states are playing and thus are a primary determinant of which systemic theory is appropriate and how it should be specified. Variation in state preferences often influences the way in which states make calculations about their strategic environment, whereas the converse— that the strategic situation leads to variation in state preferences—is inconsistent with the rationality assumption shared by all three theories.[110] *In short, liberal theory*

---

108. See Keohane 1990, 192; and Matthew and Zacher 1996, 46.

109. See Waltz 1989, 1996, 57. There is "something particularly satisfying about systemic explanations and about the structural forms of [systemic and structural] explanations"; see Keohane 1986, 193.

110. To be sure, as some constructivists and neofunctionalists argue, a reverse effect might occur by feedback over time from previous decisions, but such a dynamic process still presupposes an underlying liberal theory of state action.

explains when and why the assumptions about state preferences underlying realism or institutionalism hold, whereas the reverse is not the case. In situations where these assumptions do not hold, realism and institutionalism (as well as some variants of constructivism) are not just of limited importance, they are theoretically inappropriate and thus empirically irrelevant.

It follows that in any multicausal synthesis with realist and institutionalist theory—that is, any analysis that remains open to the possibility that variation in state preferences, as well as power and institutions, might influence state policy—liberal theory enjoys causal priority. Steven Krasner's well-known metaphor captures this insight: If institutionalism determines whether governments reach the Pareto-frontier, and realism determines which point on the Pareto-frontier governments select, liberalism defines the shape of the Pareto-frontier itself.[111] Surely the latter task is primary. This conclusion should hardly be surprising to political scientists, for it is the unambiguous lesson of the classic literature on the methodology of studying power and influence, whether in local communities or global politics. Robert Dahl's analysis of power teaches us that we cannot ascertain whether "A influenced B to do something" (that is, influence) unless we know "what B would otherwise do" (that is, preferences).[112] The implication for realism is clear: Not only do we need to know what state preferences are, but unless they are arrayed so that substantial interstate conflict of interest exists and the deployment of capabilities to achieve a marginal gain is acceptable, realist theory is powerless to explain state behavior. Similarly, institutionalist explanations of suboptimal cooperation are appropriate only under circumstances in which states have an interest in resolving particular interstate collective action problems. Kenneth Oye draws the implication: "When you observe conflict, think Deadlock—the absence of mutual interest—before puzzling over why a mutual interest was not realized."[113]

The analytical priority of liberalism is not simply an abstract requirement of theoretical consistency; it is empirically significant.[114] Realists and institutionalists alike are retreating to what Keohane terms a "fall-back position," whereby exogenous variation in the configuration of state interests defines the range of possible outcomes, *within which* capabilities and institutions explain outcomes.[115] This implicitly concedes not just the need for multicausal synthesis, but the analytical priority of liberal theory.

The popularity of the "fallback" position also defuses a practical objection often raised against "societal" or "domestic" theories, namely that research into domestic preferences is overly demanding, if not impossible. To be sure, the investigation of national motivations poses particular challenges. State preferences must be clearly distinguished from strategies and tactics and then must be inferred either by observ-

---

111. Krasner 1993.
112. See Dahl 1969; Coleman 1990, 132–35; and Baldwin 1989, 4.
113. See Oye 1986, 6; and Morrow 1994.
114. This is not to prejudge whether liberal explanations provide greater or lesser explanatory power, which is an empirical question.
115. Keohane 1986, 183.

ing consistent patterns of state behavior or by systematically analyzing stable elements internal to states, as revealed in decision-making documents, trustworthy oral histories and memoirs, patterns of coalitional support, and the structure of domestic institutions.[116] Yet the existence of such difficulties does not constitute a valid reason to neglect liberal theory. No respectable philosophy of science recognizes the difficulty of performing relevant empirical research with current techniques as a legitimate reason to abandon a promising scientific paradigm. Instead, scientific technique and training should adjust—an argument for thorough training in languages and primary-source analysis, as well as in rigorous theories of comparative politics. Moreover, the popularity of the fall-back position demonstrates that the difficulty of ascertaining preferences is not unique to liberalism. We have seen that even monocausal empirical tests of realist and institutionalist theories must control reliably for variation in underlying preferences (not just strategies) of states. *This requires precisely the same detailed research into domestic politics.* Such a baseline control is, moreover, most reliable where backed by an explicit and generalizable theory of domestic preference formation, that is, a liberal theory. In short, research into domestic preference formation is unavoidable.

The priority of liberalism in multicausal models of state behavior implies, furthermore, that collective state behavior should be analyzed as a *two-stage process* of constrained social choice. States first define preferences—a stage explained by liberal theories of state-society relations. Then they debate, bargain, or fight to particular agreements—a second stage explained by realist and institutionalist (as well as liberal) theories of strategic interaction.[117] The two-stage model offers a general structure for research design and theoretical explanation. In those cases where liberal factors only influence strategic outcomes directly, through preferences and preference intensities (*a* in Figure 1), liberalism can be tested as a monocausal hypothesis against alternative realist or institutionalist factors (*c* in Figure 1). Liberal factors may also influence outcomes indirectly, because the nature of preferences helps determine (*b* in Figure 1) the nature and strength of the causal relationship between strategic circumstances and actions (*c* in Figure 1). Recall that preferences do not simply shape outcomes, they tell us which realist or institutionalist factors are important and how they relate to state behavior. In such cases, explaining (or at least controlling for) variation in state preferences is analytically prior to an analysis of strategic interaction. Without a prior analysis of preferences, only monocausal formulations of realist or institutionalist theory can be tested.[118]

The primacy of liberal theory in such multicausal explanations may appear to be an abstract admonition, yet precisely this two-stage approach has characterized liberal theory and practice from Kant's philosophy to the practical calculations by the American architects of the post–World War II settlement. Throughout, multicausal or

---

116. On the methodological advantages of analyzing "corporate" rather than "personal" actors, see Coleman 1990, 513, 933ff.

117. See Morrow 1988; Ruggie 1982; and Legro 1996.

118. Watson and McGaw 1970, chap. 15.

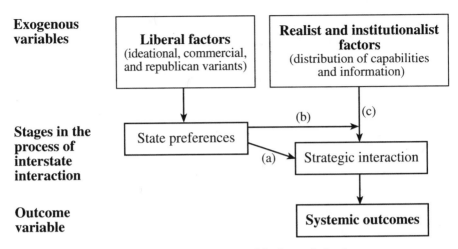

FIGURE 1. *A two-stage model of state behavior*

two-stage liberalism makes sense of what have long been considered contradictions and ambiguities in classic liberal thought and modern liberal statecraft.

Consider Wilson's proposal for the League of Nations, often cited as the epitome of liberal "legalism" and "utopianism." At first glance, Wilson's proposal seems to reflect a naive confidence in international institutions. Understood as an implicit social science theory, not ideology, we see that it was neither utopian nor fundamentally institutionalist. It rested instead on a pragmatic two-stage liberal view, and *its failure actually confirms liberal predictions.*

From the start, Wilson was skeptical about the *autonomous* influence of international institutions. He cared little about their precise form, because he viewed them as no more than "a symbolic affirmation of the 'rightness' of democracies in their mutual relations."[119] Thus, for example, his initial draft of the Covenant included no provisions for international law or a supranational court; both were eventually added only at the insistence of more conservative (and more cynical) foreign and domestic politicians. Instead what he termed the "first point" to remember about the League was not institutionalist but liberal: Its membership was to be restricted to those countries enjoying republican government and national self-determination. Insofar as the League was to rely on public opinion, it was to be solely *democratic* public opinion.

Based on a multicausal liberal analysis, Wilson explicitly identified a set of narrow preconditions under which collective security institutions could succeed. The League, he argued, would function only if nationally self-determining democracy was a nearly universal form of government among great powers, which in turn controlled an overwhelming proportion of global military power. In 1917, Wilson believed this situation to be imminent: "There are not going to be many other kinds of nations for

119. Holsti 1991, 187.

long. . . . The Hapsburgs and the Hohenzollerns are permanently out of business.''[120] Given Wilson's underlying theory, is it surprising that the League had become moribund by 1936, after twelve European countries had moved from democracy to dictatorship? Or that this shift isolated democratic France and Britain, exacerbating their oft-noted geopolitical dilemmas in Manchuria and Abyssinia? Here we again see the virtue of defining liberal theory in a nonideological manner: The failure of the League, often cited as a realist refutation of liberal *ideology*, in fact confirms liberal IR *theory*.

Multicausal liberalism helps to explain not only ambitious schemes for cooperation like collective security, but "realist" policy outcomes like power balancing and bipolar conflict. Kant, for example, recognized the balance of power as an unstable, second-best mechanism suitable only to a particular set of circumstances defined by liberal theory, namely relations among nonrepublican states. In theoretical terms, realism was embedded in a deeper and more encompassing transhistorical liberal theory of social development. The balance of power serves to limit the "vigorous . . . rivalry" among states, permitting the progressive emergence of republican government and commerce (as well as, though clearly secondary, international rules), which would in turn steadily diminish the relevance of interstate balancing. Like Wilson, Kant remained skeptical of strong international institutions, focusing instead on the development of societal preferences.[121]

A form of multicausal liberalism very similar to that espoused by Kant underlay the post–World War II U.S. policy of containment—a policy traditionally treated as the embodiment of realism. Containment was never simply power balancing. It was an integrated multicausal liberal grand strategy, as made explicit after World War I by Wilson and John Dewey, then after World War II by George Kennan. Kennan, in this regard a liberal, linked the European threat to the nature of the Soviet regime; it is often forgotten that nine-tenths of the seminal "X" article was given over to an analysis of Soviet domestic beliefs.[122] A Western military deterrent would be required, he argued, only until the Bolshevik revolution had run its course, whereupon the Soviet system would collapse of its own accord. Thus the decisive Western actions in the Cold War, according to Kennan, were the reconstruction of Germany and Japan as capitalist democracies through policies like the Marshall Plan. The goal of the policy was the transformation of social purposes and state preferences in Western countries, neither of which would assume much importance in a purely realist analysis. This multicausal liberal interpretation of containment banishes various ambiguities and tensions in Kennan's thought that have bedeviled biographers—not least his singular synthesis of balance-of-power thinking and strident antimilitarism.[123]

The conduct and conclusion of the Cold War proceeded precisely as Kennan's two-stage liberal model had predicted. Realist power balancing served throughout as

---

120. See Wilson in Foley 1923, 64–65, see also 58–59, 64–65, 74–87, 147, 198–99; Kuehl 1969, 340–44; Foley 1923, 129; and Wolfers and Martin 1956, 178.

121. Kant 1991, 49, 92, 112–14.

122. See Kennan 1947; and Gellman 1984, 37, 83–105, 130–38.

123. "To nearly everyone with an opinion on the subject, it seems plain that there have been two George Kennans. . . . Kennan the Cold Warrior [and] Kennan the peacemonger, the dovish historian"; see Gellman 1984, xiii.

a static, interim instrument to maintain the status quo, but shifting state preferences explain the outbreak and eventual passing of the conflict. By 1959, standing in a Moscow exhibit of kitchenware, Richard Nixon and Nikita Khrushchev declared that the Cold War would be won and lost not through relative military capabilities, but through the relative economic prowess and ideological attractiveness of the two superpowers. Economic stagnation and a measure of ideological change in the East predated foreign policy change. If the West, as Khrushchev rashly promised, had been buried under the superior economic performance of the East, the outcome might well have been different.[124]

These examples demonstrate the ability of multicausal liberal theory to explain critical twentieth-century foreign policy decisions, such as those taken in 1918, 1947, and 1989, even when national security interests are fully engaged.[125] In interpreting such cases, the major difference between realists and liberals lies not, as is often claimed, in the observation that states are concerned about security threats and balancing; this finding is consistent with a multicausal liberal explanation. Where the two theories genuinely differ is on the sources of security threats themselves, with realists attributing them to particular configurations of power, institutionalists attributing them to uncertainty, and liberals attributing them to ideological, institutional, and material conflict among state preferences. If liberal theory contributes to explaining core realist cases such as bipolar conflict, there is good reason to believe that the most powerful influences in world politics today are not the deployment of military force or the construction of international institutions, but the transformation of domestic and transnational social values, interests, and institutions.

Conclusion: The Virtues of Theoretical Pluralism

Liberal IR theory is not simply an ideological foil for more realistic and rigorous theories, as its critics claim, nor an eclectic collection of hypotheses linked only by common intellectual history and normative commitment, as its proponents are currently forced to concede. It is instead a logically coherent, theoretically distinct, empirically generalizable social scientific theory—one that follows from explicit assumptions and generates a rich range of related propositions about world politics that reach far beyond cases of cooperation among a minority of liberal states. By reformulating liberalism as theory rather than ideology, we have repeatedly seen that what are often treated as liberal failures become liberal predictions.

Moreover, liberalism exhibits considerable potential for theoretical extension. Aside from the myriad opportunities for empirical testing and theoretical refinement of specific hypotheses, a number of broader areas are poised for theoretical innovation. Relaxing the assumption of unitary state behavior would support a range of "two-

---

124. Jervis 1996.
125. King, Keohane, and Verba 1994, 209–12.

level" hypotheses about the differential ability of various domestic state and societal actors to pursue semiautonomous transnational activities. Relaxing the assumption that decision making is static would support analyses of change over time. Greater attention to feedback from prior decisions mediated by intervening liberal factors like domestic ideas, institutions, and interests might provide firmer microfoundations for theories of regime stability and change—an area of potential collaboration with constructivists and historical institutionalists. Finally, the rich interaction among domestic and transnational ideas, interests, and institutions is only beginning to be explored.

A final word to those readers who object to using the term *liberal* to distinguish this restatement. Such potential critics fall into two groups. One group is likely to find this formulation of liberal theory too narrow, the other too broad.

The first group of critics will protest that this restatement fails to acknowledge the full richness of the intellectual history and, in particular, the normative implications of liberalism. This criticism is correct, but the omission is deliberate. This article does not aim to provide a comprehensive intellectual history of classical liberal international thought, nor a self-sufficient guide to the normative evaluation of policy, but to distill a coherent core of social scientific assumptions for the narrower purpose of explaining international politics.[126] The project is best judged on its own terms—the four criteria outlined in the preceding section—not its fidelity to prior usage.

The second group of critics will complain that liberalism has too many definitions as it stands, most too vague to be useful. Some reject altogether the use of "isms" to designate foundational theoretical positions in IR. This criticism is semantic rather than substantive. In contrast to other fundamental divisions—for example, those between domestic and systemic "levels of analysis," optimistic and pessimistic prognoses, or realist, liberal, and Marxist ideologies—the tripartite division among realism, liberalism, and institutionalism is fully consistent with the foundation of rationalist social theory, which divides the determinants of social behavior into three categories: interests, resources, and institutions or information.[127] Those who view state behavior as the result of a process of constrained choice would do well to champion rather than criticize efforts to impose greater theoretical coherence and consistency on theories of rational state behavior.

Either type of critic may nonetheless prefer to call liberal theory a "societal," "state-society," "social purpose," or "preference-based" theory. The central claims of this article, however, remain intact. First, major IR theories should be divided into those that stress the pattern of state preferences, the distribution of resources, and the institutional provision of information. Second, greater priority should be given to the further development of the first category. This development need not proceed ad hoc, but can be achieved by grounding such efforts in the common assumptions and causal processes proposed here. Only further research can reveal their full empirical power; yet existing studies—from explanations of the democratic peace to endogenous tariff

---

126. Nonetheless, the empirical claims advanced here have normative implications; see Doyle 1997.
127. Coleman 1990.

theory to theories relating domestic institutions and ideas to foreign policy—suggest considerable promise. Third, a liberal theory of state preferences is the most fundamental type of IR theory. Hypotheses that endogenize changes in state preferences deserve equal treatment in monocausal explanations and analytical priority in multicausal ones, because liberal theory defines the theoretical and empirical domains in which it is appropriate even to consider realist and institutionalist claims. Thus those who ignore liberal theory do not simply sacrifice comprehensiveness; they undermine valid empirical evaluation of their own theories. Only by building on these three conclusions can liberals and their critics supplant debates over labels with debates over data.

References

Achen, Christopher 1995. How Can We Tell a Unitary Rational Actor When We See One? Paper presented at the Midwest Political Science Association Convention, April.

Adler, Emanuel, and Michael Barnett, eds. Forthcoming. *Security Communities Revisited*. Cambridge: Cambridge University Press.

Angell, Norman. 1933. *The Great Illusion, 1933*. New York: Putnam.

Bailey, Michael A., Judith Goldstein, and Barry R. Weingast. 1997. The Institutional Roots of American Trade Policy: Politics, Coalitions, and International Trade. *World Politics* 49 (April):309–38.

Baldwin, David A. 1989. *Paradoxes of Power*. Oxford: Basil Blackwell.

———. 1997. The Concept of Security. *Review of International Studies* 23 (1):5–26.

Baldwin, David A., ed. 1993. *Neorealism and Neoliberalism: The Contemporary Debate*. New York: Columbia University Press.

Barkin, Samuel, and Bruce Cronin. 1994. The State and the Nation: Changing Norms and Rules of Sovereignty in International Relations. *International Organization* 48 (winter):107–30.

Bueno de Mesquita, Bruce. 1996. The Benefits of a Social Scientific Approach to Studying International Relations. In *Explaining International Relations Since 1945,* edited by Ngaire Woods. Oxford: Oxford University Press.

Burley, Anne-Marie. 1992. Law Among Liberal States: Liberal Internationalism and the Act of State Doctrine. *Columbia Law Review* 92 (December):1907–96.

Burley, Anne-Marie, and Walter Mattli. 1993. Europe Before the Court: A Political Theory of Legal Integration. *International Organization* 47 (winter):41–76.

Coleman, James S. 1990. *Foundations of Social Theory*. Cambridge, Mass.: Harvard University Press.

Dahl, Robert A. 1969. The Concept of Power. In *Political Power: A Reader in Theory and Research,* edited by Roderick Bell, David V. Edwards, and R. Harrison Wagner, 79–93. New York: Free Press.

Deudney, Daniel, and G. John Ikenberry. 1994. The Logic of the West. *World Policy Journal* 10 (winter): 17–26.

Deutsch, Karl W., Sidney A. Burrell, Robert A. Kann, Maurice Lee, Jr., Martin Lichterman, Raymond E. Lindgren, Francis L. Lowenheim, and Richard W. VanRead Wagenen. 1957. *Political Community and the North Atlantic Area: International Organization in the Light of Historical Experience*. Princeton, N.J.: Princeton University Press.

DiMaggio, Paul. 1988. Interest and Agency in Institutional Theory. In *Institutional Patterns and Organizations,* edited by Lynne G. Zucker, 3–22. Cambridge, Mass: Ballinger.

Doyle, Michael. 1983. Kant, Liberal Legacies, and Foreign Affairs: Parts One and Two. *Philosophy and Public Affairs* 12 (summer–fall):205–35, 325–53.

———. 1986. Liberalism and World Politics. *American Political Science Review* 80 (December): 1151–69.

———. 1997. *Ways of War and Peace*. New York: Norton.

Elman, Colin. 1996. Horses for Courses: Why Not Neorealist Theories of Foreign Policy? *Security Studies* 6 (autumn):45–90.

Ekelund, Robert B., and Robert B. Tollison. 1981. *Mercantilism in a Rent-Seeking Society: Economic Regulation in Historical Perspective.* College Station, Tex.: Texas A&M Press.

Evans, Peter B., Harold K. Jacobson, and Robert D. Putnam, eds. 1993. *Double-Edged Diplomacy: International Bargaining and Domestic Politics.* Berkeley: University of California Press.

Fearon, James D. 1995. Rationalist Explanations of War. *International Organization* 49 (summer):379–414.

———. Forthcoming. Selection Effects and Deterrence. In *Deterrence Debates: Problems of Definition, Specification, and Estimation,* edited by Kenneth Oye.

Finnemore, Martha. 1996. *National Interests in International Society.* Ithaca, N.Y.: Cornell University Press.

Foley, Hamilton, ed. 1923. *Woodrow Wilson's Case for the League of Nations.* Princeton, N.J.: Princeton University Press.

Gellman, Barton. 1984. *Contending with Kennan: Toward a Philosophy of American Power.* New York: Praeger.

Gilpin, Robert. 1975. *U.S. Power and the Multinational Corporation: The Political Economy of Direct Foreign Investment.* New York: Basic Books.

———. 1989. *The Political Economy of International Relations.* Princeton, N.J.: Princeton University Press.

Grieco, Joseph M. 1988. Anarchy and the Limits of Cooperation: A Realist Critique of the Newest Liberal Institutionalism. *International Organization* 42 (summer):485–508.

———. 1990. *Cooperation Among Nations: Europe, America, and Non-Tariff Barriers to Trade.* Ithaca, N.Y.: Cornell University Press.

Gourevitch, Peter. 1978. The Second Image Reversed: The International Sources of Domestic Politics. *International Organization* 32 (autumn):881–912.

Gowa, Joanne. 1989. Bipolarity, Multipolarity, and Free Trade. *American Political Science Review* 83 (December):1245–56.

Haas, Ernst. 1990. *Where Knowledge Is Power: Three Models of Change in International Organizations.* Berkeley: University of California Press.

Haggard, Stephan, and Andrew Moravcsik. 1993. The Political Economy of Financial Assistance to Eastern Europe, 1989–1991. In *After the Cold War: International Institutions and State Strategies in Europe, 1989–1991,* edited by Robert O. Keohane, Joseph S. Nye, and Stanley Hoffmann, 246–85. Cambridge, Mass.: Harvard University Press.

Harsanyi, John. 1977. *Rational Behavior and Bargaining Equilibrium in Games and Social Situations.* Cambridge: Cambridge University Press.

Hellmann, Gunther, and Reinhard Wolf. 1993. Neorealism, Neoliberal Institutionalism, and the Future of NATO. *Security Studies* 3 (autumn):3–43.

Hirschleifer, Jack. 1987. On the Emotions as Guarantors of Threats and Promises. In *The Latest on the Best: Essays on Evolution and Optimality,* edited by John Dupre, 307–26. Cambridge, Mass.: MIT Press.

Hirschman, Albert. 1945. *National Power and the Structure of Foreign Trade.* Berkeley: University of California Press.

Hoffmann, Stanley. 1987. Liberalism and International Affairs. In *Essays in the Theory and Practice of International Politics,* edited by Janus and Minerva Hoffmann, 394–417. Boulder, Colo.: Westview Press.

———. 1995. The Crisis of Liberal Internationalism. *Foreign Policy* 98 (spring):159–79.

Holmes, Stephen. 1995. *Passions and Constraints: On the Theory of Liberal Democracy.* Chicago: University of Chicago Press.

Holsti, Kalevi J. 1991. *Peace and War: Armed Conflicts and International Order, 1648–1989.* Cambridge: Cambridge University Press.

Hopkins, A. J. 1980. Property Rights and Empire Building: Britain's Annexation of Lagos. *Journal of Economic History* 40:777–98.

Howard, Michael. 1978. *War and the Liberal Conscience.* New Brunswick, N.J.: Rutgers University Press.

Huntington, Samuel P. 1991. *The Third Wave: Democratization in the Late Twentieth Century.* Norman, Okla.: University of Oklahoma Press.

Huth, Paul. 1996. *Standing Your Guard: Territorial Disputes and International Conflict.* Ann Arbor, Mich.: University of Michigan Press.

Jackson, Robert H. 1990. *Quasi-States: Sovereignty, International Relations, and the Third World.* Cambridge: Cambridge University Press.

Jervis, Robert. 1996. Perception, Misperception, and the End of the Cold War. In *Witnesses to the End of the Cold War,* edited by William Wohlforth, 220–39. Baltimore, Md.: Johns Hopkins University Press.

Kant, Immanuel. 1991. *Kant: Political Writings.* 2d ed. Edited by Hans Reiss, 41–53, 61–92, 93–130. Cambridge: Cambridge University Press.

Katzenstein, Peter, ed. 1996. *The Culture of National Security: Norms and Identity in World Politics.* New York: Columbia University Press.

Kaysen, Carl. 1990. Is War Obsolete? A Review Essay. *International Security* 14 (spring):42–64.

Keeley, Lawrence H. 1996. *War Before Civilization: The Myth of the Peaceful Savage.* Oxford: Oxford University Press.

"X" [George Kennan]. 1947. The Sources of Soviet Conduct. *Foreign Affairs* 25 (July):566–82.

Keohane, Robert O. 1984. *After Hegemony: Cooperation and Discord in the World Political Economy.* Princeton, N.J.: Princeton University Press.

———. 1986. Theory of World Politics: Structural Realism and Beyond. In *Neo-Realism and its Critics,* edited by Robert O. Keohane, 158–203. New York: Columbia University Press.

———. 1989. *International Institutions and State Power: Essays in International Relations Theory.* Boulder, Colo.: Westview Press.

———. 1990. International Liberalism Reconsidered. In *The Economic Limits to Modern Politics,* edited by John Dunn. Cambridge: Cambridge University Press.

———. 1991. U.S. Compliance with Commitments: Reciprocity and Institutional Enmeshment. Paper presented at PIPES, University of Chicago, Chicago, Ill.

Keohane, Robert O., and Helen V. Milner, eds. 1996. *Internationalization and Domestic Politics.* Cambridge: Cambridge University Press.

Keohane, Robert O., and Joseph S. Nye. 1989. *Power and Interdependence: World Politics in Transition.* 2d ed. Boston: Little, Brown.

King, Gary, Robert O. Keohane, and Sidney Verba. 1994. *Designing Social Inquiry: Scientific Inference in Qualitative Research.* Cambridge: Cambridge University Press.

Krasner, Steven. 1993. Global Communications and National Power. In *Neorealism and Neoliberalism: The Contemporary Debate,* edited by David Baldwin, 234–49. New York: Columbia University Press.

Legro, Jeffrey W. 1996. Culture and Preferences in the International Cooperation Two-Step. *American Political Science Review* 90 (March):118–38.

Levy, Jack. 1988. Domestic Politics and War. *Journal of Interdisciplinary History* 18 (fall):653–73.

Lumsdaine, David. 1993. *Moral Vision in International Politics: The Foreign Aid Regime 1949–1989.* Princeton, N.J.: Princeton University Press.

Mack, Andrew J. R. 1975. Why Big Nations Lose Small Wars: The Politics of Asymmetrical Conflict. *World Politics* 27 (January):175–200.

Mansfield, Edward D., and Jack Snyder. 1995. Democratization and the Danger of War. *International Security* 20 (summer):5–38.

Martin, Lisa. 1992. *Coercive Cooperation: Explaining Multilateral Economic Sanctions.* Princeton, N.J.: Princeton University Press.

———. 1993. The Rational State Choice of Multilateralism. In *Multilateralism Matters: Theory and Praxis of an International Form,* edited by John Gerard Ruggie, 91–121. New York: Columbia University Press.

Matthew, Richard A., and Mark W. Zacher. 1995. Liberal International Theory: Common Threads, Divergent Strands. In *Controversies in International Relations Theory: Realism and the Neo-Liberal Challenge,* edited by Charles Kegley, 107–50. New York: St. Martin's Press.

Mearsheimer, John J. 1990. Back to the Future: Instability in Europe After the Cold War. *International Security* 15 (summer):5–56.

Milgrom, Paul, and John Roberts. 1990. Bargaining, Influence Costs, and Organization. In *Perspectives on Positive Political Economy,* edited by James E. Alt and Kenneth A. Schepsle, 57–89. Cambridge: Cambridge University Press.

Moravcsik, Andrew. 1993. Armaments Among Allies: Franco-German Weapons Cooperation, 1975–1985. In *Double-Edged Diplomacy: International Bargaining and Domestic Politics,* edited by Peter Evans, Harold Jacobson, and Robert Putnam, 128–68. Berkeley: University of California Press.

———. 1994. Why the European Community Strengthens the State: International Cooperation and Domestic Politics. Working Paper Series, 52. Cambridge, Mass.: Center for European Studies, Harvard University.

———. 1995. Explaining International Human Rights Regimes: Liberal Theory and Western Europe. *European Journal of International Relations* 1 (summer):157–89.

———. 1996. Federalism and Peace: A Structural Liberal Perspective. *Zeitschrift für Internationale Beziehungen* 2 (spring): 123–32.

———. Forthcoming. *The Choice for Europe: Social Purpose and State Power from Messina to Maastricht.* Ithaca, N.Y.: Cornell University Press.

Morgenthau, Hans J. 1960. *Politics Among Nations: The Struggle for Power and Peace.* 3d ed. New York: Alfred Knopf.

Morrow, James D. 1988. Social Choice and System Structure in World Politics. *World Politics* 41 (October): 75–99.

Mueller, John. 1991. Is War Still Becoming Obsolete? Paper presented at the 87th Annual Meeting of the American Political Science Association, August, Washington, D.C.

Niou, Emerson M. S., and Peter C. Ordeshook. 1994. "Less Filling, Tastes Great": The Realist–Neo-Liberal Debate. *World Politics* 46 (January):209–35.

Nolt, James. 1990. Social Order and Threat: Thucydides, Aristotle, and the Critique of Modern Realism. Unpublished manuscript, Department of Political Science, University of Chicago, Chicago, Ill.

North, Douglass C., and Robert Paul Thomas. 1973. *The Rise of the Western World: A New Economic History.* Cambridge: Cambridge University Press.

Nye, Joseph S. 1988. Neorealism and Neoliberalism. *World Politics* 40 (January):235–51

Oneal, John, Frances Oneal, Zeev Maoz, and Bruce Russett. 1996. The Liberal Peace: Interdependence, Democracy, and International Conflict, 1950–85. *Journal of Peace Research* 33 (February):11–28.

Oye, Kenneth. 1986. *Cooperation Under Anarchy.* Princeton, N.J.: Princeton University Press.

Pillar, Paul R. 1983. *Negotiating Peace: War Termination as a Bargaining Process.* Princeton, N.J.: Princeton University Press.

Powell, Robert. 1994. Anarchy in International Relations Theory: The Neorealist-Neoliberal Debate. *International Organization* 48 (spring):313–44.

Raiffa, Howard. 1982. *The Art and Science of Negotiation.* Cambridge, Mass.: Harvard University Press.

Risse-Kappen, Thomas. 1996. Collective Identity in a Democratic Community: The Case of NATO. In *The Culture of National Security: Norms and Identity in World Politics,* edited by Peter Katzenstein, 357–99. New York: Columbia University Press.

Ruggie, John Gerard. 1982. International Regimes, Transactions, and Change: Embedded Liberalism in the Postwar Economic Order. *International Organization* 36 (spring):195–231.

———. 1983. Continuity and Transformation in the World Polity: Toward a Neorealist Synthesis. *World Politics* 35 (January):261–85.

———. 1995. At Home Abroad, Abroad at Home: International Liberalization and Domestic Stability in the New World Economy. Jean Monnet Chair Paper. Fiesole, Italy: European University Institute.

Russett, Bruce. 1993. *Grasping the Democratic Peace: Principles for a Post–Cold War World.* Princeton, N.J.: Princeton University Press.

Sebenius, James K. 1991. Negotiation Analysis. In *International Negotiations: Analysis, Approaches, Issues,* edited by Victor A. Kremenyuk, 65–77. San Francisco: Jossey-Bass.

Sikkink, Kathryn. 1993. The Power of Principled Ideas: Human Rights Policies in the United States and Western Europe. In *Ideas and Foreign Policy: Beliefs, Institutions, and Political Change,* edited by Judith Goldstein and Robert Keohane. Ithaca, N.Y.: Cornell University Press.

Slaughter, Anne-Marie. 1995. Law in a World of Liberal States. *European Journal of International Law* 6 (December):503–38.

Snidal, Duncan. 1985. Coordination Versus Prisoner's Dilemma: Implications for International Cooperation and Regimes. *American Political Science Review* 79 (December):923–42.

———. 1991. Relative Gains and the Pattern of International Cooperation. *American Political Science Review* 85 (September):701–26.

Snyder, Jack. 1991. *Myths of Empire: Domestic Politics and International Ambition.* Ithaca, N.Y.: Cornell University Press.

Stein, Arthur A. 1982. Coordination and Collaboration: Regimes in an Anarchic World. *International Organization* 36 (spring):299–324.

Tetlock, Philip E., and Aaron Belkin. 1996. Counterfactual Thought Experiments in World Politics. In *Counterfactual Thought Experiments in World Politics,* edited by Philip E. Tetlock and Aaron Belkin, 3–38. Princeton, N.J.: Princeton University Press.

Van Evera, Stephen. 1990. Primed for Peace: Europe After the Cold War. *International Security* 15 (winter): 5–57.

Walt, Stephen. 1987. *The Origins of Alliances.* Ithaca, N.Y.: Cornell University Press.

Waltz, Kenneth N. 1979. *Theory of International Politics.* Reading, Mass.: Addison-Wesley.

Watson, G., and D. McGaw. 1970. *Statistical Inference.* New York: Wiley.

Wendt, Alexander. 1994. Collective Identity Formation and the International State. *American Political Science Review* 88 (June):384–96.

Wehler, Hans-Ulrich. 1985. *Bismarck und der Imperialismus.* 2d ed. Frankfurt: Suhrkamp.

Weiner, Myron. 1971. The Macedonian Syndrome: An Historical Model of International Relations and Political Development. *World Politics* 23 (July):665–83.

———. 1996. Social Theory of International Politics. Unpublished manuscript, Yale University, New Haven, Conn.

Wight, Martin. 1991. *International Theory: Three Traditions.* Leicester: Leicester University Press.

Wolfers, Arnold, and Laurence W. Martin, eds. 1956. *The Anglo-American Tradition in Foreign Affairs: Readings from Thomas More to Woodrow Wilson.* New Haven, Conn.: Yale University Press.

Wooley, John. 1992. Policy Credibility and European Monetary Institutions. In *Europolitics: Institutions and Policymaking in the New European Community,* edited by Alberta Sbragia, 157–90. Washington, D.C.: Brookings Institution.

Zacher, Mark W., and Richard A. Matthew. 1992. Liberal International Theory: Common Threads, Divergent Strands. Paper presented at the 88th Annual Meeting of the American Political Science Association, September, Chicago, Ill.

Anarchy is what states make of it: the social construction of power politics
Alexander Wendt

The debate between realists and liberals has reemerged as an axis of contention in international relations theory.[1] Revolving in the past around competing theories of human nature, the debate is more concerned today with the extent to which state action is influenced by "structure" (anarchy and the distribution of power) versus "process" (interaction and learning) and institutions. Does the absence of centralized political authority force states to play competitive power politics? Can international regimes overcome this logic, and under what conditions? What in anarchy is given and immutable, and what is amenable to change?

The debate between "neorealists" and "neoliberals" has been based on a shared commitment to "rationalism."[2] Like all social theories, rational choice directs us to ask some questions and not others, treating the identities and interests of agents as exogenously given and focusing on how the behavior of

This article was negotiated with many individuals. If my records are complete (and apologies if they are not), thanks are due particularly to John Aldrich, Mike Barnett, Lea Brilmayer, David Campbell, Jim Caporaso, Simon Dalby, David Dessler, Bud Duvall, Jean Elshtain, Karyn Ertel, Lloyd Etheridge, Ernst Haas, Martin Hollis, Naeem Inayatullah, Stewart Johnson, Frank Klink, Steve Krasner, Friedrich Kratochwil, David Lumsdaine, M. J. Peterson, Spike Peterson, Thomas Risse-Kappen, John Ruggie, Bruce Russett, Jim Scott, Rogers Smith, David Sylvan, Jan Thomson, Mark Warren, and Jutta Weldes. The article also benefited from presentations and seminars at the American University, the University of Chicago, the University of Massachusetts at Amherst, Syracuse University, the University of Washington at Seattle, the University of California at Los Angeles, and Yale University.

1. See, for example, Joseph Grieco, "Anarchy and the Limits of Cooperation: A Realist Critique of the Newest Liberal Institutionalism," *International Organization* 42 (Summer 1988), pp. 485–507; Joseph Nye, "Neorealism and Neoliberalism," *World Politics* 40 (January 1988), pp. 235–51; Robert Keohane, "Neoliberal Institutionalism: A Perspective on World Politics," in his collection of essays entitled *International Institutions and State Power* (Boulder, Colo.: Westview Press, 1989), pp. 1–20; John Mearsheimer, "Back to the Future: Instability in Europe After the Cold War," *International Security* 13 (Summer 1990), pp. 5–56, along with subsequent published correspondence regarding Mearsheimer's article; and Emerson Niou and Peter Ordeshook, "Realism Versus Neoliberalism: A Formulation," *American Journal of Political Science* 35 (May 1991), pp. 481–511.

2. See Robert Keohane, "International Institutions: Two Approaches," *International Studies Quarterly* 32 (December 1988), pp. 379–96.

International Organization 46, 2, Spring 1992, pp. 391–425

agents generates outcomes. As such, rationalism offers a fundamentally behavioral conception of both process and institutions: they change behavior but not identities and interests.[3] In addition to this way of framing research problems, neorealists and neoliberals share generally similar assumptions about agents: states are the dominant actors in the system, and they define security in "self-interested" terms. Neorealists and neoliberals may disagree about the extent to which states are motivated by relative versus absolute gains, but both groups take the self-interested state as the starting point for theory.

This starting point makes substantive sense for neorealists, since they believe anarchies are necessarily "self-help" systems, systems in which both central authority and collective security are absent. The self-help corollary to anarchy does enormous work in neorealism, generating the inherently competitive dynamics of the security dilemma and collective action problem. Self-help is not seen as an "institution" and as such occupies a privileged explanatory role vis-à-vis process, setting the terms for, and unaffected by, interaction. Since states failing to conform to the logic of self-help will be driven from the system, only simple learning or behavioral adaptation is possible; the complex learning involved in redefinitions of identity and interest is not.[4] Questions about identity- and interest-formation are therefore not important to students of international relations. A rationalist problématique, which reduces process to dynamics of behavioral interaction among exogenously constituted actors, defines the scope of systemic theory.

By adopting such reasoning, liberals concede to neorealists the causal powers of anarchic structure, but they gain the rhetorically powerful argument that process can generate cooperative behavior, even in an exogenously given, self-help system. Some liberals may believe that anarchy does, in fact, constitute states with self-interested identities exogenous to practice. Such "weak" liberals concede the causal powers of anarchy both rhetorically and substantively and accept rationalism's limited, behavioral conception of the causal powers of institutions. They are realists before liberals (we might call them "weak realists"), since only if international institutions can change powers and interests do they go beyond the "limits" of realism.[5]

3. Behavioral and rationalist models of man and institutions share a common intellectual heritage in the materialist individualism of Hobbes, Locke, and Bentham. On the relationship between the two models, see Jonathan Turner, *A Theory of Social Interaction* (Stanford, Calif.: Stanford University Press, 1988), pp. 24–31; and George Homans, "Rational Choice Theory and Behavioral Psychology," in Craig Calhoun et al., eds., *Structures of Power and Constraint* (Cambridge: Cambridge University Press, 1991), pp. 77–89.

4. On neorealist conceptions of learning, see Philip Tetlock, "Learning in U.S. and Soviet Foreign Policy," in George Breslauer and Philip Tetlock, eds., *Learning in U.S. and Soviet Foreign Policy* (Boulder, Colo.: Westview Press, 1991), pp. 24–27. On the difference between behavioral and cognitive learning, see ibid., pp. 20–61; Joseph Nye, "Nuclear Learning and U.S.–Soviet Security Regimes," *International Organization* 41 (Summer 1987), pp. 371–402; and Ernst Haas, *When Knowledge Is Power* (Berkeley: University of California Press, 1990), pp. 17–49.

5. See Stephen Krasner, "Regimes and the Limits of Realism: Regimes as Autonomous Variables," in Stephen Krasner, ed., *International Regimes* (Ithaca, N.Y.: Cornell University Press, 1983), pp. 355–68.

Yet some liberals want more. When Joseph Nye speaks of "complex learning," or Robert Jervis of "changing conceptions of self and interest," or Robert Keohane of "sociological" conceptions of interest, each is asserting an important role for transformations of identity and interest in the liberal research program and, by extension, a potentially much stronger conception of process and institutions in world politics.[6] "Strong" liberals should be troubled by the dichotomous privileging of structure over process, since transformations of identity and interest through process are transformations of structure. Rationalism has little to offer such an argument,[7] which is in part why, in an important article, Friedrich Kratochwil and John Ruggie argued that its individualist ontology contradicted the intersubjectivist epistemology necessary for regime theory to realize its full promise.[8] Regimes cannot change identities and interests if the latter are taken as given. Because of this rationalist legacy, despite increasingly numerous and rich studies of complex learning in foreign policy, neoliberals lack a systematic theory of how such changes occur and thus must privilege realist insights about structure while advancing their own insights about process.

The irony is that social theories which seek to explain identities and interests do exist. Keohane has called them "reflectivist";[9] because I want to emphasize their focus on the social construction of subjectivity and minimize their image problem, following Nicholas Onuf I will call them "constructivist."[10] Despite important differences, cognitivists, poststructuralists, standpoint and postmodern feminists, rule theorists, and structurationists share a concern with the basic "sociological" issue bracketed by rationalists—namely, the issue of identity- and interest-formation. Constructivism's potential contribution to a strong liberalism has been obscured, however, by recent epistemological debates between modernists and postmodernists, in which Science disciplines Dissent for not defining a conventional research program, and Dissent celebrates its liberation from Science.[11] Real issues animate this debate, which

---

6. See Nye, "Nuclear Learning and U.S.–Soviet Security Regimes"; Robert Jervis, "Realism, Game Theory, and Cooperation," *World Politics* 40 (April 1988), pp. 340–44; and Robert Keohane, "International Liberalism Reconsidered," in John Dunn, ed., *The Economic Limits to Modern Politics* (Cambridge: Cambridge University Press, 1990), p. 183.

7. Rationalists have given some attention to the problem of preference-formation, although in so doing they have gone beyond what I understand as the characteristic parameters of rationalism. See, for example, Jon Elster, "Sour Grapes: Utilitarianism and the Genesis of Wants," in Amartya Sen and Bernard Williams, eds., *Utilitarianism and Beyond* (Cambridge: Cambridge University Press, 1982), pp. 219–38; and Michael Cohen and Robert Axelrod, "Coping with Complexity: The Adaptive Value of Changing Utility," *American Economic Review* 74 (March 1984), pp. 30–42.

8. Friedrich Kratochwil and John Ruggie, "International Organization: A State of the Art on an Art of the State," *International Organization* 40 (Autumn 1986), pp. 753–75.

9. Keohane, "International Institutions."

10. See Nicholas Onuf, *World of Our Making* (Columbia: University of South Carolina Press, 1989).

11. On Science, see Keohane, "International Institutions"; and Robert Keohane, "International Relations Theory: Contributions of a Feminist Standpoint," *Millennium* 18 (Summer 1989), pp. 245–53. On Dissent, see R. B. J. Walker, "History and Structure in the Theory of International Relations," *Millennium* 18 (Summer 1989), pp. 163–83; and Richard Ashley and R. B. J. Walker,

also divides constructivists. With respect to the substance of international relations, however, both modern and postmodern constructivists are interested in how knowledgeable practices constitute subjects, which is not far from the strong liberal interest in how institutions transform interests. They share a cognitive, intersubjective conception of process in which identities and interests are endogenous to interaction, rather than a rationalist-behavioral one in which they are exogenous.

My objective in this article is to build a bridge between these two traditions (and, by extension, between the realist-liberal and rationalist-reflectivist debates) by developing a constructivist argument, drawn from structurationist and symbolic interactionist sociology, on behalf of the liberal claim that international institutions can transform state identities and interests.[12] In contrast to the "economic" theorizing that dominates mainstream systemic international relations scholarship, this involves a "sociological social psychological" form of systemic theory in which identities and interests are the dependent variable.[13] Whether a "communitarian liberalism" is still liberalism does not interest me here. What does is that constructivism might contribute significantly to the strong liberal interest in identity- and interest-formation and thereby perhaps itself be enriched with liberal insights about learning and cognition which it has neglected.

My strategy for building this bridge will be to argue against the neorealist claim that self-help is given by anarchic structure exogenously to process. Constructivists have not done a good job of taking the causal powers of anarchy seriously. This is unfortunate, since in the realist view anarchy justifies disinterest in the institutional transformation of identities and interests and thus building systemic theories in exclusively rationalist terms; its putative causal powers must be challenged if process and institutions are not to be subordinated to structure. I argue that self-help and power politics do not follow either logically or causally from anarchy and that if today we find ourselves in a self-help world, this is due to process, not structure. There is no

---

"Reading Dissidence/Writing the Discipline: Crisis and the Question of Sovereignty in International Studies," *International Studies Quarterly* 34 (September 1990), pp. 367–416. For an excellent critical assessment of these debates, see Yosef Lapid, "The Third Debate: On the Prospects of International Theory in a Post-Positivist Era," *International Studies Quarterly* 33 (September 1989), pp. 235–54.

12. The fact that I draw on these approaches aligns me with modernist constructivists, even though I also draw freely on the substantive work of postmodernists, especially Richard Ashley and Rob Walker. For a defense of this practice and a discussion of its epistemological basis, see my earlier article, "The Agent-Structure Problem in International Relations Theory," *International Organization* 41 (Summer 1987), pp. 335–70; and Ian Shapiro and Alexander Wendt, "The Difference That Realism Makes: Social Science and the Politics of Consent," forthcoming in *Politics and Society*. Among modernist constructivists, my argument is particularly indebted to the published work of Emanuel Adler, Friedrich Kratochwil, and John Ruggie, as well as to an unpublished paper by Naeem Inayatullah and David Levine entitled "Politics and Economics in Contemporary International Relations Theory," Syracuse University, Syracuse, N.Y., 1990.

13. See Viktor Gecas, "Rekindling the Sociological Imagination in Social Psychology," *Journal for the Theory of Social Behavior* 19 (March 1989), pp. 97–115.

"logic" of anarchy apart from the practices that create and instantiate one structure of identities and interests rather than another; structure has no existence or causal powers apart from process. Self-help and power politics are institutions, not essential features of anarchy. *Anarchy is what states make of it.*

In the subsequent sections of this article, I critically examine the claims and assumptions of neorealism, develop a positive argument about how self-help and power politics are socially constructed under anarchy, and then explore three ways in which identities and interests are transformed under anarchy: by the institution of sovereignty, by an evolution of cooperation, and by intentional efforts to transform egoistic identities into collective identities.

Anarchy and power politics

Classical realists such as Thomas Hobbes, Reinhold Niebuhr, and Hans Morgenthau attributed egoism and power politics primarily to human nature, whereas structural realists or neorealists emphasize anarchy. The difference stems in part from different interpretations of anarchy's causal powers. Kenneth Waltz's work is important for both. In *Man, the State, and War,* he defines anarchy as a condition of possibility for or "permissive" cause of war, arguing that "wars occur because there is nothing to prevent them."[14] It is the human nature or domestic politics of predator states, however, that provide the initial impetus or "efficient" cause of conflict which forces other states to respond in kind.[15] Waltz is not entirely consistent about this, since he slips without justification from the permissive causal claim that in anarchy war is always possible to the active causal claim that "war may at any moment occur."[16] But despite Waltz's concluding call for third-image theory, the efficient causes that initialize anarchic systems are from the first and second images. This is reversed in Waltz's *Theory of International Politics,* in which first- and second-image theories are spurned as "reductionist," and the logic of anarchy seems by itself to constitute self-help and power politics as necessary features of world politics.[17]

This is unfortunate, since whatever one may think of first- and second-image theories, they have the virtue of implying that practices determine the character of anarchy. In the permissive view, only if human or domestic factors cause A to attack B will B have to defend itself. Anarchies may contain dynamics that lead to competitive power politics, but they also may not, and we can argue about when particular structures of identity and interest will emerge.

14. Kenneth Waltz, *Man, the State, and War* (New York: Columbia University Press, 1959), p. 232.
15. Ibid., pp. 169–70.
16. Ibid., p. 232. This point is made by Hidemi Suganami in "Bringing Order to the Causes of War Debates," *Millennium* 19 (Spring 1990), p. 34, fn. 11.
17. Kenneth Waltz, *Theory of International Politics* (Boston: Addison-Wesley, 1979).

In neorealism, however, the role of practice in shaping the character of anarchy is substantially reduced, and so there is less about which to argue: self-help and competitive power politics are simply given exogenously by the structure of the state system.

I will not here contest the neorealist description of the contemporary state system as a competitive, self-help world;[18] I will only dispute its explanation. I develop my argument in three stages. First, I disentangle the concepts of self-help and anarchy by showing that self-interested conceptions of security are not a constitutive property of anarchy. Second, I show how self-help and competitive power politics may be produced causally by processes of interaction between states in which anarchy plays only a permissive role. In both of these stages of my argument, I self-consciously bracket the first- and second-image determinants of state identity, not because they are unimportant (they are indeed important), but because like Waltz's objective, mine is to clarify the "logic" of anarchy. Third, I reintroduce first- and second-image determinants to assess their effects on identity-formation in different kinds of anarchies.

Anarchy, self-help, and intersubjective knowledge

Waltz defines political structure on three dimensions: ordering principles (in this case, anarchy), principles of differentiation (which here drop out), and the distribution of capabilities.[19] By itself, this definition predicts little about state behavior. It does not predict whether two states will be friends or foes, will recognize each other's sovereignty, will have dynastic ties, will be revisionist or status quo powers, and so on. These factors, which are fundamentally intersubjective, affect states' security interests and thus the character of their interaction under anarchy. In an important revision of Waltz's theory, Stephen Walt implies as much when he argues that the "balance of threats," rather than the balance of power, determines state action, threats being socially constructed.[20] Put more generally, without assumptions about the structure of identities and interests in the system, Waltz's definition of structure cannot predict the content or dynamics of anarchy. Self-help is one such intersubjective structure and, as such, does the decisive explanatory work in the theory. The question is whether self-help is a logical or contingent feature of anarchy. In this section, I develop the concept of a "structure of identity and interest" and show that no particular one follows logically from anarchy.

A fundamental principle of constructivist social theory is that people act toward objects, including other actors, on the basis of the meanings that the

18. The neorealist description is not unproblematic. For a powerful critique, see David Lumsdaine, *Ideals and Interests: The Foreign Aid Regime, 1949–1989* (Princeton, N.J.: Princeton University Press, forthcoming).

19. Waltz, *Theory of International Politics*, pp. 79–101.

20. Stephen Walt, *The Origins of Alliances* (Ithaca, N.Y.: Cornell University Press, 1987).

objects have for them.[21] States act differently toward enemies than they do toward friends because enemies are threatening and friends are not. Anarchy and the distribution of power are insufficient to tell us which is which. U.S. military power has a different significance for Canada than for Cuba, despite their similar "structural" positions, just as British missiles have a different significance for the United States than do Soviet missiles. The distribution of power may always affect states' calculations, but how it does so depends on the intersubjective understandings and expectations, on the "distribution of knowledge," that constitute their conceptions of self and other.[22] If society "forgets" what a university is, the powers and practices of professor and student cease to exist; if the United States and Soviet Union decide that they are no longer enemies, "the cold war is over." It is collective meanings that constitute the structures which organize our actions.

Actors acquire identities—relatively stable, role-specific understandings and expectations about self—by participating in such collective meanings.[23] Identities are inherently relational: "Identity, with its appropriate attachments of psychological reality, is always identity within a specific, socially constructed

21. See, for example, Herbert Blumer, "The Methodological Position of Symbolic Interactionism," in his *Symbolic Interactionism: Perspective and Method* (Englewood Cliffs, N.J.: Prentice-Hall, 1969), p. 2. Throughout this article, I assume that a theoretically productive analogy can be made between individuals and states. There are at least two justifications for this anthropomorphism. Rhetorically, the analogy is an accepted practice in mainstream international relations discourse, and since this article is an immanent rather than external critique, it should follow the practice. Substantively, states are collectivities of individuals that through their practices constitute each other as "persons" having interests, fears, and so on. A full theory of state identity- and interest-formation would nevertheless need to draw insights from the social psychology of groups and organizational theory, and for that reason my anthropomorphism is merely suggestive.

22. The phrase "distribution of knowledge" is Barry Barnes's, as discussed in his work *The Nature of Power* (Cambridge: Polity Press, 1988); see also Peter Berger and Thomas Luckmann, *The Social Construction of Reality* (New York: Anchor Books, 1966). The concern of recent international relations scholarship on "epistemic communities" with the cause-and-effect understandings of the world held by scientists, experts, and policymakers is an important aspect of the role of knowledge in world politics; see Peter Haas, "Do Regimes Matter? Epistemic Communities and Mediterranean Pollution Control," *International Organization* 43 (Summer 1989), pp. 377–404; and Ernst Haas, *When Knowledge Is Power*. My constructivist approach would merely add to this an equal emphasis on how such knowledge also *constitutes* the structures and subjects of social life.

23. For an excellent short statement of how collective meanings constitute identities, see Peter Berger, "Identity as a Problem in the Sociology of Knowledge," *European Journal of Sociology*, vol. 7, no. 1, 1966, pp. 32–40. See also David Morgan and Michael Schwalbe, "Mind and Self in Society: Linking Social Structure and Social Cognition," *Social Psychology Quarterly* 53 (June 1990), pp. 148–64. In my discussion, I draw on the following interactionist texts: George Herbert Mead, *Mind, Self, and Society* (Chicago: University of Chicago Press, 1934); Berger and Luckmann, *The Social Construction of Reality;* Sheldon Stryker, *Symbolic Interactionism: A Social Structural Version* (Menlo Park, Calif.: Benjamin/Cummings, 1980); R. S. Perinbanayagam, *Signifying Acts: Structure and Meaning in Everyday Life* (Carbondale: Southern Illinois University Press, 1985); John Hewitt, *Self and Society: A Symbolic Interactionist Social Psychology* (Boston: Allyn & Bacon, 1988); and Turner, *A Theory of Social Interaction.* Despite some differences, much the same points are made by structurationists such as Bhaskar and Giddens. See Roy Bhaskar, *The Possibility of Naturalism* (Atlantic Highlands, N.J.: Humanities Press, 1979); and Anthony Giddens, *Central Problems in Social Theory* (Berkeley: University of California Press, 1979).

world," Peter Berger argues.[24] Each person has many identities linked to institutional roles, such as brother, son, teacher, and citizen. Similarly, a state may have multiple identities as "sovereign," "leader of the free world," "imperial power," and so on.[25] The commitment to and the salience of particular identities vary, but each identity is an inherently social definition of the actor grounded in the theories which actors collectively hold about themselves and one another and which constitute the structure of the social world.

Identities are the basis of interests. Actors do not have a "portfolio" of interests that they carry around independent of social context; instead, they define their interests in the process of defining situations.[26] As Nelson Foote puts it: "Motivation . . . refer[s] to the degree to which a human being, as a participant in the ongoing social process in which he necessarily finds himself, defines a problematic situation as calling for the performance of a particular act, with more or less anticipated consummations and consequences, and thereby his organism releases the energy appropriate to performing it."[27] Sometimes situations are unprecedented in our experience, and in these cases we have to construct their meaning, and thus our interests, by analogy or invent them de novo. More often they have routine qualities in which we assign meanings on the basis of institutionally defined roles. When we say that professors have an "interest" in teaching, research, or going on leave, we are saying that to function in the role identity of "professor," they have to define certain situations as calling for certain actions. This does not mean that they will necessarily do so (expectations and competence do not equal performance), but if they do not, they will not get tenure. The absence or failure of roles makes defining situations and interests more difficult, and identity

24. Berger, "Identity as a Problem in the Sociology of Knowledge," p. 111.

25. While not normally cast in such terms, foreign policy scholarship on national role conceptions could be adapted to such identity language. See Kal Holsti, "National Role Conceptions in the Study of Foreign Policy," *International Studies Quarterly* 14 (September 1970), pp. 233–309; and Stephen Walker, ed., *Role Theory and Foreign Policy Analysis* (Durham, N.C.: Duke University Press, 1987). For an important effort to do so, see Stephen Walker, "Symbolic Interactionism and International Politics: Role Theory's Contribution to International Organization," in C. Shih and Martha Cottam, eds., *Contending Dramas: A Cognitive Approach to Post-War International Organizational Processes* (New York: Praeger, forthcoming).

26. On the "portfolio" conception of interests, see Barry Hindess, *Political Choice and Social Structure* (Aldershot, U.K.: Edward Elgar, 1989), pp. 2–3. The "definition of the situation" is a central concept in interactionist theory.

27. Nelson Foote, "Identification as the Basis for a Theory of Motivation," *American Sociological Review* 16 (February 1951), p. 15. Such strongly sociological conceptions of interest have been criticized, with some justice, for being "oversocialized"; see Dennis Wrong, "The Oversocialized Conception of Man in Modern Sociology," *American Sociological Review* 26 (April 1961), pp. 183–93. For useful correctives, which focus on the activation of presocial but nondetermining human needs within social contexts, see Turner, *A Theory of Social Interaction*, pp. 23–69; and Viktor Gecas, "The Self-Concept as a Basis for a Theory of Motivation," in Judith Howard and Peter Callero, eds., *The Self-Society Dynamic* (Cambridge: Cambridge University Press, 1991), pp. 171–87.

confusion may result. This seems to be happening today in the United States and the former Soviet Union: without the cold war's mutual attributions of threat and hostility to define their identities, these states seem unsure of what their "interests" should be.

An institution is a relatively stable set or "structure" of identities and interests. Such structures are often codified in formal rules and norms, but these have motivational force only in virtue of actors' socialization to and participation in collective knowledge. Institutions are fundamentally cognitive entities that do not exist apart from actors' ideas about how the world works.[28] This does not mean that institutions are not real or objective, that they are "nothing but" beliefs. As collective knowledge, they are experienced as having an existence "over and above the individuals who happen to embody them at the moment."[29] In this way, institutions come to confront individuals as more or less coercive social facts, but they are still a function of what actors collectively "know." Identities and such collective cognitions do not exist apart from each other; they are "mutually constitutive."[30] On this view, institutionalization is a process of internalizing new identities and interests, not something occurring outside them and affecting only behavior; socialization is a cognitive process, not just a behavioral one. Conceived in this way, institutions may be cooperative or conflictual, a point sometimes lost in scholarship on international regimes, which tends to equate institutions with cooperation. There are important differences between conflictual and cooperative institutions to be sure, but all relatively stable self-other relations—even those of "enemies"— are defined intersubjectively.

Self-help is an institution, one of various structures of identity and interest that may exist under anarchy. Processes of identity-formation under anarchy are concerned first and foremost with preservation or "security" of the self. Concepts of security therefore differ in the extent to which and the manner in which the self is identified cognitively with the other,[31] and, I want to suggest, it

---

28. In neo-Durkheimian parlance, institutions are "social representations." See Serge Moscovici, "The Phenomenon of Social Representations," in Rob Farr and Serge Moscovici, eds., *Social Representations* (Cambridge: Cambridge University Press, 1984), pp. 3–69. See also Barnes, *The Nature of Power*. Note that this is a considerably more socialized cognitivism than that found in much of the recent scholarship on the role of "ideas" in world politics, which tends to treat ideas as commodities that are held by individuals and intervene between the distribution of power and outcomes. For a form of cognitivism closer to my own, see Emanuel Adler, "Cognitive Evolution: A Dynamic Approach for the Study of International Relations and Their Progress," in Emanuel Adler and Beverly Crawford, eds., *Progress in Postwar International Relations* (New York: Columbia University Press, 1991), pp. 43–88.

29. Berger and Luckmann, *The Social Construction of Reality*, p. 58.

30. See Giddens, *Central Problems in Social Theory;* and Alexander Wendt and Raymond Duvall, "Institutions and International Order," in Ernst-Otto Czempiel and James Rosenau, eds., *Global Changes and Theoretical Challenges* (Lexington, Mass.: Lexington Books, 1989), pp. 51–74.

31. Proponents of choice theory might put this in terms of "interdependent utilities." For a useful overview of relevant choice-theoretic discourse, most of which has focused on the specific case of altruism, see Harold Hochman and Shmuel Nitzan, "Concepts of Extended Preference,"

is upon this cognitive variation that the meaning of anarchy and the distribution of power depends. Let me illustrate with a standard continuum of security systems.[32]

At one end is the "competitive" security system, in which states identify negatively with each other's security so that ego's gain is seen as alter's loss. Negative identification under anarchy constitutes systems of "realist" power politics: risk-averse actors that infer intentions from capabilities and worry about relative gains and losses. At the limit—in the Hobbesian war of all against all—collective action is nearly impossible in such a system because each actor must constantly fear being stabbed in the back.

In the middle is the "individualistic" security system, in which states are indifferent to the relationship between their own and others' security. This constitutes "neoliberal" systems: states are still self-regarding about their security but are concerned primarily with absolute gains rather than relative gains. One's position in the distribution of power is less important, and collective action is more possible (though still subject to free riding because states continue to be "egoists").

Competitive and individualistic systems are both "self-help" forms of anarchy in the sense that states do not positively identify the security of self with that of others but instead treat security as the individual responsibility of each. Given the lack of a positive cognitive identification on the basis of which to build security regimes, power politics within such systems will necessarily consist of efforts to manipulate others to satisfy self-regarding interests.

This contrasts with the "cooperative" security system, in which states identify positively with one another so that the security of each is perceived as the responsibility of all. This is not self-help in any interesting sense, since the "self" in terms of which interests are defined is the community; national interests are international interests.[33] In practice, of course, the extent to which

---

Journal of Economic Behavior and Organization 6 (June 1985), pp. 161–76. The literature on choice theory usually does not link behavior to issues of identity. For an exception, see Amartya Sen, "Goals, Commitment, and Identity," *Journal of Law, Economics, and Organization* 1 (Fall 1985), pp. 341–55; and Robert Higgs, "Identity and Cooperation: A Comment on Sen's Alternative Program," *Journal of Law, Economics, and Organization* 3 (Spring 1987), pp. 140–42.

32. Security systems might also vary in the extent to which there is a functional differentiation or a hierarchical relationship between patron and client, with the patron playing a hegemonic role within its sphere of influence in defining the security interests of its clients. I do not examine this dimension here; for preliminary discussion, see Alexander Wendt, "The States System and Global Militarization," Ph.D. diss., University of Minnesota, Minneapolis, 1989; and Alexander Wendt and Michael Barnett, "The International System and Third World Militarization," unpublished manuscript, 1991.

33. This amounts to an "internationalization of the state." For a discussion of this subject, see Raymond Duvall and Alexander Wendt, "The International Capital Regime and the Internationalization of the State," unpublished manuscript, 1987. See also R. B. J. Walker, "Sovereignty, Identity, Community: Reflections on the Horizons of Contemporary Political Practice," in R. B. J. Walker and Saul Mendlovitz, eds., *Contending Sovereignties* (Boulder, Colo.: Lynne Rienner, 1990), pp. 159–85.

states' identification with the community varies, from the limited form found in "concerts" to the full-blown form seen in "collective security" arrangements.[34] Depending on how well developed the collective self is, it will produce security practices that are in varying degrees altruistic or prosocial. This makes collective action less dependent on the presence of active threats and less prone to free riding.[35] Moreover, it restructures efforts to advance one's objectives, or "power politics," in terms of shared norms rather than relative power.[36]

On this view, the tendency in international relations scholarship to view power and institutions as two opposing explanations of foreign policy is therefore misleading, since anarchy and the distribution of power only have meaning for state action in virtue of the understandings and expectations that constitute institutional identities and interests. Self-help is one such institution, constituting one kind of anarchy but not the only kind. Waltz's three-part definition of structure therefore seems underspecified. In order to go from structure to action, we need to add a fourth: the intersubjectively constituted structure of identities and interests in the system.

This has an important implication for the way in which we conceive of states in the state of nature before their first encounter with each other. Because states do not have conceptions of self and other, and thus security interests, apart from or prior to interaction, we assume too much about the state of nature if we concur with Waltz that, in virtue of anarchy, "international political systems, like economic markets, are formed by the coaction of self-regarding units."[37] We also assume too much if we argue that, in virtue of

---

34. On the spectrum of cooperative security arrangements, see Charles Kupchan and Clifford Kupchan, "Concerts, Collective Security, and the Future of Europe," *International Security* 16 (Summer 1991), pp. 114–61; and Richard Smoke, "A Theory of Mutual Security," in Richard Smoke and Andrei Kortunov, eds., *Mutual Security* (New York: St. Martin's Press, 1991), pp. 59–111. These may be usefully read alongside Christopher Jencks' "Varieties of Altruism," in Jane Mansbridge, ed., *Beyond Self-Interest* (Chicago: University of Chicago Press, 1990), pp. 53–67.

35. On the role of collective identity in reducing collective action problems, see Bruce Fireman and William Gamson, "Utilitarian Logic in the Resource Mobilization Perspective," in Mayer Zald and John McCarthy, eds., *The Dynamics of Social Movements* (Cambridge, Mass.: Winthrop, 1979), pp. 8–44; Robyn Dawes et al., "Cooperation for the Benefit of Us—Not Me, or My Conscience," in Mansbridge, *Beyond Self-Interest,* pp. 97–110; and Craig Calhoun, "The Problem of Identity in Collective Action," in Joan Huber, ed., *Macro-Micro Linkages in Sociology* (Beverly Hills, Calif.: Sage, 1991), pp. 51–75.

36. See Thomas Risse-Kappen, "Are Democratic Alliances Special?" unpublished manuscript, Yale University, New Haven, Conn., 1991. This line of argument could be expanded usefully in feminist terms. For a useful overview of the relational nature of feminist conceptions of self, see Paula England and Barbara Stanek Kilbourne, "Feminist Critiques of the Separative Model of Self: Implications for Rational Choice Theory," *Rationality and Society* 2 (April 1990), pp. 156–71. On feminist conceptualizations of power, see Ann Tickner, "Hans Morgenthau's Principles of Political Realism: A Feminist Reformulation," *Millennium* 17 (Winter 1988), pp. 429–40; and Thomas Wartenberg, "The Concept of Power in Feminist Theory," *Praxis International* 8 (October 1988), pp. 301–16.

37. Waltz, *Theory of International Politics,* p. 91.

anarchy, states in the state of nature necessarily face a "stag hunt" or "security dilemma."[38] These claims presuppose a history of interaction in which actors have acquired "selfish" identities and interests; before interaction (and still in abstraction from first- and second-image factors) they would have no experience upon which to base such definitions of self and other. To assume otherwise is to attribute to states in the state of nature qualities that they can only possess in society.[39] Self-help is an institution, not a constitutive feature of anarchy.

What, then, *is* a constitutive feature of the state of nature before interaction? Two things are left if we strip away those properties of the self which presuppose interaction with others. The first is the material substrate of agency, including its intrinsic capabilities. For human beings, this is the body; for states, it is an organizational apparatus of governance. In effect, I am suggesting for rhetorical purposes that the raw material out of which members of the state system are constituted is created by domestic society before states enter the constitutive process of international society,[40] although this process implies neither stable territoriality nor sovereignty, which are internationally negotiated terms of individuality (as discussed further below). The second is a desire to preserve this material substrate, to survive. This does not entail "self-regardingness," however, since actors do not have a self prior to interaction with an other; how they view the meaning and requirements of this survival therefore depends on the processes by which conceptions of self evolve.

This may all seem very arcane, but there is an important issue at stake: are the foreign policy identities and interests of states exogenous or endogenous to the state system? The former is the answer of an individualistic or undersocialized systemic theory for which rationalism is appropriate; the latter is the answer of a fully socialized systemic theory. Waltz seems to offer the latter and

38. See Waltz, *Man, the State, and War;* and Robert Jervis, "Cooperation Under the Security Dilemma," *World Politics* 30 (January 1978), pp. 167–214.

39. My argument here parallels Rousseau's critique of Hobbes. For an excellent critique of realist appropriations of Rousseau, see Michael Williams, "Rousseau, Realism, and Realpolitik," *Millennium* 18 (Summer 1989), pp. 188–204. Williams argues that far from being a fundamental starting point in the state of nature, for Rousseau the stag hunt represented a stage in man's fall. On p. 190, Williams cites Rousseau's description of man prior to leaving the state of nature: "Man only knows himself; he does not see his own well-being to be identified with or contrary to that of anyone else; he neither hates anything nor loves anything; but limited to no more than physical instinct, he is no one, he is an animal." For another critique of Hobbes on the state of nature that parallels my constructivist reading of anarchy, see Charles Landesman, "Reflections on Hobbes: Anarchy and Human Nature," in Peter Caws, ed., *The Causes of Quarrel* (Boston: Beacon, 1989), pp. 139–48.

40. Empirically, this suggestion is problematic, since the process of decolonization and the subsequent support of many Third World states by international society point to ways in which even the raw material of "empirical statehood" is constituted by the society of states. See Robert Jackson and Carl Rosberg, "Why Africa's Weak States Persist: The Empirical and the Juridical in Statehood," *World Politics* 35 (October 1982), pp. 1–24.

proposes two mechanisms, competition and socialization, by which structure conditions state action.[41] The content of his argument about this conditioning, however, presupposes a self-help system that is not itself a constitutive feature of anarchy. As James Morrow points out, Waltz's two mechanisms condition behavior, not identity and interest.[42] This explains how Waltz can be accused of both "individualism" and "structuralism."[43] He is the former with respect to systemic constitutions of identity and interest, the latter with respect to systemic determinations of behavior.

Anarchy and the social construction of power politics

If self-help is not a constitutive feature of anarchy, it must emerge causally from processes in which anarchy plays only a permissive role.[44] This reflects a second principle of constructivism: that the meanings in terms of which action is organized arise out of interaction.[45] This being said, however, the situation facing states as they encounter one another for the first time may be such that only self-regarding conceptions of identity can survive; if so, even if these conceptions are socially constructed, neorealists may be right in holding identities and interests constant and thus in privileging one particular meaning of anarchic structure over process. In this case, rationalists would be right to argue for a weak, behavioral conception of the difference that institutions make, and realists would be right to argue that any international institutions which are created will be inherently unstable, since without the power to

41. Waltz, *Theory of International Politics,* pp. 74–77.

42. See James Morrow, "Social Choice and System Structure in World Politics," *World Politics* 41 (October 1988), p. 89. Waltz's behavioral treatment of socialization may be usefully contrasted with the more cognitive approach taken by Ikenberry and the Kupchans in the following articles: G. John Ikenberry and Charles Kupchan, "Socialization and Hegemonic Power," *International Organization* 44 (Summer 1989), pp. 283–316; and Kupchan and Kupchan, "Concerts, Collective Security, and the Future of Europe." Their approach is close to my own, but they define socialization as an elite strategy to induce value change in others, rather than as a ubiquitous feature of interaction in terms of which all identities and interests get produced and reproduced.

43. Regarding individualism, see Richard Ashley, "The Poverty of Neorealism," *International Organization* 38 (Spring 1984), pp. 225–86; Wendt, "The Agent-Structure Problem in International Relations Theory"; and David Dessler, "What's at Stake in the Agent-Structure Debate?" *International Organization* 43 (Summer 1989), pp. 441–74. Regarding structuralism, see R. B. J. Walker, "Realism, Change, and International Political Theory," *International Studies Quarterly* 31 (March 1987), pp. 65–86; and Martin Hollis and Steven Smith, *Explaining and Understanding International Relations* (Oxford: Clarendon Press, 1989). The behavioralism evident in neorealist theory also explains how neorealists can reconcile their structuralism with the individualism of rational choice theory. On the behavioral-structural character of the latter, see Spiro Latsis, "Situational Determinism in Economics," *British Journal for the Philosophy of Science* 23 (August 1972), pp. 207–45.

44. The importance of the distinction between constitutive and causal explanations is not sufficiently appreciated in constructivist discourse. See Wendt, "The Agent-Structure Problem in International Relations Theory," pp. 362–65; Wendt, "The States System and Global Militarization," pp. 110–13; and Wendt, "Bridging the Theory/Meta-Theory Gap in International Relations," *Review of International Studies* 17 (October 1991), p. 390.

45. See Blumer, "The Methodological Position of Symbolic Interactionism," pp. 2–4.

transform identities and interests they will be "continuing objects of choice" by exogenously constituted actors constrained only by the transaction costs of behavioral change.[46] Even in a permissive causal role, in other words, anarchy may decisively restrict interaction and therefore restrict viable forms of systemic theory. I address these causal issues first by showing how self-regarding ideas about security might develop and then by examining the conditions under which a key efficient cause—predation—may dispose states in this direction rather than others.

Conceptions of self and interest tend to "mirror" the practices of significant others over time. This principle of identity-formation is captured by the symbolic interactionist notion of the "looking-glass self," which asserts that the self is a reflection of an actor's socialization.

Consider two actors—ego and alter—encountering each other for the first time.[47] Each wants to survive and has certain material capabilities, but neither actor has biological or domestic imperatives for power, glory, or conquest (still bracketed), and there is no history of security or insecurity between the two. What should they do? Realists would probably argue that each should act on the basis of worst-case assumptions about the other's intentions, justifying such an attitude as prudent in view of the possibility of death from making a mistake. Such a possibility always exists, even in civil society; however, society would be impossible if people made decisions purely on the basis of worst-case possibilities. Instead, most decisions are and should be made on the basis of probabilities, and these are produced by interaction, by what actors *do*.

In the beginning is ego's gesture, which may consist, for example, of an advance, a retreat, a brandishing of arms, a laying down of arms, or an attack.[48] For ego, this gesture represents the basis on which it is prepared to respond to alter. This basis is unknown to alter, however, and so it must make an inference or "attribution" about ego's intentions and, in particular, given that this is anarchy, about whether ego is a threat.[49] The content of this inference will largely depend on two considerations. The first is the gesture's and ego's

---

46. See Robert Grafstein, "Rational Choice: Theory and Institutions," in Kristen Monroe, ed., *The Economic Approach to Politics* (New York: Harper Collins, 1991), pp. 263–64. A good example of the promise and limits of transaction cost approaches to institutional analysis is offered by Robert Keohane in his *After Hegemony* (Princeton, N.J.: Princeton University Press, 1984).

47. This situation is not entirely metaphorical in world politics, since throughout history states have "discovered" each other, generating an instant anarchy as it were. A systematic empirical study of first contacts would be interesting.

48. Mead's analysis of gestures remains definitive. See Mead's *Mind, Self, and Society.* See also the discussion of the role of signaling in the "mechanics of interaction" in Turner's *A Theory of Social Interaction,* pp. 74–79 and 92–115.

49. On the role of attribution processes in the interactionist account of identity-formation, see Sheldon Stryker and Avi Gottlieb, "Attribution Theory and Symbolic Interactionism," in John Harvey et al., eds., *New Directions in Attribution Research,* vol. 3 (Hillsdale, N.J.: Lawrence Erlbaum, 1981), pp. 425–58; and Kathleen Crittenden, "Sociological Aspects of Attribution," *Annual Review of Sociology,* vol. 9, 1983, pp. 425–46. On attributional processes in international relations, see Shawn Rosenberg and Gary Wolfsfeld, "International Conflict and the Problem of Attribution," *Journal of Conflict Resolution* 21 (March 1977), pp. 75–103.

physical qualities, which are in part contrived by ego and which include the direction of movement, noise, numbers, and immediate consequences of the gesture.[50] The second consideration concerns what alter would intend by such qualities were it to make such a gesture itself. Alter may make an attributional "error" in its inference about ego's intent, but there is also no reason for it to assume a priori—before the gesture—that ego is threatening, since it is only through a process of signaling and interpreting that the costs and probabilities of being wrong can be determined.[51] Social threats are constructed, not natural.

Consider an example. Would we assume, a priori, that we were about to be attacked if we are ever contacted by members of an alien civilization? I think not. We would be highly alert, of course, but whether we placed our military forces on alert or launched an attack would depend on how we interpreted the import of their first gesture for our security—if only to avoid making an immediate enemy out of what may be a dangerous adversary. The possibility of error, in other words, does not force us to act on the assumption that the aliens are threatening: action depends on the probabilities we assign, and these are in key part a function of what the aliens do; prior to their gesture, we have no systemic basis for assigning probabilities. If their first gesture is to appear with a thousand spaceships and destroy New York, we will define the situation as threatening and respond accordingly. But if they appear with one spaceship, saying what seems to be "we come in peace," we will feel "reassured" and will probably respond with a gesture intended to reassure them, even if this gesture is not necessarily interpreted by them as such.[52]

This process of signaling, interpreting, and responding completes a "social act" and begins the process of creating intersubjective meanings. It advances the same way. The first social act creates expectations on both sides about each other's future behavior: potentially mistaken and certainly tentative, but expectations nonetheless. Based on this tentative knowledge, ego makes a new gesture, again signifying the basis on which it will respond to alter, and again alter responds, adding to the pool of knowledge each has about the other, and so on over time. The mechanism here is reinforcement; interaction rewards actors for holding certain ideas about each other and discourages them from holding others. If repeated long enough, these "reciprocal typifications" will create relatively stable concepts of self and other regarding the issue at stake in the interaction.[53]

---

50. On the "stagecraft" involved in "presentations of self," see Erving Goffman, *The Presentation of Self in Everyday Life* (New York: Doubleday, 1959). On the role of appearance in definitions of the situation, see Gregory Stone, "Appearance and the Self," in Arnold Rose, ed., *Human Behavior and Social Processes* (Boston: Houghton Mifflin, 1962), pp. 86–118.

51. This discussion of the role of possibilities and probabilities in threat perception owes much to Stewart Johnson's comments on an earlier draft of my article.

52. On the role of "reassurance" in threat situations, see Richard Ned Lebow and Janice Gross Stein, "Beyond Deterrence," *Journal of Social Issues*, vol. 43, no. 4, 1987, pp. 5–72.

53. On "reciprocal typifications," see Berger and Luckmann, *The Social Construction of Reality*, pp. 54–58.

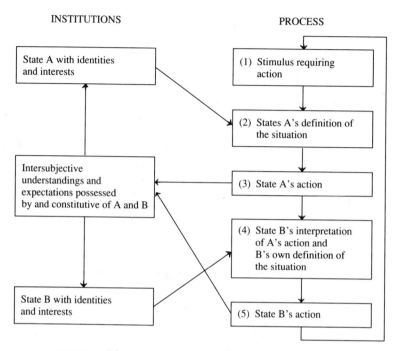

FIGURE 1. *The codetermination of institutions and process*

It is through reciprocal interaction, in other words, that we create and instantiate the relatively enduring social structures in terms of which we define our identities and interests. Jeff Coulter sums up the ontological dependence of structure on process this way: "The parameters of social organization themselves are reproduced only in and through the orientations and practices of members engaged in social interactions over time. . . . Social configurations are not 'objective' like mountains or forests, but neither are they 'subjective' like dreams or flights of speculative fancy. They are, as most social scientists concede at the theoretical level, intersubjective constructions."[54]

The simple overall model of identity- and interest-formation proposed in Figure 1 applies to competitive institutions no less than to cooperative ones. Self-help security systems evolve from cycles of interaction in which each party acts in ways that the other feels are threatening to the self, creating expectations that the other is not to be trusted. Competitive or egoistic identities are caused by such insecurity; if the other is threatening, the self is forced to "mirror" such behavior in its conception of the self's relationship to

---

54. Jeff Coulter, "Remarks on the Conceptualization of Social Structure," *Philosophy of the Social Sciences* 12 (March 1982), pp. 42–43.

that other.[55] Being treated as an object for the gratification of others precludes the positive identification with others necessary for collective security; conversely, being treated by others in ways that are empathic with respect to the security of the self permits such identification.[56]

Competitive systems of interaction are prone to security "dilemmas," in which the efforts of actors to enhance their security unilaterally threatens the security of the others, perpetuating distrust and alienation. The forms of identity and interest that constitute such dilemmas, however, are themselves ongoing effects of, not exogenous to, the interaction; identities are produced in and through "situated activity."[57] We do not *begin* our relationship with the aliens in a security dilemma; security dilemmas are not given by anarchy or nature. Of course, once institutionalized such a dilemma may be hard to change (I return to this below), but the point remains: identities and interests are constituted by collective meanings that are always in process. As Sheldon Stryker emphasizes, "The social process is one of constructing and reconstructing self and social relationships."[58] If states find themselves in a self-help system, this is because their practices made it that way. Changing the practices will change the intersubjective knowledge that constitutes the system.

Predator states and anarchy as permissive cause

The mirror theory of identity-formation is a crude account of how the process of creating identities and interests might work, but it does not tell us why a system of states—such as, arguably, our own—would have ended up with self-regarding and not collective identities. In this section, I examine an efficient cause, predation, which, in conjunction with anarchy as a permissive cause, may generate a self-help system. In so doing, however, I show the key role that the structure of identities and interests plays in mediating anarchy's explanatory role.

The predator argument is straightforward and compelling. For whatever reasons—biology, domestic politics, or systemic victimization—some states

55. The following articles by Noel Kaplowitz have made an important contribution to such thinking in international relations: "Psychopolitical Dimensions of International Relations: The Reciprocal Effects of Conflict Strategies," *International Studies Quarterly* 28 (December 1984), pp. 373–406; and "National Self-Images, Perception of Enemies, and Conflict Strategies: Psychopolitical Dimensions of International Relations," *Political Psychology* 11 (March 1990), pp. 39–82.

56. These arguments are common in theories of narcissism and altruism. See Heinz Kohut, *Self-Psychology and the Humanities* (New York: Norton, 1985); and Martin Hoffmann, "Empathy, Its Limitations, and Its Role in a Comprehensive Moral Theory," in William Kurtines and Jacob Gewirtz, eds., *Morality, Moral Behavior, and Moral Development* (New York: Wiley, 1984), pp. 283–302.

57. See C. Norman Alexander and Mary Glenn Wiley, "Situated Activity and Identity Formation," in Morris Rosenberg and Ralph Turner, eds., *Social Psychology: Sociological Perspectives* (New York: Basic Books, 1981), pp. 269–89.

58. Sheldon Stryker, "The Vitalization of Symbolic Interactionism," *Social Psychology Quarterly* 50 (March 1987), p. 93.

may become predisposed toward aggression. The aggressive behavior of these predators or "bad apples" forces other states to engage in competitive power politics, to meet fire with fire, since failure to do so may degrade or destroy them. One predator will best a hundred pacifists because anarchy provides no guarantees. This argument is powerful in part because it is so weak: rather than making the strong assumption that all states are inherently power-seeking (a purely reductionist theory of power politics), it assumes that just one is power-seeking and that the others have to follow suit because anarchy permits the one to exploit them.

In making this argument, it is important to reiterate that the possibility of predation does not in itself force states to anticipate it a priori with competitive power politics of their own. The possibility of predation does not mean that "war may at any moment occur"; it may in fact be extremely unlikely. Once a predator emerges, however, it may condition identity- and interest-formation in the following manner.

In an anarchy of two, if ego is predatory, alter must either define its security in self-help terms or pay the price. This follows directly from the above argument, in which conceptions of self mirror treatment by the other. In an anarchy of many, however, the effect of predation also depends on the level of collective identity already attained in the system. If predation occurs right after the first encounter in the state of nature, it will force others with whom it comes in contact to defend themselves, first individually and then collectively *if* they come to perceive a common threat. The emergence of such a defensive alliance will be seriously inhibited if the structure of identities and interests has already evolved into a Hobbesian world of maximum insecurity, since potential allies will strongly distrust each other and face intense collective action problems; such insecure allies are also more likely to fall out amongst themselves once the predator is removed. If collective security identity is high, however, the emergence of a predator may do much less damage. If the predator attacks any member of the collective, the latter will come to the victim's defense on the principle of "all for one, one for all," even if the predator is not presently a threat to other members of the collective. If the predator is not strong enough to withstand the collective, it will be defeated and collective security will obtain. But if it is strong enough, the logic of the two-actor case (now predator and collective) will activate, and balance-of-power politics will reestablish itself.

The timing of the emergence of predation relative to the history of identity-formation in the community is therefore crucial to anarchy's explanatory role as a permissive cause. Predation will always lead victims to defend themselves, but whether defense will be collective or not depends on the history of interaction within the potential collective as much as on the ambitions of the predator. Will the disappearance of the Soviet threat renew old insecurities among the members of the North Atlantic Treaty Organization? Perhaps, but not if they have reasons independent of that threat for identifying their security with one another. Identities and interests are relationship-specific, not intrinsic attributes of a "portfolio"; states may be competitive in some relationships and solidary in others. "Mature" anarchies are less likely than "immature" ones to be reduced by predation to a Hobbesian condition, and maturity, which is a proxy for structures of identity and interest, is a function of process.[59]

The source of predation also matters. If it stems from unit-level causes that are immune to systemic impacts (causes such as human nature or domestic politics taken in isolation), then it functions in a manner analogous to a "genetic trait" in the constructed world of the state system. Even if successful, this trait does not select for other predators in an evolutionary sense so much as it teaches other states to respond in kind, but since traits cannot be unlearned, the other states will continue competitive behavior until the predator is either destroyed or transformed from within. However, in the more likely event that predation stems at least in part from prior systemic interaction—perhaps as a result of being victimized in the past (one thinks here of Nazi Germany or the Soviet Union)—then it is more a response to a learned identity and, as such, might be transformed by future social interaction in the form of appeasement, reassurances that security needs will be met, systemic effects on domestic politics, and so on. In this case, in other words, there is more hope that process can transform a bad apple into a good one.

The role of predation in generating a self-help system, then, is consistent with a systematic focus on process. Even if the source of predation is entirely exogenous to the system, it is what states *do* that determines the quality of their interactions under anarchy. In this respect, it is not surprising that it is classical realists rather than structural realists who emphasize this sort of argument. The former's emphasis on unit-level causes of power politics leads more easily to a permissive view of anarchy's explanatory role (and therefore to a processual view of international relations) than does the latter's emphasis on anarchy as a "structural cause";[60] neorealists do not need predation because the system is given as self-help.

This raises anew the question of exactly how much and what kind of role human nature and domestic politics play in world politics. The greater and more destructive this role, the more significant predation will be, and the less amenable anarchy will be to formation of collective identities. Classical realists, of course, assumed that human nature was possessed by an inherent lust for power or glory. My argument suggests that assumptions such as this were made for a reason: an unchanging Hobbesian man provides the powerful efficient cause necessary for a relentless pessimism about world politics that anarchic structure alone, or even structure plus intermittent predation, cannot supply. One can be skeptical of such an essentialist assumption, as I am, but it does

---

59. On the "maturity" of anarchies, see Barry Buzan, *People, States, and Fear* (Chapel Hill: University of North Carolina Press, 1983).

60. A similar intuition may lie behind Ashley's effort to reappropriate classical realist discourse for critical international relations theory. See Richard Ashley, "Political Realism and Human Interests," *International Studies Quarterly* 38 (June 1981), pp. 204–36.

produce determinate results at the expense of systemic theory. A concern with systemic process over structure suggests that perhaps it is time to revisit the debate over the relative importance of first-, second-, and third-image theories of state identity-formation.[61]

Assuming for now that systemic theories of identity-formation in world politics are worth pursuing, let me conclude by suggesting that the realist-rationalist alliance "reifies" self-help in the sense of treating it as something separate from the practices by which it is produced and sustained. Peter Berger and Thomas Luckmann define reification as follows: "[It] is the apprehension of the products of human activity *as if* they were something else than human products—such as facts of nature, results of cosmic laws, or manifestations of divine will. Reification implies that man is capable of forgetting his own authorship of the human world, and further, that the dialectic between man, the producer, and his products is lost to consciousness. The reified world is . . . experienced by man as a strange facticity, an *opus alienum* over which he has no control rather than as the *opus proprium* of his own productive activity."[62] By denying or bracketing states' collective authorship of their identities and interests, in other words, the realist-rationalist alliance denies or brackets the fact that competitive power politics help create the very "problem of order" they are supposed to solve—that realism is a self-fulfilling prophecy. Far from being exogenously given, the intersubjective knowledge that constitutes competitive identities and interests is constructed every day by processes of "social will formation."[63] It is what states have made of themselves.

Institutional transformations of power politics

Let us assume that processes of identity- and interest-formation have created a world in which states do not recognize rights to territory or existence—a war of all against all. In this world, anarchy has a "realist" meaning for state action: be insecure and concerned with relative power. Anarchy has this meaning only in virtue of collective, insecurity-producing practices, but if those practices are

61. Waltz has himself helped open up such a debate with his recognition that systemic factors condition but do not determine state actions. See Kenneth Waltz, "Reflections on *Theory of International Politics:* A Response to My Critics," in Robert Keohane, ed., *Neorealism and Its Critics* (New York: Columbia University Press, 1986), pp. 322–45. The growing literature on the observation that "democracies do not fight each other" is relevant to this question, as are two other studies that break important ground toward a "reductionist" theory of state identity: William Bloom's *Personal Identity, National Identity and International Relations* (Cambridge: Cambridge University Press, 1990) and Lumsdaine's *Ideals and Interests.*

62. See Berger and Luckmann, *The Social Construction of Reality,* p. 89. See also Douglas Maynard and Thomas Wilson, "On the Reification of Social Structure," in Scott McNall and Gary Howe, eds., *Current Perspectives in Social Theory,* vol. 1 (Greenwich, Conn.: JAI Press, 1980), pp. 287–322.

63. See Richard Ashley, "Social Will and International Anarchy," in Hayward Alker and Richard Ashley, eds., *After Realism,* work in progress, Massachusetts Institute of Technology, Cambridge, and Arizona State University, Tempe, 1992.

relatively stable, they do constitute a system that may resist change. The fact that worlds of power politics are socially constructed, in other words, does not guarantee they are malleable, for at least two reasons.

The first reason is that once constituted, any social system confronts each of its members as an objective social fact that reinforces certain behaviors and discourages others. Self-help systems, for example, tend to reward competition and punish altruism. The possibility of change depends on whether the exigencies of such competition leave room for actions that deviate from the prescribed script. If they do not, the system will be reproduced and deviant actors will not.[64]

The second reason is that systemic change may also be inhibited by actors' interests in maintaining relatively stable role identities. Such interests are rooted not only in the desire to minimize uncertainty and anxiety, manifested in efforts to confirm existing beliefs about the social world, but also in the desire to avoid the expected costs of breaking commitments made to others—notably domestic constituencies and foreign allies in the case of states—as part of past practices. The level of resistance that these commitments induce will depend on the "salience" of particular role identities to the actor.[65] The United States, for example, is more likely to resist threats to its identity as "leader of anticommunist crusades" than to its identity as "promoter of human rights." But for almost any role identity, practices and information that challenge it are likely to create cognitive dissonance and even perceptions of threat, and these may cause resistance to transformations of the self and thus to social change.[66]

For both systemic and "psychological" reasons, then, intersubjective understandings and expectations may have a self-perpetuating quality, constituting path-dependencies that new ideas about self and other must transcend. This does not change the fact that through practice agents are continuously producing and reproducing identities and interests, continuously "choosing now the preferences [they] will have later."[67] But it does mean that choices may not be experienced with meaningful degrees of freedom. This could be a constructivist justification for the realist position that only simple learning is

64. See Ralph Turner, "Role-Taking: Process Versus Conformity," in Rose, *Human Behavior and Social Processes*, pp. 20–40; and Judith Howard, "From Changing Selves Toward Changing Society," in Howard and Callero, *The Self-Society Dynamic*, pp. 209–37.

65. On the relationship between commitment and identity, see Foote, "Identification as the Basis for a Theory of Motivation"; Howard Becker, "Notes on the Concept of Commitment," *American Journal of Sociology* 66 (July 1960), pp. 32–40; and Stryker, *Symbolic Interactionism*. On role salience, see Stryker, ibid.

66. On threats to identity and the types of resistance that they may create, see Glynis Breakwell, *Coping with Threatened Identities* (London: Methuen, 1986); and Terrell Northrup, "The Dynamic of Identity in Personal and Social Conflict," in Louis Kreisberg et al., eds., *Intractable Conflicts and Their Transformation* (Syracuse, N.Y.: Syracuse University Press, 1989), pp. 55–82. For a broad overview of resistance to change, see Timur Kuran, "The Tenacious Past: Theories of Personal and Collective Conservatism," *Journal of Economic Behavior and Organization* 10 (September 1988), pp. 143–71.

67. James March, "Bounded Rationality, Ambiguity, and the Engineering of Choice," *Bell Journal of Economics* 9 (Autumn 1978), p. 600.

possible in self-help systems. The realist might concede that such systems are socially constructed and still argue that after the corresponding identities and interests have become institutionalized, they are almost impossible to transform.

In the remainder of this article, I examine three institutional transformations of identity and security interest through which states might escape a Hobbesian world of their own making. In so doing, I seek to clarify what it means to say that "institutions transform identities and interests," emphasizing that the key to such transformations is relatively stable practice.

Sovereignty, recognition, and security

In a Hobbesian state of nature, states are individuated by the domestic processes that constitute them as states and by their material capacity to deter threats from other states. In this world, even if free momentarily from the predations of others, state security does not have any basis in social recognition—in intersubjective understandings or norms that a state has a right to its existence, territory, and subjects. Security is a matter of national power, nothing more.

The principle of sovereignty transforms this situation by providing a social basis for the individuality and security of states. Sovereignty is an institution, and so it exists only in virtue of certain intersubjective understandings and expectations; there is no sovereignty without an other. These understandings and expectations not only constitute a particular kind of state—the "sovereign" state—but also constitute a particular form of community, since identities are relational. The essence of this community is a mutual recognition of one another's right to exercise exclusive political authority within territorial limits. These reciprocal "permissions"[68] constitute a spatially rather than functionally differentiated world—a world in which fields of practice constitute and are organized around "domestic" and "international" spaces rather than around the performance of particular activities.[69] The location of the boundaries between these spaces is of course sometimes contested, war being one practice through which states negotiate the terms of their individuality. But this does not change the fact that it is only in virtue of mutual recognition that states have

---

68. Haskell Fain, *Normative Politics and the Community of Nations* (Philadelphia: Temple University Press, 1987).

69. This is the intersubjective basis for the principle of functional nondifferentiation among states, which "drops out" of Waltz's definition of structure because the latter has no explicit intersubjective basis. In international relations scholarship, the social production of territorial space has been emphasized primarily by poststructuralists. See, for example, Richard Ashley, "The Geopolitics of Geopolitical Space: Toward a Critical Social Theory of International Politics," *Alternatives* 12 (October 1987), pp. 403–34; and Simon Dalby, *Creating the Second Cold War* (London: Pinter, 1990). But the idea of space as both product and constituent of practice is also prominent in structurationist discourse. See Giddens, *Central Problems in Social Theory;* and Derek Gregory and John Urry, eds., *Social Relations and Spatial Structures* (London: Macmillan, 1985).

"territorial property rights."[70] This recognition functions as a form of "social closure" that disempowers nonstate actors and empowers and helps stabilize interaction among states.[71]

Sovereignty norms are now so taken for granted, so natural, that it is easy to overlook the extent to which they are both presupposed by and an ongoing artifact of practice. When states tax "their" "citizens" and not others, when they "protect" their markets against foreign "imports," when they kill thousands of Iraqis in one kind of war and then refuse to "intervene" to kill even one person in another kind, a "civil" war, and when they fight a global war against a regime that sought to destroy the institution of sovereignty and then give Germany back to the Germans, they are acting against the background of, and thereby reproducing, shared norms about what it means to be a sovereign state.

If states stopped acting on those norms, their identity as "sovereigns" (if not necessarily as "states") would disappear. The sovereign state is an ongoing accomplishment of practice, not a once-and-for-all creation of norms that somehow exist apart from practice.[72] Thus, saying that "the institution of sovereignty transforms identities" is shorthand for saying that "regular practices produce mutually constituting sovereign identities (agents) and their associated institutional norms (structures)." Practice is the core of constructivist resolutions of the agent-structure problem. This ongoing process may not be politically problematic in particular historical contexts and, indeed, once a community of mutual recognition is constituted, its members—even the disadvantaged ones[73]—may have a vested interest in reproducing it. In fact, this is part of what having an identity means. But this identity and institution remain dependent on what actors do: removing those practices will remove their intersubjective conditions of existence.

70. See John Ruggie, "Continuity and Transformation in the World Polity: Toward a Neorealist Synthesis," *World Politics* 35 (January 1983), pp. 261–85. In *Mind, Self, and Society*, p. 161, Mead offers the following argument: "If we say 'this is my property, I shall control it,' that affirmation calls out a certain set of responses which must be the same in any community in which property exists. It involves an organized attitude with reference to property which is common to all members of the community. One must have a definite attitude of control of his own property and respect for the property of others. Those attitudes (as organized sets of responses) must be there on the part of all, so that when one says such a thing he calls out in himself the response of the others. That which makes society possible is such common responses."

71. For a definition and discussion of "social closure," see Raymond Murphy, *Social Closure* (Oxford: Clarendon Press, 1988).

72. See Richard Ashley, "Untying the Sovereign State: A Double Reading of the Anarchy Problematique," *Millennium* 17 (Summer 1988), pp. 227–62. Those with more modernist sensibilities will find an equally practice-centric view of institutions in Blumer's observation on p. 19 of "The Methodological Position of Symbolic Interactionism": "A gratuitous acceptance of the concepts of norms, values, social rules and the like should not blind the social scientist to the fact that any one of them is subtended by a process of social interaction—a process that is necessary not only for their change but equally well for their retention in a fixed form. It is the social process in group life that creates and upholds the rules, not the rules that create and uphold group life."

73. See, for example, Mohammed Ayoob, "The Third World in the System of States: Acute Schizophrenia or Growing Pains?" *International Studies Quarterly* 33 (March 1989), pp. 67–80.

This may tell us something about how institutions of sovereign states are reproduced through social interaction, but it does not tell us why such a structure of identity and interest would arise in the first place. Two conditions would seem necessary for this to happen: (1) the density and regularity of interactions must be sufficiently high and (2) actors must be dissatisfied with preexisting forms of identity and interaction. Given these conditions, a norm of mutual recognition is relatively undemanding in terms of social trust, having the form of an assurance game in which a player will acknowledge the sovereignty of the others as long as they will in turn acknowledge that player's own sovereignty. Articulating international legal principles such as those embodied in the Peace of Augsburg (1555) and the Peace of Westphalia (1648) may also help by establishing explicit criteria for determining violations of the nascent social consensus.[74] But whether such a consensus holds depends on what states do. If they treat each other as if they were sovereign, then over time they will institutionalize that mode of subjectivity; if they do not, then that mode will not become the norm.

Practices of sovereignty will transform understandings of security and power politics in at least three ways. First, states will come to define their (and our) security in terms of preserving their "property rights" over particular territories. We now see this as natural, but the preservation of territorial frontiers is not, in fact, equivalent to the survival of the state or its people. Indeed, some states would probably be more secure if they would relinquish certain territories—the "Soviet Union" of some minority republics, "Yugoslavia" of Croatia and Slovenia, Israel of the West Bank, and so on. The fact that sovereignty practices have historically been oriented toward producing distinct territorial spaces, in other words, affects states' conceptualization of what they must "secure" to function in that identity, a process that may help account for the "hardening" of territorial boundaries over the centuries.[75]

Second, to the extent that states successfully internalize sovereignty norms, they will be more respectful toward the territorial rights of others.[76] This restraint is *not* primarily because of the costs of violating sovereignty norms, although when violators do get punished (as in the Gulf War) it reminds everyone of what these costs can be, but because part of what it means to be a

74. See William Coplin, "International Law and Assumptions About the State System," *World Politics* 17 (July 1965), pp. 615–34.

75. See Anthony Smith, "States and Homelands: The Social and Geopolitical Implications of National Territory," *Millennium* 10 (Autumn 1981), pp. 187–202.

76. This assumes that there are no other, competing, principles that organize political space and identity in the international system and coexist with traditional notions of sovereignty; in fact, of course, there are. On "spheres of influence" and "informal empires," see Jan Triska, ed., *Dominant Powers and Subordinate States* (Durham, N.C.: Duke University Press, 1986); and Ronald Robinson, "The Excentric Idea of Imperialism, With or Without Empire," in Wolfgang Mommsen and Jurgen Osterhammel, eds., *Imperialism and After: Continuities and Discontinuities* (London: Allen & Unwin, 1986), pp. 267–89. On Arab conceptions of sovereignty, see Michael Barnett, "Sovereignty, Institutions, and Identity: From Pan-Arabism to the Arab State System," unpublished manuscript, University of Wisconsin, Madison, 1991.

"sovereign" state is that one does not violate the territorial rights of others without "just cause." A clear example of such an institutional effect, convincingly argued by David Strang, is the markedly different treatment that weak states receive within and outside communities of mutual recognition.[77] What keeps the United States from conquering the Bahamas, or Nigeria from seizing Togo, or Australia from occupying Vanuatu? Clearly, power is not the issue, and in these cases even the cost of sanctions would probably be negligible. One might argue that great powers simply have no "interest" in these conquests, and this might be so, but this lack of interest can only be understood in terms of their recognition of weak states' sovereignty. I have no interest in exploiting my friends, not because of the relative costs and benefits of such action but because they are my friends. The absence of recognition, in turn, helps explain the Western states' practices of territorial conquest, enslavement, and genocide against Native American and African peoples. It is in *that* world that only power matters, not the world of today.

Finally, to the extent that their ongoing socialization teaches states that their sovereignty depends on recognition by other states, they can afford to rely more on the institutional fabric of international society and less on individual national means—especially military power—to protect their security. The intersubjective understandings embodied in the institution of sovereignty, in other words, may redefine the meaning of others' power for the security of the self. In policy terms, this means that states can be less worried about short-term survival and relative power and can thus shift their resources accordingly. Ironically, it is the great powers, the states with the greatest national means, that may have the hardest time learning this lesson; small powers do not have the luxury of relying on national means and may therefore learn faster that collective recognition is a cornerstone of security.

None of this is to say that power becomes irrelevant in a community of sovereign states. Sometimes states *are* threatened by others that do not recognize their existence or particular territorial claims, that resent the externalities from their economic policies, and so on. But most of the time, these threats are played out within the terms of the sovereignty game. The fates of Napoleon and Hitler show what happens when they are not.

Cooperation among egoists and transformations of identity

We began this section with a Hobbesian state of nature. Cooperation for joint gain is extremely difficult in this context, since trust is lacking, time horizons are short, and relative power concerns are high. Life is "nasty, brutish, and short." Sovereignty transforms this system into a Lockean world of (mostly) mutually recognized property rights and (mostly) egoistic rather than

---

77. David Strang, "Anomaly and Commonplace in European Expansion: Realist and Institutional Accounts," *International Organization* 45 (Spring 1991), pp. 143–62.

competitive conceptions of security, reducing the fear that what states already have will be seized at any moment by potential collaborators, thereby enabling them to contemplate more direct forms of cooperation. A necessary condition for such cooperation is that outcomes be positively interdependent in the sense that potential gains exist which cannot be realized by unilateral action. States such as Brazil and Botswana may recognize each other's sovereignty, but they need further incentives to engage in joint action. One important source of incentives is the growing "dynamic density" of interaction among states in a world with new communications technology, nuclear weapons, externalities from industrial development, and so on.[78] Unfortunately, growing dynamic density does not ensure that states will in fact realize joint gains; interdependence also entails vulnerability and the risk of being "the sucker," which if exploited will become a source of conflict rather than cooperation.

This is the rationale for the familiar assumption that egoistic states will often find themselves facing prisoners' dilemma, a game in which the dominant strategy, if played only once, is to defect. As Michael Taylor and Robert Axelrod have shown, however, given iteration and a sufficient shadow of the future, egoists using a tit-for-tat strategy can escape this result and build cooperative institutions.[79] The story they tell about this process on the surface seems quite similar to George Herbert Mead's constructivist analysis of interaction, part of which is also told in terms of "games."[80] Cooperation is a gesture indicating ego's willingness to cooperate; if alter defects, ego does likewise, signaling its unwillingness to be exploited; over time and through reciprocal play, each learns to form relatively stable expectations about the other's behavior, and through these, habits of cooperation (or defection) form. Despite similar concerns with communication, learning, and habit-formation, however, there is an important difference between the game-theoretic and constructivist analysis of interaction that bears on how we conceptualize the causal powers of institutions.

In the traditional game-theoretic analysis of cooperation, even an iterated one, the structure of the game—of identities and interests—is exogenous to interaction and, as such, does not change.[81] A "black box" is put around identity- and interest-formation, and analysis focuses instead on the relation-

---

78. On "dynamic density," see Ruggie, "Continuity and Transformation in the World Polity"; and Waltz, "Reflections on *Theory of International Politics*." The role of interdependence in conditioning the speed and depth of social learning is much greater than the attention to which I have paid it. On the consequences of interdependence under anarchy, see Helen Milner, "The Assumption of Anarchy in International Relations Theory: A Critique," *Review of International Studies* 17 (January 1991), pp. 67–85.

79. See Michael Taylor, *Anarchy and Cooperation* (New York: Wiley, 1976); and Robert Axelrod, *The Evolution of Cooperation* (New York: Basic Books, 1984).

80. Mead, *Mind, Self, and Society.*

81. Strictly speaking, this is not true, since in iterated games the addition of future benefits to current ones changes the payoff structure of the game at T1, in this case from prisoners' dilemma to an assurance game. This transformation of interest takes place entirely within the actor, however, and as such is not a function of interaction with the other.

ship between expectations and behavior. The norms that evolve from interaction are treated as rules and behavioral regularities which are external to the actors and which resist change because of the transaction costs of creating new ones. The game-theoretic analysis of cooperation among egoists is at base behavioral.

A constructivist analysis of cooperation, in contrast, would concentrate on how the expectations produced by behavior affect identities and interests. The process of creating institutions is one of internalizing new understandings of self and other, of acquiring new role identities, not just of creating external constraints on the behavior of exogenously constituted actors.[82] Even if not intended as such, in other words, the process by which egoists learn to cooperate is at the same time a process of reconstructing their interests in terms of shared commitments to social norms. Over time, this will tend to transform a positive interdependence of *outcomes* into a positive interdependence of *utilities* or collective interest organized around the norms in question. These norms will resist change because they are tied to actors' commitments to their identities and interests, not merely because of transaction costs. A constructivist analysis of "the cooperation problem," in other words, is at base cognitive rather than behavioral, since it treats the intersubjective knowledge that defines the structure of identities and interests, of the "game," as endogenous to and instantiated by interaction itself.

The debate over the future of collective security in Western Europe may illustrate the significance of this difference. A weak liberal or rationalist analysis would assume that the European states' "portfolio" of interests has not fundamentally changed and that the emergence of new factors, such as the collapse of the Soviet threat and the rise of Germany, would alter their cost-benefit ratios for pursuing current arrangements, thereby causing existing institutions to break down. The European states formed collaborative institutions for good, exogenously constituted egoistic reasons, and the same reasons may lead them to reject those institutions; the game of European power politics has not changed. A strong liberal or constructivist analysis of this problem would suggest that four decades of cooperation may have transformed a positive interdependence of outcomes into a collective "European identity" in terms of which states increasingly define their "self"-interests.[83] Even if egoistic reasons were its starting point, the process of cooperating tends to redefine those reasons by reconstituting identities and interests in terms of new intersubjective understandings and commitments. Changes in the distribution of power during the late twentieth century are undoubtedly a challenge to these new understandings, but it is not as if West European states have some

---

82. In fairness to Axelrod, he does point out that internalization of norms is a real possibility that may increase the resilience of institutions. My point is that this important idea cannot be derived from an approach to theory that takes identities and interests as exogenously given.

83. On "European identity," see Barry Buzan et al., eds., *The European Security Order Recast* (London: Pinter, 1990), pp. 45–63.

inherent, exogenously given interest in abandoning collective security if the price is right. Their identities and security interests are continuously in process, and if collective identities become "embedded," they will be as resistant to change as egoistic ones.[84] Through participation in new forms of social knowledge, in other words, the European states of 1990 might no longer be the states of 1950.

Critical strategic theory and collective security

The transformation of identity and interest through an "evolution of cooperation" faces two important constraints. The first is that the process is incremental and slow. Actors' objectives in such a process are typically to realize joint gains within what they take to be a relatively stable context, and they are therefore unlikely to engage in substantial reflection about how to change the parameters of that context (including the structure of identities and interests) and unlikely to pursue policies specifically designed to bring about such changes. Learning to cooperate may change those parameters, but this occurs as an unintended consequence of policies pursued for other reasons rather than as a result of intentional efforts to transcend existing institutions.

A second, more fundamental, constraint is that the evolution of cooperation story presupposes that actors do not identify negatively with one another. Actors must be concerned primarily with absolute gains; to the extent that antipathy and distrust lead them to define their security in relativistic terms, it will be hard to accept the vulnerabilities that attend cooperation.[85] This is important because it is precisely the "central balance" in the state system that seems to be so often afflicted with such competitive thinking, and realists can therefore argue that the possibility of cooperation within one "pole" (for example, the West) is parasitic on the dominance of competition between poles (the East–West conflict). Relations between the poles may be amenable to some positive reciprocity in areas such as arms control, but the atmosphere of distrust leaves little room for such cooperation and its transformative consequences.[86] The conditions of negative identification that make an "evolution of cooperation" most needed work precisely against such a logic.

This seemingly intractable situation may nevertheless be amenable to quite a different logic of transformation, one driven more by self-conscious efforts to change structures of identity and interest than by unintended consequences. Such voluntarism may seem to contradict the spirit of constructivism, since

---

84. On "embeddedness," see John Ruggie, "International Regimes, Transactions, and Change: Embedded Liberalism in a Postwar Economic Order," in Krasner, *International Regimes,* pp. 195–232.

85. See Grieco, "Anarchy and the Limits of Cooperation."

86. On the difficulties of creating cooperative security regimes given competitive interests, see Robert Jervis, "Security Regimes," in Krasner, *International Regimes,* pp. 173–94; and Charles Lipson, "International Cooperation in Economic and Security Affairs," *World Politics* 37 (October 1984), pp. 1–23.

would-be revolutionaries are presumably themselves effects of socialization to structures of identity and interest. How can they think about changing that to which they owe their identity? The possibility lies in the distinction between the social determination of the self and the personal determination of choice, between what Mead called the "me" and the "I."[87] The "me" is that part of subjectivity which is defined in terms of others; the character and behavioral expectations of a person's role identity as "professor," or of the United States as "leader of the alliance," for example, are socially constituted. Roles are not played in mechanical fashion according to precise scripts, however, but are "taken" and adapted in idiosyncratic ways by each actor.[88] Even in the most constrained situations, role performance involves a choice by the actor. The "I" is the part of subjectivity in which this appropriation and reaction to roles and its corresponding existential freedom lie.

The fact that roles are "taken" means that, in principle, actors always have a capacity for "character planning"—for engaging in critical self-reflection and choices designed to bring about changes in their lives.[89] But when or under what conditions can this creative capacity be exercised? Clearly, much of the time it cannot: if actors were constantly reinventing their identities, social order would be impossible, and the relative stability of identities and interests in the real world is indicative of our propensity for habitual rather than creative action. The exceptional, conscious choosing to transform or transcend roles has at least two preconditions. First, there must be a reason to think of oneself in novel terms. This would most likely stem from the presence of new social situations that cannot be managed in terms of preexisting self-conceptions. Second, the expected costs of intentional role change—the sanctions imposed by others with whom one interacted in previous roles—cannot be greater than its rewards.

When these conditions are present, actors can engage in self-reflection and practice specifically designed to transform their identities and interests and thus to "change the games" in which they are embedded. Such "critical" strategic theory and practice has not received the attention it merits from students of world politics (another legacy of exogenously given interests perhaps), particularly given that one of the most important phenomena in contemporary world politics, Mikhail Gorbachev's policy of "New Thinking," is

---

87. See Mead, *Mind, Self, and Society.* For useful discussions of this distinction and its implications for notions of creativity in social systems, see George Cronk, *The Philosophical Anthropology of George Herbert Mead* (New York: Peter Lang, 1987), pp. 36–40; and Howard, "From Changing Selves Toward Changing Society."

88. Turner, "Role-Taking."

89. On "character planning," see Jon Elster, *Sour Grapes: Studies in the Subversion of Rationality* (Cambridge: Cambridge University Press, 1983), p. 117. For other approaches to the problem of self-initiated change, see Harry Frankfurt, "Freedom of the Will and the Concept of a Person," *Journal of Philosophy* 68 (January 1971), pp. 5–20; Amartya Sen, "Rational Fools: A Critique of the Behavioral Foundations of Economic Theory," *Philosophy and Public Affairs* 6 (Summer 1977), pp. 317–44; and Thomas Schelling, "The Intimate Contest for Self-Command," *The Public Interest* 60 (Summer 1980), pp. 94–118.

arguably precisely that.[90] Let me therefore use this policy as an example of how states might transform a competitive security system into a cooperative one, dividing the transformative process into four stages.

The first stage in intentional transformation is the breakdown of consensus about identity commitments. In the Soviet case, identity commitments centered on the Leninist theory of imperialism, with its belief that relations between capitalist and socialist states are inherently conflictual, and on the alliance patterns that this belief engendered. In the 1980s, the consensus within the Soviet Union over the Leninist theory broke down for a variety of reasons, principal among which seem to have been the state's inability to meet the economic-technological-military challenge from the West, the government's decline of political legitimacy at home, and the reassurance from the West that it did not intend to invade the Soviet Union, a reassurance that reduced the external costs of role change.[91] These factors paved the way for a radical leadership transition and for a subsequent "unfreezing of conflict schemas" concerning relations with the West.[92]

The breakdown of consensus makes possible a second stage of critical examination of old ideas about self and other and, by extension, of the structures of interaction by which the ideas have been sustained. In periods of relatively stable role identities, ideas and structures may become reified and thus treated as things that exist independently of social action. If so, the second stage is one of denaturalization, of identifying the practices that reproduce seemingly inevitable ideas about self and other; to that extent, it is a form of "critical" rather than "problem-solving" theory.[93] The result of such a critique should be an identification of new "possible selves" and aspirations.[94] New

90. For useful overviews of New Thinking, see Mikhail Gorbachev, *Perestroika: New Thinking for Our Country and the World* (New York: Harper & Row, 1987); Vendulka Kubalkova and Albert Cruickshank, *Thinking New About Soviet "New Thinking"* (Berkeley: Institute of International Studies, 1989); and Allen Lynch, *Gorbachev's International Outlook: Intellectual Origins and Political Consequences* (New York: Institute for East–West Security Studies, 1989). It is not clear to what extent New Thinking is a conscious policy as opposed to an ad hoc policy. The intense theoretical and policy debate within the Soviet Union over New Thinking and the frequently stated idea of taking away the Western "excuse" for fearing the Soviet Union both suggest the former, but I will remain agnostic here and simply assume that it can be fruitfully interpreted "as if" it had the form that I describe.

91. For useful overviews of these factors, see Jack Snyder, "The Gorbachev Revolution: A Waning of Soviet Expansionism?" *World Politics* 12 (Winter 1987–88), pp. 93–121; and Stephen Meyer, "The Sources and Prospects of Gorbachev's New Political Thinking on Security," *International Security* 13 (Fall 1988), pp. 124–63.

92. See Daniel Bar-Tal et al., "Conflict Termination: An Epistemological Analysis of International Cases," *Political Psychology* 10 (June 1989), pp. 233–55. For an unrelated but interesting illustration of how changing cognitions in turn make possible organizational change, see Jean Bartunek, "Changing Interpretive Schemes and Organizational Restructuring: The Example of a Religious Order," *Administrative Science Quarterly* 29 (September 1984), pp. 355–72.

93. See Robert Cox, "Social Forces, States and World Orders: Beyond International Relations Theory," in Keohane, *Neorealism and Its Critics*, pp. 204–55. See also Brian Fay, *Critical Social Science* (Ithaca, N.Y.: Cornell University Press, 1987).

94. Hazel Markus and Paula Nurius, "Possible Selves," *American Psychologist* 41 (September 1986), pp. 954–69.

Thinking embodies such critical theorizing. Gorbachev wants to free the Soviet Union from the coercive social logic of the cold war and engage the West in far-reaching cooperation. Toward this end, he has rejected the Leninist belief in the inherent conflict of interest between socialist and capitalist states and, perhaps more important, has recognized the crucial role that Soviet aggressive practices played in sustaining that conflict.

Such rethinking paves the way for a third stage of new practice. In most cases, it is not enough to rethink one's own ideas about self and other, since old identities have been sustained by systems of interaction with *other* actors, the practices of which remain a social fact for the transformative agent. In order to change the self, then, it is often necessary to change the identities and interests of the others that help sustain those systems of interaction. The vehicle for inducing such change is one's own practice and, in particular, the practice of "altercasting"—a technique of interactor control in which ego uses tactics of self-presentation and stage management in an attempt to frame alter's definitions of social situations in ways that create the role which ego desires alter to play.[95] In effect, in altercasting ego tries to induce alter to take on a new identity (and thereby enlist alter in ego's effort to change itself) by treating alter *as if* it already had that identity. The logic of this follows directly from the mirror theory of identity-formation, in which alter's identity is a reflection of ego's practices; change those practices and ego begins to change alter's conception of itself.

What these practices should consist of depends on the logic by which the preexisting identities were sustained. Competitive security systems are sustained by practices that create insecurity and distrust. In this case, transformative practices should attempt to teach other states that one's own state can be trusted and should not be viewed as a threat to their security. The fastest way to do this is to make unilateral initiatives and self-binding commitments of sufficient significance that another state is faced with "an offer it cannot refuse."[96] Gorbachev has tried to do this by withdrawing from Afghanistan and Eastern Europe, implementing asymmetric cuts in nuclear and conventional forces, calling for "defensive defense," and so on. In addition, he has skillfully cast the West in the role of being morally required to give aid and comfort to the Soviet Union, has emphasized the bonds of common fate between the Soviet Union and the West, and has indicated that further progress in

95. See Goffman, *The Presentation of Self in Everyday Life;* Eugene Weinstein and Paul Deutschberger, "Some Dimensions of Altercasting," *Sociometry* 26 (December 1963), pp. 454–66; and Walter Earle, "International Relations and the Psychology of Control: Alternative Control Strategies and Their Consequences," *Political Psychology* 7 (June 1986), pp. 369–75.

96. See Volker Boge and Peter Wilke, "Peace Movements and Unilateral Disarmament: Old Concepts in a New Light," *Arms Control* 7 (September 1986), pp. 156–70; Zeev Maoz and Daniel Felsenthal, "Self-Binding Commitments, the Inducement of Trust, Social Choice, and the Theory of International Cooperation," *International Studies Quarterly* 31 (June 1987), pp. 177–200; and V. Sakamoto, "Unilateral Initiative as an Alternative Strategy," *World Futures,* vol. 24, nos. 1–4, 1987, pp. 107–34.

East–West relations is contingent upon the West assuming the identity being projected onto it. These actions are all dimensions of altercasting, the intention of which is to take away the Western "excuse" for distrusting the Soviet Union, which, in Gorbachev's view, has helped sustain competitive identities in the past.

Yet by themselves such practices cannot transform a competitive security system, since if they are not reciprocated by alter, they will expose ego to a "sucker" payoff and quickly wither on the vine. In order for critical strategic practice to transform competitive identities, it must be "rewarded" by alter, which will encourage more such practice by ego, and so on.[97] Over time, this will institutionalize a positive rather than a negative identification between the security of self and other and will thereby provide a firm intersubjective basis for what were initially tentative commitments to new identities and interests.[98]

Notwithstanding today's rhetoric about the end of the cold war, skeptics may still doubt whether Gorbachev (or some future leader) will succeed in building an intersubjective basis for a new Soviet (or Russian) role identity. There are important domestic, bureaucratic, and cognitive-ideological sources of resistance in both East and West to such a change, not the least of which is the shakiness of the democratic forces' domestic position. But if my argument about the role of intersubjective knowledge in creating competitive structures of identity and interest is right, then at least New Thinking shows a greater appreciation—conscious or not—for the deep structure of power politics than we are accustomed to in international relations practice.

Conclusion

All theories of international relations are based on social theories of the relationship between agency, process, and social structure. Social theories do not determine the content of our international theorizing, but they do structure the questions we ask about world politics and our approaches to answering those questions. The substantive issue at stake in debates about social theory is what kind of foundation offers the most fruitful set of questions and research strategies for explaining the revolutionary changes that seem to be occurring in the late twentieth century international system. Put simply, what should systemic theories of international relations look like? How should they conceptualize the relationship between structure and process? Should they be

97. On rewards, see Thomas Milburn and Daniel Christie, "Rewarding in International Politics," *Political Psychology* 10 (December 1989), pp. 625–45.

98. The importance of reciprocity in completing the process of structural transformation makes the logic in this stage similar to that in the "evolution of cooperation." The difference is one of prerequisites and objective: in the former, ego's tentative redefinition of self enables it to try and change alter by acting "as if" both were already playing a new game; in the latter, ego acts only on the basis of given interests and prior experience, with transformation emerging only as an unintended consequence.

based exclusively on "microeconomic" analogies in which identities and interests are exogenously given by structure and process is reduced to interactions within those parameters? Or should they also be based on "sociological" and "social psychological" analogies in which identities and interests and therefore the meaning of structure are endogenous to process? Should a behavioral-individualism or a cognitive-constructivism be the basis for systemic theories of world politics?

This article notwithstanding, this question is ultimately an empirical one in two respects. First, its answer depends in part on how important interaction among states is for the constitution of their identities and interests. On the one hand, it may be that domestic or genetic factors, which I have systematically bracketed, are in fact much more important determinants of states' identities and interests than are systemic factors. To the extent that this is true, the individualism of a rationalist approach and the inherent privileging of structure over process in this approach become more substantively appropriate for systemic theory (if not for first- and second-image theory), since identities and interests are *in fact* largely exogenous to interaction among states. On the other hand, if the bracketed factors are relatively unimportant or if the importance of the international system varies historically (perhaps with the level of dynamic density and interdependence in the system), then such a framework would not be appropriate as an exclusive foundation for general systemic theory.

Second, the answer to the question about what systemic theories should look like also depends on how easily state identities and interests can change as a result of systemic interaction. Even if interaction is initially important in constructing identities and interests, once institutionalized its logic may make transformation extremely difficult. If the meaning of structure for state action changes so slowly that it becomes a de facto parameter within which process takes place, then it may again be substantively appropriate to adopt the rationalist assumption that identities and interests are given (although again, this may vary historically).

We cannot address these empirical issues, however, unless we have a framework for doing systemic research that makes state identity and interest an issue for both theoretical and empirical inquiry. Let me emphasize that this is *not* to say we should never treat identities and interests as given. The framing of problems and research strategies should be question-driven rather than method-driven, and if we are not interested in identity- and interest-formation, we may find the assumptions of a rationalist discourse perfectly reasonable. Nothing in this article, in other words, should be taken as an attack on rationalism per se. By the same token, however, we should not let this legitimate analytical stance become a de facto ontological stance with respect to the content of third-image theory, at least not until after we have determined that systemic interaction does not play an important role in processes of state identity- and interest-formation. We should not choose our philosophical anthropologies and social theories prematurely. By arguing that we cannot derive a self-help structure of identity and interest from the principle of anarchy alone—by arguing that anarchy is what states make of it—this article has challenged one important justification for ignoring processes of identity- and interest-formation in world politics. As such, it helps set the stage for inquiry into the empirical issues raised above and thus for a debate about whether communitarian or individualist assumptions are a better foundation for systemic theory.

I have tried to indicate by crude example what such a research agenda might look like. Its objective should be to assess the causal relationship between practice and interaction (as independent variable) and the cognitive structures at the level of individual states and of systems of states which constitute identities and interests (as dependent variable)—that is, the relationship between what actors *do* and what they *are*. We may have some a priori notion that state actors and systemic structures are "mutually constitutive," but this tells us little in the absence of an understanding of how the mechanics of dyadic, triadic, and n-actor interaction shape and are in turn shaped by "stocks of knowledge" that collectively constitute identities and interests and, more broadly, constitute the structures of international life. Particularly important in this respect is the role of practice in shaping attitudes toward the "givenness" of these structures. How and why do actors reify social structures, and under what conditions do they denaturalize such reifications?

The state-centrism of this agenda may strike some, particularly postmodernists, as "depressingly familiar."[99] The significance of states relative to multinational corporations, new social movements, transnationals, and intergovernmental organizations is clearly declining, and "postmodern" forms of world politics merit more research attention than they have received. But I also believe, with realists, that in the medium run sovereign states will remain the dominant political actors in the international system. Any transition to new structures of global political authority and identity—to "postinternational" politics—will be mediated by and path-dependent on the particular institutional resolution of the tension between unity and diversity, or particularism and universality, that is the sovereign state.[100] In such a world there should continue to be a place for theories of anarchic interstate politics, alongside other forms of international theory; to that extent, I am a statist and a realist. I have argued in this article, however, that statism need not be bound by realist ideas about what "state" must mean. State identities and interests can be collectively transformed within an anarchic context by many factors—individual, domestic, systemic, or transnational—and as such are an important dependent variable. Such a

99. Yale Ferguson and Richard Mansbach, "Between Celebration and Despair: Constructive Suggestions for Future International Theory," *International Studies Quarterly* 35 (December 1991), p. 375.

100. For excellent discussions of this tension, see Walker, "Sovereignty, Identity, Community"; and R. B. J. Walker, "Security, Sovereignty, and the Challenge of World Politics," *Alternatives* 15 (Winter 1990), pp. 3–27. On institutional path dependencies, see Stephen Krasner, "Sovereignty: An Institutional Perspective," *Comparative Political Studies* 21 (April 1988), pp. 66–94.

reconstruction of state-centric international theory is necessary if we are to theorize adequately about the emerging forms of transnational political identity that sovereign states will help bring into being. To that extent, I hope that statism, like the state, can be historically progressive.

I have argued that the proponents of strong liberalism and the constructivists can and should join forces in contributing to a process-oriented international theory. Each group has characteristic weaknesses that are complemented by the other's strengths. In part because of the decision to adopt a choice-theoretic approach to theory construction, neoliberals have been unable to translate their work on institution-building and complex learning into a systemic theory that escapes the explanatory priority of realism's concern with structure. Their weakness, in other words, is a lingering unwillingness to transcend, at the level of systemic theory, the individualist assumption that identities and interests are exogenously given. Constructivists bring to this lack of resolution a systematic communitarian ontology in which intersubjective knowledge constitutes identities and interests. For their part, however, constructivists have often devoted too much effort to questions of ontology and constitution and not enough effort to the causal and empirical questions of how identities and interests are produced by practice in anarchic conditions. As a result, they have not taken on board neoliberal insights into learning and social cognition.

An attempt to use a structurationist–symbolic interactionist discourse to bridge the two research traditions, neither of which subscribes to such a discourse, will probably please no one. But in part this is because the two "sides" have become hung up on differences over the epistemological status of social science. The state of the social sciences and, in particular, of international relations, is such that epistemological prescriptions and conclusions are at best premature. Different questions involve different standards of inference; to reject certain questions because their answers cannot conform to the standards of classical physics is to fall into the trap of method-driven rather than question-driven social science. By the same token, however, giving up the artificial restrictions of logical positivist conceptions of inquiry does not force us to give up on "Science." Beyond this, there is little reason to attach so much importance to epistemology. Neither positivism, nor scientific realism, nor poststructuralism tells us about the structure and dynamics of international life. Philosophies of science are not theories of international relations. The good news is that strong liberals and modern and postmodern constructivists are asking broadly similar questions about the substance of international relations that differentiate both groups from the neorealist-rationalist alliance. Strong liberals and constructivists have much to learn from each other if they can come to see this through the smoke and heat of epistemology.

Globalization and the changing logic of collective action
Philip G. Cerny

In both modern domestic political systems and the modern international system, the state has been the key structural arena within which collective action has been situated and undertaken, as well as exercising structural and relational power as an actor in its own right. However, the state is being not only eroded but also fundamentally transformed within a wider structural context. The international system is no longer simply a states system; rather, it is becoming increasingly characterized by a plural and composite—or what I have elsewhere called "plurilateral"—structure.[1] This transformation has significant consequences for the logic of collective action. The word "globalization" often is used to represent this process of change. Globalization is neither uniform nor homogeneous; its boundaries are unclear and its constituent elements and multidimensional character have not as yet been adequately explored.[2] But by reshaping the structural context of rational choice itself,

I am particularly grateful to Louisa Gosling, formerly of the European University Institute, for having initiated a dialogue that led to the elaboration of the theoretical framework explored here. Stephen Kobrin, Ronen Palan, Geoffrey Underhill, and, of course, John Odell and two anonymous reviewers for *International Organization* have provided particularly valuable comments on the manuscript. Earlier versions were presented at the annual workshop of the International Political Economy Group of the British International Studies Association, University of Sussex, 20 February 1994; the 2d international conference of the Committee on Viable Constitutionalism, State University of New York at Albany, 17–20 March 1994; the conference on Global Politics: Setting Agendas for the Year 2000, Nottingham Trent University, 25–27 July 1994; and the annual meeting of the British International Studies Association, University of York, 19–21 December 1994. I thank a wide range of participants in those meetings for their comments.

1. P. G. Cerny, "Plurilateralism: Structural Differentiation and Functional Conflict in the Post–Cold War World Order," *Millennium: Journal of International Studies* 22 (Spring 1993), pp. 27–51.
2. The notion that transnational interpenetration is not homogeneous is essential to the concept of complex interdependence as developed in Robert O. Keohane and Joseph S. Nye, Jr., *Power and Interdependence* (Boston: Little, Brown, 1977). The implications of the growing heterogeneity of specific so-called transnational structures for domestic and international politics are more thoroughly explored in Susan Strange, *States and Markets: An Introduction to International Political Economy* (London and New York: Pinter and Basil Blackwell, 1988). For a consideration of some

International Organization 49, 4, Autumn 1995, pp. 595–625

globalization transforms the ways that the basic rules of the game work in politics and international relations and alters the increasingly complex payoff matrices faced by actors in rationally evaluating their options.

In contrast, the state has played a key role in defining the character of the global discipline of international relations and the domestic discipline of political science. The classic statement of this position is found in the first paragraph of Aristotle's *Politics:*

> Observation shows us, first, that every polis (or state) is a species of association, and, secondly, that all associations are instituted for the purpose of attaining some good—for all men do all their acts with a view to achieving something which is, in their view, a good. We may therefore hold that all associations aim at some good; and we may also hold that the particular association which is the most sovereign of all, and includes all the rest, will pursue this aim most, and will thus be directed to the most sovereign of all goods. This most sovereign and inclusive association is the polis, as it is called, or the political association.[3]

Michael Oakeshott described the state in the Western constitutional tradition as a "civil association"—the sole purpose of which is to enable other, more circumscribed social, political, and economic activities to take place and which is necessary (but not sufficient) for the pursuit of those other activities. The existence of such a civil association enables socially legitimate collective action to be undertaken in the first place. Oakeshott distinguishes this from an "enterprise association," which has particular ends and can be dissolved when those ends are no longer or are unsatisfactorily pursued.[4] In the modern study of international relations, the state has constituted the key unit of collective action, while the interaction of states has been the very object of inquiry; similarly, in the domestic arena, the state has both encompassed the political system and constituted a potentially autonomous collective agent within that field.[5]

Globalization, however, is changing all that. Globalization is defined here as a set of economic and political structures and processes deriving from the changing character of the goods and assets that comprise the base of the international political economy—in particular, the increasing structural differentiation of those goods and assets. "Structures" are more or less embedded sets—patterns—of constraints and opportunities confronting decision-making

definitional problems with the term "globalization," see Robin Brown, "The New Realities: Globalization, Culture, and International Relations," paper presented at the annual meeting of the British International Studies Association, University of Swansea, Wales, 14–16 December 1992.

3. Aristotle, *Politics,* ed. trans. Ernest Barker (New York: Oxford University Press, 1962), p. 1.

4. See Josiah Lee Auspitz, "Individuality, Civility, and Theory: The Philosophical Imagination of Michael Oakeshott," *Political Theory* 4 (August 1976), pp. 261–352; and Michael Oakeshott, "On Misunderstanding Human Conduct: A Reply to my Critics," in ibid., pp. 353–67.

5. These issues are examined at more length in P. G. Cerny, *The Changing Architecture of Politics: Structure, Agency, and the Future of the State* (London: Sage Publications, 1990), especially chap. 4.

agents ("institutions" simply being more formalized structures); "processes" are dynamic patterns of interaction and change that take place on or across structured fields of action.[6] Structural differentiation increasingly is spreading across borders and economic sectors, driving other changes and resulting in the increasing predominance of political and economic structures and processes that (1) are frequently (although not always) more transnational and multinational in scale (i.e., are in significant ways more inclusive) than the state, (2) potentially have a greater impact on outcomes in critical issue-areas than does the state (i.e., may in effect be more "sovereign"), and (3) may permit actors to be decisionally autonomous of the state. In particular, I argue that the more that the scale of goods and assets produced, exchanged, and/or used in a particular economic sector or activity diverges from the structural scale of the national state—both from above (the global scale) and from below (the local scale)—and the more that those divergences feed back into each other in complex ways, then the more that the authority, legitimacy, policymaking capacity, and policy-implementing effectiveness of states will be challenged from both without and within. A critical threshold may be crossed when the cumulative effect of globalization in strategically decisive issue-areas undermines the general capacity of the state to pursue the common good or the capacity of the state to be a true civil association; even if this threshold is not crossed, however, it is arguable that the role of the state both as playing field and as unit becomes structurally problematic.

Most of the literature on collective choice or collective action focuses on options and choices that actors (or players) make within the context of a particular payoff matrix or set of alternative payoff matrices—i.e., within existing sets of constraints and opportunities, or rewards and penalties—which confront the players. However, the focus of the analysis here is on the structural context within which collective action takes place, rather than at specific processes or outcomes of choice in a given setting. Choices are always made within specific "structured fields of action."[7] Structurally diverse fields elicit different strategies and tactics. Furthermore, such fields are themselves made up of complex multilayered structures that incorporate distinct and often asymmetric structural levels—i.e., different games with different payoff matrices. Finally, of course, their structural form can change over time.

The analysis here will focus on the changing nature and scale of public goods and private goods (expanding on the work of Manur Olson) and on the relationship between specific assets and nonspecific assets (expanding on the work of Oliver Williamson) as the bases of both political-institutional and

---

6. For an extensive discussion of the concept of structure (and of structural differentiation), see Cerny, *The Changing Architecture of Politics*.

7. Michel Crozier and Erhard Friedberg, *L'acteur et le système: Les contraintes de l'action collective* (The actor and the system: Constraints on collective action) (Paris: Éditions du Seuil, 1977).

industrial market structure.[8] "Goods" and "assets" are broadly interchange-able terms that refer to tangible or intangible property, effects, wealth, and other resources. Whereas the term "goods" is more likely to be used for items or commodities that are themselves produced and/or traded, from raw materials to final products, the term "assets" is more likely to be applied to the production facilities or systems of production by which goods are produced. However, the two terms are not easily distinguished linguistically, and the overlap between them both in the real world and in analytical usage is great. Indeed, Olson and Williamson each uses his preferred term as an overarching category or genus implicitly including the other.

This article focuses on the development of particular historical matrices or patterns of imbrication between economic-organizational and political-institutional structures; I call such composite patterns "political economies of scale." In small-scale societies, goods and assets—and the structures and institutions that stabilize and regulate them—remain relatively undifferenti-ated. However, as the scale of goods and assets expands, major structural gaps can develop between different types of assets and between public goods and private goods. In particular, as European societies and economies grew in the late feudal and early capitalist periods, such a gap was filled by the emergence of the modern nation-state as an organizational form for providing public goods across both domestic and international arenas.[9] Moreover, the develop-ment of scale economies in both the economic system and the political order during the nineteenth and early twentieth centuries dramatically reinforced and expanded the scope of this institutional isomorphism. A powerful structural convergence developed between the second industrial revolution economy, on the one hand, and the bureaucratic state, on the other. Notions of the modern state even today inordinately reify the characteristics of this period. In recent decades, however, an accelerating divergence has taken place between the structure of the state and the structure of industrial and financial markets in the complex, globalizing world of the third industrial revolution. There is a new disjuncture between institutional capacity to provide public goods and the structural characteristics of a much larger-scale, global economy. I suggest here that today's "residual state" faces crises of both organizational efficiency and institutional legitimacy. The conclusion derives a set of more complex hypotheses from the overall framework as an agenda for future research.

8. On public and private goods, see Mancur Olson, *The Logic of Collective Action* (Cambridge, Mass.: Harvard University Press, 1971). On specific and nonspecific assets, see Oliver E. Williamson, *Markets and Hierarchies* (New York: Free Press, 1975); and Oliver E. Williamson, *The Economic Institutions of Capitalism* (New York: Free Press, 1985).

9. For an effective interpretive synthesis, see Hendrik Spruyt, "Institutional Selection in International Relations: State Anarchy as Order," *International Organization* 48 (Autumn 1994), pp. 527–57.

Goods, assets, and political economies of scale

The development of the modern state and the growth of capitalism involve a complex process of interaction between cross-cutting structural dimensions: first, between politics and economics and, second, between market and hierarchy. Central to such developments are "political economies of scale," in which specific political structures—and the forms of action they ostensibly foster or dictate—appear to be more or less efficient in stabilizing, regulating, controlling, or facilitating particular economic activities. Different economic processes are said to be characterized by different minimum efficient scales, given existing technology and size of market demand. Some optimal plant sizes remain small; others exhibit increasing returns to scale—that is, greater efficiency the bigger the factory or distribution system.[10] Thus, in some cases, big is economically the most efficient, whereas in other cases small is beautiful. In the case of political economies of scale, the concept is expanded to include the scale of state structures, institutions, and processes and the economic tasks, roles, and activities they perform. Optimal political economies of scale therefore continually shift, adjusting to technological, sociological, and political change. Indeed, they have been shifting dramatically in the late twentieth century, both upward to the transnational and global levels and downward to the local level. In this more fluid environment, actors' choices have significant consequences for the changing structure of the state and, indeed, for the wider evolution of politics and society.

It is mistaken to assume that state structures are overwhelmingly hierarchical and bureaucratic in some inherent way, while economic structures are based essentially on market exchange.[11] On the contrary, both state and economy are complex compounds of market and hierarchy as well as the outcome of the interaction between politics and economics. Evolution of political-economic structures results from the interaction of independent changes along each dimension (market/hierarchy and politics/economics) and from complex feedback effects that occur as the consequence of that interaction. For a state to approximate an overarching public role of the classical type would require it to have real and effective organizational capacity to shape, influence, and/or control designated economic activities (that is, those perceived to be the most socially significant such activities). In other words, it must stabilize, regulate, promote, and facilitate economic activity generally as well as exercise other forms of politically desired and/or structurally feasible control over more-specific targeted processes of production and exchange. The core of this problematic lies in the character of the different kinds of material and

10. For the main synthesizing work on economies of scale (and economies of scope, which we will not deal with separately here), see Alfred D. Chandler, Jr., *Scale and Scope: The Dynamics of Industrial Capitalism* (Cambridge, Mass.: Harvard University Press, 1990).
11. Cerny, *The Changing Architecture of Politics,* especially chap. 3.

nonmaterial resources and values that are needed and/or desired by individuals and by society—that is, in the different kinds of goods or assets (including services) being produced and exchanged, whether through the state or through nonstate economic mechanisms. Identifying the structural characteristics of different goods and/or assets is crucial to understanding what rational players are likely to do in different situations.

I begin, like others, by distinguishing between two main polar types of good or asset. The best-known is Olson's contrast between public goods (those that are nondivisible in crucial ways and from the use of which specific people cannot be easily or effectively excluded), on the one hand, and private goods (those that are both divisible and excludable), on the other.[12] Note that "public" and "private" in this context do not refer to who *owns* the goods but to the specific structural features of the goods themselves: (1) whether the good(s) in question can in practice be divided between different users/owners, or whether they are composed of inseparable parts of a wider, inherently integrated entity; and (2) whether some people can be effectively excluded or prevented from using/owning the good(s) in question, or whether to make them available for one is to make them available to all.

A second distinction, found in institutional economics, is that which Williamson makes between specific and nonspecific assets.[13] This distinction is based upon two dimensions. The first is that of economies of scale in production, distribution, or exchange. Where returns to scale are high, then the more units of a good that are produced in a single integrated production process, the lower will be the marginal unit cost of production compared with smaller separate production processes; in asset terms, this means that the value of the entity kept as a whole would in theory be far more valuable than its "breakup" price. The second dimension is that of transaction costs, i.e., those costs incurred in the process of attempting to fix an efficiency price for an asset and actually to exchange it for another substitute asset. Transaction costs normally include negotiation costs, monitoring costs, enforcement costs, and the like. A specific asset is one for which there is no easily available substitute. Its exchange would involve high transaction costs, high economies of scale, or both, leading to difficulty in finding efficiency prices and ready markets. In turn, different types of good or asset are said to be more or less efficiently provided through distinct sets of structural arrangements or institutions, rather than simply through abstract economic processes. Markets in the real world are institutions—not spontaneous, unorganized activities.[14] Williamson refers to

---

12. Olson, *The Logic of Collective Action.* In between the two main categories, and deriving from the interaction of these polar types, stands a range of crucial intermediate categories of semipublic or quasi-private (mixed) goods.

13. See Williamson, *Markets and Hierarchies;* and Williamson, *The Economic Institutions of Capitalism.*

14. Peter A. Hall, *Governing the Economy: The Politics of State Intervention in Britain and France* (New York: Oxford University Press; London: Polity Press, 1986), chap. 1. Compare Cerny, *The Changing Architecture of Politics.*

two contrasting institutional forms: market and hierarchy. For Olson, public goods cannot be provided in optimal amounts through a market, for free riders will not pay their share of the costs. Only authoritative structures and processes make it possible for costs to be efficiently recouped from the users of public goods. For Williamson, specific assets are also more efficiently organized and managed authoritatively, through hierarchy. In his own work, of course, the authoritative unit in question is not the state but the firm. Such authoritative allocation is done through long-term contracting (keeping the same collaborators) and decision making by managerial fiat (integration, merger, cartellization, etc.) rather than through the short-term, "recurrent contracting" of marketable, easily substitutable, nonspecific assets. Whereas efficient regulation of the market for the latter merely requires post hoc legal adjudication through contract law and the courts, the former requires increasing degrees of proactive institutionalized governance in the allocation of resources and values. Different kinds of structural integration—distinct mixes of market and hierarchy—may be judged to suit particular mixes of specific and nonspecific assets.

The sort of legitimate, holistic political authority characteristic of the traditional state reflects either an institutionalized commitment to provide public goods efficiently, or the presence of extensive specific assets, or both. The latter are mainly embodied in people (human capital), immobile factors of capital such as infrastructure, and the promotion of certain types of large-scale integrated industrial processes. Of course, traditional conceptions of the state also extend to other specific factors, especially national defense (the capacity to wage war being particularly public and specific); promotion of a common culture, national ideology, or set of constitutional norms; preservation of collective unity in the face of the "other"; and maintenance of a widely acceptable and functioning legal system. These sorts of tasks and activities also would normally be more efficiently carried out through predominantly hierarchical institutions (a classic conundrum of decision making in a liberal democracy).[15] However, in the real world, most economic and political processes involve either a mix of market and hierarchy or goods having mixed public and private characteristics. In this context, it is important to remember that politics involves not only constructing relatively efficient structures within which to provide public goods and minimize transaction costs in the maintenance of specific assets but also managing the overarching system within which both types of goods and assets are produced and exchanged—this system itself constituting a public good.

---

15. For a classic statement of the predicament of how stability and effectiveness in democratic systems may depend on authoritarian institutions and processes, see Harry Eckstein, "A Theory of Stable Democracy," research monograph no. 10, Princeton University, 1961, reprinted in Eckstein, *Division and Cohesion in Democracy: A Study of Norway* (Princeton: Princeton University Press, 1966). See also Giovanni Sartori, *Democratic Theory* (New York: Praeger, 1965).

The historical evolution of political economies of scale

Such complex political-economic structures develop mainly through a continuing process of bricolage or tinkering. Occasional paradigmatic change does occur however when the requirements for providing (at its simplest) both public goods and private goods in some workable combination increase beyond the capacity of the institutional structure to reconcile the two over the medium-to-long term. Such major transformations are reflected in historical changes from small-scale to large-scale societies. At one end of the spectrum, the smaller the scale of an economy/society the more the public and private are likely to overlap and coincide. Such mechanisms remain relatively undifferentiated. The outstanding exemplar of how this management system works can be seen in the role of kinship as studied by anthropologists. Subsistence and early surplus production and reproduction in small, relatively isolated communities usually involve the emergence of a single, relatively homogeneous institutional structure in which economic and political power are part of the same more or less hierarchical system. It could even be suggested that by basing society for political and economic reasons around an extended kinship structure, the range of what Fred Hirsch calls "positional goods" (those goods that can be used only by a small number of people, such as those standing on the top rung of a ladder or, in this case, occupying a patriarchally determined position of power in a kinship hierarchy) might therefore also be constrained and controlled in one virtual natural monopoly of power.[16]

In contrast, however, the larger and more complex the structural scale of a society/economy, the more assets and goods become differentiated. The scale of existing social and political arrangements for the stabilization and regulation of production, exchange, and consumption—i.e., for the provision of public goods—is likely to be suboptimal for the scale of public goods required and of specific assets involved. Furthermore, some former public goods and specific assets may be more readily and efficiently provided by the market, given the greater range of factors of production available and the greater number of participants in larger-scale markets. A new structural settlement reflecting altered optimal political economies of scale must therefore be found—what Spruyt calls "institutional selection."[17]

Sociological theorists have long identified structural differentiation as the core process of the development of societies.[18] Analogous processes of political and economic differentiation are the key to understanding how political economies of scale shift over time. In agricultural societies, early states exhibited analogous structural characteristics whether they emerged as the result of predation by a single group or through the development of a more

16. Fred Hirsch, *Social Limits to Growth* (London: Routledge and Kegan Paul, 1976).
17. Spruyt, "Institutional Selection in International Relations."
18. Peter M. Blau, ed., *Approaches to the Study of Social Structure* (New York and London: Free Press and Open Books, 1975).

complex division of labor.[19] Later, modern states, whatever their specific historical origins, developed not only from the need to provide appropriate levels of new and more broadly defined public goods in material terms but also in order to create appropriate conditions for stabilizing and promoting rapidly expanding market processes.[20] Establishing and maintaining a stable and ordered playing field on which both private and public goods could be provided efficiently came increasingly to be seen as a public good in itself, in contrast to the quasi-private predatory state that had first succeeded feudalism.[21] These structural innovations enabled postfeudal societies to survive and compete in the fierce military and economic struggles of that period.[22]

The central process in the development of the modern capitalist nation-state thus involved a complex and interdependent shift of both political and economic structures to a broader scale.[23] Interaction between states—economic competition and military conflict—was crucial to this convergence.[24] To foster the expanding provision of private goods, the development of national markets and production processes was promoted by otherwise quite different types of states. States in general, which previously had fulfilled only limited socioeconomic functions, thereby came to undertake an increasing range of core social, economic, and political functions—notably stabilization of the social order, promotion of a national culture, the establishment and defense of more clearly defined territorial borders, increased regulation of economic activities, and the development and maintenance of a legal system to enforce contracts and private property. Although the expansion of these general functions of the state was accompanied by growing demands for constitutional and democratic government to define and secure those func-

19. Raymond Cohen and Elman R. Service, eds., *Origins of the State: The Anthropology of Political Evolution* (Philadelphia, Penn.: Institute for the Study of Human Issues, 1985).

20. See especially Douglass C. North, *Structure and Change in Economic History* (New York: Norton, 1981), especially chap. 3. Compare Perry Anderson, *Lineages of the Absolutist State* (London: New Left Books, 1974); and Spruyt, "Institutional Selection in International Relations."

21. Margaret Levi, "The Predatory Theory of Rule," *Politics and Society,* vol. 10, no. 4, 1981, pp. 431–65.

22. A similar analysis, although expressed in less social-theoretical language, is developed in Paul Kennedy, *The Rise and Fall of the Great Powers: Economic Change and Military Conflict From 1500 to 2000* (London: Unwin Hyman, 1988), chaps. 1–3.

23. This complex process—combining structural differentiation and interdependence (i.e., the increasing integration of more and more complex structures)—is essentially the same as Durkheim's conception of how "organic solidarity" develops out of a more complex division of labor (replacing "mechanical solidarity"). See Emile Durkheim, *The Division of Labor in Society,* trans. G. Simpson (New York: Free Press, 1933; original French edition, 1893). For different interpretations of how Durkheim should be applied to international relations, see Kenneth Waltz, *Theory of International Politics* (Reading, Mass.: Addison-Wesley, 1979); John Gerard Ruggie, "Continuity and Transformation in the World Polity: Toward a Neorealist Synthesis," *World Politics* 35 (January 1983), pp. 261–85; Kenneth Waltz, "Reflections on *Theory of International Politics:* A Reply to My Critics," in Robert O. Keohane, ed., *Neorealism and Its Critics* (New York: Columbia University Press, 1986), pp. 322–45; and Cerny, "Plurilateralism."

24. See Kennedy, *The Rise and Fall of the Great Powers,* especially pp. 16–30; and Cerny, *The Changing Architecture of Politics,* chaps. 1 and 4.

tions, hierarchical and authoritarian bureaucracies were set up at the same time to carry them out. In addition, states took on more specific public goods functions such as public works, promotion and protection of particular industries, development of monopolies, provision of infrastructure, and the like. The evolution of these functions was highly uneven both within and across state borders.

Only with the coming of the so-called second industrial revolution in the late nineteenth and early twentieth centuries did the process shift reach a more comprehensive stage of convergence. The second industrial revolution comprised the development of advanced forms of mass production, the increasing application of science and scientific methods to both production processes and management techniques, and the expansion of economies of scale—often called Fordism, or, in Alfred Chandler's terms, the modern industrial enterprise. This era is generally acknowledged to have taken off with the growth of railroad systems from small lines to national networks. In the United States, oligopolistic firms emerged as the core of the new heavy industrial capital as America in the 1880s became the world's largest industrial producer. In other newly industrializing countries the state took a more direct role in tying economy and society together. This process occurred not only in Europe and later Japan but to a greater or lesser extent throughout the world as emerging states sought to industrialize. First the steel, then the chemical, automobile, and other large-scale heavy industries grew up, generally in highly favorable political and bureaucratic conditions. Central to this process was the growth of large-scale finance capital, whether under the wing of the state or in a more freewheeling liberal environment, as in the United States.[25] Along with these developments came national-scale processing and packing industries, integrated distribution systems, and the emergence of chains of large retail firms. The rise of the modern corporation and "scientific management" was part and parcel of this era.[26] Despite the different absolute sizes of such new industrial states, the combination of internal hierarchization and external competition gave them a certain unitary character and relative equality compared with the patchwork of political and economic units that had characterized late feudalism and even early industrial capitalism.

State promotion of industrial development further unified the nation-state—despite the growing conflict between democratic and authoritarian forms of government and struggles among emerging economic classes—and led to an intensification of national economic competition. In the United States, with its

---

25. See P. G. Cerny, "Money and Power: The American Financial System from Free Banking to Global Competition," in Grahame Thompson, ed., *Markets,* vol. 2 of *The United States in the Twentieth Century* (London: Hodder and Stoughton, 1994), pp. 175–213; and Ron Chernow, *The House of Morgan: An American Banking Dynasty and the Rise of Modern Finance* (New York: Simon and Schuster, 1990).

26. Chandler, *Scale and Scope.* Also see Robert B. Reich, *The Next American Frontier* (New York: Times Books, 1983), part 2.

huge domestic market, this involved relatively less direct state intervention, whereas in Germany and Japan state promotion was critical to large-scale capital. Max Weber's conception of modern social organization (the development of large-scale political and economic bureaucracies) as well as Karl Marx's belief that the end result would be a top-heavy monopoly capitalism shored up by the state were essentially second industrial revolution theories.[27] Ironically, Britain's decline was inextricably intertwined with its inability to develop much beyond the structures of a first industrial revolution state.[28] The subsequent development of the second industrial revolution state can be traced forward to the intense national competition of the 1930s, most strikingly embodied in the rise of fascism and Stalinism, but also reflected in President Franklin Roosevelt's New Deal in the United States. This worldwide scale shift led to what Karl Polanyi called the great transformation: namely, a change from the first industrial revolution attempt to establish a global self-regulating market, to the corporatist, social democratic, national welfare state, which crystallized in the 1930s and became dominant after World War II.[29] Second industrial revolution states thus converged on a more or less centralized model concerned with a growing range of policy functions: promoting and maintaining large-scale mass production industries; providing the requisite levels of regulation and demand management to ensure, in particular, that their extensive specific assets would not be undermined by economic downturns; and creating not only mass markets but also a disciplined work force to keep the factories humming.

The above account of the convergence of the political and economic structures of the second industrial revolution is, of course, a schematic oversimplification. One obvious problem is that it does not take much notice of the tensions and contradictions within the political-economic structures of the second industrial revolution. A more critical problem, however, is that this account cannot anticipate those new developments that would create pressures for fundamental structural change beyond the second industrial revolution model. On the endogenous level, the principal economic pressures for change stemmed from the competition among different fractions of capital and the increasing differentiation of production and consumption processes. The "competition of capitals" did not so much concern competition between rival capitalist firms as that between sectors rooted in different asset structures, producing and marketing different types of goods. Large-scale production sectors characterized by high levels of specific assets, especially natural monopolies and sectors producing capital goods, were best placed to benefit

27. On Marx's beliefs, see Bob Jessop, *The Capitalist State: Marxist Theory and Methods* (Oxford: Martin Robertson, 1982). For Weber's, see Max Weber, *Economy and Society*, 2 vols., eds. Guenther Roth and Claus Wittich (Berkeley: University of California Press, 1978).

28. Eric J. Hobsbawm, *Industry and Empire* (Harmondsworth, England: Penguin, 1969). Chandler refers to the continuation of "personal capitalism" in Britain. See his *Scale and Scope*, part 3.

29. Karl Polanyi, *The Great Transformation: The Political and Economic Origins of Our Time* (New York: Rinehart, 1944).

structurally from state promotion and procurement and from centralized structures of public and/or private finance capital. Small-scale sectors characterized primarily by nonspecific assets were structurally oriented toward other small producers and final consumers and found their relationships with the state or with high finance nonexistent, irrelevant, or threatening to their markets. The United States was probably the only country that, because of the size of its home market, could institutionally cater to both sectors. In most countries, however, tension between these economic sectors was interwoven with political and ideological clashes across a range of social and economic groups supporting different forms and combinations of authoritarianism and democracy. The internal control span of the state qua hierarchy was continually under challenge, even in the most outwardly authoritarian of states, and failures of hierarchy to work efficiently were commonplace.

Even more important in the long run was the interaction of these endogenous tensions with exogenous ones. On the exogenous level, the principal forms of tension between different types of goods or asset structures were those between the nationalization of warfare (and the production system necessary for modern total war), on the one hand, and the gradual but uneven internationalization of civilian production and exchange, on the other. Until World War I, the dynamics of economic competition and those of military rivalry were not so different with regard to many key issues, such as the development of dual-use railway systems, steel industries, and shipbuilding industries. Additionally, the nation-state constituted the predominant (although not the only) organizational unit for both types of activities. The international economic instability of the 1920s and the Great Depression of the 1930s, however, represented a fundamental loss of control by states, both authoritarian and liberal, over international economic processes.[30] The immediate result was, of course, the attempt to reassert previously existing forms of control in more intensified forms—more potent authoritarian autarchic empires and the withdrawal of even liberal states behind trade barriers—as all major states tried to recapture hierarchical control over their economic processes.

Thus the story of capitalism in the second industrial revolution was one of uneven internationalization if not yet of globalization. Britain's relatively free-trading empire, increasingly reinforced (and later replaced) by America's open door, created productive financial and trade links that drew second industrial revolution states out of their national shell and into an international web of linkages.[31] Despite the growth of autarchic empires in the 1920s and

---

30. This general loss of control was perhaps even more significant than the loss of leadership addressed by Kindleberger (which was a key symptom of the broader phenomenon, nonetheless). See Charles P. Kindleberger, *The World in Depression, 1929–1939* (London: Allen Lane the Penguin Press, 1973).

31. A now classic analysis of the history of U.S. foreign policy in terms of the open-door approach can be found in William Appleman Williams, *The Tragedy of American Diplomacy*, 2d ed. (New York: Dell, 1972).

1930s, the internationalists who prevailed within the Roosevelt administration by the mid-to-late 1930s and who later dominated wartime planning for the peace aimed to establish an arm's-length, increasingly multinational, free-trading system after the war.[32] Postwar U.S. hegemony, furthermore, was itself based on quasi-multilateral international economics and quasi-integrated defense systems; these were not entirely dependent upon the continuance of U.S. military dominance for their survival. Free trade outlived the recession and new protectionism of the 1970s, while French President Charles de Gaulle's attempt in the 1960s to revive the notion of purely national, nonintegrated defense petered out even before his exit from power.[33]

Thus, although political consciousness remained overwhelmingly national, both security and economic structures—especially the latter—became increasingly internationalized. The later stages of the second industrial revolution itself—the so-called long boom—saw the beginnings of the decay of the second industrial revolution state. By the time John Kenneth Galbraith had published *The New Industrial State* in 1967, the relatively monolithic political-economic "technostructure" that he depicted was already out of date.[34] Existing contradictions interacted with a new phase of scale shift. Many of what constituted public goods in the second industrial revolution (national-level strategic industries and regulatory and welfare systems, for example) increasingly are integrated into a wider world marketplace. The third industrial revolution—characterized by the intensive application of information and communications technology, flexible production systems and organizational structures, market segmentation, and globalization—also has profoundly altered the way that the structure of goods and assets themselves is shaped. Differentiation within production processes and through the segmentation of markets have contributed to this newer shift, as has the globalization of finance, which increasingly has divorced finance capital from the state. Institutional capacities for political control, stabilization, regulation, promotion, and facilitation of economic activities have therefore become increasingly fragmented. From international regimes to cross-cutting local pressures, new circuits of power are emerging.[35] These circuits of power result, in effect, both from new forms of collective action and from a revival of old forms in response to the changing structural context. They have not merely challenged the state but

32. On diplomacy during the Roosevelt administration, see Lloyd C. Gardner, *Economic Aspects of New Deal Diplomacy* (Boston: Beacon Press, 1971). On the later effects of internationalism, see E. F. Penrose, *Economic Planning for the Peace* (Princeton, N.J.: Princeton University Press, 1953).

33. P. G. Cerny, *The Politics of Grandeur: Ideological Aspects of de Gaulle's Foreign Policy* (Cambridge: Cambridge University Press, 1980), especially chaps. 7–9.

34. John Kenneth Galbraith, *The New Industrial State* (Harmondsworth, England: Penguin, 1967).

35. On regimes, see Stephen Krasner, ed., *International Regimes* (Ithaca, N.Y.: Cornell University Press, 1983). The concept of circuits of power, and their increasing fragmentation in the contemporary world, was developed by Foucault. See Michel Foucault, *Power/Knowledge: Selected Interviews and Other Writings 1972–1977*, ed. Colin Gordon (New York: Pantheon Books, 1980).

instead overlap with it, cut across it, and fragment it. Forms of collective action tailored to the nation-state have proved increasingly ineffective—leading at first to political polarization and then to attempts to reinvent government.[36]

Globalization and the changing public goods problem

The most important dimension of convergence between political and economic structures in the second industrial revolution state was the dominance of national-level organizational apparatuses in each sphere and the development of complex organized interfaces cutting across and linking the two spheres. Among these interfaces was corporatism, both state and societal.[37] Expanding national bureaucracies continually took on new social and economic tasks, while national capital found that national markets (and the national state) provided a congenial and appropriate framework around which to organize. International capital, too, looked to the home state for promotion and protection while seeking to control and manipulate host states. Political consciousness and growing demands from below emerged and consolidated in practice within the arena of the national constitutional state, even when opposing that state in principle. It is still difficult today to conceive of working democratic systems other than through the lens of the nation-state. Even Marxist internationalism, especially under the revisionist influence of Lenin, became increasingly focused on taking power by appropriating the apparatuses of the state.[38] Public goods were perceived by all interested parties as national-level phenomena, even when they were externalized through imperial expansion. Nevertheless, a fundamental transformation has taken place in the structure of public goods in today's global era, making both their pursuit and their provision through the nation-state more problematic.

Those traditionally conceived public goods have been primarily of three kinds.[39] The first involves the establishment of a workable market framework for the ongoing operation of the system as a whole—regulatory public goods. These include the establishment and protection of private (and public)

36. See David Osborne and Ted Gaebler, *Reinventing Government: How the Entrepreneurial Spirit is Transforming the Public Sector, from Schoolhouse to Statehouse, City Hall to the Pentagon* (Reading, Mass.: Addison-Wesley, 1992). This book has had an enormous impact on both right and left in the United States and elsewhere.

37. The classic statement of the neocorporatist approach is that in Philippe C. Schmitter, "Still the Century of Corporatism?" in Frederick Pike and Thomas Stritch, eds., *The New Corporatism* (Notre Dame, Ind.: Notre Dame University Press, 1974), pp. 85–131.

38. See V. I. Lenin, *Imperialism, the Highest Stage of Capitalism* (1917; reprint, Moscow: Progress Publishers, 1978); and V. I. Lenin, *State and Revolution* (1918; reprint, New York: International Publishers, 1932).

39. I am here borrowing freely from Theodore Lowi's three categories of public policy: distributive, regulatory, and redistributive. See his works "American Business, Public Policy, Case Studies, and Political Theory," *World Politics* 16 (July 1964), pp. 677–715, and *The End of Liberalism: Ideology, Polity, and the Crisis of Public Authority* (New York: Norton, 1969).

property rights, a stable currency, the abolition of internal barriers to production and exchange, standardization of weights and measures, a legal system to sanction and enforce contracts and to adjudicate disputes, a more specific regulatory system to stabilize and coordinate economic activities, a system of trade protection, and other systems that could be mobilized to counteract system-threatening market failures (such as lender of last resort facilities and emergency powers provisions). The second involves specific state-controlled or state-sponsored activities of production and distribution—productive/distributive public goods. Among these are full or partial public ownership of certain industries, direct or indirect provision of infrastructure and public services, direct or indirect involvement in finance capital, and myriad public subsidies. The third type of public goods are redistributive public goods, especially those resulting from the expanding political and public policy demands of emerging social classes, economic interests, and political parties and the responses of state actors to those demands. Redistributive goods include health and welfare services, employment policies, corporatist bargaining processes (although these often have had a significant regulatory function as well), and environmental protection—indeed, the main apparatus of the national welfare state. The provision of all three kinds of public goods in second industrial revolution states was dependent on the interweaving of large-scale specific assets between bureaucratic structures and structures of capital.

In a globalizing world, however, national states have difficulty supplying or fostering all of these categories of public good. Regulatory public goods are an obvious case. In a world of relatively open trade, financial deregulation, and the increasing impact of information technology, property rights are more difficult for the state to establish and maintain. For example, cross-border industrial espionage, counterfeiting of products, copyright violations, and the like have made the multilateral protection of intellectual property rights a focal point of international disputes and a bone of contention in the Uruguay Round of the General Agreement on Tariffs and Trade (now the World Trade Organization). International capital flows and the proliferation of offshore financial centers and tax havens have rendered firm ownership and firms' ability internally to allocate resources through transfer pricing and the like increasingly opaque to national tax and regulatory authorities. Traditional forms of trade protectionism, too, are both easily bypassed and counterproductive.[40] Currency exchange rates and interest rates are increasingly set in globalizing marketplaces, and governments attempt to manipulate them at their peril.[41] Legal rules are increasingly easy to evade, and attempts to extend the legal reach of the national state through the development of extraterritoriality are

40. See Pietro S. Nivola, *Regulating Unfair Trade* (Washington, D.C.: Brookings Institution, 1993).
41. P. G. Cerny, "The Dynamics of Financial Globalization: Technology, Market Structure, and Policy Response," *Policy Sciences* 27 (November 1994), pp. 319–342.

ineffective and hotly disputed. Finally, the ability of firms, market actors, and competing parts of the national state apparatus itself to defend and expand their economic and political turf through activities such as transnational policy networking and regulatory arbitrage—the capacity of industrial and financial sectors to whipsaw the state apparatus by pushing state agencies into a process of competitive deregulation or what economists call competition in laxity—has both undermined the control span of the state from without and fragmented it from within.[42]

Furthermore, real or potential inefficiencies in the provision of regulatory public goods have much wider ramifications than merely for the provision of public goods per se, because they constitute the framework, the playing field, within which private goods as well as other public goods are provided in the wider economy and society. In other words, actors seeking to pursue regulatory public goods today are likely to see traditional state-based forms of regulation as neither efficient nor sufficient in a globalizing world. Perhaps a more familiar theme in the public goods literature, however, has been the impact of globalization on the capacity of the state to provide productive/distributive public goods. The most visible aspect of this impact has been the crisis of public ownership of strategic industries and the wave of privatization that have characterized the 1980s and 1990s. Once again, both political and economic scale factors are at work. At one level, such industries are no longer perceived as strategic. Steel, chemicals, railroad, motor vehicles, aircraft, shipbuilding, and basic energy industries were once seen as a core set of industries over which national control was necessary for both economic strength in peacetime and survival in wartime. Today, internationalization of the asset structure of these industries, of the goods they produce, and of the markets for those products—with foreign investment going in both directions—has caused the internationalization of even high-technology industries producing components for weaponry.[43]

At the same time, the state is seen as structurally inappropriate for the task of directly providing productive/distributive goods. Public ownership of industry is thought so inherently inefficient economically (the "lame duck syndrome") as to render ineffectual its once-perceived benefits of permitting national planning, providing employment, or enlarging social justice. Third World countries increasingly reject delinkage and import substitution industrialization and embrace export promotion industrialization, thereby imbricating their economies even more closely with the global economy.[44] Even where

42. For an analysis of regulatory arbitrage in the financial sector, see P. G. Cerny, ed., *Finance and World Politics: Markets, Regimes and States in the Post-hegemonic Era* (Cheltenham, England: Edward Elgar, 1993), especially chaps. 3 and 6.

43. Edward M. Graham and Paul R. Krugman, *Foreign Direct Investment in the United States* (Washington, D.C.: Institute for International Economics, 1989), chap. 5.

44. See Nigel Harris, *The End of the Third World* (Harmondsworth, England: Penguin, 1986); and Stephan Haggard, *Pathways from the Periphery: The Politics of Growth in the Newly Industrializing Countries* (Ithaca, N.Y.: Cornell University Press, 1990).

public ownership has been expanded, its ostensible rationale has been as part of a drive for international competitiveness and not an exercise in national exclusiveness, as in France in the early 1980s.[45] The same can be said for more traditional forms of industrial policy, such as state subsidies to industry, public procurement of nationally produced goods and services, or trade protectionism. Monetarist and private sector supply-side economists deny that the state has ever been in a position to intervene in these matters in an economically efficient way and argue further that the possibility of playing such a role at all in today's globalized world has utterly evaporated in the era of "quicksilver capital" flowing across borders.[46] However, even social liberal and other relatively interventionist economists nowadays regard the battle to retain the homogeneity of the national economy to be all but lost and argue that states are condemned to tinkering around the edges.[47]

The outer limits of effective action by the state in this environment are usually seen to comprise its capacity to promote a relatively favorable investment climate for transnational capital—i.e., by providing an increasingly circumscribed range of goods that retain a national-scale (or subnational-scale) public character or of a particular type of still-specific assets described as immobile factors of capital.[48] Such potentially manipulable factors include: human capital (the skills, experience, education, and training of the work force); infrastructure (from public transportation to high-technology information highways); support for a critical mass of research and development activities; basic public services necessary for a good quality of life for those working in middle- to high-level positions in otherwise footloose (transnationally mobile) firms and sectors; and maintenance of a public policy environment favorable to investment (and profit making) by such companies, whether domestic or foreign-owned. I have called this mixture the "competition state."[49]

Finally, of course, globalization has had a severe impact, both direct and indirect, on the possibility for the state efficiently to provide redistributive public goods. With regard to labor market policy, for example, corporatist bargaining and employment policies are everywhere under pressure—although somewhat unevenly, depending less on the country than on the sector concerned—in the face of international pressure for wage restraint and flexible working practices. The provision of education and training increasingly is taking priority over direct labor market intervention, worker protection, and

---

45. P. G. Cerny, "State Capitalism in France and Britain and the International Economic Order," in P. G. Cerny and M. A. Schain, eds., *Socialism, the State, and Public Policy in France* (London and New York: Pinter and Methuen, 1985), chap. 10.
46. Richard B. McKenzie and Dwight R. Lee, *Quicksilver Capital: How the Rapid Movement of Wealth Has Changed the World* (New York: Free Press, 1991).
47. Probably the best known protagonist in this field is Reich. See Robert B. Reich, *The Work of Nations: Preparing Ourselves for Twenty-first-Century Capitalism* (New York: Knopf, 1991).
48. Ibid.
49. Cerny, *The Changing Architecture of Politics,* especially chap. 8.

incomes policies.[50] With regard to the welfare state, although the developed states generally have not been able to reduce the overall weight of welfare spending in the economy, a highly significant shift from maintaining free-standing social and public services to merely keeping up with expanding existing commitments has occurred in many countries. Unemployment compensation and entitlement programs have ballooned as a consequence of industrial downsizing, increasing inequalities of wealth, homelessness, and the aging of the population in industrial societies, thereby tending to crowd out funding for other services. Finally, the most salient new sector of redistributive public goods, environmental protection, is especially transnational in character; pollution and the depletion of natural resources do not respect borders.[51] Therefore, in all three of the principal categories of second industrial revolution public goods, globalization has undercut the policy capacity of the national state in all but a few areas.

This view is contested, of course—for example by Geoffrey Garrett and Peter Lange. They argue that nationally autonomous corporatist policy approaches have been remarkably resilient in terms of developing labor-friendly supply-side alternatives for increasing international competitiveness, even though macroeconomic policy autonomy has been severely curtailed. This argument is not necessarily wholly incompatible with the approach taken here, especially in the light of Robert Reich's distinction between mobile and immobile factors of capital and the greater capacity of the state to manipulate the latter; indeed, elsewhere I provisionally explore supply-side alternatives for the left in the context of the competition state. Nevertheless, I believe Garrett and Lange's analysis does not fully capture the ongoing knock-on effects of financial globalization on other sectors—for example, in the stuttering cycle of recession and partial recovery since the October 1987 economic crash, which led to greater exposure to international constraints of many corporatist economies.[52]

Scale shift and the third industrial revolution

In addition to the changing scale of public goods, the changing technological and institutional context in which all goods are increasingly being

50. See Reich, *The Work of Nations;* and Sally Hayward, "Labor Markets: A Case for Inclusion in International Political Economy," paper presented to a colloquium on Technology, Change, and the Global Political Economy, Nottingham Trent University, Nottingham, England, 4–6 May 1994.

51. Angela Liberatore, "Problems of Transnational Policymaking: Environmental Policy in the European Community," in P. G. Cerny, ed., *The Politics of Transnational Regulation: Deregulation or Reregulation,* special issue of the *European Journal of Political Research* 19 (March/April 1991), pp. 281–305.

52. Geoffrey Garrett and Peter Lange, "Political Responses to Interdependence: What's 'Left' for the Left?" *International Organization* 45 (Autumn 1991), pp. 539–64. Garrett and Lange's conclusions may be limited by the fact that they have data only through 1987. Compare Cerny, *The Changing Architecture of Politics,* especially chap. 8 and the epilogue. See also Roy E. Allen, *Financial Crises and Recession in the Global Economy* (Aldershot, England, and Brookfield, Vt.: Edward Elgar, 1994).

produced and exchanged has been central to this transformation. The third industrial revolution has many characteristics, but those most relevant to our concern with scale shift involve five trends in particular, each bound up with the others. The first is the development of flexible manufacturing systems and their spread not only to new industries but to older ones as well. The second is the changing hierarchical form of firms (and bureaucracies) to what has been called "lean management." The third is the capacity of decision-making structures to monitor the actions of all levels of management and of the labor force far more closely through the use of information technology. The fourth is the segmentation of markets in a more complex consumer society. Finally, the third industrial revolution has been profoundly shaped by the emergence of increasingly autonomous transnational financial markets and institutions.

The issue of flexible manufacturing systems has been at the heart of the new comparative and international political economy over the past decade and a half. Given the huge amount of fixed capital advanced industrial states had inherited from the various phases of the second industrial revolution (and Britain from the first), much "creative destruction" of fixed capital stock would be required before the next phase of capital investment could take off. The first reaction of the state, still shaped by the experiences and characterized by the structures of second industrial revolution bureaucracies, was to attempt to take industry under its wing again in the traditional way. But the more open international environment has made such measures increasingly counterproductive. International competition from flexible, high-technology economies like Japan and some other newly industrializing countries (whose governments promoted such flexibility) seemed to turn decline into a vicious circle.

Flexible production itself requires not an integration but a differentiation—both of distinct stages of the production process and of increasingly complex and variable production-line tasks themselves. Rather than being managed authoritatively through the hierarchical firm, flexible production is organized through a range of processes that Williamson would call "recurrent contracting." These include: increased subcontracting (rather than direct control) of the manufacturing and supply of peripheral components of the production process; increasingly autonomous labor and management teams charged with evolving more efficient ways of carrying out specific tasks (for example, intrapreneurship and Japanese-style quality circles); and shortening process and product cycles in both technological and organizational terms—including "just in time" procurement of parts supplies and the ability to switch both machines and workers from product to product and task to task. This structure obviously requires not merely a workforce that is both flexible and highly trained but also the latest in high-technology production techniques such as robots, reprogrammable machine tools, and computerized production lines. These production facilities require a range of new conditions to operate efficiently, including such factors as the availability of greenfield sites—sites away from the decaying fixed capital and unionized work forces of the second industrial revolution industries, e.g., in the U.S. Rust Belt—and proximity to other similarly structured industries. In such locations, cross-fertilization between the experiences of workers and managers, the development of product improvements in related fields, and the learning curve of process innovation can create a virtuous circle or synergy among firms. The electronics industry is the example, and Silicon Valley the exemplar. Flexible production, not a respecter of borders, is a crucial element in internationalizing production and competition.

This trend has, of course, been analyzed at several levels since the late 1970s from neo-Marxist, center-left, and neoliberal perspectives. The right, especially in the Ronald Reagan and Margaret Thatcher years, spoke much the same language about the need for flexible structures; however, certain other groups within the right rejected this analysis in favor of a more active, pro-business industrial policy approach. In the ongoing academic debate, John Zysman showed as early as 1977 how the attempt by the French government in the 1970s to promote the development of the electronics industry (through the *Plan calcul*) just as in earlier years it successfully had promoted the oil and steel industries, failed because of the differing asset structures of the industries involved.[53] Several authors, including Reich, argued in the early 1980s that restructuring the U.S. economy would require a thoroughgoing change not only in the organization of industry and of the state but also in the economic and political culture of the country.[54] Zysman and Laura D'Andrea Tyson examined challenges to U.S. competitiveness in a range of sectors and diagnosed a lack of flexibility as the main problem; they suggested that a proactive state could manipulate competitive advantages possessed by different sectors to facilitate the necessary adjustment processes.[55] Michael Piore and Charles Sabel examined the experience of "craft" production in Europe and argued that the flexible specialization of those industries also had lessons for U.S. adjustment.[56] These approaches also were reflected in sociological analysis, partly influenced by sea changes in neo- and post-Marxism, and in economic analysis as well, from the more radical regulation school in France to the new institutional economics of Williamson and others in the United States. What have been called post-Fordist social and economic structures have been examined extensively across the social sciences.[57]

53. John Zysman, *Political Strategies for Industrial Order: Market, State, and Industry in France* (Berkeley: University of California Press, 1977).

54. See Reich, *The Next American Frontier;* and S. M. Miller and Donald Tomaskovic-Devey, *Recapitalizing America: Alternatives to the Corporate Distortion of National Policy* (Boston: Routledge and Kegan Paul, 1983).

55. John Zysman and Laura d'Andrea Tyson, eds., *American Industry in International Competition* (Ithaca, N.Y.: Cornell University Press, 1983).

56. Michael J. Piore and Charles F. Sabel, *The Second Industrial Divide: Possibilities for Prosperity* (New York: Basic Books, 1984).

57. See in particular Ash Amin, ed., *Post-Fordism: A Reader* (Oxford: Basil Blackwell, 1994), especially the editor's introductory essay.

Closely linked with the development of more flexible production processes was the structure of firms as such. In addition to experimenting with new forms of differentiation outside the core firm (as with subcontracting), managerial theorists focused on the "flexibilization" of the bureaucratic layers of the firms themselves. This did not merely require firing layers of cadres—although downsizing has become increasingly important—but it also required altering the consciousness of managers themselves. Although management literature has always been filled with exhortations to such qualities as excellence, the emphasis in the scientific management era of the second industrial revolution focused on the efficient division of responsibilities among individuals who were highly skilled at discrete tasks. In the third industrial revolution, in contrast, two sorts of individual became the totems of the new excellence: brilliant innovator/managers such as Steven Jobs or William Gates, who could singlehandedly envision and construct new processes and products from outside the established structures (the entrepreneurs), and the leaders of autonomous teams within large but more flexible organizations who could change the direction of those institutions (so-called intrapreneurs).

Even IBM, which had long attempted to incorporate new practices piece-meal without having to relinquish the specific asset base it had built (its second industrial revolution-style managerial hierarchy and its secure and reliable workforce), eventually had to adjust. It did so both by dramatically increasing subcontracting globally and locally and, more recently, by extensive downsizing. What had previously been built up as specific assets, from a skilled and loyal workforce to large-scale mass production facilities—and had been prized as such—increasingly are being destroyed or transformed into nonspecific assets that can be exchanged in more open and extensive world markets. The restructuring of firms and production processes in the developed world and the Third World alike has been dramatic, and such firms are psychologically as well as materially better prepared and more eager to participate.

At the heart of the flexibilization of both production processes and firms themselves has been the explosive development of information technology. Olson argued that a key factor making collective action difficult in large groups was the inability of such groups to monitor the behavior of members who might be tempted to ride free. Electronic computer and communications technology has of course transformed this problem. The ability to coordinate centralized and therefore coherent strategic decision making with decentralized and therefore innovative operational decision making is the principal predicament faced in experimenting with the new organizational structure of the firm. The most efficient relationship between market and hierarchy varies from sector to sector, technology to technology, and product to product. Today, workers and lower-level managers increasingly are left on their own to learn how to carry out their tasks more productively and competitively; however, at the same time, financial managers are watching ever more effectively from a distance through complex and flexible information networks, using a panoply of financial controls and performance indicators.[58] This capacity to monitor ostensibly autonomous activity bridges the gap between public and private goods within the firm, enabling central decision makers to harness the initiatives of peripheral managers and workers to the wider aims of the more amorphous organization. This monitoring capability also leaps national borders and brings firms, markets, and consumers into a single, global production process in an increasing number of sectors.

But these aspects of the third industrial revolution—flexibilization of production, firm structure, and monitoring—are only part of the picture. They represent the supply side of the equation. The demand side involves the development of ever more complex consumer societies and the resulting segmentation of markets. This reflects the convergence of two developments. The first is the technological capacity to produce flexibly—the capacity of business to produce at the appropriate scale for a much more highly differentiated structure of demand, however multilayered. The second, however, is the increasing differentiation of the class system itself in advanced capitalist societies. In the second industrial revolution, workers in particular but the middle classes too, could mainly expect to buy fairly standardized products—sometimes referred to as the one-size-fits-all approach. Growing factories technologically were capable of—and often limited to—long-run, large-scale production; at the same time, social mobility meant that first-time buyers were glad to get whatever products were available. However, by the end of the 1960s, first-time markets were becoming saturated in the advanced capitalist world. Much of the long boom had involved burgeoning first-time markets for such products as "white goods" (refrigerators, washing machines), cars, and television sets. Customers making a subsequent purchase, however, demanded higher specifications and greater choice. Differentiating demand and flexible supply thus converged on market segmentation, producing a wider range of variations on a particular product or set of products, with each variation targeted to a particular subset of consumers. This process also created consumer demand for foreign-produced goods and forced firms to internationalize. These pressures now apply to the provision of public goods by governments, as well.

The final characteristic of the third industrial revolution is the growing significance of global financial markets.[59] The abstract or "dematerialized" character of finance in a world of information technology and cutting-edge communications systems makes trading in financial instruments virtually instantaneous. Even in the 1930s, Keynes believed that financial markets were too easy to play, too readily divorced from the real economy, for socially and economically necessary production to occur; they tended to constitute a giant

---

58. Dimitris N. Chorofas, *The New Technology of Financial Management: Artificial Intelligence, Expert Systems, Intelligent Networks, Knowledge Engineering* (New York: John Wiley and Sons, 1992).
59. For a more extensive treatment of the political implications of financial globalization, see Cerny, *Finance and World Politics*.

casino. In the period since the 1950s—and especially since the breakdown of the Bretton Woods system—finance has once again become globalized, with newly deregulated markets increasingly absorbing money from the real economy.[60] Indeed, finance embodies each of the main characteristics of the third industrial revolution described above. In product terms, it has become the exemplar of a flexible industry, trading in notional and infinitely variable financial instruments. Financial innovation has been rapid and far-reaching, affecting all parts of the financial services industry and shaping every industrial sector.[61] Furthermore, product innovation has been matched by process innovation. Traders and other financial market actors and firms are expected to act like entrepreneurs (or intrapreneurs) as a matter of course. Financial globalization has been virtually synonymous with the rapid development of electronic computer and communications technology.[62] The ownership and transfer of shares and other financial instruments increasingly are recorded only on computer files, without the exchange of paper certificates—what the French call dematerialization—although written documentation can always be provided for financial controllers, auditors, or regulators (in principle, at least although in practice fraud adapts quickly). With increasing globalization of production and trade, market demand for financial services products continually is segmenting, too.

Probably the most important consequence of the globalization of financial markets is their increasing structural hegemony in wider economic and political structures and processes. In a more open world, financial balances and flows increasingly are dominant—with the volume of financial transactions variously estimated as totaling twenty to forty times the value of merchandise trade. This gap is growing rapidly as private international capital markets expand. Exchange rates and interest rates, as essential to business decision making as to public policymaking, increasingly are determined by world market conditions. In addition, as trade and production structures in the third industrial revolution go through the kinds of changes outlined earlier, they will be increasingly coordinated through the application of complex financial controls, accounting techniques, and financial performance indicators (because nonfinancial performance is complex and difficult to measure in a globalizing world). These strictures are applicable to a range of organizations, including government bureaucracies. Financial markets epitomize, in Williamson's terms, the structural ascendancy of almost purely nonspecific assets over specific assets in the global economy, pushing and pulling other economic sectors and activities unevenly into the global arena.

60. Allen, *Financial Crises and Recession in the Global Economy.*
61. Richard D. Crawford and William W. Sihler, *The Troubled Money Business: The Death of an Old Order and the Rise of a New Order* (New York: HarperBusiness, 1991).
62. The implications of technological change in the financial services industry are examined in Susan Strange, "Finance, Information, and Power," *Review of International Studies* 16 (July 1990), pp. 259–74.

Collective action and the residual state

The economic and political world of the third industrial revolution revolves around a central paradox. On the one hand, globalization would seem to entail the shift of the world economy to an even larger structural scale. This perception of globalization was what led observers a decade or two ago to misinterpret the significance of multinational corporations, which were seen as involving the worldwide integration of specific assets.[63] Of course, many such firms, and some problems like environmental pollution, do resemble this model of an upward shift in scale, potentially requiring transnational-level institutions for effective regulation. However, economic restructuring has involved a more complex process, altering the composition of public goods and specific assets and even involving the privatization and marketization of the political-economic structure itself. These processes lead in turn to the whipsawing of states between structural pressures and organizational levels that they cannot control in a complex, circular fashion. Thus economic globalization contributes not to the supersession of the state by a homogeneous world order as such but to the differentiation of the existing national and international political orders, as well. Indeed, globalization leads to a growing disjunction between the democratic, constitutional, and social aspirations of people—which continue to be shaped by and understood through the framework of the territorial state—and the increasingly problematic potential for collective action through state political processes. Certain possibilities for collective action through multilateral regimes may increase, but these operate at at least one remove from democratic accountability.[64] Indeed, the study of international regimes is expanding beyond intergovernmental institutions or public entities per se toward "private regimes" as critical regulatory mechanisms.[65] New nodes of private and quasi-public economic power are crystallizing that, in their own partial domains, are in effect more sovereign than the state.

Despite these changes, of course, states retain certain vital political and economic functions at both the domestic and international levels. Indeed, some of these have paradoxically been strengthened by globalization. But the character of these functions is changing. New collective action problems undermine the constraining character of previously dominant political and economic games. As a result, policymakers everywhere are seeking to restructure the state so that it can play new roles in the future. While the state retains

63. A more complex and sophisticated analysis of multinational corporations—how they work, how they interact with each other, and how they interact with states—can be found in John Stopford and Susan Strange (with John S. Henley), *Rival States, Rival Firms: Competition for World Market Shares* (Cambridge: Cambridge University Press, 1991).

64. On collective action, see Friedrich Kratochwil and Edward D. Mansfield, eds., *International Organization: A Reader* (New York: HarperCollins, 1994).

65. See, for example, Miroslava Filipovic, "Governments, Banks, and Global Capital: The Emergence of the Global Capital Market and the Politics of its Regulation," Ph.D. diss., City University, London, 1994.

a crucial role in the political-economic matrix of a globalizing world, however, its holistic and overarching character—as reflected in Aristotle's "most sovereign and inclusive association" or Oakeshott's "civil association"—may be increasingly compromised. The state today is a potentially unstable mix of civil association and enterprise association—of constitutional state, pressure group, and firm—with state actors, no longer so autonomous, feeling their way uneasily in an unfamiliar world.[66] At this point, I will briefly consider some of the issues facing this "residual state."

The structural coherence, power, and autonomy of states themselves clearly have become problematic in recent years. Over the past four centuries, the state has become the repository of probably the most important dimension of human society—social identity, and in this case, national identity. This sense of national identity has been reinforced both by nationalism and by the spread of democratic institutions and processes. Indeed, liberal democracy has constituted the most important linkage or interface between social identity on the one hand and state structures and processes on the other. Therefore, the first main bulwark of the state, even in a globalizing world, is found in the deep social roots of *gemeinschaftlich* national identity that have developed through the modern nation-state. Such identities are bound to decline to some extent, both through the erosion of the national public sphere from above and from the reassertion of substate ethnic, cultural, and religious identities from below. Thus the decay of the cultural underpinnings of the state—of rain-or-shine loyalty—will be uneven, and in economically stronger states this decay is likely to proceed more slowly than in weaker ones.[67]

This will be particularly true if the potential capacity of the more developed states to provide infrastructure, education systems, workforce skills, and quality-of-life amenities (usually classed among the immobile factors of capital) to attract mobile, footloose capital of a highly sophisticated kind is effectively mobilized.[68] On the one hand, the ability of states to control development planning, to collect and use their own tax revenues, to build infrastructure, to run education and training systems, and to enforce law and order gives actors continuing to work through the state a capacity to influence the provision of immobile factors of capital in many highly significant ways. If Europe, Japan, and the United States along with perhaps some others are better able to provide these advanced facilities, then *gemeinschaftlich* loyalty in those states may recede more slowly or even stabilize, maintaining the civil-associational character of the state even as many of its narrower functions

---

66. For a consideration of the problem of state autonomy and the different approaches taken to it in the neo-Marxist, neo-Weberian, and neo-pluralist debates of the 1980s, see Cerny, *The Changing Architecture of Politics,* especially chap. 4.

67. This is Almond and Verba's more familiar version of what they also call "system affect." See Gabriel A. Almond and Sidney Verba, *The Civic Culture: Political Attitudes and Democracy in Five Nations* (Princeton, N.J.: Princeton University Press, 1963).

68. Reich, *The Work of Nations.*

are eroded. On the other hand, mobile international capital may well destabilize less-favored states, whose already fragile governmental systems will be torn by groups attempting to recast those *gemeinschaftlich* bonds through claims for the ascendancy of religious, ethnic, or other grass-roots loyalties. The extent to which richer states are able to avoid such destabilization in the long run remains problematic, however.

State-based collective action continues to have a major role to play in the provision of certain crucial types of public goods and in the management of a range of significant specific assets, even if it must do so in a context where the authoritative power of the state as a whole is weaker and more circumscribed than it has been in the past. But rather than the state being directly responsible for market outcomes that guarantee the welfare of its citizens, the main focus of this competition state in the world—partly analogous to the experience of state governments in the United States—is the proactive promotion of economic activities, whether at home or abroad, that will make firms and sectors located within the territory of the state competitive in international markets.[69] The state itself becomes an agent for the commodification of the collective, situated in a wider, market-dominated playing field. In David Andrews's terms, the competition state will increasingly "cheat" or ride free on opportunities created by autonomous transnational market structures and other public goods provided not by other states or the states system but by increasingly autonomous and private transnational structures, such as financial markets.[70] The state is thus caught in a bind in which maintaining a balance between its civil-association functions and its enterprise-association functions will become increasingly problematic.

In this new context, the logic of collective action is becoming a heterogeneous, multilayered logic, derived not from one particular core structure, such as the state, but from the structural complexity embedded in the global arena. Globalization does not mean that the international system is any less structurally anarchic; it merely changes the structural composition of that anarchy from one made up of relations between sovereign states to one made up of relations between functionally differentiated spheres of economic activity, on the one hand, and the institutional structures proliferating in an ad hoc fashion to fill the power void, on the other.[71] Different economic activities—differentiated by their comparative goods/assets structures—increasingly need to be regulated through distinct sets of institutions at different levels organized at different optimal scales. Such institutions, of course, overlap and interact in complex ways, but they no longer sufficiently coincide on a single optimal scale in such a way that they could be efficiently integrated into a multitask hierarchy like the

69. The question of foreign or domestic ownership is highly problematic here. Reich argues that ownership is far less important than the ability to attract capital. See Reich, *The Work of Nations.*
70. David M. Andrews, "Capital Mobility and State Autonomy: Toward a Structural Theory of International Monetary Relations," *International Studies Quarterly* 38 (June 1994), p. 201.
71. Strange, *States and Markets.*

nation-state. Some are essentially private market structures and regimes, some are still public intergovernmental structures, and some are mixed public–private.

The paths taken in the future in terms of both democratic accountability and political legitimacy will be crucial for the reshaping of the logic of collective action, especially where the state is no longer capable of being an effective channel for democratic demands. What sort of complex overall pattern of conflict and stability, competition and cooperation, will emerge from this process—in particular, whether the state will, despite its changing roles, remain a key element in a stabilizing, plurilateral web of levels and institutions or whether its decay will exacerbate a long-term trend toward greater instability—is not yet clear. We are only now in the first stages of a complex, worldwide evolutionary process of institutional selection.[72]

Conclusions: a framework for future research

In the course of this analysis, I have examined some of the consequences that derive from my basic argument that the more economies of scale of dominant goods and assets diverge from the structural scale of the national state—and the more that those divergences feed back into each other in complex ways—then the more that the authority, legitimacy, policymaking capacity, and policy-implementing effectiveness of the state will be eroded and undermined both without and within. At this point, I will present a number of more specific hypotheses derived from this basic problematic that might form the core of a wider research agenda in this area. These hypotheses concern the impact of the increasing differentiation of goods and asset structures on the state and other cross-cutting structured fields of action in a globalizing world.

Hypothesis 1

Developments in the production, exchange, and/or use of private goods and nonspecific assets will more and more be shaped and determined primarily by transnational or global factors and trends. While the paradigmatic case is finance, an increasing range of substitutable commodities produced through easily transferred technology come into this category. A classic example is textiles and footwear; semiconductors are a more recent one.

Corollary 1a. Such global factors and trends, however, do not only exist above the nation-state on the international level; they include direct, cross-cutting linkages between the transnational and the subnational (local/regional) levels, bypassing the national level. The regional craft economies studied by

---

72. Spruyt, "Institutional Selection in International Relations."

Piore and Sabel are criss-crossed by such linkages. However, some subnational activities that are not closely linked to the transnational level may fall under corollary 2c.

Corollary 1b. Many—though not all (see corollary 2a)—of what previously have comprised public goods and specific assets will be transformed into private goods and nonspecific assets in the wider, global economic arena. Increasing sectors of the defense industry may constitute a paradigmatic case.[73]

Hypothesis 2

Developments in economic sectors characterized predominantly by the production, exchange, or use of public goods and specific assets will be increasingly shaped and determined by the particular scale of those goods and assets, whether transnational, national, local, or somewhere in between.[74] Three categories of public goods/specific assets can be distinguished, and for each of these I suggest a corollary.

Corollary 2a. With regard to those public goods and specific assets where economies of scale already or increasingly transcend the scale of the purely national economy—i.e., where public goods and specific assets require the integration of production processes and economic activities at a global or international-regional scale—then developments in such sectors and activities will be broadly shaped by global and/or transnational factors and trends. Strategic alliances among multinational corporations and the provision of environmental protection often will come into this category.[75]

Corollary 2b. At the same time, however, in those economic sectors and activities where the scale of the goods/assets structure remains broadly congruent with the territorial parameters of the national economy—and where such goods and assets are not in effect transformed into private goods or nonspecific assets in the wider global economic space (as in corollary 1b)—then developments will continue to be determined and shaped primarily by national-level factors and trends. The provision of terrestrial transportation infrastructure and public housing still are primarily organized at the national

73. Andrew Latham, "New Manufacturing Techniques and the Evolution of 'Military-Postfordism'," paper presented at the annual meeting of the International Studies Association, Washington, D.C., 28 March–1 April 1994.
74. Economies of scale recently have become more important in international trade theory, in contrast to traditional concerns with comparative advantage. See Elhanan Helpman and Paul R. Krugman, *Market Structure and Foreign Trade: Increasing Returns, Imperfect Competition, and the International Economy* (Brighton, England: Harvester Press, 1985).
75. Stephen J. Kobrin, "Strategic Alliances and State Control of Economic Actors," paper presented at the annual meeting of the International Studies Association, Chicago, 21–25 February 1995.

level, but the range of goods and assets that fall neatly into this category is shrinking. States of different sizes may of course have institutional advantages for the stabilization and regulation of particular sectors of economic activity, those characterized by optimal scale economies congruent with the institutional scale of the state. The differentiation of economic structures in general, however, is likely to mean that such congruence will be appropriate for only a limited range of activities and not for integrated, multifunctional or multitask (statelike) institutional efficiency.

Corollary 2c. As a limited exception to corollary 1a, in some of those economic activities where the goods/assets structure is locally or regionally public/specific (here in the sense of subnational rather than international regions)—rather than organized on a national scale per se—but where those activities are relatively isolated from transnational market linkages, developments may be shaped either by purely local/subnational factors and trends or by national factors and trends, where such activities are widespread within the national territory despite not being linked through markets. Subsistence farming, cooperative organizations, barter circles, and some ethnically specific activities might come into this category. The range of activities genuinely delinked from wider markets is small and shrinking.

Hypothesis 3

The authority, policymaking capacity, and policy-implementation effectiveness of national governments will be more eroded and undermined where the goods/assets structure is most globalized or transnationalized. In these circumstances, the state will be eroded from without. This is true whether globalization takes the form of nonspecific assets traded in transnational markets or of integrated specific assets operating at a transnational scale (see, for example, hypothesis 1 and corollary 2a above).

Hypothesis 4

The authority, capacity, and effectiveness of the state also will be increasingly eroded and undermined where the goods/assets structure is effectively localized—i.e., from within. This process is particularly significant, of course, where local activities are linked directly to transnational markets or asset structures (i.e., craft-based regions such as Silicon Valley), as fewer and fewer local activities can exist in isolation from wider market and asset structures.

Hypothesis 5

The combination of hypothesis 1, corollary 2a, hypothesis 3, and hypothesis 4 will take the form of a complex, nonlinear process, in effect whipsawing the state from above and below and magnifying tendencies toward its structural decay. Thinking globally but acting locally undermines the state as an arena of collective action.

Hypothesis 6

In contrast to hypothesis 1, corollary 2a, and hypotheses 3, 4, and 5, the role of the state will be maintained or even increased in sectors where the goods/assets structure or mix retains or attains a national or quasi-national scale, as in corollaries 2b and 2c. Once again, though, this is an increasingly empty category. Nevertheless, the search for such activities, especially those of a symbolic nature (e.g., representing gemeinschaft-type aspirations for cultural homogeneity or the desire to expand national-level subsidiarity in the European Union), is likely to increase as states seek to retain their legitimacy.

Hypothesis 7

After a first phase—deriving from the policy inertia that exists in the early part of a learning curve—of attempting to use traditional state policy approaches and instruments to control or reverse the processes posited in hypothesis 1, corollary 2a, and hypotheses 3, 4, and 5, state actors will attempt to engineer a restructuring of the state toward the development of a more flexible and "marketized" state form and policy process in the attempt to regain lost authority, capacity, and effectiveness (reinventing government).

Hypothesis 8

Where the combined impact of corollaries 2b and 2c and hypotheses 6 and 7, on the one hand, remains in rough balance with the cumulative impact of hypothesis 1, corollary 2a, and hypotheses 3, 4, and 5, on the other, the state will take on the character of an enterprise association. However, although states may lose some of their civil functions, they may nonetheless be able to retain a vital minimum of authority, capacity, effectiveness, and legitimacy in significant, if circumscribed, areas of economic and social life. In these circumstances, governments may begin to take on the characteristics of U.S. subnational states.

Hypothesis 9

In contrast, where the cumulative impact of the trends posited in hypothesis 1, corollary 2a, and hypotheses 3, 4, and 5 is significantly greater than the combined impact of the trends posited in corollaries 2b and 2c and hypotheses 6 and 7, the state itself will be increasingly characterized by a general loss of civil legitimacy. Under these conditions, government per se will essentially become privatized, losing much of its public character. The world will be a neofeudal one, in which overlapping and democratically unaccountable private regimes, regional arrangements, transnational market structures, "global cities," nongovernmental organizations (NGOs), quasi-autonomous NGOs, and international quasi-autonomous NGOs, with rump governments—the extreme form of the residual state—attempting to ride free on global/local trends for short-term competitive interests. Collective action will take many forms, and the state will be perceived as relatively powerless with regard to the pursuit of a wide range of collective goals.

Hypothesis 10

Finally, under these conditions the state will lose its structural primacy and autonomy as a unitary actor in the international system. The anarchy of the international system will no longer be one of states competing for power but one of neofeudal rivalries and asymmetric cooperation among a range of interests and collective agents reflecting differentiated economic activities with diverse goods/assets structures. These will operate at different institutional levels, in different issue-areas, and according to rules and payoff matrices that will vary with the structure of the particular goods and assets concerned. The interaction among these different forms and levels of collective action will be complex and nonlinear. The main question that remains to be asked is whether such a system will tend toward chaos or toward a certain stability of a plurilateral kind.

II.
International Regimes

The study of international regimes begins with two simple insights. First, in many issues, states adhere to well-understood rules. They adopt and change these rules either through formal international organizations or informal agreements, and they share some expectations about what behavior is likely to occur and what is acceptable. In short, there is patterned cooperation. Second, the specific rules and procedures differ widely across issues, as do the most important actors.

The study of regimes has systematized these insights and tried to explain the main features of order and change. This process involves (1) analyzing the rules, procedures, and patterns of cooperation in specific issues; (2) explaining why particular rule-guided arrangements develop and change; and (3) exploring what effect, if any, these arrangements have on actors' behavior and international outcomes.

This line of inquiry was advanced significantly by International Organization's 1982 publication of a special issue on international regimes. In that issue, editor Stephen Krasner defined regimes as "sets of implicit or explicit principles, norms, rules, and decision-making procedures around which actors' expectations converge in a given area of international relations."[1]

Most scholars accept Krasner's definition, but they vary in how they investigate regimes and what they seek to understand. Some see regimes mainly as outcomes to be explained. Instead of looking at countless national trade policies or bilateral trade arrangements, these analysts draw together the basic rules and procedures and explain their overall shape. For them, regimes are a concise way of summarizing the key characteristics of an issue. Why are merchandise trade, exchange rates, or foreign direct investment organized the way they are? How have the rules changed over time, and why?[2]

Other analysts look mainly at the effect of regimes on transactions or on interactions within an issue area.[3] They ask, "How do regimes matter?" That question is central to Robert O. Keohane's influential essay, "The Demand for International Regimes" (Chapter 5). States often make individual agreements about trade, oil,

---

1. Krasner 1983.
2. See Cowhey 1990; and Nayar 1995.
3. Lipson 1982.

currency, and other issues. The puzzle, he says, is why they need more comprehensive regime arrangements on top of these individual bargains. The answer centers on the high costs of negotiating each bargain from scratch. The process is much easier if states begin with some baseline rules and procedures and then negotiate individual agreements from there. By performing this baseline function, regimes reduce transaction costs, coordinate expectations, and so ease the negotiation of specific bargains. Demand for regimes will be greatest, then, when actors transact frequently and want to establish numerous individual bargains. In such issues, regimes can promote cooperation by lowering information costs.

From the beginning, this kind of analysis has had its critics. Susan Strange, for instance, offered a trenchant view in the Krasner volume itself.[4] She argued that regime theory focuses entirely too much on order and too little on change. The result, she concluded, is inherently conservative. She also criticized the research program for what she considered an overemphasis on state behavior, slighting multinational firms, private actors, and transnational networks. Her criticisms anticipated those that appeared in later work on globalization, such as the Cerny chapter included in this volume (Chapter 4).

Some critics also claim that the definition of regimes is too fuzzy and includes too many disparate elements. Most regime analysts accept at least part of this criticism. They have largely dropped consideration of broad principles that go well beyond individual issues. Instead, they focus more sharply on rules, decision-making procedures, and normative expectations. Another critique was provided by Friedrich Kratochwil and John Gerard Ruggie, who challenged the internal consistency of that focus.[5] The difficulty is that rules and procedures are about observable behavior, whereas norms and expectations are about shared beliefs. These different elements of regimes have to be studied in very different ways—a problem that regime analysts have not fully appreciated, according to Kratochwil and Ruggie, much less resolved.

Some of the most important criticisms of regime theory are drawn together and evaluated in the survey by Stephan Haggard and Beth A. Simmons (Chapter 6). They distinguish among three basic approaches to the study of regimes: game theory, functional approaches, and cognitive theories. Game theory, they conclude, has clarified the conditions for stable cooperation but says little about how regimes arise. Functional theories, like Keohane's, complement game theory and clarify regime effects. By lowering transaction costs and encouraging long-term relationships, regimes promote cooperation. But functional theories have their own generic problems. They identify "functions" after the fact and then attribute causal significance to them. How do we know they are right? Even if regimes do perform important functions, we cannot be certain that is why states constructed them.

According to Haggard and Simmons, state motivations must be studied more directly. That is the aim of cognitive theories, which focus on actors' beliefs, values, and ideologies. Unfortunately, a better understanding of cognition still does not tell

4. Strange 1982.
5. Kratochwil and Ruggie 1986.

us "at what point consensual values or knowledge will produce cooperation." Haggard and Simmons conclude by urging more research on the domestic sources of foreign policy and their relationship to regime cooperation, a program similar to that advocated by Andrew Moravcsik in Chapter 1.

The best empirical work on regimes has shown how these cooperative arrangements actually work in specific issues—how and why particular rules are devised, which actors dominate decision making, what their goals are, and, most of all, how different rules work in practice. Much of this empirical work recognizes the importance of multinational firms as well as states and explores actors' motivations in some detail.

Ronald B. Mitchell's work on pollution by oil tankers (Chapter 7) is an excellent example. Tankers can pollute by inadvertent leaks and deliberate discharges as well as catastrophic collisions. Most states agree on the need to control such pollution, even though doing so may be difficult and expensive. States have actually tried to do that with two very different sets of international rules, a kind of natural experiment that Mitchell analyzes. One method prohibits certain kinds of pollution at sea and sets penalties for violators. The other requires tankers to install expensive equipment that limits pollution.

As it turned out, the installation rules were far more successful, mainly because they were so easy to observe and reinforce with sanctions. Once the largest economies had agreed on the equipment rules, they could simply prevent noncompliant vessels from leaving port. Marine insurance agents and tanker classification groups added their own sanctions and incentives. Insurers demanded proof that the required equipment was installed before they would issue policies—and, of course, they got it. In contrast, states found tracing discharges at sea and imposing sanctions on purported violators to be far more difficult. These rules failed where the equipment rules succeeded. As Mitchell succinctly puts it, "Regime design matters."

Empirical studies like this show why regime analysis has been so important for the field of international political economy. First, it directs investigation—in a systematic and productive way—toward fundamental issues that affect states, firms, and individuals in the world economy. Second, it provides a consistent framework for analysis, one that has led to extensive empirical research. This research is especially valuable because separate contributions speak to each other and cumulate. In one issue area after another, analysts have explored similar questions and provided detailed answers. Much of this scholarship has appeared in International Organization. Examples include work by Vinod K. Aggarwal, Jack Donnelly, John S. Duffield, James A. Dunn, Mark W. Zacher, and Oran Young.[6] Taken together, these research efforts allow us to compare governance arrangements and their effect in major aspects of the world economy.

---

6. See Aggarwal 1983; Donnelly 1986; Duffield 1992; Dunn 1987; Zacher 1987; and Young 1989.

References

Aggarwal, Vinod K. 1983. The Unraveling of the Multi-Fiber Arrangement, 1981: An Examination of International Regime Change. *International Organization* 37 (4):617–45.

Cowhey, Peter F. 1990. The International Telecommunications Regime: The Political Roots of Regimes for High Technology. *International Organization* 44 (2):169–200.

Donnelly, Jack. 1986. International Human Rights: A Regime Analysis. *International Organization* 40 (3):599–642.

Duffield, John S. 1992. International Regimes and Alliance Behavior: Explaining NATO Conventional Force Levels. *International Organization* 46 (4):819–56.

Dunn, James A., Jr. 1987. Automobiles in International Trade: Regime Changes or Persistence? *International Organization* 41 (2):173–202.

Krasner, Stephen D., ed. 1983. *International Regimes*. Ithaca, N.Y.: Cornell University Press. (Originally published as *International Organization* 36 (2).)

Kratochwil, Friedrich, and John Gerard Ruggie. 1986. IO as an Art of the State: A Regime Critique. *International Organization*, 40 (4):753–76.

Lipson, Charles. 1982. The Transformation of Trade: The Sources and Effects of Regime Change. *International Organization* 36 (2):417–55.

Nayar, Baldev Raj. 1995. Regimes, Power, and International Aviation. *International Organization* 49 (1):139–70.

Strange, Susan. 1982. *Cave! Hic Dragones*: A Critique of Regime Analysis. *International Organization* 36 (2):479–96.

Young, Oran. 1989. The Politics of International Regime Formation: Managing Natural Resources and the Environment. *International Organization* 43 (3):349–76.

Zacher, Mark W. 1987. Trade Gaps, Analytical Gaps: Regime Analysis and International Commodity Trade Regulation. *International Organization* 41 (2):173–202.

The demand for
international regimes
Robert O. Keohane

We study international regimes because we are interested in understanding order in world politics. Conflict may be the rule; if so, institutionalized patterns of cooperation are particularly in need of explanation. The theoretical analysis of international regimes begins with what is at
least an apparent anomaly from the standpoint of Realist theory: the existence of many "sets of implicit or explicit principles, norms, rules, and
decision-making procedures around which actor expectations converge," in
a variety of areas of international relations.

This article constitutes an attempt to improve our understanding of international order, and international cooperation, through an interpretation of
international regime-formation that relies heavily on rational-choice analysis
in the utilitarian social contract tradition. I explore why self-interested actors in world politics should seek, under certain circumstances, to establish
international regimes through mutual agreement; and how we can account

The original idea for this paper germinated in discussions at a National Science Foundation-
sponsored conference on International Politics and International Economics held in Minneapolis, Minnesota, in June 1978.

I am indebted to Robert Holt and Anne Krueger for organizing and to the NSF for funding
that meeting. Several knowledgeable friends, particularly Charles Kindleberger, Timothy J.
McKeown, James N. Rosse, and Laura Tyson, provided bibliographical suggestions that helped
me think about the issues discussed here. For written comments on earlier versions of this
article I am especially grateful to Robert Bates, John Chubb, John Conybeare, Colin Day, Alex
Field, Albert Fishlow, Alexander George, Ernst B. Haas, Gerald Helleiner, Harold K. Jacobson, Robert Jervis, Stephen D. Krasner, Helen Milner, Timothy J. McKeown, Robert C. North,
John Ruggie, Ken Shepsle, Arthur Stein, Susan Strange, Harrison Wagner, and David Yoffie. I
also benefited from discussions of earlier drafts at meetings held at Los Angeles in October 1980
and at Palm Springs in February 1981, and from colloquia in Berkeley, California, and Cambridge, Massachusetts.

International Organization 36, 2, Spring 1982, pp. 325–55

for fluctuations over time in the number, extent, and strength of international regimes, on the basis of rational calculation under varying circumstances.

Previous work on this subject in the rational-choice tradition has emphasized the "theory of hegemonic stability": that is, the view that concentration of power in one dominant state facilitates the development of strong regimes, and that fragmentation of power is associated with regime collapse.[1] This theory, however, fails to explain lags between changes in power structures and changes in international regimes; does not account well for the differential durability of different institutions within a given issue-area; and avoids addressing the question of why international regimes seem so much more extensive now in world politics than during earlier periods (such as the late 19th century) of supposed hegemonic leadership.[2]

The argument of this article seeks to correct some of these faults of the hegemonic stability theory by incorporating it within a supply-demand approach that borrows extensively from microeconomic theory. The theory of hegemonic stability can be viewed as focusing only on the supply of international regimes: according to the theory, the more concentrated power is in an international system, the greater the supply of international regimes at any level of demand.[3] But fluctuations in demand for international regimes are not taken into account by the theory; thus it is necessarily incomplete. This article focuses principally on the demand for international regimes in order to provide the basis for a more comprehensive and balanced interpretation.

Emphasizing the demand for international regimes focuses our attention on why we should want them in the first place, rather than taking their desirability as a given. I do not assume that "demand" and "supply" can be specified independently and operationalized as in microeconomics. The same actors are likely to be the "demanders" and the "suppliers." Furthermore, factors affecting the demand for international regimes are likely simultaneously to affect their supply as well. Yet supply and demand language allows us to make a distinction that is useful in distinguishing phenomena that, in the first instance, affect the desire for regimes, on the one hand, or the ease of supplying them, on the other. "Supply and de-

---

[1] See especially Robert O. Keohane, "The Theory of Hegemonic Stability and Changes in International Economic Regimes, 1967–1977," in Ole R. Holsti, Randolph Siverson, and Alexander George, eds., *Changes in the International System* (Boulder: Westview, 1980); and Linda Cahn, "National Power and International Regimes: The United States and International Commodity Markets," Ph.D. diss., Stanford University, 1980.

[2] Current research on the nineteenth century is beginning to question the assumption that Britain was hegemonic in a meaningful sense. See Timothy J. McKeown, "Hegemony Theory and Trade in the Nineteenth Century," paper presented to the International Studies Association convention, Philadelphia, 18–21 March 1981; and Arthur A. Stein, "The Hegemon's Dilemma: Great Britain, the United States, and the International Economic Order," paper presented to the American Political Science Association annual meeting, New York, 3–6 September 1981.

[3] The essential reason for this (discussed below) is that actors that are large relative to the whole set of actors have greater incentives both to provide collective goods themselves and to organize their provision, than do actors that are small relative to the whole set. The classic discussion of this phenomenon appears in Mancur Olson Jr., *The Logic of Collective Action: Political Goods and the Theory of Groups* (Cambridge: Harvard University Press, 1965).

mand'' should be seen in this analysis as a metaphor, rather than an attempt artificially to separate, or to reify, different aspects of an interrelated process.[4]

Before proceeding to the argument, two caveats are in order. First, the focus of this article is principally on the *strength* and *extent* of international regimes, rather than on their *content* or *effects*. I hope to contribute to understanding why international regimes wax and wane, leaving to others (in this volume and elsewhere) the analysis of what ideologies they encompass or how much they affect ultimate, value-laden outcomes. The only significant exception to this avoidance of questions of content comes in Section 5, which distinguishes between control-oriented and insurance-oriented regimes. Second, no claim is made here that rational-choice analysis is the only valid way to understand international regimes, or even that it is preferable to others. On the contrary, I view rational-choice analysis as one way to generate an insightful interpretation of international regimes that complements interpretations derived from analyses of conventions and of learning (illustrated in the articles in this volume by Young and Haas). My analysis is designed to be neither comprehensive nor exclusive: I suggest hypotheses and try to make what we know more intelligible, rather than seeking to put forward a definitive theory of international regimes.

The major arguments of this article are grouped in five sections. First, I outline the analytical approach by discussing the virtues and limitations of "systemic constraint-choice analysis." Section 2 lays the basis for the development of a constraint-choice theory of international regimes by specifying the context within which international regimes operate and the functions they perform. In Section 3 elements of a theory of the demand for international regimes are presented, emphasizing the role of regimes in reducing transactions costs and coping with uncertainty. In Section 4, I use insights from theories of information and uncertainty to discuss issues of closure and communication. Section 5 suggests that control-oriented regimes are likely to be increasingly supplemented in the 1980s by insurance regimes as the dominance of the advanced industrial countries in the world political economy declines.

1. Systemic constraint-choice analysis: virtues and limitations

The argument developed here is deliberately limited to the *systemic* level of analysis. In a systemic theory, the actors' characteristics are given by assumption, rather than treated as variables; changes in outcomes are explained not on the basis of variations in these actor characteristics, but on the basis of changes in the attributes of the system itself. Microeconomic theory, for instance, posits the existence of business firms, with given utility

---

[4] I am indebted to Albert Fishlow for clarifying this point for me.

functions, and attempts to explain their behavior on the basis of environmental factors such as the competitiveness of markets. It is therefore a systemic theory, unlike the so-called "behavioral theory of the firm," which examines the actors for internal variations that could account for behavior not predicted by microeconomic theory.

A systemic focus permits a limitation of the number of variables that need to be considered. In the initial steps of theory-building, this is a great advantage: attempting to take into account at the outset factors at the foreign policy as well as the systemic level would lead quickly to descriptive complexity and theoretical anarchy. Beginning the analysis at the systemic level establishes a baseline for future work. By seeing how well a simple model accounts for behavior, we understand better the value of introducing more variables and greater complexity into the analysis. Without the systemic microeconomic theory of the firm, for instance, it would not have been clear what puzzles needed to be solved by an actor-oriented behavioral theory.

A systems-level examination of changes in the strength and extent of international regimes over time could proceed through historical description. We could examine a large number of cases, attempting to extract generalizations about patterns from the data. Our analysis could be explicitly comparative, analyzing different regimes within a common analytical framework, employing a methodology such as George's "focused comparison."[5] Such a systematic comparative description could be quite useful, but it would not provide a theoretical framework for posing questions of why, and under what conditions, regimes should be expected to develop or become stronger. Posing such fundamental issues is greatly facilitated by *a priori* reasoning that makes specific predictions to be compared with empirical findings. Such reasoning helps us to reinterpret previously observed patterns of behavior as well as suggesting new questions about behavior or distinctions that have been ignored: it has the potential of "discovering new facts."[6] This can be useful even in a subject such as international politics, where the variety of relevant variables is likely to confound any comprehensive effort to build deductive theory. Deductive analysis can thus be used in interpretation as well as in a traditional strategy of theory-building and hypothesis-testing.

This analysis follows the tradition of microeconomic theory by focusing on constraints and incentives that affect the choices made by actors.[7] We

[5] Alexander L. George, "Case Studies and Theory Development: The Method of Structured, Focused Comparison," in Paul Lauren, ed., *Diplomacy: New Approaches in History, Theory, and Policy* (New York: Free Press, 1979).

[6] Imre Lakatos, "Falsification and the Methodology of Scientific Research Programmes," in Lakatos and Alan Musgrave, eds., *Criticism and the Growth of Scientific Knowledge* (Cambridge: Cambridge University Press, 1970).

[7] Stimulating discussions of microeconomic theory can be found in Martin Shubik, "A Curmudgeon's Guide to Microeconomics," *Journal of Economic Literature* 8 (1970): 405–434; and Spiro J. Latsis, "A Research Programme in Economics," in Latsis, ed., *Method and Appraisal in Economics* (Cambridge: Cambridge University Press, 1976).

assume that, in general, actors in world politics tend to respond rationally to constraints and incentives. Changes in the characteristics of the international system will alter the opportunity costs to actors of various courses of action, and will therefore lead to changes in behavior. In particular, decisions about creating or joining international regimes will be affected by system-level changes in this way; in this model the demand for international regimes is a function of system characteristics.

This article therefore employs a form of rational-choice analysis, which I prefer to term "constraint-choice" analysis to indicate that I do not make some of the extreme assumptions often found in the relevant literature. I assume a prior context of power, expectations, values, and conventions; I do not argue that rational-choice analysis can derive international regimes from a "state of nature" through logic alone.[8] This paper also eschews deterministic claims, or the *hubris* of believing that a complete explanation can be developed through resort to deductive models. To believe this would commit one to a narrowly rationalistic form of analysis in which expectations of gain provide both necessary and sufficient explanations of behavior.[9] Such beliefs in the power of Benthamite calculation have been undermined by the insufficiency of microeconomic theories of the firm—despite their great value as initial approximations—as shown by the work of organization theorists such as Simon, Cyert, and March.[10]

Rational-choice theory is not advanced here as a magic key to unlock the secrets of international regime change, much less as a comprehensive way of interpreting reality. Nor do I employ it as a means of explaining particular actions of specific actors. Rather, I use rational-choice theory to develop models that help to explain trends or tendencies toward which patterns of behavior tend to converge. That is, I seek to account for typical, or modal, behavior. This analysis will not accurately predict the decisions of all actors, or what will happen to all regimes; but it should help to account for overall trends in the formation, growth, decay, and dissolution of regimes. The deductive logic of this approach makes it possible to generate hypotheses about international regime change on an *a priori* basis. In this article several such hypotheses will be suggested, although their testing will have to await further specification. We shall therefore be drawing on microeconomic theories and rational-choice approaches heuristically, to help us con-

---

[8] I am indebted to Alexander J. Field for making the importance of this point clear to me. See his paper, "The Problem with Neoclassical Institutional Economics: A Critique with Special Reference to the North/Thomas Model of Pre–1500 Europe," *Explorations in Economic History* 18 (April 1981).

[9] Lance E. Davis and Douglass C. North adopt this strong form of rationalistic explanation when they argue that "an institutional arrangement will be innovated if the expected net gains exceed the expected costs." See their volume, *Institutional Change and American Economic Growth* (Cambridge: Cambridge University Press, 1971).

[10] Two of the classic works are James March and Herbert Simon, *Organizations* (New York: Wiley, 1958); and Richard Cyert and James March, *The Behavioral Theory of the Firm* (Englewood Cliffs, N.J.: Prentice-Hall, 1963).

struct nontrivial hypotheses about international regime change that can guide future research.

The use of rational-choice theory implies that we must view decisions involving international regimes as in some meaningful sense voluntary. Yet we know that world politics is a realm in which power is exercised regularly and in which inequalities are great. How, then, can we analyze international regimes with a voluntaristic mode of analysis?

My answer is to distinguish two aspects of the process by which international regimes come into being: the imposition of constraints, and decision making. Constraints are dictated not only by environmental factors but also by powerful actors. Thus when we speak of an "imposed regime," we are speaking (in my terminology) of a regime agreed upon within constraints that are mandated by powerful actors.[11] Any agreement that results from bargaining will be affected by the opportunity costs of alternatives faced by the various actors: that is, by which party has the greater need for agreement with the other.[12] Relationships of power and dependence in world politics will therefore be important determinants of the characteristics of international regimes. Actor choices will be constrained in such a way that the preferences of more powerful actors will be accorded greater weight. Thus in applying rational-choice theory to the formation and maintenance of international regimes, we have to be continually sensitive to the structural context within which agreements are made. Voluntary choice does not imply equality of situation or outcome.

We do not necessarily sacrifice realism when we analyze international regimes as the products of voluntary agreements among independent actors within the context of prior constraints. Constraint-choice analysis effectively captures the nonhierarchical nature of world politics without ignoring the role played by power and inequality. Within this analytical framework, a systemic analysis that emphasizes constraints on choice and effects of system characteristics on collective outcomes provides an appropriate way to address the question of regime formation.

Constraint-choice analysis emphasizes that international regimes should not be seen as quasi-governments—imperfect attempts to institutionalize centralized authority relationships in world politics. Regimes are more like contracts, when these involve actors with long-term objectives who seek to structure their relationships in stable and mutually beneficial ways.[13] In

---

[11] For a discussion of "spontaneous," "negotiated," and "imposed" regimes, see Oran Young's contribution to this volume.

[12] For a lucid and original discussion based on this obvious but important point, see John Harsanyi, "Measurement of Social Power, Opportunity Costs and the Theory of Two-Person Bargaining Games," *Behavioral Science* 7, 1 (1962): 67–80. See also Albert O. Hirschman, *National Power and the Structure of Foreign Trade* (1945; Berkeley: University of California Press, 1980), especially pp. 45–48.

[13] S. Todd Lowry, "Bargain and Contract Theory in Law and Economics," in Warren J. Samuels, ed., *The Economy as a System of Power* (New Brunswick, N.J.: Transaction Books, 1979), p. 276.

some respects, regimes resemble the "quasi-agreements" that Fellner discusses when analyzing the behavior of oligopolistic firms.[14] In both contracts and quasi-agreements, there may be specific rules having to do with prices, quantities, delivery dates, and the like; for contracts, some of these rules may be legally enforceable. The most important functions of these arrangements, however, are not to preclude further negotiations, but to establish stable mutual expectations about others' patterns of behavior and to develop working relationships that will allow the parties to adapt their practices to new situations. Rules of international regimes are frequently changed, bent, or broken to meet the exigencies of the moment. They are rarely enforced automatically, and they are not self-executing. Indeed, they are often matters for negotiation and renegotiation; as Puchala has argued, "attempts to enforce EEC regulations open political cleavages up and down the supranational-to-local continuum and spark intense politicking along the cleavage lines."[15]

This lack of binding authority associated with international regimes has important implications for our selection of analytical approaches within a constraint-choice framework: it leads us to rely more heavily on microeconomic, market-oriented theory than on theories of public choice. Most public-choice theory is not applicable to international regime change because it focuses on the processes by which authoritative, binding decisions are made within states.[16] Yet in international politics, binding decisions, arrived at through highly institutionalized, rule-oriented processes, are relatively rare and unimportant, and such decisions do not constitute the essence of international regimes. Traditional microeconomic supply and demand analysis, by contrast, assumes a situation in which choices are made continuously over a period of time by actors for whom "exit"—refusal to purchase goods or services that are offered—is an ever-present option. This conforms more closely to the situation faced by states contemplating whether to create, join, remain members of, or leave international regimes. Since no binding decisions can be made, it is possible to imagine a market for international regimes as one thinks of an economic market: on the basis of an analysis of relative prices and cost-benefit calculations, actors decide which regimes to "buy." In general, we expect states to join those regimes in which they expect the benefits of membership to outweigh the costs. In such an analysis, observed changes in the extent and strength of international

[14] William Fellner, *Competition among the Few* (New York: Knopf, 1949).

[15] Donald J. Puchala, "Domestic Politics and Regional Harmonization in the European Communities," *World Politics* 27,4 (July 1975), p. 509.

[16] There are exceptions to this generalization, such as Tiebout's "voting with the feet" models of population movements among communities. Yet only one chapter of fourteen in a recent survey of the public-choice literature is devoted to such models, which do not focus on authoritative decision-making processes. See Dennis C. Mueller, *Public Choice* (Cambridge: Cambridge University Press, 1980). For a brilliantly innovative work on "exit" versus "voice" processes, see Albert O. Hirschman, *Exit, Voice, and Loyalty* (Cambridge: Harvard University Press, 1970).

regimes may be explained by reference to changes either in the characteristics of the international system (the context within which actors make choices) or of the international regimes themselves (about which the choices are made).

This constraint-choice approach draws attention to the question of why disadvantaged actors join international regimes even when they receive fewer benefits than other members—an issue ignored by arguments that regard certain regimes as simply imposed. Weak actors as well as more powerful actors make choices, even if they make them within more severe constraints. (Whether such choices, made under severe constraint, imply obligations for the future is another question, one not addressed here.)[17]

2. The context and functions of international regimes

Analysis of international regime-formation within a constraint-choice framework requires that one specify the nature of the context within which actors make choices and the functions of the institutions whose patterns of growth and decay are being explained. Two features of the international context are particularly important: world politics lacks authoritative governmental institutions, and is characterized by pervasive uncertainty. Within this setting, a major function of international regimes is to facilitate the making of mutually beneficial agreements among governments, so that the structural condition of anarchy does not lead to a complete "war of all against all."

The actors in our model operate within what Waltz has called a "self-help system," in which they cannot call on higher authority to resolve difficulties or provide protection.[18] Negative externalities are common: states are forever impinging on one another's interests.[19] In the absence of authoritative global institutions, these conflicts of interest produce uncertainty and risk: possible future evils are often even more terrifying than present ones. All too obvious with respect to matters of war and peace, this is also characteristic of the international economic environment.

Actors in world politics may seek to reduce conflicts of interest and risk

[17] Anyone who has thought about Hobbes's tendentious discussion of "voluntary" agreements in *Leviathan* realizes the dangers of casuistry entailed in applying voluntaristic analysis to politics, especially when obligations are inferred from choices. This article follows Hobbes's distinction between the structure of constraints in a situation, on the one hand, and actor choices, on the other; but it does not adopt his view that even severely constrained choices ("your freedom or your life") create moral or political obligations.

[18] Kenneth N. Waltz, *Theory of International Politics* (Reading, Mass.: Addison-Wesley, 1979).

[19] Externalities exist whenever an acting unit does not bear all of the costs, or fails to reap all of the benefits, that result from its behavior. See Davis and North, *Institutional Change and American Economic Growth*, p. 16.

by coordinating their behavior. Yet coordination has many of the characteristics of a public good, which leads us to expect that its production will be too low.[20] That is, increased production of these goods, which would yield net benefits, is not undertaken. This insight is the basis of the major "supply-side" argument about international regimes, epitomized by the theory of hegemonic stability. According to this line of argument, hegemonic international systems should be characterized by levels of public goods production higher than in fragmented systems; and, if international regimes provide public goods, by stronger and more extensive international regimes.[21]

This argument, important though it is, ignores what I have called the "demand" side of the problem of international regimes: why should governments desire to institute international regimes in the first place, and how much will they be willing to contribute to maintain them? Addressing these issues will help to correct some of the deficiencies of the theory of hegemonic stability, which derive from its one-sidedness, and will contribute to a more comprehensive interpretation of international regime change. The familiar context of world politics—its competitiveness, uncertainty, and conflicts of interest—not only sets limits on the supply of international regimes, but provides a basis for understanding why they are demanded.

Before we can understand why regimes are demanded, however, it is necessary to establish what the functions of international regimes, from the perspective of states, might be.[22]

At the most specific level, students of international cooperation are interested in myriads of particular agreements made by governments: to

[20] Olson, *The Logic of Collection Action;* Bruce M. Russett and John D. Sullivan, "Collective Goods and International Organization," with a comment by Mancur Olson Jr., *International Organization* 25,4 (Autumn 1971); John Gerard Ruggie, "Collective Goods and Future International Collaboration," *American Political Science Review* 66,3 (September 1972); Duncan Snidal, "Public Goods, Property Rights, and Political Organization," *International Studies Quarterly* 23,4 (December 1979), p. 544.

[21] Keohane, "The Theory of Hegemonic Stability"; Charles P. Kindleberger, *The World in Depression, 1929–1939* (Berkeley: University of California Press, 1974); Mancur Olson and Richard Zeckhauser, "An Economic Theory of Alliances," *Review of Economics and Statistics* 48,3 (August 1966), reprinted in Bruce M. Russett, ed., *Economic Theories of International Politics* (Chicago: Markham, 1968). For a critical appraisal of work placing emphasis on public goods as a rationale for forming international organizations, see John A. C. Conybeare, "International Organizations and the Theory of Property Rights," *International Organization* 34,3 (Summer 1980), especially pp. 329–32.

[22] My use of the word "functions" here is meant to designate consequences of a certain pattern of activity, particularly in terms of the utility of the activity; it is not to be interpreted as an explanation of the behavior in question, since there is no teleological premise, or assumption that necessity is involved. Understanding the function of international regimes helps, however, to explain why actors have an incentive to create them, and may therefore help to make behavior intelligible within a rational-choice mode of analysis that emphasizes the role of incentives and constraints. For useful distinctions on functionalism, see Ernest Nagel, *The Structure of Scientific Explanation* (New York: Harcourt, Brace, 1961), especially "Functionalism and Social Science," pp. 520–35. I am grateful to Robert Packenham for this reference and discussions of this point.

maintain their exchange rates within certain limits, to refrain from trade discrimination, to reduce their imports of petroleum, or progressively to reduce tariffs. These agreements are made despite the fact that, compared to domestic political institutions, the institutions of world politics are extremely weak: an authoritative legal framework is lacking and regularized institutions for conducting transactions (such as markets backed by state authority or binding procedures for making and enforcing contracts) are often poorly developed.

Investigation of the sources of specific agreements reveals that they are not, in general, made on an *ad hoc* basis, nor do they follow a random pattern. Instead, they are "nested" within more comprehensive agreements, covering more issues. An agreement among the United States, Japan, and the European Community in the Multilateral Trade Negotiations to reduce a particular tariff is affected by the rules, norms, principles, and procedures of the General Agreement on Tariffs and Trade (GATT)—that is, by the trade regime. The trade regime, in turn, is nested within a set of other arrangements—including those for monetary relations, energy, foreign investment, aid to developing countries, and other issues—that together constitute a complex and interlinked pattern of relations among the advanced market-economy countries. These, in turn, are related to military-security relations among the major states.[23]

Within this multilayered system, a major function of international regimes is to facilitate the making of specific agreements on matters of substantive significance within the issue-area covered by the regime. International regimes help to make governments' expectations consistent with one another. Regimes are developed in part because actors in world politics believe that with such arrangements they will be able to make mutually beneficial agreements that would otherwise be difficult or impossible to attain. In other words, regimes are valuable to governments where, in their absence, certain mutually beneficial agreements would be impossible to consummate. In such situations, *ad hoc* joint action would be inferior to results of negotiation within a regime context.

Yet this characterization of regimes immediately suggests an explanatory puzzle. Why should it be worthwhile to construct regimes (themselves requiring agreement) in order to make specific agreements within the regime frameworks? Why is it not more efficient simply to avoid the regime stage and make the agreements on an *ad hoc* basis? In short, why is there any demand for international regimes apart from a demand for international agreements on particular questions?

An answer to this question is suggested by theories of "market failure" in economics. Market failure refers to situations in which the outcomes of

---

[23] Vinod Aggarwal has developed the concept of "nesting" in his work on international regimes in textiles since World War II. I am indebted to him for this idea, which has been elaborated in his "Hanging by a Thread: International Regime Change in the Textile/Apparel System, 1950–1979," Ph.D. diss., Stanford University, 1981.

market-mediated interaction are suboptimal (given the utility functions of actors and the resources at their disposal). Agreements that would be beneficial to all parties are not made. In situations of market failure, economic activities uncoordinated by hierarchical authority lead to *in*efficient results, rather than to the efficient outcomes expected under conditions of perfect competition. In the theory of market failure, the problems are attributed not to inadequacies of the actors themselves (who are presumed to be rational utility-maximizers) but rather to the structure of the system and the institutions, or lack thereof, that characterize it.[24] Specific attributes of the system impose transactions costs (including information costs) that create barriers to effective cooperation among the actors. Thus institutional defects are responsible for failures of coordination. To correct these defects, conscious institutional innovation may be necessary, although a good economist will always compare the costs of institutional innovation with the costs of market failure before recommending tampering with the market.

Like imperfect markets, world politics is characterized by institutional deficiencies that inhibit mutually advantageous coordination. Some of the deficiencies revolve around problems of transactions costs and uncertainty that have been cogently analyzed by students of market failure. Theories of market failure specify types of institutional imperfections that may inhibit agreement; international regimes may be interpreted as helping to correct similar institutional defects in world politics. Insofar as regimes are established through voluntary agreement among a number of states, we can interpret them, at least in part, as devices to overcome the barriers to more efficient coordination identified by theories of market failure.[25]

The analysis that follows is based on two theoretical assumptions. First, the actors whose behavior we analyze act, in general, as rational utility-maximizers in that they display consistent tendencies to adjust to external changes in ways that are calculated to increase the expected value of outcomes to them. Second, the international regimes with which we are concerned are devices to facilitate the making of agreements among these actors. From these assumptions it follows that the demand for international regimes

---

[24] Of particular value for understanding market failure is Kenneth J. Arrow, *Essays in the Theory of Risk-Bearing* (New York: North Holland/American Elsevier, 1974).

[25] Helen Milner suggested to me that international regimes were in this respect like credit markets, and that the history of the development of credit markets could be informative for students of international regimes. The analogy seems to hold. Richard Ehrenberg reports that the development of credit arrangements in medieval European Bourses reduced transaction costs (since money did not need to be transported in the form of specie) and provided high-quality information in the form of merchants' newsletters and exchanges of information at fairs: "during the Middle Ages the best information as to the course of events in the world was regularly to be obtained in the fairs and the Bourses" (p. 317). The Bourses also provided credit ratings, which provided information but also served as a crude substitute for effective systems of legal liability. Although the descriptions of credit market development in works such as that by Ehrenberg are fascinating, I have not been able to find a historically-grounded theory of these events. See Richard Ehrenberg, *Capital and Finance in the Age of the Renaissance: A Study of the Fuggers and Their Connections,* translated from the German by H. M. Lucas (New York: Harcourt, Brace, no date), especially chap. 3 (pp. 307–333).

at any given price will vary directly with the desirability of agreements to states and with the ability of international regimes actually to facilitate the making of such agreements. The condition for the theory's operation (that is, for regimes to be formed) is that sufficient complementary or common interests exist so that agreements benefiting all essential regime members can be made.

The value of theories of market failure for this analysis rests on the fact that they allow us to identify more precisely barriers to agreements. They therefore suggest insights into how international regimes help to reduce those barriers, and they provide richer interpretations of previously observed, but unexplained, phenomena associated with international regimes and international policy coordination. In addition, concepts of market failure help to explain the strength and extent of international regimes by identifying characteristics of international systems, or of international regimes themselves, that affect the demand for such regimes and therefore, given a supply schedule, their quantity. Insights from the market-failure literature therefore take us beyond the trivial cost-benefit or supply-demand propositions with which we began, to hypotheses about relationships that are less familiar.

The emphasis on efficiency in the market-failure literature is consistent with our constraint-choice analysis of the decision-making processes leading to the formation and maintenance of international regimes. Each actor must be as well or better off with the regime than without it—given the prior structure of constraints. This does not imply, of course, that the whole process leading to the formation of a new international regime will yield overall welfare benefits. Outsiders may suffer; indeed, some international regimes (such as alliances or cartel-type regimes) are specifically designed to impose costs on them. These costs to outsiders may well outweigh the benefits to members. In addition, powerful actors may manipulate constraints prior to the formation of a new regime. In that case, although the regime *per se* may achieve overall welfare improvements compared to the immediately preceding situation, the results of the joint process may be inferior to those that existed before the constraints were imposed.

3. Elements of a theory of the demand for international regimes

We are now in a position to address our central puzzle—why is there any demand for international regimes?—and to outline a theory to explain why this demand exists. First, it is necessary to use our distinction between "agreements" and "regimes" to pose the issue precisely: given a certain level of demand for international agreements, what will affect the demand for international regimes? The Coase theorem, from the market-failure literature, will then be used to develop a list of conditions under which international regimes are of potential value for facilitating agreements in world politics. This typological analysis turns our attention toward two central problems, *transactions cost* and *informational imperfections.* Questions of information, involving uncertainty and risk, will receive particular attention, since their exploration has rich implications for interpretation and future research.

The demand for agreements and the demand for regimes

It is crucial to distinguish clearly between international regimes, on the one hand, and mere *ad hoc* substantive agreements, on the other. Regimes, as argued above, facilitate the making of substantive agreements by providing a framework of rules, norms, principles, and procedures for negotiation. A theory of international regimes must explain why these intermediate arrangements are necessary.

In our analysis, the demand for agreements will be regarded as exogenous. It may be influenced by many factors, particularly by the perceptions that leaders of governments have about their interests in agreement or nonagreement. These perceptions will, in turn, be influenced by domestic politics, ideology, and other factors not encompassed by a systemic, constraint-choice approach. In the United States, "internationalists" have been attracted to international agreements and international organizations as useful devices for implementing American foreign policy; "isolationists" and "nationalists" have not. Clearly, such differences cannot be accounted for by our theory. We therefore assume a given desire for agreements and ask: under these conditions, what will be the demand for international regimes?

Under certain circumstances defining the demand and supply of agreements, there will be no need for regimes and we should expect none to form. This will be the situation in two extreme cases, where demand for agreements is nil and where the supply of agreements is infinitely elastic and free (so that all conceivable agreements can be made costlessly). But where the demand for agreements is positive at some level of feasible cost, and the supply of agreements is not infinitely elastic and free, there may be a demand for international regimes *if* they actually make possible agreements yielding net benefits that would not be possible on an *ad hoc* basis. In such a situation regimes can be regarded as "efficient." We can now ask: under what specific conditions will international regimes be efficient?

One way to address this question is to pose its converse. To ask about the conditions under which international regimes will be *worthless* enables us to draw on work in social choice, particularly by Ronald Coase. Coase was able to show that the presence of externalities alone does not necessarily prevent Pareto-optimal coordination among independent actors: under certain conditions, bargaining among these actors could lead to Pareto-optimal solutions. The key conditions isolated by Coase were (a) a legal framework establishing liability for actions, presumably supported by governmental authority; (b) perfect information; and (c) zero transactions costs (including organization costs and costs of making side-payments).[26] If all these conditions were met in world politics, *ad hoc* agreements would be costless and regimes unnecessary. *At least one of them must not be fulfilled if international regimes are to be of value, as facilitators of agreement, to independent utility-maximizing actors in world politics.* Inverting the Coase theorem provides us, therefore, with a list of conditions, at least one of which must apply if regimes are to be of value in facilitating agreements among governments:[27]

(a) lack of a clear legal framework establishing liability for actions;
(b) information imperfections (information is costly);
(c) positive transactions costs.[28]

In world politics, of course, *all* of these conditions are met all of the time: world government does not exist; information is extremely costly and often impossible to obtain; transactions costs, including costs of organization and side-payments, are often very high. Yet the Coase theorem is useful not merely as a way of categorizing these familiar problems, but because it suggests how international regimes can improve actors' abilities to make mutually beneficial agreements. Regimes can make agreement easier if they provide frameworks for establishing legal liability (even if these are not perfect); improve the quantity and quality of information available to actors; or reduce other transactions costs, such as costs of organization or of making side-payments. This typology allows us to specify regime functions—as devices to make agreements possible—more precisely, and therefore to understand demand for international regimes. Insofar as international regimes can correct institutional defects in world politics along any of these three dimensions (liability, information, transactions costs), they may become efficient devices for the achievement of state purposes.

Regimes do not establish binding and enforceable legal liabilities in any strict or ultimately reliable sense, although the lack of a hierarchical struc-

---

[26] Ronald Coase, "The Problem of Social Cost," *Journal of Law and Economics* 3 (October 1960). For a discussion, see James Buchanan and Gordon Tullock, *The Calculus of Consent: Logical Foundations of Constitutional Democracy* (Ann Arbor: University of Michigan Press, 1962), p. 186.

[27] If we were to drop the assumption that actors are strictly self-interested utility-maximizers, regimes could be important in another way: they would help to develop norms that are internalized by actors as part of their own utility functions. This is important in real-world political-economic systems, as works by Schumpeter, Polanyi, and Hirsch on the moral underpinnings of a market system indicate. It is likely to be important in many international systems as well. But it is outside the scope of the analytical approach taken in this article—which is designed to illuminate some issues, but not to provide a comprehensive account of international regime change. See Joseph Schumpeter, *Capitalism, Socialism, and Democracy* (New York: Harper & Row, 1942), especially Part II, "Can Capitalism Survive?"; Karl Polanyi, *The Great Transformation: The Political and Economic Origins of Our Time* (1944; Boston: Beacon Press, 1957); and Fred Hirsch, *Social Limits to Growth* (Cambridge: Harvard University Press, 1976).

[28] Information costs could be considered under the category of transaction costs, but they are so important that I categorize them separately in order to give them special attention.

ture does not prevent the development of bits and pieces of law.[29] Regimes are much more important in providing established negotiating frameworks (reducing transactions costs) and in helping to coordinate actor expectations (improving the quality and quantity of information available to states). An explanation of these two functions of international regimes, with the help of microeconomic analysis, will lead to hypotheses about how the demand for international regimes should be expected to vary with changes in the nature of the international system (in the case of transactions costs) and about effects of characteristics of the international regime itself (in the case of information).

International regimes and transactions costs

Neither international agreements nor international regimes are created spontaneously. Political entrepreneurs must exist who see a potential profit in organizing collaboration. For entrepreneurship to develop, not only must there be a potential social gain to be derived from the formation of an international arrangement, but the entrepreneur (usually, in world politics, a government) must expect to be able to gain more itself from the regime than it invests in organizing the activity. Thus organizational costs to the entrepreneur must be lower than the net discounted value of the benefits that the entrepreneur expects to capture for itself.[30] As a result, international cooperation that would have a positive social payoff may not be initiated unless a potential entrepreneur would profit sufficiently. This leads us back into questions of supply and the theory of hegemonic stability, since such a situation is most likely to exist where no potential entrepreneur is large relative to the whole set of potential beneficiaries, and where "free riders" cannot be prevented from benefiting from cooperation without paying proportionately.

Our attention here, however, is on the demand side: we focus on the efficiency of constructing international regimes, as opposed simply to making *ad hoc* agreements. We only expect regimes to develop where the costs of making *ad hoc* agreements on particular substantive matters are higher than the sum of the costs of making such agreements within a regime framework and the costs of establishing that framework.

With respect to transactions costs, where do we expect these conditions to be met? To answer this question, it is useful to introduce the concept of *issue density* to refer to the number and importance of issues arising within a given policy space. The denser the policy space, the more highly interdependent are the different issues, and therefore the agreements made about

---

[29] For a discussion of "the varieties of international law," see Louis Henkin, *How Nations Behave: Law and Foreign Policy*, 2d ed. (New York: Columbia University Press for the Council on Foreign Relations, 1979), pp. 13–22.

[30] Davis and North, *Institutional Change and American Economic Growth*, especially pp. 51–57.

them. Where issue density is low, *ad hoc* agreements are quite likely to be adequate: different agreements will not impinge on one another significantly, and there will be few economies of scale associated with establishing international regimes (each of which would encompass only one or a few agreements). Where issue density is high, on the other hand, one substantive objective may well impinge on another and regimes will achieve economies of scale, for instance in establishing negotiating procedures that are applicable to a variety of potential agreements within similar substantive areas of activity.[31]

Furthermore, in dense policy spaces, complex linkages will develop among substantive issues. Reducing industrial tariffs without damaging one's own economy may depend on agricultural tariff reductions from others; obtaining passage through straits for one's own warships may depend on wider decisions taken about territorial waters; the sale of food to one country may be more or less advantageous depending on other food-supply contracts being made at the same time. As linkages such as these develop, the organizational costs involved in reconciling distinct objectives will rise and demands for overall frameworks of rules, norms, principles, and procedures to cover certain clusters of issues—that is, for international regimes—will increase.

International regimes therefore seem often to facilitate side-payments among actors within issue-areas covered by comprehensive regimes, since they bring together negotiators to consider a whole complex of issues. Side-payments in general are difficult in world politics and raise serious issues of transaction costs: in the absence of a price system for the exchange of favors, these institutional imperfections will hinder cooperation.[32] International regimes may provide a partial corrective.[33] The well-known literature on "spillover" in bargaining, relating to the European Community and other integration schemes, can also be interpreted as being concerned with side-

[31] The concept of issue density bears some relationship to Herbert Simon's notion of "decomposability," in *The Sciences of the Artificial* (Cambridge: MIT Press, 1969). In both cases, problems that can be conceived of as separate are closely linked to one another functionally, so that it is difficult to affect one without also affecting others. Issue density is difficult to operationalize, since the universe (the "issue-area" or "policy space") whose area forms the denominator of the term cannot easily be specified precisely. But given a certain definition of the issue-area, it is possible to trace the increasing density of issues within it over time. See, for example, Robert O. Keohane and Joseph S. Nye, *Power and Interdependence: World Politics in Transition* (Boston: Little, Brown, 1977), chap. 4.

[32] On questions of linkage, see Arthur A. Stein, "The Politics of Linkage," *World Politics* 33,1 (October 1980): 62–81; Kenneth Oye, "The Domain of Choice," in Oye et al., *Eagle Entangled: U.S. Foreign Policy in a Complex World* (New York: Longmans, 1979), pp. 3–33; and Robert D. Tollison and Thomas D. Willett, "An Economic Theory of Mutually Advantageous Issue Linkage in International Negotiations," *International Organization* 33,4 (Autumn 1979).

[33] GATT negotiations and deliberations on the international monetary system have been characterized by extensive bargaining over side-payments and complex politics of issue-linkage. For a discussion see Nicholas Hutton, "The Salience of Linkage in International Economic Negotiations," *Journal of Common Market Studies* 13, 1–2 (1975): 136–60.

payments. In this literature, expectations that an integration arrangement can be expanded to new issue-areas permit the broadening of potential side-payments, thus facilitating agreement.[34]

It should be noted, however, that regimes may make it more difficult to link issues that are clustered separately. Governments tend to organize themselves consistently with how issues are treated internationally, as well as vice versa; issues considered by different regimes are often dealt with by different bureaucracies at home. Linkages and side-payments become difficult under these conditions, since they always involve losses as well as gains. Organizational subunits that would lose, on issues that matter to them, from a proposed side-payment are unlikely to support it on the basis of another agency's claim that it is in the national interest. Insofar as the dividing lines between international regimes place related issues in different jurisdictions, they may well make side-payments and linkages between these issues less feasible.

The crucial point about regimes to be derived from this discussion of transactions costs can be stated succinctly: the optimal size of a regime will increase if there are increasing rather than diminishing returns to regime-scale (reflecting the high costs of making separate agreements in a dense policy space), or if the marginal costs of organization decline as regime size grows. The point about increasing returns suggests an analogy with the theory of imperfect competition among firms. As Samuelson notes, "increasing returns is the prime case of deviations from perfect competition."[35] In world politics, increasing returns to scale lead to more extensive international regimes.

The research hypothesis to be derived from this analysis is that increased issue density will lead to greater demand for international regimes and to more extensive regimes. Since greater issue density is likely to be a feature of situations of high interdependence, this forges a link between interdependence and international regimes: increases in the former can be expected to lead to increases in demand for the latter.[36]

The demand for principles and norms

The definition of international regimes provided in the introduction to this volume stipulates that regimes must embody principles ("beliefs of fact, causation, and rectitude") and norms ("standards of behavior defined in

[34] Ernst B. Haas, *The Uniting of Europe* (Stanford: Stanford University Press, 1958).

[35] Paul A. Samuelson, "The Monopolistic Competition Revolution," in R. E. Kuenne, ed., *Monopolistic Competition Theory* (New York: Wiley, 1967), p. 117.

[36] Increases in issue density could make it more difficult to supply regimes; the costs of providing regimes could grow, for instance, as a result of multiple linkages across issues. The 1970s Law of the Sea negotiations illustrate this problem. As a result, it will not necessarily be the case that increases in interdependence will lead to increases in the number, extensiveness, and strength of international regimes.

terms of rights and obligations'') as well as rules and decision-making procedures.[37] Otherwise, international regimes would be difficult to distinguish
from any regular patterns of action in world politics that create common
expectations about behavior: even hostile patterns of interactions could be
seen as embodying regimes if the observer could infer implied rules and
decision-making procedures from behavior.

Arguments about definitions are often tedious. What is important is not
whether this definition is "correct," but that principles and norms are integral parts of many, if not all, of the arrangements that we regard as international regimes. This raises the question of why, in interactions (such as those
of world politics) characterized by conflict arising from self-interest, norms
and principles should play any role at all.

The constraint-choice framework used in this article is not the best approach for describing how principles and norms of state behavior evolve
over time. The legal and sociological approaches discussed in this volume by
Young are better adapted to the task of historical interpretation of norm-
development. Nevertheless, a brief analysis of the function of principles and
norms in an uncertain environment will suggest why they are important for
fulfilling the overall function of international regimes: to facilitate mutually
advantageous international agreements.

An important principle that is shared by most, if not all, international
regimes is what Jervis calls "reciprocation": the belief that if one helps
others or fails to hurt them, even at some opportunity cost to oneself, they
will reciprocate when the tables are turned. In the Concert of Europe, this
became a norm specific to the regime, a standard of behavior providing that
statesmen should avoid maximizing their interests in the short term for the
sake of expected long-run gains.[38]

This norm requires action that does not reflect specific calculations of
self-interest: the actor making a short-run sacrifice does not know that future
benefits will flow from comparable restraint by others, and can hardly be
regarded as making precise calculations of expected utility. What Jervis calls
the norm of reciprocation—or (to avoid confusion with the concept of reciprocity in international law) what I shall call a norm of generalized
commitment—precisely forbids specific interest calculations. It rests on the
premise that a veil of ignorance stands between us and the future, but that
we should nevertheless assume that regime-supporting behavior will be
beneficial to us even though we have no convincing evidence to that effect.

At first glance, it may seem puzzling that governments ever subscribe
either to the principle of generalized commitment (that regime-supporting
behavior will yield better results than self-help in the long run) or to the
corresponding norm in a given regime (that they should act in a regime-
supporting fashion). But if we think about international regimes as devices to

---

[37] Stephen D. Krasner, article in this volume, p. 2.
[38] Robert Jervis, article in this volume, p. 180.

facilitate mutually beneficial agreements the puzzle can be readily resolved. Without such a norm, each agreement would have to provide net gains for every essential actor, or side-payments would have to be arranged so that the net gains of the package were positive for all. Yet as we have seen, side-payments are difficult to organize. Thus, packages of agreements will usually be difficult if not impossible to construct, particularly when time is short, as in a balance of payments crisis or a sudden military threat. The principle of generalized commitment, however, removes the necessity for specific clusters of agreements, each of which is mutually beneficial. Within the context of a regime, help can be extended by those in a position to do so, on the assumption that such regime-supporting behavior will be reciprocated in the future. States may demand that others follow the norm of generalized commitment even if they are thereby required to supply it themselves, because the result will facilitate agreements that in the long run can be expected to be beneficial for all concerned.

The demand for specific information

The problems of organization costs discussed earlier arise even in situations where actors have entirely consistent interests (pure coordination games with stable equilibria). In such situations, however, severe information problems are not embedded in the structure of relationships, since actors have incentives to reveal information and their own preferences fully to one another. In these games the problem is to reach some agreement point; but it may not matter much which of several is chosen.[39] Conventions are important and ingenuity may be required, but serious systemic impediments to the acquisition and exchange of information are lacking.[40]

The norm of generalized commitment can be seen as a device for coping with the conflictual implications of uncertainty by imposing favorable assumptions about others' future behavior. The norm of generalized commitment requires that one accept the veil of ignorance but act *as if* one will benefit from others' behavior in the future if one behaves now in a regime-supporting way. Thus it creates a coordination game by ruling out potentially antagonistic calculations.

Yet in many situations in world politics, specific and calculable conflicts of interest exist among the actors. In such situations, they all have an interest in agreement (the situation is not zero-sum), but they prefer different types of agreement or different patterns of behavior (e.g., one may prefer to

[39] The classic discussion is in Thomas C. Schelling, *The Strategy of Conflict* (1960; Cambridge: Harvard University Press, 1980), chap. 4, "Toward a Theory of Interdependent Decision." See also Schelling, *Micromotives and Macrobehavior* (New York: Norton, 1978).

[40] For an interesting discussion of regimes in these terms, see the paper in this volume by Oran R. Young. On conventions, see David K. Lewis, *Convention: A Philosophical Study* (Cambridge: Cambridge University Press, 1969).

cheat without the other being allowed to do so). As Stein points out in this volume, these situations are characterized typically by unstable equilibria. Without enforcement, actors have incentives to deviate from the agreement point:

> [Each] actor requires assurances that the other will also eschew its rational choice [and will not cheat, and] such collaboration requires a degree of formalization. The regime must specify what constitutes cooperation and what constitutes cheating.[41]

In such situations of strategic interaction, as in oligopolistic competition and world politics, systemic constraint-choice theory yields no determinate results or stable equilibria. Indeed, discussions of "blackmailing" or games such as "prisoners' dilemma" indicate that, under certain conditions, suboptimal equilibria are quite likely to appear. Game theory, as Simon has commented, only illustrates the severity of the problem; it does not solve it.[42]

Under these circumstances, power factors are important. They are particularly relevant to the supply of international regimes: regimes involving enforcement can only be supplied if there is authority backed by coercive resources. As we have seen, regimes themselves do not possess such resources. For the means necessary to uphold sanctions, one has to look to the states belonging to the regime.

Yet even under conditions of strategic interaction and unstable equilibria, regimes may be of value to actors by providing information. Since high-quality information reduces uncertainty, we can expect that there will be a demand for international regimes that provide such information.

Firms that consider relying on the behavior of other firms within a context of strategic interaction—for instance, in oligopolistic competition—face similar information problems. They also do not understand reality fully. Students of market failure have pointed out that risk-averse firms will make fewer and less far-reaching agreements than they would under conditions of perfect information. Indeed, they will eschew agreements that would produce mutual benefits. Three specific problems facing firms in such a context are also serious for governments in world politics and give rise to demands for international regimes to ameliorate them.

(1) Asymmetric information. Some actors may have more information about a situation than others. Expecting that the resulting bargains would be unfair, "outsiders" may therefore be reluctant to make agreements with "insiders."[43] One aspect of this in the microeconomic literature is "quality uncertainty," in which a buyer is uncertain about the real value of goods

---

[41]Arthur A. Stein, article in this volume, p. 128.

[42] Herbert Simon, "From Substantive to Procedural Rationality," in Latsis, ed., *Method and Appraisal in Economics;* Spiro J. Latsis, "A Research Programme in Economics," in ibid.; and on blackmailing, Oye, "The Domain of Choice."

[43] Oliver E. Williamson, *Markets and Hierarchies: Analysis and Anti-Trust Implications* (New York: Free Press, 1975).

being offered. In such a situation (typified by the market for used cars when sellers are seen as unscrupulous), no exchange may take place despite the fact that with perfect information, there would be extensive trading.[44]

(2) Moral hazard. Agreements may alter incentives in such a way as to encourage less cooperative behavior. Insurance companies face this problem of "moral hazard." Property insurance, for instance, may make people less careful with their property and therefore increase the risk of loss.[45]

(3) Deception and irresponsibility. Some actors may be dishonest, and enter into agreements that they have no intention of fulfilling. Others may be "irresponsible," and make commitments that they are unlikely to be able to carry out. Governments or firms may enter into agreements that they intend to keep, assuming that the environment will continue to be benign; if adversity sets in, they may be unable to keep their commitments. Banks regularly face this problem, leading them to devise standards of "creditworthiness." Large governments trying to gain adherents to international agreements may face similar difficulties: countries that are enthusiastic about cooperation are likely to be those that expect to gain more, proportionately, than they contribute. This is analogous to problems of self-selection in the market-failure literature. For instance, if rates are not properly adjusted, people with high risks of heart attack will seek life insurance more avidly than those with longer life expectancies; people who purchased "lemons" will tend to sell them earlier on the used-car market than people with "creampuffs."[46] In international politics, self-selection means that for certain types of activities—for example, sharing research and development information— weak states (with much to gain but little to give) may have greater incentives to participate than strong ones. But without the strong states, the enterprise as a whole will fail. From the perspective of the outside observer, irresponsibility is an aspect of the problem of public goods and free-riding;[47] but from the standpoint of the actor trying to determine whether to rely on a potentially irresponsible partner, it is a problem of uncertainty and risk. Either way, information costs may prevent mutually beneficial agreement, and the presence of these costs will provide incentives to states to demand international regimes (either new regimes or the maintenance of existing ones) that will ameliorate problems of uncertainty and risk.

4. Information, openness, and communication in international regimes

International regimes, and the institutions and procedures that develop in conjunction with them, perform the function of reducing uncertainty and

---

[44] George A. Ackerlof, "The Market for 'Lemons': Qualitative Uncertainty and the Market Mechanism," *Quarterly Journal of Economics* 84,3 (August 1970).

[45] Arrow, *Essays in the Theory of Risk-Bearing.*

[46] Ackerlof, "The Market for 'Lemons' "; Arrow, *Essays in the Theory of Risk-Bearing.*

[47] For an analysis along these lines, see Davis B. Bobrow and Robert T. Kudrle, "Energy R&D: In Tepid Pursuit of Collective Goods," *International Organization* 33,2 (Spring 1979): 49–76.

risk by linking discrete issues to one another and by improving the quantity and quality of information available to participants. Linking issues is important as a way to deal with potential deception. Deception is less profitable in a continuing "game," involving many issues, in which the cheater's behavior is closely monitored by others and in which those actors retaliate for deception with actions in other areas, than in a "single-shot" game. The larger the number of issues in a regime, or linked to it, and the less important each issue is in proportion to the whole, the less serious is the problem of deception likely to be.

Another means of reducing problems of uncertainty is to increase the quantity and quality of communication, thus alleviating the information problems that create risk and uncertainty in the first place. Williamson argues on the basis of the organization theory literature that communication tends to increase adherence to group goals: "Although the precise statement of the relation varies slightly, the general proposition that intragroup communication promotes shared goals appears to be a well-established empirical finding."[48] Yet not all communication is of equal value: after all, communication may lead to asymmetrical or unfair bargaining outcomes, deception, or agreements entered into irresponsibly. And in world politics, governmental officials and diplomats are carefully trained to communicate precisely what they wish to convey rather than fully to reveal their preferences and evaluations. Effective communication is not measured well by the amount of talking that used-car salespersons do to customers or that governmental officials do to one another in negotiating international regimes. Strange has commented, perhaps with some exaggeration:

> One of the paradoxes of international economic relations in the 1970s has been that the soft words exchanged in trade organizations have coexisted with hard deeds perpetuated by national governments. The reversion to economic nationalism has been accompanied by constant reiterations of continued commitment to international cooperation and consultation. The international bureaucracies of Geneva, New York, Paris and Brussels have been kept busier than ever exchanging papers and proposals and patiently concocting endless draft documents to which, it is hoped, even deeply divided states might subscribe. But the reality has increasingly been one of unilateral action, even where policy is supposedly subject to multilateral agreement.[49]

The information that is required in entering into an international regime is not merely information about other governments' resources and formal negotiating positions, but rather knowledge of their internal evaluations of the situation, their intentions, the intensity of their preferences, and their

---

[48] Oliver E. Williamson, "A Dynamic Theory of Interfirm Behavior," *Quarterly Journal of Economics* 79 (1965), p. 584.

[49] Susan Strange, "The Management of Surplus Capacity: or How Does Theory Stand Up to Protectionism 1970s Style?", *International Organization* 33,3 (Summer 1979): 303–334.

willingness to adhere to an agreement even in adverse future circumstances. As Hirsch points out with respect to the "Bagehot Problem" in banking, lenders need to know the moral as well as the financial character of borrowers.[50] Likewise, governments contemplating international cooperation need to *know* their partners, not merely know *about* them.

This line of argument suggests that governments that successfully maintain "closure," protecting the autonomy of their decision-making processes from outside penetration, will have more difficulty participating in international regimes than more open, apparently disorganized governments. "Closed" governments will be viewed with more skepticism by potential partners, who will anticipate more serious problems of bounded rationality in relations with these closed governments than toward their more open counterparts. Similarly, among given governments, politicization of issues and increases in the power of political appointees are likely to reduce the quality of information and will therefore tend to reduce cooperation. Thus as an issue gains salience in domestic politics, other governments will begin to anticipate more problems of bounded rationality and will therefore perceive greater risks in cooperation. International cooperation may therefore decline quite apart from the real intentions or objectives of the policy makers involved.

This conclusion is important: international policy coordination and the development of international regimes depend not merely on interests and power, or on the negotiating skills of diplomats, but also on expectations and information, which themselves are in part functions of the political structures of governments and their openness to one another. Intergovernmental relationships that are characterized by ongoing communication among working-level officials, "unauthorized" as well as authorized, are inherently more conducive to information-exchange and agreements than are traditional relationships between internally coherent bureaucracies that effectively control their communications with the external world.[51]

Focusing on information and risk can help us to understand the performance of international regimes over time, and therefore to comprehend better the sources of demands for such regimes. Again, reference to theories of oligopoly, as in Williamson's work, is helpful. Williamson assumes that cooperation—which he refers to as "adherence to group goals"—will be a function both of communication and of the past performance of the oligopoly; reciprocally, communication levels will be a function of cooperation. In addition, performance will be affected by the condition of the environment. Using these assumptions, Williamson derives a model that has two points of equilibrium, one at high levels and one at low levels of cooperation.

---

[50] Fred Hirsch, "The Bagehot Problem," *The Manchester School* 45,3 (1977): 241–57.

[51] Notice that here, through a functional logic, a systemic analysis has implications for the performance of different governmental structures at the level of the actor. The value of high-quality information in making agreements does not force governments to become more open, but it gives advantages to those that do.

His oligopolies are characterized by substantial inertia. Once a given equilibrium has been reached, substantial environmental changes are necessary to alter it:

> If the system is operating at a low level of adherence and communication (i.e., the competitive solution), a substantial improvement in the environment will be necessary before the system will shift to a high level of adherence and communication. *Indeed, the condition of the environment required to drive the system to the collusive solution is much higher than the level required to maintain it once it has achieved this position. Similarly, a much more unfavorable condition of the environment is required to move the system from a high to a low level equilibrium than is required to maintain it there.* [52]

It seems reasonable to suppose that Williamson's assumptions about relationships among communication, cooperation or adherence, and performance have considerable validity for international regimes as well as for cartels. If so, his emphasis on the role of information, for explaining persistent behavior (competitive or oligopolistic) by groups of firms, helps us to understand the lags between structural change and regime change that are so puzzling to students of international regimes. In our earlier work, Nye and I observed discrepancies between the predictions of structural models (such as what I later called the "theory of hegemonic stability") and actual patterns of change; in particular, changes in international regimes tend to lag behind changes in structure.[53] But our explanation for this phenomenon was essentially *ad hoc:* we simply posited the existence of inertia, assuming that "a set of networks, norms, and institutions, once established, will be difficult either to eradicate or drastically to rearrange." [54] Understanding the role of communication and information in the formation and maintenance of international regimes helps locate this observation in a theoretical context. The institutions and procedures that develop around international regimes acquire value as arrangements permitting communication, and therefore facilitating the exchange of information. As they prove themselves in this way, demand for them increases. Thus, even if the structure of a system becomes more fragmented—presumably increasing the costs of providing regime-related collective goods (as suggested by public goods theory)—increased demand for a particular, well-established, information-providing international regime may, at least for a time, outweigh the effects of increasing costs on supply.

These arguments about information suggest two novel interpretations of puzzling contemporary phenomena in world politics, as well as providing the

---

[52] Williamson, "A Dynamic Theory of Interfirm Behavior," p. 592, original italics.
[53] *Power and Interdependence,* especially pp. 54–58 and 146–53. Linda Cahn also found lags, particularly in the wheat regime; see "National Power and International Regimes."
[54] *Power and Interdependence,* p. 55.

basis for hypotheses that could guide research on fluctuations in the strength and extent of international regimes.

Understanding the value of governmental openness for making mutually beneficial agreements helps to account for the often-observed fact that effective international regimes—such as the GATT in its heyday, or the Bretton Woods international monetary regime[55]—are often associated with a great deal of informal contact and communication among officials. Governments no longer act within such regimes as unitary, self-contained actors. "Transgovernmental" networks of acquaintance and friendship develop, with the consequences that supposedly confidential internal documents of one government may be seen by officials of another; informal coalitions of like-minded officials develop to achieve common purposes; and critical discussions by professionals probe the assumptions and assertions of state policies.[56] These transgovernmental relationships increase opportunities for cooperation in world politics by providing policy makers with high-quality information about what their counterparts are likely to do. Insofar as they are valued by policy makers, they help to generate demand for international regimes.

The information-producing "technology" that becomes embedded in a particular international regime also helps us to understand why the erosion of American hegemony during the 1970s has not been accompanied by an immediate collapse of international regimes, as a theory based entirely on supply-side public goods analysis would have predicted. Since the level of institutionalization of postwar regimes was exceptionally high, with intricate and extensive networks of communication among working-level officials, we should expect the lag between the decline of American hegemony and the disruption of international regimes to be quite long and the "inertia" of the existing regimes relatively great.

The major hypothesis to be derived from this discussion of information is that demand for international regimes should be in part a function of the effectiveness of the regimes themselves in providing high-quality information to policy makers. The success of the institutions associated with a regime in providing such information will itself be a source of regime persistence.

Three inferences can be made from this hypothesis. First, regimes accompanied by highly regularized procedures and rules will provide more information to participants than less regularized regimes and will therefore, on

[55] On the GATT, see Gardner Patterson, *Discrimination in International Trade: The Policy Issues* (Princeton: Princeton University Press, 1966); on the international monetary regime, see Robert W. Russell, "Transgovernmental Interaction in the International Monetary System, 1960–1972," *International Organization* 27,4 (Autumn 1973) and Fred Hirsch, *Money International*, rev. ed. (Harmondsworth, England: Pelican Books, 1969), especially chap. 11, "Central Bankers International."

[56] Robert O. Keohane and Joseph S. Nye, "Transgovernmental Relations and International Organizations," *World Politics* 27,1 (October 1974): 39–62.

information grounds, be in greater demand. Thus, considerations of high-quality information will help to counteract the normal tendencies of states to create vague rules and poorly specified procedures as a way of preventing conflict or maintaining freedom of action where interests differ.

Second, regimes that develop norms internalized by participants—in particular, norms of honesty and straightforwardness—will be in greater demand and will be valued more than regimes that fail to develop such norms.

Third, regimes that are accompanied by open governmental arrangements and are characterized by extensive transgovernmental relations will be in greater demand and will be valued more than regimes whose relationships are limited to traditional state-to-state ties.[57]

Perhaps other nontrivial inferences can also be drawn from the basic hypothesis linking a regime's information-provision with actors' demands for it. In any event, this emphasis on information turns our attention back toward the regime, and the process of institutionalization that accompanies regime formation, and away from an exclusive concern with the power structure of world politics. The extent to which institutionalized cooperation has been developed will be an important determinant, along with power-structural conditions and issue density, of the extent and strength of international regimes.

From a future-oriented or policy perspective, this argument introduces the question of whether governments (particularly those of the advanced industrial countries) could compensate for the increasing fragmentation of power among them by building communication-facilitating institutions that are rich in information. The answer depends in part on whether hegemony is really a necessary condition for effective international cooperation or only a facilitative one. Kindleberger claims the former, but the evidence is inconclusive.[58] Analysis of the demand for international regimes, focusing on questions of information and transactions costs, suggests the possibility that international institutions could help to compensate for eroding hegemony. International regimes could not only reduce the organization costs and other transactions costs associated with international negotiations; they could also provide information that would make bargains easier to strike.

How effectively international regimes could compensate for the erosion of hegemony is unknown. Neither the development of a theory of international regimes nor the testing of hypotheses derived from such a theory is likely to resolve the question in definitive terms. But from a contemporary policy standpoint, both theory development and theory testing would at least

---

[57] These first three inferences focus only on the *demand* side. To understand the degree to which norms, for example, will develop, one needs also to look at supply considerations. Problems of organization, such as those discussed in the public goods literature and the theory of hegemonic stability, may prevent even strongly desired regimes from materializing.

[58] Kindleberger has asserted that "for the world economy to be stabilized, there has to be a stabilizer, one stabilizer." *The World in Depression,* p. 305.

help to define the dimensions of the problem and provide some guidance for thinking about the future consequences of present actions.

5. Coping with uncertainties: insurance regimes

Creating international regimes hardly disposes of risks or uncertainty. Indeed, participating in schemes for international cooperation entails risk for the cooperating state. If others fail to carry out their commitments, it may suffer. If (as part of an international growth scheme) it reflates its economy and others do not, it may run a larger-than-desired current-account deficit; if it liberalizes trade in particular sectors and its partners fail to reciprocate, import-competing industries may become less competitive without compensation being received elsewhere; if it curbs bribery by its multinational corporations without comparable action by others, its firms may lose markets abroad. In world politics, therefore, governments frequently find themselves comparing the risks they would run from lack of regulation of particular issue-areas (i.e., the absence of international regimes) with the risks of entering into such regimes. International regimes are designed to mitigate the effects on individual states of uncertainty deriving from rapid and often unpredictable changes in world politics. Yet they create another kind of uncertainty, uncertainty about whether other governments will keep their commitments.

In one sense, this is simply the old question of dependence: dependence on an international regime may expose one to risks, just as dependence on any given state may. Governments always need to compare the risks they run by being outside a regime with the risks they run by being within one. If the price of achieving short-term stability by constructing a regime is increasing one's dependence on the future decisions of others, that price may be too high.

Yet the question of coping with risk also suggests the possibility of different types of international regimes. Most international regimes are *control-oriented*. Through a set of more or less institutionalized arrangements, members maintain some degree of control over each other's behavior, thus decreasing harmful externalities arising from independent action as well as reducing uncertainty stemming from uncoordinated activity. A necessary condition for this type of regime is that the benefits of the regularity achieved thereby must exceed the organizational and autonomy costs of submitting to the rules, both for the membership as a whole and for each necessary member.

Control-oriented regimes typically seek to ensure two kinds of regularity, internal and environmental. Internal regularity refers to orderly patterns of behavior among members of the regime. The Bretton Woods international monetary regime and the GATT trade regime have focused, first of all, on members' obligations, assuming that, if members behaved according to the rules, the international monetary and trade systems would be orderly. Where all significant actors within an issue-area are members of the regime, this assumption is warranted and mutual-control regimes tend to be effective.

Yet there are probably few, if any, pure cases of mutual-control regimes. Typically, an international regime is established to regularize behavior not only among the members but also between them and outsiders. This is a side-benefit of stable international monetary regimes involving convertible currencies.[59] It was an explicit purpose of the nonproliferation regime of the 1970s, in particular the "suppliers' club," designed to keep nuclear material and knowledge from diffusing rapidly to potential nuclear powers. Military alliances can be viewed as an extreme case of attempts at environmental control, in which the crucial benefits of collaboration stem not from the direct results of cooperation but from their effects on the behavior of outsiders. Alliances seek to induce particular states of minds in nonmembers, to deter or to intimidate.

Observers of world politics have often assumed implicitly that all significant international regimes are control-oriented. The economic literature, however, suggests another approach to the problem of risk. Instead of expanding to control the market, firms or individuals may diversify to reduce risk or may attempt to purchase insurance against unlikely but costly contingencies. Portfolio diversification and insurance thus compensate for deficiencies in markets that lack these institutions. Insurance and diversification are appropriate strategies where actors cannot exercise control over their environment at reasonable cost, but where, in the absence of such strategies, economic activity would be suboptimal.[60]

In world politics, such strategies are appropriate under similar conditions. The group of states forming the insurance or diversification "pool" is only likely to resort to this course of action if it cannot control its environment effectively. Second, for insurance regimes to make sense, the risks insured against must be specific to individual members of the group. If the catastrophic events against which one wishes to insure are likely (should they occur at all) to affect all members simultaneously and with equal severity, risk sharing will make little sense.[61]

---

[59] Charles P. Kindleberger, "Systems of International Economic Organization," in David P Calleo, ed., *Money and the Coming World Order* (New York: New York University Press for the Lehrman Institute, 1978); Ronald McKinnon, *Money in International Exchange: The Convertible Currency System* (New York: Oxford University Press, 1979).

[60] Arrow, *Essays in the Theory of Risk-Bearing,* pp. 134–43.

[61] In personal correspondence, Robert Jervis has suggested an interesting qualification to this argument. He writes: "If we look at relations that involve at least the potential for high conflict then schemes that tie the fates of all the actors together may have utility even if the actors are concerned about catastrophic events which will affect them all. They can worry that if some states are not affected, the latter will be much stronger than the ones who have been injured. So it would make sense for them to work out a scheme which would insure that a disaster would no affect their relative positions, even though this would not mean that they would all not be wors off in absolute terms." The point is certainly well taken, although one may wonder whethe such an agreement would in fact be implemented by the states that would make large relativ gains in the absence of insurance payments.

International regimes designed to share risks are less common than those designed to control events, but three examples from the 1970s can be cited that contain elements of this sort of regime:

(1) The STABEX scheme of the Lomé Convention, concluded between the European Community and forty-six African, Caribbean, and Pacific states in 1975. "Under the STABEX scheme, any of the 46 ACP countries dependent for more than 7.5 percent (2.5 percent for the poorest members of the ACP) of their export earnings on one of a list of commodities, such as tea, cocoa, coffee, bananas, cotton, and iron ore, will be eligible for financial help if these earnings fall below a certain level." [62] STABEX, of course, is not a genuine mutual-insurance regime because the guarantee is made by one set of actors to another set.

(2) The emergency sharing arrangements of the International Energy Agency, which provide for the mandatory sharing of oil supplies in emergencies, under allocation rules devised and administered by the IEA. [63]

(3) The Financial Support Fund of the OECD, agreed on in April 1975 but never put into effect, which would have provided a "lender of last resort" at the international level, so that risks on loans to particular countries in difficulty would have been "shared among all members, in proportion to their quotas and subject to the limits of their quotas, however the loans are financed." [64]

Control-oriented and insurance strategies for coping with risk and uncertainty have different advantages and liabilities. Control-oriented approaches are more ambitious; when effective, they may eliminate adversity rather than simply spread risks around. After all, it is more satisfactory to prevent floods than merely to insure against them; likewise, it would be preferable for consumers to be able to forestall commodity embargoes rather than simply to share their meager supplies fairly if such an embargo should take place.

Yet the conditions for an effective control-oriented regime are more stringent than those for insurance arrangements. An effective control-oriented regime must be supported by a coalition that has effective power in the issue-area being regulated, and whose members have sufficient incentives to exercise such power. [65] Where these conditions are not met, insurance regimes may be "second-best" strategies, but they are better than no strategies at all. Under conditions of eroding hegemony, one can expect the increasing emergence of insurance regimes, in some cases as a result of the

[62] Isebill V. Gruhn, "The Lomé Convention: Inching toward Interdependence," *International Organization* 30,2 (Spring 1976), pp. 255–56.

[63] Robert O. Keohane, "The International Energy Agency: State Influence and Transgovernmental Politics," *International Organization* 32,4 (Autumn 1978): 929–52.

[64] OECD *Observer*, no. 74 (March–April 1975), pp. 9–13.

[65] The optimal condition under which such a coalition may emerge could be called the "paper tiger condition": a potential external threat to the coalition exists but is too weak to frighten or persuade coalition members to defect or to desist from effective action. OPEC has been viewed by western policy makers since 1973 as a real rather than paper tiger, although some observers keep insisting that there is less to the organization than meets the eye.

unwillingness of powerful states to adopt control-oriented strategies (as in the case of STABEX), in other cases as replacements for control-oriented regimes that have collapsed (as in the cases of the IEA emergency sharing arrangements and the OECD Financial Support Fund or "safety net"). Economic theories of risk and uncertainty suggest that as power conditions shift, so will strategies to manage risk, and therefore the nature of international regimes.

6. Conclusions

The argument of this paper can be summarized under six headings. First, international regimes can be interpreted, in part, as devices to facilitate the making of substantive agreements in world politics, particularly among states. Regimes facilitate agreements by providing rules, norms, principles, and procedures that help actors to overcome barriers to agreement identified by economic theories of market failure. That is, regimes make it easier for actors to realize their interests collectively.

Second, public goods problems affect the supply of international regimes, as the "theory of hegemonic stability" suggests. But they also give rise to demand for international regimes, which can ameliorate problems of transactions costs and information imperfections that hinder effective decentralized responses to problems of providing public goods.

Third, two major research hypotheses are suggested by the demand-side analysis of this article.

(a) Increased issue density will lead to increased demand for international regimes.
(b) The demand for international regimes will be in part a function of the effectiveness of the regimes themselves in developing norms of generalized commitment and in providing high-quality information to policymakers.

Fourth, our analysis helps us to interpret certain otherwise puzzling phenomena, since our constraint-choice approach allows us to see how demands for such behavior would be generated. We can better understand transgovernmental relations, as well as the lags observed between structural change and regime change in general, and between the decline of the United States' hegemony and regime disruption in particular.

Fifth, in the light of our analysis, several assertions of structural theories appear problematic. In particular, it is less clear that hegemony is a necessary condition for stable international regimes under all circumstances. Past patterns of institutionalized cooperation may be able to compensate, to some extent, for increasing fragmentation of power.

Sixth, distinguishing between conventional control-oriented international regimes, on the one hand, and insurance regimes, on the other, may help us to understand emerging adaptations of advanced industrialized countries to a global situation in which their capacity for control over events is much less than it was during the postwar quarter-century.

None of these observations implies an underlying harmony of interests in world politics. Regimes can be used to pursue particularistic and parochial interests, as well as more widely shared objectives. They do not necessarily increase overall levels of welfare. Even when they do, conflicts among units will continue. States will attempt to force the burdens of adapting to change onto one another. Nevertheless, as long as the situations involved are not constant-sum, actors will have incentives to coordinate their behavior, implicitly or explicitly, in order to achieve greater collective benefits without reducing the utility of any unit. When such incentives exist, and when sufficient interdependence exists that *ad hoc* agreements are insufficient, opportunities will arise for the development of international regimes. If international regimes did not exist, they would surely have to be invented.

Theories of international regimes
Stephan Haggard and Beth A. Simmons

Over the last ten years, international regimes emerged as a major focus of empirical research and theoretical debate within international relations. The interest in regimes sprang from a dissatisfaction with dominant conceptions of international order, authority, and organization. The sharp contrast between the competitive, zero-sum "anarchy" of interstate relations and the "authority" of domestic politics seemed overdrawn in explaining cooperative behavior among the advanced industrial states. The policy dilemmas created by the growth of interdependence since World War II generated new forms of coordination and organization that fit uneasily in a realist framework.

Intellectual traditions emphasizing the "societal" dimension of international politics suffered, however, from a lingering taint of idealism. Realism questioned the importance of international law as a constraint on state behavior and by the 1970s, its positive study by political scientists was virtually moribund. The subfield of international organization, and particularly the study of regional integration, generated rich theoretical debates during the 1960s.[1] Yet the field remained closely tied to the study of formal organi-

We are indebted to Don Babai, David Baldwin, Esther Barbe, Jack Donnelly, Jeff Frieden, Barbara Geddes, Joe Grieco, Ernst Haas, Peter Haas, Stanley Hoffmann, Peter Katzenstein, Robert Keohane, Stephen Krasner, Fritz Kratochwil, Charles Kupchan, David Lake, Doug Nelson, Eric Nordlinger, Helen Milner, Andy Moravcsik, Craig Murphy, Joseph Nye, Robert Putnam, John Ruggie, Raymond Vernon, and two anonymous reviewers for their comments.

1. For a review tracing the importance of the study of regional integration to later theoretical developments, see Robert Keohane and Joseph Nye, "International Integration and Interdependence," in Fred Grenstein and Nelson Polsby, eds., *Handbook of Political Science*, vol. 8 (Reading: Addison-Wesley, 1975). See also Ernst Haas, *Beyond the Nation State* (Stanford: Stanford University Press, 1964), chaps. 1–5, 13–14; Joseph Nye, ed., *International Regionalism* (Boston: Little Brown, 1968); Leon N. Lindberg and Stuart A. Scheingold, eds., *Regional Integration: Theory and Research* (Cambridge: Harvard University Press, 1971); and Ernst Haas, *The Obsolescence of Regional Integration Theory* (Berkeley: Institute for International Studies, 1975).

International Organization 41, 3, Summer 1987, pp. 491–517
© 1987 by the World Peace Foundation and the Massachusetts Institute of Technology

zations, missing a range of state behavior that nonetheless appeared regulated or organized in a broader sense. Few strong theories started from the assumption that, as John Ruggie put it in a seminal article, "international behavior is institutionalized."[2]

Regime analysis attempted to fill this lacuna by defining a focus that was neither as broad as international structure, nor as narrow as the study of formal organizations. Regime analysts assumed that patterns of state action are influenced by norms, but that such norm-governed behavior was wholly consistent with the pursuit of national interests. Hence, the regimes literature can be viewed as an experiment in reconciling the idealist and realist traditions.

After a decade of development, it is time to submit this research program to critical review. A plethora of contending theories have explained regime creation, maintenance, and transformation, but the relationship among them is unclear and empirical research has yet to determine which are the more plausible. While earlier work on regimes focused on interdependence, the widening variety of state goals, and the importance of non-state actors and international organizations, recent work on regimes and international cooperation unfortunately reverts to an approach which treats states as unified, rational actors. In addition, little research has addressed whether, and in what ways, regimes "matter."[3] Do regimes have independent influence on state behavior and, if so, how?

We begin by briefly surveying the contending definitions of international regimes, which range from patterned behavior, to convergent norms and expectations, to explicit injunctions. We then suggest a number of dimensions along which regimes vary over time or across cases; these dimensions have been or might be used to operationalize "regime change." They include strength, organizational form, scope, and allocational mode. The third section examines four theoretical approaches to regimes—structural, game-theoretic, functional, and cognitive—and attempts to clarify what each theory can and cannot tell us about regimes.

In the conclusion, we ask how and whether regimes "matter." So far, little research addresses this problem. Testing for the significance of regimes—even to verify international systemic theories—demands careful tracing of *national* level processes, structures, and values. We outline a research program that focuses greater attention on issues raised by theorists of complex interdependence; these issues have been neglected in the revival of game theory, and include the erasure of the boundaries between domestic and foreign policies, the importance of transnational coalitions, and, above

---

2. John Gerard Ruggie, "International Responses to Technology: Concepts and Trends," *International Organization* 29 (Summer 1975), p. 559.

3. Susan Strange, "Cave! Hic Dragones: A Critique of Regimes Analysis," in Stephen Krasner, ed., *International Regimes* (Ithaca: Cornell University Press, 1983), pp. 337–54.

all, the way in which domestic political forces determine patterns of international cooperation.

1. Regimes: Definitions

How do we know a regime when we see one? Three answers have been offered to this question. The most comprehensive equates regimes with patterned behavior. Donald Puchala and Raymond Hopkins argue that "a regime exists in every substantive issue-area in international relations . . . Wherever there is regularity in behavior, some kinds of principles, norms or rules must exist to account for it."[4] But the existence of patterned behavior alone should not lead one to suspect that a regime lurks below the surface. A broad definition runs the risk of conflating regularized patterns of behavior with rules, and almost certainly overestimates the level of normative consensus in international politics.[5] Deducing regimes from patterned behavior makes it difficult to decide how they mediate, constrain, or influence behavior. The term "regime" is sometimes used in a purely descriptive way to group a range of state behaviors in a particular issue-area, but since the potential for tautology is high, this approach has largely been abandoned.[6]

Stephen Krasner's influential definition seeks a middle ground between "order" and explicit commitments; it stresses the normative dimension of international politics. Krasner defines a regime as "implicit or explicit principles, norms, rules and decision-making procedures around which actors' expectations converge in a given area of international relations."[7] Despite the care with which this complex hierarchy of components is defined, "principles" (which include not only beliefs of fact and causation, but also of "rectitude") shade off into norms, "standards of behavior defined in terms of rights and obligations." Norms, in turn, are difficult to distinguish from rules, "specific prescriptions or proscriptions for action."[8]

4. Donald Puchala and Raymond Hopkins, "International Regimes: Lessons from Inductive Analysis," in ibid., pp. 61–91.

5. Friedrich Hayek, *Law, Legislation and Liberty*; vol. 1, *Rules and Order* (Chicago: University of Chicago Press, 1973), pp. 78–79. See also H. L. A. Hart, *The Concept of Law* (New York: Oxford University Press, 1961), chap. 1.

6. The concept of "system" suffered a similar fate during the 1960s. See Ernst B. Haas, "On Systems and International Regimes," *World Politics* 27 (January 1975), pp. 147–74; Jerome Stephens, "An Appraisal of Some Systems Approaches in the Study of International Systems," *International Studies Quarterly* 16 (September 1972).

7. Stephen Krasner, "Structural Causes and Regime Consequences: Regimes as Intervening Variables," in Krasner, *International Regimes*, pp. 1–21. See also Robert Keohane and Joseph Nye, *Power and Interdependence* (Boston: Little Brown, 1977), p. 19.

8. Friedrich Kratochwil makes a similar point in "The Force of Prescriptions," *International Organization* 38 (Autumn 1984), p. 685; John Ruggie and Friedrich Kratochwil, "International Organization: A State of the Art on the Art of the State," *International Organization* 40 (Autumn 1986), pp. 753–76; and Oran Young, "International Regimes: Toward A New Theory of Institutions," *World Politics* 39 (October 1986), p. 106. Robert Keohane struggles with this

Not surprisingly, analysts have had serious disagreements about how the "norms" and "principles" of a given regime should be defined; their differences have strong implications for interpretations of regime stability and change. Susan Strange, John Zysman, and Stephen Cohen argue that state practices such as selective safeguards and industrial targeting have undermined the fundamental premises of the trade regime.[9] John Ruggie, on the other hand, contends that these derogations are consistent with a broader ideological framework, which he calls "embedded liberalism," which will endure as long as there is some accommodation of economic efficiency to social stability.[10] It is exceedingly difficult to imagine any state abandoning this "norm"; the result is a bias in favor of seeing continuity and a stable order.

The explicitness of commitment required before a regime can be said to exist creates a related problem. Focusing on "implicit regimes" captures the convergence of actor expectations and may help us summarize a complex pattern of behavior. But it begs the question of the extent to which state behavior is, in fact, rule-governed. Robert Keohane's effort to trace postwar cooperation in oil and Charles Lipson's study of changes in the treatment of foreign investment exemplify unnecessary, if not misleading, uses of the regime concept.[11] In both cases, the rights and duties of different actors were open to significant question and conflict. Violations of the norms governing the treatment of foreign investment in the 19th century, for example, really violated European (and primarily British) expectations. Do we gain explanatory leverage in analyzing 20th-century investment disputes when we point out that " 'national treatment' [became] an *international* norm"?[12] The core of Lipson's argument is not normative; national policies towards

---

problem in *After Hegemony: Cooperation and Discord in the World Political Economy* (Princeton: Princeton University Press, 1985), p. 58.

9. Susan Strange, "The Management of Surplus Capacity: or How Does Theory Stand Up to Protectionism Seventies Style?" *International Organization* 33 (Summer 1979), pp. 303–34; Stephen Cohen and John Zysman, "Double or Nothing: Open Trade and Competitive Industry," *Foreign Affairs* 62 (Summer 1983), pp. 1113–39. For a careful application of the regime concept to the trade system, see J. Finlayson and Mark Zacher, "The GATT and the Regulation of Trade Barriers: Regime Dynamics and Effects," *International Organization* 35 (Autumn 1981), pp. 561–602.

10. John Ruggie, "International Regimes, Transactions and Change: Embedded Liberalism in the Postwar Economic Order," in Krasner, *International Regimes*, pp. 195–232.

11. Keohane, in *After Hegemony*, notes that a formal international regime was never established in oil (p. 140), but later refers to the postwar oil regime (p. 190). Charles Lipson, *Standing Guard: Protecting Foreign Capital in the Nineteenth and Twentieth Centuries* (Berkeley: University of California Press, 1985), p. 32, includes in his object of analysis both patterns of behavior and normative structures; the concept of regime is not central to his analysis, and is used primarily as a summary of state behaviors. This is true also of Robert E. Wood, *From Marshall Plan to Debt Crisis* (Berkeley: University of California Press, 1986). For a defense of this usage, see Jack Donnelly, "International Human Rights Regimes," *International Organization* 40 (Summer 1986), pp. 599–642.

12. Lipson, *Standing Guard*, p. 262, emphasis in original.

foreign investment are neatly explained in terms of the investing countries'· relative power and the hosts' regulatory capabilities.

The "oil regime" between 1945 and 1970 consisted of the market activities of oligopolistically interdependent firms, the national rules of the producers, and ad hoc interventions by the United States. The Seven Sisters no doubt followed certain "rules" concerning production, exploration, and marketing. But their behavior must be understood in terms of supply conditions, a particular market structure, and national regulatory environments. The behavior of the major powers seems even less constrained by international rules. How "convergent" were British, French, and American expectations during the Suez crisis, in which the United States' diplomatic use of the oil weapon played a key role? Clear American interests and the power to back them adequately explain the outcome of the crisis. By endorsing the idea of "tacit" or "implicit" regimes, Keohane overemphasizes the importance of convergent expectations, particularly among governments.

A third, more restricted definition treats regimes as multilateral agreements among states which aim to regulate national actions within an issue-area.[13] Regimes define the range of permissible state action by outlining *explicit* injunctions. Regimes often contain rules which govern or specify their own transformation, but to explain "regime change" per se is to explain why states would agree to modify the codified rights and rules that regulate their behavior. This approach risks the charge of formalism—a charge which has plagued the study of international law. On the other hand, it focuses attention on the evolution of the texts constituting international agreements; it also clearly separates normative consensus from the definition of regimes, treating it rather as a causal or constitutive variable that may be useful in explaining cooperation.[14]

This definition also allows a sharper distinction between the concept of regime and several cognates, such as cooperation.[15] Regimes are *examples* of cooperative behavior, and *facilitate* cooperation, but cooperation can take place in the absence of established regimes. A recent example was the package of measures adopted by the advanced industrial states at the 1978 Bonn summit.[16] Regimes must also be distinguished from the broader concept of "institutions," the essential feature of which is "the conjunction of

---

13. This approach to regimes is closest to that of Oran Young, *Resource Regimes: Natural Resources and Social Institutions* (Berkeley: University of California Press, 1982); p. 20; *Compliance and Public Authority* (Washington, D.C.: Resources for the Future, 1979); "International Regimes: Problems of Concept Formation," *World Politics* 32 (April 1980), pp. 331–35; and "Anarchy and Social Choice: Reflections on the International Polity," *World Politics* 30 (January 1978), pp. 241–63; and Vinod Aggarwal, *Liberal Protectionism: The International Politics of Organized Textile Trade* (Berkeley: University of California Press, 1985), chap. 2.

14. See particularly Aggarwal, *Liberal Protectionism*, p. 16.

15. On cooperation, see Keohane, *After Hegemony*, pp. 51–52.

16. Robert Putnam and Nicholas Bayne, *Hanging Together: The Seven Power Summits* (Cambridge: Harvard University Press, 1984).

convergent expectations and patterns of behavior or practice."[17] Regimes aid the "institutionalization" of portions of international life by regularizing expectations, but some international institutions such as the balance of power are not bound to explicit rights and rules. "Convergent expectations" may or may not be tied to explicit agreements—they might, in fact, arise in a milieu characterized by substantial conflict. Finally, we should distinguish between regimes and "order" or "stability." Regimes may facilitate order and stability but are not coterminus with them.[18] In some instances, regimes may unintentionally contribute to instability, as when commitments to maintain parities under the Bretton Woods regime in the late 1960s produced chaotic exchange markets.

2. Regimes: Dimensions of variance and change

Many studies fail to specify what they mean by regime transformation or treat it in a unidimensional way. Regimes may change over time or vary across cases in at least four ways: strength, organizational form, scope, and allocational mode. As we shall argue, different theoretical approaches address one or more of these variables, but are less useful in explaining others.

a. Strength

The majority of "regime change" studies try to explain why regimes eventually weaken or decay.[19] Stength is measured by the degree of compliance with regime injunctions, particularly in instances where short-term or "myopic" self-interests collide with regime rules.

b. Organizational form

In its quest to move beyond the study of concrete international organizations, recent regimes literature has largely ignored problems of organizational design and operation. Some issues are conducive to decentralized regulation: regime injunctions may only call on states to share information, or to refrain from certain actions, such as polluting, over-fishing, nuclear testing, or raising tariffs. Other regimes, such as a fixed-exchange-rate re-

17. Oran Young, *Compliance and Public Authority,* p. 16; and his "International Regimes: Toward a New Theory."

18. The dependent variable of structural analysis is often cast quite broadly. See, for example, Duncan Snidal, "Limits of Hegemonic Stability Theory," *International Organization* 39 (Autumn 1985), pp. 579–614.

19. Explaining regime strength is central to the analysis of Lipson, *Standing Guard*; Aggarwal, *Liberal Protectionism*; Keohane, *After Hegemony*; and Stephen Krasner, *Structural Conflict: The Third World Against Global Liberalism* (Berkeley: University of California, 1985).

gimes, demand positive interventions by states, but remain largely decentralized.

Most regimes, however, are likely to have at least some minimal administrative apparatus for the purpose of dispute settlement, the collection and sharing of information, or surveillance. Complex cooperative tasks require more elaborate, and potentially autonomous, organizational structures. If cooperation is already highly institutionalized, theories resting on assumptions of anarchy are highly misleading; blackboxing organizational structure and processes will lead to simplistic predictions.[20]

The principles governing representation are another dimension of organizational variance. Most universalist regimes are structured either on the "one nation, one vote" principle or, as in the International Monetary Fund (IMF) and World Bank, on weighted voting. Alternative principles of membership, however, are based on discrimination along functional or sectoral lines (the Tokyo Round codes) or regional ones (the Caribbean Basin Initiative). Principles of membership have important distributional consequences, since they affect international agendas and organizational resource allocation.

c. Scope

Scope refers to the range of issues the regime covers. Though changes in regime scope have attracted little theoretical attention, its neglect can cause misleading characterizations. The failure to comply with certain GATT (General Agreement on Tariffs and Trade) provisions signaled a weakening of the trade regime in the 1970s. Yet at the same time, the regime's scope expanded through the negotiation of the Tokyo Round codes.[21] The most contentious questions on the current trade agenda concern the regime's scope—namely, how the GATT will address new issues such as trade in services, industrial policy, and national rules governing foreign direct investment.

The jurisdictional scope of a regime is not incidental to its success. Overly broad jurisdiction raises administrative costs and complexity, but overly narrow agreements may allow little room for bargaining and issue-linkage. One important cause of regime change is the "externalities" associated with

---

20. Keohane and Nye, *Power and Interdependence*, p. 55. Neo-functionalists drew inspiration from organization theorists, including James D. Thompson, *Organizations in Action* (New York: McGraw-Hill, 1967). Robert Keohane, in *After Hegemony*, draws on neoclassical theories of organization, such as Douglass North, *Structure and Change in Economic History* (New York: Norton, 1981), and Oliver Williamson, *Markets and Hierarchies: Analysis and Antitrust Implications* (New York: Free Press, 1975). See also W. Richard Scott, *Organizations: Rational, Natural and Open Systems* (Englewood Cliffs, N.J.: Prentice-Hall, 1981), chap. 5.

21. Stephen Krasner, "The Tokyo Round: Pluralistic Interests and Prospects for Stability in the Global Trading System," *International Studies Quarterly* 23 (December 1979), pp. 491–531.

inadequate scope. GATT negotiations in the 1950s and 1960s virtually eliminated tariff barriers as an important impediment to trade. The result, however, was to expose, and even encourage, non-tariff barriers. These externalities drove the reform efforts which culminated in the Tokyo Round.

d. Allocational mode

Regimes can endorse different social mechanisms for resource allocation.[22] A market-oriented regime supports the private allocation of resources, discourages national controls, guarantees property rights, and facilitates private contracting. As Oran Young states, "free enterprise systems . . . are not institutional arrangements operating outside or in the absence of any regime. Such systems clearly require explicit structures of property or use rights."[23] At the other extreme, authoritative allocation involves the direct control of resources by regime authorities, and will demand more extensive, and potentially autonomous, organizational structures. The IMF's role in the balance-of-payments financing regime provides an example.

The nature of the issue-area and the extent of cooperation sought will partly determine the preference for market-oriented versus authoritative modes of allocation. Many issue-areas could be organized either way, however, with sharply different distributional consequences. The Group of 77's proposal for a New International Economic Order (NIEO) provides the clearest example. Virtually all of the NIEO debates centered on allocation mechanisms, with the South generally favoring authoritative ones.[24]

3. Theoretical approaches to regime change and variance

The literature on regime development and change can be grouped into four families: structural, game-theoretic, functional, and cognitive. These categories are not mutually exclusive, and the most persuasive interpretations are likely to draw from more than one theoretical tradition.[25] Yet these ap-

---

22. Stephen Krasner makes this point in *Structural Conflict.*
23. Oran Young, *Compliance and Public Authority,* p. 55.
24. On the NIEO debate over modes of resource allocation, see Juergen Donges, "The Third World Demand for a New International Economic Order," *Kyklos* 30 (no. 2, 1977) and Michael Doyle, "Stalemate in the North-South Debate: Strategies and the New International Economic Order," *World Politics* 35 (April 1983), pp. 426–64. For discussions of the NIEO in a regime context, see Jeffrey Hart, *The New International Economic Order: Conflict and Cooperation in North-South Economic Relations, 1974–77* (New York: St. Martin's Press, 1983); Robert Rothstein, "Regime Creation by a Coalition of the Weak: Lessons from the NIEO and the Integrated Program for Commodities," *International Studies Quarterly* 28 (Summer 1984) pp. 307–28; Krasner, *Structural Conflict.*
25. Structural models have been given game-theoretic treatment by David Lake, "Beneath the Commerce of Nations: A Theory of International Economic Structures," *International*

proaches often speak past one another—in part because of fundamental differences in their underlying assumptions, in part because they address different dimensions of regime change and variance. We can gain a great deal by being explicit about underlying assumptions and what each approach can and cannot explain.

Most structural, game-theoretic, and functional theories of regimes are state-centered, presuming unified rational actors, even if the assumption is relaxed to gain explanatory leverage.[26] Structural explanations, particularly including the theory of hegemonic stability, attempt to show how international conditions define the possibilities for cooperation. Structuralists argue that we cannot infer national policies from intentions because structures tend to mold state behavior "toward a common quality of outcomes even though the efforts and aims of agents and agencies vary."[27] Game-theoretic approaches incorporate exogenously determined preference orderings into the analysis. While these preference rankings, in principle, include all domestic factors that may impinge on a state's overall preferences, most research emphasizes that actors are primarily constrained by the structure of the interstate game. Functional theories, of which Robert Keohane's *After Hegemony* is a leading example, also assume rational actors, but introduce market imperfections, transactions, and information costs and uncertainty. We argue that all three approaches downplay the central insight of interdependence theorists: foreign policy is integrally related to domestic structures and processes.

A group of theorists we have labeled (for want of a better term) "cognitivists" have suggested a radically different research program. Focusing on the intersubjective meaning structures that bind actors together, they necessarily see a looser fit between structural constraints, interests, and choices. Where functional theories see regimes as more or less efficient responses to fixed needs, cognitive theories see them as conditioned by ideology and consensual knowledge and evolving as actors learn. Cognitivists argue that "there is no fixed 'national interest' and no 'optimal regime.' "[28] Presumably determinative "structural" constraints must always be understood in terms of historically conditioned, interpretive frameworks. This requirement promises some corrective to the spare assumptions of other theoretical approaches, particularly by reminding us of historical context and the substan-

---

Studies Quarterly 28 (June 1984), pp. 143–70; Duncan Snidal, "Limits of Hegemonic Stability Theory."

26. Keohane, *After Hegemony*, chap. 7, explores the implications of introducing Simon's notion of bounded rationality. Robert Axelrod argues that his own theory is not dependent on rational utility maximization in *The Evolution of Cooperation* (New York: Basic Books, 1984), p. 18.

27. Kenneth Waltz, *Theory of International Politics* (Reading, Mass.: Addison-Wesley, 1979), p. 74.

28. Ernst Haas, "Words Can Hurt You: Or Who Said What to Whom About Regimes" in Krasner, *International Regimes*, p. 57.

tive issues over which conflict and cooperation occur. Yet, to date, the cognitivists have not adequately resolved their relationship with the structuralist research program. The relationship between power, ideology, and knowledge is one of the most exciting areas of theoretical debate, but one strewn with basic methodological problems.[29]

a. Structuralism: The theory of hegemonic stability

The theory of hegemonic stability offers the most parsimonious and widely employed explanation of regime dynamics; it links regime creation and maintenance to a dominant power's existence and the weakening of regimes to a waning hegemon. Ironically, the theory's early proponents were interested primarily in the world economy's stability and openness and did not mention the role of rules or regimes.[30] In *Power and Interdependence,* Keohane and Nye first linked regime dynamics to waxing and waning state power. They argued that, since power is not wholly fungible under conditions of complex interdependence, linkage across issue-areas is not likely to be effective. Keohane and Nye proposed a more disaggregated "issue-structural" model, predicting that "stronger states in the issue system will dominate the weaker ones and determine the rules of the game."[31]

The theory of hegemonic stability has subsequently been challenged on both empirical and theoretical grounds.[32] First, the hazards of power analy-

29. The social theorist most interested in the relationship between knowledge and power is Michel Foucault. See particularly Colin Gordon, ed., *Power/Knowledge: Selected Interviews and Other Writings by Michel Foucault, 1972–1977* (New York: Pantheon, 1980).

30. In his book, *World In Depression* (Berkeley: University of California Press, 1973), Charles Kindleberger links the "stability" of the world economy to *unilateral* leadership by a dominant power; no formal international commitments or institutional machinery would be required. Robert Gilpin's *U.S. Power and the Multinational Corporation* (New York: Basic Books, 1975) and his *War and Change in International Politics* (New York: Cambridge University Press, 1981) make little reference to the role of international rules. Stephen Krasner's "State Power and the Structure of International Trade," *World Politics* 28 (April 1976), tests the correlation between the distribution of economic power, the trade preferences of states, and the openness of the international trading system. David Lake, "Beneath the Commerce of Nations," also makes no reference to the intervening role of international regimes. Rather, position within carefully specified international economic structures directly conditions trade policy preferences.

31. Keohane and Nye, *Power and Interdependence,* pp. 50–51.

32. A number of tests have been devised for the theory of hegemonic stability in recent years. Reviewing the trade, money, and oil regimes between 1967 and 1977, Keohane concluded that we lack compelling causal arguments linking hegemonic decline and regime change, particularly for trade; Keohane, "Theory of Hegemonic Stability and Changes in International Economic Regimes, 1967–1977," in Ole Holsti, ed., *Change in the International System* (Boulder: Westview Press, 1980); Keohane, *After Hegemony,* chap. 9. Krasner's "Structure of International Trade" found that hegemonic theory predicted trading patterns in some periods (1820–79, 1880–1900, 1945–60), but not in others (1900–13, 1919–39, 1960 to present). Timothy McKeown argues that Britain did not actively encourage free trade in the 19th century, "Hegemonic Stability Theory and 19th-Century Tariff Levels in Europe," *International Organization* 37 (Winter 1983), pp. 73–91. Arthur Stein argues that hegemons cannot enforce free trade, but can pay the price of asymmetric openness under certain domestic political conditions, "The Hege-

sis plague efforts to explain concisely the structure of regime dynamics. Inferring interests from capabilities implies that there is some unambiguous way to assess the distribution of capabilities. From this structure flows a greatly restricted set of possible international outcomes. The delineation of the relevant structure, however, is bound to be arbitrary. David Lake offers the most careful conceptualization of international structure within the trade area, including a measure of relative productivity as well as relative size. These measures seek to explain both the *capacity* to underwrite or support free trade and the *willingness* to do so. But as Jeff Frieden points out (using Lake's data), the shift in the United States' share of world trade is only minuscule between 1929, when the United States refused to lead, and 1960, the high point of American hegemony.[33] Can a move from 13.9 percent of world trade in the earlier period to 15.3 percent in the latter account for the sharp contrast in trade practices?

Second, since structure alone is a poor predictor of regime characteristics and national policies, "structural" theories must continually revert in an ad hoc way to domestic political variables. As Kindleberger recognized, America's refusal to lead in the interwar period had a domestic foundation.[34] Similarly, Krasner found that structure predicted the openness of the trading system in only half the cases he examined, with domestic institutional "lags" introduced to explain the rest.[35] If such "slippage" is common, or if similarly situated states tend to respond differently to international con-

---

mon's Dilemma: Great Britain, the United States, and the International Economic Order," *International Organization* 38 (Spring 1984), pp. 355–86. More positive assessments of the theory's utility can be found in William P. Avery and David P. Rapkin, eds., *America in a Changing World Political Economy* (New York: Longman, 1982), though most of the pieces address the question of U.S. policy, as opposed to regime outcomes.

Several efforts have been made to confront hegemonic stability theory with alternative explanations. Joanne Gowa resorts to domestic factors and international market conditions in "Hegemons, IOs and Markets: The Case of the Substitution Account," *International Organization* 38 (Autumn 1984), pp. 661–83. Beverly Crawford and Stephanie Lenway supplement a structural model with a cognitive approach, "Decision Modes and International Regime Change: Western Collaboration on East-West Trade," *World Politics* 37 (April 1985), pp. 375–402. In *Standing Guard*, Lipson couples a hegemonic decline argument with an analysis of the changing capabilities of "weak" states. In one of the few efforts to test the theory against a contending approach, Peter Cowhey and Edward Long find that theories of surplus capacity are superior to the theory of hegemonic stability for predicting the timing of protection in automobile trade; see Cowhey and Long, "Testing Theories of Regime Change: Hegemonic Decline or Surplus Capacity?" *International Organization* 37 (Spring 1983), pp. 157–85.

Finally some have suggested that the theory is simply misspecified. Bruce Russett and Susan Strange argue that American decline has been exaggerated; see Russett, "The Mysterious Case of Vanishing Hegemony, or is Mark Twain Really Dead?" *International Organization* 39 (Spring 1985) pp. 202–31; and Strange, "Cave! Hic Dragones." Snidal (in "Hegemonic Stability Theory") and Russett both argue that the theory has been misapplied to cases where provision of a public good is not at stake.

33. Jeff Frieden, "From Economic Nationalism to Hegemony: Social Forces and the Emergency of Modern U.S. Foreign Economic Policy, 1914–1940" (UCLA, 1986).

34. Kindleberger, *World in Depression*, pp. 297–98.

35. Krasner, "Structure of International Trade."

straints, than the primacy of structural theory is called into question. We need theories of domestic processes or theories linking the international and domestic levels.

Hegemonic interpretations of regimes are not always clear about what hegemons actually *do* to promulgate and maintain a given set of rules; structural theories are, by their nature, less useful for understanding processes than for establishing correlations. The two major schools of thought on the mechanics of hegemonic leadership stress different solutions to the provision of public goods.[36] The "malign" view, associated with Gilpin's work, sees the hegemon providing coercive leadership. The hegemon enforces regime rules with positive and negative sanctions; it even extracts payment from smaller states to maintain the regime. Thucydides describes, for example, how Athens's "leadership" of the Delian League, based on consensus, was gradually transformed into coercive empire.[37] This interpretation of hegemony would cast doubt on the assumption that regimes are "cooperative" institutions, even though benefits might accrue to the coerced actors.[38] Empirical studies suggest that we cannot assume the hegemon will enforce regime compliance, however. Timothy McKeown's study of 19th-century trade concludes that European liberalization had little to do with pressure from England, but rather was the result of national policies towards industrialization.[39] Similarly, the United States tolerated derogations from "liberal" norms in the first two postwar decades. Only when its relative power eroded did the United States insist on "reciprocity."

The "benign" view of hegemony turns realism on its head.[40] Because they benefit greatly from a well-ordered system, hegemons are willing to provide

---

36. Snidal, "Hegemonic Stability Theory."

37. Thucydides, *The Peloponnesian War* (New York: Random House, Modern Library edition), passim.

38. On the problem of "benign" coercion, see Michael Taylor, *Community, Anarchy, Liberty* (New York: Cambridge University Press, 1982), pp. 10–25.

39. McKeown, "Hegemonic Stability Theory."

40. Kindleberger, *World in Depression*, initially made no reference to the theory of collective action, but in a 1976 piece, he noted that "the provision of the world public good of economic stability is best provided, if not by world government, by a system of rules." See his "Systems of International Economic Organization," in David P. Calleo et al., eds., *Money and the Coming World Order* (New York: New York University Press, 1976). In "Hierarchy versus Inertial Cooperation," *International Organization* 40 (Autumn 1986), p. 841, he states that he borrowed his concept of leadership from Norman Frohlich and Joe Oppenheimer, "I Get Along with a Little Help from My Friends," *World Politics* 23 (October 1970), pp. 104, 120. See also his "International Public Goods without International Leadership," *American Economic Review* 76 (March 1986), pp. 1–13.

For approaches to regimes which depart from Olson's analysis of collective goods, see John A. C. Conybeare, "Public Goods, Prisoners' Dilemmas and the International Political Economy," *International Studies Quarterly* 28 (March 1984), pp. 5–22; Duncan Snidal, "Hegemonic Stability Theory," and his excellent summary and organization of the literature, "Public Goods, Property Rights and Political Organizations," *International Studies Quarterly* 23 (December 1979), pp. 532–66; Bruno Frey, *International Political Economics* (New York: Basil Blackwell, 1984), chap. 7.

international public goods. More precisely, the hegemon constitutes a "privileged group," for which the cost of supplying the public good is less than the benefit. But since the hegemon has an independent interest in supplying public goods regardless of the contributions of others, beneficiaries of the system will have an incentive to free-ride. Rather than the strong exploiting the weak, it is the weak who exploit the strong.

Two criticisms have been raised against the collective goods approach to the hegemonic theory of regimes; both point to the inappropriate application of otherwise sound theory. First, most regimes do not provide pure public goods, which are characterized not only by jointness of supply but by non-excludability. Most regimes have developed mechanisms that enhance compliance through exclusion—for example, trade reciprocity, reciprocal rights of innocent passage, and technological assistance in exchange for adherence to non-proliferation agreements.[41] Keohane and Snidal also point out that nothing in the theory of collective action suggests that a single hegemon is required to provide public goods.[42] If a privileged subgroup exists such that each member benefits from providing the good even without cooperation from other members, the public good will be provided. Individual incentives *not* to contribute will increase as the size of the privileged subgroup increases, but certain characteristics of the regimes, such as those which increase the transparency of state action, may mitigate this effect.

A broader criticism may be leveled against the theory of hegemonic stability, however. The relevant "structure" is usually defined as the distribution of power within the international capitalist system rather than within the world political system as a whole; regimes are seen primarily as responses to the problems of collective action among the advanced capitalist countries rather than as an integral part of high politics and alliance solidarity. Despite all the attention lavished on "international structure" as an explanation of regime creation and maintenance, bipolarity has been all but overlooked.[43] This hardly conforms with the views of the postwar planners who constructed the Bretton Woods order.[44] The World Bank and IMF can be seen, and indeed *were* seen by the Soviet Union, as an American effort to close capitalist ranks at the Eastern bloc's expense; contrast America's insouciant response to negotiations for the Bank for International Settlements in 1929

---

41. Trade reciprocity is not an example of an exclusionary device as long as there is a most-favored nation provision. Most reductions in tariffs are negotiated by principle suppliers, however, and discriminatory treatment couched in the language of "reciprocity" has clearly grown. For a discussion of impure public goods and so-called "club goods," which are excludable at a cost, see Richard Carnes and Todd Sandler, *The Theory of Externalities, Public Goods, and Club Goods* (New York: Cambridge University Press), chaps. 10–12.

42. Keohane, *After Hegemony;* Snidal, "Hegemonic Stability Theory."

43. Keohane, *After Hegemony*, p. 137, explicitly eschews consideration of the military-economic linkage. Ethan Kapstein develops a perspective linking economic and security cooperation in "Alliance Energy Security," *Fletcher Forum* (1984), pp. 91–116.

44. See, for example, David Calleo and Benjamin M. Rowland, *America and the World Political Economy* (Bloomington, Ind.: Indiana University Press, 1973).

and its largely uncooperative attitude towards outstanding war debts throughout the 1920s and 1930s. The link between economic and security relations is often ignored by American students of international political economy; it is, however, a recurrent theme in the writing of Europeans. It has been highlighted in new interpretations of the emergence of the postwar Pacific order, and it is an underlying theme in the work of contemporary diplomatic historians such as Paul Kennedy.[45] By ignoring grand strategy, hegemonic interpretations may have missed this century's most important "structural" cause of cooperation among the advanced industrial states.

b. Strategic and game-theoretic approaches

Game theory has recently been used to explain how cooperation can evolve under anarchic conditions which lack supranational authority to enforce compliance.[46] Again, we must distinguish regimes from cooperation, which is clearly possible in the absence of regimes. Game theory can readily explain the conditions under which regimes might arise as an instance of cooperative behavior, and it can also suggest the conditions conducive to stable compliance, but it has difficulty explaining organizational form, scope, or change.

The attraction of game theory is its spare elucidation of a strategic interaction's structure. The attendant risk is oversimplification, particularly given the daunting problems which surround the application and testing of its insights. Where multilateral interactions cannot be disaggregated into actor dyads, the 2×2 game may mislead more than it clarifies. The alternative—the n-person game—does not yield determinate outcomes.[47] The 2×2 game also radically simplifies the choice set into unambiguous categories—cooperate and defect—though choices in most areas, such as macroeconomic coordination, are continuous.[48] Games are also frequently depicted in their

---

45. See, for example, Alfred Grosser, *The Western Alliance: European American Relations Since 1945* (New York: Continuum, 1980); Bruce Cumings, "The Origins and Development of the Northeast Asian Political Economy: Industrial Sectors, Product Cycles, and Political Consequences," *International Organization* 38 (Winter 1984), pp. 1–40; Paul Kennedy, *The Realities Behind Diplomacy: Background Influences on British External Policy, 1865–1980* (Glasgow: Fontana, 1981).

46. See the special issue of *World Politics* 38 (October 1985), edited by Kenneth Oye. See also R. Harrison Wagner, "The Theory of Games and the Problem of International Cooperation," *American Political Science Review* 70 (June 1983), pp. 330–46.

47. Duncan R. Luce and Howard Raiffa, *Games and Decisions* (New York: Wiley, 1957), chap. 7.

48. For economists' efforts to model macroeconomic interdependence from a strategic perspective, see Koichi Hamada, "A Strategic Analysis of Monetary Interdependence," *Journal of Political Economy* 84 (August 1976), pp. 677–99; Gilles Oudiz and Jeffrey Sachs, "Macroeconomic Policy Coordination among the Industrial Economies," *Brookings Papers on Economic Activity* (no. 1, 1984), pp. 1–64; Richard Cooper, "Economic Interdependence and Coordination of Economic Policies," in R. Jones and Peter Kenen, eds., *Handbook of International Economics* (Amsterdam: North-Holland, 1985).

normal rather than extensive form, though game theorists have shown that this can lead one to overlook how the dynamics of bargaining and sequencing of moves can determine outcomes.[49] The game may change in the course of negotiations; indeed, bargaining is precisely an effort to re-structure preference orderings.

The greatest difficulty is in specifying preferences at the outset, which includes not only their ordering but their intensity.[50] This effort must consider all relevant factors of the game environment: economic and technological conditions, domestic politics, transnational relations, and the rules under which the game is played. Deciding what the game *is* may be as difficult as solving it. One is tempted to construct the payoff in light of the outcomes, which throws into question the predictive value of the exercise.

Game theory can cope *in principle* with a high degree of complexity. Games may be "graduated" by introducing subgames, extended out into meta- or super-games, "linked" to games in other issue-areas or modeled in an evolutionary fashion. The result, however, is to detract from the selling point, parsimony, and to question how the theory actually explains particular cases. Empirical studies too often lapse into descriptive history followed by elaborate, and perhaps redundant, translation into game theoretical argot.[51]

Most game theoretic studies of international cooperation and regimes have focused on the Prisoner's Dilemma (PD). PD is attractive since it can produce cooperative behavior under "realist" conditions.[52] If play is repeated, the costs of defecting on any single move must be calculated not only with reference to the immediate payoff, but with reference to the opportunity costs associated with future interactions. Yet under assumptions of complex interdependence, the "dilemma" of PD diminishes. The very existence of a network of regimes and transnational relations among the ad-

49. For example, Glenn Snyder and Paul Diesing, *Conflict among Nations: Bargaining, Decision Making and System Structure in International Crises* (Princeton: Princeton University Press, 1977), p. 40; Steven J. Brams and M. P. Hessel, "Threat Power in Sequential Games," *International Studies Quarterly* 28 (March 1984), pp. 33–34.

50. The intensity of players' preferences has generally been given less attention in recent applications of game theory than their ordering. As Robert Jervis notes, however, "cooperation is more probable when mutual cooperation is only slightly less attractive than exploiting the other, when being exploited is only slightly worse than mutual competition and when the latter outcome is much worse than mutual cooperation." "From Balance to Concert: A Study of International Security Cooperation," in *World Politics* 38 (October 1985), p. 64.

51. For a review of this problem, see Duncan Snidal, "The Game *Theory* of International Politics," ibid., pp. 25–57.

52. Russell Hardin, *Collective Action* (Baltimore: Johns Hopkins University Press, 1982); Robert Axelrod, *The Evolution of Cooperation* (New York: Basic Books, 1984) and "The Emergence of Cooperation among Egoists," *American Political Science Review* 75 (June 1981) 306–18; Michael Taylor, *Anarchy and Cooperation* (New York: Wiley, 1976) and *Community, Anarchy and Liberty*. For a technical review of the literature, see N. Schofield, "Anarchy, Altruism and Cooperation," *Social Choice and Welfare* 2 (December 1985), 207–19. For evidence from experimental studies, see S. Siegel and L. E. Fouraker, *Bargaining and Group Decision-Making: Experiments in Bilateral Monopoly* (New York: McGraw-Hill, 1960).

vanced industrial states facilitates communication, enhances the importance of reputation, and lengthens the "shadow of the future."[53] In its heuristic use, PD indicates why these institutions deter suboptimal outcomes; more compelling theories of how these institutions actually evolve are still in their infancy.

Most applications of game theory to the study of international cooperation have assumed unified state actors and the dominance of the international game. These presumptions are strongly challenged by earlier literature on transnational relations and bureaucratic politics. As with structural approaches, the domestic processes affecting payoff structures are frequently blackboxed as "exogenous." As we shall argue in the conclusion, one must analyze the tradeoffs a state, or more accurately, a particular political leadership, is willing and able to make between domestic and foreign games. This certainly doesn't rule out the application of game theory, but it demands that we reorient our effort towards the analysis of domestic/international linkages.

Game-theoretic approaches are strongest when they reveal the conditions which enable cooperation and stability; they say far less about whether regimes will actually arise, how they will be institutionalized, and, above all, the rules and norms which will comprise them.[54] Functionalist logic provides a useful supplement.

c. Functional theories

Functional theory explains behaviors or institutions in terms of their effects.[55] If regimes serve to reduce information and transaction costs among their adherents, for example, the rewards of compliance will *reinforce* the regime. Thus, anticipated consequences explain the persistence of the regime and compliance with its injunctions. Similarly, the modification of regimes or their weakening is likely to occur when they become "dysfunctional." Functional theories explain regime strength, particularly the puzzle of why compliance with regimes tends to persist even when the structural conditions that initially gave rise to them changes.

Functional theories have important limitations. They are not causal in a strong sense. They are better at specifying when regimes will be demanded rather than suggesting how or when they will be supplied. Regimes and

53. Joanne Gowa, "Cooperation and International Relations," *International Organization* 40 (Winter 1986), 167–86; Snyder and Diesing, *Conflict among Nations.*

54. Duncan Snidal, "Coordination versus Prisoner's Dilemma: Implications for International Cooperation and Regimes," *American Political Science Review* 79 (December 1985), pp. 923–42.

55. "Functional" here refers to a particular form of explanation, and should be distinguished from earlier functional and neofunctional theories of international organization. For a discussion of earlier work, see Ernst Haas, *Beyond the Nation State,* chaps. 1–5, 13–14. For a general discussion of functional explanatory logic, see Arthur L. Stinchcombe, *Constructing Social Theories* (New York: Harcourt Brace, 1968), pp. 80–98.

cooperation in one issue-area may arise as an unintended consequence of cooperation in some other area. For example, three countries may respond to a security threat from a fourth with a cooperative venture, yet the regime may persist because of the positive externalities generated by military cooperation. Unless functional theories suggest how a selection mechanism operates, they can easily become teleological, a problem suffered by earlier functionalist writing, which viewed international cooperation as a response to imputed "system-maintenance" or "equilibrating" functions.[56] Collective action may not occur because of the free-rider problem or if the "need" goes unperceived.[57] This criticism need not deter one from formulating a functionalism that operates through individual motivations, particularly where existing institutions mitigate the collective action dilemma. The regime's benefits are simply that it provides incentives to certain forms of cooperative action, for example, by offering forums in which reputation comes into play or where games can be iterated and linked. Regimes may be "supplied" when there is sufficient "demand" for the functions they perform, but the market analogy has obvious limitations. In any case, this approach seems little different from an intentional theory that begins from old-fashioned interests.

The specific functions that regimes perform naturally vary from issue-area to issue-area. Most functionalist theorizing suggests that some *generalized* functions are underprovided, given conditions of anarchy or market failure. Regime analysts working in this vein have drawn heavily from the economic literature on transaction costs. In this literature, organizations, or "hierarchies," evolve as solutions to the opportunism, uncertainty, information costs, measurement problems, and difficulties of contract enforcement which plague arms-length market transactions.[58] Drawing an analogy between the market and the uncoordinated actions of states, Keohane, Oye, and Aggarwal have shown that regimes reduce transactions costs and facilitate decentralized rule-making.[59] Aggarwal notes that "construction of a multilateral mechanism is organizationally less expensive than is the development of many bilateral contracts."[60] Keohane notes that the marginal cost

56. Keohane, *After Hegemony*, p. 81.

57. Jan Elster, "Marxism, Functionalism and Game Theory," *Theory and Society* 11 (July–August 1982), p. 462.

58. See Oliver Williamson, *Markets and Hierarchies: Analysis and Antitrust Implications* (New York: Free Press, 1975); "The Modern Corporation: Origins, Evolution, Attributes," *Journal of Economic Literature* 19 (December 1981), pp. 1537–68; "Transaction-Cost Economics: The Governance of Contractual Relations," *The Journal of Law and Economics* 22 (October 1979), pp. 233–61; Douglass North, "Government and the Cost of Exchange in History," *Journal of Economic History* 44 (June 1984); Andrew Schotter, *The Economic Theory of Social Institutions* (New York: Cambridge University Press, 1981).

59. Keohane, *After Hegemony*, chap. 6; Aggarwal, *Liberal Protectionism*, chap. 2; Kenneth Oye, "Explaining Cooperation under Anarchy: Hypotheses and Strategies," in *World Politics* 38 (October 1985), pp. 16–18.

60. Aggarwal, *Liberal Protectionism*, p. 28.

of dealing with an additional issue will be lower with a regime, an insight that casts light on the important question of why regimes often expand in scope.[61]

Once these functions are enumerated, the remaining positive research program which follows is unclear. Crude functionalism has been criticized for simply noting that some behavior or institution—in this case, a regime—does, in fact, perform an anticipated function. Even if we knew that every regime performed some specified set of functions, this knowledge would not explain why regimes emerge in some issue-areas and not in others.

Nor would it explain why some regimes develop impressive formal organizations, while others do not. Unlike the transactions cost literature, the institutional solution resulting from failed interstate coordination is not a "hierarchy" in Williamson's sense. Numerous institutional solutions to a given problem of cooperation are possible, and little work has been done to show how particular contracting problems may yield particular governance solutions. In general, the "new functionalism" does not distinguish clearly between institutions and organizations, nor indicate the conditions that lead to the international development of the latter.[62]

In addition, we are interested not only in the fact that regimes perform certain tasks, but the importance or weight regimes have in motivating and explaining state behavior. The proper test of a functional theory is not the mere existence of a regime, but the demonstration that actors' behavior was motivated by benefits provided uniquely, or at least more efficiently, through the regime, or by reputational concerns connected to the existence of rules.

Finally, a strong liberal bias operates in the "new functionalism" just as it did in the old. Though Keohane admits that cooperation is not, in itself, a good, he tends to emphasize the functions which enhance global welfare, or at least the collective welfare of the regime's adherents. The bias is suggested by Keohane's premise of the "suboptimality" of market failure. But the institutions "provided" may or may not be Pareto superior, let alone optimal, and can certainly result in different distributional outcomes. The institutions that emerge in world politics are certainly more likely to reflect the interests of the powerful than the interests of the weak, a complaint repeatedly raised by commodity producers against the operation of the GATT. Aggarwal argues that regimes control large states' behavior toward the small by reducing the need to exercise power directly. He demonstrates that regimes have occasionally kept domestic protectionist interests from

61. Keohane, *After Hegemony*, pp. 103–6.
62. Oran Young makes this point in ''International Regimes: Toward a New Theory of Institutions'' and Snidal grapples with it in ''Coordination versus Prisoner's Dilemma.'' The most lucid statement of variations in organizational form remains Ruggie, ''International Responses to Technology.'' See also Ernst Haas, ''Is There a Hole in the Whole? Knowledge, Technology, Interdependence and the Construction of International Regimes,'' *International Organization* 29 (Summer 1975).

achieving their preferred solutions. Yet his analysis of the textile regime also demonstrates that most of the functions which regimes perform can be used to control states when the initial discrepancies of power are large, and that stronger players frequently ignore the "restraints" placed on them. The regime changed when it could not adequately serve the interests of the developed country importers.[63] How do we decide between Cheryl Payer's Marxist functionalism, which asserts that the World Bank operates as an instrument of Northern control, and a benign, liberal functionalism, which sees it as a more-or-less optimal institutional response to "failures" in international capital markets?[64] Douglass North has outlined the problem in a trenchant review of the transaction costs literature:

> One cannot have the productivity of an industrial society with political anarchy. But while . . . a state is a necessary condition for realizing the gains from trade, it obviously is not sufficient. A state becomes the inevitable source of struggle to take control of it in the interests of one of the parties. The state then becomes the vehicle by which the costs of transacting are raised to capture the gains that will accrue to any interested party that can control the specification and enforcement of property rights.[65]

Substituting "regime" for "state" in the foregoing passage raises a problem for functionalist analysis. Functional theories emphasize how the facilitating role of regimes helps them realize common interests. But regimes are also arenas for conflict and the exercise of power. Because functional theories assume highly convergent interests and downplay divergent ones, they do not explore how regimes may institutionalize inequalities.

d. Cognitive theories: Knowledge, ideology, and regimes

"Cognitive" theories explore what structural, game-theoretic, and functional approaches bracket.[66] The core cognitive insight is that cooperation

63. Aggarwal, *Liberal Protectionism*, p. 28.

64. For a succinct example of Marxist functionalism, see Cheryl Payer, *The World Bank: A Critical Analysis* (New York: Monthly Review, 1982), pp. 19–20.

65. North, "Government and the Cost of Exchange," p. 260.

66. "Cognitive" would best be left in quotation marks throughout, since we use the term to refer to a quite disparate group of approaches. We focus on the commonalities among those writers emphasizing ideology, belief systems, and knowledge as explanations of regime change. For other cuts at "cognitive" approaches that focus more squarely on the individual decision-maker see Deborah Welch Larson, *Origins of Containment: A Psychological Approach* (Princeton: Princeton University Press, 1985); Robert Jervis, *Perception and Misperception in International Politics* (Princeton: Princeton University Press, 1976).

The critique of structuralist and game-theoretic approaches from a hermeneutic, historicist, or "dialectical" viewpoint includes Richard Ashley, "The Poverty of Neorealism," *International Organization* 38 (Spring 1984), pp. 225–86 and "Three Modes of Economism," *International Studies Quarterly* 27 (December 1983), 463–96; John Ruggie, "Continuity and Transformation in the World Polity: Toward a Neorealist Synthesis," *World Politics* 35 (January

cannot be completely explained without reference to ideology, the values of actors, the beliefs they hold about the interdependence of issues, and the knowledge available to them about how they can realize specific goals. Cooperation is affected by perception and misperception, the capacity to process information, and learning. While structural, game-theoretic, and functional theories assume that cooperation operates within an issue-area which is relatively unambiguous, cognitivists point out that issue-areas are never simply given. Cognitive approaches are therefore particularly important in explaining the substantive content of regime rules and why they evolve. By elevating the importance of actor learning, cognitive theories have a dynamic other theoretical approaches lack.

Cognitive approaches cannot predict at what point consensual values or knowledge will produce cooperation. Consensus still may not overcome problems of collective action. More importantly, "ends, or purposes, of action are not self-evidently derivable from the scientific understanding of relationships among variables."[67] The generation of new knowledge just as easily might render a game less cooperative by exposing new incentives to defect.[68] Nor can cognitive approaches argue that a particular regime is uniquely suited to realize some common values. Criticizing the hegemonic stability theory, Ruggie argues that regimes reflect not only a configuration of power, but also a configuration of dominant social purpose.[69] Ruggie's concept of "embedded liberalism" tries to describe the common social purpose that arose after the Great Depression across the advanced capitalist states—the need to reconcile the advantages of liberalism and the costs of an unfettered market system. Yet this "purpose" is elastic enough to subsume a fairly wide range of "norm-governed changes," including the move from fixed to flexible exchange rates and the rise of the new protectionism during the 1970s. For this very reason, it cannot fully explain these changes.

Cognitivists argue that learning and, in a somewhat different fashion, ideology, affect international rules and cooperation by showing the merit (or futility) of certain lines of action. Knowledge and ideology, including the knowledge provided by regimes, can alter actor interests. But the cognitive

---

1983), pp. 261–85; Ruggie and Kratochwil, "IO as an Art of the State," particularly pp. 764–66 where they discuss the conflict between an "intersubjective ontology" and a "positivist epistemology"; and Hayward Alker, "Dialectical Foundations of Global Disparities," *International Studies Quarterly* 25 (March 1981), pp. 69–98; "From Quantity to Quality: A New Research Program on Resolving Sequential Prisoner's Dilemmas" (Paper presented at the American Political Science Association annual convention, August 1985) and "The Presumption of Anarchy in World Politics," (Massachusetts Institute of Technology, 1986).

67. Ernst Haas, "Is There a Hole in the Whole?" p. 848.

68. John Odell demonstrates the disruptive effect of new ideas in *U.S. International Monetary Policy: Markets, Power and Ideas as Sources of Change* (Princeton: Princeton University Press, 1982).

69. John Ruggie, "International Regimes."

critique reaches deeper. Even this causal language—knowledge "affects" interests—is inappropriate, since the dichotomy between ideology and knowledge on the one hand, and interests on the other, is wholly artificial and misleading. "Interests" only emerge within particular normative and epistemic contexts and cannot be understood outside them. Cognitivists argue that the assumption of rational utility maximization, for example, is too spare to be of explanatory value, since it ignores the way that historically situated actors interpret their constraints. Nor is the problem solved simply by showing that rationality is "bounded" in various ways. Such a modification predicts deviations from "rational" decision-making in environments characterized by incomplete information, uncertainty, complexity, but still divorces the concept of interest from shared meanings. The recurrent structuralist fallacy is to expect different states or individuals to respond similarly to the same structural constraints and opportunities; much depends on past history, knowledge, and purpose.

It is very difficult to generalize from the central cognitive insight. The predictive value of cognitive theories is problematic, particularly when they emphasize the importance of consensual knowledge. Historical episodes of cooperation may be inexplicable without reference to shared knowledge and meanings, but since future knowledge is, by definition, impossible to foresee, prediction about the substantive content of cooperation is ruled out. Nonetheless, the *degree* of ideological consensus and agreement over causal relationships, regardless of the nature of the issue, is an important variable in explaining cooperation.

Studies taking a cognitive perspective frequently have an evolutionary, historicist, or, less kindly, post hoc flavor that highlights contingency and path-dependence. Ernst Haas summarizes the methodological biases of one cognitivist:

> The type of systems theory I find useful features the inductive method in the construction of reality and uses the perceptions and actions of concrete human beings in grappling with reality as its main data. Such systems are assumed "open" in the sense that they do not tend, by definition, toward a given state, such as equilibrium. They are "constructed" in the sense that the theorist considers them as heuristic approximations rather than networks of determinative "laws" constraining choice.[70]

Ideology and knowledge can be construed and combined in a number of ways, creating a wide range of possible research strategies. Writers emphasizing the role of consensual knowledge have naturally focused on areas of technical cooperation. Richard Cooper has shown how a slow and painful evolution of consensus on the causes of disease transmission was critical for

70. Ernst Haas, "Is There a Hole in the Whole?" p. 839.

international cooperation on public health in the 19th century.[71] Don Babai argues that structuralist models are ill-equipped to explain the types of changes which took place at the World Bank under Robert McNamara. The evolution of knowledge, as well as intellectual fashion concerning development, shaped the Bank's lending strategy.[72] Cognitive theories which explain international cooperation primarily with ideological variables are more rare. Judith Goldstein's work on U.S. trade policy, however, argues that a liberal ideology has become institutionalized in a way that systemmatically conditions the propensity to cooperate, even where defection might be more rational.[73]

Sorting out the autonomous influence of knowledge and ideology can prove extremely difficult in practice, particularly where there is a congruence between ideology and structural position. If structural theories are weak on cognitive variables, most cognitive theories cannot describe clearly how power and ideas interact. The same set of objections may even extend to knowledge-oriented "cognitivism." While few would claim that scientific knowledge is reducible to social interests, scientific evidence can be resisted. The *range* of scientific investigation, if not its content, is also shaped by social and political purposes. Cognitive theory needs to specify more clearly the types of issues and conditions under which consensual knowledge is likely to drive cooperation.[74] Are they many or few? No one would disagree that purposes, values, and knowledge matter, but when? What is the relationship between the cognitivist research program and that outlined by various forms of structuralism?

Cognitivists pose a simple, yet profound, question: can interests in an issue area be unambiguously deduced from power and situational con-

71. Richard Cooper, "International Cooperation in Public Health as a Prologue to Macroeconomic Cooperation" (Harvard University, 1986); and "International Economic Cooperation: Is It Desirable? Is It Likely?" *Bulletin of the American Academy of Arts and Sciences* 39 (1985).

72. Don Babai, "Between Hegemony and Poverty: The World Bank in the International System" (Ph.D. dissertation, University of California, Berkeley, 1984). For other work in this vein, see Beverly Crawford and Stefanie Lenway, "Decison Modes"; Ernst Haas, Mary Pat Williams, and Don Babai, *Scientists and World Order: The Uses of Technical Information in International Organizations* (Berkeley: University of California Press, 1977); Emmanuel Adler, "Ideological 'Guerillas' and the Quest for Technological Autonomy: Brazil's Domestic Computer Industry," *International Organization* 40 (Summer 1986), pp. 673–706.

73. Judith Goldstein, "The Political Economy of Trade: Institutions of Protection," *American Political Science Review* 80 (March 1986), pp. 161–84. Other analyses emphasizing the role of ideology in regime maintenance and change are Robert Cox, "Ideologies and the New International Economic Order: Reflections on Some Recent Literature," *International Organization* 33 (Spring 1979), pp. 257–302; Jason L. Finkle and Barbara Crane, "Ideology and Politics at Mexico City: The United States at the 1984 International Conference on Population," *Population and Development Review* 11 (March 1985), pp. 1–28; Charles Kindleberger, "The Rise of Free Trade in Europe, 1820–1875," *Journal of Economic History* 4 (March 1975), pp. 613–34.

74. Ernst Haas attempts this discussion in "Why Collaborate? Issue-Linkage and International Regimes," *World Politics* 32 (April 1980), pp. 357–405.

straints? Frequently they cannot. Without shifts in power position, interests change as a result of learning, persuasion, and divine revelation. Knowledge and ideology may then become an important explanation of regime change, but when posed in this fashion, the question is an empirical as much as a theoretical one. The resolution of the debate between structuralists and cognitivists will depend on tests that allow a confrontation between the two approaches without violating the epistemological tenets of either.

4. Conclusion: Recapturing politics

Current theories of international regimes have ignored domestic political processes, in part because of the lure of parsimonious systemic theory. This neglect has extended to the issue of how regimes actually influence national policy choices, a question closely related to the issue of compliance and regime strength. More broadly, there have been few studies of the domestic political determinants of international cooperation. There are both methodological and theoretical reasons to open the black-box of domestic politics. Even if one adopts a structural explanation of compliance and defection, validating such claims demands careful reconstruction of decision-making at the national level. But the neglect of the domestic political and economic realm has had deeper costs, including a neglect of the substantive issues over which states are likely to seek cooperation and the basic forces leading to regime change. To address these difficulties, we suggest a research program that views international cooperation not only as the outcome of relations among states, but of the interaction between domestic and international games and coalitions that span national boundaries.

Do regimes "matter"?

Regimes are said to affect state behavior in two ways. One, emphasized in functionalist and game-theoretic approaches, is that regimes have altered the situation or setting in which states interact so that cooperation is more likely. The literature on iterated Prisoner's Dilemma claims that altering the institutional environment—by lengthening the shadow of the future, limiting the number of players, increasing the transparency of state action, and altering the payoff structure—can increase the incentives to cooperate. Functionalist theories emphasize that regimes reduce the transactions costs associated with bilateral contracting.

How do we know if these claims are correct? More importantly, how do we know that these explanations of cooperative behavior are superior to alternative explanations? Two methods could substantiate these claims. Large-n studies could determine whether or not regimes are, in fact, associated with the institutional factors specified *ex ante* by the theory. Far more convincing, however, would be evidence that domestic policymakers were actually concerned with reputation, reducing transactions costs, the need for transparency, and so forth, when facing decisions about regime creation and compliance. Even if one advances a structural explanation, the most convincing evidence must be found in the calculations of national decision-makers. Drawing on the work of Alexander George, Vinod Aggarwal employs such a method of "process tracing" in analyzing the influence of international structure on national textile policies.[75] Surprisingly little work of this kind has been done.

An even stronger claim for regimes is that they can alter actors' interests or preferences, which are generally held constant in functional and game-theoretic formulations. Cognitivists claim that regimes may change basic definitions of reality. Over the 1970s, for example, the United Nations Conference on Trade and Development (UNCTAD) provided the institutional locus for a new Third World critique of the existing international economic order. UNCTAD virtually served as a secretariat for the Group of 77 developing countries; it provided studies and documentation that were crucial in defining individual LDC's positions in international forums.[76]

Where regimes are actually suspected of altering state preferences, the proposed research program should focus on domestic decision-making for verification, since other forces may also be at work simultaneously. This can be seen by examining the problems of compliance and defection.

A fit between regime rules and national behavior may not occur for three reasons. The first is that the norms characterizing the regime may not be *formulated* to be authoritatively binding. Some regimes, such as those governing human rights, allow self-selected national exemptions or represent only broad collective aspirations; they are, in effect, born weak.[77] Opportunism presents a second reason for disjuncture between regime norms and state behavior. States may negotiate regimes with the intention of breaking them or knowingly exploit others' compliance in order to extract higher payoffs.

A final possibility, and a more common and politically interesting one, is what Robert Putnam has called "involuntary defection."[78] This defection happens when a party reaching or supporting an international agreement is unable to sustain commitments because of domestic political constraints. Three examples suggest the pervasiveness of this phenomenon. The first is

---

75. Aggarwal, *Liberal Protectionism*, pp. 16, 19.

76. Rothstein, *Global Bargaining*.

77. Jack Donnelly shows that the international human rights regime is composed of widely accepted substantive norms and internationalized standard-setting procedures, but a very limited degree of international implementation and no international enforcement. As he concludes, "such normative strength and procedural weakness, however, is the result of conscious political decisions," "International Human Rights," p. 614.

78. Robert D. Putnam, "The Logic of Two-Level Games: International Cooperation, Domestic Politics, and Western Summitry, 1975–1986," Paper presented at the annual meeting of the American Political Science Association, Washington, D.C., 1986, p. 13.

the rise of the "new protectionism" in the advanced industrial states. Taking the form of quantitative restrictions in particular products aimed at particular exporting countries, these "orderly marketing agreements" and "voluntary export restraints" clearly violate GATT norms, especially the non-discrimination norm. Yet they are driven by efforts to diffuse political pressures, while simultaneously limiting the extent of protection, both by product and by trading partner. This practice has, in turn, affected the nature of the regime. Not surprisingly, there is little agreement on a code governing the use of selective safeguards, but the consensus seems to be moving towards a tolerance of their use.[79] Recent research on the implementation of IMF stabilization programs suggests a similar phenomenon.[80] Some programs are no doubt negotiated in bad faith, with little intention of fulfillment. More commonly, those at the negotiating table are simply unable to control those in the palace or in the streets. A final example may be drawn from the interwar period. Great Britain's strong commitment to maintaining the gold standard during the 1920s stimulated strong industrial opposition to the Bank of England's policies, contributing to the final decision to go off gold in 1931.[81]

"Defection" in such instances is not the result of calculating unified actors, but the outcome of domestic political conflicts which no single actor can control. How international agreements play into these domestic political fights is still poorly understood. Reputation has appeared in arguments against "rash" protectionist moves. Occasionally, the IMF has been used to implement programs that would have been impossible without outside pressure. The Bank of England argued that defending parity was key to British leadership in international financing affairs. On the other hand, opposition forces have used the government's compliance with regime injunctions to their own political benefit, arguing that they could have extracted a superior bargain by defecting, or that bowing to outside pressure is intolerable. Joanne Gowa shows how those defending the closing of the gold window portrayed regime rules as overly restrictive of national autonomy.[82]

Towards a new theory of international cooperation

Building a theory of cooperation and regime change demands that we return to the central insight of the interdependence literature: growing interdependence means the erasure of the boundaries separating international

79. Alan William Wolff, "The Need for New GATT Rules to Govern Safeguard Actions," in William Cline, ed., *Trade Policy in the 1980s* (Washington, D.C.: Institute for International Economics, 1983).

80. Stephan Haggard, "The Politics of Adjustment: Lessons from the IMF's Extended Fund Facility," and Robert Kaufman, "Democratic and Authoritarian Responses to the Debt Issue: Argentina, Brazil, Mexico," both in *International Organization* 39 (Summer 1986), pp. 505–34.

81. L. J. Hume, "The Gold Standard and Deflation: Issues and Attitudes in the Nineteen-Twenties," *Economica* 30 (August 1963), pp. 225–42.

82. Joanne Gowa, *Closing the Gold Window* (Ithaca: Cornell University Press, 1983).

and domestic politics. "Domestic" political issues spill over into international politics and "foreign policy" has domestic roots and consequences. Governments, when making choices about regime creation and compliance, try to preserve the benefits of cooperation while minimizing the costs that may fall on politically important groups. This insight appears to have been lost in much recent writing about regimes. One approach would be to start with the domestic-level game, and consider the conditions favorable to cooperation. This approach assumes that a state's decision to enter into and abide by international rules can be treated in the same way as any other public policy choice.[83] An institutionalist approach, for example, would suggest that the arena in which decisions are made conditions the ability of state elites to sustain commitments. Decisions made in insulated arenas may not be pulled as much by "uncooperative" forces. On the other hand, the decentralization of certain policies, such as banking regulation and tax policy in the United States, may inhibit the formation of international regimes. A coalitional approach would emphasize the constellation of domestic actors standing to benefit from cooperation. The Reagan administration's 1985 decision to seek international cooperation on the dollar and exchange rates was prodded in part by export interests and firms facing import competition.

Starting with the "unit" level is risky, since the interactive effects of international structures, bargaining, and rules on domestic politics can get lost. Peter Katzenstein's work on small European democracies attempts to capture such feedback, at least over a long historical period.[84] The position of small states in the international system influences the development of domestic institutions in predictable ways; these institutions, in turn, affect these states' ability to adjust to the dictates of a liberal international and regional order.

The next step is to develop interactive models that link domestic and international politics more closely. Robert Putnam has suggested that episodes of international cooperation must be viewed as "two-level games."[85] At one level, representatives of different countries seek to reach or sustain international agreements; at a second level, those same representatives must build the political support required to sustain commitments and establish credibility. These processes often occur simultaneously and expectations about the likelihood of gaining acceptance in one arena influence the bargaining process in the other.

Another approach focuses on the transnational coalitions that span countries. This method is adopted by Ernst Haas in his classic study *The Uniting*

---

83. For an insightful review of different approaches to public policy, see Herbert Kitschelt, "Four Theories of Public Policy Making and Fast Breeder Reactor Development," *International Organization* 40 (Winter 1986).

84. Peter Katzenstein, *Small States in World Markets* (Ithaca: Cornell University Press, 1985).

85. Putnam, "The Logic of Two-Level Games."

of Europe, but this line of research has not been adequately pursued. For example, does some synchronization of coalitional patterns or electoral cycles across states make cooperation more likely? Where a nation may lack a winning coalition domestically, can pressure or support from external actors tip policy in the direction favored by the cooperative minority? Robert Putnam and Nicholas Bayne suggest this may have occurred in the German decision to reflate in 1978.[86]

The central point is that growing interdependence means that groups at the domestic level increasingly have "regime interests." Welfare is tied not only to particular policy decisions, but to other states' compliance with regime norms, the way in which international cooperation is institutionalized, and the access regimes provide for private actors. Structural theory alerted us to the myopia of the second image. It would be a misfortune if the quest for parsimonious systemic theory displaced other research and theoretical traditions that study domestic histories and, above all, politics.

---

86. Robert D. Putnam and Nicholas Bayne, *Hanging Together* (Cambridge: Harvard University Press, 1984), pp. 88–89.

Regime design matters: intentional oil pollution and treaty compliance

Ronald B. Mitchell

Too many people assume, generally without having given any serious thought to its character or its history, that international law is and always has been a sham. Others seem to think that it is a force with inherent strength of its own. . . . Whether the cynic or sciolist is the less helpful is hard to say, but both of them make the same mistake. They both assume that international law is a subject on which anyone can form his opinions intuitively, without taking the trouble, as one has to do with other subjects, to inquire into the relevant facts.

—J. L. Brierly

Regime design matters.[1] International treaties and regimes have value if and only if they cause people to do things they would not otherwise do. Governments spend considerable resources and effort drafting and refining treaty language with the (at least nominal) aim of making treaty compliance and effectiveness more likely. This article demonstrates that whether a treaty elicits compliance or other desired behavioral changes depends upon identifiable characteristics of the regime's compliance systems.[2] As negotiators incorporate certain rules into a regime and exclude others, they are making choices that have crucial implications for whether or not actors will comply.

For decades, nations have negotiated treaties with simultaneous hope that those treaties would produce better collective outcomes and skepticism about

The research reported herein was conducted with support from the University of Oregon and the Center for Science and International Affairs of Harvard University. Invaluable data were generously provided by Clarkson Research Studies, Ltd. The article has benefited greatly from discussions with Abram Chayes, Antonia Chayes, William Clark, and Robert Keohane and from collaboration with Moira McConnell and Alexei Roginko as part of a project on regime effectiveness based at Dartmouth College and directed by Oran Young and Marc Levy. John Odell, Miranda Schreurs, David Weil, and two anonymous reviewers provided invaluable comments on earlier drafts of this article. The epigraph is from J. L. Brierly, *The Outlook for International Law* (Oxford: Clarendon Press, 1944), pp. 1–2.

1. This article summarizes the arguments made in Ronald B. Mitchell, *Intentional Oil Pollution at Sea: Environmental Policy and Treaty Compliance* (Cambridge, Mass.: MIT Press, forthcoming).

2. The term "compliance system" comes from Oran Young, *Compliance and Public Authority: A Theory with International Applications* (Baltimore, Md.: Johns Hopkins University Press, 1979), p. 3.

International Organization 48, 3, Summer 1994, pp. 425–58

the ability to influence the way governments or individuals act. Both lawyers and political scientists have theorized about how international legal regimes can influence behavior and why they often do not.[3] Interest in issues of compliance and verification has a long history in the field of nuclear arms control.[4] More recently, this interest in empirically evaluating how international institutions, regimes, and treaties induce compliance and influence behavior has broadened to include other security areas as well as international trade and finance.[5] Concern over the fate of the earth's environment recently has prompted a further extension into questions of whether and how environmental treaties can be made more effective at eliciting compliance and achieving their goals.[6]

Researchers in all these issue-areas face two critical questions. First, given that power and interests play important roles in determining behavior at the international level, is any of the compliance we observe with international treaties the result of the treaty's influence? Second, if treaties and regimes can alter behavior, what strategies can those who negotiate and design regimes use to elicit the greatest possible compliance? This article addresses both these questions by empirically evaluating the international regime controlling intentional oil pollution. Numerous efforts to increase the regime's initially low levels of compliance provide data for comparing the different strategies for eliciting compliance within a common context that holds many important

3. See, for example, Abram Chayes and Antonia Handler Chayes, "On Compliance," *International Organization* 47 (Spring 1993), pp. 175–205; Young, *Compliance and Public Authority;* Roger Fisher, *Improving Compliance with International Law* (Charlottesville: University Press of Virginia, 1981); and W. E. Butler, ed., *Control over Compliance with International Law* (Boston: Kluwer Academic Publishers, 1991).

4. See, for example, Abram Chayes, "An Inquiry into the Workings of Arms Control Agreements," *Harvard Law Review* 85 (March 1972), pp. 905–69; Coit D. Blacker and Gloria Duffy, eds., *International Arms Control: Issues and Agreements,* 2d ed. (Stanford, Calif.: Stanford University Press, 1984); and Antonia Handler Chayes and Paul Doty, *Defending Deterrence: Managing the ABM Treaty into the Twenty-first Century* (Washington, D.C.: Pergamon-Brassey's International Defense Publishers, 1989).

5. See, for example, John S. Duffield, "International Regimes and Alliance Behavior: Explaining NATO Conventional Force Levels," *International Organization* 46 (Autumn 1992), pp. 819–55; Ethan Kapstein, *Governing the Global Economy: International Finance and the State* (Cambridge, Mass.: Harvard University Press, 1994); and Joseph M. Grieco, *Cooperation Among Nations: Europe, America, and Non-tariff Barriers to Trade* (Ithaca, N.Y.: Cornell University Press, 1990).

6. For example, see Peter Haas, Robert Keohane, and Marc Levy, eds., *Institutions for the Earth: Sources of Effective International Environmental Protection* (Cambridge, Mass.: MIT Press, 1993); Peter H. Sand, *Lessons Learned in Global Environmental Governance* (Washington, D.C.: World Resources Institute, 1990); and Peter M. Haas, "Do Regimes Matter? Epistemic Communities and Mediterranean Pollution Control," *International Organization* 43 (Summer 1989), pp. 377–403. Current projects that deal with questions of regime compliance and effectiveness (and their principal investigators) include those being conducted at, or with funding from, Dartmouth College (Oran Young and Marc Levy); the European Science Foundation (Kenneth Hanf and Arild Underdal); the Foundation for International Environmental Law and Diplomacy (James Cameron); the Fridtjof Nansen Institute (Steinar Andresen); Harvard University (Abram Chayes and Antonia Chayes); Harvard University (William Clark, Robert Keohane, and Marc Levy); the International Institute for Applied Systems Analysis (David Victor and Eugene Skolnikoff); and the Social Science Research Council (Edith Brown Weiss and Harold Jacobson).

explanatory variables constant. The goal of the treaties underlying this regime has been to reduce intentional discharges of waste oil by tankers after they deliver their cargoes. Since the late 1970s, these treaties have established two quite different compliance systems, or "subregimes," to accomplish this goal. One has prohibited tanker operators from discharging oil in excess of specified limits. The other has required tanker owners to install expensive pollution-reduction equipment by specified dates. Treaty parties viewed both subregimes as equally legitimate and equally binding.[7] The two subregimes regulated similar behavior by the same nations and tankers over the same time period. The absence of differences in power and interests would suggest that compliance levels with the two subregimes would be quite similar.[8] According to collective action theory, these cases are among the least likely to provide support for the hypothesis that regime design matters: subregime provisions required the powerful and concentrated oil industry to incur large pollution control costs to provide diffuse benefits to the public at large.[9] Indeed, the lower cost of complying with discharge limits would suggest that compliance would be higher with those limits than with equipment requirements.

Not surprisingly, violations of the limits on discharges have occurred frequently, attesting to the ongoing incentives to violate the agreement and confirming the characterization of oil pollution as a difficult collaboration problem.[10] A puzzle arises, however, from the fact that contrary to expectation compliance has been all but universal with requirements to install expensive equipment that provided no economic benefits. The following analysis clearly demonstrates that the significant variance across subregimes can only be explained by specific differences in subregime design. Comparing the two compliance systems shows that the equipment subregime succeeded by ensuring that actors with incentives to comply with, monitor, and enforce the treaty were provided with the practical ability and legal authority to conduct

7. Thomas M. Franck, *The Power of Legitimacy Among Nations* (New York: Oxford University Press, 1990).

8. Case selection that holds these other factors constant avoids the notorious difficulties of measuring power and interests and allows us to "attribute variance in collective outcomes to the impact of institutional arrangements with some degree of confidence"; see Oran Young, *International Cooperation: Building Regimes for Natural Resources and the Environment* (Ithaca, N.Y.: Cornell University Press, 1989), p. 208. On difficulties in measuring power, see David A. Baldwin, "Power Analysis and World Politics: New Trends Versus Old Tendencies," *World Politics* 31 (January 1979), pp. 161–93.

9. Michael McGinnis and Elinor Ostrom, "Design Principles for Local and Global Commons," Workshop in Political Theory and Policy Analysis, Bloomington, Ind., March 1992, p. 21. Olson's argument that small groups supply public goods more often than large groups assumes that group members benefit from providing the good, which is not true in the oil pollution case; see Mancur Olson, *The Logic of Collective Action: Public Goods and the Theory of Groups* (Cambridge, Mass.: Harvard University Press, 1965), p. 34.

10. See Arthur A. Stein, *Why Nations Cooperate: Circumstance and Choice in International Relations* (Ithaca, N.Y.: Cornell University Press, 1990); and Robert Axelrod and Robert O. Keohane, "Achieving Cooperation Under Anarchy: Strategies and Institutions," in Kenneth Oye, ed., *Cooperation Under Anarchy* (Princeton, N.J.: Princeton University Press, 1986).

those key implementation tasks. Specifically, the regime elicited compliance when it developed integrated compliance systems that succeeded in increasing transparency, providing for potent and credible sanctions, reducing implementation costs to governments by building on existing infrastructures, and preventing violations rather than merely deterring them.

Compliance theory and definitions

Explaining the puzzle of greater compliance with a more expensive and economically inefficient international regulation demands an understanding of existing theories about the sources of compliance in international affairs. Realists have inferred a general inability of international regimes to influence behavior from the fact that the international system is characterized by anarchy and an inability to organize centralized enforcement. In what has been the dominant theoretical view, "considerations of power rather than of law determine compliance."[11] To explain variance in treaty compliance, look for variance in the power of those with incentives to violate it or in the interests of those with the power to violate it. Treaties are epiphenomenal: they reflect power and interests but do not shape behavior.

This view does not imply that noncompliance is rare in international affairs. Although nations will violate rules whenever they have both the incentives and ability to do so, as Hans Morgenthau notes, "the great majority of the rules of international law are generally observed by all nations."[12] For the realist, behavior frequently conforms to treaty rules because both the behavior and the rules reflect the interests of powerful states. More specifically, compliance is an artifact of one of three situations: (1) a hegemonic state forces or induces other states to comply; (2) the treaty rules merely codify the parties' existing behavior or expected future behavior; or (3) the treaty resolves a coordination game in which no party has any incentive to violate the rules once a stable equilibrium has been achieved.[13]

Treaty rules correlate with but do not cause compliance. Therefore, efforts to improve treaty rules to increase compliance reflect either the changed interests of powerful states or are misguided exercises in futility. The strength of this view has led to considerable attention being paid to whether rules influence behavior and far less being paid to design features that explain why one rule influences behavior and another does not.

---

11. The quotation is from Hans Joachim Morgenthau, *Politics Among Nations: The Struggle for Power and Peace,* 5th ed. (New York: Alfred A. Knopf, 1978), p. 299. See also Kenneth Waltz, *Theory of International Politics* (Reading, Mass.: Addison-Wesley Publishing Co., 1979), p. 204; and Susan Strange, "Cave! Hic Dragones: A Critique of Regime Analysis," in Stephen D. Krasner, ed., *International Regimes* (Ithaca, N.Y.: Cornell University Press, 1983), pp. 337–54 at p. 338. For a contrasting view, see Young, *International Cooperation,* p. 62.

12. Morgenthau, *Politics Among Nations,* p. 267.

13. On this distinction, see Stein, *Why Nations Cooperate.*

In contrast, international lawyers and institutionalists contend that the anarchic international order need not lead inexorably to nations violating agreements whenever doing so suits them. Other forces—such as transparency, reciprocity, accountability, and regime-mindedness—allow regimes to impose significant constraints on international behavior under the right conditions.[14] Implicit in the institutionalist view is the assumption that power and interests alone cannot explain behavior: a given constellation of power and interests leaves room for nations to choose among treaty rules that will elicit significantly different levels of compliance. High compliance levels can be achieved even in difficult collaboration problems in which incentives to violate are large and ongoing. Treaties can become more effective over time, and regimes may even learn.[15] Agreeing with Morgenthau that compliance will be quite common, institutionalists do not exclude the possibility that the regime, rather than mere considerations of power, causes some of that compliance.[16]

In essence, this debate revolves around whether in a realm of behavior covered by an international agreement, that behavior is ever any different than it would have been without the agreement. If we define "treaty-induced compliance" as behavior that conforms to a treaty's rules because of the treaty's compliance system, institutionalists view treaty-induced compliance as possible. In contrast, realists see all compliance as "coincidental compliance," that is, behavior that would have occurred even without the treaty rules.

The debate between these theories highlights the demands placed on research that seeks to identify those design characteristics of a regime, if any, that are responsible for observed levels of compliance. I define compliance, the dependent variable, as an actor's behavior that conforms with an explicit treaty provision. Speaking of compliance with treaty provisions rather than with a treaty captures the fact that parties may well comply with some treaty provisions while violating others. A study of "treaty compliance" would aggregate violation of one provision with compliance with another, losing valuable empirical information.[17] Restricting study to the explicit rules in a treaty-based regime allows the analyst to distinguish compliance from noncompliance in clear and replicable ways. Obviously, a focus on explicit rules ignores other potential mechanisms of regime influence, such as norms, principles, and

---

14. See, for example, Abram Chayes and Antonia Chayes, "Compliance Without Enforcement: State Behavior Under Regulatory Treaties," *Negotiation Journal* 7 (July 1991), pp. 311–30; Young, *International Cooperation;* Robert O. Keohane, "Reciprocity in International Relations," *International Organization* 40 (Winter 1986), pp. 1–27; and Krasner, *International Regimes.*

15. Joseph S. Nye, Jr., "Nuclear Learning and U.S.–Soviet Security Regimes," *International Organization* 41 (Summer 1987), pp. 371–402.

16. See, for example, Louis Henkin, *How Nations Behave: Law and Foreign Policy* (New York: Columbia University Press, 1979), p. 47; Young, *International Cooperation,* p. 62; and Chayes and Chayes, "Compliance Without Enforcement," p. 31.

17. At the extreme, if all parties violated treaty provision A and complied with treaty provision B, they could all be classified as in partial compliance, ignoring the important variance in compliance rates.

processes of knowledge creation.[18] However, this restrictive definition has the virtue of bringing the debate to a level at which research on actual treaties and actual compliance can contribute to the intellectual and policy debates.

This article evaluates the features of a regime that may determine compliance by differentiating among three parts of any compliance system: a primary rule system, a compliance information system, and a noncompliance response system. The primary rule system consists of the actors, rules, and processes related to the behavior that is the substantive target of the regime. In the choice of who gets regulated and how, the primary rule system determines the pressures and incentives for compliance and violation. The compliance information system consists of the actors, rules, and processes that collect, analyze, and disseminate information on instances of violations and compliance. Self-reporting, independent monitoring, data analysis, and publishing comprise the compliance information system that determines the amount, quality, and uses made of data on compliance and enforcement. The noncompliance response system consists of the actors, rules, and processes governing the formal and informal responses—the inducements and sanctions—employed to induce those in noncompliance to comply. The noncompliance response system determines the type, likelihood, magnitude, and appropriateness of responses to noncompliance. These categories provide the framework used in the remainder of this article to evaluate the oil pollution regime's sources of success and failure in its attempt to elicit compliance.

Two subregimes for international oil pollution control

For most people, oil pollution conjures up images of tanker accidents such as that of the *Exxon Valdez*.[19] While oil from such accidents poses a concentrated but localized hazard to the marine environment, the waste oil traditionally generated during normal oil transport has posed a more diffuse but ubiquitous threat. After a tanker delivers its cargo, a small fraction of oil remains onboard, adhering to cargo tank walls. Ballasting and tank-cleaning procedures mixed this oil—averaging about 300 tons per voyage—with seawater, creating slops. These in turn were most easily and cheaply disposed of by discharging them overboard while at sea.[20] By the 1970s, the intentional discharges made on thousands of tanker voyages were putting an estimated million tons of oil into the oceans annually.[21] While scientific uncertainty remains regarding the extent

18. See Haas, Keohane, and Levy, *Institutions for the Earth;* George W. Downs and David M. Rocke, *Tacit Bargaining, Arms Races, and Arms Control* (Ann Arbor: University of Michigan Press, 1990); Charles Lipson, "Why Are Some International Agreements Informal?" *International Organization* 45 (Autumn 1991), pp. 495–538; and Chayes and Chayes, "On Compliance," pp. 188–92.
19. The *Exxon Valdez* wrecked in Prince William Sound, Alaska, on 24 March 1989.
20. For comparison, the *Exxon Valdez* spilled thirty-five thousand tons.
21. National Academy of Sciences, *Petroleum in the Marine Environment* (Washington, D.C.: National Academy of Sciences, 1975). See also National Academy of Sciences and National Research Council, *Oil in the Sea: Inputs, Fates, and Effects* (Washington, D.C.: National Academy Press, 1985).

of damage to marine life caused by such chronic but low-concentration discharges, their impact and that of accidents on seabirds and resort beaches have produced regular international efforts at regulation.[22]

Intentional oil discharges were one of the first pollutants to become the subject of an international regulatory regime.[23] In the International Convention for the Prevention of Pollution of the Seas by Oil (OILPOL) of 1954, nations addressed the coastal oil pollution problem by limiting the oil content of discharges made near shore.[24] In what has been a regime largely focused on regulation,[25] numerous revisions were negotiated within diplomatic conferences sponsored by the Intergovernmental Maritime Consultative Organization (IMCO) or within its committees and those of its successor, the International Maritime Organization (IMO). By the late 1970s, the regime's major provisions, now contained in the International Convention for the Prevention of Pollution from Ships (MARPOL), consisted of restrictions on both tanker operations and tanker equipment that relied on quite different compliance systems.[26] Although rule-making has remained consistently international, governments and nonstate actors have played crucial roles in the implementation and enforcement of the regime: tanker owners and operators have been the targets of the regulations while maritime authorities, classification societies, insurers, and shipbuilders have monitored and enforced the regulations.

The discharge subregime

The discharge subregime of the last fifteen years evolved from the initial regulations of 1954. That agreement constituted a compromise between the United Kingdom—which wielded strong power in oil markets but had strong

22. See, for example, National Academy of Sciences and National Research Council, *Oil in the Sea;* and Joint Group of Experts on the Scientific Aspects of Marine Pollution (GESAMP), *The State of the Marine Environment,* Reports and Studies no. 39 (New York: United Nations, 1990).

23. For the history of oil pollution control from the 1920s through the 1970s, see Sonia Zaide Pritchard, *Oil Pollution Control* (London: Croom Helm, 1987); for a history from the 1950s through the 1970s, see R. Michael M'Gonigle and Mark W. Zacher, *Pollution, Politics, and International Law: Tankers at Sea* (Berkeley: University of California Press, 1979).

24. "International Convention for the Prevention of Pollution of the Sea by Oil," 12 May 1954, *Treaties and Other International Agreements Series (TIAS),* no. 4900 (Washington, D.C.: U.S. Department of State, 1954).

25. For an excellent description of a regime more focused on developing scientific understanding of an environmental problem, see Levy's description of the regime on European acid precipitation in Marc Levy, "European Acid Rain: The Power of Tote-board Diplomacy," in Haas, Keohane, and Levy, *Institutions for the Earth,* pp. 75–132.

26. See *International Convention for the Prevention of Pollution from Ships (MARPOL),* 2 November 1973, reprinted in *International Legal Materials (ILM),* vol. 12 (Washington, D.C.: American Society of International Law, 1973), p. 1319 (hereafter cited by abbreviation, volume, and year); and *Protocol of 1978 Relating to the International Convention for the Prevention of Pollution from Ships,* 17 February 1978, reprinted in *ILM,* vol. 17, 1978, p. 1546 (hereafter cited together as *MARPOL 73/78*).

environmental nongovernmental organizations pushing it to reduce coastal pollution—and Germany, the Netherlands, the United States, and other major states that viewed any regulation as either environmentally unnecessary or as harmful to their own shipping interests. Although the United Kingdom had sought to restrict tanker discharges throughout the ocean, the final agreement limited the oil content of discharges made within fifty miles of any coastline to 100 parts oil per million parts water (100 ppm). In 1962, the British pushed through an amendment applying this 100 ppm standard to discharges made by new tankers regardless of their distance from shore.

The principle underlying the 1962 amendment—that crude oil could float far enough that discharge zones would not effectively protect coastlines—had gained sufficient support by 1969 that nations agreed to limit discharges by all tankers throughout the ocean. The pressure to amend the 1954/62 agreement came from two different sources. On one side, the thirty-five million gallons of oil spilled by the grounding of the *Torrey Canyon* off Britain and France on 18 March 1967 and growing environmentalism, especially in the United States, supported a push for stronger regulations.[27] The previously resistant United States replaced the United Kingdom as the leading activist state and especially sought to ensure that amendments would address the growing evidence of enforcement problems with existing regulations.

On the other side, oil companies rightly interpreted the 1962 amendments as a wake-up call that discharge standards would soon be replaced by expensive equipment requirements. In response, Shell Marine International developed and promoted an operational means by which tankers could reduce oil discharges without any new equipment.[28] The load-on-top procedure (LOT) involved consolidating ballast and cleaning slops in a single tank, letting gravity separate out the water so it could be decanted from beneath the oil, and loading the next cargo on top of the remaining slops. The beauty of LOT was that it ensured that less cargo was wasted, thereby advancing both the environmental goal of reducing intentional oil pollution and the economic goal of reducing the amount of valuable oil discharged overboard. LOT even improved on the regime's existing standards, since its use reduced rather than merely redistributed intentional discharges. The problem was that normal operation of LOT produced discharges that exceeded the 100 ppm standard. If this criterion had remained in effect, tankers would have had to install expensive new equipment to comply with OILPOL, defeating LOT's major economic virtue. With the support of France, the Netherlands, Norway, and the now less-activist United Kingdom, oil and shipping companies therefore also sought to amend the treaty. Oil companies considered LOT so effective that they wanted diplomats to scrap the 1954/62 zonal approach altogether.

27. M'Gonigle and Zacher, *Pollution, Politics, and International Law*, p. 100.
28. J. H. Kirby, "The Clean Seas Code: A Practical Cure of Operation Pollution," in *Third International Conference on Oil Pollution of the Sea: Report of Proceedings, Rome 7–9 October 1968* (Winchester, England: Warren and Son, 1968), pp. 201–19.

The pressures for greater environmental protection, however, led them to support the more limited objective of redefining the limits on discharges from the 100 ppm "content" criterion to one that could be monitored using existing on-board equipment.[29]

In a unanimously accepted compromise in 1969, more stringent and enforceable regulations were framed in terms that averted equipment requirements. Within the fifty-mile near-shore zones, discharges could now only involve "clean ballast" that left no visible trace; outside the fifty-mile zones, discharges could not exceed 60 liters of oil per mile (60 l/m). Proponents argued that the clean ballast provision would improve enforcement by transforming any sighting of a discharge into evidence of a violation.[30] The more crucial change involved a new limit that total discharges not exceed one fifteen-thousandth of a tanker's capacity.[31] Although compliance with this standard required a tanker to reduce its average discharges by almost 98 percent, Shell's J. H. Kirby claimed that "any responsibly run ship, no matter how big, could operate" within these standards if it used LOT.[32] The low total discharge limit also allowed port authorities to assume that any tanker with completely clean tanks had blatantly violated the agreement.[33] These standards took effect in 1978 and remain in force today through their incorporation into the 1973 MARPOL agreement.

The equipment subregime

By the early 1970s, public concern was pushing environmental issues onto the international political scene with increasing frequency. The United Nations Conference on the Human Environment and negotiation of the London Dumping Convention in 1972 set the stage for a major overhaul of the OILPOL agreement. IMCO hosted a major conference in 1973 to negotiate the MARPOL treaty. Its goal was the replacement of OILPOL's rules with rules that would cover all major types of vessel-source marine pollution.

29. Kirby, "The Clean Seas Code," p. 206.

30. Assembly resolution 391, IMCO/IMO doc. resolution A.391(X), 1 December 1977, Annex, par. 5. All document citations herein refer to IMCO/IMO documents housed in the IMO Secretariat library. They are numbered similarly: according to issuing committee (abbreviated), meeting number, agenda item, and document number. Information documents are designated by "Inf." prior to the document number. Circulars are designated by "Circ.," issuing committee, and circular number only. Resolutions are designated by adopting body, resolution number, and meeting number. Conference documents are cited by abbreviated conference title, preparatory meeting number, agenda item, and document number. Hence the above resolution citation would be interpreted as the 391st resolution adopted by the 10th meeting of the (IMCO) assembly.

31. *1969 Amendments to the International Convention for the Prevention of Pollution of the Sea by Oil*, 21 October 1969, reprinted in Bernd Ruster and Bruno Simma, eds., *International Protection of the Environment: Treaties and Related Documents* (Dobbs Ferry, N.Y.: Oceana Publications, 1975).

32. Kirby, "The Clean Seas Code," p. 208.

33. See Kirby, "The Clean Seas Code," pp. 200 and 209; and William T. Burke, Richard Legatski, and William W. Woodhead, *National and International Law Enforcement in the Ocean* (Seattle: University of Washington Press, 1975), p. 129.

The U.S. government had become increasingly concerned that the ease with which tanker crews could violate discharge standards and the massive resources and diligence needed to detect violations were preventing effective mitigation of the growing oil pollution problem.[34] By 1972, Congress had adopted legislation that threatened to require all American tankers as well as all tankers entering U.S. ports to install expensive pollution-reducing equipment. The legislation included a proposal to require all large tankers to install double hulls to address accidental spills and segregated ballast tanks (SBT) to address intentional discharges. The SBT system involved arranging ballast tanks and associated piping such that ballast water could not come into contact with oil being carried as cargo. The system was expensive both in terms of capital and the reduction to cargo-carrying capacity. The United States sought international agreement to require SBT but threatened to require it unilaterally if necessary. Discharge requirements clearly were cheaper, more economically efficient, and "in theory . . . a good idea."[35] However, environmental pressures and growing evidence that LOT was neither as widespread nor as effective as had been hoped led the United States and the United Kingdom to support rules that offered easier and more effective enforcement.

The largely U.S.-based oil companies initially opposed SBT requirements but eventually supported them as preferable to threatened U.S. unilateral rules. Many shipping states also reluctantly supported SBT requirements. They believed such requirements would avert an even more costly double bottom requirement. It was also fiscally acceptable: the combination of a recent building boom and the proposed language of the requirements meant that tanker owners would only have to incur the additional costs of SBT many years in the future and then only for large tankers. However, governments representing shipbuilding interests (France and Japan) and those representing independent tanker owners (Denmark, Germany, Greece, Norway, and Sweden) opposed the requirement.[36] By a vote of thirty to seven, the conference adopted a requirement for tankers over 70,000 tons built in 1980 and later to install SBT.

By 1977, a spate of accidents in the United States and continuing enforcement concerns led President Jimmy Carter to propose that SBT requirements be applied to all tankers, not just large new tankers.[37] Given (1) that the United States was again explicitly threatening unilateral action and (2) that the 1973

---

34. M'Gonigle and Zacher, *Pollution, Politics, and International Law,* p. 108.

35. See statements submitted by the U.S. delegation to the 13th Preparatory Session for an International Conference on Marine Pollution in 1973: IMCO/IMO doc. MP XIII/2(c)/5, 23 May 1972. (Using note 30 as a guide, this would be the 5th document issued relating to agenda item 2[c]). See also doc. MP XIII/2(a)/5, 1 June 1972; G. Victory, "Avoidance of Accidental and Deliberate Pollution," in *Coastal Water Pollution: Pollution of the Sea by Oil Spills* (Brussels: North Atlantic Treaty Organization [NATO], 2–6 November 1970), p. 2.3.

36. M'Gonigle and Zacher, *Pollution, Politics, and International Law,* p. 114.

37. Jacob W. Ulvila, "Decisions with Multiple Objectives in Integrative Bargaining," Ph.D. diss., Harvard University, 1979, appendix A1.1.

MARPOL agreement still had been ratified by only three states, IMCO called a second major conference in 1978.[38] State positions reflected the fact that retrofitting existing tankers with SBT would reduce each tanker's (and the fleet's) cargo capacity by some 15 percent.[39] Greece, Norway, and Sweden saw this as a means to put scores of their laid up independent tankers back to work. However, most states saw SBT retrofitting as extremely expensive.[40] Just as the 1962 amendments had prompted LOT development, the 1973 MARPOL agreement prompted oil companies to perfect a technique known as crude oil washing (COW), which entailed spraying down cargo tanks with the cargo itself rather than with seawater. Operating COW equipment during cargo delivery transformed oil that otherwise would have been discharged as slops into usable delivered cargo, simultaneously reducing oil pollution and increasing cargo owner revenues. The industry proposal for COW as an alternative to SBT produced a compromise in which tankers built after 1982 had to install both SBT and COW, while existing tankers had to be retrofitted with either SBT or COW by 1985. The 1978 Protocol Relating to the International Convention for the Prevention of Pollution from ships was made an integral part of the 1973 MARPOL agreement. While MARPOL and its protocol, known collectively as MARPOL 73/78, did not enter into force until 1983, their standards regulated all new construction after 1979.

Observed compliance levels

Available evidence demonstrates a wide divergence in levels of compliance under these two subregimes. During the same time period in which almost every tanker owner was retrofitting existing tankers and buying new tankers to conform with MARPOL's requirements for SBT and COW, large numbers of tanker operators continued to discharge oil well in excess of legal limits. The variance between the observed compliance rates with the two subregimes is quite marked.

Violations of the clean ballast, 60 l/m, and total discharge standards in place since 1978 have been common. Oil company surveys from the 1970s show that neither oil company nor independent tankers reduced average discharge levels to the one fifteen-thousandth limit in any year between 1972 and 1977 (see Figure 1). Although oil company tankers dramatically reduced average discharges in the early 1970s, discharges remained at three times the legal limit. The two-thirds of the fleet operated by independent oil transporters did far worse, with discharges that were thirty times the legal limit and that were not

---

38. M'Gonigle and Zacher, *Pollution, Politics, and International Law*, pp. 122 and 130.
39. See Sonia Z. Pritchard, "Load on Top: From the Sublime to the Absurd," *Journal of Maritime Law and Commerce* 9 (April 1978), pp. 185–224 at p. 194.
40. For an excellent discussion of state positions during both the 1973 and 1978 conferences, see M'Gonigle and Zacher, *Pollution, Politics, and International Law*, pp. 107–42.

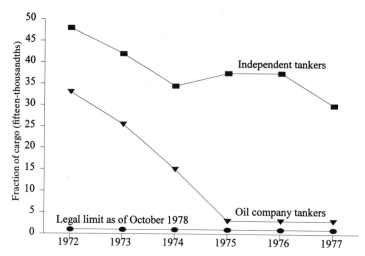

FIGURE 1. *Average tanker discharges, 1972–77*

Source. U.S. Congress, House Committee on Government Operations, *Oil Tanker Pollution: Hearings Before the Subcommittee on Government Activities and Transportation, 18 and 19 July 1978,* 95th Congress, 2d sess., p. 322.

much below levels that a tanker practicing no pollution control would have produced.[41] The trends in these discharges suggest that few tankers complied with the limit after it took legal effect in 1978.[42]

Other evidence confirms the frequency of discharge violations. A 1981 National Academy of Sciences estimate of oil pollution relied on an assumption that 50 percent of the world's tanker fleet was violating the total discharge limit.[43] A 1989 revision of that study assumed 15–20 percent of tankers were still violating this limit, although it provided no evidence to support the dramatic improvement.[44] Representatives of independent transporters admit that tankers often violate discharge limits to comply with their contracts: some charter arrangements require ships to arrive with clean tanks but many ports lack facilities to receive the slops they generate by cleaning.[45] Studies of

41. See, for example, the estimate of 0.3 percent in James E. Moss, *Character and Control of Sea Pollution by Oil* (Washington, D.C.: American Petroleum Institute, 1963), p. 47, and the estimate of 0.4 percent in IMCO/IMO doc. OP I/21, 15 January 1965, of the Oil Pollution subcommittee. (Using note 30 as a guide, this indicates the only document issued relating to agenda item 21 at the 1st meeting of the subcommittee.)

42. Unfortunately, oil companies discontinued the surveys after 1977. Personal communication from Arthur McKenzie, Tanker Advisory Center, New York, 1992.

43. Informational document of the Marine Environment Protection Committee: IMCO/IMO doc. MEPC XVI/Inf.2, 4 November 1981.

44. IMCO/IMO doc. MEPC 30/Inf.13, 19 September 1990, p. 15.

45. For example, "IMO, Tanker Owners Urge Increase in Facilities Accepting Oily Wastes," *International Environment Reporter,* 8 March 1989, p. 130.

detected oil slicks and dead seabirds as well as violation reports provided to IMO confirm that many tankers continue to discharge their slops at sea.[46]

The variety of sources pointing to violation of the discharge standards contrasts sharply with the uniformity of evidence that compliance with the equipment standards has been exceptionally high. By 1981, one shipping research firm already had evidence that new tankers were being built with SBT and existing tankers were being retrofitted with SBT and/or COW.[47] Recent national and international studies as well as industry experts reveal a common assumption that all tankers comply with the equipment standards although none provides empirical support for this assumption.[48]

Analysis of previously unavailable data on equipment installed on large tankers supports these perceptions (see Table 1).[49] Among large tankers in the fleet at the end of 1991, 94 percent of tankers built in 1979 or earlier had installed SBT or COW as required, 98 percent of those built between 1980 and 1982 had installed SBT as required, and 98 percent of those built after 1982 had installed both SBT and COW as required. The figures not only confirm remarkably high compliance rates but also document that tankers of all nations, not merely those that supported the equipment requirements during negotiation, have complied.

The variance between the subregimes is more remarkable when one considers that both international politics and private economics would lead us to expect higher compliance with the discharge standards, not the equipment standards. The discharge standards had been adopted unanimously. In contrast, several powerful nations opposed the equipment standards in both 1973 and 1978. Tankers seeking the economic benefits of conserving oil could have done so most cheaply by using the equipment-free option of LOT, not by installing COW or the even more expensive SBT. Indeed, in 1978, one

---

46. See, for example, C. J. Camphuysen, *Beached Bird Surveys in the Netherlands 1915–1988: Seabird Mortality in the Southern North Sea Since the Early Days of Oil Pollution* (Amsterdam: Werkgroep Noordzee, 1989); United States Coast Guard, *Polluting Incidents In and Around U.S. Waters* (Washington, D.C.: U.S. Department of Commerce, 1973 and 1975–86); N. Smit-Kroes, *Harmonisatie Noordzeebeleid: Brief van de Minister van Verkeer en Waterstaat* (Tweede Kamer der Staten-Generaal: 17-408) (Harmonization of North Sea policy: Letter from the Minister of Transport and Waterways; Lower House of Parliament) (The Hague: Government Printing Office of the Netherlands, 1988); IMCO/IMO doc. MEPC 21/Inf. 8, 21 March 1985; and Second International Conference on the Protection of the North Sea, *Quality Status of the North Sea: A Report by the Scientific and Technical Working Group* (London: Her Majesty's Stationery Office, 1987), p. 14.

47. Drewry Shipping Consultants, Ltd., *The Impact of New Tanker Regulations,* Drewry publication no. 94 (London: Drewry Shipping Consultants, Ltd., 1981), p. 25.

48. See IMCO/IMO doc. MEPC 30/Inf.13, 19 September 1990, p. 8; Second International Conference on the Protection of the North Sea, *Quality Status of the North Sea,* p. 57; Pieter Bergmeijer, "The International Convention for the Prevention of Pollution from Ships," paper presented at the 17th Pacem in Maribus conference, Rotterdam, August 1990, p. 12; and personal interview with E. J. M. Ball, Oil Companies International Marine Forum, London, 26 June 1991;

49. The detailed statistics in Table 1 and Figure 2 were developed from an electronic version of Clarkson Research Studies, Ltd., *The Tanker Register* (London: Clarkson Research Studies, Ltd., 1991) generously provided by Clarkson Research Studies, Ltd.

TABLE 1. *Percentage of crude oil tankers weighing over 70,000 deadweight tons with segregated ballast tanks (SBT) and/or crude oil washing equipment (COW) onboard*[a]

Equipment onboard	Tanker construction date (and MARPOL requirement)[b]		
	1979 and earlier (SBT or COW)	1980–82 (SBT only)	Post 1982 (SBT and COW)
SBT and COW	32%	94%	98%
SBT or COW	94%	99%	100%
Total SBT (alone and with COW)	36%	98%	99%
Total COW (alone and with SBT)	89%	95%	99%
SBT alone	4%	4%	1%
COW alone	58%	1%	1%
Neither SBT nor COW	6%	1%	0%
MARPOL compliance level	94%	98%	98%

[a]Data reflect tankers in the fleet as of 31 December 1991.
[b]MARPOL = International Convention for the Prevention of Pollution from Ships.

Source. Electronic version of Clarkson Research Studies, Ltd., *The Tanker Register* (London: Clarkson Research Studies, Ltd., 1991).

academic analyst, Charles Okidi, predicted that the enormous costs of SBT would make compliance "negligible."[50]

In short, the empirical evidence of higher compliance levels with the equipment subregime runs contrary to predictions based on a simple analysis of exogenous power and interests. How do we explain what appears to be a significant divergence between theory and observed outcomes? Was any of the observed compliance treaty-induced? If so, what elements of the equipment standards compliance system explain its greater success at eliciting compliance? The rest of this article answers these questions.

Was compliance treaty-induced?

Before we can explain how one subregime produced such dramatically higher compliance levels than another within the same issue-area, we need to assure ourselves that we can accurately attribute this variance to features of the

50. Charles Odidi Okidi, *Regional Control of Ocean Pollution: Legal and Institutional Problems and Prospects* (Alphen aan den Rijn, The Netherlands: Sijthoff and Noordhoff, 1978), p. 34.

regime. Taking realist analysis seriously requires that we avoid attributing causation where only spurious correlation exists. Factors other than variation in the compliance systems of the two subregimes may explain the observed behaviors. Did tanker owners and operators act any differently than they would have in the absence of international regulations? The following accounting of incentives to comply with regulations from both within and outside of the regime strongly suggests (1) that increased use of LOT owes more to economics than to international law, (2) that increased installation of COW equipment owes much to economics but also reflects the MARPOL regime's influences, and (3) that increased installation of SBT largely is due to MARPOL influences.

LOT

Several pieces of evidence indicate that the 1969 rules had little to do with the observed increase in the use of LOT by tanker operators. A large share of tankers simply did not use LOT or comply with the discharge standards. The continuing noncompliance with discharge standards did not result from an inability to use LOT—a noncomplex procedure that required no new equipment—but from insufficient incentives to use it.

The subregime itself produced few effective mechanisms for inducing operators to adopt LOT. While I discuss these failures more fully below, the discharge subregime's compliance system failed to induce the monitoring and enforcement necessary to deter violations. The subregime's failure effectively to detect, identify, prosecute, and penalize violators left tanker operators' incentives to comply with it largely uninfluenced. As the official IMO newsletter put it, "Little has changed in the three decades since [1962]. The problem is detecting a violation in the first place (which is difficult) and then collecting sufficient evidence to prove the case in court (which has all too often proved to be impossible)."[51]

Given the absence of these pathways for regime influence, it is not surprising to find that economic influences readily explain the pattern of LOT usage. A tanker operator's first-order incentives to use LOT depended on the costs of recovering waste oil, the value of that oil, and the ownership of the oil being transported. This last factor meant that oil companies had far greater incentives to adopt LOT than did independent transporters. The latter carry oil on charter to cargo owners and are paid for the amount of oil initially loaded, known as the bill-of-lading weight, not for the amount delivered. Therefore, discharging waste oil at sea costs the independent transporter nothing. Indeed, using LOT reduces the bill-of-lading weight in subsequent cargo by the amount of remaining slops, thereby reducing the payment that the independent transporter receives. In contrast, operators that own their cargoes, as oil

---

51. See p. 9 of "Cleaner Oceans: The Role of the IMO in the 1990s," *IMO News,* no. 3, 1990, pp. 6–12.

companies usually do, can offset a LOT tanker's slightly smaller cargo capacity with the benefit of having all the oil it paid for delivered. At 1976 prices, the lower bill-of-lading weight cost the tanker owner some $700, while the value of oil recovered benefited the cargo owner some $16,000.[52]

The decrease in average discharges of oil company tankers in the 1970s and the absence of a similar decrease in discharges of independent tankers correlate more with these divergent incentives and with rising oil prices than with any treaty proscription. Oil companies' greater incentives to conserve oil explain why their average discharges were lower than those of independent tankers in 1972 and why they decreased discharges more rapidly after the 1973 oil price hikes (see Figure 1). If the regime, rather than economics, were influencing oil company behavior, these decreases should have occurred only after the total discharge limits took legal effect in 1978, not after 1973. The far smaller decrease in average discharge among independents reflects the fact that conserved oil had little value to them.

Nevertheless, the OILPOL regime does appear to have been responsible for the timing of LOT development in the early 1960s and to have at least contributed to some adoption of LOT. Oil company representatives noted at the time that they had developed LOT in response to the increasing pressures for equipment requirements that were evident at the 1962 conference. The facts that (1) oil prices remained constant throughout the 1960s and (2) LOT involved a procedural—not a technological—breakthrough support this more limited claim of regime influence. Declines in discharges by both oil company and independent tankers before the oil price increases of 1973 and declines in independent tankers' discharges after 1973 also prove difficult to attribute exclusively to economic factors. Having said this, however, it remains clear that economic factors rather than the features of the subregime were the dominant factors influencing tanker operators' behavior.

COW

The almost universal installation of COW equipment initially tempts one to conclude that compliance was treaty-induced. The contrast in rates of use of LOT and COW suggest that differences in the designs of the corresponding subregimes may be responsible, given that both methods allowed a tanker operator to reduce waste oil. However, closer evaluation reveals that here, too, economic factors played an important role, although not an exclusive one.

Like LOT, COW has economic as well as environmental benefits. COW's costs include those for the washing machines and the additional time and labor needed to wash tanks in port during delivery rather than during the ballast

---

52. The following discussion of the costs of LOT, COW, and SBT draws heavily on William G. Waters, Trevor D. Heaver, and T. Verrier, *Oil Pollution from Tanker Operations: Causes, Costs, Controls* (Vancouver, B.C.: Center for Transportation Studies, 1980).

voyage.[53] As with LOT, the offsetting benefit of more delivered cargo accrues to the cargo owner. However, the tanker operator also benefits: the decrease in oil left on board increases the tanker's effective cargo capacity and reduces sludge buildup, which can lead to large repair and maintenance costs. Compared with a tanker that was not practicing pollution control, using COW produced a net savings per voyage of $9,000.

These economic incentives to adopt COW are borne out by the evidence of the timing of its adoption. In many instances, tankers adopted COW before required to do so by MARPOL. Recall that negotiators only incorporated COW requirements into MARPOL in 1978 and only made them applicable to tankers built after 1982. Yet by the mid-1970s, many oil companies had already incorporated COW as a standard operational procedure.[54] This timing does not correspond with the development of COW technology in the late 1960s or with the deadline set by MARPOL. Instead, like LOT, it corresponds with the rising oil prices of the 1970s.

The contrast to the SBT requirements also confirms the role of economics. The higher capital costs of SBT and the significant reduction to cargo-carrying capacity that SBT involved imposed a net cost per voyage on a tanker with SBT of $1,500 relative to a tanker with no pollution-control equipment. A new tanker installing both COW and SBT, as required by MARPOL, faced costs of almost $8,000 per voyage. Owners of large tankers built before 1980, who were allowed to choose between SBT and COW, installed COW equipment on 89 percent of their tankers and SBT on only 36 percent (see Table 1). Owners also installed COW equipment on 95 percent of large tankers built between 1980 and 1982, even though MARPOL only required them to install SBT. COW's economic benefits certainly appear to be a major influence on COW installations.

Several details suggest that economics were not the sole influence on behavior, however. If they were, we should expect companies to achieve the economic goal of conserving oil by the cheapest and most cost-effective means possible, that is, by LOT, not COW. We should also expect to see the same divergence between the behavior of independent carriers and oil companies as we observed in the LOT case. Yet the 99 percent compliance rate attests to the fact that all tanker owners were installing COW. The adoption of COW more frequently than SBT does not imply that the subregime was ineffective, only that when the subregime left owners with alternatives, their choices were driven by costs. In contrast to clear flaws in the compliance system supporting

53. Drewry Shipping Consultants, Ltd., *Tanker Regulations: Enforcement and Effect,* Drewry publication no. 135 (London: Drewry Shipping Consultants, Ltd., 1985), p. 25.

54. See M. G. Osborne and J. M. Ferguson, "Technology, MARPOL, and Tankers: Successes and Failures," *IMAS 90: Maritime Technology and the Environment* (London: Institute of Marine Engineers, 1990), p. 6–2; Testimony of William Gray, in U.S. Congress, House Committee on Government Operations, *Oil Tanker Pollution: Hearings Before the Subcommittee on Government Activities and Transportation, 18 and 19 July 1978,* 95th Congress, 2d sess., 1978, p. 92; and IMCO/IMO doc. MEPC V/Inf.A, 27 April 1976.

discharge standards, as I detail below, the design of the compliance system supporting equipment requirements provided several means of successfully reducing both the incentives and ability of tanker owners to violate COW requirements. Thus, an interplay among economics and subregime characteristics appears to have been the source of widespread COW adoption.

SBT

Adoption of the SBT standard provides an unambiguous example of subregime influence on behavior. Unlike COW or LOT, tanker owners had no economic incentives to install this technology. SBT's additional piping and equipment added several million dollars to the cost of a new tanker, representing almost 5 percent of total cost.[55] Installing SBT also reduced cargo capacity, especially when installed on an existing tanker. Yet these costs provided no offsetting benefits in the form of reduced cargo wastage. Even those governments that had supported the 1978 proposal that all tankers be retrofitted with SBT admitted that SBT would increase the cost of carrying oil by 15 percent; some oil company estimates ran up to 50 percent.[56] As late as 1991, oil and shipping interests opposed mandatory SBT retrofitting as being too expensive.[57]

The pattern of observed SBT installation follows that which one would predict for behavior driven by effective treaty rules rather than economics. Among tankers currently in the fleet, more than 98 percent of those required to install SBT have done so despite the significant costs involved. Compliance has been elicited even among those required to install both SBT and COW. Rates of SBT installation among older tankers bolster the argument: among tankers built before 1980, which MARPOL allowed to choose between SBT and COW, only 36 percent have installed SBT. Indeed, owners installed SBT alone on only 4 percent of older tankers but installed COW alone on 58 percent, suggesting that owners installed SBT only when a tanker was already in dock to be retrofitted with COW. Figure 2 graphs the percentages of current tankers using SBT and COW by year of construction. The timing of the increase in the number of tankers installing SBT seen in the figure reinforces the conclusion that owners installed SBT only under the regulatory threat posed by the subregime's compliance system. In short, owners have installed SBT only when MARPOL required them to do so. As one analyst noted, "If there were not a

---

55. See Philip A. Cummins, Dennis E. Logue, Robert D. Tollison, and Thomas D. Willett, "Oil Tanker Pollution Control: Design Criteria Versus Effective Liability Assessment," *Journal of Maritime Law and Commerce* 7 (October 1975), pp. 181–82; and Charles S. Pearson, *International Marine Environmental Policy: The Economic Dimension* (Baltimore, Md.: The Johns Hopkins University Press, 1975), p. 98.

56. See IMCO/IMO doc. MEPC V/Inf. 4, 8 March 1976, p. A18; and M'Gonigle and Zacher, *Pollution, Politics, and International Law*, p. 134.

57. See IMCO/IMO doc. MEPC 31/8/5, 4 April 1991; and Osborne and Ferguson, "Technology, MARPOL, and Tankers," p. 6-2.

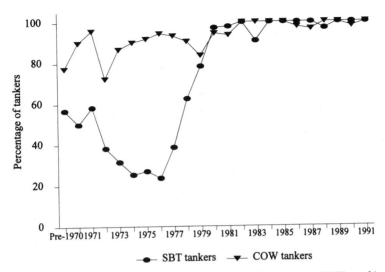

FIGURE 2. *Percentage of tankers with segregated ballast tanks (SBT) and/or crude oil washing equipment (COW) on board in 1991, by year of tanker construction*

Source. Electronic version of Clarkson Research Studies, Ltd., *The Tanker Register* (London: Clarkson Research Studies, Ltd., 1991), provided to the author.

regulatory requirement, there would not be SBT."[58] Within several years, the subregime had caused a radical change in tanker owner behavior.

One alternative explanation of SBT adoption deserves special attention. At least one analyst has claimed that hegemonic pressures exerted by the United States explain the success of MARPOL.[59] Certainly the negotiation history demonstrates that the SBT requirements of 1973 and 1978 resulted directly from threats of unilateral U.S. regulation. Indeed, the United States is the only state that adopted national legislation containing a faster schedule and broader application of equipment requirements than MARPOL.[60] Admitting that MARPOL's rules resulted from hegemonic pressures, however, does not imply that subsequent behaviors result from that same pressure. As international diplomats are all too well aware, resources adequate to elicit votes for a resolution during a conference may prove inadequate to cause corresponding changes in behavior. The relevant question is, "Could the United States,

58. Personal interview with Sean Connaughton, marine transportation analyst, American Petroleum Institute, Washington, D.C., 8 April 1992.

59. Jesper Grolin, "Environmental Hegemony, Maritime Community, and the Problem of Oil Tanker Pollution," in Michael A. Morris, ed., *North–South Perspectives on Marine Policy* (Boulder, Colo.: Westview Press, 1988).

60. Drewry Shipping Consultants, Ltd., *Tanker Regulations*, p. 11.

through unilateral measures, have induced so many tanker owners to install SBT?" Available evidence suggests not.

While the United States wields tremendous diplomatic leverage, it wields nothing near hegemonic power in oil transportation markets. Since the United States became concerned about oil pollution in the late 1960s, it has been responsible for less than 5 percent of new tankers built, less than 7 percent of tanker registrations, and less than 20 percent of world oil imports.[61] Given SBT's high costs, oil transportation companies would have been more likely to respond to unilateral U.S. equipment requirements by installing SBT on a sufficient number of tankers to service the U.S. market than by installing it on all tankers. Nor has the United States sought to link MARPOL enforcement with other issues through threats of sanctions or through side-payments.[62] Indeed, in terms of power to control oil tankers, Japan—which opposed SBT requirements in both 1973 and 1978—consistently has controlled larger shares of tanker construction, tanker registration, and oil imports than the United States. Thus, while the nation most strongly supporting universal installation of SBT could not have imposed its preferences on its own, the nation most capable of doing so consistently opposed such measures.

Mechanisms of influence

Compliance with discharge standards via the use of LOT was largely an artifact of economic factors. Compliance with requirements for SBT and COW has been both higher and more clearly the result of the treaty. Rival explanations of economic influences and international political hegemony prove incapable of adequately explaining the observed outcomes and behaviors. The equipment subregime succeeded at inducing reluctant tanker owners to spend considerable money on additional equipment that provided them with no economic benefit. The following assessment of the exact means by which it did so simultaneously reinforces the conclusion that the regime caused the change in behavior and identifies design features that might be used to improve the effectiveness of other regimes.

Which of the many differences between the two subregimes best explain the different levels of observed compliance? In what ways did the equipment subregime "get it right" where the discharge standards failed? In subsequent portions of this article, I shall show how the design of the equipment regime

---

61. See Lloyd's Register of Shipping, *Annual Summary of Merchant Ships Completed* (London: Lloyd's Register of Shipping, various years); Lloyd's Register of Shipping, *Statistical Tables* (London: Lloyd's Register of Shipping, various years); and United Nations, *Statistical Yearbook* (New York: United Nations, various years).

62. For examples of U.S. sanctions to enforce the International Convention for the Regulation of Whaling, see Gene S. Martin, Jr., and James W. Brennan, "Enforcing the International Convention for the Regulation of Whaling: The Pelly and Packwood–Magnuson Amendments," *Denver Journal of International Law and Policy* 17 (Winter 1989), pp. 271–92.

induced compliance by (1) eliciting monitoring and enforcement and (2) reducing opportunities for violation.

Enhancing transparency

The equipment subregime had one major advantage over the discharge subregime in its significantly higher transparency level. Violations of the SBT and COW requirements simply were far easier to observe than violations of any discharge standard.

Consider the two compliance information systems. Both OILPOL and MARPOL required tanker captains to note discharges in record books and to make those books available to port authorities for inspection. This obvious reliance on self-incrimination made naval and aerial surveillance programs the more common means of detecting illegal discharges. The total discharge standard of one fifteen-thousandth of cargo capacity improved on this system by providing a criterion that could be monitored by tank inspections in port without relying on information supplied by the tanker captain. Practically speaking, these inspections were restricted to ports in oil-exporting states, since discharges occurred after delivery, on a tanker's return to port to load more cargo.

In contrast, the compliance information system for equipment standards relied on the fact that buying or retrofitting a tanker requires the knowledge and consent of at least three other actors: a builder, a classification society, and an insurance company. Agents in each of these industries would know of a violation even before it was committed. MARPOL also required flag state governments, or classification societies nominated by them, to survey all tankers to ensure compliance before issuing the required International Oil Pollution Prevention (IOPP) certificate and to conduct periodic inspections thereafter.[63] As part of the process of evaluating tankers to provide insurers with the information needed to set rates, classification societies regularly monitor compliance with international construction requirements through representatives stationed in shipyards.[64] Finally, MARPOL gave all port states the legal authority to inspect a tanker's IOPP certificate and its equipment to ensure compliance with the equipment requirements.

The equipment standards subregime made violations more transparent than violations in the discharge standards subregime in several ways. To begin with, regulating the tanker builder–tanker buyer transaction yielded a drastically reduced number of events to be monitored. While several thousand tankers ply the world's oceans, they are owned, built, and classified by only a few owners, shipyards, and classification societies. A tanker making ten trips per year could

---

63. *MARPOL 73/78*, Annex I, Regulations 4 and 5.
64. Personal interview with John Foxwell, Shell International Marine, London, 27 June 1991.

violate the total discharge standard three hundred times in its thirty-year life but could only violate the equipment requirements once.

Equipment standards also required authorities to monitor far fewer locations to detect violations. The discharge process standards—100 ppm, clean ballast, and 60 l/m—required patrols of wide areas of ocean to detect slicks that often could not be linked with the responsible tanker. As early as the 1920s, experts had noted the difficulties of such a monitoring system.[65] The addition of total discharge limits allowed detection of violations while a tanker was in an oil port, a procedure involving far fewer resources. Unfortunately, most oil-exporting states had exhibited little interest in preventing marine pollution; many such states were not even parties to MARPOL.[66] Inspections to verify compliance with equipment standards could occur in developed oil-importing states, which had shown far more interest in enforcement. The shift from the 100 ppm and 60 l/m limits to total discharge limits improved dramatically the practical ability to detect violations. The shift from total discharge limits to equipment standards improved the regime further by increasing incentives for monitoring among those who already had the practical ability to monitor.

Equipment standards dramatically eased the problem of obtaining evidence needed to sanction a violator. The standards eliminated any reliance on self-incrimination by the perpetrator of a violation. Detecting an equipment violation and identifying its perpetrator also were not time-sensitive. Successful detection and identification of a violation had to occur within hours for violations of the initial standards and within days for total discharge violations but could wait for years for equipment violations. Authorities also faced several difficulties in transforming detection of a discharge at sea into a case worthy of prosecution. In what can be called "passive voice" violations, often a tanker could not be identified as responsible for a detected slick: authorities could only say a violation "had been committed." Even if a responsible tanker could be identified, determining whether the 100 ppm or 60 l/m criterion had been exceeded generally was difficult. The total discharge standard could have eliminated this problem, but oil-exporting states never established inspection programs. These flaws in the design of the discharge standards compliance system were not necessarily inherent or insurmountable. For example, some analysts proposed placing observers on all tankers to verify compliance with discharge standards.[67] Even without such a system, governments could have established enough ocean patrol and in-port inspection programs to make detection of discharge violations likely. However, such programs would have

---

65. Charles Hipwood, United Kingdom Marine Department, cited in Pritchard, *Oil Pollution Control*, p. 23.

66. While Iran and Iraq never have signed either agreement, Kuwait, Libya, Nigeria, Qatar, Saudi Arabia, the United Arab Emirates, and Venezuela have never signed MARPOL.

67. Cummins et al., "Oil Tanker Pollution Control," p. 171.

involved huge expenditures of resources to produce only a low probability of successful deterrence.

In the first years after OILPOL was signed, evidence quickly demonstrated that only the Federal Republic of Germany and the United Kingdom were making any significant efforts to monitor compliance with discharge standards.[68] By the late 1970s, the Americans, British, Dutch, and French had instituted aerial surveillance programs.[69] Many other countries used aerial surveillance during the 1980s.[70] However, these programs were most often small and nonsystematic. The Dutch program flew more surveillance flights per year in the late 1970s than at any time in the 1980s, and the United States discontinued its program in the 1980s due to budgetary pressures.[71] Reports to IMO from 1983 to 1990 show that only one-quarter of the sixty-seven MARPOL signatories had any programs to detect discharges at sea.[72] British and Dutch data confirm the problems of identifying perpetrators: the British could link detected spills to tankers in only 22 percent of cases and the Dutch, in only 14 percent.[73]

The entry into force of total discharge standards in 1978 allowed inspectors in oil-loading ports to assume that any incoming tanker with all tanks free of slops had violated the very low limit placed on total discharges. However, even those oil-exporting states that were party to MARPOL had strong disincentives to inspect ships in their ports: ports that were conducting inspections were less attractive loading sites than neighboring ports that were not conducting inspections. Not surprisingly, most governments did not alter their enforcement strategies in response to the greater potential for enforcement provided by the promulgation of total discharge standards. In contrast, considerable evidence confirms that the equipment regime significantly changed the ways in which nations and classification societies conducted tanker inspections. Many of the states that originally had opposed the 1973 and 1978 U.S. proposals for equipment regulations subsequently have conducted the in-port inspections needed to detect violations. In 1982, the maritime authorities of fourteen European states signed a Memorandum of Understanding on Port State Control, committing themselves annually to inspect 25 percent of ships

68. IMCO/IMO doc. OP/CONF/2, 1 September 1961.

69. See James Cowley, "IMO and National Administrations," *IMO News*, no. 4, 1988, pp. 6–11; Smit-Kroes, *Harmonisatie Noordzeebeleid;* and IMCO/IMO doc. MEPC 21/Inf.9, 25 March 1985.

70. James McLoughlin and M. J. Forster, *The Law and Practice Relating to Pollution Control in the Member States of the European Communities: A Comparative Survey* (London: Graham and Trotman, 1982).

71. Personal interview with Daniel Sheehan, U.S. Coast Guard, Washington, D.C., 9 April 1992.

72. Gerard Peet, *Operational Discharges from Ships: An Evaluation of the Application of the Discharge Provisions of the MARPOL Convention by Its Contracting Parties* (Amsterdam: AIDEnvironment, 1992), annexes 5 and 10.

73. See United Kingdom Royal Commission on Environmental Pollution, *Eighth Report: Oil Pollution of the Sea* (London: Her Majesty's Stationery Office, 1981), p. 195; and Smit-Kroes, *Harmonisatie Noordzeebeleid.*

entering their ports for violations of maritime treaties, including MARPOL.[74] Notably, until 1992, the memorandum of understanding explicitly excluded inspections for discharge violations from its mandate, limiting cooperation to inspection for equipment violations. Even though several member states had voted against SBT, all fourteen have included checks of IOPP certificates in the thousands of inspections they conduct each year. In reports to the IMO secretariat, five additional countries and the United States have reported finding discrepancies in tankers' oil pollution certificates. Canada, Japan, Poland, and Russia have major port inspection programs, and ten Latin American states have recently signed an agreement similar to the European memorandum.[75] While these countries undoubtedly vary widely in how frequently and carefully they conduct inspections, all have made inspections for MARPOL-required equipment a standard element of their inspection programs.

The effectiveness of these governmental inspections depends at least in part on the initial issue of accurate IOPP certificates by flag states or classification societies designated by them. Reports to IMO for 1984 to 1990 show that missing and inaccurate pollution certificates declined steadily from 9 percent to 1 percent; the memorandum of understanding secretariat reports similar declines—from 11 percent to 3 percent.[76] These trends suggest that after an initial period of learning how to issue and inspect certificates, classification societies and governments both now issue thorough and accurate certifications. Like port state governments, flag states and classification societies appear to have altered their behavior to become active participants in the equipment subregime's compliance information system. It would seem unlikely that classification societies and flag states would have responded in the same fashion to U.S.-only legislation.

The greater transparency of violations of equipment requirements served perhaps most importantly to reassure other tanker owners that their own compliance would not place them at a competitive disadvantage in the marketplace. An environmentally concerned tanker operator inclined to comply with the discharge standards could not escape the knowledge that others probably would not comply. The economic incentives to discharge oil at sea, the absence of transparency about who was and who was not complying, and the attendant inability of enforcement efforts to effectively deter dis-

74. "Memorandum of Understanding on Port State Control," reprinted in *ILM*, vol. 21, 1982, p. 1.

75. *Acuerdo de Viña del Mar: Acuerdo Latinoamericano Sobre Control de Buques por el Estado Rector Del Puerto* (Viña del Mar Accord: Latin American Accord on Port State Control of Vessels), 5 November 1992. The text of the agreement is almost identical to the text of the "Memorandum of Understanding on Port State Control," cited above. Reference to the agreement can be found in Secretariat of the Memorandum of Understanding on Port State Control, *Annual Report* (The Hague: The Netherlands Government Printing Office, 1992).

76. Secretariat of the Memorandum of Understanding on Port State Control, *Annual Report* (The Hague: The Netherlands Government Printing Office, various years).

charges precluded any assumption other than that many competitors would violate the discharge standards to reduce their costs. The greater transparency of equipment requirements assured a tanker owner installing SBT and COW that all other owners also were doing so. Each company could rest assured that its competitors also would have to incur equipment costs or be sanctioned for not doing so.

The equipment standards provided the foundation for a compliance information system far more transparent than was possible under the discharge subregime. In response, even governments that had opposed the adoption of the requirements conducted inspections for compliance. The subregime's compliance information system channeled the behavior of both governments and classification societies into monitoring activities that supported the regime. It did so by ensuring that those actors with incentives to monitor compliance also had the practical ability and legal authority to do so. The transparency of the system improved the ability to deter violations and simultaneously reassured tanker owners that their own compliance would not place them at a competitive disadvantage with respect to other owners.

Facilitating potent but low-cost sanctions

Greater transparency translated into higher levels of compliance with equipment standards only because the compliance system also induced likely and potent sanctions. The noncompliance response system of the discharge subregime failed to do the same. Even after a violation was detected, tanker operators were unlikely to be successfully prosecuted and equally unlikely to receive a stiff penalty. In contrast, the equipment subregime authorized governments to use the administrative sanction of detention, which made both the likelihood and the cost of being penalized far higher for the equipment standards than for discharge standards. The incentives and abilities of governments to prosecute and to impose large penalties for violation were far lower under the discharge standards than under the equipment standards.

Detected discharge violations frequently remained unprosecuted because the subregime relied on customary international law with its deference to enforcement by flag states. Both OILPOL and MARPOL required a government that detected a discharge violation at sea to forward all evidence to the flag state for prosecution. Only if a tanker discharged illegally within a state's twelve-mile territorial sea and then entered a port of that state could that state prosecute a tanker registered elsewhere. Flag states have generally been less than aggressive in following up on evidence referred to them.[77] Flag states often lack the ability to prosecute, since tankers flying their flag may rarely enter their ports. They also have few incentives to prosecute because vigorous enforcement on their part would induce owners to take their registrations, and the

77. See Organization for Economic Cooperation and Development (OECD), "OECD Study on Flags of Convenience," *Journal of Maritime Law and Commerce* 4 (January 1973), pp. 231–54.

large associated fees, to a less scrupulous state.[78] The fact that pollution occurred off another state's coastline and that many developing flag states lack vocal environmental constituencies only reinforced these disincentives to prosecute. In short, the flag states with the authority to prosecute lacked incentives to do so, and the coastal states with the incentives to prosecute lacked the authority to do so.

Under the discharge standards, even states sincerely seeking to prosecute and convict a violator faced major obstacles to success. As already noted, evidence of a violation often failed to produce a violator, and otherwise convincing evidence often failed to meet the legal standards of proof needed for conviction. Evidentiary hurdles should have decreased with the prohibition of discharges that produced visible traces. However, even with aerial photographs of discharges, tankers frequently avoid conviction.[79] Between 1983 and 1990, port and coastal states discarded for lack of evidence an average of 36 percent of cases occurring in territorial seas and successfully convicted and fined less than 33 percent of all detected violators.[80] An additional 20 percent of high-seas cases referred to flag states were not prosecuted for the same reason, and less than 15 percent of all referrals resulted in fines being imposed.[81] Indeed, according to Paul Dempsey, from 1975 through 1982 "ninety-two percent of all fines were imposed through port state enforcement."[82] Many experts had hoped that the clearer evidence from inspections for total discharge violations would overcome these problems, but, according to E. J. M. Ball, there is no record "of a single case where the one fifteen-thousandth rule was used for prosecution."[83]

When conviction was successful, governments rarely imposed penalties adequate to deter future discharge violations as required by MARPOL.[84] Although governments have the ability and legal authority to impose high fines, the conflicting goals of the judiciary often inhibit them from doing so. Most states' courts are reluctant to impose fines disproportionate to the offense to compensate for low detection and conviction rates. The principle that "the punishment should fit the crime" places an upper bound on fines that may be too low to successfully deter violation, if detection and prosecution is difficult.

---

78. Paul Stephen Dempsey, "Compliance and Enforcement in International Law—Oil Pollution of the Marine Environment by Ocean Vessels," *Northwestern Journal of International Law and Business* 6 (Summer 1984), pp. 459–561 and p. 576 in particular.

79. See ibid., p. 526; and personal interview with Ronald Carly, Ministry of Transportation, Brussels, 10 June 1991.

80. Peet, *Operational Discharges from Ships*, pp. 17–18, Tables 11 and 12; and Marie-Jose Stoop, *Olieverontreiniging door schepen op de noordzee over de periode 1982–1987: opsporing en vervolging* (Oil pollution by ships on the North Sea 1982–1987: Investigations and prosecution) (Amsterdam: Werkgroep Noordzee, July 1989).

81. Ronald Bruce Mitchell, "From Paper to Practice: Improving Environmental Treaty Compliance," Ph.D. diss., Harvard University, Cambridge, Mass., 1992, Table 5-1.

82. Dempsey, "Compliance and Enforcement in International Law," p. 537.

83. Personal interview with E. J. M. Ball.

84. *MARPOL 73/78*, Article 4(4).

Since 1975, the average fine imposed by states never has exceeded $7,000 and actually has decreased over time.[85] A Friends of the Earth International study concluded that fines have remained "very low in comparison to the price the vessel would have to pay for using port reception facilities."[86] Even when a large penalty is assessed, the delays between initial violation and final sentencing and the reluctance of most states to detain tankers for minor discharge violations often mean that the responsible tanker and crew have long since left the state's jurisdiction, making fine collection difficult. Owen Lomas points out that the problem is further exacerbated by the fact that "shipowners and their insurers routinely indemnify the masters of their ships against fines imposed upon them for oil pollution."[87]

In place of the discharge subregime's legal system of prosecution, conviction, and fines, the equipment subregime relied on quite different responses to noncompliance. The most immediate sanctions involved the ability of classification societies, insurers, and flag state governments to withhold the classification, insurance, and pollution prevention certificates that a tanker needed to conduct international trade. As John Foxwell put it, tankers "cannot get insurance without certification, and can't get certification without compliance."[88] These sanctions amounted to preventing any illegally equipped tanker from doing business. Even if an owner could devise a means to avoid these direct economic effects, a noncompliant tanker that could not trade to all ports would still bring a far lower price in the large tanker resale market.[89]

Besides these market-based sanctions, the equipment subregime obligated port states either to detain tankers with false pollution prevention certificates or inadequate equipment or to bar them from port.[90] As administrative sanctions, these responses skirted both flag state and port state legal systems—and the associated sensitivities regarding legal sovereignty. Paradoxically, this strategy made port states more likely to use detention and flag states more willing to accept it. Detention also had the virtue that even low usage by a few major oil-importing states forced tanker owners to choose between risking detention and the more costly option of not trading to those lucrative markets. Authorizing developed states to detain violating tankers effectively moved the right to sanction to countries that had far greater domestic political pressures to use it.

Coupling the equipment requirements themselves with these administrative sanctions completely eliminated the legal and evidentiary problems that make

85. Mitchell, "From Paper to Practice," Table 4–5.

86. IMCO/IMO doc. MEPC 29/10/3, 15 January 1990.

87. Owen Lomas, "The Prosecution of Marine Oil Pollution Offences and the Practice of Insuring Against Fines," *Journal of Environmental Law,* vol. 1, no. 1, 1989, p. 54. See also IMCO/IMO doc. MEPC 32/14/3, 17 January 1992.

88. Personal interview with John Foxwell, Shell International Marine, London, 27 June 1991.

89. Bergmeijer, "The International Convention for the Prevention of Pollution from Ships," p. 12.

90. *MARPOL 73/78,* Articles 5(2) and 5(3).

even clear violations of discharge standards difficult to prosecute successfully. Detention imposed opportunity costs on a tanker operator of several thousand dollars per day, and forced retrofitting could cost millions of dollars—far exceeding the fines for discharge violations.[91] Detention had the positive quality that it was not so costly as to be considered a disproportionate response to the crime but was costly enough to deter other violations. In short, detention was simultaneously more likely and more costly.

While many states inspected tankers for compliance with equipment requirements, most have not detained noncompliant ships frequently. IMO records from 1984 to 1990 reveal that seven of fifteen states, including Japan, have detained ships at least once. Only Germany, the United Kingdom, and the United States have detained ships often. This undoubtedly reflects a reluctance on the parts of some states to detain foreign tankers as well as the fact that most tankers were equipped appropriately in the first place.

Although few states detained ships, available evidence supports the conclusion that the subregime altered enforcement behavior. Not one of the states that detained ships began to do so until after MARPOL took effect in 1983.[92] Even the United States waited until that year—ten years after the detention provision had been accepted. Consider the counterfactual: it is unlikely that the United States would have detained tankers for breaching U.S.-only requirements for SBT, even though it had the practical ability to do so. Without MARPOL, such detentions would have constituted a major infringement of flag state sovereignty. If the use of the more costly detention sanction had reflected an exogenous increase in the interests of states in environmental enforcement, fines for discharge violations should have increased at the same time. Yet, as states began to use detention, fines did not increase dramatically.[93] Finally, public goods theory predicts that actors will tend not to enforce rules that supply benefits to other parties.[94] Contrary to theory, however, European states and the United States spend far more on enforcing equipment standards—a public good that improves the global ocean environment—than on enforcing discharge standards off their own coastlines—the benefits of which would be more "private."

The equipment subregime operated not by convincing reluctant actors to enforce rules with which they disagreed but by removing the legal barriers that inhibited effective enforcement by those states and nonstate actors willing to enforce them. Classification societies had interests in ensuring that the tankers they classified were able to trade without fear of detention. The incorporation of equipment requirements into their classification criteria provided the

---

91. Personal interviews with John Foxwell; and with Richard Schiferli, Memorandum of Understanding Secretariat, Rijswijk, The Netherlands, 17 July 1991.

92. Personal interview with Daniel Sheehan.

93. See Peet, *Operational Discharges from Ships,* annex 15; and Dempsey, "Compliance and Enforcement in International Law."

94. Axelrod and Keohane, "Achieving Cooperation Under Anarchy."

foundation for insurers to penalize noncompliant tankers. The willingness of a few environmentally concerned oil-importing states to inhibit tankers that lacked the required equipment from trading freely posed an extremely potent threat to a tanker owner. However, the ability and willingness of these states to threaten this sanction depended on removing international legal barriers to its use. Once these barriers were removed, imposing sanctions involved few costs to those imposing them, whether classification societies, insurers, or port state authorities. It thereby made detention more likely, even though it created no new incentives for states to impose sanctions. In a case of "nothing succeeds like success," the various threats of the equipment subregime's noncompliance system led to initial compliance by almost all tankers, making it rare that sanctions ever needed to be imposed.

Building on existing institutions

The oil pollution control regime induced implementation of those provisions that involved few direct costs to governments. Monitoring and enforcement proved especially likely when their costs were pushed "off-budget" by deputizing private, nonstate actors to issue certificates and conduct inspections. Piggy backing monitoring and enforcement efforts onto existing government programs also has been successful in accomplishing the regime's objectives with only minor program modifications and minimal cost. Governments have tended to ignore or put little effort into those stipulations that require significant new expenditure of government resources.

MARPOL's equipment subregime fostered monitoring by allowing governments to delegate responsibility for surveys to classification societies. This in turn increased the likelihood that tankers would be initially surveyed and subsequently inspected; additionally, the quality of inspections increased. Delegation also helps developing flag states, many of which lack the resources, the practical ability, and the incentives to conduct such inspections. MARPOL allowed such states to fulfill their treaty commitments by assigning classification and inspection responsibilities to actors who often had greater access to and more resources with which to conduct such inspections. Classification societies also had strong incentives to conduct accurate surveys as a means of protecting their business reputations and avoiding problems with insurance companies. The strategy thus simultaneously removed these tasks and the resources they required from the hands of governments and placed them in the hands of actors who could more easily accomplish them. Classification societies already had infrastructures to monitor tanker purchases for safety, financing, and insurance purposes. Adding pollution control to their long inspection checklists required only marginal changes to existing procedures.

The many inspection programs operated by developed port states parallel this pattern. Like classification societies, the maritime authorities of the European memorandum of understanding states, the United States, and other states interested in enforcing the equipment requirements could make simple, low-cost alterations to port state inspections already being conducted for safety, customs, and other purposes. The recent establishment of a Latin American memorandum and current negotiations for an Asian-Pacific memorandum suggest that the equipment subregime has provided states with a low-cost means to implement their international commitments as their interests in enforcement increase. In contrast, where states have had to incur significant new costs to implement treaty provisions, they have proved highly unlikely to do so. Detection of discharge violations required development of completely new surveillance programs. Most developed states have not established large, ongoing surveillance programs. Even in environmentally concerned states, aerial surveillance programs have tended to be relatively small and subject to the vagaries of domestic budget battles.

In the realm of compliance, the tendency for governments to push implementation costs onto nonstate actors is obvious. Compliance with the equipment standards has involved significant costs to tanker owners and no direct costs to governments. Yet, the treaty also required member states to ensure that their ports had facilities to receive the slops that tankers traditionally had discharged overboard. Although developed states have built more reception facilities, ports in the oil-loading states where they are most needed still largely lack any facilities. IMO participants consistently have failed to adopt proposals for developed states to fund reception facilities in developing states. Even in many developed states, facilities are sorely inadequate relative to the demands of their tanker traffic.[95] Additionally, the task of determining which ports have adequate facilities and which do not largely has fallen on the shoulders of nonstate actors.[96] National governments consistently have argued that providing reception facilities is the responsibility of either the ports themselves or of the oil industry.

Coercing compliance rather than deterring violation

The compliance systems of the two subregimes differ most strikingly in the fundamental model underlying their regulatory strategies. The equipment standards subregime relied on a "coerced compliance" strategy, which sought to monitor behavior to prevent violations from occurring in the first place. The discharge standards subregime was deterrence-oriented, attempting to detect, prosecute, and sanction violations after they occurred to deter future violations.[97] This basic difference in orientation made the compliance task facing the

95. IMCO/IMO doc. MEPC 30/Inf.32, 12 October 1990.
96. See IMCO/IMO docs. MEPC 19/5/2, 21 October 1983; MEPC 22/8/2, 8 October 1985; and MEPC 30/Inf.30, 15 October 1990.
97. Neither strategy was incentive-based, as was the funding of compliance under the Montreal Protocol and Framework Convention on Climate Change. For development of the distinction between these three strategies, see Albert J. Reiss, Jr., "Consequences of Compliance and Deterrence Models of Law Enforcement for the Exercise of Police Discretion," *Law and Contemporary Problems* 47 (Fall 1984), pp. 83–122; and Keith Hawkins, *Environment and Enforcement: Regulation and the Social Definition of Pollution* (Oxford: Clarendon Press, 1984).

equipment standards subregime more manageable than that facing the discharge standards subregime. The underlying strategy choice had important consequences for the level of compliance achieved: inhibiting the ability to violate treaty provisions proved far more effective than increasing the disincentives for violating them.

MARPOL's equipment standards created a remarkably effective system for detecting and sanctioning violations. Even if this compliance system had relied exclusively on the threat of oil-importing states detecting and detaining noncompliant tankers, most tankers would have installed COW and SBT. However, the equipment subregime's strength really came from the fact that it rarely had to use the more potent sanctions it made possible. Involving shipbuilders, classification societies, and insurers in the regulatory process could well have produced the same outcome even without the additional threat of detention. The subregime relied on surveying behavior and preventing violations rather than detecting and investigating them afterwards.[98] By regulating the business transaction of a tanker purchase rather than the autonomous action of a discharge, the equipment rules allowed identification of potential violators and made it harder to actually commit a violation. Tanker captains faced many regular autonomous decisions about whether to violate discharge standards. In contrast, tanker owners only had to decide once between violating or complying with equipment standards, and their decision required cooperation from other actors and involved major economic consequences. Even before construction began, classification societies and insurance companies were pressing for and monitoring compliance with international standards, helping avert violations before they occurred. Classification societies, insurance companies, and flag state inspectors could withhold the papers necessary to conduct business in international oil markets, thereby frustrating any tanker owner's attempt to reap the benefits of sidestepping these standards.

Experience with the discharge standards had shown that many states would not enforce pollution standards; indeed, even detention was used regularly by only a few states. Given the costs of SBT, if deterrence had been the major source of compliance, one would expect some tankers initially to have violated the equipment standards in an attempt to identify which and how many states actually would enforce the rules. Especially in light of their votes against the requirements, owners might well have assumed less than rigorous enforcement in places like France and Japan. Yet, compliance levels did not follow a pattern of initial noncompliance followed by stiff sanctions and subsequent compliance. The compliance system of the equipment subregime succeeded by effectively restricting the opportunities to violate it rather than making the

---

98. Reiss, "Consequences of Compliance and Deterrence Models of Law Enforcement for the Exercise of Police Discretion."

choice of violation less attractive. The very low noncompliance levels suggest that in most cases an owner simply decided it would be impossible to convince a tanker builder, a classification society, and an insurer to allow the purchase of a tanker without COW and SBT. Likewise, tankers coming in for repairs and maintenance undoubtedly would have found it difficult to explain why they were not planning on installing SBT or COW, as required. The low levels of detected violations of the equipment standards reveal that obstacles to committing a violation played a major role in preventing such violations. New tankers have been built initially to MARPOL standards, not retrofitted later in response to deterrence threats. Even before MARPOL's equipment deadlines passed, owners were building new and retrofitting older tankers to meet the requirements.

The equipment subregime may have been as successful as it was precisely because it produced a redundant regulatory system. It established compliance information and noncompliance response systems that prevented most violations but could successfully deter any actors who might otherwise have considered violating it. As the experience with discharge standards clarifies, deterrence-based strategies often require the successful completion of a complex chain of actions to be effective. The initial discharge standards subregime faced problems at almost every step of the process: detecting violations, identifying violators, prosecuting violators, and imposing potent sanctions. The shift to total discharge standards eliminated or mitigated some of these problems, but the problems remaining left overall deterrent levels essentially unchanged. A tanker captain evaluating the expected costs of violating OILPOL's or MARPOL's discharge standards could only conclude that the magnitude and likelihood of a penalty were quite small. Successful deterrence strategies must ensure that the whole legal chain operates smoothly, since the breakdown of any link can significantly impair its effectiveness.

Conclusions

Nations can design regime rules to improve compliance. This article has demonstrated that, even within a single issue-area, reference to design features of compliance systems surrounding particular provisions is necessary to explain observed variance in compliance. In the regime regulating intentional oil pollution, the same governments and corporations with the same interests during the same time period complied far more frequently with rules requiring installation of expensive equipment than they did with rules limiting total discharges of oil. Where theories of hegemonic power and economic interests fail to explain this variance, differences in the subregime's compliance systems readily explain why the former subregime led powerful actors to comply with it while the latter did not.

The equipment standards elicited significantly higher compliance because they selected a point for regulatory intervention that allowed for greater transparency, increased the likelihood of forceful responses to detected violations, built on existing institutions, and coerced compliance by preventing actors from violating them rather than merely deterring actors from doing so. In any regime, the distribution of state power and interests and the traits of relevant economic sectors constrain, but fail to fully explain, the regulations to which states will agree and the degree of possible compliance. By acknowledging these limits and realizing that the same goal often may be achieved by regulating quite different activities, policymakers can improve compliance by regulating those sectors more vulnerable to pressures for compliance and by facilitating the efforts of those governments and nonstate actors more likely to implement and enforce such regulations. This matching of regulatory burdens to expected behavior places the careful choice of the regime's primary rules at the center of any effective compliance system.

Once such primary rules have been established, careful crafting of the compliance information system and the noncompliance response system can further increase the likelihood of compliance. Oil pollution regulations succeeded by facilitating the goals of, placing responsibilities on, and removing the legal and practical barriers limiting those governments and private actors predisposed to monitor and enforce agreements, not by imposing obligations on recalcitrant actors. Inducing compliance required an integrated system of rules and processes that placed actors within a strategic triangle of compliance so that they had the political and economic incentives, practical ability, and legal authority to perform the tasks necessary to implement the treaty.[99] When such efforts succeeded, governments and private actors acted differently than they would have in the absence of the regime. When such efforts failed, opportunities to increase compliance were missed. We should not expect treaties to achieve perfect compliance.[100] Nevertheless, negotiators can and should design and redesign them to maximize compliance within the constraints that power and interests impose.

Eliciting compliance is only one of the criteria on which we would want to judge a regime's rules. Indeed, the value of compliance itself rests on the assumption that more compliance makes the treaty itself more effective. In the oil pollution case, compliance with the equipment rules involved at least as great a reduction in intentional discharges as did compliance with the discharge standards. Thus, we can safely infer that the higher compliance levels under the former rules also led to increased treaty effectiveness, a fact confirmed by a consensus among most experts that intentional oil discharges have declined since MARPOL took effect.[101] However, I am not arguing here for "command and control" regulations but for considering compliance levels—along with efficiency, cost, and equity—as an important evaluative criteria in regime design. The cheaper, more flexible, and more efficient discharge standards simply failed to induce the level of compliance needed to achieve a socially

99. I am indebted to Robert O. Keohane for the notion of a strategic triangle of compliance.
100. Chayes and Chayes, "On Compliance."
101. See Ronald B. Mitchell, "Intentional Oil Pollution of the Oceans," in Haas, Keohane, and Levy, *Institutions for the Earth*, pp. 183–248.

desired outcome; yet the costs of the equipment standards may have exceeded the benefits of that outcome. In cases in which more efficient solutions elicit compliance sufficient to achieve a policy goal, they are clearly preferable. If expected compliance with such solutions appears low, effective regime design requires evaluating whether the benefits of higher compliance outweigh the expense and inefficiency of alternative solutions.

Can we apply the findings developed from studying these two oil pollution cases to other issue-areas? Initial selection of a difficult collaborative problem with characteristics common to many international collaboration problems provides some confidence that we can do so. Other treaties provide anecdotal support for some of the findings reported herein. Nuclear powers consistently have sought to increase the transparency of arms control treaties through progressively tighter provisions for data exchange and on-site inspections. Although the experience with Iraq provides a dramatic example of failure, the nuclear materials and missile technology control regimes rely primarily on coerced compliance models of regulation, seeking to prevent countries from violation in the first instance. Human rights regimes frequently have used information from nongovernmental organizations to monitor compliance with their provisions. These design features seem likely to be the source of some regime compliance, but confirming that conclusion requires considerably more research. The solutions adopted in the oil pollution regime also undoubtedly cannot be applied to all regimes or even to all environmental regimes. Wildlife and habitat protection, for example, can rarely be achieved through technological solutions or quantitative requirements that can be easily monitored. In other instances, the solutions to new problems will not be able to build on existing infrastructures and institutions. The strategies available to international regulators will depend at least in part on features unique to the problem being addressed. Analysts have already shown how regimes influence behavior in realms involving security.[102] How the impacts of similar compliance systems vary across security, economic, human rights, or environmental regimes remains one of many important future questions.

Whether the nations of the world can collaborate to resolve the many international problems, both environmental and otherwise, that face them will depend not on merely negotiating agreements requiring new behaviors but on ensuring that those agreements succeed in inducing governments, industry, and individuals to adopt those new behaviors. We can hope and work for a day when all nations and their citizens are sufficiently concerned about peace, economic well-being, human rights, and the environment that we will not need international law to criminalize the behavior threatening those values and to dictate more benign behaviors. Until then, however, careful crafting and recrafting of international treaties provides one valuable means of managing the various problems facing the nations of the world.

---

102. See Robert Jervis, "Security Regimes," in Krasner, *International Regimes,* pp. 173–94; and Duffield, "International Regimes and Alliance Behavior."

III.
Multilateralism and
International Leadership

For several decades now, international organizations have played a major role in world politics. On most important issues, from trade to human rights, organizations with multiple members (that is, multilateral organizations) have played a crucial role in debate and diplomacy. Beyond their obvious role as sounding board, they have also facilitated cooperation by providing better information, established bargaining procedures, and mechanisms for dispute settlement. Naturally, these organizations have attracted interest from scholars and policymakers, who want to understand how they work and how they fit into the wider world of international politics.[1]

Perhaps the most fundamental question is whether multilateral institutions make a significant difference in international politics. What roles do they play, and how effective are they? Who benefits from them, and how evenly are those benefits spread? Are these organizations durable enough to withstand major global changes such as a deep depression or a prolonged decline in the power of key states such as the United States? What about regional organizations, such as the European Union and the North American Free Trade Agreement (NAFTA), which seem to be increasing in importance? Do they complement and reinforce global arrangements, or do they threaten them? These are central questions of interest to both theorists and policymakers.

In answering these questions, we need to remember the uneven history of multilateral organizations since World War I. Woodrow Wilson's effort to create a League of Nations ended in catastrophic failure. The United States actually chose to remain outside the very organization it created. Wilson refused to compromise with the Senate, which then voted down the Versailles Treaty and U.S. participation in the League. Worse yet, the League of Nation's plans for "collective security" proved worthless in the face of military aggression by Imperial Japan, Fascist Italy, and Nazi Germany in the 1930s.

The United States was determined not to repeat these failures after the next great war. Instead of abandoning the idea of multilateral cooperation, it actually began serious planning for new and better organizations in the early 1940s. The goal was

1. See Ruggie 1992; Caporaso 1992; and Kahler 1992.

to create a whole network of international organizations to deal not only with political questions but also with trade, investment, and monetary relations.

The U.S. role in establishing these organizations has been a major source of research and debate, as the chapters in this section show. John Gerard Ruggie (Chapter 8) is particularly interested in how the enormous postwar power of the United States was joined to its specific vision of political order, at home and abroad. Certainly American leaders wanted a more open system of trade and investment. But these were not its only goals. Ruggie concludes that the United States always intended to pursue liberalization in ways consistent with its basic New Deal social and political policies. Nor did it expect its European partners to abandon their newly erected social safety nets, the heart of political reconstruction after World War II. The goal of the United States, in other words, was to create a liberal world economy firmly embedded in the basic political arrangements of western Europe and North America.

How do these policies compare with those of the other great international economic power of modern times, nineteenth-century Britain? One of the most prominent theories, that of "hegemonic stability," underscores the similarities. According to hegemonic stability theory, a liberal world economy rested firmly on British leadership in the late 1800s, just as it rested on U.S. leadership after 1945. According to this argument, the Depression of the 1930s was so deep and prolonged because no global leader was willing (and able) to keep its markets open or to provide essential loans in times of trouble. By the same token, any decline in U.S. power today would shake the foundations of the world economy—a prospect hegemonic theorists have worried about since the 1970s.

Although this theory has an appealing simplicity, it has been subjected to telling critiques by Timothy J. McKeown, Bruce Russett, Duncan Snidal, and Susan Strange.[2] They show that (1) Britain's role in promoting international liberalization has been exaggerated; (2) the relative economic position of the United States has not declined since the 1950s, at least by some measures; and (3) multiple states, and not just a hegemon, can sustain well-functioning multilateral institutions.

Ruggie's own approach is to return to the fusion of political power and purpose, which he argues is far different today than it was in the nineteenth century. He argues that the comparison between Britain and the United States is forced and distorted because the two countries pursued such different purposes. Victorian Britain's policies were based on a principled commitment to free trade and minimal state interference, a far cry from the goals of modern welfare states. It is hardly surprising, then, that trade liberalization has such a different meaning in the two periods.

Arthur Stein takes up a another aspect of the comparison between Britain and the United States (Chapter 9). He examines the bilateral treaties Britain negotiated to promote nondiscriminatory trade. His central point is that Britain's deep-seated com-

---

2. See McKeown 1983; Russett 1985; Snidal 1985; and Strange 1987.

mitment to trade liberalization created an environment in which other major economies could prosper disproportionately—so much so that Britain actually lost its edge
as the leading industrial economy. The problem Britain faced was whether to stick
with its basic policies even though they hastened the rise of competing economies
and contributed to Britain's own relative decline. That hard choice is what Stein
terms "the hegemon's dilemma."

Lisa L. Martin (Chapter 10) takes a very different approach to the analysis of
multilateralism. In contrast to Ruggie's and Stein's historical interpretations, Martin
uses simple games, deliberately stripped of their wider political context. Her aim is
to show that multilateral institutions take on very different characteristics as they
confront different problems of strategic interaction. States do not always face the
problems of international leadership that Ruggie, Stein, and others analyze. Nor can
their strategic interactions be reduced to the familiar game of Prisoners' Dilemma,
as they so often are.

The actual design of multilateral organizations reflects the varied problems
states face. Martin's chapter highlights several. If, for example, states or firms
are concerned about setting common standards, their organizations will be
designed mainly to spread information. In coordination problems like these, enforcement is rarely an issue. In many other circumstances, however, participants are
tempted to cheat. To succeed in these cases, multilateral organizations must somehow enforce their agreements. They can do so in a number of ways. One way is to
create a strong central authority—a choice that most states reject because it might
undermine their sovereignty. Another possibility is to limit membership to a small
group that is already joined by cooperative ties, perhaps a regional grouping. Still
another possibility is to delegate enforcement tasks to aggrieved members. Dispute
panels at the World Trade Organization can authorize countries to retaliate against
members who have violated specific treaty commitments. The commitments that sustain these multilateral organizations, Martin notes, are quite distinct from general
(and diffuse) norms of reciprocity and nondiscrimination and may even contradict
them.

The overriding point here is that multilateral organizations vary enormously in
their tasks, their design, and their effectiveness. For students of international political economy, the challenge is to explain this enormous variety and to relate it systematically to larger conceptions of international politics.

References

Caporaso, James A. 1992. International Relations Theory and Multilateralism: The Search for Foundations. *International Organization* 46 (2):599–632.

Kahler, Miles. 1992. Multilateralism with Small and Large Numbers. *International Organization* 46 (2):
681–708.

McKeown, Timothy J. 1983. Hegemonic Stability Theory and 19th Century Tariff Levels in Europe. *International Organization* 37 (1):73–91.

Ruggie, John Gerard. 1992. Multilateralism: The Anatomy of an Organization. *International Organization* 46 (2):561–98

Russett, Bruce. 1985. The Mysterious Case of Vanishing Hegemony; or, Is Mark Twain Really Dead? *International Organization* 39 (2):207–32.

Snidal, Duncan. 1985. The Limits of Hegemonic Stability Theory. *International Organization* 39 (4):579–614.

Strange, Susan. 1987. The Persistent Myth of Lost Hegemony. *International Organization* 41 (4):551–74.

International regimes, transactions, and change: embedded liberalism in the postwar economic order
John Gerard Ruggie

> A philosopher is someone who goes into a dark room at night, to look for a black cat that isn't there. A theologian does the same thing, but comes out claiming he found the cat.
>
> Nick Philips, "The Case of the Naked Quark," *TWA Ambassador Magazine*, October 1980.

One of our major purposes in this volume is to establish whether we, as students of international regimes, most resemble the philosopher, the theologian or, as most of us would like to believe, the social scientist—suspecting from the beginning that there is a black cat in there somewhere, and emerging from the room with scratches on the forearm as vindication. This article consists of another set of scratches, together with what I hope will be persuasive reasoning and demonstration that a black cat put them there.

My focus is on how the regimes for money and trade have reflected and affected the evolution of the international economic order since World War II. Let me state my basic approach to this issue at the outset, for, as Krasner shows in the Introduction, a good deal of the disagreement and confusion

I have benefited from the comments and suggestions of a large number of friends, colleagues, and fellow travelers, and am particularly indebted to the detailed written remarks of Catherine Gwin, Ernst Haas, Robert Keohane, Stephen Krasner, and Susan Strange, as well as to Albert Fishlow's constructive criticism at the Palm Springs conference. Research for this article was made possible by financial support from the Rockefeller Foundation and the Ira D. Wallach Chair of World Order Studies at Columbia University.

International Organization 36, 2, Spring 1982, pp. 379–415
© 1982 by the Massachusetts Institute of Technology

about international regimes stems from deeper epistemological and even ontological differences among observers.

International regimes have been defined as social institutions around which actor expectations converge in a given area of international relations.[1] Accordingly, as is true of any social institution, international regimes limit the discretion of their constituent units to decide and act on issues that fall within the regime's domain. And, as is also true of any social institution, ultimate expression in converging expectations and delimited discretion gives international regimes an intersubjective quality. To this extent, international regimes are akin to language—we may think of them as part of "the language of state action."[2] The constituent units of a regime, like speakers of a common language, generally have little difficulty in determining what even an entirely new usage signifies. Should it be technically inappropriate or incorrect, they nevertheless may still "understand" it—in the dual sense of being able to comprehend it and willing to acquiesce in it. In sum, we know international regimes not simply by some descriptive inventory of their concrete elements, but by their generative grammar, the underlying principles of order and meaning that shape the manner of their formation and transformation. Likewise, we know deviations from regimes not simply by acts that are undertaken, but by the intentionality and acceptability attributed to those acts in the context of an intersubjective framework of meaning.[3]

The analytical components of international regimes we take to consist of principles, norms, rules, and procedures. As the content for each of these terms is specified, international regimes diverge from social institutions like language, for we do not normally attribute to language any specific "consummatory" as opposed to "instrumental" values.[4] Insofar as international regimes embody principles about fact, causation, and rectitude, as well as political rights and obligations that are regarded as legitimate, they fall closer to the consummatory end of the spectrum, into the realm of political authority. Thus, the formation and transformation of international regimes may be said to represent a concrete manifestation of the internationalization of political authority.[5]

[1] Oran R. Young, "International Regimes: Problems of Concept Formation," *World Politics* 32 (April 1980); and Stephen D. Krasner's introduction to this volume.

[2] This phrase is taken from Bruce Andrews's application of the linguistic metaphor to the study of foreign policy: "The Language of State Action," *International Interactions* 6 (November 1979).

[3] Cf. Noam Chomsky, *Current Issues in Linguistic Theory* (The Hague: Mouton, 1964), chap. 1.

[4] These are derived from the standard Weberian distinction between *Wert-* and *Zweckrational*. Max Weber, *Economy and Society*, ed. by Guenther Roth and Claus Wittich (Berkeley: University of California Press, 1978), pp. 24–26.

[5] Discussions of political authority often fuse the very meaning of the concept with one of its specific institutional manifestations, that expressed in super-subordinate relations. But, as demonstrated repeatedly in organization theory and recognized by Weber, authority rests on a form of legitimacy that ultimately can derive only from a community of interests. Chester Barnard has carried this line of reasoning the furthest: "Authority is another name for the willingness and capacity of individuals to submit to the necessities of cooperative systems." *The*

What is the "generative grammar" that shapes the internationalization of political authority? The most common interpretation has been stated succinctly by Kenneth Waltz: the elements of international authority, he maintains, "are barely once removed from the capability that provides [their] foundation. . . ."[6] On this interpretation others, in turn, have built what now amounts to a prevalent model of the formation and transformation of international economic regimes. In its simplest form, the model makes this prediction: if economic capabilities are so concentrated that a hegemon exists, as in the case of Great Britain in the late 19th century and the U.S.A. after World War II, an "open" or "liberal" international economic order will come into being.[7] In the organization of a liberal order, pride of place is given to market rationality. This is not to say that authority is absent from such an order. It is to say that authority relations are constructed in such a way as to give maximum scope to market forces rather than to constrain them. Specific regimes that serve such an order, in the areas of money and trade, for example, limit the discretion of states to intervene in the functioning of self-regulating currency and commodity markets. These may be termed "strong" regimes, because they restrain self-seeking states in a competitive international political system from meddling directly in domestic and international economic affairs in the name of their national interests. And the strength of these regimes, of course, is backed by the capabilities of the hegemon. If and as such a concentration of economic capabilities erodes, the liberal order is expected to unravel and its regimes to become weaker, ultimately being replaced by mercantilist arrangements, that is, by arrangements under which the constituent units reassert national political authority over transnational economic forces. If the order established by British economic supremacy in the 19th century and that reflecting the supremacy of the United States after World War II illustrate liberal orders with strong regimes, the interwar period illustrates the darker corollary of the axiom.

I do not claim that this model is fundamentally wrong. But it does not take us very far in understanding international economic regimes, and, by extension, the formation and transformation of international regimes in gen-

Functions of the Executive (Cambridge: Harvard University Press, 1968), p. 184. See also the important statement by Peter Blau, "Critical Remarks on Weber's Theory of Authority," *American Political Science Review* 57 (June 1963). An illustration (though unintended) of how *not* to think of authority if the concept is to be at all useful in a discussion of international relations is provided by Harry Eckstein, "Authority Patterns: A Structural Basis for Political Inquiry," *American Political Science Review* 67 (December 1973). More elaborate typologies of forms of authority relations in international regimes may be found in my papers, "International Responses to Technology: Concepts and Trends," *International Organization* 29 (Summer 1975), and "Changing Frameworks of International Collective Behavior: On the Complementarity of Contradictory Tendencies," in Nazli Choucri and Thomas Robinson, eds., *Forecasting in International Relations* (San Francisco: W. H. Freeman, 1978).

[6] *Theory of International Politics* (Reading, Mass.: Addison-Wesley, 1979), p. 88.

[7] The relevant literature is cited in Robert O. Keohane, "The Theory of Hegemonic Stability and Changes in International Economic Regimes, 1967–1977," in Ole Holsti et al., eds., *Change in the International System* (Boulder, Col.: Westview Press, 1980).

eral.[8] This is so precisely because it does not encompass the phenomeno-logical dimensions of international regimes.

From this vantage point, I develop three theoretical arguments; each yields an interpretation of central features of the postwar international economic order that is distinct from the prevailing view.

The first concerns the "generative grammar" or what I shall call the "structure" of the internationalization of political authority. Whatever its institutional manifestations, political authority represents a fusion of power with legitimate social purpose. The prevailing interpretation of international authority focuses on power only; it ignores the dimension of social purpose.[9] The problem with this formulation is that power may predict the *form* of the international order, but not its *content*. For example, in the era of the third hegemon in the complex of modern state-system and capitalist-world-economy, the Dutch in the 17th century, the condition of hegemony coexisted with mercantilist behavior,[10] and it would be straining credulity to attribute this difference solely or even mainly to differences in the relative economic supremacy of the three hegemons without discussing differences in social purpose. Moreover, had the Germans succeeded in their quest to establish a "New International Order" after World War II, the designs Hjalmar Schacht would have instituted were the very mirror image of Bretton Woods[11]—obviously, differences in social purpose again provide the key. Lastly, the common tendency to equate the 19th century liberal international economic order and its post–World War II counterpart itself obscures exceedingly important differences in their domestic and international organization, differences that stem from the fact that the one represented laissez-faire liberalism and the other did not. In sum, to say anything sensible about the *content* of international economic orders and about the regimes that serve them, it is necessary to look at how power and legitimate social purpose become fused to project political authority into the international system. Applied to the post–World War II context, this argument leads me to characterize the international economic order by the term "em-

---

[8] Nor should it be expected to. As Waltz makes clear, his is a theory intended to predict that certain conditioning and constraining forces will take effect within the international system as a whole depending upon variation in its structure, not to account for such "process-level" outcomes as international regimes. Some of the literature cited by Keohane attempts to do more than this, however, though Keohane himself reaches a conclusion that is not at variance with my own.

[9] More accurately, it either assumes social purpose (as in Waltz, *Theory of International Politics*), or seeks to deduce it from state power (as in Krasner, "State Power and the Structure of International Trade," *World Politics* 28 [April 1976]).

[10] To my knowledge, the case of Dutch supremacy in the world economy has not been addressed in the "hegemonic stability" literature; but see Immanuel Wallerstein, *The Modern World System*, vol. 2 (New York: Academic Press, 1980), chap. 2.

[11] A brief description may be found in Armand Van Dormael, *Bretton Woods: Birth of a Monetary System* (London: Macmillan, 1978), chap. 1. The classic statement of how it actually worked remains Albert O. Hirschman, *National Power and the Structure of Foreign Trade*, expanded ed. (Berkeley: University of California Press, 1980).

bedded liberalism,'' which I show to differ from both its classical ancestor and its ignominious predecessor even as it has systematically combined central features of both.

My second theoretical argument concerns the relationship between international economic regimes and developments in the international economy, particularly at the level of private transaction flows.[12] Conventional structural arguments, whether Realist or Marxist, see transnationalization as a direct reflection of hegemony: high levels of trade and capital flows obtain under the *pax Britannica* and the *pax Americana*. The regimes for trade and money are largely epiphenomenal adjuncts that may be invoked to legitimate this outcome, but they have little or no real bearing on it. Conventional liberals, on the other hand, hold that high levels of trade and capital flows will obtain only if there is strict adherence to open international economic regimes, so that these become virtually determinative. Neither formulation is satisfactory.

The relationship between economic regimes and international transaction flows is inherently problematical, because the domain of international regimes consists of the behavior of states, vis-à-vis one another and vis-à-vis the market-place, *not* the market-place itself. Nevertheless, simply on *a priori* grounds we may argue that because there is no direct relationship, it is highly unlikely that the character of international regimes would have a determinative impact on international transaction flows; and yet, because international regimes do encompass the behavior of states vis-à-vis the market-place, it stands to reason that they would have some effect on international transaction flows. I contend that the nature of this relationship, at least in the first instance, is one of complementarity. That is to say, international economic regimes provide a permissive environment for the emergence of *specific kinds* of international transaction flows that actors take to be complementary to the particular fusion of power and purpose that is embodied within those regimes.[13] The contextual specificity of this complementarity makes equations of the variety ''pax Britannica is equal to pax Americana,'' as well as insistence on universal regime formulae to achieve a given outcome, extremely dubious propositions.

Applying this argument to the postwar international economic order, I conclude that the emergence of several specific developments in transnational economic activities can be accounted for at least in part by their perceived first-order contribution to the regimes for trade and money.[14] These regimes, then, are neither determinative nor irrelevant, but provide part of the context that shapes the character of transnationalization.

[12] In this connection, see also Charles Lipson's chapter in this volume.
[13] This is not to ignore the possibility that the same developments may have second-order consequences or long-term effects that pose stresses or even contradictions for international economic regimes, a problem which I take up in a later section.
[14] The present formulation of this conclusion owes much to Albert Fishlow's commentary on an earlier version at the Palm Springs Conference, for which I am obliged to him.

My third theoretical argument concerns the occurrence of change in and of regimes. The prevailing model postulates one source of regime change, the ascendancy or decline of economic hegemons, and two directions of regime change, greater openness or closure. If, however, we allow for the possibility that power and purpose do not necessarily covary, then we have two potential sources of change and no longer any simple one-to-one correspondence between source and direction of change. For example, we could have a situation in which there exists a predominant economic power whose economic program differs fundamentally from that of its leading rivals (e.g., Dutch supremacy in the 17th century). Or, we could have a situation in which power and purpose covary negatively, that is, in which neither a hegemon nor a congruence of social purpose exists among the leading economic powers (the interwar period approximates this case). We could have a situation in which power and purpose covary positively (e.g., Bretton Woods). There remains the situation of no hegemon but a congruence of social purpose among the leading economic powers (albeit imperfectly, the post–1971 international economic order illustrates this possibility).

It is the last possibility that interests me most. It suggests the need for a more nuanced formulation of regime change than is currently available. If and as the concentration of economic power erodes, and the "strength" of international regimes is sapped thereby, we may be sure that the *instruments* of regimes also will have to change.[15] However, as long as purpose is held constant, there is no reason to suppose that the *normative framework* of regimes must change as well. In other words, referring back to our analytical components of international regimes, rules and procedures (instruments) would change but principles and norms (normative frameworks) would not. Presumably, the new instruments that would emerge would be better adapted to the new power situation in the international economic order. But insofar as they continued to reflect the same sense of purpose, they would represent a case of norm-governed as opposed to norm-transforming change.

Applying this argument to the post–1971 period leads me to suggest that many of the changes that have occurred in the regimes for money and trade have been norm-governed changes rather than, as is often maintained, reflecting the collapse of Bretton Woods and a headlong rush into mercantilism. Indeed, in certain cases earlier acts by the hegemon had violated the normative frameworks of these regimes, so that some post–1971 changes may be viewed as adaptive restorations of prior sets of norms in the context of a new and different international economic environment. Both occurrences may to taken to demonstrate what we might call "the relative autonomy" of international regimes (with due apologies to the appropriate quarters).

The various parts of my argument clearly stand or fall together. Ulti-

---

[15] The "hegemonic stability" school effectively demonstrates why this is so. See Keohane, "Theory of Hegemonic Stability."

mately, they lead back to my depiction of international authority as reflecting a fusion of power and legitimate social purpose. An historical illustration of this interpretation of the "structure" of international authority therefore serves as my point of departure.

1. The structure of international authority

Karl Polanyi's magisterial work, *The Great Transformation*, was first published in 1944. In it, he developed a distinction between "embedded" and "disembedded" economic orders: "normally, the economic order is merely a function of the social, in which it is contained. Under neither tribal, nor feudal, nor mercantile conditions was there, as we have shown, a separate economic system in society. Nineteenth century society, in which economic activity was isolated and imputed to a distinctive economic motive, was, indeed, a singular departure."[16] The best known international forms taken by this "singular departure" were, of course, the regimes of free trade and the gold standard. What were their bases?

The internationalization of domestic authority relations

Charles Kindleberger, who is justly accorded a leading role in having established the efficacy of the "hegemonic stability" model in his book on the Great Depression,[17] subsequently managed to write an account of the rise of free trade in western Europe without even mentioning British economic supremacy as a possible source of explanation.[18] He focused instead on a fundamental reordering of the relationships between domestic political authority and economic processes. Free trade, he reminds us, was due first of all to the general breakdown of the manor and guild system and the so-called policy of supply, through which a complex structure of social regulations rather than market exchange determined the organization of economic activity at home and abroad. Indeed, the earliest measures undertaken in order to free trade were to dismantle prohibitions on exports, prohibitions that had restricted the outward movement of materials, machinery, and artisans. The bulk of these prohibitions was not removed until well into the 1820s and 1830s, and in some instances even later. A second part of the stimulus "came from the direct self-interest of particular dominant groups.

[16] Boston: Beacon Press, 1944, p. 71. The historical claims are backed up in Polanyi et al., eds., *Trade and Markets in the Early Empires* (Glencoe, Ill.: Free Press, 1957).
[17] Charles P. Kindleberger, *The World in Depression, 1929–1939* (Berkeley: University of California Press, 1973), esp. chaps. 1 and 14.
[18] "The Rise of Free Trade in Western Europe, 1820–1875," *Journal of Economic History* 35 (March 1975): 20–55.

. . ."[19] In the Netherlands, these were merchants, shipowners, and bankers; in Great Britain, the manufacturing sectors backed by the intellectual hegemony established by the Manchester School; in France, largely industrial interests employing imported materials and equipment in production, though they would not have succeeded against the weight of countervailing interests had not Louis Napoleon imposed free trade for unrelated reasons of international diplomacy; in Prussia, grain and timber exporters, though Bismarck was not adverse to using trade treaties in the pursuit of broader objectives and free trade treaties seemed to be *au courant;* in Italy, the efforts of Cavour, which prevailed over disorganized opposition. Equally particularistic factors were at work in Belgium, Denmark, Norway, Sweden, Spain, and Portugal. But how did such diverse forces come to converge on the single policy response of free trade? In a certain sense, Kindleberger contends, Europe in this period should be viewed not as a collection of separate economies, but "as a *single entity* which moved to free trade for ideological or perhaps better doctrinal reasons."[20] The image of the market became an increasingly captivating social metaphor and served to focus diverse responses on the outcome of free trade. And unless one holds that ideology and doctrine exist in a social vacuum, this ascendancy of market rationality in turn must be related to the political and cultural ascendance of the middle classes. In Polanyi's inimitable phrase, "*Laissez-faire* was planned. . . ."[21]

In sum, this shift in what we might call the balance between "authority" and "market" fundamentally transformed state-society relations, by redefining the legitimate social purposes in pursuit of which state power was expected to be employed in the domestic economy. The role of the state became to institute and safeguard the self-regulating market. To be sure, this shift occurred unequally throughout western Europe, and at uneven tempos. And of course nowhere did it take hold so deeply and for so long a period as in Great Britain. Great Britain's supremacy in the world economy had much to do with the global expansion of this new economic order, and even more with its stability and longevity. But the authority relations that were instituted in the international regimes for money and trade reflected a new balance of state-society relations that expressed a *collective* reality.

These expectations about the proper scope of political authority in economic relations did not survive World War I. Despite attempts at restoration, by the end of the interwar period there remained little doubt about how thoroughly they had eroded. Polanyi looked back over the period of the "twenty years' crisis" from the vantage point of the Second World War—at the emergence of mass movements from the Left and the Right throughout Europe, the revolutionary and counterrevolutionary upheavals in central

[19] Ibid., p. 50.

[20] Ibid., p. 51, italics added.

[21] Polanyi describes the parallel movements, in the case of Great Britain, of the middle class into the political arena and the state out of the economic arena.

and eastern Europe in the 1917–20 period, the General Strike of 1926 in Great Britain, and, above all, the rapid succession of the abandonment of the gold standard by Britain, the instituting of the Five Year Plans in the Soviet Union, the launching of the New Deal in the United States, unorthodox budgetary policies in Sweden, *corporativismo* in Fascist Italy, and *Wirkschaftslenkung* followed by the creation of both domestic and international variants of the "new economic order" by the Nazis in Germany. Running throughout these otherwise diverse events and developments, he saw the common thread of social reaction against market rationality. State-society relations again had undergone a profound—indeed, the *great*—transformation, as land, labor, and capital had all seized upon the state in the attempt to reimpose broader and more direct social control over market forces. Once this domestic transformation began, late in the 19th century, international liberalism of the orthodox kind was doomed. Thus, it was the singular tragedy of the interwar period, Polanyi felt, to have attempted to restore internationally, in the form of the gold-exchange standard in particular, that which no longer had a corresponding social base domestically. The new international economic order that would emerge from World War II, Polanyi concluded, on the one hand would mark the end of "capitalist internationalism," as governments learned the lesson that international automaticity stands in fundamental and potentially explosive contradiction to an active state domestically, and, on the other hand, the emergence of deliberate management of international economic transactions by means of collaboration among governments.[22]

Some of Polanyi's thoughts about the future had already been entertained by the individuals who would come to be directly responsible for negotiating the monetary component of the postwar international economic order. In the depth of the Depression, Harry Dexter White had pondered the problem of how to buffer national economies from external disturbances without, at the same time, sacrificing the benefits of international economic relations. "The path, I suspect, may lie in the direction of centralized control over foreign exchanges and trade."[23] Indeed, in 1934 White had applied for a fellowship to study planning techniques at the Institute of Economic Investigations of Gosplan in Moscow. Instead, he accepted an offer to go to Washington and work in the New Deal. For his part, one of the first assignments that Keynes undertook after he joined the British Treasury in 1940 was to draft the text of a radio broadcast designed to discredit recent propaganda proclamations by Walther Funk, minister for economic affairs and president of the Reichsbank in Berlin, on the economic and social benefits that the "New Order" would bring to Europe and the world. Keynes was instructed to stress the traditional virtues of free trade and the gold standard. But this, he felt, "will not have much propaganda value." Britain would have to offer

[22] *The Great Transformation,* esp. chaps. 2 and 19–21.
[23] Quoted in Van Dormael, *Bretton Woods,* p. 41.

"the same as what Dr. Funk offers, except that we shall do it better and more honestly."[24] He had reached the conclusion that only a refinement and improvement of the Schachtian device would restore equilibrium after the war. "To suppose that there exists some smoothly functioning automatic mechanism of adjustment which preserves equilibrium if only we trust to methods of *laissez-faire* is a doctrinaire delusion which disregards the lessons of historical experience without having behind it the support of sound theory."[25]

Polanyi's prediction of the end of capitalist internationalism does not stand up well against the subsequent internationalization of production and finance; White's views were altered considerably over the years as a result of negotiations within the bureaucracy and the adversarial process with Congress, before he was driven from Washington altogether in an anticommunist witch-hunt; and American resistance scaled down even the multilateral variants of Keynes's ambitious vision. Yet each had been correct in the essential fact that a new threshold had been crossed in the balance between "market" and "authority," with governments assuming much more direct responsibility for domestic social security and economic stability. The extension of the suffrage and the emergence of working-class political constituencies, parties, and even governments was responsible in part; but demands for social protection were very nearly universal, coming from all sides of the political spectrum and from all ranks of the social hierarchy (with the possible exception of orthodox financial circles). Polanyi, White, and Keynes were also correct in their premise that, somehow, the postwar international economic order would have to reflect this change in state-society relations if the calamities of the interwar period were not to recur.

Transformations in power versus purpose

Changes in the distribution of power and in the structure of social purpose covaried from the pre–World War I era through to the interwar period, so that we cannot say with any degree of certainty what might have happened had only one changed. However, by looking at the relationship between the two in greater detail in a single, circumscribed domain, we may get closer to a firm answer. I focus on the monetary regime under the gold standard before World War I, and its attempted approximation in the gold-exchange standard of the interwar period.

I begin with the domestic side of things, though this distinction itself would barely apply to currencies under a "gold specie" standard[26] where

[24] Quoted in ibid., p. 7.
[25] Quoted in ibid., p. 32.
[26] Unless otherwise noted, this paragraph is based on League of Nations [Ragnar Nurkse], *International Currency Experience: Lessons of the Inter-War Period* (League of Nations, Economic, Financial and Transit Department, 1944), chap. 4. (Hereafter referred to as Nurkse.)

both domestic circulation and international means of settlement took the form largely of gold, and the domestic money supply therefore was determined directly and immediately by the balance of payments. Under the more familiar "gold bullion" standard prior to World War I, where the bulk of domestic money took the form of bank notes and deposits, backed by and fixed in value in terms of gold, there still existed a strong relationship between domestic money supply and the balance of payments, but it was more indirect. In theory, it worked via the effects of gold movements on the domestic credit supply: an expansion of credit in the gold-receiving country, and a contraction in the gold-losing country, affected prices and incomes in such a way as to close the balance of payments discrepancy that had triggered the gold movement in the first place. This was reinforced by an attending change in money rates, which would set off equilibrating movements in short-term private funds. In practice, gold movements among the major economies were relatively infrequent and small. Temporary gaps to a large extent were filled by short-term capital movements, responding to interest differentials or slight variations within the gold points.[27] More fundamental adjustments were produced by the impact of the balance of payments not only on domestic money stock and the volume of credit, but also through the direct effects of export earnings on domestic income and effective demand.

In sum, even in its less than pristine form, the pre–World War I gold standard was predicated upon particular assumptions concerning the fundamental purpose of domestic monetary policy and the role of the state in the process of adjusting imbalances in the level of external and internal economic activity. With respect to the first, in Bloomfield's words, the "dominant and overriding" objective of monetary policy was the maintenance of gold parity. "The view, so widely recognized and accepted in recent decades, of central banking policy as a means of facilitating the achievement and maintenance of reasonable stability in the level of economic activity and prices was scarcely thought about before 1914, and certainly not accepted, as a formal objective of policy."[28] Second, insofar as the adjustment process ultimately was geared to securing external stability, state abstinence was prescribed so as not to undermine the equilibrating linkages between the balance of payments, changes in gold reserves and in domestic credit supply,

[27] Note, however, Bloomfield's cautionary remark: "While this picture is broadly accurate, the nature and role of private short-term capital movements before 1914 have usually been oversimplified and their degree of sensitivity to interest rates and exchange rates exaggerated. At the same time these movements have been endowed with a benign character that they did not always possess." Arthur I. Bloomfield, "Short-Term Capital Movements Under the Pre-1914 Gold Standard," *Princeton Studies in International Finance* 11 (1963), p. 34. Bloomfield presents a more complex and balanced picture, which, however, does not contradict the basic generalization.

[28] Arthur I. Bloomfield, *Monetary Policy Under the International Gold Standard* (New York: Federal Reserve Bank of New York, 1959), p. 23. Bloomfield shows that central banks did attempt partially to "sterilize" the effects of gold flows.

income, and demand. This was not incompatible with partial efforts at sterilization. As Nurkse put it, "all that was required for this purpose was that countries should not attempt to control their national income and outlay by deliberate measures—a requirement which in the age of laissez-faire was generally fulfilled."[29]

It is impossible to say precisely when these assumptions ceased to be operative and their contraries took hold. But it is clear that after World War I there was a growing tendency "to make international monetary policy conform to domestic social and economic policy and not the other way round."[30] The proportion of currency reserves held in the form of foreign exchange more than doubled between 1913 and 1925, to 27 percent; in 1928, it stood at 42 percent. And international reserves increasingly came to serve as a "buffer" against external economic forces rather than as their "transmitter"; Nurkse found that throughout the interwar period the international and domestic assets of central banks moved in opposite directions far more often than in the same direction.[31] After the collapse of the gold-exchange standard in 1931, exchange stabilization funds were established in the attempt to provide more of a cushion than "neutralization" had afforded. Mere stabilization was followed by direct exchange controls in many instances, with the gold bloc countries attempting to achieve analogous insulation through import quotas. Governments everywhere had developed increasingly active forms of intervention in the domestic economy in order to affect the level of prices and employment, and to protect them against external sources of dislocation.[32] The international monetary order disintegrated into five more or less distinct blocs, each with its own prevailing currency arrangement.

On the international side, there is little doubt that the pre–World War I gold standard functioned as it did because of the central part Great Britain played in it. In general terms, "if keeping a free market for imports, maintaining a flow of investment capital, and acting as lender of last resort are the marks of an 'underwriter' of an international system, then Britain certainly fulfilled this role in the nineteenth-century international economy."[33] More specifically, in the domain of monetary policy it was the role of sterling as the major vehicle currency, held by foreign business, banks, and even central banks, that gave the Bank of England the influence to shape international monetary conditions consistent with the fundamental commitments and

[29] Nurkse, *International Currency Experience*, p. 213.

[30] Ibid., p. 230.

[31] Ibid., pp. 68–88.

[32] For a good global overview of these policy shifts, see Asa Briggs, "The World Economy: Interdependence and Planning," in C. L. Mowat, ed., *The New Cambridge Modern History*, vol. 12 (Cambridge: Cambridge University Press, 1968).

[33] Robert J. A. Skidelsky, "Retreat from Leadership: The Evolution of British Economic Foreign Policy, 1870–1939," in Benjamin M. Rowland, ed., *Balance of Power or Hegemony: The Interwar Monetary System* (New York: New York University Press, 1976), p. 163. Cf. Kindleberger, *The World in Depression*, chap. 1.

dynamics of the regime. And yet, the critical issue in the stability of this regime was not simply some measure of material "supremacy" on the part of Britain, but that "national monetary authorities were inclined to *'follow the market'*—and indirectly the Bank of England—rather than to assert independent national objectives of their own."[34] Thus, the international gold standard rested on both the special position of Great Britain and prevailing attitudes concerning the role of the state in the conduct of national monetary policy. It reflected a true "hegemony," as Gramsci used the term.

What of the interwar period? Counterfactual historiography is little better than a parlor game under ideal circumstances; it should be especially suspect when an outcome is as overdetermined as institutional failure in the international economy between the wars.[35] It seems reasonable to assume, though, that with the end of monetary laissez-faire, "the monetary leader would need to dispose of more monetary influence and political authority than Britain ever possessed, except within its own imperial system."[36] And where British hegemony lingered on, as in the Financial Committee of the League of Nations, the outcome was not salutary. For example, the eastern European countries that had their currencies stabilized by the League and were put under the gold-exchange standard before the major countries had fixed their currency rates did so at considerable domestic social cost.[37] And virtually every effort at constructing a viable international monetary regime in the interwar period, in which Britain took a leading role, did little more than decry the newly prevailing social objectives of state policy while pleading for a speedy return to the principles of "sound finance."[38] The consequences of course were counterproductive: just as the rhetoric of the

[34] Harold van B. Cleveland, "The International Monetary System in the Interwar Period," in Rowland, *Balance of Power*, p. 57, emphasis added. Note, in addition, that major primary-producing countries, who may well have borne more than their share of the international adjustment process under the gold standard, by and large did not establish their own central banks until the 1930s—this includes Argentina, Canada, India, New Zealand, and Venezuela. The argument that the adjustment process worked disproportionately on primary-producing countries is made by Robert Triffin, "National Central Banking and the International Economy," in Lloyd A. Metzler et al., eds., *International Monetary Policies* (Washington, D.C.: Board of Governors of the Federal Reserve System, 1947).

[35] There is almost no end to the number of dislocating features of the post–World War I international economy that can be adduced as part of the explanation for its institutional failure. Kindleberger, *The World in Depression*, chap. 1, briefly recounts most of them.

[36] Cleveland, "International Monetary System," p. 57.

[37] "The deflationist's ideal came to be 'a free economy under a strong government'; but while the phrase on government meant what it said, namely, emergency powers and suspension of public liberties, 'free economy' meant in practice the opposite of what it said: . . . while the inflationary governments condemned by Geneva subordinated the stability of the currency to stability of incomes and employment, the deflationary governments put in power by Geneva used no fewer interventions in order to subordinate the stability of incomes and employment to the stability of the currency." Polanyi, *The Great Transformation*, p. 233. For French skepticism concerning the "dogma of Geneva," see Judith L. Kooker, "French Financial Diplomacy: The Interwar Years," in Rowland, *Balance of Power*.

[38] For summary descriptions of the major conferences, see Dean E. Traynor, *International Monetary and Financial Conferences in the Interwar Period* (Washington, D.C.: Catholic Universities Press of America, 1949).

League concerning collective security and disarmament sought and in some measure served morally to undermine the balance of power system, without providing a viable alternative, so too did the League and successive international gatherings in the monetary sphere seek to undermine the legitimacy of domestic stabilization policies while offering only the unacceptable gold-exchange standard in their place.[39]

It is hardly surprising, therefore, that apart from Britain, seized by its own ideology and institutional past and willing to pay the domestic social cost, there were few takers among the major countries.[40] In sum, efforts to construct international economic regimes in the interwar period failed not because of the lack of a hegemon. They failed because, even had there been a hegemon, they stood in contradiction to the transformation in the mediating role of the state between market and society, which altered fundamentally the social purpose of domestic and international authority. As Ragnar Nurkse observed in 1944,

> There was a growing tendency during the inter-war period to make international monetary policy conform to domestic social and economic policy and not the other way round. Yet the world was still economically interdependent; and an international currency mechanism for the multilateral exchange of goods and services, instead of primitive bilateral barter, was still a fundamental necessity for the great majority of countries. The problem was to find a system of international currency relations compatible with the requirements of domestic stability. Had the period been more than a truce between two world wars, the solution that would have evolved would no doubt have been in the nature of a compromise.[41]

Ultimately, it was. The liberalism that was restored after World War II differed in kind from that which had been known previously. My term for it is "embedded liberalism."

---

[39] The most trenchant critique of the moral failure of the League remains that of Edward Hallett Carr, *The Twenty Years' Crisis, 1919–1939* (1939, 1946; New York: Harper Torchbooks, 1964).

[40] For example, France decided in 1928 to accept only gold in settlement of the enormous surplus it was accruing; and in 1929 the U.S. "went off on a restrictive monetary frolic of its own" even though it was in surplus" (Cleveland, "International Monetary System," p. 6). Four years later, in his inaugural address, President Roosevelt proclaimed the primacy of domestic stabilization, as he did again a few months later when, on the eve of the World Economic Conference of 1933, he took the U.S. off gold.

[41] *International Currency Experience*, p. 230. Note that Nurkse was speaking of "the great majority of countries." Those who chose bilateralism as an instrument of economic warfare and imperialism were unlikely to be accommodated within any multilateral regime. However, mere state trading or even the participation of centrally planned economies, while posing special problems, were not seen to be insuperable obstacles to multilateralism; see Herbert Feis, "The Conflict Over Trade Ideologies," *Foreign Affairs* 25 (July 1947), and Raymond F. Mikesell, "The Role of the International Monetary Agreements in a World of Planned Economies," *Journal of Political Economy* 55 (December 1947). I think it is fair to say, though, that reconciling the many variants and depths of state intervention would have been a difficult task in the best of times, which the 1930s of course weren't. We are justified, therefore, in "coding" the interwar period as "no hegemon, no agreement on purpose."

2. The compromise of embedded liberalism

Liberal internationalist orthodoxy, most prominent in New York financial circles, proposed to reform the old order simply by shifting its locus from the pound to the dollar and by ending discriminatory trade and exchange practices.[42] Opposition to economic liberalism, nearly universal outside the United States, differed in substance and intensity depending upon whether it came from the Left, Right, or Center, but was united in its rejection of unimpeded multilateralism.[43] The task of postwar institutional reconstruction, as Nurkse sensed, was to maneuver between these two extremes and to devise a framework which would safeguard and even aid the quest for domestic stability without, at the same time, triggering the mutually destructive external consequences that had plagued the interwar period. This was the essence of the embedded liberalism compromise: unlike the economic nationalism of the thirties, it would be multilateral in character; unlike the liberalism of the gold standard and free trade, its multilateralism would be predicated upon domestic interventionism.

If this was the objective of postwar institutional reconstruction for the international economy, there remained enormous differences among countries over precisely what it meant and what sorts of policies and institutional arrangements, domestic and international, the objective necessitated or was compatible with. This was the stuff of the negotiations on the postwar international economic order. The story of these negotiations has been told by others, in detail and very ably.[44] I make no attempt to repeat it here. I simply summarize the conjunction of the two themes that constitutes the story's plot. The first, which we tend to remember more vividly today, concerned

[42] Professor John H. Williams, vice-president of the Federal Reserve Bank of New York, was a leading spokesman for the New York financial community, which resented having lost control over international monetary affairs when authority shifted from the FRBNY to the U.S. Treasury under Secretary Morgenthau. Their plan, which had some support in Congress, called simply for a resurrection of the gold-exchange standard, with the dollar performing the role that sterling had played previously. They opposed the New Deal "gimmickry" of the White Plan, and of course they liked Keynes's Clearing Union even less. See Van Dormael, *Bretton Woods*, chap. 9.

[43] In the case of Britain, the other major actor in the negotiations concerning postwar economic arrangements, opposition from the Left was based on the desire to systematize national economic planning, which would necessarily entail discriminatory instruments for foreign economic policy. Opposition from the Right stemmed from a commitment to imperial preferences and the imperial alternative to a universal economic order. Speaking for many moderates, Hubert Henderson was opposed because he doubted the viability of a "freely working economic system," that is, of laissez-faire. "To attempt this would be not to learn from experience but to fly in its face. It would be to repeat the mistakes made last time in the name of avoiding them. It would be to invite the same failure, and the same disillusionment; the same economic chaos and the same shock to social and political stability; the same discredit for the international idea." (Richard N. Gardner, *Sterling-Dollar Diplomacy in Current Perspective* [New York: Columbia University Press, 1980], chap. 1; the quotation is from a memorandum prepared by Henderson in December 1943, while serving in the British Treasury; reproduced in Gardner, p. 30.)

[44] The following account draws heavily on Gardner's classic study, as supplemented by the greater detail on the monetary side presented in Van Dormael.

multilateralism versus discrimination. It was an achievement of historic proportions for the United States to win adherence to the principle of multilateralism, particularly in trade. It required the expenditure of enormous resources. Still, it would not have succeeded but for an acceptable resolution of the dilemma between internal and external stability, the story's second theme. Here, history seemed not to require any special agent. True, the United States from the start of the negotiations was far less "Keynesian" in its positions than Great Britain. Within the United States, the social and economic reforms of the New Deal had lacked ideological consistency and programmatic coherence, and opposition had remained firmly entrenched. The transformation of the full-employment bill into the Employment Act of 1946 demonstrated the country's continuing ambivalence toward state intervention. This, of course, affected the outcome of the negotiations. Indeed, the United States would come to use its influence abroad in the immediate postwar years, through the Marshall Plan, the Occupation Authorities in Germany and Japan, and its access to transnational labor organizations, for example, to shape outcomes much more directly, by seeking to moderate the structure and political direction of labor movements, to encourage the exclusion of Communist Parties from participation in governments, and generally to discourage collectivist arrangements where possible or at least contain them within acceptable Center-Left bounds.[45] But these differences among the industrialized countries concerned the forms and depth of state intervention to secure domestic stability, not the legitimacy of the objective.[46]

In the event, on the list of Anglo-American postwar economic objectives, multilateralism was joined by collaboration to assure domestic economic growth and social security as early as the Atlantic Charter, issued in August 1941. Indeed, progress on multilateralism seemed to be made contingent upon progress in expanding domestic production, employment, and the exchange and consumption of goods in Article VII of the Mutual Aid Agreement (Lend Lease), which was signed in February 1942.

On the monetary side, however different White's Stabilization Fund may have been from Keynes's Clearing Union (and there were considerable differences on instrumentalities), they shared a common purpose: intergov-

---

[45] Charles S. Maier, "The Politics of Productivity: Foundations of American International Economic Policy After World War II," *International Organization* 31 (Autumn 1977), and Robert W. Cox, "Labor and Hegemony," *International Organization* 31 (Summer 1977).

[46] Interesting in this regard is the role played by Leon Keyserling, appointed in 1949 as the first Keynesian on the Council of Economic Advisers, in helping to undermine the previous "economy-in-defense" policy by providing economic support for the proposed rearmament program contained in NSC-68 (Fred M. Kaplan, "Our Cold-War Policy, Circa '50," *New York Times Magazine*, 18 May 1980). Radicals have implied that "military Keynesianism" was the only kind of Keynesianism acceptable in the U.S. at that time (cf. Fred L. Block, *The Origins of International Economic Disorder* [Berkeley: University of California Press, 1977], pp. 102–8). But this interpretation slights the substantial state involvement in the U.S. in the postwar years in infrastructural investment (interstate highways, for example), agricultural price supports, and even in social expenditures, well before the full impact of Keynesian thinking was felt on monetary and fiscal policy in the 1960s.

ernmental collaboration to facilitate balance-of-payments equilibrium, in an international environment of multilateralism and a domestic context of full employment. Early in 1943, Adolf Berle foresaw that the compromise on the means to achieve these ends would have to "free the British people from their fear that they might have to subordinate their internal social policy to external financial policy, and to assure the United States that a share of its production was not claimable by tender of a new, 'trick' currency, and that the economic power represented by the US gold reserves would not be substantially diminished."[47] By the time of the Anglo-American "Joint Statement of Principles," issued not long before the Bretton Woods Conference, the consensus that had emerged provided for free and stable exchanges, on the one hand, and, on the other, the erection of a "double screen," in Cooper's words,[48] to cushion the domestic economy against the strictures of the balance of payments. Free exchanges would be assured by the abolition of all forms of exchange controls and restrictions on current transactions. Stable exchanges would be secured by setting and maintaining official par values, expressed in terms of gold. The "double screen" would consist of short-term assistance to finance payments deficits on current account, provided by an International Monetary Fund, and, so as to correct "fundamental disequilibrium," the ability to change exchange rates with Fund concurrence. Governments would be permitted to maintain capital controls.

In devising the instruments of the monetary regime, the most intense negotiations were occasioned by the functioning of the "double screen." On the question of the Fund, Keynes had argued for an international overdraft facility. This would have created some $25 billion to $30 billion in new liquidity, with the overall balance of credits and debits in the Fund being expressed in an international unit of account, which was to be monetized. The arrangement would have been self-clearing unless a country were out of balance with the system as a whole, in which case corrective measures were called for on the part of creditors and debtors alike. The White plan originally called for a $5 billion Fund, though the U.S. ultimately agreed to $8.8 billion. However, these funds would have to be paid in by subscription. Access to the Fund as well as total liability were strictly limited by quotas, which in turn reflected paid-in subscriptions—the initial U.S. contribution was $3.175 billion. And a country that sought to draw on the Fund had to make "representations" that the particular currency was needed for making payments on current account. Thus, with the United States, the sole major creditor country, seeking to limit its liabilities, the first part of the "double screen" was both more modest and more rigid than the United Kingdom and other potential debtor countries would have liked. But there was no question about its being provided. On the second part, exchange rate changes, the

---

[47] Paraphrased by Van Dormael, *Bretton Woods*, p. 103.

[48] Richard N. Cooper, "Prolegomena to the Choice of an International Monetary System," *International Organization* 29 (Winter 1975), p. 85.

U.K. was more successful in assuring automaticity and limiting intrusions into the domain of domestic policy. The Fund was required to concur in any change necessary to correct a "fundamental disequilibrium," and if the change was less than 10 percent the Fund was given no power even to raise objections. Most important, the Fund could not oppose *any* exchange rate change on the grounds that the domestic social or political policies of the country requesting the change had led to the disequilibrium that made the change necessary. Lastly, the final agreement did include a provision to shift at least some of the burden of adjustment onto creditor countries. This was by means of the "scarce currency" clause, which Keynes, in the end, thought to be quite important. It empowered the Fund, by decision of the Executive Directors, to ration its supply of any currency that had become scarce in the Fund and authorized members to impose exchange restrictions on that currency.

Once negotiations on postwar commercial arrangements got under way seriously, in the context of preparations for an International Conference on Trade *and* Employment, the principles of multilateralism and tariff reductions were affirmed, but so were safeguards, exemptions, exceptions, and restrictions—all designed to protect the balance of payments and a variety of domestic social policies. The U.S. found some of these abhorrent and sought to limit them, but even on so extraordinary an issue as making full employment an international obligation of governments it could do no better than to gain a compromise. The U.S. Senate subsequently refused to ratify the Charter of the International Trade Organization (ITO), as a result of which a far smaller domain of commercial relations became subject to the authority of an international regime than would have been the case otherwise. The regulation of commodity markets, restrictive business practices, and international investments were the most important areas thereby excluded.[49] But within this smaller domain, consisting of the more traditional subjects of commercial policy, the conjunction of multilateralism and safeguarding domestic stability that had evolved over the course of the ITO negotiations remained intact.[50]

Jacob Viner summarized the prevailing consensus in 1947, at the time of the negotiations for a General Agreement on Tariffs and Trade (GATT): "There are few free traders in the present-day world, no one pays any attention to their views, and no person in authority anywhere advocates free trade."[51] The United States, particularly the State Department, was the

[49] The provisions of the ITO Charter became internally so inconsistent that it is difficult to say just what sort of a regime it would have given rise to. See William Diebold Jr., "The End of the ITO," *Princeton Essays in International Finance* 16 (Princeton, N.J., October 1952).

[50] The following account draws heavily on Gardner, *Sterling-Dollar Diplomacy,* and on Gerard and Victoria Curzon, "The Management of Trade Relations in the GATT," in Andrew Shonfield, ed., *International Economic Relations of the Western World, 1959–1971,* vol. I (London: Oxford University Press for the Royal Institute of International Affairs, 1976).

[51] Jacob Viner, "Conflicts of Principle in Drafting a Trade Charter," *Foreign Affairs* 25 (January 1947), p. 613.

prime mover behind multilateralism in trade. But this meant nondiscrimination above all. The reduction of barriers to trade of course also played a role in American thinking, but here too the concern was more with barriers that were difficult to apply in a nondiscriminatory manner. Tariff reduction was subject to much greater domestic constraint. For their part, the British made it clear from the beginning that they would countenance no dismantling of imperial preferences unless the U.S. agreed to deep and linear tariff cuts. The proposed Commercial Union, put forward by James Meade on behalf of Britain, contained such a formula, together with an intergovernmental code of conduct for trade and machinery to safeguard the balance of payments. But the U.S. Congress could not be expected to accept linear tariff cuts.[52]

The General Agreement on Tariffs and Trade made obligatory the most-favored-nation rule, but a blanket exception was allowed for all existing preferential arrangements, and countries were permitted to form customs unions and free trade areas. Moreover, quantitative restrictions were prohibited, but were deemed suitable measures for safeguarding the balance of payments—*explicitly* including payments difficulties that resulted from domestic policies designed to secure full employment. They could also be invoked in agricultural trade if they were used in conjunction with a domestic price support program. The substantial reduction of tariffs and other barriers to trade was called for; but it was not made obligatory and it was coupled with appropriate emergency actions, which were allowed if a domestic producer was threatened with injury from import competition that was due to past tariff concessions. The Agreement also offered a blanket escape from any of its obligations, provided that two-thirds of the contracting parties approved. Lastly, procedures were provided to settle disputes arising under the Agreement and for the multilateral surveillance of the invocation of most (though not all) of its escape clauses. The principle of reciprocity was enshrined as a code of conduct, to guide both tariff reductions and the determination of compensation for injuries suffered.

To repeat my central point: that a multilateral order gained acceptance reflected the extraordinary power and perseverance of the United States.[53]

---

[52] In the spring of 1947, the U.S. delegation arrived in Geneva armed with congressional authorization for an overall tariff reduction to 50% of their 1945 levels (which, however, would still have left U.S. tariffs relatively high), in return for elimination of preferences. But, at the same time, the United States entered into preferential trade agreements with Cuba and the Philippines. Though mutual concessions on several important items were made in Geneva, in the end some 70% of existing British preferences remained intact (Gardner, *Sterling-Dollar Diplomacy*, chap. 17).

[53] At the Palm Springs Conference, Peter Kenen argued that this is true more for trade than for money. He maintains that, with the exception of the particulars of the credit arrangement (and the future role of the dollar, which I take up below), the general outlines of Bretton Woods would not have differed appreciably had there not been an American hegemon present. This is so because the basic design rested on a widely shared consensus. However, in trade, Kenen suggests, it is unlikely that nondiscrimination would have been accepted as a guiding principle had it not been for American "muscle." Keep in mind that even here the U.S. was forced to accept the indefinite continuation of all existing preferential trade agreements.

But that multilateralism and the quest for domestic stability were coupled and even conditioned by one another reflected the shared legitimacy of a set of social objectives to which the industrial world had moved, unevenly but "as a single entity." Therefore, the common tendency to view the postwar regimes as liberal regimes, but with lots of cheating taking place on the domestic side, fails to capture the full complexity of the embedded liberalism compromise.[54]

3. Complementary transaction flows

The postwar regimes for trade and money got off to a slow start. The early GATT rounds of tariff negotiations were modest in their effects. As a lending institution, the IMF remained dormant well into the 1950s. Meanwhile, bilateral currency arrangements in the late 1940s and early 1950s became far more extensive than they had ever been in the 1930s, doubling to some four hundred between 1947 and 1954.[55] But by the late 1950s, the Europeans had "the worst of their post-war problems behind them—and new ones had not yet come to take their place." Both Europe and the United States were poised "on the brink of a decade of phenomenal expansion which imperiously demanded wider markets through freer trade."[56] This in turn demanded the elimination of exchange restrictions on current account. Liberalization in trade and money soon followed.

Preoccupation with the fact of subsequent liberalization has tended to detract from consideration of its precise characteristics, at least on the part of political scientists.[57] The questions that have dominated discussion concern the impact of liberalization on the expansion of international economic transactions, or the effects on both of U.S. hegemony (with a time lag), operating directly by means of the exercise of American state power or indi-

---

[54] The third panel of the Bretton Woods triptych was the World Bank, which to some extent may also be said to reflect this conjunction of objectives. True, the grandiose concept of an international bank to engage in countercyclical lending and to help stabilize raw materials prices, which both White and Keynes had entertained at one point, was shelved due to opposition on both sides of the Atlantic. Nevertheless, for the first time, international *public* responsibility was acknowledged for the provision of investment capital, supplementing the market mechanism. For Secretary Morgenthau's strong views on this subject, see Gardner, *Sterling-Dollar Diplomacy*, p. 76.

[55] Of the 1954 total, 235 existed in Europe. Margaret G. De Vries and J. Keith Horsefield, *The IMF, 1945–1965*, vol. 2 (Washington, D.C.: International Monetary Fund, 1969), chap. 14.

[56] Curzon and Curzon, "Management of Trade," pp. 149–50.

[57] A notable exception is Kenneth N. Waltz, "The Myth of National Interdependence," in Charles P. Kindleberger, ed., *The International Corporation* (Cambridge: MIT Press, 1970). However, Waltz considers the characteristics of an international division of labor at any given point in time to be a product solely of international polarity. And this, in turn, requires that he consider Great Britain in the 19th century to have been but one among several coequal members of a plural system. He concludes that the international division of labor in the present era has been less extensive in kind and degree than in the pre–World War I setting *because of* bipolarity today and multipolarity then.

rectly through the internationalization of American capital. These of course are interesting questions, but they are not the questions that concern me here. Having argued that the postwar regimes for trade and money institutionalized the normative framework of embedded liberalism, I now examine whether and how this framework is reflected in the character of the international economic transactions that emerged when imminent expansion "imperiously" demanded liberalization.

I proceed by way of hypothesis. Imagine a world of governments seized by the compelling logic of David Ricardo; following a bout with mercantilism, this world is poised "on the brink" of liberalization. What kinds of international economic transactions are governments likely to encourage?

> Under a system of perfectly free trade each country naturally devotes its capital and labour to such employments as are most beneficial to each. This pursuit of individual advantage is admirably connected with the universal good of the whole. By stimulating industry, by rewarding ingenuity, and by using most efficaciously the peculiar powers bestowed by nature, it distributes labour most effectively and most economically; while, by increasing the general mass of productions, it diffuses general benefit, and binds together, by one common tie of interest and intercourse, the universal society of nations throughout the civilised world. It is this principle which determines that wine shall be made in France and Portugal, that corn shall be grown in America and Poland, and that hardware and other goods shall be manufactured in England.[58]

In short, our governments are likely to encourage an international division of labor based on the functional differentiation of countries that reflects their comparative advantage. Trade among them therefore would be socially highly profitable.

Now imagine the same governments under similar circumstances, the only difference being that they are committed to embedded liberalism rather than to laissez-faire. What sorts of international economic transactions would we expect them to favor? The essence of embedded liberalism, it will be recalled, is to devise a form of multilateralism that is compatible with the requirements of domestic stability. Presumably, then, governments so committed would seek to encourage an international division of labor which, while multilateral in form and reflecting *some* notion of comparative advantage (and therefore gains from trade), *also* promised to minimize socially disruptive domestic adjustment costs as well as any national economic and political vulnerabilities that might accrue from international functional differentiation. They will measure collective welfare by the extent to which these objectives are achieved. However, as neoclassical trade theory defines the term, the overall social profitability of this division of labor will be lower than of the one produced by laissez-faire.

[58] David Ricardo, *Works,* ed. by Piero Sraffa (Cambridge: Cambridge University Press, 1955), 1:133–34.

Let us return from the world of hypothesis and review briefly the character of postwar transaction flows.[59]

The great bulk of international economic transactions since the 1950s shows very definite patterns of concentration. The growth in trade has exceeded the growth in world output, and the most rapidly growing sector of trade has been in manufactured products among the industrialized countries. Within this general category, some two-thirds of the increase in trade from 1955 to 1973 is accounted for by "intracontinental" trade, that is, trade within western Europe and within North America.[60] What is more, it appears that trade in products originating in the same sector, or "intra-industry" trade, is growing far more rapidly than trade involving products of different sectors.[61] This in turn reflects a secular decline of specialization in different sectors of manufacturing activity among the industrialized countries.[62] Lastly, there is evidence to suggest that trade among related corporate parties, or "intrafirm" trade, accounts for an ever-larger portion of total world trade.[63] On the financial side, international investments have been rising even more rapidly than world trade, and they conform roughly to the same pattern of geographical, sectoral, and institutional concentration.[64] This is also true of international transfers of short-term funds.[65]

What kind of division of labor among the industrialized countries do these patterns portray? It is, in Cooper's words, one characterized by a

[59] The facts are well enough known, but not enough is made of them. For example, I find that much of what I have to say is implied in if not anticipated by the *locus classicus* of liberal interdependence theorists: Richard N. Cooper, *The Economics of Interdependence* (1968; New York: Columbia University Press, 1980). However, Cooper was concerned with telling a different story, so he chose not to take up issues and conclusions that, from the present vantage point, appear more scintillating. To cite but one illustration, Cooper demonstrates a converging cost structure among the industrialized countries. His major concern is to argue that this contributes to the increasing marginal price sensitivity of rapidly growing foreign trade—that is, to interdependence as he defines the term. In passing, he mentions another implication of this convergence, but one "which will not much concern us here." It is "that international trade becomes less valuable from the viewpoint of increasing economic welfare" (pp. 75–76). This striking departure from the textbook case for free trade, amidst an explosion in world trade, is left unexplored.

[60] Richard Blackhurst, Nicolas Marian, and Jan Tumlir, "Trade Liberalization, Protectionism and Interdependence," *GATT Studies in International Trade* 5 (November 1977), pp. 18–19.

[61] Ibid., pp. 10–11, 15–16; and Charles Lipson's article in this volume.

[62] Richard Cooper has traced this back to 1938, and finds that ten of thirteen manufacturing sectors show declines in variation among countries, and none shows a sharp increase. Cooper, *Economics of Interdependence*, pp. 74–78. In a further refinement, Blackhurst, Marian, and Tumlir, "Trade Liberalization," add that the proportion of imports and exports consisting of intermediate manufactured goods, as opposed to goods destined for final use, is rising rapidly, particularly in the category of engineering products. This reflects, among other things, "the growth in intra-branch specialization, foreign processing and sub-contracting" (pp. 15–16).

[63] Gerald K. Helleiner, "Transnational Corporations and Trade Structure: The Role of Intra-Firm Trade," in Herbert Giersch, ed., *Intra-Industry Trade* (Tübingen: J. C. B. Mohr, Paul Siebeck, 1979).

[64] For a historical overview, see John H. Dunning, *Studies in International Investments* (London: Allen & Unwin, 1970).

[65] A recent survey may be found in Joan Edelman Spero, *The Failure of the Franklin National Bank* (New York: Columbia University Press, 1980), chap. 2.

"narrowing of the economic basis" on which international transactions rest.[66] By this he means that international economic transactions increasingly reflect the effects of marginal cost and price differentials of similar activities and products, rather than the mutual benefits of divergent investment, production, and export structures. Moreover, within this division of labor there is a critical shift in functional differentiation *from* the level of country and sector *to* the level of product and firm. And the economic gains from trade are correspondingly smaller.[67]

All of this stands in stark contrast to the half-century prior to 1914. Intercontinental trade was higher.[68] Intersectoral trade dominated.[69] Long-term capital movements favored capital-deficient areas, and were concentrated overwhelmingly in the social-overhead capital sector of the borrowing countries.[70] Marginal cost and price differentials appear to have had only limited bearing on the pattern of trade and investment flows;[71] the requirements of international functional differentiation and, later, absorptive capacity, account for much more of the variance.[72] Lastly, the large dif-

---

[66] *Economics of Interdependence*, p. 68.

[67] Ibid., p. 76. Cooper adds that both product differentiation and economies of scale may modify this conclusion, "but several of the countries under consideration have sufficiently large domestic markets to reap most benefits likely to flow from large scale production even without trade."

[68] A. G. Kenwood and A. L. Lougheed, *The Growth of the International Economy, 1820–1960* (London: Allen & Unwin, 1971), chap. 5.

[69] For example, in 1913 Great Britain imported 87% of the raw materials it consumed (excluding coal), and virtually as much of its foodstuffs. Moreover, the share of primary products in world trade from 1876–1913 remained steady at about 62%, even though total world trade trebled. And right up to World War I, Germany, Great Britain's main industrial rival, remained a major source of supply of manufactured materials for Great Britain, including chemicals and dyestuffs. Kenwood and Lougheed, *Growth of International Economy*, chap. 5, and Briggs, "World Economy," p. 43.

[70] During the fifty years preceding 1914, the Americas received 51% of British portfolio foreign investment (North America 34%, South America 17%); overall, some 69% of British portfolio foreign investment went into transportation, public utilities, and other public works; 12% into extractive industries; and only 4% into manufacturing. Matthew Simon, "The Pattern of New British Portfolio Foreign Investment, 1865–1914," in A. R. Hall, ed., *The Export of Capital from Britain* (London: Methuen, 1968), p. 23; cf. A. K. Cairncross, *Home and Foreign Investment, 1870–1913* (Cambridge: Cambridge University Press, 1953). A broader survey of the various forms of investment from all sources may be found in Kenwood and Lougheed, *Growth of International Economy*, chap. 2.

[71] For trade, see ibid., chap. 5; for investment, A. I. Bloomfield, "Patterns of Fluctuations in International Investment Before 1914," *Princeton Studies in International Finance* 21 (1968), esp. pp. 35–40. Cooper (*Economics of Interdependence,* pp. 151–52), concerned to show that interdependence in the pre-1914 world economy "was something of an illusion," argues that despite the freedom of capital to move, "it did not in fact move in sufficient volume *even* to erase differences in short-term interest rates." (Emphasis added, to underscore his looking at the pre-1914 world through post-1960 lenses).

[72] "The industrialization of Europe and the growth of its population created a steadily growing demand for raw materials and foodstuffs, much of which had to be imported. At the same time, important advances in technical knowledge, especially in transportation and communications, and the existence of underpopulated and land-rich countries in other continents provided the means whereby these demands could be met. The greater part of the foreign investment undertaken during the nineteenth century was concerned with promoting this international specialization between an industrial centre located in Europe (and, later, in the United States) and a

ferences in comparative cost structures meant that trade was socially very profitable.[73]

To explain fully the differences between the pre–1914 and the post–1950s international division of labor would require linking them to a number of potentially causal factors. Among these, the most frequently invoked are differences in the relative levels of economic and technological development of the major countries concerned;[74] the evolution of the global organization of capital over the course of the past century;[75] the effects of differences in the configuration of interstate power in the two eras;[76] and the respective external consequences of shifts in domestic state-society relations.[77] International regimes thus do not determine these outcomes. At the same time, however, the close similarity between our hypothesized expectations of laissez-faire liberalism and embedded liberalism and actual patterns of transaction flows suggests that regimes do play a mediating role.

This mediating role of the postwar regimes for trade and money, and the complementary transaction flows to which they gave rise, have come to be recognized even by those most consistently espousing conventional liberal orthodoxies. As Charles Lipson points out, GATT negotiations have strongly favored intra-industry specialization.[78] And a recent GATT study notes that liberalization has produced "surprisingly few adjustment problems" among the industrialized countries because there has been "no abandonment of whole industrial sectors." Instead, specialization is "achieved mainly by individual firms narrowing their product range. . . ."[79] As a result, national export structures among the industrialized countries are becoming ever more alike.[80] On reflection, however, this outcome should not cause surprise. For governments pursuing domestic stabilization, it is quite safe to liberalize this kind of trade. Adjustment costs are low. It poses none of the vulnerabilities that a true Ricardian specialization among sectors would pose. Whatever political vulnerabilities might arise from it are more or less shared by all parties to it, so that it is unlikely to lead to a contest for political

---

periphery of primary producing countries." Kenwood and Lougheed, *Growth of International Economy*, p. 48.

[73] Cooper, *Economics of Interdependence*, p. 152.

[74] This is generally considered to be the driving force by liberal economists, as exemplified by Cooper, ibid.

[75] Marxists have tended to stress this factor; see, for example, Christian Palloix, "The Self-Expansion of Capital on a World Scale," *Review of Radical Political Economy* 9 (Summer 1977), which is drawn from his larger work, *L'internationalisation du capital* (Paris: Maspero, 1975).

[76] This is the realists' explanandum, as developed in Waltz, "Myth of National Interdependence," though most realists, unlike Waltz, would characterize the distribution of power in the pre–1914 world political economy as having been hegemonic. Cf. Robert Gilpin, *U.S. Power and the Multinational Corporation* (New York: Basic Books, 1975).

[77] See Polanyi's *Great Transformation* for one expression of this social-organicist position; for another, from a different location on the political spectrum, see Gunnar Myrdal, *Beyond the Welfare State* (New Haven: Yale University Press, 1960).

[78] His article in this volume.

[79] Blackhurst, Marian, and Tumlir, "Trade Liberalization," p. 11.

[80] See Lipson's article in this volume, and the references he cites.

advantage among them. And all the while it offers gains from trade. In contrast, there has been no progress in liberalizing agricultural trade. Furthermore, where trade in industrial products is based on a more classical notion of comparative advantage, as it is with imports from the so-called newly industrializing countries, the trade regime has encountered difficulty.[81] Apart from oil, North-South raw materials trade has posed few problems for the industrialized countries, both because of their overall domination of world trade and because of the characteristics of the raw materials sector.[82]

International financial flows may be expected to follow closely the evolving patterns of production and trade. Since the liberalization of payments facilities at the end of the 1950s and the loosening of capital controls in the early 1960s, they have done so. Two additional features of international financial transactions bear on my argument. First, international investments in social overhead capital, which provided the great bulk of private flows in the 1865–1914 period, now are almost the exclusive domain of national and international public institutions, acting alone or in cofinancing arrangements with private capital.[83] This has meant a welcome supplement to the vagaries of the market mechanism for recipient countries, and for donor countries as well, though in a different sense. For the donor countries, it has meant an ability to exercise far greater discretion over patterns of investment decisions in this leading sector than governments in the 19th century either enjoyed or sought. Second, the international financial markets that emerged in the 1960s, above all the Euromarkets, offered governments an important supplement to the monetary regime. Under Keynes's Clearing Union, capital controls were combined with generous overdraft allowances and parity changes as needed. In their absence or, more accurately, under the more modest forms of each that came to prevail in the 1960s, these markets offered the prospect of an adjustment mechanism to cushion both surplus and deficit countries (at least in the short run). Accordingly, governments did little to control and much to encourage the formation and growth of these markets.[84] Today, they constitute the main source of balance-of-payments financing.[85]

[81] This is not to suggest that the trade regime has encountered no other difficulties. One of the more serious is surplus capacity, which shows that the apparent ease with which liberalization has been accommodated was also dependent upon unprecedented rates of economic growth.

[82] Paul Bairoch, *The Economic Development of the Third World since 1900* (Berkeley: University of California Press, 1975), chap. 5.

[83] Dunning, *International Investments*, chap. 1. Governmental loans were largely confined to Continental Europe in the 19th century, and were small in comparison with private loans. Today, the situation is reversed in each respect.

[84] A good discussion of the role of governments in triggering the expansion of these markets may be found in Susan Strange, *International Monetary Relations*, vol. 2 of Shonfield, ed., *International Economic Relations of the Western World*, esp. chap. 6. Strange's primary concern is to show how the Euromarkets transformed from "good servant" to "bad master," by making difficult the conduct of domestic monetary policy and generally eroding national monetary sovereignty. The good servant role received rather more attention again in the mid to late 1970s, following the enormous payments imbalances produced by oil price increases. More on this general problem below.

[85] Benjamin J. Cohen's article in this volume.

In sum, international economic regimes do not determine international economic transactions. For determinants we have to look deeper into basic structural features of the world political economy. But, as we have seen, nor are international economic regimes irrelevant to international economic transactions. They play a mediating role, by providing a permissive environment for the emergence of certain kinds of transactions, specifically transactions that are perceived to be complementary to the normative frameworks of the regimes having a bearing on them. This conclusion does not imply that perceptions are never mistaken, that "good servants" never go on to become "bad masters," that complementarity is never condemned to coexist with contradiction—or, indeed, that international regimes have a bearing on the entire range of international transactions. Nor does it suggest that the effectiveness of international regimes may not become undermined by such disjunctions. The question of possible responses to second-order consequences of this sort takes us into a different analytical realm, that of regime change.

4. Norm-governed change

The 1970s witnessed important changes in central features of the postwar regimes for money and trade. Among political scientists and some economists, the decline of U.S. hegemony is most often adduced as the *causa causans* of these changes. Terms such as "erosion" and even "collapse" are most often invoked to describe them. Triffin depicted the Jamaica Accords as "slapstick comedy" rather than monetary reform, while for a former U.S. trade official the Tokyo Round "performed the coup de grace" on liberal trade.[86] The sense of discontinuity is pervasive. Is it justified?

Once again I take temporary refuge in hypothesis. If we allow that international regimes are not simply emanations of the underlying distribution of interstate power, but represent a fusion of power and legitimate social purpose, our cause and effect reasoning becomes more complex. For then the decline of hegemony would not necessarily lead to the collapse of regimes, provided that shared purposes are held constant. Instead, one ought to find changes in the instrumentalities of regimes, which, under hegemony, are likely to have relied on disproportionate contributions by and therefore reflected the preferences of the hegemon.[87] At the same time, one ought to find continuity in the normative frameworks of regimes, which would still

---

[86] Robert Triffin, "Jamaica: 'Major Revision' or Fiasco," in Edward M. Bernstein et al., "Reflections on Jamaica," *Princeton Essays in International Finance* 115 (Princeton, N.J., 1976), as cited in Benjamin J. Cohen, *Organizing the World's Money* (New York: Basic Books, 1977), chap. 4, fn. 24; and Thomas Graham, "Revolution in Trade Politics," *Foreign Policy* 36 (Fall 1979), p. 49.

[87] Supporters of the hegemonic stability position speak of "burdens of leadership"; critics, of "exorbitant privileges." The empirical referents are the same.

reflect shared purposes. And the new instrumentalities ought to be more appropriate to the new power distribution while remaining compatible with the existing normative framework. In short, the result would be "norm-governed" change.

Let us turn back to the post–1971 changes in the regimes for money and trade. On the monetary side, the major changes at issue are the end of the dollar's convertibility into gold and the adoption of floating rates of exchange, both in violation of the original Articles of Agreement. On the trade side, no discrete event fully symbolizes the perceived discontinuities, though they are characterized generally as "the new protectionism" and include the proliferation of nontariff barriers to trade and violations of the principle of nondiscrimination, in the form of domestic interventions as well as internationally negotiated export restraints. In both cases a weakening of the central institutions, the IMF and the GATT, is taken to reflect the same syndrome.

It is my contention that, on balance, the hypothesis of norm-governed change accounts for more of the variance than claims of fundamental discontinuity.

Base-line

The base-line against which change is here to be compared consists of two parts. First, if we compare changes in the monetary and trade regimes against some ideal of orthodox liberalism, then we are bound to be disappointed if not shocked by recent trends. But we are also bound to be misled. For orthodox liberalism has not governed international economic relations at any time during the postwar period. My starting point, of course, is the institutional nexus of embedded liberalism. Within this framework, it will be recalled, multilateralism and domestic stability are linked to and conditioned by one another. Thus, movement toward greater openness in the international economy is likely to be coupled with measures designed to cushion the domestic economy from external disruptions. At the same time, measures adopted to effect such domestic cushioning should be commensurate with the degree of external disturbance and compatible with the long-term expansion of international transactions. Moreover, what constitutes a deviation from this base-line cannot be determined simply by the "objective" examination of individual acts in reference to specific texts. Rather, deviation will be determined by the "intersubjective" evaluation of the intentionality and consequences of acts within the broader normative framework and prevailing circumstances.

The second component of my base-line is the peculiar relation of the United States to the institutionalization of embedded liberalism immediately after the war. The United States was, at one and the same time, the paramount economic power *and* the country in which the domestic state-society shift remained the most ambivalent. This had several complex consequences, with differential effects on the two regimes. The United States would have to provide the bulk of the material resources required to translate the negotiated compromises into institutional reality. This would give the U.S. influence that it could be expected to exercise in keeping not only with its own interests, but also with its preferred interpretations of both the compromises and how they were to be realized. The impact on the institutionalization of the trade agreement, once the ITO was abandoned, on the whole supported the basic design and need not detain us. But the institutionalization of the monetary agreement was profoundly skewed by the asymmetrical position of the U.S.[88] At Bretton Woods, through a combination of stealth and inevitability, the dollar had become equated with gold and was recognized officially but apparently without the knowledge of Keynes as the key currency.[89] Once the IMF came into existence, the U.S. insisted on terms of reference and a series of "interpretations" of the Articles, as well as decisions of the Executive Directors, that had the effect of launching what would come to be known as "IMF orthodoxy" and, inadvertently or otherwise, guaranteeing that there would be no intergovernmental alternative to U.S. payments deficits as the major instrument of international liquidity creation.[90] Thus, the monetary regime that emerged in the 1950s already differed in several important respects from the intent of Bretton Woods.

It is against this starting point that subsequent developments must be assessed.

[88] The differential impact on the two regimes is explained largely by the total asymmetry that prevailed in the monetary domain and the relatively more balanced configuration in trade. In the case of money, the U.S. possessed the fungible resources that everyone required, including some two-thirds of the world's monetary gold supply, which it acquired as an unbalanced creditor country before World War II. At the same time, the U.S. saw no situation in which it might become dependent upon the regime as a debtor. The case of trade is inherently somewhat more symmetrical, since the mutual granting of access to markets is the key resource. It is also a domain in which the domestic constraints within the United States differed little from domestic constraints elsewhere.

[89] Harry Dexter White and his staff had complete control over the organization of meetings, scheduling of subjects, rules of procedure, and drafting of all official documentation including daily minutes and the Final Act. In addition, White headed the so-called special committee, which resolved ambiguities and elaborated operational details. According to Van Dormael, on whose account I draw here, this committee "prepared for inclusion in the Final Act a number of provisions that were never discussed nor even brought up" (*Bretton Woods*, pp. 202–3). Even senior members of the American delegation were not always fully aware of what White was up to; Dean Acheson, normally no slouch, expressed confusion, and what he suspected he didn't much care for (ibid., pp. 200–203). In any case, Van Dormael attributes several features of the Fund to these organizational and procedural manipulations, the most important of which was an equation that no one else became aware of until after the fact, between gold and the U.S. dollar. This was in clear violation of the Joint Statement of Principles. Keynes had rejected any special role for the dollar; he favored the monetization of an international unit of account, and he assumed a multiple-currency reserve system. But in the final analysis, the major consequence of White's maneuverings on this issue was simply to give *de jure* expression to what surely would have occurred *de facto* and have been sanctified by subsequent practice.

[90] At the inaugural meeting of the Boards of Governors of the IMF and IBRD, held in Savannah, Georgia, the United States succeeded in having both institutions located in Washington, which could be expected to amplify day-to-day influence by Congress and the Administration,

The evolving monetary regime

The post–1971 inconvertibility of the dollar into gold may be usefully framed within the broader rubric of liquidity problems and floating rates of exchange within adjustment problems. I take up each in turn, and conclude with a comment on the IMF.

As noted, the liquidity provisions of Bretton Woods proved inadequate, even though, as Cohen points out elsewhere in this volume, an adequate supply of international liquidity was one of its cardinal principles. The growing volume of international trade increased liquidity requirements, as did the growing magnitude of speculative pressure on exchange rates. The dollar exchange standard, which had "solved" this problem in the short run, was already in trouble when the monetary regime first began to function without the protective shield of the postwar transitional arrangements. In 1958, just as the Europeans were resuming full convertibility of their currencies, U.S. gold reserves fell permanently below U.S. overseas liabilities. And before the next year was out, Professor Triffin had articulated his famous dilemma.[91] Throughout the 1960s, a seemingly endless series of stopgap measures was tried in an effort to devise what Robert Roosa, former

---

and in having the Executive Directors be full-time and highly paid officials, which was seen by the British as assuring greater Fund meddling in the affairs of members when they applied for assistance. They were not mistaken. In May 1947, the United States pushed through a meeting of the Executive Directors an "interpretation" of the Articles of Agreement, to the effect that the Fund could "challenge" the representations made by governments that a currency was presently needed for balance-of-payments purposes, *and* that the Fund had the authority to "postpone or reject the request, *or accept it subject to conditions.* . . ." (Reproduced in Horsefield, *The IMF*, 3: 227, emphasis added.) This interpretation was confirmed by decision of the Executive Directors in 1948. And thus was IMF conditionality born. In a further decision, taken in 1952, conditionality was elaborated to include "policies the member will pursue" to overcome payments deficits. (Ibid., 3: 228.) In the meantime, once the Marshall Plan went into effect, the United States secured further agreement that recipients of Marshall Plan aid could not also draw on the Fund. With the Europeans effectively excluded from the Fund, its only clients were developing countries. And it was during this period, on initiatives by the United States and in response to requests for assistance by developing countries, that the Fund developed its program of "stabilization" measures: exchange depreciation, domestic austerity measures, reduced public spending, rigid conditionality. Total drawings from the Fund dropped to zero in 1950, and did not exceed 1947 levels again until 1956. With respect to liquidity, the provisions of Bretton Woods were modest and proved inadequate. The European Reconstruction Program took care of Europe's needs. But the IMF repeatedly turned aside requests for new measures to increase its own capacity to supply liquidity, maintaining that the real need was for adjustment. The dollar exchange standard emerged as a "solution" to this problem. (Strange, *International Monetary Relations,* pp. 93–96; Block, *Origins of International Economic Disorder*, chap. 5; Richard Cooper, "Prolegomena to the Choice," p. 86; and Benjamin J. Cohen, in this volume.)

[91] In essence, Triffin argued that if the United States corrected its balance of payments deficit, the result would be world deflation because gold production at $35 an ounce could not adequately supply world monetary reserves. But if the United States continued running a deficit, the result would be the collapse of the monetary standard because U.S. foreign liabilities would far exceed its ability to convert dollars into gold on demand. Robert Triffin, *Gold and the Dollar Crisis* (New Haven: Yale University Press, 1960), which was largely a reprint of two journal articles that appeared the year before.

under-secretary of the treasury, called "outer perimeter defenses" for the dollar. Roughly speaking, these measures were designed to make gold conversion financially unattractive, to increase the capacity of the IMF to supply liquidity, and to increase the capacity of central banks to neutralize the flow of speculative capital. The U.S. also undertook limited domestic measures to reduce its payments deficits and pressured surplus countries to revalue their currencies. By 1968, however, the dollar had become in effect inconvertible into gold; it was declared formally inconvertible in 1971.

The rise and fall of the gold-convertible dollar has placed the monetary regime in a paradoxical predicament from beginning to end. It has altered profoundly central instruments of the regime having to do with the creation of international liquidity, the system of currency reserves, and the means of ultimate settlement. It has also violated procedural norms, as unilateral action usurped collective decision. But, at the same time, it seems to have been understood and acknowledged all around that, under the material and political conditions prevailing, the substantive norms of Bretton Woods, the compromise of embedded liberalism, would not have been realized in the first place by any other means. So the regime today remains stuck with the undesired consequences of means that helped bring about a desired end. What of the long-term alternatives? Several have emerged in embryonic form. Were they to be instituted more fully, all would imply a reduced official role for the dollar and a return to the kinds of mechanisms anticipated by Bretton Woods. An internationally created reserve asset exists in the form of the special drawing right (SDR). A multiple-currency reserve system is slowly coming into being, and a dollar-substitution account has been under negotiation in the IMF. The U.S. views the SDR with disfavor and actively opposes the substitution account. It has no objection to other currencies playing a larger reserve role. As they do, however, the pressure may be expected to increase both for a substitution facility covering all reserve currencies and for a noncurrency reserve asset.

With respect to the problem of adjustment, as we saw, few provisions for international measures to affect the economic policies of deficit or surplus countries survived the Bretton Woods negotiations. And once the new creditor-debtor relationships became established in the late 1950s, the mechanism of exchange rate changes also failed to operate effectively. There existed no means to compel surplus countries to appreciate, and among the largest deficit countries, Great Britain resisted depreciation fiercely in a vain attempt to preserve an international role for sterling while the United States, as the "Nth country," necessarily remained passive. Thus, the only real international leverage for adjustment was the conditionality provision developed by the Fund. The burden of domestic adjustment measures, therefore, fell disproportionately on the developing countries. The adjustable peg system became intolerable when imbalances in the external trade account came to be overshadowed, both as a source of problems and as a response to them, by massive movements of short-term speculative funds. This made it increasingly difficult for governments to conduct domestic macroeconomic policy, and to support exchange rates under pressure. When, in the late 1960s, the full attention of these funds came to be focused on the dollar as a result of dramatic deficits in the U.S. trade balance and current account, the system of fixed rates of exchange was doomed.

Shifting to floating rates required formal amendment of the Articles of Agreement of the Fund, the "slapstick comedy" act of which Triffin spoke. This is prima facie evidence of discontinuity. However, living within the Articles provided the international monetary system with an adjustment mechanism that neither functioned effectively nor fulfilled the expectations of Bretton Woods. What of the present arrangement? Three aspects bear on the argument. First, it is important to keep distinct the instrument of fixed rates from the norm of outlawing competitive currency depreciation and thus providing a framework for relatively stable exchanges. There is a good case to be made that the norm had become sufficiently well institutionalized and recourse to competitive depreciation sufficiently unnecessary given other means of influencing domestic macroeconomic factors that reliance on an increasingly burdensome instrument, which itself had begun to contribute to currency instability, could no longer be justified.[92] Moreover, experience since has shown the managed float to be capable of avoiding serious disorderliness—the early months of new administrations in Washington providing the major exceptions—and to have few if any deleterious consequences for international trade. Second, floating rates were widely perceived to provide a greater cushion for domestic macroeconomic policy, which was increasingly subjected to dislocation from speculative capital flows that were often quite out of proportion to underlying economic reality. It is clear now that the degree of insulation is less than was advertised, but in the absence of uniform and fairly comprehensive capital controls it is probably as much as can be secured. Third, as an adjustment mechanism, the managed float appears to function more symmetrically than fixed rates did. Not only have surplus countries been forced to take notice, but the precipitous depreciation of the U.S. dollar caught the attention of American policy makers in the autumn of 1978 more effectively than past balance-of-payments deficits had done.

On the evolution of the IMF we can be brief; its tendency seems to be to come full circle. One does not want to exaggerate recent changes in the Fund, especially in relation to the developing countries. Nevertheless, its financing facilities have been considerably expanded, repayment periods lengthened, and conditionality provisions relaxed somewhat as well as now requiring the Fund "to pay due regard to the domestic social and political objectives" of borrowing countries.[93] Moreover, decision-making power within the Fund has been reapportioned, at least to the extent of distributing

---

[92] Richard Cooper enumerates the pros and cons of these and related issues in "Prolegomena to the Choice," esp. pp. 80–81.

[93] Reported in *The New York Times*, 5 February 1980. In exploring the reasons for this change, the *Times* cites a "Washington wit" who "once said that the monetary fund had toppled more governments than Marx and Lenin combined."

veto power more equitably. These changes began in the late 1950s, to make the Fund more acceptable to the Europeans once they accepted the full obligations of IMF membership; they continued in the 1960s to reflect the economic status of the European Community and Japan; and they were accelerated and aimed increasingly at the developing countries in the 1970s, as a result of the massive payments imbalances produced by new energy terms of trade and subsequent fears about the stability of the international financial system.

The evolution of the trade regime

The sense of discontinuity concerning the international trade regime is illustrated in the following excerpt from a *Wall Street Journal* article, entitled "Surge in Protectionism Worries and Perplexes Leaders of Many Lands":

> After three decades of immense increase in world trade and living standards, exports and imports are causing tense pressures in nearly every nation and among the best of allies. The U.S. sets price floors against Japanese steel, Europe accuses the U.S. of undercutting its papermakers, the Japanese decry cheap textiles from South Korea, French farmers have smashed truckloads of Italian wine, and AFL-CIO President George Meany rattles exporters world-wide by calling free trade—'a joke.'[94]

By now, even its most severe critics realize that "the new protectionism" is not simply the latest manifestation of "old-style" protectionism. "The emergence of the new protectionism in the Western world reflects the victory of the interventionist, or welfare, economy over the market economy."[95] However, they continue to have difficulty appreciating that the new protectionism is not an aberration from the norm of postwar liberalization, but an integral feature of it.

Today, tariffs on products traded among the industrialized countries are an insignificant barrier to trade. The Tokyo Round managed to institute further tariff cuts, and began to cope with nontariff barriers for the first time. It produced codes to liberalize such barriers resulting from domestic subsidies and countervailing duties, government procurement, product standards, customs valuation, and import licensing. All barriers to trade in civil aircraft and aircraft parts were removed. And preparations for a new GATT round, on investment and services, have commenced. What is more, the volume of world trade continues to increase and its rate of growth, though declining, still exceeds economic growth rates in several OECD countries. In sum, liberalization and growth have continued despite the erosion of postwar

---

[94] 14 April 1978, as cited in Melvyn B. Krauss, *The New Protectionism: The Welfare State in International Trade* (New York: New York University Press, 1978), pp. xix-xx.
[95] Ibid., p. 36.

prosperity, and despite the erosion of American willingness to absorb disproportionate shares of liberalized trade.[96]

Restraints on trade have also grown. Much of the time they take one of two forms: domestic safeguards, and "voluntary" or negotiated export restraints. Under the GATT, domestic safeguards may be invoked for balance-of-payments reasons (Article XII), or to prevent injury to domestic producers caused by a sudden surge of imports that can be attributed to past tariff concessions (Article XIX). The first of these has caused little difficulty, notwithstanding several deviations from prescribed procedure.[97] Article XIX lends itself to greater abuse. It permits alteration or suspension of past tariff concessions in a nondiscriminatory manner, provided that interested parties are consulted. It has been invoked with growing frequency, particularly by the U.S. and Australia. It is quite clumsy, however, because bystanders are likely to be affected and because it may involve renegotiation or even retaliatory suspension of concessions. As a result, "most governments, on most occasions, have simply short-circuited Article XIX altogether, going straight to the heart of the problem by negotiating a minimum price agreement, or a 'voluntary' export restraint with the presumably reluctant exporter who has previously been 'softened' by threats of emergency action under GATT."[98] Many of these agreements do not involve governments at all, but are reached directly between the importing and exporting industries concerned. They take place beyond the purview of the GATT and therefore are not subject to official multilateral surveillance. An attempt, made during the Tokyo Round, to conclude a safeguards code that would have provided detailed rules and procedures was unsuccessful, though negotiations are continuing. However, these problems do not afflict the entire trading order, but are sectorally specific, and a close sectoral analysis will show that there is *not* "any decisive movement toward protectionism. . . ."[99] Lastly, so-

---

[96] Stephen D. Krasner, "The Tokyo Round: Particularistic Interests and Prospects for Stability in the Global Trading System," *International Studies Quarterly* 23 (December 1979).

[97] For example, Article XII calls for quantitative restrictions, but as time has passed import surcharges have usually been imposed. In an extremely peculiar "non-use" of Article XII, France imposed emergency measures against imports after the 1968 disturbances, while enjoying a strong reserve position and only fearing a potential balance-of-payments problem. France asked for "sympathy and understanding" from its partners in the GATT and got it. The exceptional circumstances were stressed all around, the danger of precedent was flagged, and the measures were approved and soon thereafter discontinued. The case shows, according to Curzon and Curzon, "the complicity which exists between governments when one of them is forced to take unpopular trade measures because it has a domestic problem on its hands" ("Management of Trade," p. 222). Their characterization of the reaction of others as complicitous captures the very essence of an international regime.

[98] Ibid., p. 225.

[99] Krasner, "Tokyo Round," p. 507. Krasner examines sectoral crosspressures and finds roughly this pattern: little pressure for protectionism where there is high intrasectoral trade, and even less if the sector is highly internationalized; protectionist pressures from import-competing sectors, which, however, may be balanced off by countervailing pressure from export sectors; high protectionist pressure when import competition is largely asymmetrical (pp. 502–7). Lipson, elsewhere in this volume, relates protectionist pressures to the production characteristics of sectors and finds that "sectoral protectionism is most likely in standardized, basic industries,

called orderly marketing arrangements, of which the Longterm Textile Agreement of 1962 was the first multilateral variant, have also proliferated vastly. However, each of these has provided for a regular expansion of exports, though of course more limited than would have been obtained under conditions of "free" trade. In sum, the impact of these restraints on international trade, even by the GATT's own reckoning, has been relatively modest.[100] Their purpose, moreover, has not been to freeze the international division of labor but to slow down structural change and to minimize the social costs of domestic adjustment.

With respect to the institutional role of the GATT, legal scholars in particular have lamented the passing of "effective and impartial" dispute settlement mechanisms.[101] However, these mechanisms had begun to fall into disuse by the late 1950s—that is, just as production and trade began to soar and serious tariff reductions were contemplated. Bilateral consultations and negotiations among instructed representatives of the disputants have since been the norm.[102] It requires an extremely optimistic view of the possibilities for international law and conciliation to expect interventionist governments to behave otherwise.

Assessment

This review does not argue that the world it describes is the best of all possible worlds. I have only argued that the world has to be looked at as it is: when the regimes for money and trade are viewed in this light, the hypothesis of norm-governed change accounts for more of the variance than claims of fundamental discontinuity. Much of the observed change has been at the level of instrument rather than norm. Moreover, in most cases the new instruments are not inimical to the norms of the regimes but represent adaptations to new circumstances. And in some cases the collective response by governments to changing circumstances reflects a greater affinity to the ex-

---

or those with high capital requirements. It is least likely in industries where R&D is high and is oriented to changing market opportunities, where innovation in products and processes is rapid, and where the rents attributable to proprietary knowledge are short-lived" (draft manuscript).

[100] Two figures are pertinent here. First, the GATT estimated in the late 1970s that import restrictions already in place or seriously threatened would affect some 3%–5% of world trade—which its Director General took to represent a threat to "the whole fabric of postwar cooperation in international trade policy." *IMF Survey,* 12 December 1977, p. 373. The second concerns the declining portion of world trade subject to MFN principles; here it must be pointed out that the overwhelming share of this decline is accounted for by customs unions and free trade areas, which, for better or for worse, have been sanctioned by the GATT. A more fundamental problem could emerge as a result of the Tokyo Round, insofar as the codes for government procurement, subsidies, and safeguards (if the last materializes) will apply only to signatories of each individual code. At this point, however, the long-term significance of this proviso remains unclear.

[101] See the literature cited in Lipson's article in this volume.

[102] Curzon and Curzon, "Management of Trade," chap. 3.

pectations of original regime designs than did the arrangements that prevailed in the interval.

This analysis suggests that far more continuity can attend hegemonic decline than would be predicted by the hegemonic stability thesis, provided that social purposes are held constant.[103] And, since social purposes in turn reflect particular configurations of state-society relations, it suggests further that fundamental discontinuity in these regimes *would* be effected by an erosion in the prevailing balance of state-society relations among the major economic powers. Ironically, then, the foremost force for discontinuity at present is not "the new protectionism" in money and trade, but the resurgent ethos of liberal capitalism.

5. Stress, contradiction, and the future

One question remains. How enduring is embedded liberalism? Specifically, will it survive the current domestic and international economic malaise? A central ingredient in the success of embedded liberalism to date has been its ability to accommodate and even facilitate the externalizing of adjustment costs. There have been three major modes of externalization: an intertemporal mode, via inflation; an intersectoral mode, whereby pressure on domestic and international public authorities is vented into the realm of private markets; and what, for the sake of congruity, we might call an interstratum mode, through which those who are "regime makers" shift a disproportionate share of adjustment costs onto those who are "regime takers." Each of these has emerged virtually by default as a means to avoid a still worse outcome.[104] The accumulated effects of these practices, however, have produced severe stresses in the world political economy. As a result, some manner of renegotiating the forms of domestic and international social accommodation reflected in embedded liberalism is inevitable. Its future, then, depends on how this is brought about. I take up the three modes of externalization in reverse order.

The compromise of embedded liberalism has never been fully extended to the developing countries. They have been disproportionately subject to the orthodox stabilization measures of the IMF, often with no beneficial results in export earnings but substantial increases in import bills and con-

---

[103] The fit between hypothesis and real world obviously is not perfect, because factors other than those examined here are also at work in the evolution of the postwar regimes. Moreover, the notion of declining American hegemony itself is very imprecise and, indeed, easy to exaggerate. See, respectively, Keohane, "Theory of Hegemonic Stability," and Susan Strange, "Still an Extraordinary Power," in Ray Lombra and Bill Witte, eds., *The Political Economy of International and Domestic Monetary Relations* (Ames: Iowa State University Press, 1982).

[104] I am here generalizing from Fred Hirsch's brilliant dissection of the social functions of inflation: "The Ideological Underlay of Inflation," in Fred Hirsch and John H. Goldthorpe, eds., *The Political Economy of Inflation* (Cambridge: Harvard University Press, 1978), esp. p. 278.

sequent increases in domestic prices. Moreover, the liberalization produced by the GATT has benefited relatively few among them. On the whole, the developing countries did well in the 1960s, as an adjunct to expansion in the OECD area; in the 1970s, they suffered as much from export losses to OECD markets as they did from the direct impact of increased oil prices. For a time in the mid 1970s, the developing countries managed to sustain both rates of growth and imports from the industrialized countries through additional private borrowing (their upper tranches in the IMF were left virtually untouched). However, neither could be continued indefinitely. Recent IMF reforms are important, as we have noted, but they cannot initiate economic recovery in the Third World. Nor are other means forthcoming in abundance. Thus, unlike the pattern under laissez-faire liberalism in the 19th century, under embedded liberalism lending and investment in the peripheral areas has been both relatively lower and positively correlated with core expansion rather than counterpoised to it. From the point of view of the future of embedded liberalism, the accumulated effects of this practice are not fatal—though they may prove to be very nearly fatal for some of the poorer developing countries.[105] From the point of view of the established system as a whole, these effects are more in the nature of lost opportunities whose realization could have contributed to the resolution of the current economic malaise.

A second mode of externalizing adjustment costs in recent decades has been to channel pressure away from domestic and international public authorities into the domain of private markets. A prime example is the vastly increased role of international financial markets in balance-of-payments lending, as analyzed by Cohen in this volume. I argued above that the success of the monetary and trade regimes may be said to have depended in some measure on this practice, even before the recycling problems of the 1970s. But it has also come to pose a source of serious stress and potential contradiction for the monetary regime, particularly as the control of inflation has become the leading economic objective of governments. One of its consequences, discussed by Cohen, is at least a partial loss of control by governments over the process of international liquidity creation. Perhaps even more important, in attempting to achieve significant restraint in the expansion of credit and money stock effected by these markets, governments may find that the domestic economy now must shoulder a disproportionate share of the burden of adjustment. Higher domestic interest rates may have to be employed than would be warranted by domestic conditions alone, in order to compensate for the more rapid rate of expansion of the Eurofund component of the consolidated domestic and international markets. "Today the mass is still relatively small, but the speed is high. Mass times speed, as the physi-

---

[105] Hollis B. Chenery notes this exception in his otherwise optimistic outlook, "Restructuring the World Economy: Round II," *Foreign Affairs* 59 (Summer 1981).

cists like to say, equals momentum."[106] From the vantage point of our concerns, then, what has served as a handy and even necessary vent is threatening to undergo a means-ends reversal, with potentially serious consequences for domestic and international financial stability.

Lastly, I turn to the most pervasive and the most serious mode by which adjustment costs have been externalized, inflation. It is the most serious because it is the most likely to lead to a direct renegotiation of the modus vivendi that has characterized embedded liberalism. The international regimes for money and trade have increasingly accommodated inflation, in parallel with inflation's becoming the dominant domestic means of dealing with distributional strife in advanced capitalist societies.[107] On the monetary side, the release of domestic and international money supplies from their metallic base established the essential permissive condition, facilitated by subsequent developments in the monetary regime. The primacy of domestic objectives over external financial discipline was established in the interwar period. The Bretton Woods adjustment process, when it worked, worked primarily to devalue the currencies of deficit countries and consequently to increase their domestic prices. With inconvertible reserve currencies and floating rates, whatever counterforce may have existed in the pressures that previously led to gold outflows now leads to a fall in exchange rates and thus to increases in prices and costs. On the side of the trade regime, the structure of trade that it has encouraged and the minimization of domestic adjustment costs that it allows have both had inflationary consequences, by sacrificing economic efficiency to social stability. Hirsch's conclusion concerning the monetary regime is equally applicable to both: "Critics who see these international . . . arrangements as embodying a ratchet effect for world inflation are probably right. But the relevant question is whether a liberal international economy could have been purchased at any more acceptable price."[108] This dilemma will not be easily resolved.[109] However, so long as it remains understood that it is a dilemma, both parts of which have to be accommodated, the normative framework of embedded liberalism will endure as a central institutional feature of the international economic order.

[106] Henry C. Wallich, "Why the Euromarket Needs Restraint," *Columbia Journal of World Business* 14 (Fall 1979), p. 17. Wallich estimates that the Euromarkets are expanding at two to three times the rate of growth of the domestic markets of major countries (p. 23).

[107] Hirsch and Goldthorpe, *Political Economy of Inflation*, especially the chapters by Hirsch; Goldthorpe, "The Current Inflation: Towards a Sociological Account," pp. 186–214; and Charles S. Maier, "The Politics of Inflation in the Twentieth Century," pp. 37–72. The following discussion of the monetary regime draws heavily on Hirsch.

[108] Ibid., p. 279.

[109] Recent enthusiasm for simply discrediting Keynesian management and reverting to earlier monetary and fiscal "discipline" has begun to dampen under the weight of its apparent consequences. For example, in a postmortem of the 1981 summer riots across England, a junior member of the Tory government chose words that could have been taken directly from Polanyi: "This is what happens when you separate economic theory from social policy and pursue the one at the expense of the other." (Cited by David S. Broder, "Britain Offers a Grim Reminder," *Manchester Guardian Weekly*, 26 July 1981, p. 16.)

The hegemon's dilemma: Great Britain, the United States, and the international economic order
Arthur A. Stein

In the past decade, the "theory of hegemonic stability" has become the conventional but inadequate wisdom for assessing both international economic relations in the 1970s and 1980s and the broader history of such interactions during the last 150 years.[1] It asserts that a hegemonic power creates a stable international economic order and that the hegemon's decline leads to global instability.[2] As applied specifically to international trade, the

The author gratefully acknowledges the extensive comments provided by Amy Davis, Peter Gourevitch, Roger Haydon, Robert Jervis, Peter Katzenstein, Robert Keohane, Stephen Krasner, George Modelski, and two anonymous referees. Earlier versions of this paper were presented at the 1981 annual meeting of the American Political Science Association and a 1981 meeting of the Politics Colloquium of the UCLA Department of Political Science. The author is grateful for the financial assistance of the UCLA Council on International and Comparative Studies and the UCLA Academic Senate. The author also thanks the Brookings Institution, where, as a Guest Scholar, he revised this paper.

1. Its major proponents are Charles P. Kindleberger, Robert Gilpin, and Stephen Krasner. For Kindleberger's arguments, see *The World in Depression, 1929–1939* (Berkeley: University of California Press, 1973), "Systems of International Economic Organization," in David P. Calleo, ed., *Money and the Coming World Order* (New York: New York University Press, 1976), and "Dominance and Leadership in the International Economy: Exploitation, Public Goods, and Free Rides," *International Studies Quarterly* 25 (June 1981): 242–54. For Gilpin's arguments, see *U.S. Power and the Multinational Corporation: The Political Economy of Foreign Direct Investment* (New York: Basic Books, 1975), and "Economic Interdependence and National Security in Historical Perspective," in Klaus Knorr and Frank N. Trager, eds., *Economic Issues and National Security* (Lawrence: Regents Press of Kansas, 1977), pp. 19–66. Also see Krasner, "State Power and the Structure of International Trade," *World Politics* 28 (April 1976): 317–47. Robert Keohane coined the phrase now in common use in his application of their work to three current issues; see "The Theory of Hegemonic Stability and Changes in International Economic Regimes, 1967–1977," in Ole R. Holsti, Randolph M. Siverson, and Alexander George, eds., *Change in the International System* (Boulder, Colo.: Westview Press, 1980).

2. It bears some resemblance to A. F. K. Organski's "power transition." Organski disagrees with most international relations theorists and argues that an imbalance of power (i.e., a system with a hegemonic power) is more stable and peaceful than one with a true balance of power. Curiously, most international political economists are unaware of Organski's work. See Organski, *World Politics*, 2d ed. (New York: Knopf, 1968), and Organski and Jacek Kugler, *The War Ledger* (Chicago: University of Chicago Press, 1980). It also resembles George Modelski's "long cycles," which Modelski has applied to explain international economic as well as political orders. See Modelski, "The Long Cycle of Global Politics and the Nation-State," *Comparative Studies*

International Organization 38, 2, Spring 1984, pp. 355–86
© 1984 by the Massachusetts Institute of Technology and the World Peace Foundation

argument holds that hegemony leads to open markets and that its decline brings about their renewed closure. Although no author defines hegemony precisely, all agree that Britain provided hegemonic leadership in the 19th century and that the United States played a similar role in the years following World War II. The rise and decline of British hegemony thus explain the existence and collapse of the "era of free trade." Changes in America's relative power not only explain the postwar growth of global trade but also portend the imminent demise of the current trading regime. In this article I provide an alternative formulation of the formation, maintenance, and collapse of liberal trading orders as well as a revised account of the evolution of the global trading order.

Charles P. Kindleberger sparked the current debate with his book *The World in Depression*. He argues that a hegemon can provide the collective good of global stability, and that the absence of such hegemonic leadership worsened the Great Depression. Recognizing that the existence of a hegemon is not in itself sufficient to insure stability, he stresses the selflessness and far-sightedness required if such a leader is to serve world interests. He describes the problems of the 1930s, therefore, as stemming not only from Britain's decline, which made it unable to provide direction, but from the unwillingness of the United States to accept new responsibility by maintaining open markets in a time of economic downturn.

Given his characterization of international economic stability as a collective good, Kindleberger recognizes that various combinations of nations might provide the requisite leadership. He argues, however, that the incentives to cheat and become a free rider are great enough that any international regime which depends on collective provision is inherently unstable. Stability can only be assured when a hegemon both bears the costs of providing the collective good and extracts the support of others.[3] Kindleberger does not deal with the formation of regimes, but his argument that hegemony is prerequisite to international economic stability relies both on his characterization of international economic regimes as collective goods and on the presumption that only a hegemonic provision of a collective good is in itself stable.[4]

Political scientists have both extended and altered his thesis. Kindleberger's emphasis on stability leads him to consider questions about the nature and

in Society and History 20 (April 1978): 214–35, and "Long Cycles and the Strategy of U.S. International Economic Policy," in William P. Avery and David P. Rapkin, eds., *America in a Changing World Political Economy* (New York: Longman, 1982).

3. In "Systems" and "Dominance and Leadership," he argues that even hegemony is subject to entropy and, therefore, unstable.

4. Kindleberger's "The Rise of Free Trade in Western Europe, 1820–1875," *Journal of Economic History* 35 (March 1975): 20–55, is an exception; its implicit argument is quite at odds with his general thesis. The point is made by John Gerard Ruggie, "International Regimes, Transactions, and Change: Embedded Liberalism in the Postwar Economic Order," *International Organization* 36 (Spring 1982): 385.

substance of the international economic order only implicitly, but they treat these issues far more directly. They have also changed Kindleberger's focus with their explicit interest in the rise and fall of liberal free trade regimes in the 19th and 20th centuries. Most importantly, they argue that hegemons create liberal international economic orders not from altruism but from their own interest in open markets.

Robert Gilpin and Stephen Krasner have contributed most to the evolution of this literature. Both stress the hegemon's interest in and ability to create a liberal trading order. Gilpin argues that there are two dimensions to a hegemon's power: economic efficiency and political and military strength. Having the world's most efficient economy, the hegemon has the most to gain from free trade.[5] Given its political power, it has the resources to force or induce others to adopt liberal practices in their foreign trade. Krasner arrives at the same conclusion somewhat differently. He assesses the set of state interests that are affected by the international trading order and then deduces that only a large hegemonic state would find free trade both desirable and achievable. Thus, for Gilpin and Krasner, hegemony is prerequisite to the emergence of a liberal trade regime.

None of these authors describes how a free trade regime is established, maintained, and abandoned.[6] Kindleberger's focus is on the endurance and breakdown of an extant order rather than on its establishment. Gilpin and Krasner are concerned with regime formation as well as change, but they move from the assertion of a hegemonic state's interest in liberal trade to the presumption of a regime's emergence. All three mention that a hegemon uses inducements and force to create or maintain open markets, yet none provides a sense of how this occurs. Because they argue that a hegemon is essential to the existence of a regime, Gilpin and Krasner see its decline as leading to the collapse of the order.

All three scholars use Britain's international economic role in the 19th century, and America's in the 20th, to illustrate the argument that a hegemon creates an open world and that its decline leads to closure. Yet Gilpin and Krasner recognize the empirical problems with this exercise. The golden age of free trade in the 19th century began decades after Britain's emergence as a hegemonic power. The return to protectionism started in the latter part of the 19th century, when Britain, despite the beginning of a decline in its relative power, was still the hegemon. Global trade reached its greatest levels in the years just preceding World War I, when many European nations had

5. Gilpin draws on the collective goods argument yet believes that only the most efficient nation finds open markets in its interest. David Lake points out that Gilpin must mean relative productivity rather than efficiency, in "International Economic Structures and American Foreign Economic Policy, 1887–1934," *World Politics* 35 (July 1983): 517–43.

6. This point is made by Timothy J. McKeown, "Hegemonic Stability and 19th Century Tariff Levels in Europe," *International Organization* 37 (Winter 1983): 73–91.

supposedly reverted to protectionist policies.[7] The United States emerged from the war as the new hegemon but adopted prohibitive tariffs rather than pursuing free trade. The collapse of the current liberal trading order, predicted in the wake of America's relative decline, has not yet come to pass. Political scientists, to whatever extent they address these anomalies, tend to explain them as peculiar to the specific hegemons.[8]

I argue here that liberal international trade regimes did not, and indeed will not, emerge from the policies of one state. A hegemon cannot alone bring about an open trading order. It can unilaterally reduce its own tariffs, but this does not create an international trading order of lower tariffs. It can impose an open trading regime on weak countries, but this too does not create a global regime. Trade liberalization among major trading states is, rather, the product of tariff bargains. The hegemon must get others to agree to lower their tariffs as well.[9] Without agreements, there can be no regime.[10]

Such accords typically require the hegemon to make important concessions. Indeed, in both the 19th and 20th centuries, the hegemonic power accepted compromises and deviated from the ideal of free trade. Hegemons may lead, but they need followers, and they must make concessions to gain others' assent. In other words, the liberal trade regimes that emerged in both centuries

7. Openness is typically measured by trade flows, liberalization by tariff rates and tariff legislation. The interrelationships among the indicators and the concepts themselves are usually not assessed. These indicators are not always coincident and neither are the constructs. This article, however, is not the place to discuss these issues.

8. Several explanations attempt to deal with these empirical problems. None provides complete alternative explanations for the creation, maintenance, and decline of liberal trade regimes; they address only their decline. Timothy McKeown, for example, sketches a "political business cycle" explanation for foreign economic policies. The theory can explain closure during a hegemon's dominance but cannot explain why (or how) a hegemon pursues openness during good times. A similarly problematic example is the "surplus capacity" explanation of Peter F. Cowhey and Edward Long, who apply the hegemonic stability argument to a specific sector, the automobile industry. But it is not clear that the theory should be seen in sector-specific terms, nor that surplus capacity is independent of hegemonic decline. See Cowhey and Long, "Testing Theories of Regime Change: Hegemonic Decline or Surplus Capacity?" *International Organization* 37 (Spring 1983): 157–88.

9. Lake, "International Economic Structures," argues that medium-size states with high productivity will support a liberal regime, but that medium-size states with low productivity will act as spoilers. He goes on to describe the fitful movement toward lower tariffs by the United States during the latter 19th century and the early 20th. Lake characterizes the United States as a "supporter" of the liberal trade regime, but it never became part of that regime in the 19th century, and it did not adopt an unconditional most-favored-nation clause, which was at the heart of that regime, until the early 1920s. Indeed, the United States continually sought exclusive favors. Often it not only insisted that negotiated concessions were not subject to most-favored-nation treatment but also refused to allow other countries to generalize the concessions they had granted to it. By Lake's criteria, France and Germany were "spoilers" *throughout* the latter 19th century; thus he cannot explain any liberalization among the major European trading states during this period. His argument regarding France and German policy would neither square with the interpretation offered below nor with the standard interpretation of a shift in French and German policy in the 1880s and 1890s.

10. International regimes emerge not from the actions of one power, even a hegemonic one, but from the interactions of major powers, even if they are not even roughly equal in power. Strategic interaction is as important in a hegemonic system as in a balance-of-power one.

were founded on asymmetric bargains that permitted discrimination, especially against the hegemon. The agreements that lowered tariff barriers led not to free trade, but freer trade. In the process, they legitimated a great deal of mercantilism and protectionism.

The hegemon's willingness to accept asymmetric trade agreements is not a function of its economic interests alone. Both trade agreements and trade disputes have inherently international political underpinnings; their foundations are not solely economic. Great Britain and the United States had important political objectives for which they were prepared to make economic concessions.

Yet hegemonic states interested in the economic benefits of liberalized trade and desiring improved political relations with other nations may still cling to tariffs for domestic reasons. An interest in trade liberalization presumes not only certain international economic and political interests but also a certain internal strength on the part of the government. A government that lowers tariffs must have both alternative sources of revenue and either a winning political coalition arrayed in its support or the ability to prevent the coalescence of a blocking one. Domestic interests may not determine a state's foreign economic policy, but they certainly do constrain it.

Just as the existence of a hegemonic power does not necessarily imply the emergence of a liberal trading order, so its decline does not necessarily presage the end of such a regime. The decline of hegemony is a result of differential rates of economic growth, which surely affect the nature of the international trade regime. Markets can change rapidly and alter the nature of goods traded, the price level, and the terms of trade. Domestic and international economic developments thus modify the interests both of groups within nations and of whole nations. Protectionist policies, legitimated and accepted by trade liberalization agreements, will ebb and flow with such economic developments. Tariff bargains can become irrelevant with changing circumstances and may have to be renegotiated. Indeed, 19th-century trade agreements were temporary ones that required periodic renegotiation. (Such renegotiations may also be one result of the decline of hegemony; in any case, they will be marked by jockeying and conflict.) Nevertheless, international trade can be, and historically has been, sustained without a complete political rupturing of relations. When such breaks have occurred, they have typically been a result of major war.

Finally, the international economic orders that have been created by trade agreements have been subsystemic rather than global; not all states became parties to such agreements and many were effectively excluded from them. Moreover, they did not provide collective goods because nonsignatory states could be effectively excluded. At best, subsystemic regimes only indirectly provide collective goods to nonsignatories. The use of a most-favored-nation clause implies the existence of less or least favored nations. Thus the systems allowed for discrimination and exclusion, and cannot be considered to have provided a collective good.[11]

These interrelated arguments are developed below in a narrative reconstruction of the international trading order's evolution since 1820. The analytic arguments recast the hegemon's interests, the role that it plays, the process by which trade relationships change, the nature of those changes, and the implications of hegemonic decline. In developing these analytic points and presenting a historical narrative, I also correct the blithe historical generalizations often made about the evolution of the international trading order.

State strength and the British move to freer trade

My first argument is that the hegemon's ability to adopt openness is an issue not only of its external strength but also of its internal strength. To characterize a nation or state as an economic hegemon is to describe its economic power vis-à-vis other states. Yet an internationally powerful state may still not be able to afford free trade, even when free trade is in its interest, because it needs to control access to its domestic market in order to generate revenue.[12] A fully protectionist state, because it allows no foreign goods at all to cross its borders, must be not only self-sufficient but also able to survive without customs duties. Similarly, a state that permits entirely free trade accrues no revenues from customs. Thus, free trade and no trade are the luxuries of strong states, states able to extract resources from their domestic societies; weak states, on the other hand, often depend on import duties as their primary source of revenue. In order to lower or do away with tariffs, the state must be able to depend on other sources of income.

Although generally considered the prototype of a hegemon that establishes free trade, Great Britain, the globe's leading economic power as it emerged from the Napoleonic Wars, was a fully protectionist state. Still not strong enough to be able to afford free trade, it abolished the income tax it had imposed during wartime but kept import duties at their wartime heights.[13]

11. However, one can argue that subsystemic trade liberalization provides a global collective good in its effect on general economic conditions, for the growth in global trade triggered by trade liberalization is likely to spill over and include nonsignatories.

12. Compare this view of a hegemon's interest with that presented by Krasner, "State Power." The ability to extract resources directly from the society may be only one element of internal state strength. Even a state that can afford free trade may be able neither to persuade certain societal elements to accept free trade nor to impose it upon them. For an analysis that uses state strength relative to the society to explain commercial policy, see Stephen D. Krasner, "U.S. Commercial and Monetary Policy: Unravelling the Paradox of External Strength and Internal Weakness," *International Organization* 31 (Autumn 1977): 635–71.

13. Indeed, Kenneth Fielden argues that "the British tariff of 1815 was harsher than the eighteenth century's." See Fielden, "The Rise and Fall of Free Trade," in C. J. Bartlett, ed., *Britain Pre-eminent: Studies of British World Influence in the Nineteenth Century* (New York: St. Martin's Press, 1969), p. 81.

(This customs revenue was required to pay for the national debt, which in the 1820s constituted 59% of public expenditures.) In addition, Britain maintained other protectionist measures. The Navigation Acts prohibited foreign ships from trading in British colonies and required that only British ships or those of the exporting nation carry goods to Britain. Britain, "the first industrial nation," prohibited the export of machinery and forbade the emigration of artisans and technicians who might practice or teach their craft abroad. (The concern with technology transfer thus began with the very beginnings of the technological revolution.)[14] Finally, Britain permitted the export of gold only under government license.

Britain's retreat from these highly protectionist policies took decades. William Huskisson, president of the Board of Trade, made a start during the 1820s when he persuaded Parliament to allow the free export of gold, "a token of the availability of financial credit without political interference." At roughly the same time, Britain first allowed the free emigration of artisans and the licensed export of machinery, "symbols that the secrets of the Industrial Revolution were not to be made another subject of division and competition between nations."[15] Many outright prohibitions were also abolished.

British policy was moving from prohibitionism to protectionism—from no trade to the freer trade of some goods—but hardly to free trade. There were revisions in the Corn Laws and in the colonial system, and some reduction in duties. But import duties still accounted for 44.2 percent of all government revenues in 1840 (see Table 1). Without an alternative source of income, the British could not abolish their tariffs. Further tariff reduction would await a British state strong enough to institute a peacetime income tax.

The British government, unable unilaterally to adopt free trade, was also unable to reach commercial agreements with other governments to lower tariffs. Great Britain was, in this period, the premier economic power, the foremost trading nation, and the first country to industrialize. Freer trade, if not free trade, was in its national interest: British industry needed markets and raw materials. Yet other nations, scrambling to catch up, were hardly going to adopt free trade simply because British political economists suggested that it was in the best interests of all to do so. Although able to obtain concessions from some non-European countries, "in dealing with her equals in Europe, Britain failed to make headway."[16] Between 1831 and 1841, for

14. For a fascinating history, see David J. Jeremy, "Damming the Flood: British Government Efforts to Check the Outflow of Technicians and Machinery, 1780–1943," *Business History Review* 51 (Spring 1977): 1–34.

15. Albert H. Imlah, *Economic Elements in the Pax Britannica: Studies in British Foreign Trade in the Nineteenth Century* (Cambridge: Harvard University Press, 1958), p. 14.

16. A. A. Iliasu, "The Cobden-Chevalier Commercial Treaty of 1860," *Historical Journal* 14 (March 1971): 69.

TABLE 1. *Government reliance on customs revenue (customs revenue as %
of total government revenue)*

Year	United Kingdom	France	Germany	United States[a]
1820	20.0%			
1830	35.2			
1840	44.2			
1850	38.6	9.9%		
1860	32.9	7.8		
1870	29.4	4.9	52.2%[b]	
1880	23.2	8.9	55.8	
1890	20.6	11.0	55.7	
1900	19.3	10.9	52.5	37.2%
1910	16.2	13.7	44.2	32.2
1920	9.4	8.5	4.1	7.5
1930	14.1	12.1	16.3	11.8
1940	20.4	19.0	5.2	4.7
1950	21.8	7.2	3.8	0.9
1960	23.0	11.7	4.9	1.1
1970		8.3	2.1	1.2
1975		6.1	1.5	1.4

a. Early figures are for 1902, 1913, 1922, and 1932 respectively.
b. Figure is for 1872.
Sources. B. R. Mitchell, *European Historical Statistics 1750–1975*, 2d ed. (New York: Facts on File, 1980), pp. 742–69; U.S. Bureau of the Census, *Historical Statistics of the United States, Colonial Times to 1970* (Washington, D.C.: GPO, 1976), pp. 1121–22, series Y567, Y573, and *Statistical Abstract of the United States: 1977*, 98th ed. (Washington, D.C.: GPO, 1977), p. 283, Table 463.
Notes. "United Kingdom" includes Southern Ireland through 1920. Figures for France are based on receipts by the customs administration through 1868 and on receipts from import duties thereafter. German data for 1950 and later are for West Germany (figure for 1950 excludes West Berlin and the Saar). Figures for Germany are based on total tax revenue. U.S. data are as a percentage of Federal government revenue.

example, it failed to reach agreement through four sets of commercial negotiations with France.[17]

Britain took further steps toward freer trade in the 1840s, a series of reforms made possible by two events. First, a parliamentary report pointed

17. Barrie M. Ratcliffe, "Great Britain and Tariff Reform in France, 1831–36," in W. H. Chaloner and Ratcliffe, eds., *Trade and Transport: Essays in Economic History in Honour of T. S. Willan* (Manchester: Manchester University Press, 1977). Other nations perceived a British strategy to prevent them from industrializing and were thus quite wary; see P. J. Cain and A. G. Hopkins, "The Political Economy of British Expansion Overseas, 1750–1914," *Economic History Review*, 2d ser., 33 (November 1980): 477. For the limited impact of the reciprocity treaties that Britain did sign in the mid 1820s, see Iliasu, "Cobden-Chevalier Commercial Treaty."

out that only a few commodities produced almost all of the nation's import revenue. Fewer than twenty articles, in fact, generated 95 percent of the customs duties.[18] Then, in 1842, Parliament reinstituted the income tax. For the first time, the British state had the fiscal freedom to lower tariffs substantially, although it preserved some duties to use as bargaining chips in commercial negotiations. As these negotiations with various nations dragged on, however, the British abandoned their attempts to establish bilateral reciprocity treaties as a means to open foreign markets, and, in the late 1840s, Britain reduced its tariffs unilaterally, a move symbolized by the repeal of the Corn Laws. In 1849, Britain abolished the Navigation Acts. Excepting only a half-dozen still dutiable items, Britain had opened its doors to the goods of all nations on equal terms.

The reliance of governments on import duties for revenue continued to constrain their pursuit of freer trade. Although the British government's moves toward freer trade followed its lessened dependence on duties, as shown in Table 1, it is striking that Britain continued to depend on import duties for over 20 percent of its revenue during the heyday of the lower tariff era of the 1860s, and even during the lower tariff period following World War II.[19] The Germans were similarly constrained from pursuing freer trade. Prior to unification, the German states had belonged to a customs union, the Zollverein, and had adopted relatively low tariffs. But the new federal government did not have the sources of revenue available to the component states, and thus it depended on customs duties for over 50 percent of its revenue. Ironically, during the middle of the 19th century, France was better able to afford freer trade. In 1850, when customs duties accounted for 38.6 percent of British state income, the French government relied on import levies for only 9.9 percent of its revenue.[20]

18. Peter Mathias, *The First Industrial Nation: An Economic History of Britain 1700–1914* (London: Methuen, 1969), p. 300.

19. Fiscal concerns were prominent in the unsuccessful campaigns from 1900 to 1914 for tariff reform in Britain. Revenue needs increased by the Boer War led to the temporary reimposition of agricultural duties. The prewar Liberal government introduced new economic and social programs, and tariff reformers advocated duties to generate the necessary revenue. See Peter Cain, "Political Economy in Edwardian England: The Tariff-Reform Controversy," in Alan O'Day, ed., *The Edwardian Age: Conflict and Stability, 1900–1914* (Hamden, Conn.: Archon, 1979); and Barry J. Eichengreen, "The Eternal Fiscal Question: Free Trade and Protection in Britain, 1860–1929," Harvard Institute for Economic Research Discussion Paper no. 949 (Cambridge, Mass., December 1982).

20. American reliance on customs revenue was dramatically reduced by the institution of the income tax in 1913 and, therefore, did not constrain American initiatives in the 1930s. In the 19th century, the tariff was usually the major source of federal revenue; see Asher Isaacs, *International Trade: Tariff and Commercial Policies* (Chicago: Richard D. Irwin, 1948), pp. 283–85. Import duties remain an important source of central government revenue for many nations. An analysis of 94 countries (excluding the OECD nations) shows that in 1970, 10 depended on customs for 10% or less of total government revenue, 15 depended on customs for 11–20%, 21 for 21–30%, 22 for 31–40%, 13 for 41–50%, 9 for 51–60%, and 4 for 61% or more. Those least dependent on duties were primarily oil-producing countries, which relied largely on royalties instead. For non-oil LDCs, government reliance on customs represents a

Cobden-Chevalier: the asymmetric bargain for freer trade

The freer trade era only started in 1860. Earlier, Britain had been unable either to impose free trade or to reach agreements with others mutually to reduce tariffs.[21] As it could better afford to do so, however, it unilaterally opened its borders to trade. But free trade is not a game at which only one can play—more than a single country must lower its tariffs before a free trade regime can be said to exist. Only when Britain and France signed the Cobden-Chevalier Commercial Treaty in 1860 did the free trade era begin.

Britain's willingness to pursue negotiations for a trade agreement in 1859 represented a departure from its recent commercial policy. As it became able to do so, however, Britain unilaterally lowered its barriers to trade. (Although it still depended on duties for one-third of its revenues, those tariffs were on only a small number of goods.) Having unilaterally adopted a largely free trade policy, the British had little left to concede in negotiations. Moreover, many in Britain believed that such bilateral treaties were "incompatible with the principles of free trade."[22]

It is important to understand, therefore, that political rather than commercial or philosophical considerations motivated Britain's shift in its commercial practices. Both Britain and France looked to a commercial agreement as a basis for improving their relations, which might in turn prevent a European war over Italy.[23] The French wanted to associate Britain with their desire to replace Austria in dominating Italy. The British hoped for a free and unified Italy that could act as a counterweight to both France and Austria. In other words, political considerations underlay the desire of both for a

---

major impediment to liberalization. (Figures calculated from data provided by the Inter-University Consortium for Political and Social Research, Cross-National Socio-Economic Time Series, 1950–1975 [ICPSR 7592]).

21. A hegemon can impose free trade on weak states. Britain forced its way into Turkey in 1838 and finally opened China in 1842. See Michael Greenberg, *British Trade and the Opening of China 1800–42* (Cambridge: Cambridge University Press, 1951). This is part of what I take to be the "imperialism of free trade"; see John Gallagher and Ronald Robinson, "The Imperialism of Free Trade," *Economic History Review*, 2d ser., 6 (1953): 1–15. An interesting recent discussion links British expansionism with the course of British modernization: Cain and Hopkins, "Political Economy of British Expansion." The trade agreements forced on small countries were often asymmetrical ones that did not entail mutual liberalization, however; these "Capitulations" often included extraterritoriality clauses as well. The British could not even impose free trade on their colonies. When the British lifted commercial restrictions on trade with the colonies, the colonies were free to choose their own trade policies. Some picked free trade, others opted for protective tariffs.

22. Frank Arnold Haight, *A History of French Commercial Policies* (New York: Macmillan, 1941), p. 36.

23. Britain and France both departed from their past practices in signing the 1860 agreement, and they did so for political reasons. See Iliasu, "Cobden-Chevalier Commercial Treaty," and Barrie M. Ratcliffe, "The Origins of the Anglo-French Commercial Treaty of 1860: A Reassessment," in Ratcliffe, ed., *Great Britain and Her World, 1759–1914: Essays in Honour of W. O. Henderson* (Manchester: Manchester University Press, 1975), and Ratcliffe, "Napoleon III and the Anglo-French Commercial Treaty of 1860: A Reconsideration," *Journal of European Economic History* 2 (1973): 582–613.

commercial agreement. Even the committed free trader Richard Cobden saw political considerations as central to his diplomatic mission. After visiting Gladstone, he wrote to his French negotiating counterpart, Chevalier, that

> there is always a latent suspicion that I, as an Englishman, in recommending other Governments to adopt Free Trade principles, am merely pursuing a selfish British policy. Thus my advice is deprived of all weight, and even my facts are doubted. But, on totally different grounds, I should be glad to see a removal of the impediments which our foolish legislation interposes to the intercourse between the two countries. I see no other hope but in such a policy for any permanent improvements in the *political* relations of France and England. I utterly despair of finding peace and harmony in the efforts of Governments and diplomatists. The people of the two nations must be brought into mutual dependence by the supply of each other's wants. There is no other way of counteracting the antagonism of language and race. It is God's own method of producing an *entente cordiale*, and no other plan is worth a farthing.[24]

In fact, earlier British and French attempts to reach a trade agreement in the 1830s had also been based in part on political concerns.[25] Although the French recognized that free trade with an economic hegemon such as Britain would be economically devastating, they wanted to break out of the diplomatic isolation to which the Congress of Vienna had consigned them. Britain hoped to improve relations with France in part because its relations with Russia were deteriorating. The failure of these earlier attempts had led Britain to abandon trade negotiations as a tool of foreign economic policy. Thus, the talks that resulted in the Cobden-Chevalier Treaty represented a reversion to earlier British tactics, a return based on political calculations.

The 1860 treaty was quite asymmetrical, which is not surprising given how little Britain had left to barter away. Although France thus conceded more than Britain, the treaty nonetheless affirmed and legitimated French protectionism. Britain's major concession was to reduce duties on French wines and spirits; except for duties on a few items, Britain maintained no other tariffs. France agreed to remove all of its outright prohibitions, but the treaty did permit it to retain reduced tariff barriers, to be lowered to a maximum of 25 percent within five years. For the interim, the treaty des-

24. J. A. Hobson, *Richard Cobden: The International Man* (New York: Henry Holt, 1919), p. 244. Emphasized there.

25. See Ratcliffe, "Great Britain and Tariff Reform in France," and his "The Tariff Reform Campaign in France, 1831–1836," *Journal of European Economic History* 7 (Spring 1978): 61–138. Attempts to create customs unions have historically also had political motivations and repercussions. A good starting point is Fritz Machlup, *A History of Thought on Economic Integration* (New York: Columbia University Press, 1977). Obviously, political unification requires an economic unity that minimally requires the absence of internal barriers to trade; not surprisingly, the U.S. Constitution forbids individual states from imposing "any imposts or duties on imports and exports."

ignated a commission to set specific duties using the principle of cost equalization.[26] This allowed France to retain such duties as would bring the price of foreign goods up to the price of domestically produced goods, and thus insured domestic producers protection from foreign competition. Remaining faithful to their free trade principles, the British unilaterally granted to all nations the concessions they had made to France. France did not generalize its concessions but retained its old tariffs for other nations. To protect Britain from future discrimination, however, the treaty included an unconditional most-favored-nation clause requiring each nation to grant to the other any tariff concessions it might later give any third state. Thus, the treaty was itself a departure from the standard form of bilateral agreements, which usually excluded certain areas, typically colonies, from the scope of most-favored-nation clauses. "Britain had achieved Free Trade," but for France, the treaty "only replaced a frankly prohibitionist with a moderately protective system."[27]

Thus, the Cobden-Chevalier Treaty, generally regarded as ushering in the era of free trade, actually legitimated discriminatory liberalization. Britain and France liberalized the exchanges between them, but the treaty allowed them to retain (as France did) higher duties or prohibitions against other countries. Freer trade requires both liberalization and nondiscrimination; fully free trade only follows the complete abolition of protection and discrimination. The Cobden-Chevalier Treaty, despite its inclusion of an unconditional most-favored-nation clause, accepted discriminatory liberalization in preference to nondiscriminatory prohibition. Thus, bilateral discriminatory liberalization, a hallmark of mercantilism, was conjoined with unconditional most-favored-nation clauses as a means to lower tariff barriers.

Leaders and followers

Many scholars have emphasized the hegemon's leadership in establishing an international economic order. But establishing liberalized trade requires not only leaders but followers. Both are critical in determining the nature of the outcome. This is illuminated by the 1860s, when the Cobden-Chevalier Treaty, itself a simple bilateral agreement, became the basis for a wider liberalization of trade.

The most-favored-nation clause in the Cobden-Chevalier Treaty provided a basis for lower trade barriers worldwide. By itself, the treaty was a bilateral mercantilistic agreement. It had the potential for multilateral liberalization, however, in that it committed Britain and France to give each other any

---

26. Haight, *History of French Commercial Policies*, pp. 32–33.
27. Fielden, "Rise and Fall of Free Trade," p. 89; and Marcel Rist, "A French Experiment with Free Trade: The Treaty of 1860," in Rondo Cameron, ed., *Essays in French Economic History* (Homewood, Ill.: Richard D. Irwin, 1970), p. 289.

concessions they obtained from any agreement with a third party. For it to become more than a merely mercantilist agreement thus required Britain and France to pursue accords with other nations. In fact, they did negotiate such additional bilateral treaties with other states; they then extended the tariff reductions they granted other nations to each other. Because they had already lowered tariffs unilaterally and thus extended to all nations the concessions that they had given the French in 1860, however, the British had great difficulty concluding additional bilateral treaties. They had signed a treaty legitimating discrimination, but they were unprepared to discriminate themselves. Thus, they had little to offer others in trade negotiations. They were able only to conclude four more trade treaties, with Belgium, Italy, Austria, and the Zollverein, in the five years following the Cobden-Chevalier Treaty. The French, who had in fact initiated the talks that led to the 1860 agreement, played the key role in expanding the bilateral treaty into a multilateral freer trade area. By 1867, France had signed eleven more trade agreements, turning British doctrine into a working system of lower tariff barriers that linked thirteen European nations. France also adopted legislation in the mid 1860s that reduced restrictions on trade with its colonies.

The 1860s also illuminate the subsystemic nature of the freer trade regime. Although often characterized as "the era of free trade," this "free international" trading system did not include most of the world's nations and even omitted some major nations, among them the United States. Indeed, most international economic orders are *sub*systemic. Although typically referred to as "the international economic order," the system created by the United States following the Second World War is, in fact, a subsystem that excludes the Soviet bloc. Similarly, those who emphasize Britain's role in creating and maintaining an international economic system in the 19th century refer to a subsystem that did not include most nations.

These discriminatory and subsystemic freer trade regimes both do and do not provide a collective good. Nations outside the system are discriminated against and can be effectively denied its benefits. The criterion of nonexcludability, central to the definition of a collective good, is not met: states can be prevented from benefiting from lower tariffs and hence, they cannot be true free riders. On the other hand, within the freer trade subsystem, any concession made to any state is indeed a collective good from which others who have been granted most-favored-nation status cannot be excluded.

The decline of British hegemony

The reverse of the argument that a hegemon establishes an open economic system is that the decline of hegemony results in economic closure and renewed protectionism. Scholars point to the period from 1873 to 1896 as one of continuous British decline and renewed protectionism.[28] Yet the empirical evidence suggests a more ambiguous picture. There was a change in the general European attitude toward free trade, and the decline of economic growth rates throughout the continent did generate increased pressures for protectionism in most countries. Nonetheless, the British economy's relative decline, especially compared to the French and German and American economies, did not lead to the closure of the European trading system.

Indeed, the last quarter of the 19th century brought no widespread increase in protectionism within the freer trade system. The atmosphere of the later period was less liberal, and domestic protectionist forces were evident in all countries. But the gains of the 1860s were not surrendered. Moreover, much of what has been interpreted as a rebirth of protectionism was the direct outgrowth of the sorts of practices legitimated during the establishment of freer trade in the 1860s.

The protectionist pressures that grew within many European nations in the late 19th century were largely generated by the general decline in growth rates and especially the recessions that marked the century's last quarter. Over the entire period, however, the European economy continued to grow, if at a much slower rate.[29] Some nations fared better than others, of course, as did some industries. Britain, for example, had one of the slower-growing economies of the major nations: its average per capita economic growth just about equaled the European average and was below that of France and Germany. Throughout Europe, one response to slower growth was pressure, especially during periods of actual recession, to adopt protectionist policies.

Those who argue that there was a return to closure point to the tariff legislation passed in various countries. France, Germany, Switzerland, Italy, Russia, and the United States all passed major revisions in their tariff laws. In many cases a nation passed more than one set of revisions between 1870 and the beginning of World War I. Tariff legislation in Russia and the United

---

28. Succinctly demonstrated by Cain, "Political Economy in Edwardian England," pp. 36–38. For the most extensive recent work on the British decline, called the British climacteric, see W. Arthur Lewis, *Growth and Fluctuations, 1870–1913* (London: Allen & Unwin, 1978), chap. 5. A sector-specific analysis of this decline is Robert C. Allen, "International Competition in Iron and Steel, 1850–1913," *Journal of Economic History* 39 (December 1979): 911–37.

29. The most recent data set is provided by Paul Bairoch, "Europe's Gross National Product: 1800–1975," *Journal of European Economic History* 5 (Autumn 1976): 273–340. Bairoch assesses average annual European GNP growth as 2% between 1842–44 and 1867–69, 1% between 1867–69 and 1889–91, and 2.4% between 1889–91 and 1913. These figures are significantly lower than those provided by Angus Maddison, "Growth and Fluctuation in the World Economy, 1870–1960," *Banca Nazionale del Lavoro Quarterly Review* 15 (June 1962): 127–95. Maddison places average European growth at 2.2% between 1870 and 1890 and at 2.1% between 1890 and 1913. Both authors show that the average growth in trade exceeded that of GNP. For Bairoch's trade figures see his "European Foreign Trade in the XIX Century: The Development of the Value and Volume of Export (Preliminary Results)," *Journal of European Economic History* 2 (Spring 1973): 5–36. He calculates the average growth in exports as 5% between 1846–47 and 1865–68, as 2% between 1865–68 and 1896–97, and as 5% between 1896–97 and 1913.

States can hardly be cited as evidence of the decline of the liberal order of the 1860s; the two nations were never part of it. Here, therefore, I focus on the legislation passed in those major trading states which were part of that order.[30]

Such legislation, irrespective of its domestic support, epitomized the system emplaced in the 1860s and typically represented no departure from it. The earlier bilateral trade treaties, which had legitimated discrimination and tariff bargaining as appropriate means to achieve liberalization, required regular renegotiation. In those treaties, states had offered one another concessions from the general tariffs maintained against states that did not join the network of bilateral treaties. Thus, nations had every incentive to raise their general tariff in order to provide themselves with bargaining chips.[31] Moreover, they wanted the most possible while giving up the least possible. Governments could use new tariff laws both to buy off domestic protectionist forces and to increase their own bargaining power vis-à-vis outsiders. The net impact of each piece of legislation depended, therefore, primarily on the extent to which it constrained the nation's executive in negotiating subsequent treaties.

Some of the so-called protectionist legislation passed in Europe during the latter part of the century was, in fact, anything but protectionist. France, for example, passed a major tariff act in 1881, which many argue marked the start of a French return to protectionism. The new general tariff rates set by this legislation were, indeed, higher than those that applied to nations with which France had trade agreements. Yet the legislation actually reduced the general rates then prevailing for countries with which France had not signed treaties—older rates that had been on the books since before 1860. In other words, the legislation was a liberalizing step. Its net impact would depend, however, on the outcome of France's renegotiation of expired treaties, and, in fact, France did go on to sign new agreements, extending those treaties for another decade. In addition, France concluded agreements with states with which it had had no previous treaties. Thus, the legislation, when seen in conjunction with the trade agreements, resulted in a net liberalization of French commercial policy.[32]

30. The liberal trade regime of the 1860s was based on a network of states linked by trade agreements containing unconditional most-favored-nation clauses. Thus, to argue that this regime collapsed requires evidence that a state in the network took protectionist measures aimed at others within the network. Increased tariffs on agricultural goods provide no such evidence. Most scholars attribute declining European growth rates to the flooding of European markets by cheap American and Russian wheat. The response in many European states was higher agricultural duties, but mostly aimed at states with whom most European states had no trade agreements (i.e., the United States).

31. For the underlying bargaining purposes of tariff legislation, see Isaacs, *International Trade*, pp. 336, 347–48.

32. France's original move away from prohibitionism in the 1860s had greater staying power than many suggest; see Michael S. Smith, "Free Trade Versus Protection in the Early Third Republic: Economic Interests, Tariff Policy, and the Making of the Republican Synthesis," *French Historical Studies* 10 (Autumn 1977): 293–314, and Smith, "The Free Trade Revolution Reconsidered: Economic Interests and the Making of French Tariff Policy under the Second Empire," *Proceedings of the Annual Meeting of the Western Society for French History* 6 (1978):

The treaties of the 1860s were reciprocal tariff bargains, and the need to renegotiate them when they expired generated strategic behavior. Nations not only had an incentive to raise general tariffs to provide themselves with bargaining chips but also had an incentive to make maximal demands. The very existence of a network of states linked by trade treaties containing unconditional most-favored-nation clauses made this shrewd policy. The British, for example, demanded in 1882 that the French do more than extend the terms of the Cobden-Chevalier Treaty. With a few exceptions, France offered terms equal to or better than those of 1860, but the British wanted rates 20 percent lower.[33] The British said that without such concessions they would only sign a most-favored-nation agreement that did not include any specific concessions by either party. They would make specific concessions only if the French were prepared to improve on the terms of the status quo. Although no new accord was reached, the British knew that French treaties with other states insured them at least the continuation of the status quo as long as the French continued to grant them most-favored-nation status.

The French passed still another general tariff law, the Meline Tariff of 1892, which is generally considered to mark the high point of French protectionism. Indeed, this legislation was passed by protectionist forces unhappy with the net results of the 1881 legislation. In addition to specifying the maximum general tariff to be charged all states with whom France had no trade treaty, the legislature added a new wrinkle by stipulating the minimum tariff that could be granted in trade negotiations. In other words, the legislature attempted to specify the maximum concession that the executive could make during negotiations. Because the protectionists failed to obtain adoption of a clause expressly forbidding negotiating duties below the legislated minimum, however, the government was once again able to sign new treaties with those nations with which it had prior agreements; this time, it even extended the minimum rates to states with which it had no treaties.[34] The freer trade system was largely maintained. Higher general tariffs were combined with a continuation and extension of past trade treaties to maintain the freer trade system.

327–35. Even in the early 1870s, when the new Third Republic was saddled with indemnity payments to Germany, attempts to use tariffs to generate revenue were rebuffed (this was the reason for the resignation of Thiers, the president of the Republic, in 1873).

33. Michael Stephen Smith, *Tariff Reform in France, 1860–1900: The Politics of Economic Interest* (Ithaca: Cornell University Press, 1980), p. 188.

34. France even negotiated some treaties that stipulated duties lower than the legislatively mandated minimum; see Smith, *Tariff Reform in France,* p. 209. The maximum rates continued to apply only to Portuguese goods throughout the entire period of the Meline Tariff. Other nations each paid those rates only for short periods of time while negotiating new trade agreements with France. The French tariff war with Switzerland resulted in part from the latter's refusal to grant most-favored-nation status merely in return for a legislated minimum tariff. The Swiss maintained that they would grant such status only in a negotiated agreement and insisted in some cases on rates lower than the minimum.

Nor was the famous German turn to protectionism in 1879 a wholesale departure from the 1860s. When Germany was united in 1871, it had relatively low tariffs, and these were reduced further in the following lustrum. The Tariff Act of 1879, dubbed the marriage of iron and rye, raised some duties and restored others. Yet these duties, although higher than those of the mid 1870s, were no higher than those of the 1860s.[35] Only the unilateral reductions of the early 1870s were eliminated, as Germany returned to the level of protection it had maintained in the 1860s.[36] Furthermore, the impact of these duties was weaker than in the 1860s because four free ports, Hamburg, Cuxhaven, Bremerhaven, and Geestemunde, were excluded from the German customs area.[37] With the coming to power of Caprivi, twelve years after the 1879 Tariff Act, the German government would retreat from even this degree of protectionism and sign a series of bilateral commercial agreements to lower tariffs and which, in some cases, included a most-favored-nation clause.

The celebrated tariff wars of the 1880s and 1890s are also cited as evidence of a return to protectionism. Yet they were really a stage in the maintenance of trade agreements. States sometimes increased tariffs as bargaining chips and held out for maximalist positions, and thus "the concessional method of tariff bargaining [led] by its very nature to bickerings and tariff wars."[38] All the tariff wars began after negotiations collapsed, as one state raised general tariffs and sometimes slapped on surcharges in order to induce another state to conclude a new trade agreement.[39] They ended with the signing of

35. W. O. Henderson, *The Rise of German Industrial Power 1834–1914* (Berkeley: University of California Press, 1975), p. 220.

36. The German Tariff Act of 1879 was not just the product of the marriage of iron and rye. It also resulted from the political leadership of the newly unified German nation needing an independent source of revenue. As Bismarck told the Reichstag in 1872, "An empire that is dependent upon the contributions of individual states lacks the bonds of a strong and common financial institution" (Henderson, *Rise of German Industrial Power*, p. 219). Bismarck supported higher duties in order to generate more central government revenues directly (see Table 1). Thus, the state's fiscal needs combined with protectionist interests to increase German tariffs, though only to moderate levels.

37. They became part of the German customs union in 1906. The impact of duties on specific industries has been overstated. Germany was not keeping out goods to protect weak domestic industries: it exported 19% of iron and steel production in 1879, and "German costs were clearly low enough for the iron and steel industry to compete at world prices" (Allen, "International Competition," p. 928).

38. W. S. Culbertson, "Commercial Treaties," in *Encyclopedia of the Social Sciences*, vol. 4 (New York: Macmillan, 1931), p. 29.

39. Some also had political overtones. The French-Italian tariff war was not unrelated to French unhappiness with Italy's alliance with Germany and Austria. A model of tariff wars is developed by Michael Nicholson, "Tariff Wars and a Model of Conflict," *Journal of Peace Research* 4 (1967): 27–38. An important source is *Reports on Tariff Wars between Certain European States* (London: HMSO, 1904). As these tariff wars demonstrate, commercial policy can reflect the international political needs of the state, and commercial agreements, such as the Cobden-Chevalier Treaty, often have similar political underpinnings. As argued in the text, commercial policy may also reflect the state's fiscal needs. Commercial policy is thus more than the mere expression of different domestic economic interests. For examples of that argument, see Charles P. Kindleberger, "Group Behavior and International Trade," *Journal of Political Economy* 59 (1951): 30–47; and Peter A. Gourevitch, "International Trade, Domestic Coalitions, and Liberty: Comparative Responses to the Crises of 1873–1896," *Journal of Interdisciplinary History* 8 (Autumn 1977): 281–313.

new trade agreements. Thus, they were a critical bargaining chip; at times, especially in periods of slow growth, a nation could obtain greater access to the markets of others only by denying access to its own.

The aggregate data for the period also fail to demonstrate any widespread return to protectionism. During the entire period from 1873 to the turn of the century, international trade continued to grow, although more slowly than in earlier periods. Indeed, the rate of trade growth, averaged annually over the entire period, exceeded that of domestic growth for many countries, and the degree of openness (the ratio of imports and exports to gross national product) was remarkably stable for the United Kingdom, Germany, and France. French external trade, for example, constituted less than 10 percent of GNP prior to 1850, shot up to over 25 percent of GNP by the 1870s, and stayed at that level through the remainder of the century. Germany imported and exported about one-third of its net national product both in the "protectionist" 1880s and in Caprivi's more liberal 1890s (see Table 2). During the last two decades of the 19th century, these countries did not decrease their engagement in foreign trade.

Still another, and more direct, aggregate indicator of the degree of protectionism—customs duties as a proportion of the value of imports—does not demonstrate any wholesale return to protectionism. Although this measure is imperfect, because it does not capture truly prohibitive tariffs, it does give some indication of overall trends. It clearly shows the liberalization of the 1860s: British duties, which constituted more than a fifth of the value of imports in 1850, constituted less than a twentieth in 1890 (see Table 3). The degree of French protection in 1850 was 16.2 percent in a context that included many prohibitions; it dropped to 3 percent by 1870 and included no prohibitions. There was some growth in French customs duties as a percentage of the value of all imports from 1880 to 1900, but French tariffs remained quite low and quite stable. (Indeed, French tariff levels were lower between 1880 and 1913 than those between 1950 and the middle 1970s.) When France and Germany's tariff levels are compared with those of such truly protectionist states as the United States and Russia, it is clear that neither country reverted to wholesale protectionism.

The various pieces of tariff legislation did not prevent world trade from growing at unprecedented rates when domestic growth rates increased after 1896. Despite the passage of a German tariff law in 1902, which, scholars argue, marked the end of the liberal Caprivi period and a return to Bismarckian commercial policy, and despite the Meline Tariff of 1892 and the French Tariff Act of 1910, the greatest levels of international trade were achieved in the years immediately preceding the First World War.[40] Indeed, those heights would not be recaptured until the 1970s.

---

40. Such levels would not be seen again until the early 1970s. See Richard Rosecrance and Arthur Stein, "Interdependence: Myth or Reality?" *World Politics* 26 (October 1973): 1–27.

TABLE 2. *Openness of four major trading nations, 1820–1975 (imports plus exports divided by production)*

Year	United Kingdom	France	Germany	United States
1820		7.6%		
1830	21.5%	7.65		
1840	28.3	9.2		
1850	32.5	11.2		
1860	49.4	18.2		
1870	52.8 43.5[a]	24.1		
1880	45.7	28.8	33.9%	
1890	44.2	27.6	31.7	
1900	39.6	28.3	32.0	
1910	46.1	33.0	35.8	9.0%
1920	50.4	33.1		15.2
1930	33.0	25.4	31.1	7.6
1940	20.7	17.5	11.1	6.6
1950	35.9	2.1	20.2	6.7
1960	31.5	21.5	30.0	7.1
1970	33.2	25.2	34.6	8.5
1975	41.8	35.3[b]	39.4	13.5

a. The second figure for 1870 is comparable with those below.

b. Figure for 1974.

Sources. B. R. Mitchell, *European Historical Statistics 1750–1975*, 2d ed. (New York: Facts on File, 1980), pp. 507–22, 817–39; U.S. Bureau of the Census, *Historical Statistics of the United States, Colonial Times to 1970* (Washington, D.C.: GPO, 1976), p. 887, series U201, U202, and *Statistical Abstract of the United States: 1977*, 98th ed. (Washington, D.C.: GPO, 1977), pp. 428, 865, tables 688, 1469.

Notes. French figures are based on gross domestic product at current prices; German figures are based on net national product at market prices; and the figures for the United Kingdom are based on gross national product at factor cost to 1870, and at market prices thereafter. The French figure for 1820 is for general trade. The figures for the United Kingdom are based on domestic exports. The German figures for 1920–35 and 1945–59 exclude the Saar. British trade with Southern Ireland has been external since 1923. The French figures for 1871–1918 exclude Alsace-Lorraine.

The First World War and the return to protectionism

These high levels of exchange and presumed interdependence did not prevent the nations of Europe from going to war with one another, and it was the First World War, not the depression of the last quarter of the 19th century or the relative decline of British hegemony, that sounded the death knell for liberalized international trade. Only the Netherlands did not change its commercial policy during the war; all other states, including Britain, raised or

TABLE 3. *Degree of protection: customs revenue as a percentage of total value of imports*

Year	United Kingdom	France	Germany	United States	Russia
1830	33.9%			57.3%	33.3%
1840	25.3			17.6	33.3
1850	21.4	16.2%		24.5	31.9
1860	10.9	7.1		15.7	21.4
1870	6.6	2.9		44.9	12.8
1880	4.6	5.2	5.8%	29.1	15.4
1890	4.75	8.0	8.8	29.6	34.9
1900	5.2	8.8	8.1	27.6	32.6
1910	4.9	8.2	7.4	21.1	27.8
1920	6.9	3.8		6.4	
1930	11.6	11.7	10.5	14.8	
1940	26.5	29.8	28.2	12.5	
1950	34.7	14.0	5.4	6.0	
1960	32.1	23.3	6.5	7.4	
1970		13.7	2.6	6.5	
1975		8.4	1.8	3.9	

Sources. B. R. Mitchell, *European Historical Statistics 1750–1975*, 2d ed. (New York: Facts on File, 1980), pp. 507–22, 742–69; U.S. Bureau of the Census, *Historical Statistics of the United States, Colonial Times to 1970* (Washington, D.C.: GPO, 1976), p. 888, series U211, and *Statistical Abstract of the United States: 1977*, 98th ed. (Washington, D.C.: GPO, 1977), p. 876, Table 1482.

instituted barriers to trade.[41] Wartime protectionism destroyed an only somewhat liberal economic order.

During the 1920s, numerous attempts to reconstruct the prewar system of trade and finance failed. All of the nations that had restricted commerce during the war found it difficult to dismantle protection, whose continuation many of their producers had come to expect. Quite simply, protection generates interests demanding its preservation.[42] Other legacies of World War I hampered postwar attempts to liberalize trade, among them the structure of international debt and residual antipathy toward Germany. Hostility to Germany manifested itself not only in the victors' demands for large reparations but also in a Versailles Treaty clause requiring Germany to provide others with most-favored-nation treatment even when unreciprocated.[43] Even

41. Isaacs, *International Trade.*
42. Indeed, one legacy of war is greater state involvement in economy and society. See Arthur A. Stein, *The Nation at War* (Baltimore: Johns Hopkins University Press, 1980).
43. Germany had every incentive to restrict imports and attempt to run regular balance-of-trade surpluses in order to pay for its war debt.

the British could not eschew such an opportunity and imposed a special tariff aimed solely at restricting German imports.[44] Thus the prewar network of trade agreements had bound together the otherwise competitive states of Europe, but it proved impossible to reconstruct this network after 1918 on the basis of nondiscrimination.

The onset of the Great Depression dealt a fatal blow to attempts to restore the prewar international economic order. States reacted to the Depression by further raising their tariffs and devaluing their currencies. This reversion to greater protection was predicated on the assumption that Britain would remain open, as it had before. Depression left Britain unable and unwilling to accept an increasingly asymmetric bargain. The hegemon's relative decline had not left it unable to enforce free trade (something it had never done anyway). But its absolute decline did leave it unable to carry the burden of others' increasing defections.

Britain's departure from its long-standing freer trade policy came only after it failed to restructure the asymmetric bargain that had underlain the prewar trading order. Before restoring general duties, the British proposed to the International Conference with a View to Concerted Economic Action, held in 1930, that other states reduce tariffs by 25 percent in return for Britain's continued adherence to a policy of predominantly free trade. There were no takers. The British then fully and formally abandoned free trade in 1932 with the reintroduction of across-the-board tariffs and the creation of the Imperial Preference System. They adopted the Import Duties Act, which levied a minimum tariff of 10 percent on all imports and exempted products from the Empire. In that same year, at the Ottawa Imperial Conference, the nations of the Empire signed fifteen bilateral agreements that restored preferential discrimination and clearly stipulated their precedence over any other agreements, even those including most-favored-nation clauses. Empowered by the 1932 Act to negotiate trade agreements with other countries, the British government concluded with non-Imperial nations a series of strictly bilateral agreements intended purely to balance bilateral trade.[45] These accords included no requirements that equal treatment be extended to other nations.

Britain only retreated from free trade and systemic leadership after others had refused to continue following its lead or even to compromise. Even then, Britain saw its reconstitution of tariffs and its reluctance to extend concessions without reciprocity as strengthening its hand in commercial negotiations. A nation unilaterally committed to free trade could not, after all, extract negotiated concessions. Furthermore, the British did no more than contract their free trading sphere to an economic bloc that included Canada, Australia,

44. F. Benham, *Great Britain under Protection* (New York: Macmillan, 1941).

45. Richard N. Kottman, *Reciprocity and the North Atlantic Triangle, 1932–1938* (Ithaca: Cornell University Press, 1968). For an aggregate analysis of commercial policy during the 1930s, see Richard C. Snyder, "Commercial Policy as Reflected in Treaties from 1931 to 1939," *American Economic Review* 30 (December 1940): 787–802.

South Africa, India, and the rest of the Commonwealth. The British system of free trade, already subsystemic, got smaller.

Scholars point to these events as evidence of a British retreat from leadership and suggest that the Americans' adoption of the ultraprotectionist Smoot-Hawley Tariff in 1930 represented their reluctance to assume the mantle of leadership. The American tariff increase of 1930 certainly represented an unwillingness to go along with the British and the recommendations of various international bodies. But the American action was not unusual in that the nation had a history of alternating between high and moderate tariffs. Furthermore, the new American tariff corresponded to actions already taken by others; it represented not an unwillingness to lead but a reluctance to follow the British.

The freer trade order was undone during the First World War when its constituent states went to war with one another; the war's legacy would not allow the restoration of the prewar order, and the Depression cut into the ranks of Britain's followers. The system was sustained only as long as the British had followers—as long as both the hegemon and its followers accepted the asymmetric bargain originally reached, and as long as the hegemon maintained its relatively liberal policies. In the end, the fate of the trading order was sealed when the British departed from it. The collapse came not from Britain's inability to continue imposing that order on others but from its inability to continue accepting the degree of asymmetry in trade relationships.

The period of American hegemony

It is commonly presumed that the United States refused to assume international economic leadership until the end of the Second World War. Its assumption of leadership actually began in 1933, however, when Secretary of State Cordell Hull enunciated an American commitment to liberalized international trade based on a general application of the unconditional most-favored-nation principle.[46] The general U.S. position was that bilateral accords should include unrestricted and unconditional most-favored-nation clauses, and that quotas should be used to insure that the flow of goods was disturbed as little as possible.[47] The American commitment to the principle of equal treatment did include an exception for economic blocs, however, and rep-

46. For a discussion of the impact of European noncooperation on Roosevelt's economic policies, see James R. Moore, "Sources of New Deal Economic Policy: The International Dimension," *Journal of American History* 61, 3 (1974): 728–44. Not until 1923 did the United States accept the unconditional most-favored-nation clause, see Vladimir N. Pregelj, " 'Most-Favored-Nation' Principle: Definition, Brief History, and Use by the United States," in *Studies in Taxation, Public Finance and Related Subjects: A Compendium*, vol. 2 (Washington, D.C.: Fund for Public Policy Research, 1978).

47. Kottman, *Reciprocity*, p. 72. See also I. Lang, "The Conflict between American and British Commercial Policies prior to World War II," *Acta Historica* 25 (1979): 267–96.

resented America's reconciliation to the reality of the British Imperial Preference System.

For the American executive to pursue such a policy required congressional authorization. In 1934, Congress passed the Reciprocal Trade Agreements Act, empowering the president to negotiate agreements reducing American duties by as much as 50 percent.[48] The United States could now play the same leadership role as the British did in the 19th century. Yet the Act was similar in spirit to the Meline Tariff of 1892, in that Congress stipulated a minimum tariff and constrained the executive's bargaining position. In the following years, agreements embodying the unconditional most-favored-nation principle extended tariff reductions to all but those who discriminated against the United States.

The American assumption of the mantle of leadership in liberalizing the trading order retained and expanded the mercantilistic and protectionist elements of earlier decades. The United States accepted liberalized discrimination as the path to free trade. It assured nondiscrimination within a liberal network by the inclusion of a most-favored-nation clause. The legislation upon which American policy was founded legitimated a minimum tariff. Finally, the United States, unlike Britain, enshrined reciprocity as central to the liberalization of trade. It was not willing to lower its own very high tariff barriers unilaterally.

For the Reciprocal Trade Agreements Act to have any impact required that the United States sign agreements with important followers, and that these states also sign trade agreements with others. By the end of 1937 the American government had signed sixteen such agreements, covering only one-third of U.S. foreign trade. The United States did not even try to reach agreements with Germany or Japan and was unable to conclude negotiations with either Spain or Italy. It had learned what the British had discovered in the 19th century—that a leader can only make a difference when it has followers.

It soon became clear that the United States would have to reach an agreement with Great Britain if it were to reduce barriers to world trade.[49] Indeed, the United States was eager for Britain to become its "junior partner." It wanted a British commitment to nondiscrimination that would require the dismantling of the Imperial Preference System and a renewed British commitment to the unconditional most-favored-nation clauses that would serve to multilateralize bilateral agreements. After three years of informal talks

48. Lowering trade barriers requires a domestic institutional arrangement to insulate executive power from particularistic societal interests. See Cynthia Hody, "From Protectionism to Free Trade: The Politics of Trade Policy" (Ph.D. diss., University of California, Los Angeles, in progress).

49. For a discussion of political considerations underpinning American-British trade discussions in the mid 1930s, see Arthur W. Schatz, "The Anglo-American Trade Agreement and Cordell Hull's Search for Peace 1936–1938," *Journal of American History* 57 (June 1970): 85–103.

and almost a year of official negotiations, the two nations finally concluded an agreement in which Britain acceded to most substantive American demands about commodities and duties. The British stood firm on Imperial Preference, however, and, while the United States met its immediate economic objectives, it was forced to accept continued British discrimination against non-Imperial nations.

The Anglo-American trade agreement of 1938 was quite similar to the Anglo-French agreement of 1860. Both agreements accepted discriminatory liberalization. In each case, the economic hegemon, unable to promote free trade and nondiscrimination by itself, was willing to accept a bilateral treaty as the best way to liberalize trade—as long as the treaty included an unconditional most-favored-nation clause. In each case, the hegemon was able to exercise leadership only upon compromising its nondiscrimination principles in order to reach agreement with a major follower. In each case, this involved striking a reciprocal tariff bargain.

Although World War II put certain issues on hold, the United States continued to press for nondiscriminatory unrestricted trade and maintained its opposition to Imperial Preference. In exchange for Lend-Lease aid, for example, the United States forced the British to agree to discuss the postwar dismantling of Imperial Preference.[50] American wartime documents suggest a government often as concerned with British economic policy as with the political and military policies of Germany and Japan.[51] During the discussions on postwar reconstruction that began during the war itself, the United States urged all of its allies to adopt free trade at the war's end. Forced to compromise, however, the United States accepted a long list of exceptions. Thus, in return for general acceptance of the principle of nondiscrimination, it effectively acquiesced in the continuation of discrimination and quantitative restrictions.

Following the Second World War, bilateral agreements with unconditional most-favored-nation clauses again became the basis for liberalizing global trade. A new wrinkle, however, was to negotiate as many bilateral agreements as possible at the same time and place, immediately creating an entire web of states committed to liberalized trade. In 1947, twenty-three nations convened at Geneva and created the General Agreement on Tariffs and Trade (GATT), a package of 123 bilateral trade agreements intended to expand international trade. Because each agreement contained a most-favored-nation clause, each signer was extended the same concessions that the other nation

---

50. Winston Churchill called Lend-Lease "the most unsordid act" for precisely this reason. Indeed, Imperial preferences were the only point of major disagreement between the United States and Great Britain in drafting the Atlantic Charter. See Lloyd C. Gardner, *Economic Aspects of New Deal Diplomacy* (Boston: Beacon Press, 1964). For British Labour's commitment to Imperial preference, see Amy E. Davis, "The Foreign Policy of British Labour Party Leaders: Postwar Planning, Continuity of Foreign Policy, and the Origins of the Cold War, 1939–1946" (Honors Thesis, Cornell University, 1974).

51. Gabriel Kolko, *The Politics of War: The World and United States Foreign Policy, 1943–1945* (New York: Random House, 1968).

had conceded to all the countries at the conference with which it had concluded agreements. The United States concluded nineteen such bilateral agreements, but the conference's successful outcome depended on its ability to reach an agreement with Britain. The American delegation had congressional authorization to negotiate reductions of 50 percent in all U.S. tariffs, in return for which the United States wanted the elimination of the Imperial Preference System. When Britain refused to commit itself even to an eventual dismantling of the system, the success of the Geneva Conference hung in the balance; because it was too important to jeopardize, the United States gave up the entire 50 percent in return for only a slight reduction in the preferences.[52]

Despite the presumed commitment of its signers to multilateralism, the GATT did allow other exceptions to free trade. It permitted the use of tariffs, for example, when they were intended to create customs unions or free trade areas. It was assumed that either would eventually lead to both increased and liberalized trade. Similarly, it accepted those quantitative restrictions (quotas) that protected agriculture, fostered economic growth, or were intended to help nations deal with balance-of-payments deficits.

Rebuilding Europe after the Second World War proved so difficult that the United States, understanding that worldwide recovery depended on the reconstruction of intra-European trade, insisted that the European states reduce discrimination against one another but discriminate as a group against non-European states in return for aid under the Marshall Plan.[53] Thus, the Europeans lifted quantitative restrictions against one another and maintained them against the United States.

By the late 1950s, the creation of the European Economic Community (EEC) and the European Free Trade Association had led to the use of tariff barriers as well as quotas against the United States, again justified on the grounds of increasing and liberalizing trade. In addition, in establishing preferences for associated states the EEC maintained and expanded discriminatory preferences in which the United States, a staunch supporter of European integration, acquiesced. In other words, the Europeans used the exceptions permitted by the GATT in the late 1940s to institute additional discrimination in the later postwar period.

The American role as economic hegemon, like the British in the 19th century, was to make an asymmetric bargain. The United States opened its own borders substantially in return for an easing of protectionism by others, and it assured it would not retaliate against others' departures from free

52. The United States also had preferences, which were grandfathered in these agreements. The United States had given preferences to Cuba in 1903 and to the Philippines in 1946 upon granting each their independence. The United States was allowed to retain these preferences.
53. Otto Hieronymi, *Economic Discrimination against the United States in Western Europe (1945–1958): Dollar Shortage and the Rise of Regionalism* (Geneva: Droz, 1973).

trade as long as these exceptions remained within specified bounds.[54] Like the liberal trading order of the 19th century, the new international trading system was actually subsystemic; it excluded fascist states in the 1930s and the Soviet bloc beginning in the late 1940s.

There were differences between the two orders, however. First, the political motivations were quite different. Trade agreements and trade disputes in the 19th century reflected political competition among rival European states. Since World War II, on the other hand, both commercial disagreements and commercial accords have reflected the political requisites of alliance formation and maintenance within a group of states for whom the greatest threat came from outside its ranks. In the 19th century, the European states were political rivals using commercial agreements to improve political relations when that seemed to be in their interest. When political relations deteriorated, economic ones also suffered. Ultimately, the First World War severed their economic links. After World War II, the United States used commercial agreements to knit together a political coalition of liberal, democratic, capitalist societies. European and Japanese economic recovery was essential to America's political interests, both short and long term. Thus, America's commercial strategy hinged on its interest in the economic resuscitation of its former allies and enemies.

Although both were willing to enter into asymmetric trade arrangements, Britain and the United States were quite different economic hegemons. I have already emphasized that commercial policy serves to further a government's domestic and foreign policy interests, and that these are reflected in its foreign economic policy. Britain did not initiate nor was it the driving force behind the trade liberalization of the 1860s. It adopted a largely free trade commercial policy unilaterally once the government found alternative sources of revenue. The United States was a more activist promoter of trade liberalization, yet it was not willing to lower tariffs except through reciprocal arrangement. Furthermore, its successive tariff reductions were from the highs established in 1930, and thus included large interindustry variations. Moreover, the American commitment to trade liberalization was heavily qualified. The United States obtained an exceptionally broad waiver from the GATT in the mid 1950s for its agricultural quotas. Congressional opposition insured that the planned international trade institutions, the International Trade Organization and later the Organization for Trade Cooperation, never came into being.[55] Indeed, the trade agreements that the United States

---

54. The United States has even been prepared to tolerate cheating on the already asymmetrical bargain it had accepted and has rarely resorted to its right to retaliate. A sense of the extent to which the United States has turned the other cheek can be seen in Judith Lynn Goldstein, "A Re-examination of American Trade Policy: An Inquiry into the Causes of Protectionism" (Ph.D. diss., University of California, Los Angeles, 1983).

55. On the nature of these stillborn organizations, see George Bronz, "The International Trade Organization Charter," *Harvard Law Review* 62 (May 1949): 1089–1125, and Bronz, "An International Trade Organization: The Second Attempt," *Harvard Law Review* 69 (January

made in the two decades following 1945 were executive agreements never presented to Congress for its approval. The executive obtained negotiating authority through successive extensions of the 1934 Reciprocal Trade Agreements Act; these extensions often included declarations stating that the bill's enactment did not imply approval of the GATT itself. In short, despite its active promotion of trade agreements, American acceptance of liberal trade was more qualified than Britain's from the very outset.

Part of the difference is attributable to differences in the role of government in the 19th and 20th centuries. The mercantilistic and protectionist elements of the liberal trading order of the 19th century were rooted in government's felt responsibility for a nation's economic development.[56] Governmental responsibilities have been transformed in the 20th century to include maintenance of economic growth, price stability, and full employment.[57] Thus, governments impose much greater constraints on the workings of the international marketplace and are much less willing to adjust to changes in trade. A government's commercial policy still has foreign policy implications and incorporates foreign policy interests, but domestic interests constrain tariff bargains more in the latter 20th century. The tariff bargains that result are more protectionist and may need to be renegotiated more often.

The decline of American hegemony

The decline of American economic hegemony became fully manifest in 1971, when the United States transformed the postwar economic order by simultaneously instituting an import surcharge and refusing to exchange gold

---

1956): 440–82. For the problems in drafting a charter for such an organization, see Jacob Viner, "Conflicts of Principle in Drafting a Trade Charter," *Foreign Affairs* 25 (July 1947): 612–28. Viner points out the extent to which the United States could not fully accept free trade. The ITO was opposed in the United States not only by protectionists but by perfectionists who felt that it accepted too much protectionism; see William Diebold Jr., "The End of the I.T.O.," *Princeton Essays in International Finance* no. 16 (Princeton, N.J., October 1952). The ITO charter institutionalized the subsystemic nature of the hoped-for liberal regime. It specified that member countries were not permitted to generalize concessions to nonmembers.

56. For an important corrective to the prevalent view that government policy has been successful in this role, see Frank B. Tipton Jr., "Government Policy and Economic Development in Germany and Japan: A Skeptical Reevaluation," *Journal of Economic History* 41 (March 1981): 139–50.

57. This is what I take to be, at bottom, the argument made by Ruggie, "International Regimes, Transactions, and Change." This argument is also used to explain current trade concerns in Arthur A. Stein, "Freer Trade: Problems and Prospects," manuscript (1983). Yet it is inappropriate to impose modern motivations and concerns upon past generations. Barry J. Eichengreen points out that the British decision to adopt the General Tariff in 1932 was primarily motivated by a concern not about unemployment but about hyperinflation and exchange depreciation. Politicians adopted the tariff knowing it would worsen domestic unemployment, but deeming the price acceptable for price and exchange-rate stability. See Eichengreen, "Sterling and the Tariff, 1929–32," *Princeton Studies in International Finance* no. 48 (Princeton, N.J., September 1981).

for dollars. With these measures, it knocked out the monetary and commercial underpinnings of postwar international economic relationships. The rest of the decade was marked by constant fears that protectionism was once more on the rise. In the early 1970s, many were afraid of a return to economic blocs, protectionism, autarky, and the collapse of international trade—that the decline of American hegemony would mean a return to a closed economic world. The anticipated collapse did not materialize, and the doomsayers retreated only a little: whatever the reason for its failure to occur thus far, they argued, it would still do so.

The postwar world had been one of constrained protectionism during which the United States had assured others it would not retaliate against trade barriers that remained within agreed limits, and during which international trade grew rapidly. Protectionist policies were not intended to prohibit or reduce trade but were adopted either as temporary measures to speed reconstruction (similar to those intended to protect infant industries) or, in the case of quotas, orderly marketing agreements, and voluntary export agreements, as ways to freeze trade at a given level and thus prevent further domestic adjustment. Thus, the collapse of international trade would require not only increased protectionism but a retaliation against such practices by the world's major trading power.

In other words, the real trade issue of the 1970s was not whether other nations would increase protection but whether the United States would maintain its commitment to nonretaliation. The relative decline in American economic power did not mean it had a lessened ability to impose openness (something it had never done). Rather, the increased relative strength of others might lead to an American unwillingness to continue carrying so large a burden. The import surcharge of 1971 demonstrated that the United States would not maintain that commitment at any price; rather, it would require a renegotiation of the original asymmetric bargain.

Thus, the 1960s and 1970s have seen movement by others toward greater openness under American pressure. The Tokyo Round trade negotiations of the late 1970s further lowered tariff barriers and included codes limiting nontariff barriers. Because the Tokyo agreements also maintained and relegitimated certain exceptions to free trade, however, scholars have differed in their assessments of the final package. Some have concluded that it actually signaled a return to protectionism. But besides concluding a new basic agreement along the lines of earlier multilateral trade packages, the conferees showed a willingness to tackle new problems and agree on solutions to them—a major breakthrough.[58] It seems clear, therefore, that the agreements are a step toward greater openness.

The current trading order is more open than that of the late 1940s and

---

58. Stephen D. Krasner, "The Tokyo Round: Particularistic Interests and Prospects for Stability in the Global Trading System," *International Studies Quarterly* 23 (December 1979): 491–531.

1950s, and the critical issue for economic liberals now is more complicated than discrimination and protection. Governments are competing not so much by raising barriers to trade as in the amount and forms of assistance they provide to various domestic industries. Success in liberalization (lowering tariffs) has served to expose other governmental policies that distort the marketplace. The 19th century liberals who promoted free trade did not foresee the growth of governmental involvement in the economy. All governmental policies generate positive and negative externalities for producers, and, because they affect competitiveness, they can become the basis for international disagreements.

The general concern of the early 1980s, one that first appeared in the global recession of 1974–75, is how the major trading nations will respond to a downturn in the global economy. Those states which have pursued constrained protectionism all along will likely increase protection. The issue then becomes whether the former hegemon is able to accept not only the original asymmetric bargain but also the increased cheating of others at a time when it is experiencing an absolute economic downturn. The collapse of the order comes not because of the increased cheating of others. Rather, it follows the refusal of the former hegemon, still the world's leading trader, to keep a bargain it can no longer afford. Even then, its departure only comes after others have failed to comply with its demands that they undo their restrictions on trade.

Free trade and the hegemon's dilemma

The periods dubbed "free trade eras" certainly saw years of rapid trade expansion, but they were hardly periods of free trade. Rather, they were periods of *freer* trade. The trade agreements that comprised the more liberal trade system permitted some internal discrimination, but they discriminated far more severely against those who remained outside the system altogether. These systems of freer trade were based on asymmetric tariff bargains in which a hegemon substantially opened its own borders and accepted the tariff barriers of other states, which gave up their prohibitions but retained moderate tariffs. The system was hardly open, but it was *more* open, and the self-abnegation of the hegemon provided a degree of certainty. In both periods, this greater certainty, together with lower tariffs and the outright abolition of prohibitions, resulted in a tremendous growth in trade.

Great Britain and the United States accepted systems for which they bore higher costs than did others, and scholars have thus questioned whether those systems were in their own interests. Neomercantilists, for example, argue that the hegemon undercut its relative position. Liberals, on the other hand, point out that freer trade improves efficiency and global welfare, and hence probably increases the hegemon's absolute wealth.

Both arguments are correct, and the debate is really about the decision criteria that states do and should employ. The realist injunction to maximize power can be seen as an imperative to maximize either one's absolute power over time or one's power relative to others at any given point in time. The liberal suggests that a rational actor should employ an individualistic decision criterion intended strictly to maximize its own returns. The mercantilist, however, recommends a competitive decision criterion meant to maximize relative gains. The use of strict maximization to guide one's choice does not preclude working with others out of common interests, but for the relative maximizer there exist no common interests, and the mutual use of difference maximization transforms any situation into a zero-sum game. Sometimes, an actor is confronted by a difficult choice between the dominant strategies suggested by the different decision criteria.

This is "the hegemon's dilemma," the situation that confronted Great Britain in the 19th century and the United States in the 20th. To maximize one's own returns requires a commitment to openness regardless of what others do. To maximize one's relative position, on the other hand, calls for a policy of continued closure irrespective of others' policies. Each strategy is dominant, but for a different decision rule.[59]

The policies the hegemons adopted actually insured that they would experience a relative economic decline and in time, therefore, a decline in their hegemonic position. Each could, of course, have attempted to maintain its hegemony. The British might have tried to tighten their grip on the secrets of the industrial revolution, and the United States could have closed itself off and attempted to prevent the recovery of nations devastated during the Second World War. It is not clear, however, that either could have maintained its relative hegemony with such policies. It may be that hegemony is a historical accident and is inherently unstable—that Britain, for example, achieved its hegemonic position because it was first to industrialize, but that others would eventually have done so as well. Similarly, the United States may have achieved its position only because of the devastation suffered in two world wars by other major powers whose eventual recovery was only a matter of time. Yet whether Britain and the United States could have pursued policies that would have sustained their hegemony, and for how long, is academic, because both hegemons chose to adopt policies that undercut their relative positions.

The relative decline of the hegemon's position threatens the trading order

59. A dominant strategy is one that maximizes returns no matter the course of action taken by others. It is deductively true that a situation in which one course of action is dominant for one decision criterion but another is dominant for the other decision criterion is one in which the hegemon has a greater effect on others' returns than on its own. Choosing to maximize its absolute returns means that others will gain more and, therefore, that the hegemon undercuts its relative position. Choosing to maximize its relative returns, on the other hand, means that the hegemon gives up the possibility of greater absolute wealth.

only when the hegemon stops accepting others' departures from free trade and retaliates against them. But given that the original asymmetric bargain represented the choice of strict maximization rather than relativistic competition, it seems unlikely that a hegemon would break the agreement when others' positions improve. It is possible, however, that a strictly maximizing hegemon might retaliate and pay short-term absolute costs in the hope of obtaining greater openness and, therefore, longer-term absolute gains.

In fact, some in Britain did press for a restructured bargain, for "fair trade," as the nation's relative position declined and the position of others improved in the late 19th century.[60] Yet the British stuck by the bargain, sustaining their commitment to free trade until World War I. They were able to do so in part because the so-called return to protectionism by others in the last quarter of the 19th century was at most a *defensive* reaction intended to freeze trade levels in a period of declining growth. That reaction also exemplified the logic of the system as it had been established in the 1860s. Trade did not grow, but neither did it diminish. Beginning to expand rapidly after the decades of stagnation, international commerce reached its greatest heights at the beginning of the 20th century.

The real dangers to a relatively liberal trading order are wars that destroy political relationships and disrupt economic ones, or major sustained downturns—real depressions in the global economy. In such situations, nations that regularly pursue some protection will increase the degree to which they do so. The crucial question is whether the former hegemon, now facing domestic economic collapse, will be able to forgo retaliation. The death of the system of global trade established in the 19th century resulted from World War I and the Great Depression. Britain had sustained its commitment to free trade across decades of relative economic decline and was even prepared to continue these policies during the 1930s, although it required more in the tariff bargain from others in return.

Britain's willingness to keep leading in the early 1930s should alert us that liberalizing policies also have more staying power than many believe. There is an inertia in such governmental policies. Producers accustomed to protection and regulation find it difficult to wean themselves from governmental support. Similarly, once a nation begins to liberalize its foreign trade, interests develop that favor continuing and expanding the process. Ironically, the growth of trade and interdependence generates pressure for protection as well as for greater openness. Typically, the more a nation imports, the more some domestic producers suffer, especially during periods of recession. On the other hand, the more a nation exports, the more domestic producers are liable to be hurt by others' retaliation against protectionist policies. Thus protectionism is viable only as long as others do not retaliate. Not surprisingly,

---

60. Cain, "Political Economy in Edwardian England," argues that the tariff-reform strategy would have been an inappropriate one for Britain's problems.

innovative protectionist measures are rarely unilateral. Rather, they are negotiated agreements intended to freeze trade levels or roll them back only slightly. Protectionists are bought off and the relatively liberal system is maintained. International trade has continued to grow alongside such policies.

Hegemons do not create openness. They can open themselves up, and they can assure others of nonretaliation as long as others only impose trade barriers within specified constraints and under specified conditions. Hegemons need followers in order to liberalize international exchanges. Moreover, their decline does not insure closure, for they can close only their own borders, not those of others. Rather, their decline undermines the certainty of nonretaliation and thus makes possible greater openness (though with more uncertainty) through a restructured and more reciprocal foundation.[61] The collapse of international trade comes not only from their retaliation (i.e., their return to closure) but also from the unwillingness of others to modify the original tariff bargain. Followers who do not move toward greater openness run the risk of the hegemon's retaliation.

Hegemons do not impose openness, they bear its costs. No system is completely open, and departures from openness come at the hegemon's expense. Thus, the decline of hegemony does not suddenly insure closure, because the hegemon was never able to enforce openness in the first place. Rather, the hegemon's decline makes it more difficult for it to continue paying the price of asymmetric openness. Closure comes when the hegemon, which will no longer bear the burden, defects because others refuse to redistribute the costs. Finally, the hegemon's decline does not signify that it has become irrelevant. Rather, the former hegemon remains a major, perhaps still *the* major, trading power, and its participation and agreement are necessary if relative openness is to be maintained. The lesson of the 1930s is that Britain needed followers to remain open, and that the American assumption of leadership was insignificant until Britain became willing to follow. The continued agreement of the United States remains essential for the maintenance of the postwar trading order it made possible by its willingness to bear the costs of openness.

---

61. Such reciprocal agreements are likely to be formal and institutionalized. When a hegemon bears the burden, the arrangement can be tacit, but a more reciprocal arrangement between relatively more equal powers requires explicit collaboration. These distinctions are developed in Arthur A. Stein, "Coordination and Collaboration: Regimes in an Anarchic World," *International Organization* 36 (Spring 1982): 299-324.

Interests, power, and multilateralism
Lisa L. Martin

Within the European Community (EC), member states increasingly accept the results of majoritarian voting procedures as constraints on their foreign policies, particularly on economic issues. At the same time, the United States is turning more frequently to bilateral negotiations to solve its international trade dilemmas. Some international organizations involve all members in important decisions through regularized, weighted voting mechanisms; others—for example, the United Nations (UN)—delegate some decision-making powers to a subset of actors (such as the UN Security Council). Some organizations have gained widespread monitoring powers and have developed dispute resolution mechanisms; others are primarily talking shops or negotiating arenas. This article considers the functional imperatives that contribute to such variance in patterns of international cooperation and uses the concept of multilateralism as a metric with which to characterize the patterns thus observed.

States can choose from a wide array of organizing forms on which to base their interactions; among these is multilateralism. A number of recent works have explored situations in which states have used varying degrees of multilateralism to structure their relations.[1] This article argues that studies of

This article was originally prepared for the Ford Foundation West Coast Workshop on Multilateralism, organized by John Gerard Ruggie. The author gratefully acknowledges the Ford Foundation's financial support for this project. My thanks also to Robert Keohane and Stephen Krasner, as well as to the participants in this project, for their valuable comments on this research.

1. See Geoffrey Garrett, "International Cooperation and Institutional Choice: The European Community's Internal Market," *International Organization* 46 (Spring 1992), pp. 533–60; John Gerard Ruggie, "Multilateralism: The Anatomy of an Institution," *International Organization* 46 (Summer 1992), pp. 561–98; James A. Caporaso, "International Relations Theory and Multilateralism: The Search for Foundations," *International Organization* 46 (Summer 1992), pp. 599–632; Steve Weber, "Shaping the Postwar Balance of Power: Multilateralism in NATO," *International Organization* 46 (Summer 1992), pp. 633–80; Miles Kahler, "Multilateralism with Small and Large Numbers," *International Organization* 46 (Summer 1992), pp. 681–708; and John Gerard Ruggie, ed., *Multilateralism Matters: The Theory and Praxis of an Institutional Form* (New York: Columbia University Press, forthcoming). See also *International Journal* 45 (Autumn 1990), which is a special issue on multilateralism.

International Organization 46, 4, Autumn, 1992, pp. 765–92
© 1992 by the World Peace Foundation and the Massachusetts Institute of Technology

state choice can achieve high payoffs by giving serious consideration to functional arguments that view institutions as a solution to dilemmas of strategic interaction.[2] Consideration of the power and interests of state actors in different situations leads to hypotheses about the modal tendencies in the types of norms and organizations that states create to facilitate pursuit of their interests—what Beth Yarbrough and Robert Yarbrough term the "form of successful cooperation."[3]

The first section of this article briefly defines multilateralism as used throughout. The second section discusses a typology of cooperation problems and the potential roles of the institution of multilateralism (IM) and multilateral organizations (MOs) in helping states to overcome these problems. Each of four ideal types of cooperation problems—collaboration, coordination, suasion, and assurance—presents states with unique challenges. In some, the functions performed by formal organizations, such as monitoring and enforcement, will be essential to the achievement of cooperation. In others, multilateral norms, such as nondiscrimination, will be more efficient. The functional considerations behind alternative institutional solutions for different types of games will be illuminated. To structure this analysis, I have treated multilateralism as a strict, ideal type and will consider whether multilateral norms will facilitate cooperation. Thus, a claim that states may choose to compromise multilateral norms does not imply any normative judgment; it is only a statement about the likely form of cooperation.

However, at this abstract, functional level of analysis, outcomes remain indeterminate. Multiple feasible solutions exist for each problem. Therefore, the third section takes into consideration two key elements of international structure in the postwar era: U.S. hegemony within the Western subsystem and the bipolar distribution of power in the international system as a whole. These factors lead us to consider the strengths and weaknesses of multilateralism from the hegemon's point of view and the impact of a bipolar security structure. Considerations of power and time horizons suggest likely choices among functional solutions.

The final section turns from comparative statics and introduces a dynamic element to the analysis by inquiring about changes in institutions in the face of changing distributions of power and other exogenous changes. Some solutions to cooperation problems are preferable to others because certain structures can adapt to changes in relative power; this feature is one of the main advantages of a multilateral architecture. Other forms of cooperation will be brittle and susceptible to challenge as the hegemon declines relative to other members. Changes in the distribution of power can lead to shifts in the kind of game being played, in addition to affecting the outcome within specified games.

2. Robert O. Keohane, "Multilateralism: An Agenda for Research," *International Journal* 45 (Autumn 1990), pp. 731–64.
3. Beth V. Yarbrough and Robert M. Yarbrough, "Cooperation in the Liberalization of International Trade: After Hegemony, What?" *International Organization* 41 (Winter 1987), p. 4.

The concept of multilateralism

John Gerard Ruggie presents a precise and useful definition of the "institution of multilateralism" in his recent article entitled "Multilateralism: The Anatomy of an Institution." According to this definition, IM consists of three principles: (1) indivisibility, (2) nondiscrimination, or generalized organizing principles, and (3) diffuse reciprocity.[4] Indivisibility is illustrated by collective security arrangements wherein an attack on one is considered an attack on all. Nondiscrimination implies that all parties be treated similarly, as in the use of most-favored nation (MFN) status in trade agreements. Diffuse reciprocity implies that states do not rely on specific, quid-pro-quo exchanges, but on longer-term assurances of balance in their relations.

In this article, I inquire into the instrumental value of multilateral norms under different configurations of state interests, i.e., in different types of "cooperation problems." By treating multilateralism as a means rather than a goal, we open the possibility that alternative organizing devices will be equal to or superior to IM in their utility for reaching higher-level ends, such as liberalization. The choice of tools depends, at least in part, on the configuration of state power and interests in particular issue-areas. Thus, I assume that states are self-interested and turn to multilateralism only if it serves their purposes, whatever those may be.

A belief in the utility of multilateralism was expressed after World War II in a drive to create many international organizations. MOs must be distinguished from IM: MOs are formal organizations with more than two members. However, we see a great deal of variation in the degree to which actual organizations conform to the norms of multilateralism. This article attempts to explain variation in the organizing principles and strength of these organizations on the basis of the strategic problems facing states. In addition, it suggests hypotheses about relationships among norms, formal organizations, and behavioral outcomes.

Multilateralism is used here as a metric by which to gauge patterns of interaction, not as a normative standard. Thus, claims that multilateralism is not efficient under some conditions are not meant to imply that states will refuse to cooperate; rather, such claims imply only that alternative architectures will promote international cooperation more efficiently under those conditions. The concept of multilateralism provides a language with which to describe variation in the character of the norms governing international cooperation and the formal organizations in which it occurs. Thus, this article is less about whether multilateralism "matters" than an exploration of the comparative utility of multilateralism and alternative organizational forms.

In the following analysis, I find it useful to differentiate among the roles of multilateralism at three separate points in the cooperation process. The first

---

4. Ruggie, "Multilateralism," pp. 569–74.

stage is that of arriving at decisions. States can reach decisions through genuinely multilateral discussions, a series of bilateral agreements, or the imposition of decisions on a unilateral basis. Second, we need to specify the scope of state decisions. Decisions may only apply to those directly involved in their negotiation, or they may be extended to a broader range of actors. Finally, norms of multilateralism may apply at the stage of implementation. Central problems at that stage involve the monitoring and enforcement of agreements. States may utilize mechanisms ranging from the highly centralized to the completely decentralized to solve such problems. Multilateral norms, for example, may apply to the scope of agreements but not to their negotiation or enforcement. The questions I address are about the utility of multilateral norms and organizations (which need to be carefully distinguished from one another) at each stage, and thus about expectations for the multilateral character of the forums within which specific instances of cooperation are embedded. The conclusions I draw should be seen as hypotheses for the purpose of future empirical examination.

Strategic interaction and multilateralism

Multilateralism, as defined by Ruggie, requires that states sacrifice substantial levels of flexibility in decision making and resist short-term temptations in favor of long-term benefits. Therefore, it is unrealistic to expect state behavior to conform to pure multilateralism. Instead, we need to ask about the role IM and MOs can play under specified conditions. Here, I suggest that focusing on the fundamental problem of strategic interaction within an issue-area provides answers to questions about the likelihood of successful use of IM and MOs.

Drawing on the work of Duncan Snidal, Arthur Stein, and others, I present a simple four-category typology of cooperation problems. Each of these problems—collaboration, coordination, suasion, and assurance—uniquely challenges states considering cooperation. Thus, the problems lead to expectations about variance in the roles of norms and organizations. Consideration of the strategic dilemmas underlying particular issue-areas in their simplest forms suggests particular relationships between IM and MOs. In addition, each situation leads to different relations between IM or MOs and behavioral outcomes. Snidal and Stein differentiate between two prototypical cooperation problems.[5] Snidal refers to these as "coordination" and "prisoners' dilemma," while Stein discusses "coordination games" and "collaboration games." In this article, I use Stein's terminology, as it is more general than Snidal's. I also argue

---

5. See Duncan Snidal, "Coordination Versus Prisoners' Dilemma: Implications for International Cooperation and Regimes," *American Political Science Review* 79 (December 1985), pp. 923–42; and Arthur A. Stein, "Coordination and Collaboration: Regimes in an Anarchic World," in Stephen D. Krasner, ed., *International Regimes* (Ithaca, N.Y.: Cornell University Press, 1983), pp. 115–40.

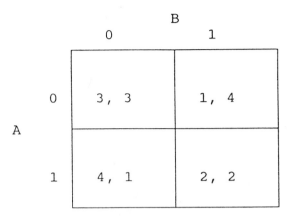

FIGURE 1. *A collaboration game (prisoners' dilemma)*

that two additional game types require consideration. Coordination and collaboration both assume symmetrical interests. In a "suasion game," defined below, states have asymmetrical interests, so the equilibrium outcome leaves one of them dissatisfied. Although analysts have downplayed the significance of regimes or institutions in such asymmetrical situations, I argue that the postwar distribution of power often created precisely this kind of problem and that institutions could, nevertheless, facilitate cooperation. In "assurance games," institutions have little to contribute to cooperation under conditions of complete information. However, given the structural uncertainty of international relations, states may find some modest level of institutionalization in these situations conducive to their ability to achieve mutual gains.

Collaboration problems

Collaboration games are characterized by situations in which equilibrium outcomes are suboptimal. These games, and the nature of potential solutions to them, have been the subject of extensive discussion among economists and political scientists, who often consider them "the" collective action problem.[6] Prisoners' dilemma, as shown in Figure 1, is the most thoroughly studied collaboration game in the international relations literature.[7]

Resolving the dilemma of collaboration games is a matter of mutual policy adjustment, since both players must agree to move away from the suboptimal equilibrium, thus rejecting their dominant strategy. Many authors have identified factors that allow states to overcome collaboration problems. Such

6. Michael Laver, "Political Solutions to the Collective Action Problem," *Political Studies* 28 (June 1980), pp. 195–209.

7. I illustrate only two-person games here. Obviously, situations of multilateralism involve more players. However, many of the fundamental dilemmas of cooperation appear in these simple two-person illustrations.

factors focus on (1) using the proper strategy, (2) extending the shadow of the future, and (3) reliance on centralized mechanisms, such as formal international organizations. MOs can play a role in facilitating cooperation in the above types of problems. However, the norms of multilateralism do not meet the functional demands of collaboration games, in that they do not overcome state incentives to defect. This leads us to expect divergence between IM and MOs in such cases. The remainder of this section identifies those functional demands and the ways in which multilateral norms fail to resolve, or may even exacerbate, collaboration dilemmas.

Collaboration problems contain strong incentives to defect from established cooperative patterns of behavior, since defection results in immediate payoffs. Therefore, mechanisms to promote cooperation must focus on *maintenance* of agreements. As Snidal argues, the need for maintenance mechanisms suggests that solutions to collaboration problems will be centralized, creating a significant role for formal organizations.

Two factors in particular promote cooperation in collaboration games. First, states will demand extensive information on others' behavior, since undetected defection will be costly for those who continue to cooperate and will complicate attempts at retaliation. Thus, we should expect extensive monitoring and assessment of compliance in successfully resolved collaboration problems. Such activity contrasts to that of coordination games, in which exchange of information should take the form of notification of intentions in order to avoid a mutually disliked outcome. According to the logic of strategic interaction, in collaboration, states will exchange information retrospectively; in coordination, prospectively.

Second, in collaboration problems, states should search for mechanisms to increase the shadow of the future in order to assure that the immediate costs associated with cooperation will be offset by the long-term benefits of mutual assistance.[8] Formal organizations can perform such functions.[9] Conventions alone, without monitoring or enforcement, cannot ensure cooperation. The solution to collaboration problems in the absence of a state acting as an entrepreneur and in the presence of large numbers of players requires centralization, leading to expectations of relatively strong formal organizations.

Research on current problems of international cooperation supports the plausibility of this argument. Analyses have suggested that the completion of

---

8. The folk theorem demonstrates that cooperation can be maintained as an equilibrium in repeated prisoners' dilemmas, conditional on a low discount rate (i.e., the future is valued highly) and credible retaliatory threats. See Dilip Abreu, "On the Theory of Infinitely Repeated Games with Discounting," *Econometrica* 56 (March 1988), pp. 383–96; James Friedman, "A Noncooperative Equilibrium for Supergames," *Review of Economic Studies* 38 (January 1971), pp. 1–12; and Robert Axelrod, *The Evolution of Cooperation* (New York: Basic Books, 1984).

9. For an example, see Paul Milgrom, Douglass North, and Barry Weingast, "The Role of Institutions in the Revival of Trade: The Medieval Law Merchant, Private Judges, and the Champagne Fairs," *Economics and Politics* 1 (Spring 1989), pp. 1–23.

the internal market in the EC can be understood in these terms.[10] The removal of internal trade barriers presents a typical collaboration problem. EC members have responded by replacing their previous pattern of bilateral, self-enforcing trade arrangements with a pattern of third-party enforcement mechanisms on an increasingly large range of issues. As expected, the liberalizing process involves a higher degree of both centralization and surrender of individual states' decision-making power than is often found in international relations. In fact, the necessary surrender of sovereignty by EC member states has been a significant impediment to even more rapid movement toward a unified economic region.

This finding about the important role of MOs, however, does not extend to the norms of multilateralism. In collaboration problems, multilateral norms may complicate attempts to cooperate. The norms of diffuse reciprocity and indivisibility, in particular, are not conducive to the solution of collaboration problems. Theoretical and experimental studies of repeated prisoners' dilemmas show the value of strategies of specific reciprocity, such as tit-for-tat and trigger strategies, for maintaining cooperation. Diffuse reciprocity, with its lack of direct retaliation for defections, is unlikely to maintain cooperation in demanding collaboration problems effectively, although it may be efficient in less demanding situations.[11] Under diffuse reciprocity, members rely on generalized norms of obligation to promote cooperation. However, if cheating is not punished, states will face short-term incentives to do so in spite of a longer-term sense of obligation. Although ongoing mutual cooperation provides benefits over mutual defection, without the threat of specific retaliation, the temptation to cheat in order to maximize immediate payoffs rises substantially. Strict adherence to the norm of diffuse reciprocity, particularly at the enforcement stage, would encourage free riding in collaboration situations. Therefore, beyond mechanisms to increase the sense of obligation among states caught in such a dilemma, we might expect to find some compromise of diffuse reciprocity to allow issue-specific sanctioning of egregious free riders. The General Agreement on Tariffs and Trade (GATT), for example, provides for direct retaliation for unfair trading practices, a clear example of specific reciprocity at the enforcement stage.

Similarly, the multilateral norm of indivisibility, taken in its strictest sense, is antithetical to the solution of collaboration dilemmas. Indivisibility, when combined with diffuse reciprocity, implies nonexclusion and creates publicness. If all threats and decisions apply equally to all members of the regime, and all members must be treated equally, the regime will create public goods where

---

10. Beth V. Yarbrough and Robert M. Yarbrough, "International Institutions and the New Economics of Organization," paper delivered to the University of California, Berkeley, Institutional Analysis Workshop, May 1990; and Garrett, "International Cooperation and Institutional Choice."

11. Robert O. Keohane, "Reciprocity in International Relations," *International Organization* 40 (Winter 1986), pp. 1–27.

private goods existed previously. Multilateral security arrangements, for example, make exclusion from protection extremely difficult, since states view a threat to one as a threat to all. Dilemmas of collective choice arise when dealing with public goods. Strict adherence to multilateral principles, rather than solving such dilemmas, would create public goods from private ones. Regime members, under a strict interpretation of such norms, could not be excluded from benefits created by the regime without compromising the indivisibility and diffuse reciprocity principles. Thus, multilateralism creates huge incentives to free ride.

One way around the dilemma of public goods would involve sacrificing some indivisibility and diffuse reciprocity, making regime benefits excludable. Organizations could sanction states that free ride by denying them "entitlements" according to the norms of the regime. One example of such a compromise occurred during the Tokyo Round in the GATT: states that refused to sign the government procurement and other protocols were denied the benefits provided to the signatory states.[12] The previous GATT practice of multilateralism in the scope of agreements was modified, making some regime benefits excludable and contingent on policy commitments. In general, we should expect formal organizations to reflect compromises of the indivisibility and diffuse reciprocity norms to allow for privatization of benefits and sanctioning of free riders in collaboration games. As Snidal argues, "The possibility of exclusion will be especially important in mitigating the adverse effects of increased numbers of states on the prospects for international cooperation."[13] Thus, regimes in issue-areas characterized by collaboration will likely depart significantly from the norms of indivisibility and diffuse reciprocity at the scope and implementation stages, allowing for specific reciprocity and exclusion. IM will appear weak in collaboration cases, while MOs should be strong.

Thus far, the logic of collaboration has suggested a limited role for multilateralism at the scope and implementation stages. I turn now to the decision-making stage. Making decisions on a multilateral basis may save transaction costs during periods of "normal politics," when a group of states is faced with only routine decisions. However, open, egalitarian processes will become cumbersome when a group confronts major decisions. For example, multilateral decision making will create problems for an organization attempting to determine members' budget contributions or to respond quickly to some exogenous crisis. In a distributive or crisis situation, multilateral decision making will entail higher transaction costs than centralized mechanisms. In addition, the collective choice literature points to the problem of cycling. When confronted with a set of choices, majoritarian voting procedures may not lead

---

12. John H. Jackson, "GATT Machinery and the Tokyo Round Agreements," in William R. Cline, ed., *Trade Policy in the 1980s* (Washington, D.C.: Institute for International Economics, 1983), pp. 159–87.

13. Snidal, "Coordination Versus Prisoners' Dilemma," pp. 929–30.

to a conclusive outcome, as each new option receives majority approval.[14] An organization may find itself unable to settle on any specific proposal unless some form of agenda control is imposed, again suggesting a role for centralized or hierarchical decision making.

Groups can overcome the difficulties of multilateral decision making by delegating urgent issues to a smaller group of actors or by allowing such a subset to exercise agenda control under certain conditions. The UN Security Council is one such example. It is a compromise of pure multilateralism that fulfills the above functions and helps account for the UN's ability to act quickly and decisively, as in the Iraqi invasion of Kuwait. Without such delegation, it is difficult to imagine swift, successful cooperation in crises. By delegating difficult decisions and agenda control to smaller groups of states, organizations can avoid some of the transaction-cost problems caused by multilateral decision making. The logic of delegation in international organizations mirrors that in legislatures, which develop systems such as committees to overcome the problems of multilateralism.[15]

MOs typically have a large number of members. As many authors have pointed out, large numbers create problems for states attempting to cooperate.[16] Having many players can increase the conflicts of interest among them, uncertainty about others' preferences, and opportunities for undetected free riding. An MO could deal with some of these difficulties by devoting substantial resources to surveillance and sanctioning of free riders, as discussed above. However, a less expensive tactic might be to sacrifice some degree of multilateralism by decomposing conflictual issues. For example, the GATT has adopted strategies of allowing major trading powers to negotiate agreements rather than mandating negotiations with the entire membership.[17] By focusing on just a few important actors for specific issues, members avoid some of the problems of numerous participants. Negotiations on arms control have followed a similar pattern of decomposition and de facto delegation to those with the most at stake.[18]

This discussion has so far stressed the role that MOs can play in solving collaboration problems, although these MOs will be weak on IM; i.e., they will not strictly reflect the principles of multilateralism. However, analysts have

---

14. See Kenneth J. Arrow, *Social Choice and Individual Values,* 2d ed. (New Haven, Conn.: Yale University Press, 1963), pp. 2–3; and Richard P. McKelvey, "Intransitivities in Multidimensional Voting: Models and Some Implications for Agenda Control," *Journal of Economic Theory* 12 (June 1976), pp. 472–82.

15. Barry R. Weingast and William J. Marshall, "The Industrial Organization of Congress; or, Why Legislatures, Like Firms, Are Not Organized as Markets," *Journal of Political Economy* 96 (February 1988), pp. 132–63.

16. For example, see Kenneth A. Oye, "Explaining Cooperation Under Anarchy: Hypotheses and Strategies," in Oye, ed., *Cooperation Under Anarchy* (Princeton, N.J.: Princeton University Press, 1986), pp. 18–22.

17. Jock A. Finlayson and Mark W. Zacher, "The GATT and the Regulation of Trade Barriers: Regime Dynamics and Functions," in Krasner, ed., *International Regimes,* pp. 273–314.

18. I am grateful to Patrick Morgan for suggesting this example.

noted that at least two other solutions to collaboration problems exist: hegemony and self-enforcing agreements among smaller numbers of players. The argument about the possibility for a single, dominant state to provide public goods and to thus enforce a solution to collaboration problems has been thoroughly explored under the rubric of hegemonic stability theory.[19] The logical and empirical weaknesses of this theory have also been subject to extensive discussion.[20] For the purposes of this article, I will simply note that if a hegemon has incentives to provide a public good and/or undertake the costs of enforcement, the strategic situation has changed from one of collaboration to one of suasion. The hegemon's size creates the incentives to provide public goods, thus changing the player's preference ordering and creating a new type of cooperation problem (one which is discussed below). Also, the hegemonic solution to collaboration problems is available only when a specific configuration of state power obtains. Thus, insofar as no single state is dominant or makes up a "uniquely privileged group," the hegemonic solution is not available.

Another potential response to collaboration problems involves the use of bilateralism at the stage of decision making but multilateralism in the scope of those decisions. In other words, states reach bilateral agreements and then, through application of the norm of nondiscrimination, extend these agreements to other members of the system. In contrast, use of IM at the negotiation stage would imply participation of far more members of the regime. The bilateral negotiating solution has been used in international trade, in both the nineteenth and twentieth centuries, through the application of unconditional MFN treatment.[21]

However, the temptation to cheat on these agreements still exists, suggesting that multilateral norms will not extend to implementation. States could perhaps make such agreements self-enforcing, for example through an "exchange of hostages" in the form of asset-specific investments.[22] If such a solution is to work, the calculation that continued cooperation is more profitable than cheating must hold for every state to which MFN treatment is extended, creating complications when large numbers of states are involved. Another numbers problem arises simply through the high transaction costs of negotiating a series of bilateral treaties, which a self-enforcing agreements

19. See Charles P. Kindleberger, *The World in Depression* (Berkeley: University of California Press, 1973); Steven D. Krasner, "State Power and the Structure of International Trade," *World Politics* 38 (April 1976), pp. 317–43; and Robert O. Keohane, "The Theory of Hegemonic Stability and Changes in International Regimes, 1967–1977," in Ole Holsti, ed., *Change in the International System* (Boulder, Colo.: Westview Press, 1980), pp. 131–62.

20. For example, see John A. C. Conybeare, *Trade Wars: The Theory and Practice of International Commercial Rivalry* (New York: Columbia University Press, 1987), pp. 55–72.

21. Arthur A. Stein, "The Hegemon's Dilemma: Great Britain, the United States, and the International Economic Order," *International Organization* 38 (Spring 1984), pp. 355–86.

22. Beth V. Yarbrough and Robert M. Yarbrough, "Reciprocity, Bilateralism, and Economic 'Hostages': Self-enforcing Agreements in International Trade," *International Studies Quarterly* 30 (March 1986), pp. 7–21.

B

0   1

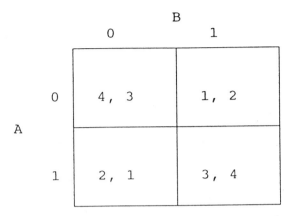

		B 0	**B** 1
A	0	4, 3	1, 2
	1	2, 1	3, 4

FIGURE 2. *A coordination game with divergent interests (battle of the sexes)*

model for collaboration requires.[23] Thus, if the MFN-type of solution is to lead to stable cooperation without the use of international organizations that have enforcement power, we should expect to find it only on a regional or subregional basis.[24] As GATT membership and the complexity of issues with which GATT deals grow, we find increasing use of centralized mechanisms for dispute resolution and of specific reciprocity. Thus, the ghost of collaboration dilemmas increasingly haunts the multilateral trading regime.[25]

Coordination problems

Figure 2 shows a typical coordination problem, the battle of the sexes. This game has two possible equilibrium outcomes, one of which is preferred by each of the players. Neither has a dominant strategy, so the best course of action is dependent on how the other player behaves. The central dilemma in this situation is deciding which of the two equilibria will prevail. The two players disagree on this and bargaining over the outcome might be quite intense, especially if players expect the result to hold far into the future. Coordination games can have major distributional implications, which sometimes make cooperative solutions difficult to achieve.[26] However, once an equilibrium has been established either by convention or by agreement, neither player has an incentive to defect from it.

23. Conybeare, *Trade Wars,* p. 278.
24. See Yarbrough and Yarbrough, "Cooperation in the Liberalization of International Trade."
25. The strategic problems states confront in international monetary affairs differ substantially from those in commercial activities. Under the Bretton Woods regime, for example, the central role of the United States prevented the cooperation problem from being one of collaboration. Instead, we saw a significant asymmetry of interests, perhaps creating a suasion game as discussed below.
26. See Stephen D. Krasner, "Global Communications and National Power: Life on the Pareto Frontier," *World Politics* 43 (April 1991), pp. 336–66.

Thus, coordination games do not require institutions with strong mechanisms for surveillance and enforcement. Since no state would gain by deviating from the established outcome, each need devote little attention to the prevention of cheating. However, structures that facilitate bargaining and allow states to identify a focal point will contribute to cooperative outcomes.[27] General multilateral principles (namely, IM) may play a central role in allowing states to settle on a particular outcome. In such cases, the benefits of multilateralism in reducing the costs of arriving at an agreement suggest that IM will contribute to cooperative outcomes if used at the negotiation stage. The logic of coordination suggests that a series of bilateral negotiations would be highly inefficient. Thus, in coordination situations (in contrast to collaboration situations) IM may be quite strong.

There is, however, no reason to expect that the strength of multilateral norms will be reflected in strong formal organizations. The roles such organizations can play (e.g., providing information about others' actions and sanctioning free-riders) are not essential to the maintenance of cooperation in coordination games. We have little reason to expect that states will choose to devote scarce resources to formal organizations that will be superfluous. Thus, while IM may be most efficacious in coordination games, MOs will not have strong enforcement powers.

Why might states create formal organizations at all under these conditions? The answer lies in transaction-cost savings on the prospective collection of information about state intentions. Consider a case in which players are choosing frequencies for radio transmissions. As long as a sufficient number of frequencies exist to satisfy everyone, the case represents a pure coordination problem. To avoid confusion and the mutually disliked outcome of two players attempting to use the same frequency, players will likely set up a centralized system of notification to advise each how the others plan to behave. Nevertheless, this system will only be an efficient means of distributing information, and states will not delegate to it unnecessary monitoring powers since no player has an incentive to cheat by deviating from his or her announced intention.[28] Although information is important to the solution of coordination games, it is signaling information about future plans, rather than retrospective information about compliance, that states need. In coordination problems, there is no incentive for surreptitious cheating. Since the point of diverging from an established equilibrium is to force joint movement to a new one, defection must be public. Under these conditions, secret defection makes as little sense as

27. See Geoffrey Garrett and Barry Weingast, "Ideas, Interests, and Institutions: Constructing the EC's Internal Market," presented at the annual meeting of the American Political Science Association, Washington, D.C., 28 August–1 September, 1991.

28. For another perspective on the functions regimes can perform in coordination games under conditions of imperfect information, see James D. Morrow, "Modelling International Regimes," paper presented at the annual meeting of the Public Choice Society, New Orleans, La., 20–22 March 1991.

undertaking terrorist operations while attempting to prevent publicity about them. In both cases, the point is to impose high costs on others in order to force them to change their policies in a specified manner—which requires publicity about the reasons for and nature of defection.

In coordination games, the primary instrumental value of multilateral norms appears during the negotiation stage, when states are attempting to reach agreements and set conventions. As in collaboration cases, however, alternative solutions exist. A primary one is action by a dominant player to establish a focal point. If a single, powerful state can commit itself to a particular equilibrium, others will find it in their interest simply to go along with this decision. Such a solution obviates the need for extensive discussions. It may have occurred, for example, during the transition from an allocative to a market-based regime in telecommunications, when the United States forced others to move to a new basis for regulation.[29] U.S. actions in the establishment of the postwar monetary order could be interpreted in a similar manner.[30]

In problems of standardization, such as transborder data flows, state preferences approach the ideal type of coordination problem. Although each actor has a preferred standard, there is a strong common interest in avoiding the use of conflicting standards. In such cases, the major analytical puzzle is the establishment of a convention, which typically follows extensive multilateral discussions. Negotiations focus on the creation of new standards rather than on arguments about whether members are violating old ones, since there is nothing to gain from concealed deviation from the focal point. States will find it easier to maintain cooperation, once established, in coordination games than in collaboration or suasion games, although some actors will inevitably have preferred a different outcome. Thus, in issues that reflect coordination preferences, IM will contribute more to cooperative outcomes than will the more formal MOs.

Suasion problems

Both coordination and collaboration problems embody a symmetry of interests among states. However, in reality, many multilateral institutions have been established under conditions of significant asymmetry. Because the United States far exceeded others in power and wealth, it frequently formed a "privileged group" of one, willing unilaterally to supply public goods. The control of technology sales to the Soviet bloc through the Coordinating Committee on Export Controls (COCOM) illustrates just such a situation, inasmuch as the United States often had a dominant strategy to control

---

29. Peter F. Cowhey, "The International Telecommunications Regime: The Political Roots of Regimes for High Technology," *International Organization* 44 (Spring 1990), pp. 169–99.
30. Barry Eichengreen, "Hegemonic Stability Theories of the International Monetary System," in Richard N. Cooper et al., *Can Nations Agree? Issues in International Economic Cooperation* (Washington, D.C.: The Brookings Institution, 1989), pp. 255–98.

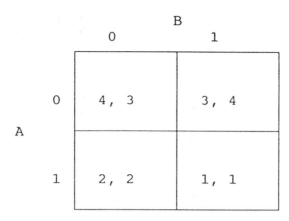

FIGURE 3. *A suasion game*

technology regardless of the policies of other states.[31] In this situation, smaller states have a strong incentive to free ride, knowing that public goods, such as control of significant technologies, will nevertheless be provided. In the COCOM case, while the United States controlled most production of high-technology goods, Europeans could reap the benefits of exports while being assured that their sales were insufficient in quantity and quality to change the overall balance of power. Such a situation presents the United States, or any hegemon, with a dilemma. The hegemon would prefer others' cooperation and is dissatisfied with the equilibrium outcome of unilateral action. I call this kind of asymmetric situation a "suasion" game, since the dilemma facing the hegemon is to persuade or coerce others to cooperate. Figure 3 shows a typical suasion game.

Suasion problems have equilibrium outcomes that leave one actor dissatisfied. In the situation shown in Figure 3, player A (perhaps the United States) has a dominant strategy to cooperate. Knowing this, player B can achieve its most favored outcome by defecting. Faced with this situation, the United States has, in the abstract, two ways to convince the other to cooperate, both of which go beyond the confines of the game illustrated here. First, it could threaten to act irrationally in the short term, defecting if player B does. This would lead to player B's least favored outcome, and, if credible, convince him to cooperate. The problem with such a strategy, of course, is establishing credibility. The United States would have to be willing to bear high short-term costs if player B did not respond to that threat. To make the threat credible, a mechanism to make U.S. defection automatic would be needed. This would involve a

31. See Michael Mastanduno, "Trade as a Strategic Weapon: American and Alliance Export Control Policy in the Early Postwar Period," *International Organization* 42 (Winter 1988), pp. 121–50; and Lisa L. Martin, *Coercive Cooperation: Explaining Multilateral Economic Sanctions* (Princeton, N.J.: Princeton University Press, 1992).

significant surrender of control over decision making and seems an unlikely course of action.

More frequently, the aggrieved actor will choose the second path—tactical issue linkage.[32] This linkage could take the form of either threats or promises (e.g., side-payments). By linking issues, the hegemon can either decrease player B's payoff associated with unilateral defection (threats) or increase the payoff for mutual cooperation (side payments). In either case, understanding the emergence of cooperation requires that we look beyond the single issue supposedly at stake. In the nuclear nonproliferation regime, for example, the goal of nonproliferation has been pursued by offering various forms of technical assistance to those who comply with regime rules.[33] Private, linked benefits contribute to the supply of a public good (nonproliferation) in suasion games.[34]

What role can multilateralism play? For the smaller states (those being either bribed or threatened into submission), maintaining the appearance of multilateralism may be quite important. Governments that give in to U.S. pressure, for example, may need to conceal this behind a veil of "multilateral agreement," for domestic purposes. Thus, we should expect that actual decision making processes in these situations are obscured, i.e., not transparent to the public. In fact, COCOM was the most secretive of international organizations; its very existence was concealed in many countries. At least prior to the Korean War, and for some period thereafter, U.S.–European efforts to control technology exports fit the suasion pattern.

While smaller states may benefit from a velvet glove of multilateralism in the above situations, there is little reason to expect that multilateral norms will play a significant role in constraining state behavior. Actual control over the agenda and decisions will likely be maintained by the hegemonic state, with face-saving arrangements to isolate others from domestic pressure. Strong asymmetries of interests and power may lead to widespread disregard of the nondiscrimination norm, since the functions performed by the hegemonic state will differ significantly from those of the smaller members. In addition, the threats or promises that lead to mutual cooperation will need to be implemented on a basis of specific reciprocity. For example, threats to retaliate against all due to

---

32. For discussions of this strategy, see James K. Sebenius, "Negotiation Arithmetic: Adding and Subtracting Issues and Parties," *International Organization* 37 (Spring 1983), pp. 281–316; Arthur A. Stein, "The Politics of Linkage," *World Politics* 33 (October 1980), pp. 62–81; and Michael D. McGinnis, "Issue Linkage and the Evolution of Cooperation," *Journal of Conflict Resolution* 30 (March 1986), pp. 141–70.

33. Benjamin N. Schiff, "Dominance Without Hegemony: U.S. Relations with the International Atomic Energy Agency," in Margaret P. Karns and Karen A. Mingst, eds., *The United States and Multilateral Institutions: Patterns of Changing Instrumentality and Influence,* Mershon Center Series on International Security and Foreign Policy, vol. 5 (Boston, Mass.: Unwin Hyman, 1990), pp. 57–89.

34. Mancur Olson, *The Logic of Collective Action* (Cambridge, Mass.: Harvard University Press, 1965).

the defection of individuals will be costly and lack credibility. Thus, IM—the embodiment of multilateral principles—suffers in suasion situations.

Even if the dominant state adopts a linkage strategy, it faces a credibility problem. Carrying out either threats or promises is costly. Thus, the hegemonic actor needs to establish a credible commitment to linkage. For the United States, making tactical linkages credible presents the major challenge in suasion situations. In the COCOM case, for example, a linkage between control of technology and Marshall Plan aid was established by Congress, thus improving the administration's bargaining position within the regime. The United States also looked to MOs to make its threats or promises credible.[35] From this perspective, one role of formal organizations in suasion games is to tie together issues that have no substantive rationale for linkage.[36] In addition to their role in tactical linkage, organizations can provide the hegemon with information on others' behavior, allowing it to respond quickly to defections.

A useful typology of cooperation problems must include suasion games if only because the conditions of the early postwar period made this asymmetric type of strategic interaction common. The asymmetry of suasion games suggests that IM may provide cover for smaller states but will have little impact on actual decision making. Formal organizations, on the other hand, may facilitate the dominant state's attempts at issue linkage. There is no reason to expect, however, that the organizations thus formed will operate on the basis of multilateral principles.

Assurance problems

For the sake of completeness, I include a fourth type of cooperation problem in this typology: the assurance game, as shown in Figure 4. In an assurance game, the sole preferred outcome is mutual cooperation. Thus, in equilibrium, rational states with complete information will cooperate within the confines of this single issue-area, one-time game. As long as all players cooperate, there are no gains to be derived from cheating; hence, there are no incentives to defect. Although mutual defection is also an equilibrium in this game, mutual cooperation is Pareto-superior and so should quite easily become a focal point—differentiating assurance from the coordination problem discussed above. On this basis, studies of regimes have concluded that institutions have little role to play in assurance games; states will therefore not waste resources to construct them.[37]

35. Domestic strategies can also influence the credibility of commitments to international agreements. See Peter Cowhey's chapter in Ruggie, *Multilateralism Matters*.

36. See Robert O. Keohane, *After Hegemony: Cooperation and Discord in the World Political Economy* (Princeton, N.J.: Princeton University Press, 1984), pp. 91–92, for a general discussion of the role of institutions in issue linkage.

37. Stein, "Coordination and Collaboration," p. 119.

B

0   1

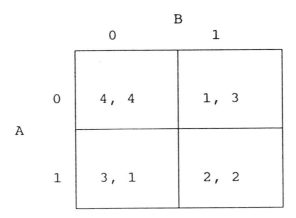

FIGURE 4. *An assurance game (stag hunt)*

The above conclusion, however, is sensitive to changes in assumptions about the information available to states and about the ability of states to behave as unitary actors. Although mutual cooperation makes all players happy, unilateral cooperation is disastrous in assurance games. Thus, two kinds of problems could cause states to fail to reach their preferred outcome: (1) uncertainty about others' payoffs and (2) suspicion that others may not actually be rational, unitary actors.

If country A has assurance preferences but believes that there is some probability that country B has collaboration preferences, for example, country A will be reluctant to take the risk of cooperation. If country B did, in fact, see benefits from unilateral defection, country A may need to protect itself by preemptive defection. Similar concerns by country B could lead to mutual defection in spite of the fact that mutual cooperation is a Pareto-superior equilibrium. This is Robert Jervis's analysis of the security dilemma, suggesting why defensive, rational states in a world of uncertainty may behave in a manner that appears quite irrational.[38]

A second problem involves the question of whether the other player is, in fact, acting as a rational, unitary actor. Although the story underlying this concern differs from the previous scenario, its formal expression is equivalent: a probability distribution over the type of game being played. Here, state A's concern is that state B is not in control of its actions. One explanation may simply be a lack of rationality on B's part, leading to some probability that B will defect regardless of its preferences.[39] A second, perhaps more plausible,

38. Robert Jervis, "Cooperation Under the Security Dilemma," *World Politics* 30 (January 1978), pp. 58–79.

39. The impact of small deviations from intended strategies has led to the concept of trembling-hand equilibria. See Reinhard Selten, "Re-examination of the Perfectness Concept for Equilibrium Points in Extensive Games," *International Journal of Game Theory,* vol. 4, no. 1, 1975, pp. 25–55.

rendering is that B's policies are the result of a domestic game being played out between factions with different preference orderings. Perhaps the chief executive has assurance preferences, for example, while the legislative branch sees immediate benefits from cheating. In that case, if the outcome of the domestic struggle is unclear, state A will want to protect itself against the possibility that the legislature will prevail in the domestic game. The outcome here is the same as in the case of uncertainty about preferences. Suboptimal, mutual defection can result and will be an equilibrium since neither player has an incentive unilaterally to change strategies.

Admitting uncertainty into the assurance problem may have, at first glance, created a situation analogous to that of a collaboration game, in which rational, self-interested behavior leads to a suboptimal outcome. However, the solution to the problem of suboptimal, mutual defection is much less demanding in the assurance than in the collaboration case. In collaboration, stringent systems of monitoring and enforcement are required to prevent cheating. In assurance games, the problem is simply one of assuring all players that each sees no benefits from unilateral defection and is in control of domestic policymaking processes. An efficient solution in this case is provided by transparency in domestic arrangements: open democratic governments may see little need for complex international arrangements to solve assurance problems.

Democracies, however, are also especially subject to the problem of divided control over policymaking. Analysts often explain U.S. problems with foreign policy, for instance, by reference to the weaknesses of divided control. Thus, governments may choose to bolster their commitment to cooperation through the use of international arrangements. The primary function of these arrangements under assurance conditions would be exchange of information about the preferences of various domestic groups with access to the decision-making process. Multilateral norms—with their emphasis on collective decision making and extensive consultation and with their transaction-cost savings—will enhance governments' knowledge about one anothers' preferences. States may even centralize information exchange to economize further on transaction costs, as in coordination cases. However, the logic of the assurance situation does not suggest a need for centralized enforcement mechanisms. Although we should expect to see extensive cooperation in assurance games when information is not scarce, it would be a mistake to credit strong organizations or regimes with this success.

In sum, different cooperation problems lead us to expect different solutions. While there is no unique solution to any problem, a functional analysis does suggest that certain norms or types of formal organizations will be either dysfunctional or inefficient under specified conditions. In collaboration games with many actors, high incentives to engage in undetected cheating lead us to expect the emergence of strong organizations, unless enforcement and monitoring are taken over by a hegemon. Thus, in collaboration games, multilateral norms cannot promote cooperation except under the restricted circumstances of self-enforcing agreements among a small number of states (minilateralism).[40] Coordination problems, on the other hand, do present room for the use of multilateral norms, since states see no advantages in concealed defection from established conventions. In suasion games, cooperation is achieved through issue linkages. MOs can play some role in this process through committing the dominant power and making agreements easier to sell domestically for smaller states; however, these MOs are unlikely to embody IM to any extensive degree. Finally, assurance games, like coordination games, lead us to expect that IM will encourage transparency. However, also as in coordination cases, the role of formal organizations will be limited to exchange of information.

The effects of state power

Thus far, this article has employed a functional approach as it has inquired into the effects of potential solutions to a variety of cooperation problems. The analysis has adopted a systemic perspective, asking about the "correct" solutions to problems on a macro level. However, more than one solution exists for each type of problem. In addition to the problem of multiple equilibria, we have yet to address the micro-level foundations of various solutions to ask why individual states would choose to adopt them. To address these concerns, in this section I examine cooperation problems from the perspective of a hegemon, relying on a fundamental characteristic of the period in which postwar institutions were established. Bipolarity in the security realm also distinguished this period. The benefits of various solutions from the perspective of a hegemon in a bipolar system provide further insight into the types of solutions states prefer to adopt, and can be generalized to develop propositions about the form of cooperation in other systems.

Hegemonic interests

As Ruggie points out, the United States played a leading role in establishing multilateral institutions after World War II.[41] For this historical reason, the potential benefits of multilateral institutions for a dominant state, such as the United States, deserve attention. These benefits fall primarily into three categories: (1) lower transaction costs, (2) the deflection of challenges to the institution by its weaker members, and (3) increased stability under conditions of changes in relative power. These are benefits from the perspective of any type of hegemon, liberal or illiberal, although different types of regimes may put different weights on these benefits relative to the costs associated with

---

40. See Kahler, "Multilateralism with Small and Large Numbers."
41. Ruggie, "Multilateralism," p. 586.

cooperation. Any type of state gains from either reducing its costs of interacting with other countries or preventing challenges to the regimes it establishes.

Multilateralism can lower the transaction costs of interaction among states, particularly when they are attempting to overcome coordination problems. Ruggie uses the example of the International Telegraph Union to illustrate this dynamic.[42] When the distributional implications of agreements are minimal and the major problem is standardization, the transaction cost savings of multilateral institutions may be sufficient to explain why a hegemon would choose the multilateral form. Because a hegemonic power would face higher costs in negotiating a series of bilateral agreements than in negotiating a single, multilateral agreement, it should prefer multilateralism. However, the hegemon may be able to choose a particular equilibrium in coordination games simply through unilateral action.[43] If so, there are few short-term gains from multilateralism. Only a long-term, risk-averse perspective, anticipating future challenges to unilateral action, could explain hegemonic reliance on multilateralism in such a situation. These incentives are discussed below.

Multilateralism may also have advantages when greater conflicts of interest arise. From the hegemon's perspective, the maintenance costs of IM will be lower than those of an organizational form with more concentrated decision-making power. As long as patterns of state interests and power do not change abruptly, a hegemon can expect fewer challenges to an institution in which smaller states have a say in joint decisions than to a unilaterally imposed arrangement. As Miles Kahler has argued regarding the early years of the International Monetary Fund (IMF), "Even in these years of American predominance, the United States found it valuable to veil its power through conventions that convinced other countries that the rules of the game were reasonably fair or at least better than no rules at all."[44]

We could consider the establishment of IM as a transfer of resources in the form of decision-making power from the hegemon to other actors.[45] This transfer legitimates the organization's decisions in the eyes of weaker states, thus reducing the chance that they will continually challenge the regime.[46] As Margaret Levi has argued in a domestic context, institutionalized bargaining under conditions of asymmetry of power is less costly and risky for the dominant actor than constant expenditure of resources to quell rebellions.[47]

42. Ibid., p. 577.
43. See Krasner, "Global Communications and National Power."
44. Miles Kahler, "The United States and the International Monetary Fund: Declining Influence or Declining Interest?" in Karns and Mingst, *The United States and Multilateral Institutions,* p. 97.
45. Giulio M. Gallarotti, "Revisions in Realism: The Political Economy of Domination," paper presented at the Annual Meeting of the American Political Science Association, Atlanta, Georgia, September 1989.
46. Stephen D. Krasner, *Structural Conflict: The Third World Against Global Liberalism* (Berkeley: University of California Press, 1985), p. 62.
47. Margaret Levi, *Of Rule and Revenue* (Berkeley: University of California Press, 1988), p. 28.

Careful institutional design can create "quasi-voluntary compliance," reducing the transaction costs embodied in bargaining, monitoring, and enforcement.

Uncertainty about the actual distribution of benefits will also help to make a multilateral institution resistant to challenges from below. All else being equal, we should expect multilateral decision making to result in a more egalitarian distribution of benefits than decision making in a regime dominated by one or a few powers. Thus, smaller states should more willingly comply with multilateral decisions than commands from above, reducing the need for the hegemon to expend resources policing behavior and enforcing rules. By investing in MOs, the United States could expect fewer challenges to its activities and thus lower maintenance costs. As discussed above, a multilateral institution does create incentives to free ride in some situations. However, from the perspective of smaller states, taking advantage of such opportunities might threaten the institution as a whole, leading to the creation of one more detrimental to their interests. When asymmetry of interests and power allow for the possibility of decision making dominated by a hegemon, others may rationally comply with a more egalitarian, though demanding, arrangement.

On a related note, MOs with some IM may be more resistant to shifts in the balance of power than forums with concentrated decision-making powers. Because the major power is not overtly privileged in multilateral structures, diffusion of power will not necessarily lead to a challenge to the organization's structure. Crises resulting from changes in the distribution of power that might destroy other types of institutions can be weathered by multilateral arrangements. In this sense, multilateralism makes sense from the perspective of a far-sighted hegemon. It requires short-term sacrifices of control over decision making but can result in more stable arrangements over the long term.

As studies of U.S. foreign policy in the 1940s have shown, many key officials adopted a long-term perspective. They saw themselves engaged in the construction of a world order that they wanted to last for more than a few years and were willing to bear short-term costs in pursuit of long-term goals.[48] In addition, there was a widespread belief that U.S. hegemony was an ephemeral situation, and there were even efforts to speed up the inevitable diffusion of power.[49] Under these conditions, when a multilateral solution was a feasible option, the United States could rationally prefer it to more brittle solutions, such as overt coercion. For a far-sighted actor, attempts to exploit power in the short run could be more costly than the design of a durable decision-making structure.[50] Overall, multilateralism provides a relatively inexpensive and

---

48. Robert A. Pollard, *Economic Security and the Origins of the Cold War, 1945–1950* (New York: Columbia University Press, 1985).

49. Weber, "Shaping the Postwar Balance of Power."

50. Joanne Gowa, "Rational Hegemons, Excludable Goods, and Small Groups: An Epitaph for Hegemonic Stability Theory?" *World Politics* 41 (April 1989), pp. 307–24. Gowa also emphasizes the point made earlier in this article that the excludibility of free trade is an essential element of its maintenance.

stable organizational form. In exchange for a loss of some power over decision making and probably some decrease in distributional benefits, the hegemon gains a stable decision-making forum. The choice between unilateral action—a feasible solution—and multilateralism depends heavily on the hegemon's discount rate. The longer the time horizon, the more attractive multilateralism.

The effects of bipolarity

While the United States was the dominant economic and security power within the Western subsystem in the 1950s, that grouping was nested in a larger, bipolar security structure. Examination of the effects of bipolarity gives further insight into the kinds of choices a rational hegemon might make when confronted with a range of feasible solutions to cooperation problems.

Neorealist analyses of the effects of bipolarity agree on one central point: a bipolar distribution of power makes exit from cooperative arrangements a less credible threat than it is in multipolar systems.[51] Given the power and threat of the Soviet Union, neither the United States nor Western Europe could credibly threaten to realign and thus destroy the Western alliance. Although within the bipolar alliance structure numerous conflicts of interest arose, the fundamental stability of alignment was guaranteed by bipolarity. In fact, the very publicity of policy differences between Western alliance members likely resulted from the understanding that such differences could not lead to defections to the Soviet bloc.[52]

The central question, in both security and economics issue-areas, is why the United States did not take advantage of its unique position to exploit the other members of these regimes. Above, I argued that the more far-sighted the hegemon, the less attractive that option becomes. One of the most important impacts of bipolarity is to encourage far-sighted behavior on the part of the hegemon toward its allies. Joanne Gowa argues that in a bipolar system the security externalities of exploitation decrease the utility of exploitation among allies: "The discount factors of allies in a bipolar system, in contrast [to a multipolar system], are not subject to the same downward bias: the greater stability of bipolar coalitions allows the value of future to approximate present benefits more closely."[53]

---

51. See Glenn H. Snyder, "The Security Dilemma in Alliance Politics," *World Politics* 36 (July 1984), pp. 461–95; Joanne Gowa, "Bipolarity, Multipolarity, and Free Trade," *American Political Science Review* 83 (December 1989), pp. 1245–56; and Kenneth N. Waltz, *Theory of International Politics* (Reading, Mass.: Addison-Wesley, 1979).

52. Snyder, "The Security Dilemma in Alliance Politics," p. 473. The question of burden sharing within the alliance, however, is an entirely different issue. Here, the asymmetry of power within the alliance put the United States into a suasion game whereby it contributed a disproportionately high level of resources to the alliance. See also Mancur Olson and Richard Zeckhauser, "An Economic Theory of Alliances," *Review of Economics and Statistics* 48 (August 1966), pp. 266–79; and John R. Oneal, "Testing the Theory of Collective Action: NATO Defense Burdens, 1950–1984," *Journal of Conflict Resolution* 34 (September 1990), pp. 426–48.

53. Gowa, "Bipolarity, Multipolarity, and Free Trade," p. 1250.

Thus, within both international economic regimes and the North Atlantic Treaty Organization (NATO), the United States was unlikely to prefer solutions that sacrificed long-term aggregate benefits for short-term relative gains at the expense of its allies. This tradeoff is the heart of the hegemon's dilemma, namely, whether to pursue its own immediate gains at the expense of its allies, or to accept a smaller share of the benefits in exchange for long-term growth and stability. A bipolar system creates incentives to pursue the latter solution, pushing a hegemon toward a multilateral rather than discriminatory solution to cooperation problems.

Although exit is a less attractive option in bipolar than in multipolar systems, significant variations in the credibility of the exit option remain even within bipolar systems. Within the bipolar structure of the cold war, in particular, exit from the Soviet bloc was a credible threat. While Western European states had no credible exit option, creating U.S. incentives as just described, Eastern European countries could credibly threaten to leave the sphere of Soviet dominance, since the alternative was attractive to them. This variation within the bipolar structure can only be explained by domestic differences between the United States and the Soviet Union, not by power differentials. Bipolarity thus creates the possibility of multilateralism but does not require it.

In the aggregate, structural approaches lead us to expect observable differences between the behavior of hegemons in bipolar and multipolar systems; bipolarity favors multilateralist policies on the part of a hegemon. However, it is not a sufficient condition. If allies have a credible exit option, as Eastern European states did, the hegemon rationally will avoid the sharing of decision-making power and benefits implied by multilateralism. The credibility of threats to exit determine the long-term costs and benefits of multilateralism. Credibility depends in the first instance on structural considerations, as threats to exit are typically quite credible in multipolarity. Bipolarity creates the possibility that such threats will become incredible, but does not assure it.[54]

According to this logic, the current movement toward multipolarity should lead powerful states to favor solutions other than multilateralism. For example, we might expect to see greater use of self-enforcing agreements among smaller numbers of players, as those who see a move toward regionalism in the global economy argue is happening. Note, however, that changing preferences over organizational form do not imply that the goal of liberalization will disappear but simply that solutions other than multilateralism will become more important for its realization. The clearest example of this trend seems to be in U.S. trade policy. The increasing reliance on retaliatory bilateral threats and negotiation of bilateral free trade agreements signal a significant change in

---

54. Current changes in the structure of security arrangements in Europe bear out this logic. East European states are turning to NATO for security. However, NATO, wary of the reliability and stability of the new East European regimes, is insisting on a series of bilateral arrangements rather than formal incorporation into the multilateral framework.

U.S. tactics to pursue the goal of freer trade.[55] While the goals espoused in the GATT remain firmly embedded, the structure used to further them appears to be in transformation, largely due to U.S. initiatives.[56]

The discussion in this section has assumed a powerful state making choices in the absence of pre-existing institutional constraints, in the sort of "blank slate" condition that confronted the United States in the early postwar era. However, ongoing events in Europe should caution us against applying these hypotheses without modification to more highly institutionalized settings. Two fundamental sets of decisions by powerful actors will provide grist for future analysts' mills: (1) Germany's dealings with the rest of Europe, and (2) Russia's dealings with the other former Soviet republics. Both are, in a highly simplified sense, situations of powerful states making decisions about institutional design. However, the context in which each is making such decisions varies greatly, creating different incentives.

Germany, as the most powerful economic actor in Europe, faces two general sets of decisions about the form of relations with its neighbors. To the west, Germany is involved in restructuring the EC. These negotiations are taking place within an unusually well-developed institutional framework. By 1991, the scope and depth of the benefits provided by the EC established it as a central piece of German foreign policy. These benefits and the dense network of relationships built within the EC over the last few decades encourage long-term thinking with respect to dealings with other EC members. Thus, in spite of the end of the cold war, Germany continues to pursue multilateral arrangements within this context.

However, bargains within the EC contrast sharply to those between Germany and Eastern European states. While the new democracies of Eastern Europe struggle to present a common front to the West in hopes of gaining political and economic support, and are searching for access to MOs—including the EC, the GATT, the IMF, and others—bargains have thus far taken on primarily bilateral forms. High levels of uncertainty and constant change contribute to reluctance to rely on multilateral forums.[57] Within the former Soviet Union, the collapse of Soviet institutions has created opportunities and demands for new arrangements. Russia, in its dealings with the other republics, confronts a situation of even more uncertainty than that in Eastern Europe, but also one of relatively high levels of interdependence. No clear pattern has yet emerged, since attempts to organize multilateral arrangements

55. For an example, see Rudiger W. Dornbusch, "Policy Options for Freer Trade: The Case for Bilateralism," in Robert Z. Lawrence and Charles L. Schultze, eds., *An American Trade Strategy* (Washington, D.C.: The Brookings Institution, 1990), pp. 106–34.

56. For a discussion of embedded goals, see John Gerard Ruggie, "International Regimes, Transactions, and Change: Embedded Liberalism in the Postwar Economic Order," in Krasner, ed., *International Regimes,* pp. 195–231.

57. For an example, see Debora L. Spar, "The Political Economy of Foreign Direct Investment in Eastern Europe," prepared for the Center for International Affairs project on International Institutions after the Cold War, Harvard University, Cambridge, Mass., November 1991.

coexist with both reliance on bilateral mechanisms to meet immediate and pressing needs and unilateral Russian actions.

Overall, consideration of the incentives and constraints created by hegemony and bipolarity gives greater precision to the earlier functional analysis, suggesting how a hegemonic state might choose from among a set of feasible solutions. From a hegemon's perspective, the primary choice is from among discriminatory bilateralism, unilateral dominance, and the use of institutions that cede greater decision-making power to other states.

Multilateralism provides benefits of transaction-cost savings and greater stability. However, these advantages are offset by the loss of short-term direct benefits, since a greater share of the immediate gains of cooperation will accrue to states other than the hegemon. The discount rate of the hegemon, therefore, influences the choice among these options: a far-sighted state will value the benefits of multilateralism more highly than a short-sighted one. It might be that bipolarity creates stability and thus encourages far-sighted behavior.

Institutional change

The previous sections of this article adopted a comparative statical approach to institutional choice, asking about the likelihood of finding different patterns of norms and organizations under certain configurations of interests and power. This section turns to the question of change. I do not attempt to develop a fully dynamic theory of change, which would require endogenizing the factors that lead to observable changes in institutions. Instead, I treat the causes of change as exogenous. Thus, this discussion does not address the possibility that participation in a multilateral regime may itself change states' conceptions of their interests. The explanatory puzzle addressed here involves the most likely causes of change in each type of cooperation problem discussed above. Assuming that a pattern of cooperation has been established in an issue-area, what factors are likely to upset it?

In collaboration situations, crises will result from constant temptations to defect in order to reap short-term benefits. Two factors in particular can lead to crises in collaboration: (1) developments that decrease the shadow of the future for individual states, and (2) changes that decrease states' ability to remain informed about the behavior of others. Numerous factors—impending change of government, threats to national security, domestic strife, increasing multipolarity—can lead to a shrinking of states' relevant time horizons. Any of these could increase states' temptation to defect sufficiently to lead to crisis within an issue-area. Similarly, if institutions' ability to provide information is threatened—for example, by technical innovations that make verification of agreements more difficult—the likelihood of defection will increase. Relative to coordination cases, crises are likely to occur frequently in collaboration situations.

In coordination cases, crises will arise when one state whose actions matter to other participants develops a particularly strong interest in changing the established equilibrium. This may occur for a number of reasons, such as domestic political change or a change in technology that makes maintenance of the existing equilibrium more costly. It is interesting to note that changes that give rise to a *longer* time horizon will likely lead to attempts to change the regime. As states value the future more highly, the short-term costs of forcing movement to a new equilibrium may be outweighed by the long-term benefits of a new outcome. Thus, in contrast to collaboration cases, cooperation is threatened rather than enhanced by a longer shadow of the future.

The state desiring change, if it believes its participation is important enough to other actors that they can be influenced by its actions, may challenge the existing equilibrium. If this state is a major player, the challenge could eventually succeed in spite of the short-term costs in deviating from the established standard. U.S. actions in challenging the telecommunications regime could be interpreted this way, as changes in technology and domestic politics led the U.S. government to challenge the existing regime, looking for an outcome more conducive to its interests in the long run.[58] Because the United States was an important player in the regime, its defection was costly to other states and eventually forced them to a new outcome, one based more on market principles.

In sum, crises arise in coordination games when some exogenous force leads an important state to challenge the existing conventions, even though this challenge will be costly in the short term. An important difference from collaboration cases lies in the fact that such challenges will be public. Since there is nothing to gain from unilaterally moving to a different standard, any challenge will be a public attempt to force others to accommodate. Thus, technological developments that threaten cooperation in coordination problems are not those that decrease transparency, but those that change the costs and benefits of specific outcomes for key members of the regime.

Regimes that rely on tactical issue linkage to foster cooperation in suasion games will face crises as the power of the hegemon declines. In this situation, the threats and promises that maintain cooperation will become less credible, increasing others' temptation to defect. This effect may be offset, however, by changing patterns of interests that result directly from changes in power relationships. A declining hegemon may no longer find it worthwhile unilaterally to provide any public goods, thus changing the cooperation problem from one of suasion to one of collaboration.[59] We should expect a fundamental shift in the nature of the regime under these conditions, although we may not see a significant decline in overall cooperation. As asymmetries of power and interest

---

58. See Cowhey, "The International Telecommunications Regime."
59. Duncan Snidal, "The Limits of Hegemonic Stability Theory," *International Organization* 39 (Autumn 1985), pp. 579–614.

decline, the de facto monopoly of decision making by the hegemon should give way to more genuinely multilateral behavior. Organizations that merely collected information may gain monitoring and enforcement powers. The International Atomic Energy Agency seems to illustrate this pattern, since it has continued to function even as U.S. power has declined.[60] Overall, crises in suasion situations will typically arise from changes in the distribution of power.

Assurance problems, in spite of their high degree of common interest, are not immune from crises. Changes in the domestic political arrangements of key actors or technological innovations that create uncertainty about preference orderings will create a desire to protect oneself from the defection of others. Thus, the kinds of factors that threaten collaboration also challenge cooperation in assurance games. Such threats to stable cooperation, however, will be moderated by the existence of viable multilateral institutions. If states have created international arrangements for the exchange of information, whether formal or informal, they will ease the adjustment process to exogenous changes in assurance games.

Conclusion

Will rational, self-interested states ever see instrumental value in multilateral norms? Consideration of the functional demands of various cooperation problems and the benefits of various patterns of cooperation for powerful states leads to a mixed answer. On the one hand, there is never an absolute need for IM, nor for formal MOs. A hegemonic actor could feasibly construct a series of bilateral arrangements, or assert its own preferences as the prerogatives of power, thus avoiding the use of IM or MOs. On the other hand, while such behavior may bring a powerful state immediate benefits, it is likely to prove highly inefficient and difficult to sustain in the long term. Thus, a far-sighted actor may choose to rely on IM or MOs in specified circumstances, rather than simply using its power to enforce a solution to cooperation problems. The extent to which a powerful state will sacrifice control over international decision making in exchange for stability depends on the degree to which conditions allow it to value future interactions as highly as it values today's. Conditions of instability and uncertainty may impair a powerful state's ability to adopt a multilateral approach to international cooperation.

This article has outlined a rational-choice approach to the relationships among IM, MOs, and international cooperation. The analysis here developed expectations about institutional and state behavior by focusing on specific cooperation problems and considering functional constraints. I argued that the relationships between principles, formal organizations, and behavior depend on the nature of strategic interaction in particular issue-areas. The next step in

60. Schiff, "Dominance without Hegemony," p. 78.

this research program should involve similar development of hypotheses from competing perspectives and systematic collection of empirical evidence that will allow us to evaluate their respective explanatory power.

Collaboration should lead to relatively strong organizations but also to the disregard of multilateral principles, particularly diffuse reciprocity and indivisibility. In coordination situations, on the other hand, IM may be strong but formal organizations are hardly necessary and will be quite weak. IM will be weak in suasion situations. In suasion games, formal organizations will probably play a larger role than they play in coordination games but less so than in collaboration games. The potential role of IM and MOs in assurance games is similar to that in coordination. The central problem in both is provision of information about preferences and intentions, and multilateral norms provide an efficient means of information exchange. However, there is no reason to expect strong organizations with enforcement power, and unilateral action by a hegemon may constitute a functional substitute for multilateralism.

Although we can rule out certain kinds of solutions for each type of cooperation problem with such functional analysis, more than one potential solution usually remains. Analysis can further narrow the range of feasible solutions, however, by considering the structural characteristics of the international system. The third section of this article examined preferred solutions from the perspective of a hegemon, asking why multilateralism might ever be preferred to an architecture where the hegemon could more directly exercise dominance. The stability of the Western alliance under conditions of bipolarity led the United States to behave as a far-sighted hegemon, often willing to bypass exploitative solutions in favor of long-term benefits and stability.

In the final section I argued that any "crisis of multilateralism" will result from different factors in each of the four situations. Changes in the distribution of power will be most threatening to cooperation in suasion games. Factors that reduce transparency will challenge both assurance and collaboration games, while increasing discount rates will be most troubling for collaboration. Coordination games are most likely to be upset by technological innovations that alter the cost-benefit calculus of existing conventions for key players. Given the urgency of decisions about institutional design in the post–cold war world, an understanding of the incentives underlying the use or non-use of multilateral norms and/or organizations has both historical and practical significance.

IV.
International Economy and
Domestic Politics

Domestic politics is closely linked to the world economy, and vice versa. Economic decisions in major economies—whether to protect an important industry, devalue a currency, allow a large bank to fail, or embargo a vital raw material—have immediate and profound repercussions abroad. By the same token, global conditions can and do have a powerful effect on domestic institutions.[1] They not only affect which policies are chosen but may also shape the institutions themselves. The question is, "How do these reciprocal influences work?"

To answer that question, we must penetrate the "black box" of national politics and delve into domestic policymaking and political structure. Inevitably, any serious inquiry adds another layer of complexity to our theories of international political economy. Although that line of analysis may produce a more complete description, it is not likely to be simpler or more elegant. There is an unavoidable trade-off here between richness and parsimony.

Scholars approach this trade-off in several ways. The most common approach is to abstract away from domestic politics entirely. For simplicity's sake, international relations theorists assume that states act like coherent units and that we already know their preferences and beliefs. Another approach turns those assumptions on their heads. It takes the international context as given in order to concentrate on the domestic sources of foreign economic policy. The goal here is to understand exactly how state preferences are formed, why actors form the ideas and beliefs they do, and ultimately why certain policies are chosen.[2] Scholars taking this approach may concentrate on one country or compare several (see, for example, the special issues of International Organization edited by Peter J. Katzenstein and by G. John Ikenberry, David A. Lake, and Michael Mastanduno; see also Peter Gourevitch's review of work on this topic).[3]

Finally, some analysts focus directly on the complex intersection between domestic and international affairs. With so many variables involved, the problem is one of formulating tractable theories and clear, sharp hypotheses. The usual response is to

---

1. See Gourevitch 1978; and Weatherford and Fukui 1989.
2. See Goldstein 1989; Pastor and Wise 1994; Garrett and Lange 1991; and Garrett 1995.
3. See Katzenstein 1977; Ikenberry, Lake, and Mastanduno 1988; and Gourevitch 1996.

analyze one key element of the interaction, such as the transmission of economic shocks or the spread of ideas and norms across national boundaries.[4]

The most influential recent effort to deal with these analytic problems is Robert Putnam's work on two-level games (Chapter 11). Putnam observes that international bargains, if they are to survive, must also win approval at home. This requirement means that political leaders must negotiate simultaneously on two levels: international and domestic. What Putnam does, in effect, is to narrow the tangle of variables by concentrating specifically on policymaking, on the connection between domestic and international bargains. In doing so, he sets aside larger structural connections between domestic and international affairs as well as the role played by ideas, norms, and identities.

Putnam's fundamental insight is that most diplomatic agreements have to pass muster at home—and the negotiators know that in advance. Likewise, if domestic policy choices need agreement from other countries, they must win that support at the diplomatic negotiating table. Gaining that agreement may require changes in policy—some give and take with foreign partners. In short, domestic and international negotiations may be closely connected, even mutually dependent.[5]

By focusing on negotiations, Putnam has opened an important research agenda. But he has also left unanswered questions about the role of domestic political structures, including systematic differences across states and across issues within individual states. In Chapter 12, Joanne Gowa offers one way to explore such questions. She shows that collective-action problems are generally more severe in monetary politics than in trade and that this difference profoundly affects coalition politics in the two areas. Gowa downplays what many consider the most characteristic feature of monetary politics: the use of autonomous bodies like the Federal Reserve Board to insulate policymaking from public pressures. She also downplays the arcane language of monetary policy, which obscures the subject matter and shelters it from public debate.

Those are not the real obstacles to interest group influence in monetary affairs, according to Gowa. The real obstacle, she says, lies in the "public character and invulnerability to small group action of some issue areas within monetary policy." She is careful to note that trade and monetary politics are both broad issues and that subissues within them may differ. But, in general, trade politics is more amenable to small-group influence than monetary politics because the collective-action problem is inherently more severe in monetary politics.

Like Gowa, Peter Cowhey is interested in comparing economic policymaking. But rather than compare across issues within a single state, Cowhey wants to compare policymaking across states. In Chapter 13, he concentrates on one major theme: What makes some international commitments more believable and reliable than others? His question is important because most international bargains must be enforced by the parties themselves. If states are to forge stable agreements, they must be able

---

4. See Sikkink 1993; and Price 1998.
5. See Paarlberg 1997; and Schoppa 1993.

to exchange credible promises. Some states, Cowhey says, are better placed to do so than others. (Kurt Taylor Gaubatz makes a similar point about democratic states.[6])

Cowhey uses a comparative approach to understand how states make international promises credible and why some are better at this than others. The key, he argues, lies in the fundamental structure of domestic political institutions.

Comparing the United States with Japan, he concludes that the United States is better placed to make credible promises, thanks to two basic features of American politics: the constitutional division of powers and single-member congressional districts. Compared to parliamentary systems like Japan's, the division of powers in the United States between Congress and the president makes it difficult to initiate international promises. For exactly the same reason, however, overturning those promises is also difficult. Single-member districts work in the same direction but for a different reason. They favor parties that appeal to the median voter and make it risky for any party "to reverse positions if they are close to those of the median voter. Brand name identities mean that parties have a tough time reversing a position once they have made a major public commitment."

Cowhey's work suggests another reason why modern multilateral institutions have been so durable in the years since World War II. Their chief source of political support, the United States, has been credible as well as powerful.

What emerges from the contributions of Putnam, Gowa, Cowhey, and others is a common recognition that domestic politics matter for international outcomes. What also emerges is a rich debate over how best to understand that important connection and whether to make our theories of international political economy complex enough to include it.

References

Garrett, Geoffrey. 1995. Capital Mobility, Trade, and the Domestic Politics of Economic Policy. *International Organization* 49 (4):657–88.

Garrett, Geoffrey, and Peter Lange. 1991. Political Responses to Interdependence: What's Left for the Left? *International Organization* 45 (4): 539–64.

Gaubatz, Kurt Taylor. 1996. Democratic States and Commitment in International Relations. *International Organization* 50 (1):109–40.

Goldstein, Judith. 1989. The Impact of Ideas on Trade Policy: The Origins of U.S. Agricultural and Manufacturing Policies. *International Organization* 43 (1):31–72.

Gourevitch, Peter. 1978. The Second Image Reversed: The International Sources of Domestic Politics. *International Organization* 32 (4):881–912.

———. 1996. Squaring the Circle: The Domestic Sources of International Cooperation. *International Organization* 50 (2):349–73.

Ikenberry, G. John, David A. Lake, and Michael Mastanduno, eds. 1988. The State and American Foreign Economic Policy. *International Organization* 42 (1). Special issue.

Katzenstein, Peter J., ed. 1977. Between Power and Plenty: Foreign Economic Policies of Advanced Industrial States. *International Organization* 31 (4). Special issue.

6. Gaubatz 1996.

Paarlberg, Robert. 1997. Agricultural Policy Reform and the Uruguay Round: Synergistic Linkage in a Two-Level Game? *International Organization* 51 (3):413–44.

Pastor, Manuel, and Carol Wise. 1994. Mexico's Free Trade Policy. *International Organization* 48 (3): 459–89.

Price, Richard. 1998. Transnational Civil Society Targets Land Mines. *International Organization* 52 (3):613–44.

Schoppa, Leonard J. 1993. Two-Level Games and Bargaining Outcomes: Why Gaiatsu Succeeds in Japan in Some Cases but Not Others. *International Organization* 47 (3):353–86.

Sikkink, Kathryn. 1993. Human Rights, Principled Issue-Networks, and Sovereignty in Latin America. *International Organization* 47 (3):411–41.

Weatherford, Stephen M., and Haruhiro Fukui. 1989. Domestic Adjustment to International Shocks in Japan and the United States. *International Organization* 43 (4):585–623.

Diplomacy and domestic politics: the logic of two-level games
Robert D. Putnam

Introduction: the entanglements of domestic and international politics

Domestic politics and international relations are often somehow entangled, but our theories have not yet sorted out the puzzling tangle. It is fruitless to debate whether domestic politics really determine international relations, or the reverse. The answer to that question is clearly "Both, sometimes." The more interesting questions are "When?" and "How?" This article offers a theoretical approach to this issue, but I begin with a story that illustrates the puzzle.

One illuminating example of how diplomacy and domestic politics can become entangled culminated at the Bonn summit conference of 1978.[1] In the mid-1970s, a coordinated program of global reflation, led by the "locomotive" economies of the United States, Germany, and Japan, had been proposed to foster Western recovery from the first oil shock.[2] This proposal

An earlier version of this article was delivered at the 1986 annual meeting of the American Political Science Association. For criticisms and suggestions, I am indebted to Robert Axelrod, Nicholas Bayne, Henry Brady, James A. Caporaso, Barbara Crane, Ernst B. Haas, Stephan Haggard, C. Randall Henning, Peter B. Kenen, Robert O. Keohane, Stephen D. Krasner, Jacek Kugler, Lisa Martin, John Odell, Robert Powell, Kenneth A. Shepsle, Steven Stedman, Peter Yu, members of research seminars at the Universities of Iowa, Michigan, and Harvard, and two anonymous reviewers. I am grateful to the Rockefeller Foundation for enabling me to complete this research.

1. The following account is drawn from Robert D. Putnam and C. Randall Henning, "The Bonn Summit of 1978: How Does International Economic Policy Coordination Actually Work?" *Brookings Discussion Papers in International Economics,* no. 53 (Washington, D.C.: Brookings Institution, October 1986), and Robert D. Putnam and Nicholas Bayne, *Hanging Together: Cooperation and Conflict in the Seven-Power Summits,* rev. ed. (Cambridge, Mass.: Harvard University Press, 1987), pp. 62–94.

2. Among interdependent economies, most economists believe, policies can often be more effective if they are internationally coordinated. For relevant citations, see Putnam and Bayne, *Hanging Together,* p. 24.

had received a powerful boost from the incoming Carter administration and was warmly supported by the weaker countries, as well as the Organization for Economic Co-operation and Development (OECD) and many private economists, who argued that it would overcome international payments imbalances and speed growth all around. On the other hand, the Germans and the Japanese protested that prudent and successful economic managers should not be asked to bail out spendthrifts. Meanwhile, Jimmy Carter's ambitious National Energy Program remained deadlocked in Congress, while Helmut Schmidt led a chorus of complaints about the Americans' uncontrolled appetite for imported oil and their apparent unconcern about the falling dollar. All sides conceded that the world economy was in serious trouble, but it was not clear which was more to blame, tight-fisted German and Japanese fiscal policies or slack-jawed U.S. energy and monetary policies.

At the Bonn summit, however, a comprehensive package deal was approved, the clearest case yet of a summit that left all participants happier than when they arrived. Helmut Schmidt agreed to additional fiscal stimulus, amounting to 1 percent of GNP, Jimmy Carter committed himself to decontrol domestic oil prices by the end of 1980, and Takeo Fukuda pledged new efforts to reach a 7 percent growth rate. Secondary elements in the Bonn accord included French and British acquiescence in the Tokyo Round trade negotiations; Japanese undertakings to foster import growth and restrain exports; and a generic American promise to fight inflation. All in all, the Bonn summit produced a balanced agreement of unparalleled breadth and specificity. More remarkably, virtually all parts of the package were actually implemented.

Most observers at the time welcomed the policies agreed to at Bonn, although in retrospect there has been much debate about the economic wisdom of this package deal. However, my concern here is not whether the deal was wise economically, but how it became possible politically. My research suggests, first, that the key governments at Bonn adopted policies different from those that they would have pursued in the absence of international negotiations, but second, that agreement was possible only because a powerful minority within each government actually favored on domestic grounds the policy being demanded internationally.

Within Germany, a political process catalyzed by foreign pressures was surreptitiously orchestrated by expansionists inside the Schmidt government. Contrary to the public mythology, the Bonn deal was not forced on a reluctant or ''altruistic'' Germany. In fact, officials in the Chancellor's Office and the Economics Ministry, as well as in the Social Democratic party and the trade unions, had argued privately in early 1978 that further stimulus was domestically desirable, particularly in view of the approaching 1980 elections. However, they had little hope of overcoming the opposition of the Finance Ministry, the Free Democratic party (part of the government coalition), and the business and banking community, especially the leadership of the Bundesbank. Publicly, Helmut Schmidt posed as reluctant to the end. Only his closest advisors suspected the truth: that the chancellor "let himself be pushed" into a policy that he privately favored, but would have found costly and perhaps impossible to enact without the summit's package deal.

Analogously, in Japan a coalition of business interests, the Ministry of Trade and Industry (MITI), the Economic Planning Agency, and some expansion-minded politicians within the Liberal Democratic Party pushed for additional domestic stimulus, using U.S. pressure as one of their prime arguments against the stubborn resistance of the Ministry of Finance (MOF). Without internal divisions in Tokyo, it is unlikely that the foreign demands would have been met, but without the external pressure, it is even more unlikely that the expansionists could have overridden the powerful MOF. "Seventy percent foreign pressure, 30 percent internal politics," was the disgruntled judgment of one MOF insider. "Fifty-fifty," guessed an official from MITI.[3]

In the American case, too, internal politicking reinforced, and was reinforced by, the international pressure. During the summit preparations American negotiators occasionally invited their foreign counterparts to put more pressure on the Americans to reduce oil imports. Key economic officials within the administration favored a tougher energy policy, but they were opposed by the president's closest political aides, even after the summit. Moreover, congressional opponents continued to stymie oil price decontrol, as they had under both Nixon and Ford. Finally, in April 1979, the president decided on gradual administrative decontrol, bringing U.S. prices up to world levels by October 1981. His domestic advisors thus won a postponement of this politically costly move until after the 1980 presidential election, but in the end, virtually every one of the pledges made at Bonn was fulfilled. Both proponents and opponents of decontrol agree that the summit commitment was at the center of the administration's heated intramural debate during the winter of 1978–79 and instrumental in the final decision.[4]

In short, the Bonn accord represented genuine international policy coordination. Significant policy changes were pledged and implemented by the key participants. Moreover—although this counterfactual claim is necessarily harder to establish—those policy changes would very probably not have been pursued (certainly not the same scale and within the same time frame) in the absence of the international agreement. Within each country, one faction supported the policy shift being demanded of its country inter-

---

3. For a comprehensive account of the Japanese story, see I. M. Destler and Hisao Mitsuyu, "Locomotives on Different Tracks: Macroeconomic Diplomacy, 1977–1979," in I. M. Destler and Hideo Sato, eds., *Coping with U.S.–Japanese Economic Conflicts* (Lexington, Mass.: Heath, 1982).

4. For an excellent account of U.S. energy policy during this period, see G. John Ikenberry, "Market Solutions for State Problems: The International and Domestic Politics of American Oil Decontrol," *International Organization* 42 (Winter 1988).

nationally, but that faction was initially outnumbered. Thus, international pressure was a necessary condition for these policy shifts. On the other hand, without domestic resonance, international forces would not have sufficed to produce the accord, no matter how balanced and intellectually persuasive the overall package. In the end, each leader believed that what he was doing was in his nation's interest—and probably in his own political interest, too, even though not all his aides agreed.[5] Yet without the summit accord he probably would not (or could not) have changed policies so easily. In that sense, the Bonn deal successfully meshed domestic and international pressures.

Neither a purely domestic nor a purely international analysis could account for this episode. Interpretations cast in terms either of domestic causes and international effects ("Second Image"[6]) or of international causes and domestic effects ("Second Image Reversed"[7]) would represent merely "partial equilibrium" analyses and would miss an important part of the story, namely, how the domestic politics of several countries became entangled via an international negotiation. The events of 1978 illustrate that we must aim instead for "general equilibrium" theories that account simultaneously for the interaction of domestic and international factors. This article suggests a conceptual framework for understanding how diplomacy and domestic politics interact.

Domestic–international entanglements: the state of the art

Much of the existing literature on relations between domestic and international affairs consists either of ad hoc lists of countless "domestic influences" on foreign policy or of generic observations that national and international affairs are somehow "linked."[8] James Rosenau was one of the first scholars to call attention to this area, but his elaborate taxonomy of "linkage politics" generated little cumulative research, except for a flurry of work correlating domestic and international "conflict behavior."[9]

A second stream of relevant theorizing began with the work by Karl

5. It is not clear whether Jimmy Carter fully understood the domestic implications of his Bonn pledge at the time. See Putnam and Henning, "The Bonn Summit," and Ikenberry, "Market Solutions for State Problems."

6. Kenneth N. Waltz, *Man, the State, and War: A Theoretical Analysis* (New York: Columbia University Press, 1959).

7. Peter Gourevitch, "The Second Image Reversed: The International Sources of Domestic Politics," *International Organization* 32 (Autumn 1978), pp. 881–911.

8. I am indebted to Stephan Haggard for enlightening discussions about domestic influences on international relations.

9. James Rosenau, "Toward the Study of National–International Linkages," in his *Linkage Politics: Essays on the Convergence of National and International Systems* (New York: Free Press, 1969), as well as his "Theorizing Across Systems: Linkage Politics Revisited," in Jonathan Wilkenfeld, ed., *Conflict Behavior and Linkage Politics* (New York: David McKay, 1973), especially p. 49.

Deutsch and Ernst Haas on regional integration.[10] Haas, in particular, emphasized the impact of parties and interest groups on the process of European integration, and his notion of "spillover" recognized the feedback between domestic and international developments. However, the central dependent variable in this work was the hypothesized evolution of new supranational institutions, rather than specific policy developments, and when European integration stalled, so did this literature. The intellectual heirs of this tradition, such as Joseph Nye and Robert Keohane, emphasized interdependence and transnationalism, but the role of domestic factors slipped more and more out of focus, particularly as the concept of international regimes came to dominate the subfield.[11]

The "bureaucratic politics" school of foreign policy analysis initiated another promising attack on the problem of domestic–international interaction. As Graham Allison noted, "Applied to relations between nations, the bureaucratic politics model directs attention to intra-national games, the overlap of which constitutes international relations."[12] Nevertheless, the nature of this "overlap" remained unclarified, and the theoretical contribution of this literature did not evolve much beyond the principle that bureaucratic interests matter in foreign policymaking.

More recently, the most sophisticated work on the domestic determinants of foreign policy has focused on "structural" factors, particularly "state strength." The landmark works of Peter Katzenstein and Stephen Krasner, for example, showed the importance of domestic factors in foreign economic policy. Katzenstein captured the essence of the problem: "The main purpose of all strategies of foreign economic policy is to make domestic policies compatible with the international political economy."[13] Both authors stressed the crucial point that central decision-makers ("the state") must be concerned simultaneously with domestic and international pressures.

10. Karl W. Deutsch et al., *Political Community in the North Atlantic Area: International Organization in the Light of Historical Experience* (Princeton: Princeton University Press, 1957) and Ernst B. Haas, *The Uniting of Europe: Political, Social, and Economic Forces, 1950–1957* (Stanford, Calif.: Stanford University Press, 1958).

11. Robert O. Keohane and Joseph S. Nye, *Power and Interdependence* (Boston: Little, Brown, 1977). On the regime literature, including its neglect of domestic factors, see Stephan Haggard and Beth Simmons, "Theories of International Regimes," *International Organization* 41 (Summer 1987), pp. 491–517.

12. Graham T. Allison, *Essence of Decision: Explaining the Cuban Missile Crisis* (Boston: Little, Brown, 1971), p. 149.

13. Peter J. Katzenstein, ed., *Between Power and Plenty: Foreign Economic Policies of Advanced Industrial States* (Madison: University of Wisconsin Press, 1978), p. 4. See also Katzenstein, "International Relations and Domestic Structures: Foreign Economic Policies of Advanced Industrial States," *International Organization* 30 (Winter 1976), pp. 1–45; Stephen D. Krasner, "United States Commercial and Monetary Policy: Unravelling the Paradox of External Strength and Internal Weakness," in Katzenstein, *Between Power and Plenty*, pp. 51–87; and Krasner, *Defending the National Interest: Raw Materials Investments and U.S. Foreign Policy* (Princeton: Princeton University Press, 1978).

More debatable, however, is their identification of "state strength" as the key variable of interest. Given the difficulties of measuring "state strength," this approach courts tautology,[14] and efforts to locate individual countries on this ambiguous continuum have proved problematic.[15] "State strength," if reinterpreted as merely the opposite of governmental fragmentation, is no doubt of some interest in the comparative study of foreign policy. However, Gourevitch is quite correct to complain that "the strong state–weak state argument suggests that . . . the identity of the governing coalition does not matter. This is a very apolitical argument."[16] Moreover, because "state structures" (as conceived in this literature) vary little from issue to issue or from year to year, such explanations are ill-suited for explaining differences across issues or across time (unless "time" is measured in decades or centuries). A more adequate account of the domestic determinants of foreign policy and international relations must stress *politics:* parties, social classes, interest groups (both economic and noneconomic), legislators, and even public opinion and elections, not simply executive officials and institutional arrangements.[17]

Some work in the "state-centric" genre represents a unitary-actor model run amok. "The central proposition of this paper," notes one recent study, "is that the state derives its interests from and advocates policies consistent with the international system at all times and under all circumstances."[18] In fact, on nearly all important issues "central decision-makers" disagree about what the national interest and the international context demand. Even if we arbitrarily exclude the legislature from "the state" (as much of this literature does), it is wrong to assume that the executive is unified in its views. Certainly this was true in *none* of the states involved in the 1978 negotiations. What was "the" position of the German or Japanese state on macroeconomic policy in 1978, or of the American state on energy policy? If the term "state" is to be used to mean "central decision-makers," we should treat it as a plural noun: not "the state, it . . ." but "the state, they . . ." Central executives have a special role in mediating domestic and international pressures precisely because they are directly exposed to both spheres, not because

14. For example, see Krasner, "United States Commercial and Money Policy," p. 55: "The central analytic characteristic that determines the ability of a state to overcome domestic resistance is its strength in relation to its own society."

15. Helen Milner, "Resisting the Protectionist Temptation: Industry and the Making of Trade Policy in France and the United States during the 1970s," *International Organization* 41 (Autumn 1987), pp. 639–65.

16. Gourevitch, "The Second Image Reversed," p. 903.

17. In their more descriptive work, "state-centric" scholars are often sensitive to the impact of social and political conflicts, such as those between industry and finance, labor and business, and export-oriented versus import-competing sectors. See Katzenstein, *Between Power and Plenty*, pp. 333–36, for example.

18. David A. Lake, "The State as Conduit: The International Sources of National Political Action," presented at the 1984 annual meeting of the American Political Science Association, p. 13.

they are united on all issues nor because they are insulated from domestic politics.

Thus, the state-centric literature is an uncertain foundation for theorizing about how domestic and international politics interact. More interesting are recent works about the impact of the international economy on domestic politics and domestic economic policy, such as those by Alt, Evans, Gourevitch, and Katzenstein.[19] These case studies, representing diverse methodological approaches, display a theoretical sophistication on the international-to-domestic causal connection far greater than is characteristic of comparable studies on the domestic-to-international half of the loop. Nevertheless, these works do not purport to account for instances of reciprocal causation, nor do they examine cases in which the domestic politics of several countries became entangled internationally.

In short, we need to move beyond the mere observation that domestic factors influence international affairs and vice versa, and beyond simple catalogs of instances of such influence, to seek theories that integrate both spheres, accounting for the areas of entanglement between them.

Two-level games: a metaphor for domestic-international interactions

Over two decades ago Richard E. Walton and Robert B. McKersie offered a "behavioral theory" of social negotiations that is strikingly applicable to international conflict and cooperation.[20] They pointed out, as all experienced negotiators know, that the unitary-actor assumption is often radically misleading. As Robert Strauss said of the Tokyo Round trade negotiations: "During my tenure as Special Trade Representative, I spent as much time negotiating with domestic constituents (both industry and labor) and members of the U.S. Congress as I did negotiating with our foreign trading partners."[21]

19. James E. Alt, "Crude Politics: Oil and the Political Economy of Unemployment in Britain and Norway, 1970–1985," *British Journal of Political Science* 17 (April 1987), pp. 149–99; Peter B. Evans, *Dependent Development: The Alliance of Multinational, State, and Local Capital in Brazil* (Princeton: Princeton University Press, 1979); Peter Gourevitch, *Politics in Hard Times: Comparative Responses to International Economic Crises* (Ithaca, N.Y.: Cornell University Press, 1986); Peter J. Katzenstein, *Small States in World Markets: Industrial Policy in Europe* (Ithaca, N.Y.: Cornell University Press, 1985).

20. Richard E. Walton and Robert B. McKersie, *A Behavioral Theory of Labor Negotiations: An Analysis of a Social Interaction System* (New York: McGraw-Hill, 1965).

21. Robert S. Strauss, "Foreword," in Joan E. Twiggs, *The Tokyo Round of Multilateral Trade Negotiations: A Case Study in Building Domestic Support for Diplomacy* (Washington, D.C.: Georgetown University Institute for the Study of Diplomacy, 1987), p. vii. Former Secretary of Labor John Dunlop is said to have remarked that "bilateral negotiations usually require three agreements—one across the table and one on each side of the table," as cited in Howard Raiffa, *The Art and Science of Negotiation* (Cambridge, Mass.: Harvard University Press, 1982), p. 166.

The politics of many international negotiations can usefully be conceived as a two-level game. At the national level, domestic groups pursue their interests by pressuring the government to adopt favorable policies, and politicians seek power by constructing coalitions among those groups. At the international level, national governments seek to maximize their own ability to satisfy domestic pressures, while minimizing the adverse consequences of foreign developments. Neither of the two games can be ignored by central decision-makers, so long as their countries remain interdependent, yet sovereign.

Each national political leader appears at both game boards. Across the international table sit his foreign counterparts, and at his elbows sit diplomats and other international advisors. Around the domestic table behind him sit party and parliamentary figures, spokespersons for domestic agencies, representatives of key interest groups, and the leader's own political advisors. The unusual complexity of this two-level game is that moves that are rational for a player at one board (such as raising energy prices, conceding territory, or limiting auto imports) may be impolitic for that same player at the other board. Nevertheless, there are powerful incentives for consistency between the two games. Players (and kibitzers) will tolerate some differences in rhetoric between the two games, but in the end either energy prices rise or they don't.

The political complexities for the players in this two-level game are staggering. Any key player at the international table who is dissatisfied with the outcome may upset the game board, and conversely, any leader who fails to satisfy his fellow players at the domestic table risks being evicted from his seat. On occasion, however, clever players will spot a move on one board that will trigger realignments on other boards, enabling them to achieve otherwise unattainable objectives. This "two-table" metaphor captures the dynamics of the 1978 negotiations better than any model based on unitary national actors.

Other scholars have noted the multiple-game nature of international relations. Like Walton and McKersie, Daniel Druckman has observed that a negotiator "attempts to build a package that will be acceptable both to the other side and to his bureaucracy." However, Druckman models the domestic and international processes separately and concludes that "the interaction between the processes . . . remains a topic for investigation."[22] Robert Axelrod has proposed a "Gamma paradigm," in which the U.S. president pursues policies vis-à-vis the Soviet Union with an eye towards maximizing his popularity at home. However, this model disregards domestic

---

22. Daniel Druckman, "Boundary Role Conflict: Negotiation as Dual Responsiveness," in I. William Zartman, ed., *The Negotiation Process: Theories and Applications* (Beverly Hills: Sage, 1978), pp. 100–101, 109. For a review of the social–psychological literature on bargainers as representatives, see Dean G. Pruitt, *Negotiation Behavior* (New York: Academic Press, 1981), pp. 41–43.

cleavages, and it postulates that one of the international actors—the Soviet leadership—cares only about international gains and faces no domestic constraint while the other—the U.S. president—cares only about domestic gains, except insofar as his public evaluates the international competition.[23] Probably the most interesting empirically based theorizing about the connection between domestic and international bargaining is that of Glenn Snyder and Paul Diesing. Though working in the neo-realist tradition with its conventional assumption of unitary actors, they found that, in fully half of the crises they studied, top decision-makers were *not* unified. They concluded that prediction of international outcomes is significantly improved by understanding internal bargaining, especially with respect to minimally acceptable compromises.[24]

Metaphors are not theories, but I am comforted by Max Black's observation that "perhaps every science must start with metaphor and end with algebra; and perhaps without the metaphor there would never have been any algebra."[25] Formal analysis of any game requires well-defined rules, choices, payoffs, players, and information, and even then, many simple two-person, mixed-motive games have no determinate solution. Deriving analytic solutions for two-level games will be a difficult challenge. In what follows I hope to motivate further work on that problem.

Towards a theory of ratification: the importance of "win-sets"

Consider the following stylized scenario that might apply to any two-level game. Negotiators representing two organizations meet to reach an agreement between them, subject to the constraint that any tentative agreement must be ratified by their respective organizations. The negotiators might be heads of government representing nations, for example, or labor and management representatives, or party leaders in a multiparty coalition, or a finance minister negotiating with an IMF team, or leaders of a House–Senate conference committee, or ethnic-group leaders in a consociational democracy. For the moment, we shall presume that each side is represented by a single leader or "chief negotiator," and that this individual has no indepen-

23. Robert Axelrod, "The Gamma Paradigm for Studying the Domestic Influence on Foreign Policy," prepared for delivery at the 1987 Annual Meeting of the International Studies Association.

24. Glenn H. Snyder and Paul Diesing, *Conflict Among Nations: Bargaining, Decision Making, and System Structure in International Crises* (Princeton: Princeton University Press, 1977), pp. 510–25.

25. Max Black, *Models and Metaphors* (Ithaca, N.Y.: Cornell University Press, 1962), p. 242, as cited in Duncan Snidal, "The Game *Theory* of International Politics," *World Politics* 38 (October 1985), p. 36n.

dent policy preferences, but seeks simply to achieve an agreement that will be attractive to his constituents.[26]

It is convenient analytically to decompose the process into two stages:

1. bargaining between the negotiators, leading to a tentative agreement; call that Level I.

2. separate discussions within each group of constituents about whether to ratify the agreement; call that Level II.

This sequential decomposition into a negotiation phase and a ratification phase is useful for purposes of exposition, although it is not descriptively accurate. In practice, expectational effects will be quite important. There are likely to be prior consultations and bargaining at Level II to hammer out an initial position for the Level I negotiations. Conversely, the need for Level II ratification is certain to affect the Level I bargaining. In fact, expectations of rejection at Level II may abort negotiations at Level I without any formal action at Level II. For example, even though both the American and Iranian governments seem to have favored an arms-for-hostages deal, negotiations collapsed as soon as they became public and thus liable to de facto "ratification." In many negotiations, the two-level process may be iterative, as the negotiators try out possible agreements and probe their constituents' views. In more complicated cases, as we shall see later, the constituents' views may themselves evolve in the course of the negotiations. Nevertheless, the requirement that any Level I agreement must, in the end, be ratified at Level II imposes a crucial theoretical link between the two levels.

"Ratification" may entail a formal voting procedure at Level II, such as the constitutionally required two-thirds vote of the U.S. Senate for ratifying treaties, but I use the term generically to refer to any decision-process at Level II that is required to endorse or implement a Level I agreement, whether formally or informally. It is sometimes convenient to think of ratification as a parliamentary function, but that is not essential. The actors at Level II may represent bureaucratic agencies, interest groups, social classes, or even "public opinion." For example, if labor unions in a debtor country withhold necessary cooperation from an austerity program that the government has negotiated with the IMF, Level II ratification of the agreement may be said to have failed; ex ante expectations about that prospect will surely influence the Level I negotiations between the government and the IMF.

Domestic ratification of international agreements might seem peculiar to democracies. As the German Finance Minister recently observed, "The limit of expanded cooperation lies in the fact that we are democracies, and we

---

26. To avoid unnecessary complexity, my argument throughout is phrased in terms of a single chief negotiator, although in many cases some of his responsibilities may be delegated to aides. Later in this article I relax the assumption that the negotiator has no independent preferences.

need to secure electoral majorities at home.''[27] However, ratification need not be "democratic" in any normal sense. For example, in 1930 the Meiji Constitution was interpreted as giving a special role to the Japanese military in the ratification of the London Naval Treaty;[28] and during the ratification of any agreement between Catholics and Protestants in Northern Ireland, presumably the IRA would throw its power onto the scales. We need only stipulate that, for purposes of counting "votes" in the ratification process, different forms of political power can be reduced to some common denominator.

The only formal constraint on the ratification process is that since the identical agreement must be ratified by both sides, a preliminary Level I agreement cannot be amended at Level II without reopening the Level I negotiations. In other words, final ratification must be simply "voted" up or down; any modification to the Level I agreement counts as a rejection, unless that modification is approved by all other parties to the agreement.[29] Congresswoman Lynn Martin captured the logic of ratification when explaining her support for the 1986 tax reform bill as it emerged from the conference committee: "As worried as I am about what this bill does, I am even more worried about the current code. The choice today is not between this bill and a perfect bill; the choice is between this bill and the death of tax reform."[30]

Given this set of arrangements, we may define the "win-set" for a given Level II constituency as the set of all possible Level I agreements that would "win"—that is, gain the necessary majority among the constituents—when simply voted up or down.[31] For two quite different reasons, the contours of the Level II win-sets are very important for understanding Level I agreements.

First, **larger win-sets make Level I agreement more likely,** *ceteris paribus.*[32] By definition, any successful agreement must fall within the Level II win-

27. Gerhardt Stoltenberg, *Wall Street Journal Europe*, 2 October 1986, as cited in C. Randall Henning, *Macroeconomic Diplomacy in the 1980s: Domestic Politics and International Conflict Among the United States, Japan, and Europe*, Atlantic Paper No. 65 (New York: Croom Helm, for the Atlantic Institute for International Affairs, 1987), p. 1.

28. Ito Takashi, "Conflicts and Coalition in Japan, 1930: Political Groups and the London Naval Disarmament Conference," in Sven Groennings et al., eds, *The Study of Coalition Behavior* (New York: Holt, Rinehart, & Winston, 1970); Kobayashi Tatsuo, "The London Naval Treaty, 1930," in James W. Morley, ed., *Japan Erupts: The London Naval Conference and the Manchurian Incident, 1928–1932* (New York: Columbia University Press, 1984), pp. 11–117. I am indebted to William Jarosz for this example.

29. This stipulation is, in fact, characteristic of most real-world ratification procedures, such as House and Senate action on conference committee reports, although it is somewhat violated by the occasional practice of appending "reservations" to the ratification of treaties.

30. *New York Times*, 26 September 1986.

31. For the conception of win-set, see Kenneth A. Shepsle and Barry R. Weingast, "The Institutional Foundations of Committee Power," *American Political Science Review* 81 (March 1987), pp. 85–104. I am indebted to Professor Shepsle for much help on this topic.

32. To avoid tedium, I do not repeat the "other things being equal" proviso in each of the propositions that follow. Under some circumstances an expanded win-set might actually make practicable some outcome that could trigger a dilemma of collective action. See Vincent P. Crawford, "A Theory of Disagreement in Bargaining," *Econometrica* 50 (May 1982), pp. 607–37.

sets of each of the parties to the accord. Thus, agreement is possible only if those win-sets overlap, and the larger each win-set, the more likely they are to overlap. Conversely, the smaller the win-sets, the greater the risk that the negotiations will break down. For example, during the prolonged pre-war Anglo–Argentine negotiations over the Falklands/Malvinas, several tentative agreements were rejected in one capital or the other for domestic political reasons; when it became clear that the initial British and Argentine win-sets did not overlap at all, war became virtually inevitable.[33]

A brief, but important digression: The possibility of failed ratification suggests that game theoretical analyses should distinguish between *voluntary* and *involuntary defection*. Voluntary defection refers to reneging by a rational egoist in the absence of enforceable contracts—the much-analyzed problem posed, for example, in the prisoner's dilemma and other dilemmas of collective action. Involuntary defection instead reflects the behavior of an agent who is unable to deliver on a promise because of failed ratification. Even though these two types of behavior may be difficult to disentangle in some instances, the underlying logic is quite different.

The prospects for international cooperation in an anarchic, "self-help" world are often said to be poor because "unfortunately, policy makers generally have an incentive to cheat."[34] However, as Axelrod, Keohane, and others have pointed out, the temptation to defect can be dramatically reduced among players who expect to meet again.[35] If policymakers in an anarchic world were in fact constantly tempted to cheat, certain features of the 1978 story would be very anomalous. For example, even though the Bonn agreement was negotiated with exquisite care, it contained no provisions for temporal balance, sequencing, or partial conditionality that might have protected the parties from unexpected defection. Moreover, the Germans and the Japanese irretrievably enacted their parts of the bargain more than six months before the president's action on oil price decontrol and nearly two years before that decision was implemented. Once they had done so, the temptation to the president to renege should have been overpowering, but in fact virtually no one on either side of the decontrol debate within the administration dismissed the Bonn pledge as irrelevant. In short, the Bonn "promise" had political weight, because reneging would have had high political and diplomatic costs.

33. The Sunday Times Insight Team, *The Falklands War* (London: Sphere, 1982); Max Hastings and Simon Jenkins, *The Battle for the Falklands* (New York: Norton, 1984); Alejandro Dabat and Luis Lorenzano, *Argentina: The Malvinas and the End of Military Rule* (London: Verso, 1984). I am indebted to Louise Richardson for these citations.

34. Matthew E. Canzoneri and Jo Anna Gray, "Two Essays on Monetary Policy in an Interdependent World," International Finance Discussion Paper 219 (Board of Governors of the Federal Reserve System, February 1983).

35. Robert Axelrod, *The Evolution of Cooperation* (New York: Basic Books, 1984); Robert O. Keohane, *After Hegemony: Cooperation and Discord in the World Political Economy* (Princeton: Princeton University Press, 1984), esp. p. 116; and the special issue of *World Politics*, "Cooperation Under Anarchy," Kenneth A. Oye, ed., vol. 38 (October 1985).

On the other hand, in any two-level game, the credibility of an official commitment may be low, even if the reputational costs of reneging are high, for the negotiator may be unable to guarantee ratification. The failure of Congress to ratify abolition of the "American Selling Price" as previously agreed during the Kennedy Round trade negotiations is one classic instance; another is the inability of Japanese Prime Minister Sato to deliver on a promise made to President Nixon during the "Textile Wrangle."[36] A key obstacle to Western economic coordination in 1985–87 was the Germans' fear that the Reagan administration would be politically unable to carry out any commitment it might make to cut the U.S. budget deficit, no matter how well-intentioned the president.

Unlike concerns about voluntary defection, concern about "deliver-ability" was a prominent element in the Bonn negotiations. In the post-summit press conference, President Carter stressed that "each of us has been careful not to promise more than he can deliver." A major issue throughout the negotiations was Carter's own ability to deliver on his energy commitments. The Americans worked hard to convince the others, first, that the president was under severe domestic political constraints on energy issues, which limited what he could promise, but second, that he could deliver what he was prepared to promise. The negotiators in 1978 seemed to follow this presumption about one another: "He will do what he has promised, so long as what he has promised is clear and within his power."

Involuntary defection, and the fear of it, can be just as fatal to prospects for cooperation as voluntary defection. Moreover, in some cases, it may be difficult, both for the other side and for outside analysts, to distinguish voluntary and involuntary defection, particularly since a strategic negotiator might seek to misrepresent a voluntary defection as involuntary. Such behavior is itself presumably subject to some reputational constraints, although it is an important empirical question how far reputations generalize from collectivities to negotiators and vice versa. Credibility (and thus the ability to strike deals) at Level I is enhanced by a negotiator's (demonstrated) ability to "deliver" at Level II; this was a major strength of Robert Strauss in the Tokyo Round negotiations.[37]

Involuntary defection can only be understood within the framework of a two-level game. Thus, to return to the issue of win-sets, the smaller the win-sets, the greater the risk of involuntary defection, and hence the more applicable the literature about dilemmas of collective action.[38]

---

36. I. M. Destler, Haruhiro Fukui, and Hideo Sato, *The Textile Wrangle: Conflict in Japanese–American Relations, 1969–1971* (Ithaca, N.Y.: Cornell University Press, 1979), pp. 121–57.

37. Gilbert R. Winham, "Robert Strauss, the MTN, and the Control of Faction," *Journal of World Trade Law* 14 (September–October 1980), pp. 377–97, and his *International Trade and the Tokyo Round* (Princeton: Princeton University Press, 1986).

38. This discussion implicitly assumes uncertainty about the contours of the win-sets on the part of the Level I negotiators, for if the win-sets were known with certainty, the negotiators would never propose for ratification an agreement that would be rejected.

The second reason why win-set size is important is that **the relative size of the respective Level II win-sets will affect the distribution of the joint gains from the international bargain.** The larger the perceived win-set of a negotiator, the more he can be "pushed around" by the other Level I negotiators. Conversely, a small domestic win-set can be a bargaining advantage: "I'd like to accept your proposal, but I could never get it accepted at home." Lamenting the domestic constraints under which one must operate is (in the words of one experienced British diplomat) "the natural thing to say at the beginning of a tough negotiation."[39]

This general principle was, of course, first noted by Thomas Schelling nearly thirty years ago:

> The power of a negotiator often rests on a manifest inability to make concessions and meet demands. . . . When the United States Government negotiates with other goverments . . . if the executive branch negotiates under legislative authority, with its position constrained by law, . . . then the executive branch has a firm position that is visible to its negotiating partners. . . . [Of course, strategies such as this] run the risk of establishing an immovable position that goes beyond the ability of the other to concede, and thereby provoke the likelihood of stalemate or breakdown.[40]

Writing from a strategist's point of view, Schelling stressed ways in which win-sets may be manipulated, but even when the win-set itself is beyond the negotiator's control, he may exploit its leverage. A Third World leader whose domestic position is relatively weak (Argentina's Alfonsin?) should be able to drive a better bargain with his international creditors, other things being equal, than one whose domestic standing is more solid (Mexico's de la Madrid?).[41] The difficulties of winning congressional ratification are often exploited by American negotiators. During the negotiation of the Panama Canal Treaty, for example, "the Secretary of State warned the Panamanians several times . . . that the new treaty would have to be acceptable to at least sixty-seven senators," and "Carter, in a personal letter to Torrijos, warned that further concessions by the United States would seriously threaten chances for Senate ratification."[42] Precisely to forestall such tactics, opponents may demand that a negotiator ensure himself "negotiating room" at Level II before opening the Level I negotiations.

The "sweet-and-sour" implications of win-set size are summarized in Figure 1, representing a simple zero-sum game between X and Y. X_M and

39. Geoffrey W. Harrison, in John C. Campbell, ed., *Successful Negotiation: Trieste 1954* (Princeton: Princeton University Press, 1976), p. 62.

40. Thomas C. Schelling, *The Strategy of Conflict* (Cambridge, Mass.: Harvard University Press, 1960), pp. 19–28.

41. I am grateful to Lara Putnam for this example. For supporting evidence, see Robert R. Kaufman, "Democratic and Authoritarian Responses to the Debt Issue: Argentina, Brazil, Mexico," *International Organization* 39 (Summer 1985), pp. 473–503.

42. W. Mark Habeeb and I. William Zartman, *The Panama Canal Negotiations* (Washington, D.C.: Johns Hopkins Foreign Policy Institute, 1986), pp. 40, 42.

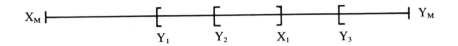

FIGURE 1. *Effects of reducing win-set size*

Y_M represent the maximum outcomes for X and Y, respectively, while X_1 and Y_1 represent the minimal outcomes that could be ratified. At this stage any agreement in the range between X_1 and Y_1 could be ratified by both parties. If the win-set of Y were contracted to, say, Y_2 (perhaps by requiring a larger majority for ratification), outcomes between Y_1 and Y_2 would no longer be feasible, and the range of feasible agreements would thus be truncated in Y's favor. However, if Y, emboldened by this success, were to reduce its win-set still further to Y_3 (perhaps by requiring unanimity for ratification), the negotiators would suddenly find themselves deadlocked, for the win-sets no longer overlap at all.[43]

Determinants of the win-set

It is important to understand what circumstances affect win-set size. Three sets of factors are especially important:

43. Several investigators in other fields have recently proposed models of linked games akin to this "two-level" game. Kenneth A. Shepsle and his colleagues have used the notion of "interconnected games" to analyze, for example, the strategy of a legislator simultaneously embedded in two games, one in the legislative arena and the other in the electoral arena. In this model, a given action is simultaneously a move in two different games, and one player maximizes the sum of his payoffs from the two games. See Arthur Denzau, William Riker, and Kenneth Shepsle, "Farquharson and Fenno: Sophisticated Voting and Home Style," *American Political Science Review* 79 (December 1985), pp. 1117–34; and Kenneth Shepsle, "Cooperation and Institutional Arrangements," unpublished manuscript, February 1986. This approach is similar to models recently developed by economists working in the "rational expectations" genre. In these models, a government contends simultaneously against other governments and against domestic trade unions over monetary policy. See, for example, Kenneth Rogoff, "Can International Monetary Policy Cooperation be Counterproductive," *Journal of International Economics* 18 (May 1985), pp. 199–217, and Roland Vaubel, "A Public Choice Approach to International Organization," *Public Choice* 51 (1986), pp. 39–57. George Tsebelis ("Nested Games: The Cohesion of French Coalitions," *British Journal of Political Science* 18 [April 1988], pp. 145–70) has developed a theory of "nested games," in which two alliances play a competitive game to determine total payoffs, while the individual players within each alliance contend over their shares. Fritz Sharpf ("A Game-Theoretical Interpretation of Inflation and Unemployment in Western Europe," *Journal of Public Policy* 7 [1988], pp. 227–257) interprets macroeconomic policy as the joint outcome of two simultaneous games; in one, the government plays against the unions, while in the other, it responds to the anticipated reactions of the electorate. James E. Alt and Barry Eichengreen ("Parallel and Overlapping Games: Theory and an Application to the European Gas Trade," unpublished manuscript, November 1987) offer a broader typology of linked games, distinguishing between "parallel" games, in which "the same opponents play against one another at the same time in more than one arena," and "overlapping" games, which arise "when a particular player is engaged at the same time in games against distinct opponents, and when the strategy pursued in one game limits the strategies available in the other." Detailed comparison of these various linked-game models is a task for the future.

- Level II preferences and coalitions
- Level II institutions
- Level I negotiators' strategies

Let us consider each in turn.

1. The size of the win-set depends on the distribution of power, preferences, and possible coalitions among Level II constituents.

Any testable two-level theory of international negotiation must be rooted in a theory of domestic politics, that is, a theory about the power and preferences of the major actors at Level II. This is not the occasion for even a cursory evaluation of the relevant alternatives, except to note that the two-level conceptual framework could in principle be married to such diverse perspectives as Marxism, interest group pluralism, bureaucratic politics, and neo-corporatism. For example, arms negotiations might be interpreted in terms of a bureaucratic politics model of Level II politicking, while class analysis or neo-corporatism might be appropriate for analyzing international macroeconomic coordination.

Abstracting from the details of Level II politics, however, it is possible to sketch certain principles that govern the size of the win-sets. For example, the lower the cost of "no-agreement" to constituents, the smaller the win-set.[44] Recall that ratification pits the proposed agreement, *not* against an array of other (possibly attractive) alternatives, but only against "no-agreement."[45] No-agreement often represents the status quo, although in some cases no-agreement may in fact lead to a worsening situation; that might be a reasonable description of the failed ratification of the Versailles Treaty.

Some constituents may face low costs from no-agreement, and others high costs, and the former will be more skeptical of Level I agreements than the latter. Members of two-wage-earner families should be readier to strike, for example, than sole breadwinners, and small-town barbers should be more isolationist than international bankers. In this sense, some constituents may offer either generic opposition to, or generic support for, Level I agreements, more or less independently of the specific content of the agreement, although naturally other constituents' decisions about ratification will be closely conditioned on the specifics. The size of the win-set (and thus the negotiating

44. Thomas Romer and Howard Rosenthal, "Political Resource Allocation, Controlled Agendas, and the Status Quo," *Public Choice* 33 (no. 4, 1978), pp. 27–44.

45. In more formal treatments, the no-agreement outcome is called the "reversion point." A given constituent's evaluation of no-agreement corresponds to what Raiffa terms a seller's "walk-away price," that is, the price below which he would prefer "no-deal." (Raiffa, *Art and Science of Negotiation*.) No-agreement is equivalent to what Snyder and Diesing term "breakdown," or the expected cost of war. (Snyder and Diesing, *Conflict Among Nations*.)

room of the Level I negotiator) depends on the relative size of the "isolationist" forces (who oppose international cooperation in general) and the "internationalists" (who offer "all-purpose" support). All-purpose support for international agreements is probably greater in smaller, more dependent countries with more open economies, as compared to more self-sufficient countries, like the United States, for most of whose citizens the costs of no-agreement are generally lower. *Ceteris paribus,* more self-sufficient states with smaller win-sets should make fewer international agreements and drive harder bargains in those that they do make.

In some cases, evaluation of no-agreement may be the *only* significant disagreement among the Level II constituents, because their interests are relatively homogeneous. For example, if oil imports are to be limited by an agreement among the consuming nations—the sort of accord sought at the Tokyo summit of 1979, for example—then presumably every constituent would prefer to maximize his nation's share of the available supply, although some constituents may be more reluctant than others to push too hard, for fear of losing the agreement entirely. Similarly, in most wage negotiations, the interests of constituents (either workers or shareholders) are relatively homogeneous, and the most significant cleavage within the Level II constituencies is likely to be between "hawks" and "doves," depending on their willingness to risk a strike. (Walton and McKersie refer to these as "boundary" conflicts, in which the negotiator is caught between his constituency and the external organization.) Other international examples in which domestic interests are relatively homogeneous except for the evaluation of no-agreement might include the SALT talks, the Panama Canal Treaty negotiations, and the Arab-Israeli conflict. A negotiator is unlikely to face criticism at home that a proposed agreement reduces the opponents' arms too much, offers too little compensation for foreign concessions, or contains too few security guarantees for the other side, although in each case opinions may differ on how much to risk a negotiating deadlock in order to achieve these objectives.

The distinctive nature of such "homogeneous" issues is thrown into sharp relief by contrasting them to cases in which constituents' preferences are more heterogeneous, so that any Level I agreement bears unevenly on them. Thus, an internationally coordinated reflation may encounter domestic opposition *both* from those who think it goes too far (bankers, for example) *and* from those who think it does not go far enough (unions, for example). In 1919, some Americans opposed the Versailles Treaty because it was too harsh on the defeated powers and others because it was too lenient.[46] Such patterns are even more common, as we shall shortly see, where the negotiation involves multiple issues, such as an arms agreement that involves tradeoffs between seaborne and airborne weapons, or a labor agreement that

46. Thomas A. Bailey, *Woodrow Wilson and the Great Betrayal* (New York: Macmillan, 1945), pp. 16–37.

involves tradeoffs between take-home pay and pensions. (Walton and McKersie term these "factional" conflicts, because the negotiator is caught between contending factions within his own organization.)

The problems facing Level I negotiators dealing with a *homogeneous* (or "boundary") conflict are quite different from those facing negotiators dealing with a *heterogeneous* (or "factional") conflict. In the former case, the more the negotiator can win at Level I—the higher his national oil allocation, the deeper the cuts in Soviet throw-weight, the lower the rent he promises for the Canal, and so one—the better his odds of winning ratification. In such cases, the negotiator may use the implicit threat from his own hawks to maximize his gains (or minimize his losses) at Level I, as Carter and Vance did in dealing with the Panamanians. Glancing over his shoulder at Level II, the negotiator's main problem in a homogeneous conflict is to manage the discrepancy between his constituents' expectations and the negotiable outcome. Neither negotiator is likely to find much sympathy for the enemy's demands among his own constituents, nor much support for his constituents' positions in the enemy camp. The effect of domestic division, embodied in hard-line opposition from hawks, is to raise the risk of involuntary defection and thus to impede agreement at Level I. The common belief that domestic politics is inimical to international cooperation no doubt derives from such cases.

The task of a negotiator grappling instead with a heterogeneous conflict is more complicated, but potentially more interesting. Seeking to maximize the chances of ratification, he cannot follow a simple "the more, the better" rule of thumb; imposing more severe reparations on the Germans in 1919 would have gained some votes at Level II but lost others, as would hastening the decontrol of domestic oil prices in 1978. In some cases, these lines of cleavage within the Level II constituencies will cut across the Level I division, and the Level I negotiator may find silent allies at his opponent's domestic table. German labor unions might welcome foreign pressure on their own government to adopt a more expansive fiscal policy, and Italian bankers might welcome international demands for a more austere Italian monetary policy. Thus transnational alignments may emerge, tacit or explicit, in which domestic interests pressure their respective governments to adopt mutually supportive policies. This is, of course, my interpretation of the 1978 Bonn summit accord.

In such cases, domestic divisions may actually improve the prospects for international cooperation. For example, consider two different distributions of constituents' preferences as between three alternatives: A, B, and no-agreement. If 45 percent of the constituents rank these A > no-agreement > B, 45 percent rank them B > no-agreement > A, and 10 percent rank them B > A > no-agreement, then both A and B are in the win-set, even though B would win in a simple Level-II-only game. On the other hand, if 90 percent rank the alternatives A > no-agreement > B, while 10 percent still rank them B > A > no-agreement, then only A is in the win-set. In this sense, a government that is internally divided is more likely to be able to strike a deal internationally than one that is firmly committed to a single policy.[47] Conversely, to impose binding ex ante instructions on the negotiators in such a case might exclude some Level I outcomes that would, in fact, be ratifiable in both nations.[48]

Thus far we have implicitly assumed that all eligible constituents will participate in the ratification process. In fact, however, participation rates vary across groups and across issues, and this variation often has implications for the size of the win-set. For example, when the costs and/or benefits of a proposed agreement are relatively concentrated, it is reasonable to expect that those constituents whose interests are most affected will exert special influence on the ratification process.[49] One reason why Level II games are more important for trade negotiations than in monetary matters is that the "abstention rate" is higher on international monetary issues than on trade issues.[50]

The composition of the active Level II constituency (and hence the character of the win-set) also varies with the politicization of the issue. Politicization often activates groups who are less worried about the costs of no-agreement, thus reducing the effective win-set. For example, politicization of the Panama Canal issue seems to have reduced the negotiating flexibility on both sides of the diplomatic table.[51] This is one reason why most professional diplomats emphasize the value of secrecy to successful negotiations. However, Woodrow Wilson's transcontinental tour in 1919 reflected the opposite calculation, namely, that by expanding the active constituency he could ensure ratification of the Versailles Treaty, although in the end this strategy proved fruitless.[52]

Another important restriction of our discussion thus far has been the

47. Raiffa notes that "the more diffuse the positions are within each side, the easier it might be to achieve external agreement." (Raiffa, *Art and Science of Negotiation,* p. 12.) For the conventional view, by contrast, that domestic unity is generally a precondition for international agreement, see Michael Artis and Sylvia Ostry, *International Economic Policy Coordination,* Chatham House Papers: 30 (London: Routledge & Kegan Paul, 1986), pp. 75–76.

48. "Meaningful consultation with other nations becomes very difficult when the internal process of decision-making already has some of the characteristics of compacts between quasi-sovereign entities. There is an increasing reluctance to hazard a hard-won domestic consensus in an international forum." Henry A. Kissinger, "Domestic Structure and Foreign Policy," in James N. Rosenau, ed., *International Politics and Foreign Policy* (New York: Free Press, 1969), p. 266.

49. See James Q. Wilson, *Political Organization* (New York: Basic Books, 1975) on how the politics of an issue are affected by whether the costs and the benefits are concentrated or diffuse.

50. Another factor fostering abstention is the greater complexity and opacity of monetary issues; as Gilbert R. Winham ("Complexity in International Negotiation," in Daniel Druckman, ed., *Negotiations: A Social-Psychological Perspective* [Beverly Hills: Sage, 1977], p. 363) observes, "complexity can strengthen the hand of a negotiator vis-à-vis the organization he represents."

51. Habeeb and Zartman, *Panama Canal Negotiations.*

52. Bailey, *Wilson and the Great Betrayal.*

assumption that the negotiations involve only one issue. Relaxing this assumption has powerful consequences for the play at both levels.[53] Various groups at Level II are likely to have quite different preferences on the several issues involved in a multi-issue negotiation. As a general rule, the group with the greatest interest in a specific issue is also likely to hold the most extreme position on that issue. In the Law of the Sea negotiations, for example, the Defense Department felt most strongly about sea-lanes, the Department of the Interior about sea-bed mining rights, and so on.[54] If each group is allowed to fix the Level I negotiating position for "its" issue, the resulting package is almost sure to be "non-negotiable" (that is, non-ratifiable in opposing capitals).[55]

Thus, the chief negotiator is faced with tradeoffs across different issues: how much to yield on mining rights in order to get sea-lane protection, how much to yield on citrus exports to get a better deal on beef, and so on. The implication of these tradeoffs for the respective win-sets can be analyzed in terms of iso-vote or "political indifference" curves. This technique is analogous to conventional indifference curve analysis, except that the operational measure is vote loss, not utility loss. Figure 2 provides an illustrative Edgeworth box analysis.[56] The most-preferred outcome for A (the outcome which wins unanimous approval from both the beef industry and the citrus industry) is the upper right-hand corner (A_M), and each curve concave to point A_M represents the locus of all possible tradeoffs between the interests of ranchers and farmers, such that the net vote in favor of ratification at A's Level II is constant. The bold contour A_1-A_2 represents the minimal vote necessary for ratification by A, and the wedge-shaped area northeast of A_1-A_2 represents A's win-set. Similarly, B_1-B_2 represents the outcomes that are minimally ratifiable by B, and the lens-shaped area between A_1-A_2 and B_1-B_2 represents the set of feasible agreements. Although additional subtleties (such as the nature of the "contract curve") might be extracted from this sort of analysis, the central point is simple: the possibility of package deals opens up a rich array of strategic alternatives for negotiators in a two-level game.

One kind of issue linkage is absolutely crucial to understanding how domestic and international politics can become entangled.[57] Suppose that a majority of constituents at Level II oppose a given policy (say, oil price

53. I am grateful to Ernst B. Haas and Robert O. Keohane for helpful advice on this point.
54. Ann L. Hollick, *U.S. Foreign Policy and the Law of the Sea* (Princeton: Princeton University Press, 1981), especially pp. 208–37, and James K. Sebenius, *Negotiating the Law of the Sea* (Cambridge, Mass.: Harvard University Press, 1984), especially pp. 74–78.
55. Raiffa, *Art and Science of Negotiation*, p. 175.
56. I am indebted to Lisa Martin and Kenneth Shepsle for suggesting this approach, although they are not responsible for my application of it. Note that this construction assumes that each issue, taken individually, is a "homogeneous" type, not a "heterogeneous" type. Constructing iso-vote curves for heterogeneous-type issues is more complicated.
57. I am grateful to Henry Brady for clarifying this point for me.

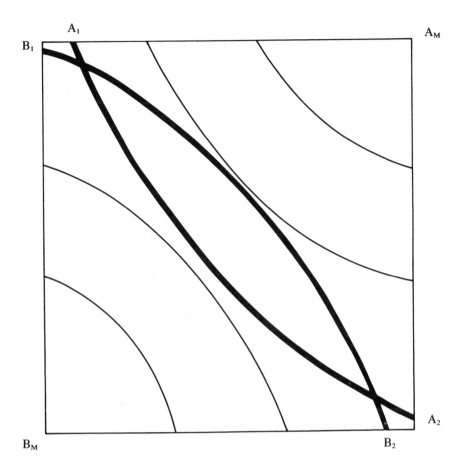

FIGURE 2. *Political indifference curves for two-issue negotiation*

decontrol), but that some members of that majority would be willing to switch their vote on that issue in return for more jobs (say, in export industries). If bargaining is limited to Level II, that tradeoff is not technically feasible, but if the chief negotiator can broker an international deal that delivers more jobs (say, via faster growth abroad), he can, in effect, overturn the initial outcome at the domestic table. Such a transnational issue linkage was a crucial element in the 1978 Bonn accord.

Note that this strategy works not by changing the preferences of any domestic constituents, but rather by creating a policy option (such as faster export growth) that was previously beyond domestic control. Hence, I refer to this type of issue linkage at Level I that alters the feasible outcomes at Level II as *synergistic linkage*. For example, "in the Tokyo Round . . . nations used negotiation to achieve internal reform in situations where constituency pressures would otherwise prevent action without the pressure (and tradeoff benefits) that an external partner could provide.''[58] Economic interdependence multiplies the opportunities for altering domestic coalitions (and thus policy outcomes) by expanding the set of feasible alternatives in this way—in effect, creating political entanglements across national boundaries. Thus, we should expect synergistic linkage (which is, by definition, explicable only in terms of two-level analysis) to become more frequent as interdependence grows.

2. The size of the win-set depends on the Level II political institutions.

Ratification procedures clearly affect the size of the win-set. For example, if a two-thirds vote is required for ratification, the win-set will almost certainly be smaller than if only a simple majority is required. As one experienced observer has written: "Under the Constitution, thirty-four of the one hundred senators can block ratification of any treaty. This is an unhappy and unique feature of our democracy. Because of the effective veto power of a small group, many worthy agreements have been rejected, and many treaties are never considered for ratification."[59] As noted earlier, the U.S. separation of powers imposes a tighter constraint on the American win-set than is true in many other countries. This increases the bargaining power of American negotiators, but it also reduces the scope for international cooperation. It raises the odds for involuntary defection and makes potential partners warier about dealing with the Americans.

The Trade Expansion Act of 1974 modified U.S. ratification procedures in an effort to reduce the likelihood of congressional tampering with the final deal and hence to reassure America's negotiating partners. After the American Selling Price fiasco, it was widely recognized that piecemeal congressional ratification of any new agreement would inhibit international negotiation. Hence, the 1974 Act guaranteed a straight up-or-down vote in Congress. However, to satisfy congressional sensitivities, an elaborate system of private-sector committees was established to improve communication between the Level I negotiators and their Level II constituents, in effect coopting the interest groups by exposing them directly to the implications of their demands.[60] Precisely this tactic is described in the labor-management case by Walton and McKersie: "Instead of taking responsibility for directly persuading the principals [Level II constituents] to reduce their expectations, [the Level I negotiator] structures the situation so that they (or their more immediate representatives) will persuade themselves."[61]

58. Gilbert R. Winham, "The Relevance of Clausewitz to a Theory of International Negotiation," prepared for delivery at the 1987 annual meeting of the American Political Science Association.

59. Jimmy Carter, *Keeping Faith: Memoirs of a President* (New York: Bantam Books, 1982), p. 225.

60. Winham (see note 37); Twiggs, *The Tokyo Round.*

61. Walton and McKersie, *Behavioral Theory of Labor Organizations,* p. 321.

Not all significant ratification practices are formalized; for example, the Japanese propensity for seeking the broadest possible domestic consensus before acting constricts the Japanese win-set, as contrasted with majoritarian political cultures. Other domestic political practices, too, can affect the size of the win-set. Strong discipline within the governing party, for example, increases the win-set by widening the range of agreements for which the Level I negotiator can expect to receive backing. For example, in the 1986 House-Senate conference committee on tax reform, the final bill was closer to the Senate version, despite (or rather, *because of*) Congressman Rosten-kowski's greater control of his delegation, which increased the House win-set. Conversely, a weakening of party discipline across the major Western nations would, *ceteris paribus*, reduce the scope for international cooperation.

The recent discussion of "state strength" and "state autonomy" is relevant here. The greater the autonomy of central decision-makers from their Level II constituents, the larger their win-set and thus the greater the likelihood of achieving international agreement. For example, central bank insulation from domestic political pressures in effect increases the win-set and thus the odds for international monetary cooperation; recent proposals for an enhanced role for central bankers in international policy coordination rest on this point.[62] However, two-level analysis also implies that, *ceteris paribus*, the stronger a state is in terms of autonomy from domestic pressures, the weaker its relative bargaining position internationally. For example, diplomats representing an entrenched dictatorship are less able than representatives of a democracy to claim credibly that domestic pressures preclude some disadvantageous deal.[63] This is yet another facet of the disconcerting ambiguity of the notion of "state strength."

For simplicity of exposition, my argument is phrased throughout in terms of only two levels. However, many institutional arrangements require several levels of ratification, thus multiplying the complexity (but perhaps also the importance) of win-set analysis. Consider, for example, negotiations between the United States and the European Community over agricultural trade. According to the Treaty of Rome, modifications of the Common Agricultural Policy require unanimous ratification by the Council of Ministers, representing each of the member states. In turn, each of those governments must, in effect, win ratification for its decision within its own national arena, and in coalition governments, that process might also require ratification within each of the parties. Similarly, on the American side, ratification would (informally, at least) necessitate support from most, if not all, of the major agricultural organizations, and within those organizations, further ratification by key interests and regions might be required. At each stage, cleavage patterns, issue linkages, ratification procedures, side-payments, negotiator

---

62. Artis and Ostry, *International Economic Policy Coordination*. Of course, whether this is desirable in terms of democratic values is quite another matter.

63. Schelling, *Strategy of Conflict*, p. 28.

strategies, and so on would need to be considered. At some point in this analytic regress the complexity of further decomposition would outweigh the advantages, but the example illustrates the need for careful thought about the logic of multiple-level games.

3. The size of the win-set depends on the strategies of the Level I negotiators.

Each Level I negotiator has an unequivocal interest in maximizing the other side's win-set, but with respect to his own win-set, his motives are mixed. The larger his win-set, the more easily he can conclude an agreement, but also the weaker his bargaining position vis-à-vis the other negotiator. This fact often poses a tactical dilemma. For example, one effective way to demonstrate commitment to a given position in Level I bargaining is to rally support from one's constituents (for example, holding a strike vote, talking about a "missile gap," or denouncing "unfair trading practices" abroad). On the other hand, such tactics may have irreversible effects on constituents' attitudes, hampering subsequent ratification of a compromise agreement.[64] Conversely, preliminary consultations at home, aimed at "softening up" one's constituents in anticipation of a ratification struggle, can undercut a negotiator's ability to project an implacable image abroad.

Nevertheless, disregarding these dilemmas for the moment and assuming that a negotiator wishes to expand his win-set in order to encourage ratification of an agreement, he may exploit both conventional side-payments and generic "good will." The use of side-payments to attract marginal supporters is, of course, quite familiar in game theory, as well as in practical politics. For example, the Carter White House offered many inducements (such as public works projects) to help persuade wavering Senators to ratify the Panama Canal Treaty.[65] In a two-level game the side-payments may come from unrelated domestic sources, as in this case, or they may be received as part of the international negotiation.

The role of side-payments in international negotiations is well known. However, the two-level approach emphasizes that the value of an international side-payment should be calculated in terms of its marginal contribution to the likelihood of ratification, rather than in terms of its overall value to the recipient nation. What counts at Level II is not total national costs and benefits, but their *incidence, relative to existing coalitions and proto-coalitions*. An across-the-board trade concession (or still worse, a concession on a product of interest to a committed free-trade congressman) is less effective than a concession (even one of lesser intrinsic value) that tips the balance with a swing voter. Conversely, trade retaliation should be targeted,

---

64. Walton and McKersie, *Behavioral Theory of Labor Organizations*, p. 345.
65. Carter, *Keeping Faith*, p. 172. See also Raiffa, *Art and Science of Negotiation*, p. 183.

neither at free-traders nor at confirmed protectionists, but at the uncommitted.

An experienced negotiator familiar with the respective domestic tables should be able to maximize the cost-effectiveness (to him and his constituents) of the concessions that he must make to ensure ratification abroad, as well as the cost-effectiveness of his own demands and threats, by targeting his initiatives with an eye to their Level II incidence, both at home and abroad. In this endeavor Level I negotiators are often in collusion, since each has an interest in helping the other to get the final deal ratified. In effect, they are moving jointly towards points of tangency between their respective political indifference curves. The empirical frequency of such targeting in trade negotiations and trade wars, as well as in other international negotiations, would be a crucial test of the relative merits of conventional unitary-actor analysis and the two-level approach proposed here.[66]

In addition to the use of specific side-payments, a chief negotiator whose political standing at home is high can more easily win ratification of his foreign initiatives. Although generic good will cannot guarantee ratification, as Woodrow Wilson discovered, it is useful in expanding the win-set and thus fostering Level I agreement, for it constitutes a kind of "all-purpose glue" for his supporting coalition. Walton and McKersie cite members of the United Auto Workers who, speaking of their revered leader, Walter Reuther, said, "I don't understand or agree with this profit-sharing idea, but if the Red Head wants it, I will go along."[67] The Yugoslav negotiator in the Trieste dispute later discounted the difficulty of persuading irredentist Slovenes to accept the agreement, since "the government [i.e., Tito] can always influence public opinion if it wants to."[68]

Note that each Level I negotiator has a strong interest in the popularity of his opposite number, since Party A's popularity increases the size of his win-set, and thus increases both the odds of success and the relative bargaining leverage of Party B. Thus, negotiators should normally be expected to try to reinforce one another's standing with their respective constituents.

---

66. The strategic significance of targeting at Level II is illustrated in John Conybeare, "Trade Wars: A Comparative Study of Anglo-Hanse, Franco-Italian, and Hawley-Smoot Conflicts," *World Politics* 38 (October 1985), p. 157: Retaliation in the Anglo-Hanse trade wars did not have the intended deterrent effect, because it was not (and perhaps could not have been) targeted at the crucial members of the opposing Level II coalition. Compare Snyder and Diesing, *Conflict Among Nations*, p. 552: "If one faces a coercive opponent, but the opponent's majority coalition includes a few wavering members inclined to compromise, a compromise proposal that suits their views may cause their defection and the formation of a different majority coalition. Or if the opponent's strategy is accommodative, based on a tenuous soft-line coalition, one knows that care is required in implementing one's own coercive stretegy to avoid the opposite kind of shift in the other state."

67. Walton and McKersie, *Behavioral Theory of Labor Negotiations*, p. 319.

68. Vladimir Velebit, in Campbell, *Trieste 1954*, p. 97. As noted earlier, our discussion here assumes that the Level I negotiator wishes to reach a ratifiable agreement; in cases (alluded to later) when the negotiator's own preferences are more hard-line than his constituents, his domestic popularity might allow him to resist Level I agreements.

Partly for this reason and partly because of media attention, participation on the world stage normally gives a head of government a special advantage vis-à-vis his or her domestic opposition. Thus, although international policy coordination is hampered by high transaction costs, heads of government may also reap what we might term "transaction benefits." Indeed, the recent evolution of Western summitry, which has placed greater emphasis on publicity than on substance, seems designed to appropriate these "transaction benefits" without actually seeking the sort of agreements that might entail transaction costs.[69]

Higher status negotiators are likely to dispose of more side-payments and more "good will" at home, and hence foreigners prefer to negotiate with a head of government than with a lower official. In purely distributive terms, a nation might have a bargaining advantage if its chief negotiator were a mere clerk. Diplomats are acting rationally, not merely symbolically, when they refuse to negotiate with a counterpart of inferior rank. America's negotiating partners have reason for concern whenever the American president is domestically weakened.

Uncertainty and bargaining tactics

Level I negotiators are often badly misinformed about Level II politics, particularly on the opposing side. In 1978, the Bonn negotiators were usually wrong in their assessments of domestic politics abroad; for example, most American officials did not appreciate the complex domestic game that Chancellor Schmidt was playing over the issue of German reflation. Similarly, Snyder and Diesing report that "decision makers in our cases only occasionally attempted such assessments, and when they tried they did pretty miserably. . . . Governments generally do not do well in analyzing each other's internal politics in crises [and, I would add, in normal times], and indeed it is inherently difficult."[70] Relaxing the assumption of perfect information to allow for uncertainty has many implications for our understanding of two-level games. Let me illustrate a few of these implications.

Uncertainty about the size of a win-set can be both a bargaining device and a stumbling block in two-level negotiation. In purely distributive Level I bargaining, negotiators have an incentive to understate their own win-sets. Since each negotiator is likely to know more about his own Level II than his opponent does, the claim has some plausibility. This is akin to a tactic

---

69. Transaction benefits may be enhanced if a substantive agreement is reached, although sometimes leaders can benefit domestically by loudly rejecting a proffered international deal.

70. Snyder and Diesing, *Conflict Among Nations*, pp. 516, 522–23. Analogous misperceptions in Anglo-American diplomacy are the focus of Richard E. Neustadt, *Alliance Politics* (New York: Columbia University Press, 1970).

that Snyder and Diesing describe, when negotiators seek to exploit divisions within their own government by saying, in effect, "You'd better make a deal with me, because the alternative to me is even worse."[71]

On the other hand, uncertainty about the opponent's win-set increases one's concern about the risk of involuntary defection. Deals can only be struck if each negotiator is convinced that the proposed deal lies within his opposite number's win-set and thus will be ratified. Uncertainty about party A's ratification lowers the expected value of the agreement to party B, and thus party B will demand more generous side-payments from party A than would be needed under conditions of certainty. In fact, party B has an incentive to feign doubt about party A's ability to deliver, precisely in order to extract a more generous offer.[72]

Thus, a utility-maximizing negotiator must seek to convince his opposite number that his own win-set is "kinky," that is, that the proposed deal is certain to be ratified, but that a deal slightly more favorable to the opponent is unlikely to be ratified. For example, on the energy issue in 1978, by sending Senator Byrd on a personal mission to Bonn before the summit and then by discussing his political problems in a length tête-à-tête with the chancellor, Carter sought successfully to convince Schmidt that immediate decontrol was politically impossible, but that decontrol by 1981 was politically doable. Kinky win-sets may be more credible if they pivot on what Schelling calls a "prominent" solution, such as a 50–50 split, for such outcomes may be distinctly more "saleable" at home. Another relevant tactic is for the negotiator actually to submit a trial agreement for ratification, in order to demonstrate that it is not in his win-set.

Uncertainty about the contours of the respective "political indifference curves" thus has strategic uses. On the other hand, when the negotiators are seeking novel packages that might improve both sides' positions, misrepresentation of one's win-set can be counterproductive. Creative solutions that expand the scope for joint gain and improve the odds of ratification are likely to require fairly accurate information about constituents' preferences and points of special neuralgia. The analysis of two-level games offers many illustrations of Zartman's observation that all negotiation involves "the controlled exchange of partial information."[73]

71. Synder and Diesing, *Conflict Among Nations*, p. 517.

72. I am grateful to Robert O. Keohane for pointing out the impact of uncertainty on the expected value of proposals.

73. I. William Zartman, *The 50% Solution* (Garden City, N.J.: Anchor Books, 1976), p. 14. The present analysis assumes that constituents are myopic about the other side's Level II, an assumption that is not unrealistic empirically. However, a fully informed constituent would consider the preferences of key players on the other side, for if the current proposal lies well within the other side's win-set, then it would be rational for the constituent to vote against it, hoping for a second-round proposal that was more favorable to him and still ratifiable abroad; this might be a reasonable interpretation of Senator Lodge's position in 1919 (Bailey, *Wilson and the Great Betrayal*). Consideration of such strategic voting at Level II is beyond the scope of this article.

Restructuring and reverberation

Formally speaking, game-theoretic analysis requires that the structure of issues and payoffs be specified in advance. In reality, however, much of what happens in any bargaining situation involves attempts by the players to restructure the game and to alter one another's perceptions of the costs of no-agreement and the benefits of proposed agreements. Such tactics are more difficult in two-level games than in conventional negotiations, because it is harder to reach constituents on the other side with persuasive messages. Nevertheless, governments do seek to expand one another's win-sets. Much ambassadorial activity—wooing opinion leaders, establishing contact with opposition parties, offering foreign aid to a friendly, but unstable government, and so on—has precisely this function. When Japanese officials visit Capitol Hill, or British diplomats lobby Irish-American leaders, they are seeking to relax domestic constraints that might otherwise prevent the administration from cooperating with their governments.

Another illuminating example of actions by a negotiator at the opposing Level II to improve the odds of ratification occurred during the 1977 negotiations between the International Monetary Fund and the Italian government. Initial IMF demands for austerity triggered strong opposition from the unions and left-wing parties. Although the IMF's bargaining position at Level I appeared strong, the Fund's negotiator sought to achieve a broader consensus within Italy in support of an agreement, in order to forestall involuntary defection. Accordingly, after direct consultations with the unions and leftist leaders, the IMF restructured its proposal to focus on long-term investment and economic recovery (incidentally, an interesting example of targeting), without backing off from its short-term demands. Ironically, the initial Communist support for this revised agreement subsequently collapsed because of conflicts between moderate and doctrinaire factions within the party, illustrating the importance of multilevel analysis.[74]

In some instances, perhaps even unintentionally, international pressures "reverberate" within domestic politics, tipping the domestic balance and thus influencing the international negotiations. Exactly this kind of reverberation characterized the 1978 summit negotiations. Dieter Hiss, the German sherpa and one of those who believed that a stimulus program was in Germany's own interest, later wrote that summits change national policy

only insofar as they mobilize and/or change public opinion and the attitude of political groups. . . . Often that is enough, if the balance of

---

74. John R. Hillman, "The Mutual Influence of Italian Domestic Politics and the International Monetary Fund," *The Fletcher Forum* 4 (Winter 1980), pp. 1–22. Luigi Spaventa, "Two Letters of Intent: External Crises and Stabilization Policy, Italy, 1973–77," in John Williamson, ed., *IMF Conditionality* (Washington, D.C.: Institute for International Economics, 1983), pp. 441–73, argues that the unions and the Communists actually favored the austerity measures, but found the IMF demands helpful in dealing with their own internal Level II constituents.

opinion is shifted, providing a bare majority for the previously stymied actions of a strong minority. . . . No country violates its own interests, but certainly the definition of its interests can change through a summit with its possible tradeoffs and give-and-take.[75]

From the point of view of orthodox social-choice theory, reverberation is problematic, for it implies a certain interconnectedness among the utility functions of independent actors, albeit across different levels of the game. Two rationales may be offered to explain reverberation among utility-maximizing egoists. First, in a complex, interdependent, but often unfriendly world, offending foreigners may be costly in the long run. "To get along, go along" may be a rational maxim. This rationale is likely to be more common the more dependent (or interdependent) a nation, and it is likely to be more persuasive to Level II actors who are more exposed internationally, such as multinational corporations and international banks.

A second rationale takes into account cognitive factors and uncertainty. It would be a mistake for political scientists to mimic most economists' disregard for the suasive element in negotiations.[76] Given the pervasive uncertainty that surrounds many international issues, messages from abroad can change minds, move the undecided, and hearten those in the domestic minority. As one reluctant German latecomer to the "locomotive" cause in 1978 explained his conversion, "In the end, even the Bank for International Settlements [the cautious Basle organization of central bankers] supported the idea of coordinated relation." Similarly, an enthusiastic advocate of the program welcomed the international pressure as providing a useful "tailwind" in German domestic politics.

Suasive reverberation is more likely among countries with close relations and is probably more frequent in economic than in political–military negotiations. Communiqués from the Western summits are often cited by participants to domestic audiences as a way of legitimizing their policies. After one such statement by Chancellor Schmidt, one of his aides privately characterized the argument as "not intellectually valid, but politically useful." Conversely, it is widely believed by summit participants that a declaration contrary to a government's current policy could be used profitably by its opponents. Recent congressional proposals to ensure greater domestic publicity for international commentary on national economic policies (including hitherto confidential IMF recommendations) turn on the idea that reverberation might increase international cooperation.[77]

75. Dieter Hiss, "Weltwirtschaftsgipfel: Betrachtungen eines Insiders [World Economic Summit: Observations of an Insider]," in Joachim Frohn and Reiner Staeglin, eds., *Empirische Wirtschaftsforschung* (Berlin: Duncker and Humblot, 1980), pp. 286–87.

76. On cognitive and communications explanations of international cooperation, see, for example, Ernst B. Haas, "Why Collaborate? Issue-Linkage and International Regimes," *World Politics* 32 (April 1980), pp 357–405; Richard N. Cooper, "International Cooperation in Public Health as a Prologue to Macroeconomic Cooperation," *Brookings Discussion Papers in International Economics* 44 (Washington, D.C.: Brookings Institution, 1986); and Zartman, *50% Solution*, especially Part 4.

77. Henning, *Macroeconomic Diplomacy in the 1980s*, pp. 62–63.

Reverberation as discussed thus far implies that international pressure expands the domestic win-set and facilitates agreement. However, reverberation can also be negative, in the sense that foreign pressure may create a domestic backlash. Negative reverberation is probably less common empirically than positive reverberation, simply because foreigners are likely to forgo public pressure if it is recognized to be counterproductive. Cognitive balance theory suggests that international pressure is more likely to reverberate negatively if its source is generally viewed by domestic audiences as an adversary rather than an ally. Nevertheless, predicting the precise effect of foreign pressure is admittedly difficult, although empirically, reverberation seems to occur frequently in two-level games.

The phenomenon of reverberation (along with synergistic issue linkage of the sort described earlier) precludes one attractive short-cut to modeling two-level games. If national preferences were exogenous from the point of view of international relations, then the domestic political game could be molded separately, and the "outputs" from that game could be used as the "inputs" to the international game.[78] The division of labor between comparative politics and international relations could continue, though a few curious observers might wish to keep track of the play on both tables. But if international pressures reverberate within domestic politics, or if issues can be linked synergistically, then domestic outcomes are not exogenous, and the two levels cannot be modeled independently.

The role of the chief negotiator

In the stylized model of two-level negotiations outlined here, the chief negotiator is the only formal link between Level I and Level II. Thus far, I have assumed that the chief negotiator has no independent policy views, but acts merely as an honest broker, or rather as an agent on behalf of his constituents. That assumption powerfully simplifies the analysis of two-level games. However, as principal-agent theory reminds us, this assumption is unrealistic.[79] Empirically, the preferences of the chief negotiator may well diverge from those of his constituents. Two-level negotiations are costly and

78. This is the approach used to analyze the Anglo–Chinese negotiations over Hong Kong in Bruce Bueno de Mesquita, David Newman, and Alvin Rabushka, *Forecasting Political Events: The Future of Hong Kong* (New Haven: Yale University Press, 1985).

79. For overviews of this literature, see Terry M. Moe, "The New Economics of Organization," *American Journal of Political Science* 28 (November 1984), pp. 739–77; John W. Pratt and Richard J. Zeckhauser, eds., *Principals and Agents: The Structure of Business* (Boston, Mass.: Harvard Business School Press, 1985); and Barry M. Mitnick, "The Theory of Agency and Organizational Analysis," prepared for delivery at the 1986 annual meeting of the American Political Science Association. This literature is only indirectly relevant to our concerns here, for it has not yet adequately addressed the problems posed by multiple principals (or constituents, in our terms). For one highly formal approach to the problem of multiple principals, see R. Douglas Bernheim and Michael D. Whinston, "Common Agency," *Econometrica* 54 (July 1986), pp. 923–42.

risky for the chief negotiator, and they often interfere with his other priorities, so it is reasonable to ask what is in it for him.

The motives of the chief negotiator include:

1. Enhancing his standing in the Level II game by increasing his political resources or by minimizing potential losses. For example, a head of government may seek the popularity that he expects to accrue to him if he concludes a successful international agreement, or he may anticipate that the results of the agreement (for example, faster growth or lower defense spending) will be politically rewarding.

2. Shifting the balance of power at Level II in favor of domestic policies that he prefers for exogenous reasons. International negotiations sometimes enable government leaders to do what they privately wish to do, but are powerless to do domestically. Beyond the now-familiar 1978 case, this pattern characterizes many stabilization programs that are (misleadingly) said to be "imposed" by the IMF. For example, in the 1974 and 1977 negotiations between Italy and the IMF, domestic conservative forces exploited IMF pressure to facilitate policy moves that were otherwise infeasible internally.[80]

3. To pursue his own conception of the national interest in the international context. This seems the best explanation of Jimmy Carter's prodigious efforts on behalf of the Panama Canal Treaty, as well as of Woodrow Wilson's ultimately fatal commitment to the Versailles Treaty.

It is reasonable to presume, at least in the international case of two-level bargaining, that the chief negotiator will normally give primacy to his domestic calculus, if a choice must be made, not least because his own incumbency often depends on his standing at Level II. Hence, he is more likely to present an international agreement for ratification, the less of his own political capital he expects to have to invest to win approval, and the greater the likely political returns from a ratified agreement.

This expanded conception of the role of the chief negotiator implies that he has, in effect, a veto over possible agreements. Even if a proposed deal lies within his Level II win-set, that deal is unlikely to be struck if he opposes it.[81] Since this proviso applies on both sides of the Level I table, the actual international bargaining set may be narrower—perhaps much narrower—than the overlap between the Level II win-sets. Empirically, this additional constraint is often crucial to the outcome of two-level games. One momentous example is the fate of the Versailles Treaty. The best evidence suggests, first, that perhaps 80 percent of the American public *and* of the Senate in 1919 favored ratification of the treaty, if certain reservations were attached, and second, that those reservations were acceptable to the other key sig-

---

80. Hillman, "Mutual Influence," and Spaventa, "Two Letters of Intent."

81. This power of the chief negotiator is analogous to what Shepsle and Weingast term the "penultimate" or "ex post veto" power of the members of a Senate-House conference committee. (Shepsle and Weingast, "Institutional Foundations of Committee Power.")

natories, especially Britain and France. In effect, it was Wilson himself who vetoed this otherwise ratifiable package, telling the dismayed French Ambassador, "I shall consent to nothing."[82]

Yet another constraint on successful two-level negotiation derives from the leader's existing domestic coalition. Any political entrepreneur has a fixed investment in a particular pattern of policy positions and a particular supporting coalition. If a proposed international deal threatens that investment, or if ratification would require him to construct a different coalition, the chief negotiator will be reluctant to endorse it, even if (judged abstractly) it could be ratified. Politicians may be willing to risk a few of their normal supporters in the cause of ratifying an international agreement, but the greater the potential loss, the greater their reluctance.

In effect, the fixed costs of coalition-building thus imply this constraint on the win-set: How great a realignment of prevailing coalitions at Level II would be required to ratify a particular proposal? For example, a trade deal may expand export opportunities for Silicon Valley, but harm Aliquippa. This is fine for a chief negotiator (for example, Reagan?) who can easily add Northern California yuppies to his support coalition and who has no hope of winning Aliquippa steelworkers anyhow. But a different chief negotiator with a different support coalition (for example, Mondale?) might find it costly or even impossible to convert the gains from the same agreement into politically usable form. Similarly, in the 1978 "neutron bomb" negotiations between Bonn and Washington, "asking the United States to deploy [these weapons] in West Germany might have been possible for a Christian Democratic Government; for a Social Democratic government, it was nearly impossible."[83] Under such circumstances, simple "median-voter" models of domestic influences on foreign policy may be quite misleading.

Relaxing the assumption that the chief negotiator is merely an honest broker, negotiating on behalf of his constituents, opens the possibility that the constituents may be more eager for an agreement (or more worried about "no-agreement") than he is. Empirical instances are not hard to find: in early 1987, European publics were readier to accept Gorbachev's "double-zero" arms control proposal than European leaders, just as in the early 1970s the American public (or at least the politically active public) was more eager for a negotiated end to the Vietnam War than was the Nixon administration. As a rule, the negotiator retains a veto over any proposed agreement in such cases. However, if the negotiator's own domestic standing (or indeed, his incumbency) would be threatened if he were to reject an agreement that falls within his Level II win-set, and if this is known to all parties, then the other side at Level I gains considerable leverage. Domestic U.S. discontent about

---

82. Bailey, *Wilson and the Great Betrayal*, quotation at p. 15.
83. Robert A. Strong and Marshal Zeringue, "The Neutron Bomb and the Atlantic Alliance," presented at the 1986 annual meeting of the American Political Science Association, p. 9.

the Vietnam War clearly affected the agreement reached at the Paris talks.[84] Conversely, if the constituents are (believed to be) hard-line, then a leader's domestic weakness becomes a diplomatic asset. In 1977, for example, the Americans calculated that "a delay in negotiating a treaty . . . endangered [Panamanian President Omar] Torrijos' position; and Panama without Torrijos most likely would have been an impossible negotiating partner."[85] Similarly, in the 1954 Trieste negotiations, the weak Italian government claimed that "'Unless something is done in our favor in Trieste, we can lose the election.' That card was played two or three times [reported the British negotiator later], and it almost always took a trick."[86]

My emphasis on the special responsibility of central executives is a point of affinity between the two-level game model and the "state-centric" literature, even though the underlying logic is different. In this "Janus" model of domestic-international interactions, transnational politics are less prominent than in some theories of interdependence.[87] However, to disregard "cross-table" alliances at Level II is a considerable simplification, and it is more misleading, the lower the political visibility of the issue, and the more frequent the negotiations between the governments involved.[88] Empirically, for example, two-level games in the European Community are influenced by many direct ties among Level II participants, such as national agricultural spokesmen. In some cases, the same multinational actor may actually appear at more than one Level II table. In negotiations over mining concessions in some less-developed countries, for example, the same multinational corporation may be consulted privately by both the home and host governments. In subsequent work on the two-level model, the strategic implications of direct communication between Level II players should be explored.

Conclusion

The most portentous development in the fields of comparative politics and international relations in recent years is the dawning recognition among practitioners in each field of the need to take into account entanglements between the two. Empirical illustrations of reciprocal influence between domestic and international affairs abound. What we need now are concepts

84. I. William Zartman, "Reality, Image, and Detail: The Paris Negotiations, 1969–1973," in Zartman, *50% Solution*, pp. 372–98.

85. Zbigniew Brzezinski, *Power and Principle* (New York: Farrar, Straus and Giroux, 1983), p. 136, as quoted in Habeeb and Zartman, *Panama Canal Negotiations*, pp. 39–40.

86. Harrison in Campbell, *Trieste 1954*, p. 67.

87. Samuel P. Huntington, "Transnational Organizations in World Politics," *World Politics* 25 (April 1973), pp. 333–68; Keohane and Nye, *Power and Interdependence*; Neustadt, *Alliance Politics*.

88. Barbara Crane, "Policy Coordination by Major Western Powers in Bargaining with the Third World: Debt Relief and the Common Fund," *International Organization* 38 (Summer 1984), pp. 399–428.

and theories that will help us organize and extend our empirical observations.

Analysis in terms of two-level games offers a promising response to this challenge. Unlike state-centric theories, the two-level approach recognizes the inevitability of domestic conflict about what the "national interest" requires. Unlike the "Second Image" or the "Second Image Reversed," the two-level approach recognizes that central decision-makers strive to reconcile domestic and international imperatives simultaneously. As we have seen, statesmen in this predicament face distinctive strategic opportunities and strategic dilemmas.

This theoretical approach highlights several significant features of the links between diplomacy and domestic politics, including:

- the important distinction between voluntary and involuntary defection from international agreements;

- the contrast between issues on which domestic interests are homogeneous, simply pitting hawks against doves, and issues on which domestic interests are more heterogeneous, so that domestic cleavage may actually foster international cooperation;

- the possibility of synergistic issue linkage, in which strategic moves at one game-table facilitate unexpected coalitions at the second table;

- the paradoxical fact that institutional arrangements which strengthen decision-makers at home may weaken their international bargaining position, and vice versa;

- the importance of targeting international threats, offers, and side-payments with an eye towards their domestic incidence at home and abroad;

- the strategic uses of uncertainty about domestic politics, and the special utility of "kinky win-sets";

- the potential reverberation of international pressures within the domestic arena;

- the divergences of interest between a national leader and those on whose behalf he is negotiating, and in particular, the international implications of his fixed investments in domestic politics.

Two-level games seem a ubiquitous feature of social life, from Western economic summitry to diplomacy in the Balkans and from coalition politics in Sri Lanka to legislative maneuvering on Capitol Hill. Far-ranging empirical research is needed now to test and deepen our understanding of how such games are played.

Public goods and political institutions: trade and monetary policy processes in the United States
Joanne Gowa

Basic analytic premises are an issue in contemporary debates about the U.S. foreign economic policy process. In dispute are the power structures alleged to govern the formation of American trade and international monetary policy. Thus, the literature supports both of these assumptions: the distribution of power is skewed towards private actors in the issue-area generally; the distribution of power varies according to issue-area. Within the camp of issue-specific power structures, as I shall discuss in more detail, support can be found for almost any assumption about the distribution of power prevailing, in the language of current debate, between "state and society."[1]

This debate echoes the long and still unresolved community power debate not only because of its manifest confusion about essential issues. The debate is as fundamental to larger issues in international relations as the community power debate was to central issues in American politics. The power structure governing U.S. foreign economic policymaking is assumed to have a strong influence on policy itself: state-centered structures, it is assumed, produce liberal trade policy; society-centered structures produce protection. As a consequence, reliable predictions about the U.S. commit-

Earlier versions of this article were presented at the 1985 annual meeting of the American Political Science Association, New Orleans, 29 August–1 September 1985, and at a UCLA conference on The American State in the International Political Economy, November 1985. For comments on the article, I am grateful to Frederick W. Frey, Avery Goldstein, Stephan Haggard, Robert O. Keohane, Jack Nagel, Paul Quirk, Peter Swenson, the participants in the UCLA conference, and four *IO* referees.

1. Despite its rapid growth, the state and society literature still lacks rigorous and consistent definitions of both of its critical variables. In general, of course, they are meant to distinguish public and private actors. This distinction is adequate for the purposes of this article, which largely challenge the microanalytic foundations of this literature. Successful research in comparative politics oriented along state and society lines, however, depends on the development of much more precise analytic and empirical referents for both variables than currently exist.

International Organization 42, 1, Winter 1988, pp. 15–32

ment to a liberal world-trading order depend partly on a better understanding of policy structures than we currently have.

In an effort to clarify ongoing debate, this article applies to the arena of U.S. foreign economic policymaking the logic of collective action, as affected by the specific institutions of the U.S. policy process. This approach requires a conception of American trade and international monetary policy as political goods whose susceptibility to collective action is a function both of characteristics inherent in those goods and of the institutional framework within which they are produced. As such, this article employs and extends arguments linking issue-areas and political processes that have been advanced in different contexts by Theodore J. Lowi, William Zimmerman, and James Q. Wilson.[2] To the extent that this analysis is persuasive, it suggests the need for a differentiation of political process in foreign economic policy based on variables associated with organizational choice within politically determined constraints.

As will become apparent, an analysis of the collective action problems posed by monetary and trade policy seems to challenge fundamentally the logic of the existing state and society literature. Paradoxically, however, this logic is partly resurrected when attention shifts to the institutional framework within which collective action occurs. Some discussion of the state of the art in explanations of foreign economic policymaking and of the logic of collective action must precede this argument.

The U.S. policy process: divergent views

In *Between Power and Plenty,* Peter J. Katzenstein argues that the relationship between state and society determines foreign economic policy in some historical periods. "The domestic structure of the nation-state," he contends, "is a critical intervening variable without which the interrelation between international interdependence and political strategies cannot be understood." Katzenstein arrays six advanced industrialized nations along a continuum from strong to weak states in relation to their societies, and places the United States at the weak-state end of the continuum. There (and in Britain), he asserts, ". . . the coalition between business and the state is relatively unfavorable to state officials and the policy network linking the public with the private sector is relatively fragmented."[3]

2. Theodore J. Lowi, "American Business, Public Policy, Case-Studies, and Political Theory," *World Politics* 16 (July 1964), pp. 677–715; James Q. Wilson, *Political Organizations* (New York: Basic, 1973), chap. 16; William Zimmerman, "Issue Area and Foreign-Policy Process: A Research Note in Search of a General Theory," *The American Political Science Review* 67 (December 1973), pp. 1204–12. For a recent typology that explicitly includes public goods, see Leonard Champney, "Public Goods and Policy Types," paper prepared for the annual meeting of the American Political Science Association, New Orleans, 29 August–1 September, 1985.

3. Peter J. Katzenstein, ed., *Between Power and Plenty: Foreign Economic Policies of*

Although Katzenstein maintains that "state power . . . varies according to whether one analyzes the definition of objectives or the implementation of foreign economic policy," he does not distinguish state strength along the more conventional issue-area lines.[4] Some of the contributors to his book, however, do. In discussing the American case, Stephen D. Krasner, for example, asserts that the state is much stronger in the arena of international monetary policy than in the arena of foreign trade policy. "The laws and practices affecting America's foreign commercial policy." he observes, "illustrate the fragmentation and diffusion of power that can exist for particular issue-areas in the American political system. The problem has been much less acute for monetary policy," where, according to Krasner, "U.S. leaders . . . have had a relatively free hand. . . ."[5]

Neither Katzenstein's emphasis on domestic structures nor Krasner's insistence on distinguishing between money and trade has been universally acclaimed. Arguing that power is not a highly fungible resource, John Zysman objects to Katzenstein's approach: ". . . a government's ability to act in one policy arena will be very different from its ability to act in another. . . . The policy tasks in each sector vary, as does the pattern of interest organization. Consequently, a state's 'strength'—the ability to formulate and implement policy—varies with its capacity to execute these different tasks."[6]

Krasner has been attacked from both sides: although they agree that the power of the state varies across issue areas, some scholars dispute his view that the U.S. state is weak in trade, while others object to his view that it is strong in international monetary policy.[7] Thus, Judith Goldstein argues, for example, that the weakness of the American state in foreign commercial policy has been exaggerated: the persistence of a liberal U.S. trade policy, despite domestic opposition to that stance, she maintains, "suggests an ability on the part of the U.S. government to retain its autonomy from society. That autonomy is a result of the ideological adherence of central decision makers to the tenets of free trade."[8] A detailed study of the politics

---

Advanced Industrialized States (Madison: University of Wisconsin Press, 1978), pp. 3, 21. In a more recent work, Katzenstein applies a similar analytic framework to Switzerland and Austria, arguing that "liberal capitalism" in the former and "democratic socialism" in the latter condition the different responses of each to changing international markets. See his *Corporatism and Change: Switzerland, Austria, and the Politics of Industry* (Ithaca and London: Cornell University Press, 1984).

4. Katzenstein, *Between Power and Plenty,* p. 20.

5. Stephen D. Krasner, "United States Commercial and Monetary Policy: Unravelling the Paradox of External Strength and Internal Weakness," in ibid., pp. 64, 66.

6. John Zysman, *Governments, Markets, and Growth: Financial Systems and the Politics of Industrial Change* (Ithaca and London: Cornell University Press, 1983), p. 297.

7. Krasner himself has argued that the U.S. state is strong in the area of foreign raw materials investment. See his *Defending the National Interest: Raw Materials Investment and U.S. Foreign Policy* (Princeton, N.J.: Princeton University Press, 1978).

8. Judith L. Goldstein, "A Domestic Explanation for Regime Formation and Maintenance: Liberal Trade Policy in the U.S.," paper prepared for delivery at the annual meeting of the

of U.S. trade from 1953 to 1962 also demonstrated to the satisfaction of its authors that the influence of special interest groups on American trade policy has been overstated.[9]

On the monetary side, conversely, some observers contend that the U.S. state has evidenced less autonomy than might be expected of a strong state. They do not agree among themselves, however, on the factors that allegedly limit the American state's power in this policy arena. Thus, Jeff Frieden asserts that bankers, in particular, have played a large role in setting U.S. international monetary policy; I have argued that the size and structure of the domestic economy constrains the freedom of American officials in this sphere of policy.[10]

Were Krasner's original argument compelling or the counterarguments it provoked consistent with each other, both heat and light might have been shed on the character of the U.S. foreign economic policymaking process. Neither, however, has been wholly the case. Krasner argues that the American state is more powerful in establishing monetary than trade policy in large part because the monetary policymaking process is more insulated. "Decisions about monetary policy," he contends, "have been taken in the White House, the Treasury Department, and the Federal Reserve Board, arenas that are well insulated from particular societal pressures."[11] Yet, in the next breath, Krasner seems to suggest that institutional insularity *per se* is less significant in explaining the difference than the relatively greater activity of pressure groups in trade: "Private actors rarely saw how monetary decisions related to their specific interests and therefore did not press for greater access to the decision-making system."[12]

Krasner attributes the observed activity pattern of pressure groups partly to their inability to relate international monetary policy easily to their own tangible economic interests.[13] Krasner's emphasis on the intellectual barriers to interest group activity in monetary policy is typical of other work on U.S. foreign economic policy formation. John S. Odell observes, for example:

American Political Science Association, Washington, D.C., 30 August–2 September 1984, pp. 13–14. For a further development of her general argument and an empirical test of it, see her "The Political Economy of Trade: Institutions of Protection," *American Political Science Review* 80 (March 1986), pp. 161–84.

9. Raymond A. Bauer, Ithiel DeSola Pool, and Lewis Anthony Dexter, *American Business and Public Policy: The Politics of Foreign Trade,* 2d ed. (Chicago: Aldine-Atherton, 1972).

10. Jeff Frieden, "The Internationalization of U.S. Finance and the Transformation of U.S. Foreign Policy, 1890–1940," paper prepared for delivery at the annual meeting of the American Political Science Association, Washington, D.C., 30 August–2 September, 1984; Joanne Gowa, *Closing the Gold Window: Domestic Politics and the End of Bretton Woods* (Ithaca and London: Cornell University Press, 1983).

11. Krasner, "United States Commercial and Monetary Policy," p. 65.

12. Ibid.

13. Krasner also notes, however, the role of the norm of fixed exchange rates in establishing the pattern of interest group activity, an important observation to which I will return.

Here we have [three] counterintuitive cases in which interested groups did not act on behalf of their supposed interests. What accounts for these cases? One ready explanation would be the esoteric nature of the subject of international monetary policy and ignorance on the part of group leaders. Put another way, the causal chains from dollar devaluation to group welfare are multiple and difficult for even specialists to weigh, contrary to simple assumptions about group interest. In contrast, group leaders more readily grasp the net consequences of raising and lowering trade barriers for their sectors, and they are therefore far more active on trade policy.[14]

Robert O. Keohane, Joseph S. Nye, and I have also linked the scarcity of interest groups in the international monetary policy process to the nature of monetary policy itself.[15]

When interest groups are routinely engaged on other issues as seemingly arcane as international monetary issues, however, it is not easy to attribute the absence of pressure group activity to the esoteric nature of its subject. The Occupational Safety and Health Administration (OSHA), for example, is beset by group pressures whenever it proposes changing the permissible level of industrial chemicals in the workplace; congressional representatives contemplating seemingly obscure details of banking deregulation also experience interest group pressures. International monetary policy should be no more intellectually inaccessible to the groups it affects than other issues, which are hopelessly obscure only to those without a clear stake in them. The rise in the dollar exchange rate during the early 1980s, moreover, provided anecdotal evidence that export- and import-competing industries clearly understood the relationship between their shrinking market shares and U.S. exchange-rate policy.

Thus it seems unlikely that intellectual barriers to entry can explain the differences that are alleged to exist between the U.S. trade and monetary policy processes. Nor, in fact, does it seem likely that the conventional distinction between commercial and financial policy actually distinguishes correspondingly different political processes: these can vary not only *between* money and trade but also among issue-areas *within* monetary and trade policymaking. Frieden's observations of a weak state in the arena of international debt, for example, may be perfectly consistent with Krasner's emphasis on a strong state in exchange-rate policy. Similarly, state strength in American commercial policy may be a function of the particular trade

---

14. John S. Odell, *U.S. International Monetary Policy: Markets, Power, and Ideas as Sources of Change* (Princeton, N.J.: Princeton University Press, 1982), p. 347. As is true of Krasner, however, Odell's explanation is not monocausal: he also attributes the relative scarcity of pressure group activity to norms that established a "taboo" against pressures for devaluation, to the availability of alternatives to devaluation, and to the nature of the U.S. economy. See ibid., p. 347.

15. Robert O. Keohane and Joseph S. Nye, *Power and Interdependence: World Politics in Transition* (Boston: Little, Brown, 1977); Gowa, *Closing the Gold Window*, p. 134.

policy at issue. We can distinguish these issues and structures analytically by relying on insights that are drawn from the literature on collective action and embedded within the institutional framework of U.S. foreign economic policymaking.

The logic of collective action

Contrary to at least the conventional interpretation of pluralist theory, Mancur Olson argued in 1965 that the expectation that groups would act effectively on their shared interests rested on a fallacious assumption.[16] Interest groups supposedly exist to secure collective goods for their members. Paradoxically, however, collective goods greatly inhibit group activity. Olson points out that this occurs because collective or public goods possess two attributes that distinguish them from private goods: 1) they exhibit "non-rivalry" in consumption (that is, one individual's consumption of the good does not interfere with any other individual's ability to consume it); and 2) they are "non-excludable" (that is, it is either "impossible, or at least very costly" to prevent any individual from consuming the good, once it is supplied, whether or not he has paid for it[17]).

These characteristics imply, Olson observed, that each potential member of a large group will refuse to pay his share of the costs of producing the group's good. Rational individuals will seek to "free ride" on the contributions of others in the group, and the collective good, without certain countervailing conditions, is therefore unlikely to be provided at all. This sometimes unfortunate outcome is attributable to two factors: the cost of an individual's contribution is likely to exceed the benefit returned to him as a result of his contribution; and the "inconsequentiality problem" or the assumed independence of individual decisions in large groups.[18]

Thus, large groups are unlikely to successfully provide themselves with collective goods unless they can overcome the free-rider problem. This can occur, Olson asserts, through two routes: the use of selective incentives or coercion. Large groups can induce individuals to contribute to common purposes if group membership makes the individual eligible to receive selec-

16. Mancur Olson, *The Logic of Collective Action: Public Goods and the Theory of Groups* (Cambridge: Harvard University Press, 1965).
17. Robin W. Boadway and David E. Wildasin, *Public Sector Economics*, 2d ed. (Boston: Little, Brown, 1984), p. 57.
As Duncan Snidal argues, non-excludability implies non-rivalry. See Snidal, "Public Goods, Property Rights, and Political Organizations," *International Studies Quarterly*, 23 (December 1979), pp. 534–44.
18. For Olson's discussion of large groups, see his *Logic of Collective Action*.

tive incentives—"gains that are private or subject to some form of exclusion"[19]—that exceed the cost of contribution. Large groups can also induce contributions if group membership is compulsory: the introduction of closed shops, for example, led to a rapid increase in unionization.[20]

Small groups encounter less difficult collective action problems. Brian Barry observes that "where the beneficiaries form a small group in close contact with one another, the assumption that . . . [individuals'] decisions are independent of one another cannot be upheld."[21] Moreover, in a small group, the individual's share of the incremental increase in the collective good his contribution produces may exceed the costs of that contribution. Thus, a small group may successfully organize itself for collective action, although the level of collective goods produced is likely to be suboptimal.

Basing an analysis even in part on the logic of collective action requires some sensitivity to the weaknesses of this analytic framework. The utility function that Olson attributes to individuals deciding whether to contribute to the production of collective goods is clearly too narrow to capture the interests of actors in all political and social situations.[22] Olson is vulnerable as well on the issue of selective incentives: if members join an organization that supplies collective goods because of the selective incentives it offers, it seems reasonable to assume that another organization not burdened with supplying collective goods would be able to supply the private goods more cheaply.[23] Russell Hardin points out, in addition, that while the provision of selective incentives or the "by-product theory . . . can make sense of contributions to an ongoing political organization, it does not seem to explain how it is that many groups got started in the first place," nor does "political entrepreneurship" provide a suitable substitute.[24]

More fundamental, perhaps, is the charge that the logic of collective ac-

19. V. Kerry Smith, "A Theoretical Analysis of the Green Lobby," *American Political Science Review* 79 (March 1985), p. 132.

20. Olson, *The Logic of Collective Action*, p. 68.

21. Brian Barry, *Sociologists, Economists, and Democracy* (London: Macmillan, 1970), p. 25.

22. See Russell Hardin, *Collective Action* (Baltimore: Johns Hopkins University Press for Resources for the Future, 1982), p. 72; and John Mark Hansen, "The Political Economy of Group Membership," *American Political Science Review* 79 (March 1985), p. 82.

23. George J. Stigler, "Free Riders and Collective Action: An Appendix to Theories of Economic Regulation," *Bell Journal of Economics and Management Science* 5 (Autumn 1974), p. 360.

24. Hardin, *Collective Action*, pp. 34, 36. Hardin comments:

. . . the incentive of personal career may seem more suited to explaining ongoing than newly emerging organizations. Jimmy Hoffa owed his great power in the Teamsters Union in large part to his efforts to strengthen and expand the union, thereby enhancing the prosperity of its members. One may be less inclined to suppose that, say Joe Hill, the 'poet laureate' of the Wobblies who was executed in Utah in 1915 on a murder charge that was believed by many to be a frame-up for his strike activities, was motivated by his own career prospects as an eventual union leader (p. 36).

tion predicts much more severe social and political problems than actually exist. The "basic 'economic man' model . . . correctly identifies the 'free rider' problem as absolutely crucial," notes Howard Margolis, "but it rather overkills this issue. The conventional economic model not only predicts (correctly) the existence of problems with free riders but also predicts (incorrectly) such severe problems that no society we know could function if its members actually behaved as the conventional model implies they will."[25] Analogously, Barry argues that such relatively widespread phenomena as voting make no sense when viewed in terms of Olson's logic; similar arguments could be made about social revolutions and urban riots.[26]

Although "the logic" of collective action, at least as Olson expressed it, does not seem to hold universally across all contexts, it nonetheless does provide a powerful explanation of collective action (or its absence) in some important situations. The theory seems least vulnerable to criticism when we apply it to the context within which it was originally advanced: economic interest groups. Since these groups are the focus of this article, an application of even a theory of collective action that is somewhat limited empirically may prove useful.

Collective action in money and trade

We can easily explain prevailing patterns of interest group activity in the U.S. foreign economic policy process by examining the very different collective action problems presented by trade and monetary policy. The concentration ratios in U.S. industry that permit small groups to organize successfully for collective action does not by itself distinguish commercial from financial policy. Because it is more excludable, however, trade policy presents fewer problems for collective action than does monetary policy. As a consequence, interest groups are far more active in it, and the trade policy process appears more fragmented than does its financial counterpart.

Industrial concentration in the United States potentially offers a small group solution to the collective action problems that confront interests with a stake in foreign economic policy. This conclusion follows from the definition of a small group, in which the number of potential members of any group is less critical to determining whether it is "small" or "large" than is the size of any subgroup that would benefit if it alone provided all of the group's good—the size of what Thomas Schelling refers to as a "k" group.[27]

25. Howard Margolis, *Selfishness, Altruism, and Rationality: A Theory of Social Choice* (Cambridge: Cambridge University Press, 1982), p. 6.
26. Barry, *Sociologists, Economists, and Democracy,* chap. 2. For an attempt to explain contributions to urban riots within a collective action framework, see T. David Mason, "Individual Participation in Collective Racial Violence: A Rational Choice Synthesis," *American Political Science Review* 78 (December 1984), pp. 1040–56.
27. See Hardin, *Collective Action,* p. 41.

Thus, as George Stigler points out, "the small number solution has a wider scope than a literal count of numbers would suggest. The size distribution of individuals is highly skewed when these individuals have a size dimension (sales of firm, property of family). The large individuals in a group may therefore properly view themselves as members of a small number industry if their aggregate share of the group's resources is large." For industry, using the Herfindahl measure of concentration, Stigler adds that "many, many industries fulfill in good measure the small number condition."[28]

Highly concentrated industries may satisfy the small number condition conducive to collective action, but this fact does not by itself distinguish the monetary from the trade arena in terms of predictions of pressure group activity. *A priori,* there is no reason to expect that industries with an interest in trade policy would be more highly concentrated than industries affected by international monetary policy: indeed, in many cases, the sets of industries affected by either policy would be identical. Observable variations in pressure group activity must instead be a function partly of differences in the "excludability" of political goods sought in each issue-area.

The excludability of non-rivalrous goods can vary: as Michael Laver notes, "goods may be more or less excludable, the degree of 'excludability' being measured by the costs of exclusion, relative to the benefits to the excluder." Laver asserts that control over exclusion can theoretically be exercised, even over the service provided by a lighthouse, which is a frequently cited example of a pure public good: ". . . I could surround the entire area within which the lighthouse was visible with a minefield, and issue the directions for safe passage only to those whom I wished to use it. . . ."[29]

The political goods an industry receives as a result of collective action may be excludable partly as a consequence of variations among firms in the product mixes they produce. As Stigler observes:

28. Stigler, "Free Riders and Collective Action: An Appendix to Theories of Economic Regulation," p. 362.

The Herfindahl index is "the sum of squares of the sizes of firms in an industry where size is the percentage of total industry assets." See Kenneth W. Clarkson and Roger Leroy Miller, *Industrial Organization: Theory, Evidence, and Public Policy* (New York: McGraw-Hill, 1982), p. 72.

29. Michael Laver, "Political Solutions to the Collective Action Problem," *Political Studies* 28 (June 1980), p. 198. Laver adds about the lighthouse, however: ". . . in practice, this would probably be unfeasible, and almost certainly not economically worthwhile."

In fact, lighthouses once produced private goods in England: shipowners were "assessed . . . at the docks. Ordinarily only one ship was in sight of the lighthouse at a particular point in time. The light would not be shown if the ship (which was identified by its flag) had not paid." Edwin Mansfield, *Microeconomics: Theory/Applications,* 5th ed. (New York: Norton, 1985), p. 494.

For an extensive discussion of the early British lighthouse system that allegedly demonstrates that economists are wrong when they point to a lighthouse as an example of a public good requiring government supply, see R. H. Coase, "The Lighthouse in Economics," *Journal of Law and Economics* 17 (1974), pp. 357–76. quotation at 376.

The smaller firms in an industry seldom make the full range of products: they specialize in a narrower set of products. Hence, if they are not represented in the coalition, they may find that their cheap ride is to a destination they do not favor. The proposed tariff structure may neglect *their* products; the research program may neglect *their* processes; the labor negotiations may ignore *their* special labor mix.[30]

Trade legislation in the United States provides another route to excludability. This legislation routinely incorporates several provisions sanctioning protection against imports that, in effect, transform the public good (or ill) of free trade into a partly excludable good. Escape clauses, peril points, and national security clauses, for example, have all been written into legislation at various times in the postwar period. All these provisions permit protection against import competition to be extended on an industry basis.[31] In addition, specific trade acts sometimes prohibit tariff concessions on the products of particular industries: the Trade Expansion Act of 1962, for example, "actually exempted a small number of industries from [tariff] cuts, mainly the 14 industries which had received escape clause treatment before 1962 . . . , and petroleum and certain petroleum products which had received special status under the national security clause in 1959. . . ."[32]

The avenues of protection provided by Congress and implemented by the executive branch suggest that trade policy can be and has become in some instances a highly excludable good. The Short Term Arrangement on textiles concluded in 1961 specified sixty-four categories of cotton textiles; the orderly marketing agreements (OMAs) concluded in footwear in the late 1970s covered "all nonrubber footwear except zoris, disposable paper footwear, and wool felt footwear."[33] That small or even privileged groups are, as a consequence, empowered to pursue their collective interests in import protection is also suggested by the experience with voluntary export restraints (VERs) in steel: in 1984, Bethlehem Steel and the United Steelworkers of America filed an escape clause petition, opposed by other steel producers, that resulted eventually in the government's approval of relief to the steel industry.[34] The successful petition for import protection filed in 1982 by

---

30. Stigler, "Free Riders and Collective Action," p. 362. Emphasis in original.

31. The escape clause (introduced in 1951) permits tariff concessions to be withdrawn if they increase imports, causing, or threatening to cause, serious injury to an industry; the peril point (introduced in 1948, eliminated in 1949, reintroduced in 1951, and eliminated again in 1962) required the establishment of a level below which tariffs for a particular industry could not be reduced; the national security clause (introduced in 1955) allows almost any measure necessary to protect national security. Réal P. Lavergne, The Political Economy of U.S. Tariffs: *An Empirical Analysis* (Toronto: Academic, 1983), p. 34.

32. Ibid., p. 28.

33. David B. Yoffie, *Power and Protectionism: Strategies of the Newly Industrializing Countries* (New York: Columbia University Press, 1983), pp. 85, 189.

34. A privileged group is one in which one member has enough interest in the collective good that he will supply it even if he bears its entire cost.

Other producers opposed escape clause action because they were concerned that it might end

Harley-Davidson, the only American manufacturer of large motorcycles, suggests that control over exclusion can sometimes be extensive enough to transform trade policy into a private good.[35]

I am not suggesting that collective action by industries seeking protection from imports is easily achieved or ultimately successful. Control over exclusion is rarely extensive enough to eliminate the public character of trade policy: a protectionist coalition's ability to keep free-riding firms from consuming the benefits of import protection, for example, will vary with the extent to which the products of those firms are substitutes for the products of firms within the coalition.[36] It will also vary with the height of barriers to entry into the industry.[37]

Nor do opportunities for small group action guarantee the successful organization of those groups. Even in theory, small groups may fail to act effectively because their members cannot agree on an acceptable distribution of the costs or benefits of collective action. A small group also almost inevitably confronts free-rider problems, making the group itself unstable unless discount rates and valuations of the good do not vary at all among its members.[38] In practice, moreover, small groups in industry may be more difficult to organize than concentration ratios suggest, in part because industries (and even individual firms) are not always homogeneous with respect to interests in trade protection: highly competitive and declining firms within a single industry will not find common ground in import protection. Nor, as empirical studies demonstrate, is the political process responsive solely to interest group pressures.[39]

---

the 1982 U.S.-EEC steel trade agreement. See Robert S. Walters, "Industrial Crises and U.S. Public Policies: Patterns in the Steel, Automobile, and Semiconductor Experiences," in W. Ladd Hollist and F. LaMond Tullis, eds., *International Political Economy Yearbook*, vol. 1. (Boulder: Westview, 1985), p. 164.

35. Technically, because any manufacturer of large motorcycles gained the same protection, trade policy in this instance was not a private good. In practice, however, the only consumer of the protection granted was Harley-Davidson.

36. As observed by Robert E. Baldwin in remarks at a National Bureau of Economic Research (NBER) Conference on the Political Economy of Trade Policy, Dedham, Mass., 10–11 January, 1986.

37. For an analysis of the underexplored issue of the life cycle of import protection that emphasizes the influence on that cycle of the height of entry barriers, see Vinod Aggarwal, Robert O. Keohane, and David B. Yoffie, "The Evolution of Cooperative Protectionism," paper presented at a NBER Conference on the Political Economy of Trade Policy, Dedham, Mass., 10–11 January 1986.

38. Laver, "Political Solutions," pp. 203–4.

39. In a recent attempt to explain the inter-industry pattern of U.S. import protection, Robert E. Baldwin tests five different models against various indicators of U.S. protection. He concludes that the pattern cannot be adequately explained by models that are based on short-run self-interest, including pressure group models. He emphasizes, however, that "an eclectic approach to understanding [U.S. trade policy] . . . is the most appropriate one currently." The relative explanatory power of different models, he argues, cannot be accurately assessed "until the various models are differentiated more sharply analytically and better empirical measures for distinguishing them are obtained. . . ." See his *The Political Economy of U.S. Import Policy* (Cambridge, Mass: MIT Press, 1985), p. 180.

On the other hand, the contrast between trade and international monetary policy in terms of ease of organization for collective action remains instructive. Consider exchange rates, for example. For those groups hurt by the rise in the effective exchange rate of the dollar—whether under Bretton Woods or the subsequent floating-rate system—a dollar devaluation was a distinctly non-excludable good: no individual could be prevented from benefiting from the change, whether or not he had contributed to it. Thus, there was no conceivable excludability for groups adversely affected by the overvaluation of the dollar.

Nor does it seem possible that any small group could organize for collective action on exchange rates: it seems highly implausible that the benefits to members of any small group would exceed their costs in seeking the public good of a lower dollar exchange rate. Given that particular groups can seek import relief to compensate for exchange-rate change, action on exchange rates seems even less probable. Again, although there has been some pressure group activity on U.S. exchange-rate policy in the very recent past, what remains most impressive—as perhaps with riots and revolutions—is not how much, but how little activity has occurred, given the damage that the rise of the dollar during the early 1980s inflicted on export and import-competing industries.

A first cut suggests, then, that the relative costs of collective action might explain why interest groups more strongly impact U.S. trade than U.S. international monetary policy. Deeper analysis makes it clear, however, that a sharp distinction between costs of group action in trade and money is misleading: neither policy arena, in reality, imposes homogeneous opportunities or constraints on collective action by groups that have a stake in the process. This heterogeneity offers some leverage for explaining why observers differ among themselves about the power of actors in the U.S. foreign economic policy process.

Disaggregating trade policy, for example, suggests that the costs of collective action can vary widely even in an arena some observers consider a paradigmatic case of interest group vulnerability. Logically, barriers to pressure-group entry into the policy process should be much higher when a major shift in trade policy is under consideration than when a more narrowly drawn policy is at stake. Proposed shifts from protection to free trade or from a unilateral to a multilateral process of tariff determination should impose prohibitive costs on group activity, because they confront affected interests with the classic problems of collective action that afflict large groups. OMAs, VERs, and similarly scaled trade issues, on the other hand, seem expressly designed to facilitate pressure-group formation. As a consequence, the trade process will not be populated uniformly by pressure

---

Baldwin also provides an excellent review of recent empirical efforts to explain U.S. tariffs in his "The Political Economy of Protection," in Jagdish N. Bhagwati, ed., *Import Competition and Response* (Chicago: University of Chicago Press, 1982), pp. 263–86.

groups, and the roles that public and private actors play, even within the realm of trade policy, will vary. Thus, Goldstein can accurately attribute "essentially liberal" policy to the major role of the state in the U.S. policy process, while, with equal accuracy, Krasner can insist that interest groups enjoy easy access to, and significant influence over, the policy process.

We can apply a similar analysis to international monetary policy. Thus, exchange rates, international reserve creation, and the nature of the monetary system are high-cost collective action issues: each affords few opportunities for excluding free riders or for organizing small groups. This is not true, however, of either capital controls or international debt. For example, capital controls need not be applied uniformly: when the United States imposed the Interest Equalization Tax in 1964, it exempted Canada, Japan, and the less developed countries. Although no firm evidence exists on this point, investment banks with large stakes in these markets might have contributed to this outcome.[40] International debt also presents opportunities for exclusion, as the lead banks may exclude from subsequent loan consortia banks that refuse to participate in collective action in this area. In addition, the concentration of foreign lending among U.S. banks permits small groups to form on issues related to foreign lending.[41]

In general, then, the costs of collective action presented by specific issues would appear to provide a more compelling basis for distinguishing the power of actors in the foreign economic policy process than would either institutional insularity or intellectual barriers to group action. On logical grounds alone, "weak" states should be no more pervasive in trade than "strong" states are in monetary policy: the power of actors will vary instead as the public character of political goods varies. However sparse, available data do suggest that the political processes relevant to specific issues may less resemble others *within* than across the conventional divide of trade versus monetary policy.[42]

Implicit in this argument is a fundamental challenge to the state and society literature. The argument suggests that the state–society relationship is not as fundamental to political analysis as is the potential for collective action that inheres in particular political goods. Because the power of state

40. This example should not be weighted heavily. The exemptions seem to have been more closely related to national security than to industry interests.

41. In the United States, "the 25 largest banks account for over three-quarters of U.S. overseas bank lending. For these banks, foreign business averages nearly half of total business." Jeff Frieden, "International Finance and Domestic Politics: Financial Internationalization and the United States," mimeo, May 1985, p. 13, cited by permission.

42. Some evidence suggests, for example, that both capital controls and international debt issues have precipitated more interest group activity than have other issues within the sphere of international monetary policy. See Odell, *U.S. International Monetary Policy*; Keohane and Nye, *Power and Interdependence*; and Gowa, *Closing the Gold Window*. Although much more evidence is available on the relationship between interest groups and trade policy (see note 39), few definitive conclusions have emerged, and attempts to compare rigorously trade and monetary policy processes seem nonexistent.

and society apparently derives from existing collective action problems that vary widely across issues, the logic of state and society interpretations appears flawed. The distribution of power over policy becomes a function not of macro but of microanalysis: power can be inferred less accurately from domestic structures than from the degree of publicness inhering in particular political goods.

As with other issue-area typologies, however, this one cannot stand alone. In reality, whether a political good is public, private, or somewhere in between does not inhere only in the good: it is also a function of existing markets in these goods, and these are established by political institutions.

Institutions and markets for political goods

Because they typically analyze choice among available alternatives, most economists and rational choice theorists do not closely examine how any given set of alternatives is itself determined.[43] Among the more powerful determinants of any particular array of choices are institutions—the rules organizing, as Alexander James Field puts it, "the interaction of two or more individuals. A hospital, school, army, firm, or church is an institution, but the essence of these organizations lies not in the physical buildings associated with these entities, but in the rules, formal and conventional, which organize the behavior of individuals within them."[44]

Institutions strongly influence the character of political goods and associated patterns of interest group activity. Whether a good is public or private is not only a function of its attributes; it is also a function of the institutional framework that produces it. Political rules of the game, in part, establish whether the government controls exclusion over what could be treated as non-excludable goods. As Duncan Snidal argues, few goods are unalterably non-excludable: "Shipping lanes, lighthouse beams, or TV signals seem to display extreme publicness. But techniques ranging from demands for tribute by Barbary Coast pirates to ship licenses to cable television reveal our ingenuity in assigning property rights and achieving some degree of exclusion."[45] Whether potentially public goods are treated as such is determined

43. Douglass C. North observes that institutions "establish the cooperative and competitive relationships which constitute a society and more specifically an economic order. When economists talk about their discipline as a theory of choice and about the menu of choices being determined by opportunities and preferences, they simply have left out that it is the institutional framework which constrains people's choice sets." *Structure and Change in Economic History* (New York: Norton, 1971), p. 201.

44. Alexander James Field, "The Problem with Neoclassical Institutional Economics: A Critique with Special Reference to the North-Thomas Model of Pre-1500 Europe," *Explorations in Economic History* 18 (April 1981), p. 183, note 13.

45. Snidal, "Political Organizations," p. 545.

by political institutions, or what Snidal refers to as the prevailing system of property rights: that *"system of mechanisms which serves to permit exclusion of goods and uniquely to determine the beneficiaries of (and losers from) that exclusion."*[46]

Brief reflection clearly shows that the public character of the specific goods of trade and monetary policy resides as much in the political institutions that produce them as in the goods themselves. Foreign economic policy can be administered as a public good, from which exclusion is impossible, or as, in Snidal's term, a "quasi-public good," "an erstwhile public good [that] has had payment and exclusion mechanisms attached to it by a central authority structure."[47] Thus, we can imagine a political universe in which trade policy is not excludable at all, just as it is possible to imagine a regime in which excludability is pervasive. The former would not sanction any exceptions to free trade, for example, and the latter would provide protection against import competition on demand. Similarly, we can conceive of domestic political regimes in which exchange-rate policy is administered as a public good, and of regimes in which exchange controls transform it into a highly excludable good.

Nor need imagination serve as the only way to examine the influence of institutional variation on the public character of political goods, even within a single country. In the United States in 1930, the concentration of power over tariffs in Congress suppressed the public character of "national" trade policy: the Smoot–Hawley tariff of that year came close to the sum of individual industry demands, accurately mirroring dominant attitudes at the time.[48] By 1934, however, Congress had shifted much of its tariff authority to the executive branch and sanctioned a negotiated approach to tariff-setting; both moves restored some of the public character to trade policy and thus "substantially reduced the probable impact of pressure groups" on U.S. tariff levels.[49]

On a smaller scale, we can also observe changes over time in the political market for U.S. international monetary policy, with corresponding changes in the costs to affected interests of collective action on particular issues. The public character of monetary policy was enhanced when the Nixon administration abandoned the capital controls used by successive administrations in the 1960s and early 1970s, which eliminated a feasible target for interest group activity. But costs of collective action in other areas—notably exchange rates—have fallen in the recent past, although for reasons that em-

46. Ibid., emphasis in original.
47. Ibid., pp. 558–59.
48. Similarly, in the 1820s, congressional responses to claims for protection were "conditioned by belief [sic] in the efficacy of protection and its proper place in the development and defense of the nation." Jonathan J. Pincus, *Pressure Groups and Politics in Antebellum Tariffs* (New York: Columbia University Press, 1977), p. 169.
49. Lavergne, *Political Economy*, p. 20.

phasize the importance of international, rather than domestic institutions as the source of variation in the public character of political goods. Almost until the collapse of the Bretton Woods system, its fixed exchange rates and the dollar's value were regarded as immutable: as Krasner observes, ". . . until the late 1960s, virtually all sectors of the American elite regarded both the value of the dollar and fixed exchange rates as graven in stone and beyond the tampering of mere mortals."[50] In contrast, under a floating exchange-rate system, the value of the dollar came to be considered of legitimate concern to both Congress and industry. Thus, the costs of collective action in exchange-rate policy have fallen over time within the United States—however, because that policy is largely the residual of domestic macro-economic policy, they remain prohibitive for interest groups other than those "piggybacking" on the activities of other groups.

Because of their influence on the public or less-than-public character of political goods, institutions strongly impact interest groups' potential for effective action. Within the United States, the public or private character of trade and monetary policy has shifted over time, as institutional structures have changed. This shift implies that, while an analysis of incentives for collective action may yield information about the distribution of power prevailing in various areas of foreign economic policy at any time, it will not address other important questions about the process: the pattern of incentives itself, for example, can be explained only by understanding the creation and evolution of the political institutions that establish incentives for collective action as a by-product of public goods definition.[51]

This emphasis on institutions as a determinant of collective action costs partially restores the logic of state and society analyses with, however, some significant caveats. The power of states and societies to determine foreign economic policy is conditioned by constraints on the publicness of political goods that either inhere in or are imposed on the goods by international and domestic political institutions. If issues cannot stand alone as predictors of foreign economic policy processes, neither can states and societies.

Conclusion

Because of important variations within each broad issue-area, efforts to distinguish power structures in U.S. foreign economic policy exclusively on the basis of differences between trade and monetary policy are destined to

---

50. Krasner, "Commercial and Monetary Policy," pp. 65–66.

51. For an analysis that emphasizes the fundamental changes in appropriate conceptions of and policy responses to issues that occur when they are seen over rather than at a single point in time, see John Gerard Ruggie, "Social Time and International Policy: Conceptualizing Global Population and Resource Issues," in Margaret P. Karns, ed., *Persistent Patterns and Emergent Structures in a Waning Century* (New York: Praeger, 1986), pp. 211–36.

prove futile. The alleged intellectual inaccessibility of international monetary policy is not the critical barrier to interest group activity: it is much more likely that the insuperable obstacles are the public character and invulnerability to small group action of *some* issue-areas within monetary policy. Analogously, debates about power structures in trade need to focus more closely on particular issues within the broad category of commercial policy. Major decisions on national trade policy present very different incentives for collective action than do more narrowly drawn decisions. This implies a weak logical foundation to any argument that posits a uniform distribution of political power across the entire U.S. trade policy process.

In short, an analysis of incentives for collective action seems likely to identify power structures in foreign economic policymaking more accurately than either institutional insularity or subject matter. Largely anecdotal evidence from the United States suggests that policy processes do conform to expectations generated by this analytic framework: thus, interest groups are active on international debt and banking issues, as Frieden observes; they appear virtually nonexistent in U.S. exchange-rate policy, as Krasner and others observe; their presence is marked in escape clause actions. Some cross-national data also suggest a relationship between incentives for group activity and foreign economic policy processes: Katzenstein's study of seven small European states, for example, effectively links highly public liberal trade policies to high degrees of democratic corporatism.[52] Whether the hypotheses that can be derived from this framework can be successfully operationalized and tested remains to be seen, but no insuperable obstacles are apparent.

Even as it stands, however, an analysis of incentives for organizational action raises red flags both for issue-area typologies and for state and society models. Emphasis on the variable publicness of trade and monetary policy tends to vitiate the logic of state and society distinctions; attention to the role of political institutions in establishing the public or "quasi" public character of goods in the political marketplace partly—but only partly—resurrects it. The U.S. case raises warning flags for both because it reveals that the defining characteristics of issues are neither obvious nor immutable, and it simultaneously demonstrates how easily "weak" states can metamorphose into "strong" states as the public character of political goods varies.

Because we assume that power structures influence policy content, their clarification is of more than academic interest. By rendering trade policy an excludable good, the current U.S. system awards interest groups an influence over public policy that, predictably, leads to a host of exceptions to liberal trade; these exceptions are not found in systems that constrain interest groups more heavily. The future of the U.S. commitment to a liberal

---

52. Peter J. Katzenstein, *Small States in World Markets: Industrial Policy in Europe* (Ithaca and London: Cornell University Press, 1985).

world trading order consequently depends in part on the evolution of its foreign economic policymaking system. As long as U.S. presidents remain committed to the existing international economic order, and as long as Congress does not radically change prevailing exclusionary mechanisms, the United States is unlikely to abandon the premise of free trade that constrains, however imperfectly, protectionist pressures. Changes in either, however, would alter the U.S. commitment to liberal trade.

Thus, foreign economic policy processes in the United States, and elsewhere to a less significant extent, play a more significant role in determining the nature of the international economic order than is sometimes acknowledged. Complex interactions among domestic policy processes, international power, and political outcomes create high risks for hypotheses, including those described in this article, whose explanatory or predictive power rests almost exclusively on variables that look either outward to the international system or inward to the domestic policy process.

Domestic institutions and the credibility of international commitments: Japan and the United States

Peter F. Cowhey

The domestic politics of great powers shape the credibility and substance of multilateral regimes. The electoral system, division of governmental powers, and transparency of the political system of great powers are the determinants of how domestic politics shape multilateral regimes. These variables explain why the domestic politics of the United States facilitated the significant global impact of multilateralism after 1945.[1] They also suggest why Japanese politics augur less favorably for multilateralism's future.

Multilateral regimes emphasize generalized principles of conduct that include significant degrees of indivisibility, nondiscrimination, and diffuse reciprocity.[2] That the General Agreement on Tariffs and Trade (GATT) obliges signatories to offer one another the same trade concessions and that the premise of the North Atlantic Treaty Organization (NATO) is that its members' security is inseparable exemplify nondiscrimination and indivisibility, respectively. These principles, in turn, force acceptance of diffuse reciprocity's rough balancing of benefits and concessions over time on many fronts.[3]

The first part of the article argues that effective multilateralism requires countries to trust that the participating great powers will adhere in good faith to the multilateral regime. International guarantees alone, however, are insufficient because great powers often can afford to renege. This article

I thank Jonathan Aronson, Deborah Avant, John Campbell, Gary Cox, Jeff Frieden, Gary Jacobson, Robert Keohane, Samuel Kernell, Stephen Krasner, Mathew McCubbins, John Odell, Paul Papayoanou, Frances Rosenbluth, John Ruggie, Edwin Smith, Steve Weber, and the reviewers of *International Organization* for their comments.
1. John Gerard Ruggie, "Multilateralism: The Anatomy of an Institution," *International Organization* 46 (Summer 1992), pp. 561–98.
2. Many regimes are not multilateral. The definition is from Ruggie, "Multilateralism."
3. If benefits extended to one country must apply to all, and countries accept that all members are reasonably important for a successful solution (e.g., Greece cannot fall while France survives), then it is harder to rely on specific reciprocity's narrow balancing of benefits. See Robert O. Keohane, "Reciprocity in International Relations," *International Organization* 40 (Winter 1986), pp. 1–27.

International Organization 47, 2, Spring 1993, pp. 299–326

examines a second determinant of great power credibility—the impact of domestic political institutions on international commitments. National electoral systems and the divisions of power in governments influence the ability to make major international commitments, the difficulty of reversing those commitments, and the capability of other countries to monitor adherence to the commitments. The second part argues that certain U.S. political institutions (namely, the division of power between the legislative and executive branches and winner-takes-all, single-member districts for federal elections) enhanced the credibility of its multilateral commitments after 1945. (This argument stands in contrast to that of several analysts.[4]) The third part of the article claims that the Japanese mix of parliamentary government tied to an electoral system based on multimember districts and a single nontransferable vote hinders its credibility today.

Domestic politics and credible commitments

International regimes face the "top dog" problem. Compared with lesser powers, great powers have numerous options for foreign policy; so, how can other countries trust the good faith of the great powers?[5] Lesser powers certainly have to be more flexible about the international order, but they have little reason to support a noxious or fickle one. It is hard to execute a smart "follower strategy" (i.e., playing for advantages within the rules) if great powers can freely rewrite the rules.[6] This problem plagues all great power commitments, but it is especially serious for multilateral regimes because they impose fewer external checks than the sharply controlled obligations of bilateral and minilateral regimes.

The great powers can reduce their burdens and improve regime performance if lesser powers give those regimes more than token support. This support is most likely if other countries trust the resolve of the great powers to support the multilateral regime. Unfortunately, the enduring advantages for a great power from a reputation for credibility are not sufficient to convince other states that it may not renege for reasons of short-term expediency.[7]

4. For example, Henry A. Kissinger, "Domestic Structures and Foreign Policy," *Daedulus* 59 (Spring 1966), pp. 503–29.

5. This article explores both a hegemonic power (the United States after 1945) and a nonhegemonic power (the future role of Japan). The hegemonic stability thesis suggests why the strong might support collective goods disproportionately, but hypotheses about the fragility and desirability of hegemonic orders differ. See Robert O. Keohane, *After Hegemony: Cooperation and Discord in the World Political Economy* (Princeton, N.J.: Princeton University Press, 1984).

6. Lesser powers also have a domestic political problem when ratifying regime bargains. If political leaders cannot point to specific credible promises by great powers, then it is harder to show concrete benefits to offset complaints by political opponents of multilateral bargains.

7. Countries can also limit the number of participants or introduce specialized checks and balances in a regime. There is, however, a limit on how far this can go without abandoning multilateralism. See Miles Kahler, "Multilateralism with Small and Large Numbers," *International Organization* 46 (Summer 1992), pp. 681–708.

The great power's problem is no different than the one faced by Europe's warring "new monarchs" in the eighteenth century when they borrowed money. The monarchs were legally untouchable. Without any enforceable curb on unrealistic borrowing and spending, sources of private capital were wary of lending except at premium rates. When the rise of power of the English Parliament created a new institutional check on the King's spending policies, it lowered the cost of borrowing for the British monarch. In short, proper checks and balances on political leaders can reduce transaction costs by making their promises believable.[8]

Similarly, a country's rise to great power does not assure a conversion from international free riding. Increased power may make it logical for a country to become a "good citizen" internationally, but its political institutions may not support that position.[9] Other countries will worry about whether it is politically profitable for government leaders in the new powers to "do the right thing."

In short, making foreign policy commitments credible poses a problem common to all institutions: how to match the "private" incentives of leaders with their policy obligations. The common solutions are to (1) create specialized incentives to match public and self-interests (e.g., appoint an American as head of NATO to make the U.S. military value NATO); (2) alter the divisions of power in an organization (e.g., institute a new check on the leader, like Parliament's budgetary powers); and/or (3) permit others to monitor the behavior of leaders (e.g., "sunshine laws" for administrative proceedings in democracies).

How does this logic apply to domestic political systems and the credibility of multilateral commitments by great powers? Three factors determine the impact of domestic political institutions on credibility.[10] First, does domestic politics make it easier (or no harder) to hold power if multilateral promises are made and kept? This is the issue of specialized leadership incentives. A great

8. Douglas C. North and Barry R. Weingast, "Constitution and Commitment: The Evaluation of Institutions Governing Public Choice in Seventeenth-century England," *Journal of Economic History* 49 (December 1989), pp. 803–32. The Folk Theorem of noncooperative games suggests that cooperation can occur so long as each party can judge the other's good faith *ex post* and can refuse to cooperate after a defection. Unfortunately, the Folk Theorem is often hard to implement. The game has multiple equilibria; many include frequent defection because it is hard to define defection. See David Kreps, "Corporate Culture and Economic Theory," in James E. Alt and Kenneth A. Shepsle, eds., *Perspectives on Positive Political Economy* (Cambridge: Cambridge University Press, 1990) pp. 90–143.

9. A good example of such a theory is found in Richard Rosecrance and Jennifer Taw, "Japan and the Theory of International Leadership," *World Politics* 42 (January 1990), pp. 184–209.

10. Diplomacy can also tailor multilateral regimes to reinforce the compatibility of everyday politics and foreign policy in the great powers. Lesser powers should accept this tactic (within commonsense boundaries) because it reinforces the commitment of great powers. A good example is that Britain recognized that the world order would suit special U.S. priorities, but London tried to seize the initiative in order to improve its bargaining hand. See David Reynolds, "Roosevelt, Churchill, and the Wartime Anglo–American Alliance, 1939–1945: Towards a New Synthesis," in Wm. Roger Louis and Hedley Bull, eds., *The "Special Relationship": Anglo–American Relations Since 1945* (Oxford: Clarendon Press, 1986), pp. 17–41; and Frederick W. Mayer, "Managing Domestic Differences in International Negotiations: The Strategic Use of Internal Side-payments," *International Organization* 46 (Autumn 1992), pp. 793–818.

power's place in the international structure makes foreign policy a salient political issue. In democracies the electoral incentives for how politicians win offices and the control of government strongly influence how they frame the politics of foreign policy. Some electoral systems, such as that in Britain, reward politicians for organizing support for the production of collective goods (such as clean air or the fruits of multilateralism) on major issues.[11] Others, such as in Japan, disproportionately reward the supply of private goods (such as constituent services). Electoral systems favoring an emphasis on collective goods bolster multilateralism.

Second, does the political system's structure make it harder or easier to make or reverse promises? This depends especially on the division of power within government. Is it a parliamentary government, or does it divide power between independent legislative and executive branches (as in the United States)? The structure of policymaking influences how preferences become policy. Divided powers make it harder to initiate commitments and also harder to reverse them. Parliamentary power makes it easier to initiate and reverse commitments. Dilemmas created by the interaction of electoral systems and divisions of power often force countries to modify government institutions to facilitate foreign policy commitments.

Third, do other countries believe that they can monitor and perhaps influence the choices of the great powers? Can they find out in a timely way (i.e., early enough to limit damage to themselves) that a great power is defecting? Can they do anything to influence the decision? These are the issues of monitoring and of transparency.[12] A great power also has to make the workings of its domestic economic institutions credible to other countries because of their importance for global prosperity and competition. Transparency is easiest to achieve in a country with a divided government and an electoral system favoring collective goods.

Ideally, a test of these three variables (emphasis on collective goods, division of power, and transparency) would include careful controls for comparing each combination of them. However, even a crude dichotomization of each variable would require fourteen cases for study.[13] Instead, this article examines two countries that are the opposite on each dimension—the United States after

---

11. The voting system of Westminster democracies (those with British parliamentary and electoral structures) are prone to produce parliamentary majorities for parties that can enact sweeping platforms involving many collective goods. See Arend Lijphart, *Democracies* (New Haven, Conn.: Yale University Press, 1984); Rein Taagepeta and Matthew Shugart, *Seats and Votes: The Effects and Determinants of Electoral Systems* (New Haven, Conn.: Yale University Press, 1989); and Gary Cox, *The Efficient Secret* (New York: Cambridge University Press, 1987).

12. The secrecy of Soviet politics posed a consistent problem for its credibility on such issues as arms control and détente before *perestroika*. Domestic politics influence transparency, which influences the resolution of prisoners' dilemma games. See Keohane, *After Hegemony*. I thank Steve Weber for this point.

13. Dichotomization would not work. Electoral systems vary widely in their significant details. The present article uses the cases to illustrate the variables that distinguish electoral systems. Although this article cannot determine the relative importance of domestic and international variables, the first section explains why international variables do not suffice.

World War II and contemporary Japan—to demonstrate the plausibility and consequences of the three variables.

In brief, the U.S. electoral system makes majoritarian politics featuring positions on collective goods profitable. Its division of powers makes it harder to initiate commitments and easier to prevent reversals of commitments. Electoral incentives plus the division of powers make it easier for other countries to monitor the United States. In contrast, Japan's electoral system penalizes politicians if they emphasize issues concerning collective goods. Its parliamentary system concentrates political power, thereby making it easier to initiate and reverse major commitments. Finally, electoral incentives plus concentrated power make it hard for foreign governments to monitor the Japanese system.

The two countries also are "least likely cases" in the sense that common interpretations of the countries assume that the U.S. political system permits less coherent pursuit of collective goods than does Japan's.[14] The emphasis on multilateral regimes has the further advantage of putting the politics of credibility into sharp relief because multilateralism is a "demanding" form of cooperation.[15]

The United States after 1945

The relationship between domestic politics and credibility emerges clearly in three prominent arguments about why the U.S. political system hindered its multilateral commitments. First, Congress worried more about local constituencies than about foreign policy, thus muddling foreign policy. Second, a powerful strain of isolationism in American politics, especially in the Republican party, made multilateralism a precarious product of bipartisanship, largely through the White House courting of the Republican Senator Arthur Vandenberg of Michigan.[16] Third, the executive branch's control of foreign policy was weak because the U.S. division of powers hobbled policy innovation and adaptation.[17] These arguments underscore the importance of electoral dynamics and the division of power in government.[18]

14. See the careful review of the literature in Richard Samuels, *The Business of the Japanese State: Energy Markets in Comparative and Historical Perspective* (Ithaca, N.Y.: Cornell University Press, 1987). Another difficulty for testing this framework is that several rival theories offer predictions of equivalent behavior on some dimensions. On testing statist theories, see Peter F. Cowhey, " 'States' and 'Politics' in American Foreign Economic Policy," in John S. Odell and Thomas D. Willett, eds., *International Trade Policies—The Gains from Exchange Between Economics and Political Science* (Ann Arbor: University of Michigan Press, 1990), pp. 225–51.

15. The term is taken from Ruggie, "Multilateralism," p. 572.

16. James M. Jones, *The Fifteen Weeks* (New York: Viking Press, 1955).

17. Stephen Krasner, *Defending the National Interest* (Princeton, N.J.: Princeton University Press, 1978).

18. An analysis of a nondemocratic country would ask how the pursuit of power works outside an electoral system. The impact of the division of power is in principle no different, although discovering the division may be hard. See the discussion of national security policy in Philip G. Roeder, *Red Sunset: Origins of the Soviet Constitutional Revolution* (Princeton, N.J.: Princeton University Press, forthcoming), chap. 7.

A Model of U.S. Politics and Foreign Policy

This section argues that domestic political structures made U.S. foreign policy commitments credible for three reasons. These reasons have to do with the incentives created by the electoral systems and the institutional arrangements of the U.S. government after 1945. (Although much of this argument still applies, some may question whether the voter preferences described here may have started to shift after the 1970s. This case study focuses on the period from 1945 until the early 1970s.)

First, national electoral systems vary in what constitutes a winning vote and in the number of elected representatives from each district. The single-member district (with victory going to the candidate with the highest vote count), as is the case for the U.S. Congress, has two consequences. It favors a two-party system built around pursuit of the median voter to build a majority.[19] (The median voter is a shorthand term for the range of policy preferences around which most voters cluster. Parties have to cover a significant part of this cluster if they want to attract a majority.) It also makes party positions on matters of broad public policy very salient.

The electoral system rewards a political party known for policies designed to build the public good as understood by its voters. Parties emphasize differing mixes of collective goods, such as welfare versus defense, but majoritarian politics force them to include most of the same items. Party identification is like a brand name—it creates general expectations about identity and quality (so the appellation "tax-and-spend Democrats," a Republican favorite, creates a certain expectation about the Democratic "brand"). Promoting the salience of public goods (such as parks or national security) to voters is advantageous because majoritarian politics require rewarding many voters at once. Collective goods have the capacity to offer those rewards at a lower marginal cost per voter than does targeting specialized benefits for each voter.

The importance of positions on collective goods does not end distributional politics. Elected officials choose policies that disproportionately favor their supporters and emphasize particularistic benefits for which they can take clear credit when designing collective goods. The United States had a potent national defense for forty-odd years and a bloated budget to fund it. Congressional members and Presidents also emphasize their individual electoral identity through constituent service. Nonetheless, party identification remains important for electoral fortunes.[20]

---

19. The presidential system is a variation of the model.

20. Hypotheses differ about the respective roles of Congress and the President in defining party reputation. All the approaches suggest that positions matter for electoral success, and parties act on policy agendas. See Samuel Kernell, "The Primacy of Politics in Economic Policy," in Samuel Kernell, ed., *Parallel Politics—Economic Policymaking in Japan and the United States* (Washington, D.C.: Brookings Institution, 1991), pp. 325–78. The mix of collective goods and constituency services emphasized by politicians may vary over time. Constituency services have grown in importance since the 1960s, but their rising marginal costs may again favor more reliance on

The logic of the U.S. electoral system also makes it risky for a party to reverse positions if they are close to those of the median voter. Brand name identities mean that parties have a tough time reversing a position once they have made a major public commitment.[21] Unless the position of the median voter has changed radically, a major shift in party position leaves significant openings for the opposition. Thus, shifts in the ideological position of particular officeholders are unlikely to produce major changes because the party as a whole has few incentives to move dramatically. If it does, it will strengthen the opposition. After 1945 the rejection of the presumed causes of the Depression (autarky and isolationism) and the opposition to communism kept the electorate extremely focused until at least the early 1970s.

Does foreign policy matter much to voters? The traditional literature on voting and U.S. foreign policy held that the low level of information on international affairs possessed by voters means that foreign policy is not important. The voting literature now rejects the equation between information and importance and that between information and rationality. Voters make judgments on issues about which they have little information (including many pocketbook domestic issues) but do so in ways that make sense given limited information.[22] Foreign policy may matter less consistently to voters, but foreign policy issues can always ignite powerful retrospective punishment by voters.[23] Although congressional members may not know the specifics of foreign policy, they delegate power to members who are willing to pay attention to and accommodate the political dictates of the party.[24]

---

collective goods. See Gary Cox and Frances Rosenbluth, "The Structural Determinants of Electoral Cohesiveness: England, Japan, and the United States," presented to a workshop on the comparison of U.S. and Japanese politics, University of California, Irvine, 21 February 1992.

21. Other models of the politics of credibility overlook this issue. See Bruce Bueno de Mesquita and David Lalman, "Domestic Opposition and Foreign War," *American Political Science Review* 84 (September 1990), pp. 747–66; and James D. Morrow, "Electoral and Congressional Incentives and Arms Control," *The Journal of Conflict Resolution* 35 (June 1991), pp. 245–65.

22. Voters are rational free riders who invest too few resources in gathering information about a public good (a better informed vote), but they reason rationally in ways consistent with the limited resources devoted to the task. Attributable benefits (or persuasive denial of blame) are the keys to a politician's success. Presidents like foreign policy especially because they have clear claims to control. Nonetheless, party identification is an important "default" value on issues that voters care about but about which they lack other information. This is especially true in congressional races. Party identification in turn is based on retrospective assessment of performance, and voters will change their assessment of party competence on major issues fairly rapidly. See Samuel Popkin, *The Reasoning Voter* (Chicago: University of Chicago Press, 1991).

23. A powerful case for retrospective accountability is made by John H. Aldrich, John L. Sullivan, and Eugene Borgida, "Foreign Affairs and Issue Voting: Do Presidential Candidates 'Waltz Before a Blind Audience?'," *American Political Science Review* 83 (March 1989), pp. 123–41. Other important work on opinion overlooks political parties and Congress. See Miroslav Nincic, "U.S. Soviet Policy and the Electoral Connection," *World Politics* 42 (April 1990), pp. 370–96.

24. U.S. foreign policy officials regale listeners with tales of congressional ignorance. However, the same sort of congressional delegation takes place around issues such as the mechanics of social security administration and tax legislation, where congressional influence is indisputable. On delegation to committee chairpersons who represent the views of the party caucus, see Gary W. Cox and Mathew D. McCubbins, *Parties and Committees in the U.S. House of Representatives* (Berkeley: University of California Press, 1991).

Second, governments differ in how they structure the division of powers. The most fundamental division in democracies is between parliamentary government and those with coequal legislative and executive branches. The U.S. division of powers—where each branch has veto power over policy—makes it potentially harder to initiate major new commitments but easier to maintain them. Divided government has two forms—the potential of different parties controlling the legislative and executive branches and the perennial differences in interests of Congress and the President irrespective of who governs.[25]

In one, the presidency and the Congress can be under the control of different parties. This makes reversal of major policies harder, a source of stability in commitments.[26] For example, congressional rebellions against any standing commitment require new legislation that the President can veto. Thus, the division of power can increase continuity and credibility, although it also can make new initiatives considerably harder. The success of an initiative hinges on whether both parties believe that voters favor the basic policy.

In another form of U.S. governmental division, irrespective of which party is in control the different electoral incentives for the President, the Senate, and the House of Representatives lead to diverging approaches to foreign policy. House members are the most parochial and have the shortest time horizons for judging programs; Senate members are less so; and the President has to be the most cosmopolitan because he or she is directly identified with broad swings in national well-being. Accordingly, the House should most strongly view foreign policy through the lens of local distributional impacts and specialized voter groups in districts (e.g., the Nissan automobile manufacturing plant in her district or German Americans in Milwaukee).[27]

Even if one party controls both legislative and executive branches, Congress (which benefits less directly than the President from diffuse national benefits) should be even more sensitive than the President about such issues creating visible burdens for constituents such as the military draft, taxes due to higher government budgets, and import competition for weak industries; assuring regional (and multidistrict) distribution of benefits by choosing measures to stabilize international monetary markets and foreign economies that do not favor New York-based banks (long unpopular in the heartland) or promote competitors to U.S. enterprises; and catering to ethnic voters' personal

---

25. Morris P. Fiorina, "Coalition Governments, Divided Governments, and Electoral Theory," *Governance* 4 (July 1991), pp. 236–49.

26. After making multilateral commitments, shifts in both the U.S. presidential party and the majority congressional party are required to obtain a major policy reversal. For example, many critical commitments to multilateralism are the products of laws and treaties. Although treaties may become attenuated in practice (as with some regional security treaties), that requires de facto congressional acquiescence.

27. Gary Jacobson, *The Electoral Origins of Divided Government* (Boulder, Colo.: Westview Press, 1990).

interests about foreign policy by creating a U.S. military policy that also protects foreign countries important to them.

The division of power and differences in electoral incentives should lead to institutional innovations for major new commitments (e.g., the Federal Reserve system for central banking) to reconcile the differing time horizons and sizes of constituencies. These innovations will include (1) new bureaucracies to advocate and safeguard each policy innovation in return for advocates accepting less initially; (2) institutional "fire alarms" (devices making it easy for the disgruntled to get information and complain); (3) "trip wires" (requirements for explicit authorization of certain uses of a general authority) to satisfy critics about contingent dangers of an innovation; (4) "time limits" on authority to force executors of the policy to pay attention to critics; and (5) "stacking the decision process" to make sure that all key interests are represented.[28] Political leaders just after World War II used these methods to reinforce multilateralism by making it more consistent with the electoral imperative.[29] The innovations did not end legislative power over foreign policy.

Third, countries differ in how easily foreign governments may monitor their choices. Intricate combinations of electoral incentives and divisions of power influence transparency. The U.S. political-economic system is relatively open and transparent to any partner committed enough to invest resources in monitoring it. The United States has its secrets, but the rivalry between the executive and the legislature favors the disclosure of information, especially about economic policy. This made America's internal market and its regulation relatively transparent and credible to other countries after 1945. Markets were generally open to foreign firms, information was readily available, and according to Jeffrey Frieden, "markets were free enough from major government manipulation to overcome investors' and borrowers' fears of political risk."[30]

In summary, political parties will back collective goods concerning foreign policy to bolster their political reputations. Once made, these commitments are hard to reverse unless there is a massive shift in voter preferences. The division of power forces institutional innovation (including tinkering with the multilateral regimes) to reconcile new foreign policy commitments with electoral considerations.

28. See Sharyn O'Halloran, "Politics, Process, and American Trade Policy: Congress and the Regulation of Foreign Commerce," Ph.D. diss., University of California, San Diego, 1990; and David Brady and Jongryn Mo, "The U.S. Congress and Trade Policy: An Institutional Approach," *Pacific Focus* 5 (Autumn 1990), pp. 5–26.

29. The Marshall Plan was more credible because its administration was removed from the State Department, put in an office with a temporary life cycle, and led by a corporate executive from Indiana (the head of Studebaker automobiles), whose mission was to deliver a viable program that Congress would not deem harmful to the industrial Midwest.

30. Jeffrey A. Frieden, "Capital Politics: Creditors and the International Political Economy," *Journal of Public Policy,* 8 (July–December 1988), p. 274.

The United States and the creation of multilateralism

Did the political party leadership think that the party would do well in elections by supporting multilateralism after World War II? The evidence shows that support for internationalism was strong, and multilateralism was a politically attractive version of internationalism, especially after receiving an American twist.

Internationalism was good politics. The restructuring of Europe and Japan to avoid another war was a critical U.S. mission consistent with voter preferences. As Michael Barone trenchantly notes, the consensus on foreign policy existed by 1944. Although isolationists had run well in some congressional districts in 1942 (when the news on the war was bad), both potential candidates of the Republican party, Wendell Willkie and Thomas Dewey, strongly supported an "internationalist" platform in 1944. The internationalist Dewey coalition subsequently held control over the presidential nomination until 1964.[31] Moreover, although Franklin Roosevelt had short coattails in 1944, Representative Hamilton Fish (Republican of New York) and Senator Gerald Nye (Republican of North Dakota) lost on isolationist platforms. Robert Taft only squeaked by in Ohio. Then, in 1946, a good year for Republicans, its two leading isolationists lost their Senate seats. And in the 1948 Presidential campaign both parties backed the emerging multilateral policy.[32]

The Republican congressional membership clearly did not want to fight over internationalism when the Republicans took control of Congress in 1946. They chose Vandenberg to be chairperson of the Foreign Relations Committee, even though he had already backed an internationalist order.[33] The glue that bound the two parties was President Truman's willingness to identify internationalism with anticommunism, the one horror that even Midwest conservatives could not stomach.[34]

A two-fold bedrock message from the electorate drove both parties: government was not to repeat mistakes that led to the Depression and the

31. The Eastern states were critical for winning the nomination, and their leadership backed the Dewey wing. See Michael Barone, *Our Country: The Shaping of America from Roosevelt to Reason* (New York: Free Press, 1990), pp. 167–81.

32. Barone and Donovan both note that the bipartisan tone benefited Truman but argue that domestic, not foreign, policy was the key to victory. See Barone, *Our Country;* and Robert J. Donovan, *Conflict and Crisis, the Presidency of Harry S. Truman* (New York: W. W. Norton, 1977).

33. Vandenberg defined the terms by which the Midwestern wing of the Republican party would join the Eastern wing in accepting multilateralism championed by Democrats. Cox and McCubbins show that the party caucus used House committee chairmanships (including that of the Foreign Affairs Committee) to exercise control over committee actions. See Cox and McCubbins, *Parties and Committees in the U.S. House of Representatives.*

34. Humanitarian appeals for European aid did not move congressional leaders. President Truman and Secretary of State Acheson then linked aid to fighting communism, and the Republicans turned positive. See Daniel Yergin, *Shattered Peace—The Origins of the Cold War and the National Security State* (Boston: Houghton Mifflin, 1977); and Timothy P. Ireland, *Creating the Entangling Alliance—The Origins of the North Atlantic Treaty Organization* (Westport, Conn.: Greenwood Press, 1981).

United States would intervene when necessary to avoid a security threat. American political leaders had further concluded that protectionism, autarky, and trading blocks were exactly the kinds of threats to prosperity and peace that could trigger punishment by voters.[35] Moreover, neither congressional party supported a strictly laissez-faire economic policy. With widespread fears of a possible depression, not even conservatives wanted a reaffirmation of former President Hoover's philosophy.

The battle was over the precise economic philosophy and terms of internationalism. The 1946 electoral resurgence of Republicans checked the growing power of labor unions (which were widely blamed for inflation). This led to less spending and rejection of detailed micromanagement of the economy (by wage and price controls, for example).[36] The election also reinforced the middle-of-the-road wing of the Democratic party in Congress that was skeptical of government planning. The Democrats did not become advocates of laissez-faire economics, but they rejected any industrial policy or corporatism based on a troika of much strengthened unions, big business, and big government.

This political mix meant that U.S. foreign economic policy would permit measures to stimulate general global recovery and open markets but would stumble on plans to have the government administer markets. Ironically, this skepticism of planning enhanced the credibility of the U.S. commitment to open world markets.

The quick passage of the huge Marshall Plan (which comprised more than 2 percent of government spending) testified to the potency of anticommunism and the fears of rising protectionism in Europe despite protests about its New Deal overtones and the bleeding of America for the benefit of foreigners. The Marshall Plan represented a dramatic yet nonmilitary response to communism just when American voters were thoroughly wary of the Soviet Union.[37] More crucially, even though the aid did not reward U.S. voters directly, it strongly boosted all U.S. exporters. Republican farmers sold wheat to Europe, and Democratic union workers got job security based on manufactured exports.

Why did internationalism become multilateralism, and why did multilateralism endure? In part, it represented the influence of ideas on U.S. leadership.[38] Yet, there was also significant disagreement about many of these ideas, and

---

35. Stephen Haggard, "The Institutional Foundations of Hegemony: Explaining the Reciprocal Trade Agreements Act of 1934," *International Organization* 42 (Winter 1988), pp. 91–120, shows how this worked for trade. Multilateralism was not the only internationalist option, but, as Odell notes, an alternative is attractive if it is well known and apparently "predicts" the failure of past policy. See John S. Odell, "From London to Bretton Woods: Sources of Change in Bargaining Strategies and Outcomes," *Journal of Public Policy* 8 (July–December 1988), pp. 287–316.

36. Barone argues that the Taft-Hartley Act virtually froze union expansion and limited growth in union power; see Barone, *Our Country*. Nau notes the conservative overtones to American commitments; see Henry R. Nau, *The Myth of America's Decline* (New York: Oxford, 1990).

37. Even Senator Robert Taft voted for aid to Greece and Turkey. See Robert Pollard, *Economic Security and the Origins of the Cold War, 1945–1950* (New York: Columbia University Press, 1985); and Jones, *The Fifteen Weeks*.

38. Ruggie, "Multilateralism."

some institutional designs flopped. Multilateralism also succeeded in part because it avoided some political problems that had plagued other internationalist initiatives, including those after 1919.

The politics of multilateralism meant that it bore the strong imprint of America's political leadership, as opposed simply to dreams of the executive branch's planners. These political roots show up in the multilateral security system for Europe, the Eurocentric bias of the multilateral order, the reliance on public international institutions for economic affairs, and the significant national controls and restrictions on the purview of those institutions.

Multilateralism in Europe solved a fundamental political dilemma for both parties because it included the homelands of all Americans of European descent. Therefore, it avoided the crossfire created by the politics of continuing ethnic ties to Europe by American voters. For example, Irish Americans always resented relying primarily on Britain; German Americans had been isolationist because internationalism traditionally had been defined as anti-German until the Marshall Plan was initiated and NATO was formed. Dean Acheson recognized these realities and ordered the end of all internal State Department studies organized around a special relationship with Britain.[39] The United States rejected the United Kingdom's effort to structure the defense of Europe in a dumbbell structure (the U.K.–France–Benelux pact on one side and a U.K.–Canada–U.S. pact on the other with the United Kingdom as the special link. The United States only wanted to negotiate about a multilateral North Atlantic pact.[40] Multilateralism favored everybody's homeland, unless the Soviets forbade it.

Indeed, the global order after 1945 was mainly a Eurocentric order. Just as U.S. voters in 1945 were largely of European descent, so the practical thrust of multilateral innovations was European based.[41] To be sure, the U.S. political and policy debate could not easily ignore the fundamentals of international power. The United States was the world's leading power. Its global interests dictated European and Asian roles. The interpretation of its own role, however, was contestable. American politics favored a multilateral approach for Europe. Largely bilateral, ad hoc commitments to Asia were acceptable

39. Ryan reports that Britain tracked U.S. opinion polls taken in 1944 that showed 71 percent approval in the Midwest for the United Nations. He suggests that anti–United Kingdom feeling among Irish American and German American voters may have bolstered the U.S. position on decolonization. See Henry Butterfield Ryan, *The Vision of Anglo-America: The U.S.–U.K. Alliance and the Emerging Cold War, 1943–1946* (New York: Cambridge University Press, 1987), pp. 31–41; and Dean Acheson, *Present at the Creation* (New York: Norton, 1969), p. 387.

40. Bradford Perkins, "Unequal Partners: The Truman Administration and Great Britain," pp. 57–58, in Louis and Bull, *The "Special Relationship."* Ireland shows why bargaining logic favored multilateralism; see Ireland, *Creating the Entangling Alliance.*

41. Reynolds notes that 20 to 30 percent of all Americans favored a negotiated peace with Germany in 1942, while the same polls showed no sympathy to Japan; see Reynolds, "Roosevelt, Churchill, and the Wartime Anglo–American Alliance, 1939–1945." My thanks to Edwin Smith for this hypothesis.

because there was less intensive common ground to bind together allies, and U.S. voters' concern with the area rested primarily with China.[42]

The practice of multilateralism also ameliorated concerns over the possibility of the economic bleeding of America while other countries shirked their duties. Collective public institutions (e.g., NATO and the World Bank) with clear conditions on access to their benefits and contributions by other countries addressed U.S. fears about burden sharing.[43] At the same time, standardized multilateral criteria for aid permitted performance conditions on aid without risking charges of bias toward any one ethnic homeland.

Even though multilateralism had political appeal, inevitable tensions over its precise character required institutional innovation to reconcile the differing political interests of the executive and legislature. At the same time, the acquiescence of other countries to the American stamp on the multilateral order further solidified political support in the United States.[44]

The well-known story of tinkering with the trade policy process illustrates how Congress can delegate power to the executive branch to resolve collective goods problems. Congress retained oversight by enfranchising selected interest groups in the trade advisory process ("stacking the decision process"), by requiring the executive to issue regular reports on its plans, by putting short time limits on each authorization for negotiations, and by retaining veto rights over agreements. In addition, trade agreements had an escape clause for dealing with temporary surges in imports. These measures let Congress keep trade policy responsive to electoral interests without degenerating to the lowest common denominator.[45]

The congressional battle over the International Trade Organization also shaped the scope of the multilateral trading regime. The struggle between the executive branch and Congress produced a commitment to free trade in manufactured goods and processed commodities but not raw commodities or

42. Republicans chose to bargain over the form of multilateralism and its geopolitical priorities. In 1948, thirty of the fifty-one Republican senators were reliable supporters of Truman's policies, a comfortable majority. Republican conservatives favored limiting commitments to Europe (especially resisting placement of U.S. troops in Europe) in order to redeem the United States' "destiny in Asia," a position popular with conservative Christians; see Gary W. Reichard, "The Domestic Politics of National Security," in Norman Graebner, ed., *The National Security: Its Theory and Practice, 1945–1960* (New York: Oxford University Press, 1986), pp. 243–74. Still, Taft did not use the Korean War to urge an anticommunist campaign in Asia because he wanted the 1952 nomination. The Dewey wing blocked Taft by turning to Dwight Eisenhower, who was an adamant multilateralist and a "Europe-first" candidate; see Barone, *Our Country.*

43. Vandenberg cast NATO as an organization stressing "mutual aid and self help" precisely to assure Congress that NATO was not a one-sided bargain. See Ireland, *Creating the Entangling Alliance,* p. 89.

44. The logic is similar to that in Mayer, "Managing Domestic Differences in International Negotiations."

45. They also allowed Congress to retain coequal power. See O'Halloran, "Politics, Process, and American Trade Policy."

services. It also excluded multilateral management of commodity markets except in very specialized cases.[46]

Multilateral regimes concerning money and aid also reflect institutional tinkering. U.S. politics created incentives for the emphasis on public international institutions (the International Monetary Fund [IMF] and the World Bank) in the new multilateralism. The alternative was to streamline the delegation of power to the private sector, much as the British Government had chosen the Bank of England as the private manager of the gold standard or the Morgan Bank had done occasionally for the U.S. Treasury Department. However, there was no way to delegate those powers in a politically acceptable manner. For example, when the Morgan Bank conducted stabilization operations, it could—and did—reap windfall profits from its role as the agent of the Treasury. Such conflicts of interest were not sustainable, especially because the average Democrat was no fan of Wall Street.[47] Public institutions were the only viable solution.

Another feature was the insistence on more explicit national control over some multilateral economic institutions than the executive branch envisioned. Organizing the IMF governance around voting by national executive directors was a direct outgrowth of congressional intervention to assure accountability (and stop Europe from upsetting U.S. interests on monetary policy).[48] Congressional authorization also "stacked the decision process" by insisting that the U.S. executive director get prior authority on key congressional concerns from a cabinet committee set up by Congress.[49] The World Bank only received U.S. funding by keeping its role targeted initially on Europe (which was popular in a European-descended, U.S. voting population) and strictly tied to businesslike investments in infrastructure of the type long supported in the United States and beneficial to U.S. engineering and manufacturing firms.

Multilateral security policy also accommodated domestic politics. The early emphasis on economic recovery and the psychological shoring up of European military security (by creating a NATO that entailed no troop commitments) and the later emphasis on building regional military groupings reflected both strategic thinking and executive–legislative dickering. Congress wanted to

---

46. Congressional committees overseeing commodity policies most resembled iron-triangle models. These committees greatly strengthened the cabinet agencies most sympathetic to the commodity producers. See Cox and McCubbins, *Parties and Committees in the U.S. House of Representatives.*

47. According to Gardner, Secretary of Treasury Henry Morgenthau told one audience that the Bretton Woods agreement would "drive the usurious money lenders from the temple of international finance." See Richard N. Gardner, "Sterling–Dollar Diplomacy in Current Perspective," in Louis and Bull, *The "Special Relationship";* and Ron Chernow, *The House of Morgan* (New York: Atlantic Monthly Press, 1990), p. 192.

48. The negotiators weakened the power of the IMF to supervise domestic economic policies in order to please Congress. The majority of Republicans supported the Bretton Woods agreement in Congress. See Gardner, *Sterling–Dollar Diplomacy* (New York: Oxford University Press, 1969), pp. 129–43.

49. Pollard, *Economic Security and the Origins of the Cold War,* pp. 15–17.

avoid the draft if possible, keep tight fire alarms on any executive branch thinking that might threaten war, and hold down spending.

A few specifics show how institutional tinkering and the movement in voter opinion resolved those problems. Some checks came through controlling the means to provide defense. Congress consistently refused Truman's appeals for the draft until the Korean War changed public opinion about conscription. Other controls involved approval procedures for military actions. The NATO accord explicitly included the right of each member to follow its constitutional processes in determining how to fulfill its commitment. The emphasis on regional security efforts also allayed fears about the budget and the possibility that foreign allies would entrap the United States without risking their own forces.

Congress also increased the fire alarms and restacked the decision process for making foreign security policy. The National Security Council (NSC) was created in part to hem in Truman with a set of senior officials representing diverse constituencies that would predictably leak contentious plans.[50] The act establishing the NSC followed the approach of the Administrative Procedures Act of the previous year, which had regularized the decision making process to make it accountable to Congress. The act also extended similar procedures to intelligence operations for the first time, a significant choice because of escalating covert action in Europe.[51] Finally, Congress denied the President most tools (including control over personnel and how the military forged its budget) that might have let the executive redefine the mission and strategy of the U.S. military to turn it away from Europe.[52]

In short, political leaders reorganized institutions to reconcile differing incentives for the legislature and executive by changing decision making to enhance accountability to the legislative branch and disgruntled constituents. They also designed program mandates to preclude (or discourage) projects that challenged congressional priorities. These measures moved the policies closer to the median position of voter support. This made commitments more credible. If one party had abandoned them, the other would have reason to turn that abandonment into an electoral issue.

Even if U.S. politics were compatible with credible promises, other countries still had to understand them. Fortunately, American politics are relatively transparent to motivated foreign observers. Political debate, regulatory policies, and executive decision making are open and accessible. Foreign political

---

50. Truman understood the challenge and maneuvered to reassert his independence. See I. M. Destler, Leslie H. Gelb, and Anthony Lake, *Our Own Worst Enemy—The Unmaking of American Foreign Policy* (New York: Simon and Schuster, 1984).

51. Harold Jongju Koh, *The National Security Constitution* (New Haven, Conn.: Yale University Press, 1990), pp. 84–99.

52. Deborah Avant, "The Institutional Sources of Military Doctrine: The United States in Vietnam and Britain in the Boer War and Malaya," Ph.D. diss., Department of Political Science, University of California, San Diego, 1991.

and economic interests can most often figure out where policy is going and how to influence it.

The multilateral regime also got an important boost because foreign economic interests shared equal standing in law and practice with U.S. interests. Although foreign lobbying in 1950 was small change compared with lobbying in Washington today, foreign economic operations inside the United States also were not subject to much attack. The embassies were quite competent to keep track of, and lobby, U.S. economic policy choices. Most fundamentally, there were no mysteries about the U.S. market. The voters' rejection of the more interventionist wing of the Democratic party in the late 1940s meant that foreign countries did not have to unravel an apparatus for central planning. The same devices designed to assist Congress in overseeing national security affairs also aided interested foreign governments.

In summary, the political terrain for multilateralism was better in the 1940s than often supposed. Once made, commitments were hard to reverse. Hence, there were both private electoral incentives to keep commitments and institutional checks on changing the U.S. commitment to multilateralism. Still, multilateralism cut different ways politically for the President and the Congress. Therefore, the political leadership tailored programs (including the design of multilateral regimes) and designed institutional innovations to reconcile executive and legislative political incentives. At the same time, the political economy of the U.S. market stabilized around a consensus that enhanced U.S. transparency and credibility.

Japan: private goods and multilateral credibility

This discussion assumes that Japan will become a great power by acquiring greater military capability (though not parity with the United States) to supplement its coleadership of the world economy. The question then becomes whether Japan will alter its international policies enough to permit multilateralism to thrive.

An evolving multipolar world already generates pressure for greater conditionality and selectivity in commitments, but multilateral regimes are adapting.[53] However, other countries doubt whether Japan will vigorously support multilateralism. Japan has a vanishingly small profile on most security matters. Most countries question the transparency and openness of Japanese markets even though Japan has fewer formal trade barriers than most countries. There is little more confidence in the transparency or accessibility of the Japanese political process for foreign interests.[54]

---

53. Ruggie, "Multilateralism."

54. Kent E. Calder, "Japanese Foreign Economic Policy Formation: Explaining the Reactive State," *World Politics* 40 (July 1988), pp. 517–41.

Japan's international performance may simply be a residue of free riding during its rise to power. However, as this article's first part showed, it cannot be assumed that domestic politics will respond to a changing international position. This analysis looks at Japan's past performance for clues about the future.

Is the evidence on the prior politics of Japan pertinent to conduct after greater international power has been gained? One advantage of this article's approach is that the dynamics attributed to political incentives and institutions cut across issues and specific circumstances. The institutional logic is basically the same for clean air or foreign policy, as well as for small or great powers. The political logic of prior foreign policy choices should remain constant. Of course, if the preferences of voters or interest groups change enough, changes in political institutions might likewise ensue—a contingency discussed shortly.

A model of Japanese politics and foreign policy

Neither current electoral incentives nor the division of power bolsters the credibility of Japanese commitments to multilateralism.[55] However, just as institutional innovation and the tailoring of multilateralism built support in the United States, perhaps adaptation will work in Japan. The analysis below examines two possible routes: shifts in interest group preferences and structural reform of the political system.

The Japanese system is parliamentary. It is easier to undertake major policy initiatives in a parliamentary system under control of a majority party than it is in a U.S.-style electoral system.[56] However, there are no built-in checks on reversals of policy promises. Thus, in theory, it is easier both to initiate and to reverse major foreign policy promises.

Parliamentary leaders can also delegate extensive authority to bureaucracies more easily than can U.S. political leaders because in the parliamentary form of government there is no rivalry between the legislature and executive. Unified control lets political leadership design quiet but effective controls over the bureaucracy. This is especially true when one party holds power continuously (in Japan, this is the Liberal Democratic party [LDP]) because the bureaucracy has learned its preferences.[57]

---

55. This model assumes that Japanese political leaders in fact are in charge. Many analysts disagree with that premise and therefore imply different paths toward domestic reforms necessary for international credibility. The classic work on bureaucratic leadership is Chalmers Johnson, *MITI and the Japanese Miracle* (Stanford, Calif.: Stanford University Press, 1982).

56. The Japanese Diet has a lower and an upper house. The lower house holds most of the power. The Liberal Democratic party (LDP) has not lost control of the lower house since 1955 and usually controls the upper chamber, as well. However, currently, it is narrowly in the minority in the upper house.

57. The political leadership does not give the bureaucracy detailed guidelines; often it only signals the outer limits for policy directions and provides a series of detailed expectations about whom policy will reward.

Delegation does not abolish political control. If important constituents complain, politicians intervene. Political leaders also settle ministerial feuds over turf precisely because the choice of the lead ministry implies which types of policy preferences (and constituents) will prevail.

In comparison to that of the United States, the Japanese electoral system rewards cautious leadership built around particularistic politics in the executive branch.[58] It does not reward risks to initiate broad policies for the collective good. Foreign policy is a much less desirable business for politicians than it is in the United States.[59]

Japan elects members to the dominant legislative body (the Diet's House of Representatives) in multimember districts (each having two to six seats) with each voter having a single nontransferable vote. (No matter how many seats are being filled in the district, the citizen can vote for only one candidate.) A party can only win a majority by running several candidates in each district. No party wanting majority status can easily run on broad policy issues because members of the party could undercut each other in the same district. (For example, imagine that all LDP candidates ran on similar issues but that one of them was the best at explaining the issues. This candidate might attract most LDP voters and cause all other LDP candidates to lose.) Instead, candidates win by building a dedicated minority block of voters cultivated largely by extensive campaign spending and lavish patronage politics.[60] Personal favors, not policies, cater to the household. This in turn leads to the notorious money politics of Japan.

Members have little pressing concern to run issue-oriented campaigns, so those seeking party leadership do not emphasize positions on broad policies unless absolutely necessary. To be sure, no political party is totally without an electoral identity, but the LDP makes the United States' Republican party look like a philosopher's club. Still, the LDP is the party of economic growth and

---

58. The following analysis of Japan draws heavily on Kent E. Calder, *Crisis and Compensation— Public Policy and Political Stability in Japan* (Princeton, N.J.: Princeton University Press, 1988), especially pp. 63–70; Frances Rosenbluth, "Japan's Response to the Strong Yen: Party Leadership and the Market for Political Favors," manuscript, Graduate School of International Relations and Pacific Studies, University of California, San Diego, December, 1990; Cox and Rosenbluth, "The Structural Determinants of Electoral Cohesiveness"; and Gary W. Cox, "SNTV and d'Hondt are 'equivalent,' " *Electoral Studies* 10 (1992), pp. 118–32.

59. Van Wolferen notes that foreign policy and defense are among the worst specialties for electoral security or party advancement because they do not generate large flows of campaign moneys; see Karel van Wolferen, *The Enigma of Japanese Power: People and Politics in a Stateless Nation* (New York: Knopf, 1989).

60. The opposition can run on issues if it does not seek majority status. The Japan Socialist party (JSP) normally fields only one candidate per constituency. This strategy enhances the chance of one candidate finding a targeted minority in the district to support his or her election. Current officeholders do not encourage a second candidate because there is strong job security with the present strategy. This strategy dooms the JSP to minority status. See Gerald Curtis, *Election Campaigning Japanese Style* (New York: Columbia University Press, 1971); and Kernell, "The Primacy of Politics in Economic Policy."

global competitive success.[61] The party's general message of growth and international economic prestige reinforced the incentives to give key industries what they wanted in return for their political and monetary support.[62]

Japanese industrial policy after 1945 inherited an economy centered on a well-defined group of large industries and banks. Even after "trust busting" by the Occupation, politicians catered to those firms with policies to boost savings and investment and to increase economic rents by protectionism. Once the domestic economy reignited, an export-oriented policy most easily harmonized the interests of those firms.[63] The bureaucracies nurtured "industrial visions" to improve coordination among oligopolistic firms, although they faltered when dealing with less concentrated industries.[64]

Politicians also catered to small businesses, which were numerous and spread across most Diet districts. For example, laws sheltered "mom and pop" shops from competition by larger stores. Conservatives also prized the rural vote and hence protected farmers from the world market.[65] Household voters benefited mainly as employees of growing firms or through personal favors from politicians.

What does Japan now do when tough choices are necessary, as when the United States threatens the Japanese export strategy in a trade dispute? When critical issues arise that can harm the LDP, the faction leaders pull together a collective policy response that goes beyond routine politics. The leadership then pressures the rank and file members to follow by using two types of control—nominations for Diet seats and large sums of campaign funds.

The LDP is divided into factions, each led by a senior politician, that emphasize money and campaigns, not policy.[66] Factions vie for control over the party by building their numbers in the Diet and their patronage powers. So, they recruit members from every *zoku* (specialized study groups that provide LDP Diet members with their closest counterpart to the policy expertise and

---

61. Takashi Inoguchi, "The Political Economy of Conservative Resurgence Under Recession: Public Policies and Political Support in Japan, 1977–1983," in T. J. Pempel, ed., *Uncommon Democracies: The One-Party Dominant Regimes* (Ithaca, N.Y.: Cornell University Press, 1990), pp. 189–225.

62. John Creighton Campbell, "Democracy and Bureaucracy in Japan," in Takeshi Ishida and Ellis S. Krauss, eds., *Democracy in Japan* (Pittsburgh, Penn.: University of Pittsburgh Press, 1989), pp. 113–37.

63. The standard discussion is found in Johnson, *MITI and the Japanese Miracle*. Many doubt the efficacy of industrial policy. However, a policy driven by narrow demands for protection that also favored investment policy could have yielded virtuous outcomes, given the Japanese industrial structure. Itoh and Kiyono largely agree with Johnson on the role of protection in triggering growth. See Motoshige Itoh and Kazuhara Kiyono, "Foreign Trade and Direct Investment," in Ryutaro Kumiya, Masahiro Okuno, and Kotaro Suzumura, eds., *Industrial Policy of Japan* (Tokyo: Academic Press, 1988), pp. 155–81.

64. Samuels, *The Business of the Japanese State*.

65. The dominance of the LDP further slanted the system because it continued massive malapportionment that favored conservative rural voters. This muted shifts in public policy associated with the rising power of urban districts (e.g., reduced protection for farmers).

66. Masaru Kohno, "Rational Foundations for the Organization of the Liberal Democratic Party," *World Politics* 44 (April 1992), pp. 369–97, especially note 30.

patronage opportunities of congressional subcommittees). Therefore, the factions are relatively cosmopolitan and representative of the party as a whole. Their leaders came to power by raising money and bargaining skillfully across issues; they value the privileges of majority rule more than particular issues and so have an incentive to compromise to save the party.

Even when the leadership acts to defuse a foreign policy crisis, there is no political incentive to rework policy broadly on behalf of foreign policy, consumers, or any other diffuse interest that cuts across election districts. Indeed, analysts often argue that the only opposition party capable of backing systematic reform is the U.S. diplomatic establishment.[67]

The following sections show why political institutions make it hard to adjust to multilateral obligations regarding security and the economy. They also examine two possibilities for making the politics of multilateralism more tractable—shifts in the preferences of interest group coalitions supporting the LDP and modification of the electoral system itself.

Defense and peacekeeping policies

Although Japan has built a substantial conventional military capability, it largely has shunned multilateral obligations.[68] After 1945 the Japanese political leadership deliberately portrayed security politics to the Japanese public so as to resist foreign pressure to extend the scope of security commitments. Now it is hard to shift the political terms of the debate.

The international position of the country certainly influences its strategic options. Japanese leaders acknowledged that Japan could not easily check the Soviet Union on its own, and the Soviet Union was a relatively close geographic threat. So, the U.S. defense connection was essential (unless Japan opted to gamble on some version of neutrality). This meant that the main question about strategy and capability was the structure of the security relationship to the United States.[69] The key questions until the 1990s were twofold: (1) would Japan have a firm security guarantee from the United States including tangible deployment of forces? and (2) how much could the United States press Japan to take an extended perimeter defense (i.e., how narrowly would Japan constitute its theater of self-defense operations) and develop massive military assets?

If this captures the security game, then the first political question for Japan's conservative political leaders was whether they wanted to gamble on neutrality. Their suspicions of Communists prompted them to reject neutrality. If the

---

67. Calder, "Japanese Foreign Economic Policy Formation."
68. Japan has cooperated on multilateral nonproliferation and antiterrorism measures.
69. See Donald Hellmann, *Japanese Domestic Politics and Foreign Policy* (Berkeley: University of California Press, 1969); and Martin E. Weinstein, *Japan's Postwar Defense Policy, 1947–1968* (New York: Columbia University Press, 1971).

alliance with the United States was the cornerstone of policy, then would Japan bow to American pressure for an extended defense perimeter?

Although conservative in its politics, the government found defense politics especially unrewarding. The leadership wanted to minimize the scope and prominence of defense issues. This task was easier because Japan's Asian neighbors were skittish about a Japanese military resurgence. The United States also supported a smaller role for the Japanese military. Nonetheless, the United States had a constant temptation to ask Japan to undertake more security tasks; so, the Japanese leadership developed preemptive policy commitments about security as a tactic for defusing its political opposition at home while fending off the United States.

If Japanese leaders rejected neutrality, they had to pay the U.S. price for a major defense alliance. As an antidote, the political leadership stacked the political cards against the development of force capabilities that could invite U.S. pressure (or Japanese military claims) for extended obligations. They interpreted Article 9 of their constitution as a "trip wire" to limit commitments and used "custom tailoring" of the defense agencies to limit capabilities.

On the face of it, the Japanese constitution preempted U.S. claims for an extended security perimeter. J.A.A. Stockton notes that "the 'no war' clause (Article 9) of the 1947 constitution would seem, according to a literal interpretation, to render armed forces . . . illegal."[70] Moreover, the opposition and some parts of the LDP have continued to block the two-thirds majority necessary to amend Article 9. Nonetheless, the practical import of the article left maneuvering room. For example, Article 9 did not prevent the creation of a self-defense force and its subsequent development into a sophisticated military force.

If the LDP wanted to do more under Article 9, it could have. Why didn't it? Its restrictive interpretation of Article 9 always let the LDP say to the United States that the constitution limited its options and that the United States would create a political imbroglio if it demanded much more.

Why didn't the LDP want to touch security? The legacy of World War II in Japanese politics was a continuing suspicion among many voters of the power of the military and a strong dislike of nuclear weapons. In the 1950s the Socialists recruited then-militant unions to form an alliance that attacked the conservative LDP by rejecting the U.S.–Japan Security Treaty. The treaty's revision in 1960 provoked the largest mass protests in contemporary Japanese history. No one was eager to revisit the issue. LDP members found that it was more appealing to emphasize economic growth and its adjunct for grand security strategy: economic strength as the key to security.[71]

70. J. A. A. Stockton, "Political Parties and Political Opposition," in Ishida and Krauss, *Democracy in Japan,* p. 105.

71. The Korean War came as the Occupation ended. The war reinforced popular views in Japan against neutrality and strengthened the military's supporters. The consolidation of conservative groups into a unified LDP (with its cautious policies) in 1955 weakened the military's sympathizers. See Calder, *Crisis and Compensation.*

Article 9 also shaped options for civilian control over the military. War planning is a complicated realm, and effective civilian oversight normally takes a major effort.[72] There is little evidence of such a political effort in Japan. However, a narrow interpretation of Article 9 makes ex ante control of military strategy relatively easy because Diet members must give full prior approval to even a limited military effort.[73] For example, in the Persian Gulf war the government had to substitute large financial contributions for military action because the Diet had rejected military participation.

The LDP also used other devices to keep tight political limits on security policy. The Japanese parliamentary system permits expert bureaucracies to do the policy work while political leaders stack the decision process to require consultation with, or aid to, preferred political clients and programs. The bureaucratic standing of the Self-Defense Force (SDF) and the Japan Defense Agency (JDA) is striking in this light.

The SDF reports to the JDA, but the JDA does not have full ministerial status. A member of Ministry of Finance, not a JDA bureaucrat, holds the critical post of budget chief. The legacy of its rivalry with the military before World War II assured that the Ministry of Finance would cast a critical eye on the SDF. Similarly, a member of the Ministry of International Trade and Industry (MITI) directs military procurement. The budget staffing makes sure that the JDA does not become demanding early in the budgetary process. The JDA can only boost its share of Japanese government spending by obtaining approval at the budget reconciliation talks directly overseen by the Prime Minister.[74] Excessive military lobbying for new missions would likely alienate the LDP Prime Minister and result in budgetary penalties.[75]

The Japanese problem in participating in the Persian Gulf war signaled how small the Japanese role may be in any future multilateral security system. The diplomatic embarrassment over that war tarnished the LDP's reputation as the party of international success. Japan's inability to join peacekeeping forces might even block acquisition of a permanent seat on the United Nations (UN) Security Council, a big setback to rising Japanese expectations at home.

72. Stephen Van Evera, "Why Cooperation Failed in 1914," *World Politics* 38 (October 1985), pp. 80–117.

73. *Ex ante* controls and commitments shape outcomes by putting significant constraints on future choices. Of course, they can be broken, as in the "no new taxes" pledge of the 1988 U.S. presidential campaign, but at a cost.

74. Calder, *Crisis and Compensation,* pp. 425–26.

75. The Japanese government's tax revenues are the lowest (as a share of gross domestic product [GDP]) of the industrial world due to business pressure. Hence, moneys for programs are tight. Moreover, big business largely has not accorded top importance to defense projects. High rates of civilian growth even divert the interests of smaller firms who might otherwise become dependent on defense spending. See Davis B. Bobrow and Stephen R. Hill, "Non-Military Determinants of Military Budgets: The Japanese Case," *International Studies Quarterly* 35 (March 1991), pp. 39–62. The LDP pledge to limit Japanese defense spending to no more than 1 percent of GDP was another political invention to limit options for defense. See Calder, *Crisis and Compensation,* pp. 437–38.

The political embarrassment finally prompted the LDP to propose a modest change in security policy to reduce international criticism. The Policy Committee of the LDP suddenly declared that Article 9 did not block extensive participation in UN peacekeeping forces. However, Prime Minister Miyazawa deemed this revisionist view too controversial for consensus in the LDP, much less in the upper house of the Diet (the House of Councillors) where Miyazawa needed some votes from the centrist Komeito and Democratic Socialist parties for any peacekeeping legislation. The final legislation permitted Japanese troops to participate solely at the request of the UN after a cease-fire was in place. Japanese peacekeepers may make only minimal use of weapons. Moreover, it forbids Japanese participation in any mission to separate warring parties forcibly (e.g., in Bosnia and Herzegovina) without prior approval of the Diet. In practice, Japan will field only small-scale logistical and medical assistance for less violent UN missions. Even the Somali peacekeeping operation was outside its scope.[76]

In short, Japan's limited multilateral commitments on security show little chance of changing despite single-party control in a parliamentary system. Electoral incentives favor the status quo. The only hint of a multilateral formula of any political viability comes from Japanese discussions of Asian security. Japan has urged building consensus through preventive diplomacy and commercial initiatives for Asia, perhaps on the model of the European Cooperation and Security Conference, but has ruled out formal military arrangements. Japan's caution is partly out of deference to the United States. It also reflects Japan's sensitivity to its neighbors' doubts about its plans and intentions.[77] But, it also grows out of the perennial problem for Japanese foreign policy: no political leader benefits significantly (nor does the LDP as a whole) from dwelling on issues beyond patronage politics or commercial diplomacy to fuel export expansion.

---

76. Ichiro Ozawa and other senior LDP leaders endorsed the more permissive view of the constitution. See Hisao Takagi, "LDP Panel Backs Active Role for Troops," *Nikkei Weekly,* 29 February 1992, p. 2. Any departure from these rules will lead to Japanese withdrawal from UN peacekeeping forces. See "Outdated Security System is in Need of Overhaul," *The Nikkei Weekly,* 27 June 1992, p. 6; and Andrew Pollack, "Japanese Say They Cannot Send Troops to Somalia," *New York Times,* 19 December 1992, p. Y3.

77. This is the logic of Akihiko Tanaka, "International Security and Japan's Contribution in the 1990s," *Japan Review of International Affairs* 4, Fall/Winter, 1990, pp. 187–208. *Asiaweek* argues that a Miyazawa doctrine emerged that emphasizes Japanese contributions to leading political and security affairs in Asia for the first time, perhaps using the Association of Southeast Asian Nations as a vehicle. The plan still features a major role for the United States, however. See "The Miyazawa Doctrine," *Asiaweek,* 24 July 1992, pp. 21–23. For alternative scenarios, see Takashi Inoguchi, "Four Japanese Scenarios for the Future," in Kathleen Newland, ed., *The International Relations of Japan* (London: Macmillan, 1992), pp. 206–23, and Tsuneo Akaha, "Japan's Security Policy after U.S. Hegemony," in ibid, pp. 147–73. If Japan adopts a more active military profile, it may be tied to the emergence of an Asian bloc that excludes roles for the United States or Europe, hardly a boon for multilateralism. See Chalmers Johnson, *Japan in Search of a 'Normal' Role,* Policy Paper no. 3 (San Diego, Calif.: Institute on Global Conflict and Cooperation: July 1992).

Trade and political innovations for multilateralism

Is there any chance that the political incentives about multilateralism will shift? This section examines one alternative for economic diplomacy—U.S. pressure coupled with a shift in the preferences of the economic coalition tied to the LDP.

How can the LDP protect Japanese industry now that its exporting and foreign investment strategies are under attack overseas? If the export sectors force a shift in policy, even at the cost of alienating some LDP supporters, then a change in policy may follow a realignment in the interest-group coalition working with the LDP.[78]

Large Japanese multinational corporations, and the smaller suppliers who follow them overseas, support selective changes in economic protection and industrial policies at home to buy peace abroad. Also, as these firms globalize, they dislike some of the rigidities imposed by industrial policies at home. As a result, they may favor a more open and cosmopolitan home economy and urge a more genuine commitment to multilateral trade practices by Japan.[79] In short, ad hoc changes in the economic interests of influential firms could indirectly shift the political agenda.

How far would the agenda shift? Would it strengthen support for multilateralism? So far, large Japanese firms with international interests have backed only very selective compromises on liberalizing competition at home.[80] This strategy—slowing entry into the market while accepting it—fits the optimal regulatory strategy for accommodating change by a dominant incumbent in any market.[81] Moreover, even the changes backed by exporters clash with the demands of smaller firms, of import competing large firms (e.g., steel), and of agriculture. The LDP only reluctantly liberalizes an industry in cases where many companies object to allowing more foreign imports and foreign investments.

The cautious LDP leadership largely has shunned any sweeping effort at trade reform. Fulfillment of multilateral obligations to liberalize investment controls and traditional trade barriers only came after they were no longer vital for Japanese competitive success. Even when business favors increased competition, Japanese political leaders still want to collect political rents by arbitrating the terms of market competition, thereby significantly reducing the

78. Peter Alexis Gourevitch, *Politics in Hard Times* (Ithaca, N.Y.: Cornell University Press, 1986).

79. The political logic is akin to that offered by Milner about U.S. and French firms. See Helen Milner, "Trading Places: Industries for Free Trade," *World Politics* 40 (April 1988), pp. 350–76.

80. Dennis J. Encarnation and Mark Mason, "Neither MITI nor America: The Political Economy of Capital Liberalization in Japan," *International Organization* 44 (Winter 1990), pp. 25–54.

81. Roger Noll and Bruce Owen, *The Political Economy of Deregulation* (Washington, D.C.: The American Enterprise Institute, 1983).

market's transparency and forcing endless appeals to the political leadership.[82] For example, in 1985 the United States had to battle over Japan's use of research and development projects to mask commercial projects from foreign bidding. With a handful of Japanese business allies the United States got the LDP to overrule the policy that forebade purchases of foreign communications satellites in order to promote use of government research satellites. Did this mean the government had liberalized the market? No. In 1989 foreign suppliers learned they would have to refight the same battle.[83]

The refusal to set clear principles raises questions about Japanese credibility and promotes tensions over trade. The American diplomatic record, however, underscores the discouraging political conditions for change. U.S. demands initially tried to limit Japanese "export offenses" in key markets. This led to voluntary export restraint agreements (VERs) for such industries as automobiles and machine tools that were administered by MITI. Japan accepted the VERs because they were better than trade retaliation and because they indirectly boosted profit margins for Japanese producers. Just as importantly, VERs reinforced the LDP's power by getting MITI into the business of organizing export cartels. This made the Japanese export industry dependent on the government for its allocation of the quotas.[84] The possibilities for political profit were endless, but VERs are not conducive to multilateralism.[85]

The more innovative and challenging test of Japanese politics started with U.S. demands for transparency in the Japanese administrative process, a vital condition for multilateral credibility. Complaints centered on the prevalence of unwritten regulations, insufficient periods to meet government administrative deadlines, and inaccessibility of key administrative organs to foreign participation. U.S. negotiators pressed Japan with occasional success for more uniform administrative procedures.[86] However, almost every dispute over transparency has required intervention by the LDP to bolster MITI and the Ministry of Foreign Affairs, which represent the interests of Japanese industry in moderating trade disputes.

---

82. One example of collecting rents from telecommunications and software firms is discussed in Kent Calder, *International Pressure and Domestic Policy Response: Japanese Informatics Policy in the 1980s,* Research Monograph no. 51 (Princeton, N.J.: Center of International Studies, Princeton University, 1989).

83. The LDP had approved continuation of the Japanese research program. See Michael Mastanduno, "Do Relative Gains Matter? America's Response to Japanese Industrial Policy," *International Security* 16 (Summer 1991), pp. 73–113.

84. Kenneth Flamm, "Managing New Rules: High-tech Trade Friction and the Semiconductor Industry," *The Brookings Review* (Spring 1991), pp. 22 and 29.

85. Peter F. Cowhey and Jonathan David Aronson, *Managing the World Economy: The Consequences of Corporate Alliances* (New York: The Council on Foreign Relations, 1993), chap. 8.

86. Uniform codes assist newcomers and consumers unless they are explicitly designed to retard them. See Yuko Inuoe, "Ministries Rapped for Excessive Guidance," *Japan Economic Journal,* 2 December 1989, p. 1.

A third U.S. focus was the organization of capital markets. The multilateral economic system envisioned evolution to a relatively free flow of funds across national borders and competition in the international banking business. Japan largely restricted such flows and lagged in liberalization. This pleased Japanese banks (because it limited competition) and served Japanese manufacturers because it lowered their cost of capital dramatically by restricting capital exports. (The savings rate of Japan was high, so capital immobility meant low interest rates.) The policies penalized household investors and the securities industry, but Japanese politics were not sensitive to consumer interests. The LDP had given the securities industry its own specialized protection in return for not poaching on banking. As a result, the LDP stalled on reform despite bitter foreign complaints. So, the United States campaigned hard to force Japan to meet its multilateral obligations. Its partial success depended on bargaining among Japanese firms over the terms of liberalization.[87]

In short, each piece of liberalization comes on a case-by-case basis. This makes the agenda for change ad hoc, slow, and very prone to rent seeking. It also provides only limited redress about problems of transparency.

On a brighter note, ad hoc erosion of government protection of markets lowers the credibility of continued government protection to Japanese business.[88] If firms begin to doubt the credibility of protection, they may shift toward greater support of multilateral regimes. Such a change could influence the LDP. The political problem for Japan, after all, is not in the division of power; it is in the incentives of the electoral system. However, such a subtle shift in interest-group politics may not be enough to reassure countries that doubt Japan's multilateral pledges.[89] As the next section shows, some Japanese leaders think other reforms are necessary.

Political institutional reform

Even the LDP leadership wonders if the current political system is viable. Perhaps the strongest effort to articulate a new multilateral vision of the world came from Prime Minister Nakasone in the mid-1980s. Although Nakasone

87. See Encarnation and Mason, "Neither MITI nor America"; and Frances Rosenbluth, *Financial Politics in Contemporary Japan* (Ithaca, N.Y.: Cornell University Press, 1989).

88. Japanese import policy has been liberalized since 1985, despite exclusionary practices by Japanese *keiretsu*. See Robert Lawrence, *Efficient or Exclusionist? The Import Behavior of Japanese Corporate Groups* Brookings Papers on Economic Activity, no. 1, 1991, pp. 311–41.

89. Could a modification of the multilateral regime strengthen Japanese support? Japan has begun to question the efficacy of the U.S. model for development. It has hinted that its support for multilateral financial institutions may depend on adjusting their strategies to Japanese development strategy and business practices. The United States criticized the Japanese approach as "wasteful." See "Japan Urges World Bank to Change Course," *Los Angeles Times,* 11 December 1991, p. D2; and James Clay Moltz, "Commonwealth Economics in Perspective: Lessons from the East Asian Model," *Soviet Economy,* vol. 7, 1991, pp. 342–63.

attempted an unusually activist form of leadership, the basic incentives for LDP leadership (money and factions, not popular support) undercut him.[90]

Since that effort, the mounting pressures to increase agricultural imports, bolster access for foreign products, and address security obligations have triggered an LDP debate about whether to reform the Japanese electoral system. The younger, more sophisticated urban voters who represent the dominant demographic wave are not so easily moved by the traditional politics of personal favors; they want second bedrooms, not an extra tatami mat. As the costs of direct favors to voters rise, the LDP is pondering whether to woo those voters with such substitutes as consumer policies. Collective goods become politically attractive because they benefit more voters at a lower cost per voter. However, the current electoral system makes it difficult to emphasize collective goods issues in elections, thereby negating many of the political benefits. As a result, the LDP has toyed with electoral reform.[91]

The Kaifu government backed a proposal in 1990 to reduce the number of seats in the Diet from 512 to 501, switch 301 of the seats to single-member districts, and undertake significant reapportionment. The redistricting would have dropped the value of rural votes from 3.18 to two times the value of urban votes.[92] Restructuring the political system would increase the importance of urban interests favoring better infrastructure, more competitive pricing, and other consumer interests. It would have reduced the power of farmers just as trade reforms began to alienate the farmers from the LDP. More fundamentally, the single-member district would change incentives about how to run for office because positions on issues not only would become compatible with a strategy to win a parliamentary majority, but also they would become desirable.

Support of the reform, however, cost Prime Minister Kaifu dearly in the LDP. His successor, Mr. Miyazawa, quietly scrapped all but a modest package to reduce the ratio of value of rural to urban votes to 3:1. This was the bare minimum that the Japanese constitutional court had declared necessary for the next election to be valid.[93] The *de minimis* plan undercut a strategy of reform based on urban support, and it completely abandoned the effort to change the basic incentives for how parties compete in Japan.

---

90. The Prime Minister has neither the staff nor sufficient time in office to do much more than engage in infighting over policy issues. See Kernell, "The Primacy of Politics in Economic Policy."

91. This is an example of the logic in Ronald Rogowski, "Trade and the Variety of Democratic Institutions," *International Organization* 41 (Spring 1987), pp. 203–24.

92. Sam Nakagama, "In Japan, Farm Supports Prop Up More than Farms," *New York Times,* 13 August 1990, p. A15. Roughly two hundred LDP Diet members are active supporters of the farm lobby, and about sixty of those seats are from agricultural districts. See *Nikkei Weekly,* 19 October 1991, p. 2.

93. Reform would initially favor the LDP, but eventually a consolidated opposition might take on the LDP successfully. This was a key reason for passing Kaifu over for a second term as Prime Minister. The Miyazawa cabinet retreated to smaller reforms to put more seats in urban areas and tidy up bits of campaign financing. A coalition of LDP dissenters and the opposition parties in the upper house delayed even that package. See *The Economist,* 1 February 1992, p. 38; and Itaru Oishi, "Diet Leaves Reform Proposals Pending," *Nikkei Weekly,* 27 June 1992, p. 2.

Summary

The credibility of all foreign policy commitments to multilateral regimes is sensitive to domestic political considerations. When the great powers are democracies the nature of the electoral system, the structure of governing institutions (including the fine tuning of institutions), and the transparency of the political system especially influence the credibility of foreign policy promises.

The analysis herein showed that U.S. political institutions bolstered the credibility of the multilateral order after 1945. Japanese politics, however, promise to hinder the credibility of Japanese commitments in the 1990s. Analysts expend enormous energy judging the degree of Japanese trade and financial concessions or the size of its military effort. This article argues that our attention should focus equally on the reform of its domestic political institutions. Although international economic negotiations may be one route leading to change in Japan, significant reform of the Japanese electoral system may be a better way to change the fit between foreign policy and domestic politics.

It is difficult to know what vision of multilateralism might emerge, if any, from political changes in Japan. Multilateral regimes are stronger if they cater selectively to the domestic political profiles of the great powers, as happened in response to American politics in the 1940s. As the ranks of great powers change, some features of the multilateral regimes should shift in response to the domestic political imperatives of the new powers. This in turn implies some adjustment burdens, and accompanying domestic political quarrels, for the existing great powers.[94] This raises the challenging question of what happens when regimes have to accommodate several distinct styles of domestic politics at once? Even if there are ways to harmonize "national interests," can great powers mutually adjust their political institutional structures sufficiently to permit the successful adaptation of multilateralism to multipolarity?

---

94. This argument holds even if there are no losses for the incumbent country as a whole from the accommodation. For a review of U.S. restructuring as part of trade diplomacy, see Cowhey and Aronson, *Managing the World Economy*.